GENERAL INDUSTRY
SECOND EDITION

DR. JOHN L. FEIRER
Editor

GENERAL INDUSTRY
SECOND EDITION

DR. JOHN R. LINDBECK
Professor Industrial Education
Western Michigan University
Kalamazoo, Michigan

and

DR. IRVIN T. LATHROP
Professor Industrial Arts
California State University
Long Beach, California

Chas. A. Bennett Co., Inc.
Peoria, Illinois 61614

Second Edition Copyright © 1977
Copyright 1969

**By Dr. John R. Lindbeck
and Dr. Irvin T. Lathrop**

All rights reserved.

79 80 81   V-H   5 4 3

ISBN 87002-185-0

Library of Cong. Cat. No. 76-12711

Printed in the United States of America

Plan of This Book

A general course should be an integral part of all modern industrial arts programs. Such a course has the following major objectives:

1. Students learn about the fields of graphic communications, metalworking, plastics, woodworking, building construction, power, and transportation at the introductory level. Furthermore they are led to explore these areas in order to learn how products are designed and manufactured.

2. Students learn how to design and make projects related to these areas. They are encouraged to experiment and do further study to increase their understanding of the principles which underlie materials processing.

3. Students learn basic hand, machine, and drawing skills which are helpful to all people living in an industrial society.

4. Students are encouraged to think seriously about their futures by familiarizing themselves with the various opportunities in industry. Such an exploratory program aids students both vocationally and avocationally.

5. Students learn how industries function and that industries are essentially the same with respect to planning and manufacturing. They also are helped to understand how such areas as power and electricity relate to the broad field of industry.

One of the features of this book is an attempt to outline for both students and teachers the basic elements of industry. The book treats this subject systematically, explaining such functions as research and development, production tooling, production control, quality control, personnel management, manufacturing, and marketing. This approach presents a clear picture of precisely what an industry is. Because manufacturing involves the processing of materials from the raw state into the finished product, this book includes sections on metals, woods, and plastics to further the student's understanding of the concepts of cutting, fastening, forming, and finishing materials.

Every attempt has been made to point out similarities and close relationships among the industrial areas covered, so that the student can realize how much the major American industries have in common. Sub-concepts are listed under each major concept to show further the many similarities among the methods of transforming materials into products. The sub-concepts of mechanical linkage, adhesion, and cohesion which fall under the major concept of metal-fastening theory are examples of this.

The authors realize that the information in this book could have been organized in various ways; they feel, however, that the organization they have chosen is valid, functional, and understandable.

GENERAL INDUSTRY is a textbook designed to be used in a first course and can be used effectively by almost any age group. The content and style, however, are directed to the early teenager. The illustrations, experiments, and examples are all planned with the interest of the adolescent in mind. Sentence structure and vocabulary have been checked especially to meet the reading abilities of this age group.

The authors wish to thank all of the many individuals and companies who have made valuable contributions to this book. (Specific acknowledgments are listed on pages 6 through 8.) It would have been difficult, if not impossible, to realize this publication without the generous assistance of those named. The authors also welcome any suggestions or comments from individuals who may use this book.

Acknowledgments

Ace-Sycamore, Incorporated
Addressograph-Multigraph
Aluminum Company of America
America House
American Electrical Heater Corporation
American Forest Products Industries
American Honda Motor Company, Incorporated
American Machine and Foundry, Inc.
American Seating Company
American Trucking Association
American Welding Society
Amtrak
Anaconda Company
Association of American Railroads
A T & T
Baldor Electric
Bell Aerospace Division of Textron
Bell & Howell
Bell System News Features
The Beloit Corporation
Bendix Corporation
Besly-Welles Corporation
Bethlehem Steel Corporation
The Beverly Shear Mfg. Corp.
Billings and Crescent Tools
Binks Manufacturing
Boeing Company
Branson
British Airways
Bruning Division, Addressograph Multigraph Corporation
Burlington Northern
California Ink Co.
Canadian National Corporation
Carpenter Technology
Caterpillar Tractor Company
Central Vermont Public Service Corp.
Cessna Aircraft Company
Civil Aeronautics Board
Clausing Corporation
Collins Radio Company
Columbian Vise and Manufacturing Company
Creative Packaging Co.

Crescent Tool Company
Department of the Air Force
Design Center, Copenhagen
Di-Acro Houdaille
A B Dick Co.
Sally Dickson Associates
The Dow Chemical Company
Dunbar Furniture
E.I. duPont de Nemours & Co., Inc.
DuPont Magazine
Eagle Manufacturing Company
Eastman Kodak
Edwards Laboratories
Electric Storage Battery Company
Federal Aviation Administration
The Firestone Tire & Rubber Company
Ford Motor Company
Frederick Post Company
Fry Plastics International
GAF
General Electric Corporation
General Motors Corporation
Genevro Machine Company
Gilmore Racing Team, Inc.
GMC Truck & Coach Public Relations
Graphic Systems Group, Rockwell International
Great Lakes Screw Corporation
Great Northern Railway
Greyhound Bus Lines, Inc.
Gulf Oil Corporation
Hall Enterprises
H. M. Harper Company
Harvey Hubbell, Incorporated
Honeywell Photographic Products
Hossfeld Manufacturing Company
Hughes Electronics
IBM
Jackson Products Company
Georg Jensen Silversmiths, Ltd., Copenhagen, Denmark
Johnson Gas Appliance Company
Jones & Lamson
Kaiser Aluminum
Kawasaki Motors Corporation

Kennecott Copper Corporation
Kester Solder Company
Keuffel and Esser Company
Lead Industries Association
Lea Manufacturing Company
Leatherwood Manufacturing Company, Incorporated
James F. Lincoln Arc Welding Foundation
The Lincoln Electric Company
Lindberg Company
Lockheed Corporation
Lufkin Rule Company
Lyon Metal Products, Incorporated
McCullough Corporation
McDonnell Douglas Corporation
McEnglevan Heat Treating and Manufacturing Company
Malleable Founders Society
Manufacturers Brush Company
Matson Navigation Company
Mazda Motor Car Company
Millers Falls Company
Murray Ohio Manufacturing Company
NASA
National Particleboard Association
National Safety Council
National Welding Equipment Company
New Jersey Zinc Company
Niagara Tools
Nicholson File Company
Nordson Corporation
Northland Ski Company
Northwest Orient Airlines
Norton Company
Pacific Far East Lines
Pacific Gas and Electric Company
Pan American
Peck, Stow and Wilcox Company
Port of Long Beach
Precast/Schokbeton, Inc.
Remington Rand Univac
Republic Steel Corporation
Reynolds Aluminum
Jens Risom Design, Inc.
Rockwell-Delta Company
Rockwell International
Rockwell Manufacturing Power Tool Division
Rohm and Haas

Rotor Way, Inc.
Sandia Laboratories
San Diego Gas and Electric Company
Santa Fe Railway
The Science Museum, London
Scott Foresman and Company
Sea-Land Service
Sears, Roebuck and Company
Seattle Center
Simonds File Company
Simonds Saw and Steel Company
Simpson Timber Company
Smithsonian Institution
Smith Welding Equipment Company
Snap-on Tools Corporation
The Society of the Plastics Industry, Inc.
Soiltest, Inc.
Southern California Edison
Southern Pacific Company
SpaN Magazine, a publication of Standard Oil of Indiana
Standard Tool Company
Stanley Tools
The L.S. Starrett Company
Teledyne Post, Des Plaines, IL
Texas Instruments
Thomas C. Thompson Company
3M Company
Todd Shipyard Corporation
Union Carbide
Union Mechling Corporation
United Airlines
United States Navy
U.S. Divers Company
U.S. Office of Education
U.S. Steel Corporation
Vandercook Co.
The Vecta Group, Inc.
Welch Scientific Company
Western Electric Corporation
Weston Instruments
Weyerhaeuser Company
Wheelabrator Corporation
Whirlpool Corporation
Willard Storage Battery Co.
J. H. Williams and Company
Wisconsin Division of Highways
Worktite Products Co.
Xerox

The authors' thanks are particularly due to the following persons for their valued assistance:
Kalman J. Chany
Mrs. Esther Cowdery
Terry Dykstra
Osmer Gorton
Charles Honeywell
Daniel Kurmas
Marshall La Cour
Jerold Harmon Saper
Floyd Stannard

Table of Contents

Plan of This Book 5
Acknowledgments 6
PART ONE—GENERAL INDUSTRY 15
    Unit 1—Introduction to Industry and Technology 16
    Unit 2—Product Design 18
        What is Design, 19; Elements of Design, 22; Design-Analysis Method, 23.
    Unit 3—Measurement 26
        The Meaning of Measurement, 26; Measuring Devices, 31; Accuracy, 32.
    Unit 4—Planning Procedures 35
    Unit 5—Safety 38
    Discussion Topics and Activities 42

PART TWO—GRAPHIC COMMUNICATIONS 44

Section 1—Drawing 44
    Unit 6—Introduction to Drawing 45
    Unit 7—Tools and Instruments 48
    Unit 8—Lines, Symbols, and Geometry 56
        Alphabet of Lines, 56; Symbols, 56; Drawing Practice, 56.
    Unit 9—Sketching 61
        Tools for Sketching, 61; Sketching Techniques, 62.
    Unit 10—Lettering 65
    Unit 11—Multiview Drawings 68
        Laying Out a Three-View Drawing, 69.
    Unit 12—Sectional and Auxiliary View 72
    Unit 13—Pictorial Drawings 74
        Perspective Drawing, 74; Isometric Drawing, 75; Oblique Drawing, 75.
    Unit 14—Dimensioning 78
    Unit 15—Metric Dimensioning 82
        Metric Dimensioning Methods, 82; Metric Dimensioning Rules, 84; Designing in Metrics, 85.
    Unit 16—Detail and Assembly Drawings 88
    Unit 17—Building Construction Drawing 91
        Planning a Building, 91; Steps in Drawing House Plans, 92.
    Unit 18—Printmaking 98
    Discussion Topics and Activities 100

Section 2—Graphic Arts 102
    Unit 19—Introduction to Graphic Arts 104
        Paper, 105; Ink, 105.
    Unit 20—Printing Processes and Materials 107
        Relief Printing, 107; Offset Lithography, 108; Gravure Printing, 109; Silk-Screen Printing, 110.
    Unit 21—Composing Type 111
        Hand-Setting Type, 112.
    Unit 22—Printing by Letterpress 115
        Making the Proof, 115; Locking Up the Form, 116; Preparing the Press, 118; Printing, 119; Linoleum Block Printing, 120.
    Unit 23—Offset Lithography 121
        Preparing Copy for Photography, 121; Photographing Copy, 122; Preparing the Offset Plate, 122; Printing, 123.

Contents

Unit 24—Silk-Screen Printing..................................125
    Equipment, 125; Stencil, 126; Making a Silk-Screen Print, 126.
Unit 25—Taking and Developing Pictures..................128
    Types of Cameras, 128; Taking Pictures, Developing Film, 130.
Unit 26—Printing Pictures...133
    Contact Printing, 133; Projection Printing, 135.
Unit 27—Office Duplicating......................................138
    Electrostatic Duplicating, 138; Spirit Duplicating, 139; Mimeograph, 140.
Discussion Topics...142

PART THREE—MANUFACTURING: PRINCIPLES, MATERIALS, AND PROCESSES.........144

Section 1—Metalworking.........144

Unit 28—Introduction to Metalworking.....................147
Unit 29—Mining and Refining Metals........................149
    Steel, 149; Aluminum, 150; Copper, 152.
Unit 30—Metal Materials..154
    Alloys, 154; Properties of Metals, 155; Metal Shapes and Sizes, 156; Kinds of Metals, 156.
Unit 31—Metal Layout and Pattern Development........163
    Layout Tools, 163; Measuring Heavy Stock, 165; Developing Sheet Metal Patterns, 167; Enlarging Patterns, 169.
Unit 32—Modern Metalworking.................................171
    Metal Cutting—Ultrasonic Machining, 171; Metal Cutting—Electrical Discharge Machining, 171; Other Cutting Developments, 172; Metal Forming—Explosive Forming, 172; Metal Forming—Hydrospinning, 172; Other Forming Developments, 173; Metal Fastening—Explosive Bonding, 173; Other Fastening Developments, 174; Metal Finishing—Electrostatic Spraying, 174; Other Finishing Developments, 174.
Unit 33—Metal Cutting Principles..............................175
Unit 34—Sawing Metal...178
    Hacksaws, 178; Metal-Cutting Band Saw, 180; Jeweler's Saw, 181.
Unit 35—Shearing Metal...182
    Tin Snips, 182; Squaring Shears, 183; Punches, 184; Chisels, 184; Bench Shears, 185.
Unit 36—Abrading Metal..187
    Kinds of Abrasives, 187; Grading Abrasives, 187; Using Abrasives, 188.
Unit 37—Shaping Metal..193
Unit 38—Drilling Metal...194
    Drilling Tools, 194; Drilling Holes, 196; Sharpening Drills, 196; Reaming, 196.
Unit 39—Milling and Filing Metal..............................200
    Filing, 200.
Unit 40—Turning Metal..205
    Lathe Accessories, 207; Measuring Tools, 208; Using the Lathe, 208.
Unit 41—Etching and Flame Cutting of Metal............214
    Etching, 214; Flame Cutting, 215.
Unit 42—Metal Forming Principles............................216
Unit 43—Bending Metal...220
    Bending Light Metals, 220; Bending Heavy Metals, 224; Machines for Bending, 224.
Unit 44—Casting Metal..227
    Sand Casting, 227.
Unit 45—Forging and Heat-Treating Metal................232
    Forging, 232; Heat-Treating, 233.

Contents

Unit 46—Pressing Metal.................................236
    Sinking, 236; Raising, 238; Tooling, 239; Stamping, 241; Chasing, 241; Spinning, 243.
Unit 47—Drawing Metal.................................244
Unit 48—Extruding Metal................................245
Unit 49—Rolling Metal..................................246
Unit 50—Metal Fastening Principles.....................248
Unit 51—Mechanical Fastening of Metal..................250
    Threaded Fasteners, 250; Rivets, 255; Sheet Metal Joints, 256.
Unit 52—Adhesive Fastening of Metal....................259
    Soldering, 259; Brazing, 262; Hard Soldering, 264; Cementing, 265.
Unit 53—Cohesive Fastening of Metal....................266
    Gas Welding, 266; Arc Welding, 267; Resistance Welding, 269.
Unit 54—Metal Finishing Principles......................271
Unit 55—Coat Finishing of Metal........................273
    Lacquers, 273; Paints, 274; Wax, 274; Electroplating, 274; Enameling, 274.
Unit 56—Remove Finishing of Metal......................277
    Polishing, 277; Buffing, 277; Abrasive Blasting, 279.
Unit 57—Displacement Finishing of Metal.................281
Unit 58—Color Finishing of Metal.........................282
    Chemicals, 282; Heat, 282; Safety Rules, 283.
Discussion Topics and Activities.........................283

Section 2—Plastics 288

Unit 59—Introduction to Plastics.........................289
    The Plastics Industry, 289; The Family of Plastics, 291.
Unit 60—Industrial Processing of Plastics................292
    Extrusion, 292; Calendering, 292; Coating, 293; Blow Molding, 293; Compression Molding, 294; Transfer Molding, 294; Thermoforming, 294; Injection Molding, 295; Rotational Molding, 295; Solvent Molding, 296; Casting, 296; High-Pressure Laminating, 296; Reinforcing, 297; Foamed Plastics, 297; Forming Plastics in the School Shop, 297.
Unit 61—Forming Plastics in the School Shop.............298
    Bending, 298; Casting, 300; Other Forming Processes, 300.
Unit 62—Cutting Plastic.................................302
Unit 63—Fastening Plastic...............................304
    Mechanical Fasteners, 304; Adhesion, 304; Cohesion, 304; Laminated Plastics, 306.
Unit 64—Finishing Plastic...............................308
    Coloring, 309; Coating, 310.
Discussion Topics......................................310

Section 3—Woodworking 312

Unit 65—Introduction to Woodworking....................315
Unit 66—Lumbering.....................................316
    Lumbering Processes, 316; Wood Identification, 318.
Unit 67—Wood Products and Occupations.................321
    Veneers and Plywood, 321; Other Wood Products, 322; Occupations in the Wood Industry, 324.
Unit 68—Estimating and Laying Out Stock.................325
    Using Metric Measurements, 326; Marking Stock for Length, 327; Marking for Width, 327.
Unit 69—New Developments in Woodworking..............328
    Wood Finishing, 328; Airless Spraying, 329; Wood Bonding, 329.
Unit 70—Woodcutting Principles.........................331

Contents

Unit 71—Sawing Wood 333
    Cutting to Length, 333; Cutting to Width, 334; Cutting Plywood, 334; Cutting Curves, 334; Cutting with the Band Saw, 337; Circular Saw, 337.

Unit 72—Planing and Chiseling Wood 338
    Parts and Types of Planes, 338; Planing a Surface, 340; Using the Chisel, 341.

Unit 73—Abrading Wood 343
    Sanding Wood, 344; Power Sanders, 345.

Unit 74—Drilling Holes in Wood 346
    Boring Holes, 346; Drilling Holes, 348.

Unit 75—Milling, Shaping, and Filing Wood 349
    Files and Rasps, 349; Cutting with the Jointer, 350; Shaping with the Router, 350.

Unit 76—Wood Turning 352

Unit 77—Wood Forming Principles 355
    Steam Bending, 355; Bending without Heat, 355; Laminating Wood, 356.

Unit 78—Wood Fastening Principles 358

Unit 79—Woodworking Joints 359

Unit 80—Mechanical Fasteners for Wood 362
    Nails and Nailing, 362; Screws, 364; Drilling Holes for Wood Screws, 366.

Unit 81—Adhesive Fastening of Wood 366
    Clamps, 367; Gluing Up Stock, 367.

Unit 82—Wood Finishing Principles 368
    Basic Finishing Steps, 370; Texturing Wood, 370.

Unit 83—Color Finishing of Wood 371
    Stains and Bleaches, 371.

Unit 84—Coat Finishing of Wood 373
    Shellac, 373; Varnish, 374; Lacquer, 375; Painting, 375; Brushes, 375.

Discussion Topics 376

PART FOUR—BUILDING CONSTRUCTION 379

Unit 85—Introduction to Building Construction 380

Unit 86—Foundations 381
    Beginning the Project, 381; Foundations, 381.

Unit 87—Framing and Roofing the Building 385

Unit 88—Utilities and Finishing 389
    Heating, 389; Plumbing, 389; Electricity, 390; Finishing, 391.

Discussion Topics 394

PART FIVE—POWER AND ENERGY 395

Section 1—Electricity 395

Unit 89—Introduction to Electricity 396

Unit 90—Electricity and Magnetism 397
    Magnetism, 397; Laws of Magnetism, 400; Care of Magnets, 401.

Unit 91—Forms of Electricity 402
    Static Electricity, 402; Current Electricity, 403.

Unit 92—Sources of Electricity 404
    Electricity by Chemical Action, 404; Electricity from Heat, 409; Electricity from Pressure, 409; Electricity from Light, 410; Electricity from Magnetism, 411.

Unit 93—Conductors and Circuits 412
    Simple Electircal Circuit, 412; Cords, Plugs, Lamp Sockets, 414.

Unit 94—Electromagnetism 417
    Generators, 418; Motors, 419.

Contents

Unit 95—Converting Electricity to Heat 421
  Fuses, 422; Heat from Electricity for Industry, 423.
Unit 96—Converting Electricity to Light 424
  Reading Meters, 426; Lighting Circuits, 426; Other Lighting Methods, 427; House Wiring, 427.
Unit 97—Communication 432
  The Telegraph, 432; The Telephone, 433; Computers and Calculators, 434; Wireless Communication, 436; Television, 437.
Discussion Topics 438

Section 2—Power 440
Unit 98—Introduction to Power 441
Unit 99—Power and Machines 442
  Simple Machines, 442; Water Power, 443; Steam Power, 444; Gasoline Engines, 444; Rotary Engines, 445; Diesel Engines, 447; Fluid Power, 447; Jet Engines, 448; Rockets, 449; Alternate Sources of Motor Power, 449; Atomic Power, 450; Sun Power, 451.
Unit 100—Small Gasoline Engines 452
  Four-Cycle Engine, 452; Two-Cycle Engine, 454; Operation of Gasoline Engines, 455; Small Engine Maintenance, 459.
Discussion Topics 460

PART SIX—TRANSPORTATION 461
Unit 101—Introduction to Transportation 463
  The Transportation System, 463.
Unit 102—Rail Transport Systems 466
  The Railway, 467; Railroad Operations, 467; Railway Vehicles, 471; New Directions in Railroad Vehicle Technology, 477.
Unit 103—Air Transport Systems 478
  Airways, 478; Air Traffic Control, 478; Aircraft, 481.
Unit 104—Sea Transport Systems 490
  Materials Transport, 490; Passenger Transport, 492; Ships, 492; Special Purpose Vessels, 495.
Unit 105—Automotive Transport Systems 497
  The Automobile, 497; Trucks and Buses, 498; The Modern Automobile, 500; Environmental Impact, 500.
Discussion Topics 503

PART SEVEN—MODERN INDUSTRY 504
Unit 106—What Is Modern Industry? 505
  People and Technology, 507; People and Ecology, 510.
Unit 107—The Essentials of Industry 513
  Material Resources, 515; Human Resources, 517; Capital Resources, 519; The Manufacturing Corporation, 521.
Unit 108—The Elements of Industry 527
  The Elements of Industry, 528; Studying Occupations, 546.
Unit 109—Mass Production in the School 547
  Research and Development (RD), 548; Production Tooling (PT), 549; Production Control (PC), 551; Quality Control (QC), 551; Personnel Management (PM), 551; Manufacturing (MF), 551; Marketing (MK), 553.
Unit 110—Careers 556
  Crafts, 556; Technical Careers, 560; Engineering and Science, 561; The Production Team, 563; Business Careers, 564; Leaning about Yourself, 566; Studying Occupations, 567.
Discussion Topics and Activities 568
Technology Report 1—Welding 570

Contents

    Technology Report 2—Composite Materials 571
    Technology Report 3—Automatic Harvesting of Trees 573
    Technology Report 4—Modified Wood 575
    Technology Report 5—Numerical Control 577
    Technology Report 6—Alternate Power Sources 579
    Technology Report 7—Automotive Engines 582

Appendix **586**
Index **592**

PART I
General Industry

Unit 1 Introduction to Industry and Technology

Unit 2 Product Design

Unit 3 Measurement

Unit 4 Planning Procedures

Unit 5 Safety

Discussion Topics and Activities

UNIT 1

Introduction to Industry and Technology

The purpose of this book is to introduce you to industry, its products, and the world of work. Fig. 1-1. Through this book you will be given a beginning course in general industry. You will gain an appreciation of craftsmanship and industrial products. You will also have a chance to explore your interests in making and

1-1. *In this course, you will learn much about the products of industry. These recreational vehicles are typical industrial products.*

Unit 1: Introduction to Industry and Technology

doing things. In addition, you will learn about career opportunities in industry and how your interests may lead you to a challenging job.

Every learning activity has objectives or aims. The objectives of a general industry course are as follows:

1. To develop an understanding of industry. You will learn of the marvels of modern technology as well as some of industry's problems. It is important for you to gain an appreciation of the place of industry in our society.

2. To develop technical skill and knowledge. As a part of your work in this course, you will learn skills in metalwork, woodwork, drafting, graphic arts, and other areas. You will explore the materials and measuring devices used. You will learn safe hand and tool skills and how to make project drawings. This exploration can help you become aware of your talents and interests. Finding out about your abilities can aid in directing your schoolwork toward a satisfying and meaningful career.

3. To develop creative problem-solving skills using the materials and processes of industry. The joys of craftsmanship are important to you as a human being. You should explore, design, create, and invent. You will be faced with many problems in your work which require intelligent solutions. Through shop experimentation and planning you can know the pleasure of successful solutions. These skills can lead to satisfying hobbies as well as successful careers.

4. To explore career opportunities in industry. Industry needs people trained in a variety of skills. Skilled craftsmen, technicians, engineers, scientists, managers and clerical workers—these are all typical of the kinds of jobs available in business and industry.

5. A general industry course requires that you work safely and in cooperation with both the teacher and other students. Good work habits and attitudes are important if you are to get as much as possible from your shopwork experiences. Fig. 1-2.

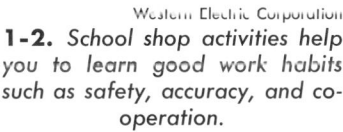

Western Electric Corporation
1-2. *School shop activities help you to learn good work habits such as safety, accuracy, and cooperation.*

17

UNIT 2

Product Design

2-1. New products are developed through research and experimentation. This experimental gasoline-electric vehicle has a power system which consists of a 12-cubic-inch gasoline engine coupled with a series DC electric motor through an electro-magnetic clutch. With the clutch energized, the gasoline engine and electric motor operate together at the same speed. Electrical energy is supplied by a 72-volt power battery pack with an additional 12-volt accessory battery. The vehicle is shown here with its canopy raised to permit entry.

General Motors Corporation

The next time you use a tool to do a job around the house, take the time to study it. Does the tool work as it should? Does the wrench hold the nut securely, or the chisel cut as it should? Have the right materials been used to make the tool strong enough? Is the tool comfortable to hold and well balanced? If you answer *yes,* the object is probably well designed.

Tools, like all other products of industry—sports equipment, automobiles, chairs, knives and forks, and dozens of other items that you use each day—were planned and made to do certain jobs and to make your life better. Fig. 2-1. The people who plan these products are called *designers.* They work in the research and development departments of industries. Their job is to design new and better products and to improve old ones. If these products work as they should, if they are made of the right materials and are interesting to look at, they are well designed. If not, the products will be poor. You will be doing some design work in this general industry course. It is important that you learn something about design so that you will be proud of the things you make.

Homes and other buildings are also designed. The people who design these structures are called *architects.* The homes they design are planned to meet the needs of the families who are to use them. A home must be planned for a family of a certain size. The structure must reflect their interests and tastes. The family may want a home made of wood or

Unit 2: Product Design

Lead Industries Association
2-2. Homes are also a result of design activities. House designers are called architects.

of brick. They may live in a warm climate or a cold one. All these facts must be studied as the architect designs the comfortable, usable home the family wants. Fig. 2-2. In the same way, other buildings must be planned to meet certain needs.

WHAT IS DESIGN?

Very simply, designing is planning. To do it well you must think carefully about the product you wish to make. You must decide what *you* wish it to be. It should be original work—your work and not someone else's. In other words, you must be creative. Designing is creative planning to meet some special human need.

In order to be good the product that you are designing should meet three requirements:

- It should work properly.
- It must be made of the correct materials.
- It should be pleasing to look at.

These are called the *functional, material,* and *visual* requirements.

Look at the canoe paddle in Fig. 2-3. This is a functional object. The paddle will be used to move and steer a canoe

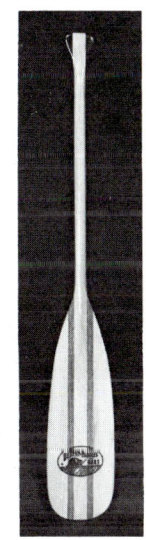

2-3. The canoe paddle is designed to steer and move a canoe. It, along with the canoe, is a well-designed product—functional, made of good material, and pleasing in form.

McCullough Corporation

19

Part I: General Industry

through water. Its shape and size are right to help you do this comfortably and with ease. The paddle is made of wood, a material that is light, strong, and durable, and it will float if accidentally dropped overboard. You will notice that it also has a nice appearance. The shape is clean and graceful—it has to be in order to perform as a paddle should. This canoe paddle is a good example of an object which is functionally, materially, and visually correct—a well-designed product of industry. Let's take a closer look at these three requirements as they apply to other kinds of products.

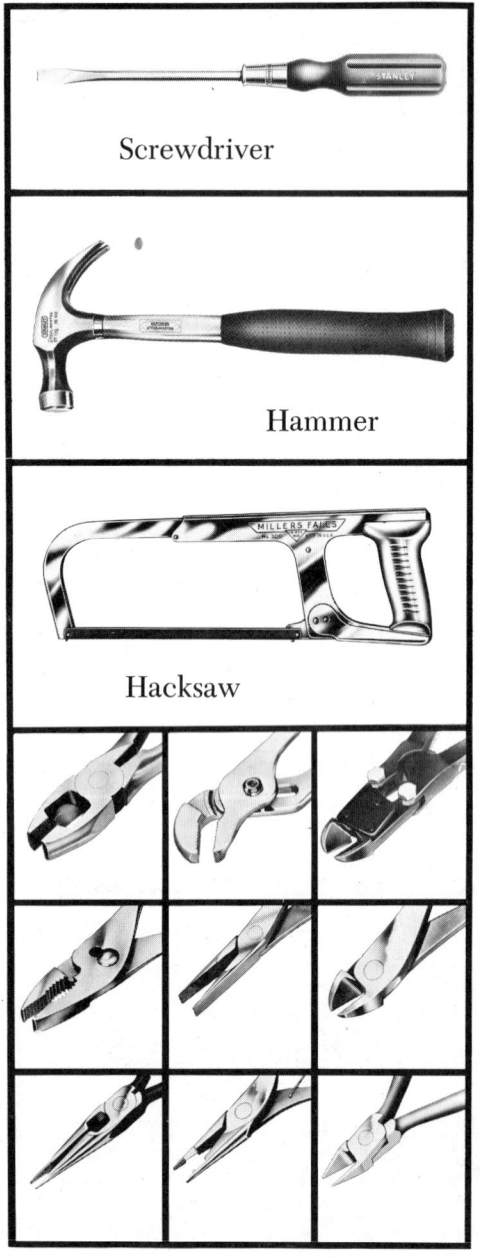

2-4. Tools are designed for function—the right tool for the right job.

Function

A product is functional if it works as it is supposed to work.

Tool handles must be functional in order to be held easily and safely. The tools are used and held differently; so their handles must be different. Fig. 2-4.

The same is true of other things you hold. Knives and forks, fishing poles, baseball bats, golf clubs, and steering wheels should all be easy to grip.

Since plier jaws also have special uses, or functions, they must be designed with these uses in mind. Some are used for holding delicate parts, some for cutting heavy or thin wire, still others for heavy gripping and turning. They must differ in design so that they can perform different functions.

Chairs must be designed or planned for different uses. They must be comfortable and be right for each use. Think how different it would be to work at a drafting table while sitting at a tablet armchair! Function in design means making sure a product works as it is supposed to work. Fig. 2-5.

These are just a few examples of the part function plays in product design. You can probably think of many others. While you are designing, you should be thinking about the purpose or use for your product. You must design it to be functional.

Materials

A product must be made from the proper kind and amount of material. If you design something to be used outdoors, it must be made to withstand water, wind,

Unit 2: Product Design

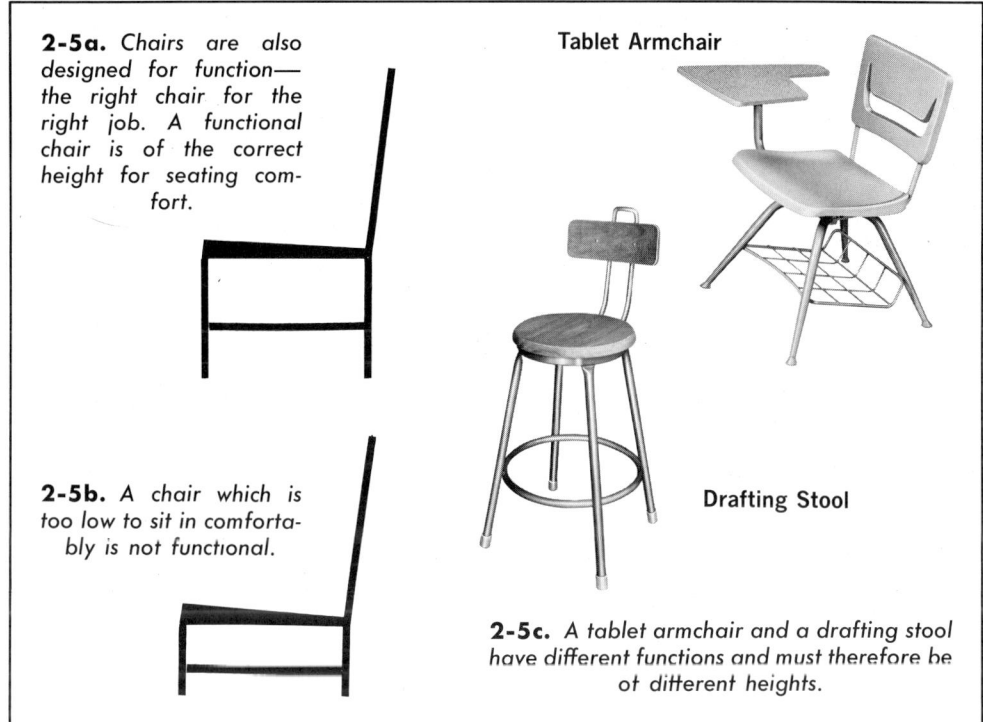

2-5a. Chairs are also designed for function— the right chair for the right job. A functional chair is of the correct height for seating comfort.

2-5b. A chair which is too low to sit in comfortably is not functional.

2-5c. A tablet armchair and a drafting stool have different functions and must therefore be of different heights.

and sun. Materials must be chosen according to the product's use.

Many kinds of materials are used to make products. You must know something about the materials before you start designing with them. Find out about such things as cost, durability, and strength.

Every material has certain characteristics all its own. You should take full advantage of this fact as you design. Fig. 2-6.

Learn what to do and what not to do with a material. For example, plastic should not automatically be used as a substitute for wood. It is expensive and

2-6. This fiberglass desk-table and matching cabinet are functional, strong, and attractive. The plastic material is used very well.

The Vecta Group, Inc.

Part I: General Industry

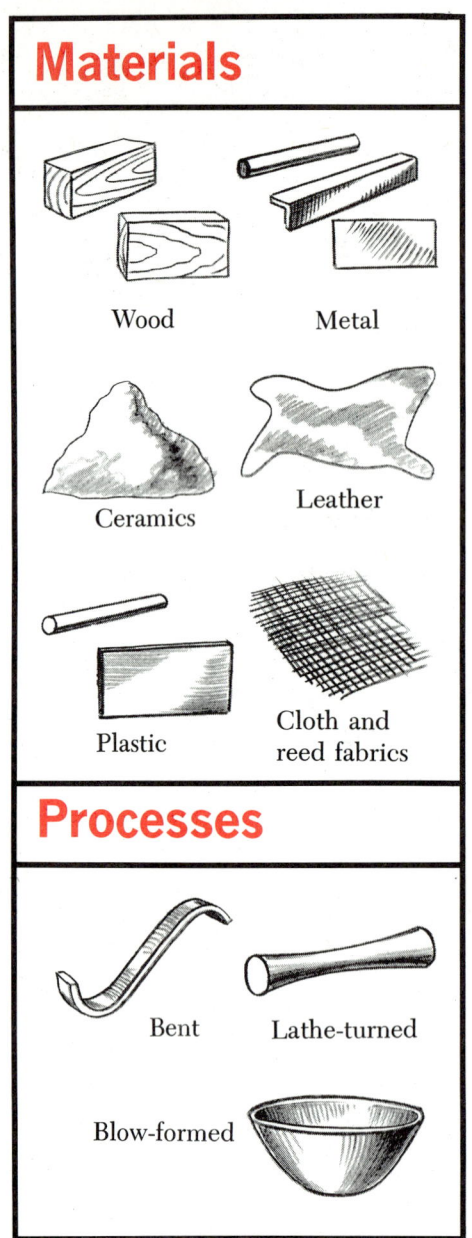

2-7. Materials should be studied so that they are used wisely in designing products. Which of the materials can be worked by the three process examples?

2-8. All the design elements are present here—line, shape, form, and texture.

counters) are strong and heat-resistant. Other plastics can be bent, lathe-turned, or blow-formed to make a bowl. Fig. 2-7.

Some plastic is tough and transparent, while other kinds scratch easily and are opaque (can't be seen through). These are the kinds of things you should know about materials.

Remember also that you should use only enough material to do the job and no more. Don't waste material. Your project will not only cost less but will also look better if material is used in proper amounts.

Appearance

A good product is pleasing to the eye. Everyone prefers things which are beautiful to those which are ugly. Designers must keep this in mind as they design products.

ELEMENTS OF DESIGN

A designer must know certain design elements and principles. The "building blocks" of design are called the *design elements*. These are the lines, the forms, the shapes (spatial forms, or solids), and the surface treatment (color, texture) that make up any three-dimensional product. The lines can appear as graceful curves or straight and strong. These grow into forms and solid shapes which display color and texture. Fig. 2-8.

The following principles of design should help you create products that will have a nice appearance.

will not be as good as wood for some projects. Instead, plastic should be used in ways that take advantage of its own characteristics. For instance, plastic laminates (the materials used to cover kitchen

Unit 2: Product Design

2-9. *This table is attractive because the designer paid attention to design principles.*

Dunbar Furniture

2-10. *This table is an excellent design example. It is functional, shows a good use of glass and metal, and is beautiful.*

1. The parts of a product should look well together. This is called *unity*.

The salt shaker in Fig. 2-8 has unity because the bowl and the cap flow together in a clean, unbroken curve.

2. The shaker also has *variety* since the cap is made of stainless steel and the bowl of teakwood. The two materials are of different colors and textures, which makes the product more interesting in appearance.

3. Products should be *well proportioned*, as is the table in Fig. 2-9. Notice that the legs are of a proper size compared with the top. The table does not look awkward, as it would if the top were very heavy and supported by thin, spindly legs.

4. If all parts of the table are well proportioned, this product will have *balance*.

Unity, variety, proportion, and balance are called *principles of design* because they deal with ways of organizing the shapes and materials of products. Fig. 2-10.

DESIGN-ANALYSIS METHOD

As stated earlier, designing is a kind of planning. You should plan a project as you would plan any other kind of work. The project that you are designing should be thought of as a problem to be solved as you would solve a problem in mathematics or science. It is helpful to break the work into a series of steps to make it easier to solve. A good way of doing this is to use the design-analysis method. In order to explain this method more clearly, let's take a certain problem. Imagine that you will be designing a rack to hold a few books on your study desk. You must first state your problem so that you know exactly what you are trying to solve.

Step 1. Statement of the problem. To design a bookrack to be used on a desk.

You must next ask some questions about function and materials for the bookrack. How many books must it hold? How large are the books? Are there any

23

Part I: General Industry

special materials you should use? (Perhaps you would want to match a note pad holder or a pen set.)

Step 2. Analysis and research. (List ideas pertaining to function and materials.)

   a. Should hold six books.
   b. My books measure about 1" thick, 9" high, and 6" wide.
   c. Make of material to match my desk set.
   d. Should be easy to remove and replace books.
   e. Books shouldn't topple over when one or two are removed.
   f. Should not scratch desk top.

Step 3. Possible solutions. (Sketch four or five ideas on paper. What might this rack look like? Improve your sketches and rework some of them. Think of the visual requirements of the unit. Be inventive and original.)

These are some possibilities—

Bookends—simple, but books might fall over when one is removed.

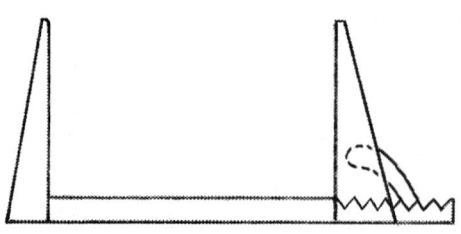

Special ratchet-locking device—good idea but complicated.

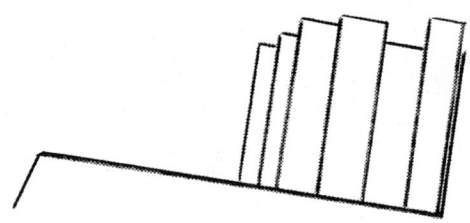

A sloping rack is a good device—gravity holds the books in place.

More ideas for the sloping bookrack—

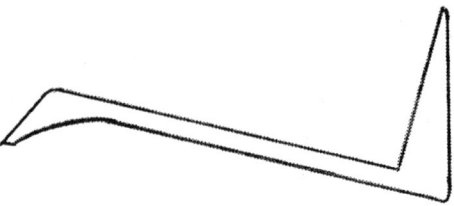

Wood—band-sawed and carved.

Carved wood and cast metal.

Bent band iron, laminated wood, or plastic.

Step 4. Experimentation. (Make a paper or wooden model of the rack. Try out some of the ideas to see if they will work.)

Step 5. Final solution. (This should be a final working sketch or drawing. From this sketch you will proceed to make the rack. Feel free to make changes in the drawing—and in the rack—as you are making the project, if you feel you can improve it. When you are finished, go back and correct the drawing. The illustration in Fig. 2-11 is the final solution for the bookrack problem.)

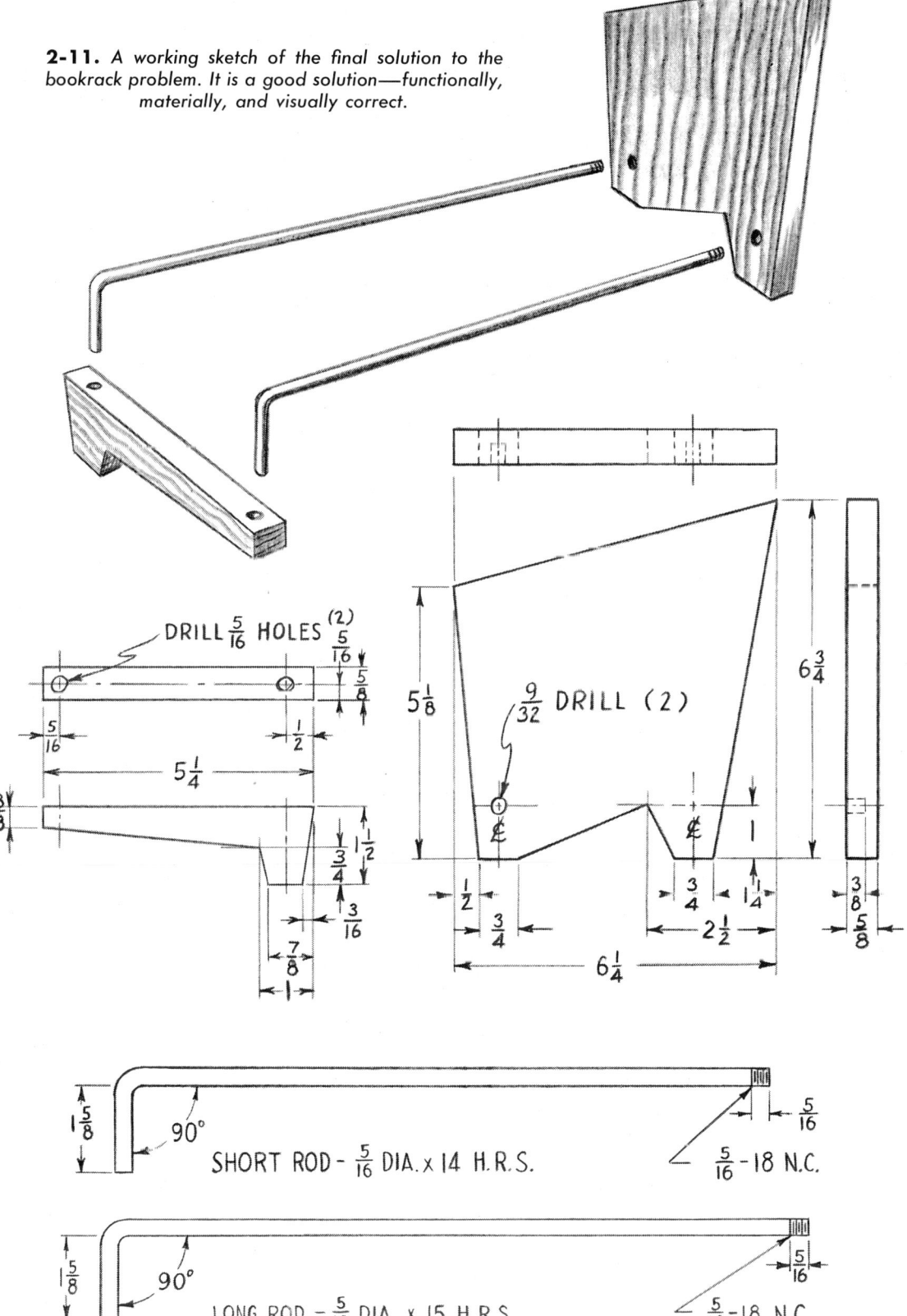

2-11. A working sketch of the final solution to the bookrack problem. It is a good solution—functionally, materially, and visually correct.

UNIT 3

Measurement

Measurement is important in daily living. All the products you use involve measurements: lumber for houses, metal in bicycles, paper in books—all must be measured before the product is sold. Milk is measured in quarts, fishing line in yards, and butter in pounds.

THE MEANING OF MEASUREMENT

Measurements are made to answer questions such as the following: How heavy is this steel bar? How long is it? How much carbon does it contain? To learn these answers, we must compare the bar to fixed, standard quantities. To measure something is to compare it with a standard unit.

Standard Units—Customary

In order to make measurements, we must have suitable units of measurement. The weight of the steel bar will be in pounds or ounces, the length in feet (') or inches ("). These are units of the *customary* (or English) system used in a few countries. All other countries including the United States, use, or are planning to use, the *metric* system, described later in this unit.

In ancient times the standard units were based upon the human body. Fig. 3-1. A cubit was the distance from the tip of the middle finger to the end of the elbow, about 18". A digit was the width of the middle finger, about $\frac{3}{4}$". But because human measurements were different from person to person, more accurate systems had to be invented.

Because of the need for accuracy, standard units of measurement were set. At the National Bureau of Standards in Washington, D.C., the standards for the inch, foot, and yard measures are available. Some other standard units are the ounce, the pound, and the gallon. The crude measuring devices of ancient times have been replaced by more accurate instruments such as the steel rule, the micrometer, and the weighing scale.

Standard Units—Metric

As said earlier, most of the world uses the metric system of measurement. This

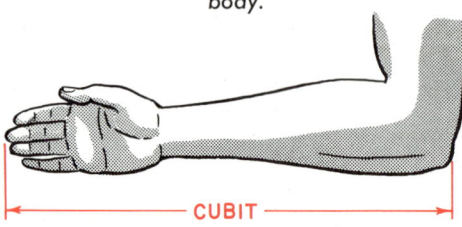

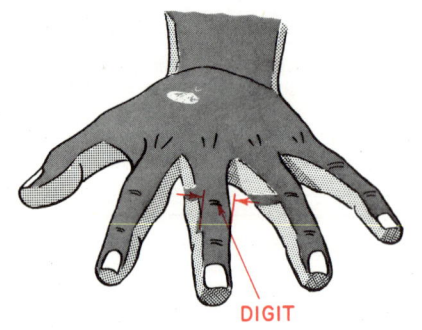

3-1. *When people first started to measure, standard units were based upon the human body.*

Unit 3: Measurement

system began in France in 1790 and is based upon the *metre*.* Originally the metre was one ten-millionth of the distance from the North Pole to the equator. Today a more accurate measure of the metre is used.

The metre is the metric unit for length. It equals about 40 inches. Units of volume (capacity) and area are based upon this unit of length. The larger and smaller measures of each unit are made by multiplying or dividing the basic units by 10 and its multiples. This feature is convenient because such calculations as dividing by 16 (to convert ounces to pounds) or by 12 (to convert inches to feet) are no longer necessary. Similar calculations in the metric system can be made by simply shifting the decimal point. Thus the metric system is a "base-10" or "decimal" system.

However, even this metric system was not perfect. Some of the measures were confusing and were not convenient for modern technology. In addition, many metric countries created their own different metric units. In 1960 a simplified metric system was developed. The name International System of Units, abbreviated "SI" (for the French, "Système International d'Unités"), was adopted for this modernized metric system.

The SI system is built upon a foundation of seven base units: metre, kilogram, second, kelvin, ampere, candela, and mole. Fig. 3-2. There are also two supplementary units, the radian and steradian, used to measure plane and solid angles. However, geometric plane angles will ordinarily continue to be measured in degrees and their decimal fractions. There are also many derived units such as the newton (to measure force) and the pascal (to measure pressure). These derived units are based upon combinations of

---

*In this book the spelling *metre* is used. It is recognized that many authors prefer the *er* spelling. There are a number of good arguments supporting both spellings. However spelled, the important thing to remember is that the symbol, *m*, remains the same.

3-2. *The metric system is built on these seven base units.*

Base Units of the SI Metric System

Unit	Symbol	Definition
metre (length)	m	The metre is equal to a specific number of wavelengths of the light given off by the atom krypton-86. Commonly used related measures are the kilometre (km) = 1000 metres; the centimetre (cm) = 0.01 (one-hundredth) metre; and the millimetre (mm) = 0.001 (one-thousandth) metre.
kilogram (mass)	kg	The kilogram is equal to the mass of the standard kilogram cylinder located at the International Bureau of Weights and Measures in France. A copy of this kilogram is located at the National Bureau of Standards in Washington, D.C. The kilogram is often used to measure what we commonly call weight. However, a weight is actually based upon mass and the pull of gravity. Common related measures are the gram (g) = 0.001 (one-thousandth) kilogram; and the milligram (mg) = 0.001 (one-thousandth) gram.

(Continued on page 28)

Part I: General Industry

Base Units of the SI Metric System (Continued)

Unit	Symbol	Definition
second (time)	s	The second is equal to a specific number of movements of the cesium atom in a device known as an atomic clock. A common related measure is the millisecond (ms) = 0.001 (one-thousandth) second. The minute, hour, day, and year are also used, although they are not SI units because they are not based upon ten.
kelvin (temperature)	K	The kelvin is equal to a specific fraction of the temperature at which water exists as a solid, liquid and vapor. This is called the triple point of water. The kelvin is used mainly for scientific measurements. For practical, everyday purposes, the degree Celsius (°C) is used. Water boils at 100°C, and it freezes at 0°C. The Celsius scale is equal to, but replaces, the old Centigrade temperature scale.
ampere (electric current)	A	The ampere is equal to the amount of current in two parallel wires one metre apart, that results in a specific force between the two wires. The milliampere (mA) = 0.001 (one-thousandth) ampere, is a common related measurement.
candela (luminous intensity)	cd	The candela is equal to the amount of light given off by platinum at its freezing point, under pressure. At this freezing point, platinum is glowing hot. The candela is used to measure an amount of light.
mole (amount of substance)	mol	The mole is equal to the number of particles contained in a specific amount of carbon. This unit is used mainly in special scientific measurements.

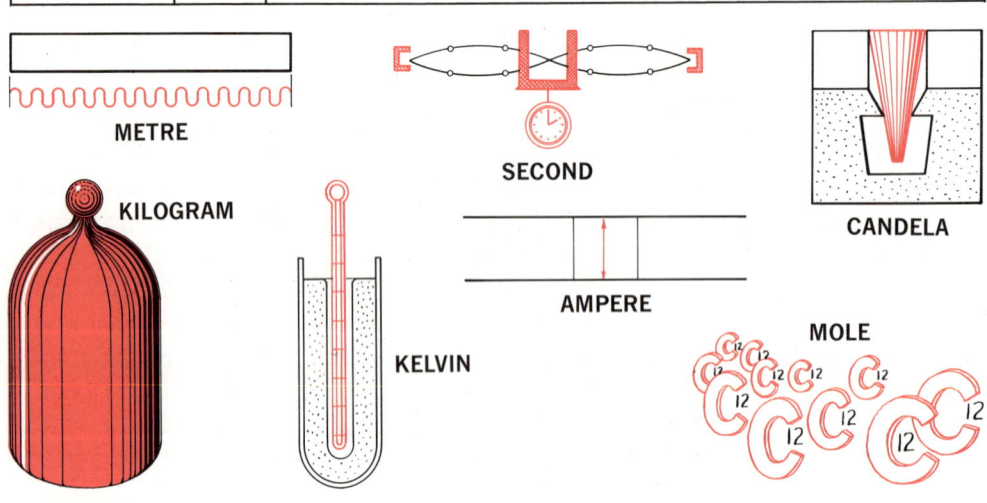

METRE

KILOGRAM

SECOND

CANDELA

KELVIN

AMPERE

MOLE

Unit 3: Measurement

base and supplementary units. But for everyday use, only four measurements are important. Fig. 3-3.
- The *metre* for length.
- The *litre* and the *cubic metre* for volume.
- The *kilogram* for mass (weight).

- Degree *Celsius* (formerly centigrade) for temperature.

Other metric measures are described and used throughout this book.

In the metric system, there are special terms or prefixes used to make calculations easier. Fig. 3-4. These are the same

3-3. *These are the units used most often in everyday life.*

Conversion Chart for Common Units

Length	1 metre (m) = 39.37 inches 25.4 millimetres (mm) = 1 inch 304 mm = 1 foot 1 kilometre (km) = 0.6 mile
Volume	1 litre (L) = 1.05 quarts [1 litre is the same as one cubic decimetre (dm^3)] 1 gallon = 3.79 litres 1 quart = 0.9 litre 1 cubic metre (m^3) = 35.3 cubic feet or 1.3 cubic yards
Weight	1 ounce = 28.35 grams (g) 1 kilogram (kg) = 2.20 pounds 1 pound = 0.45 kg 1 000 kg = 1 metric ton (t) 1 metric ton = 2204 pounds
Temperature	degree Celsius (°C) = °F x 1.8, plus 32 degree Fahrenheit (°F) = °C −32, times 0.6

3-4. *Some multiples and prefixes. These may be used with all SI metric units.*

Table of SI Unit Prefixes

Multiple or Submultiple	Prefix	Symbol	Pronunciation	Means
1 000 000 000 = 10^9	giga	G**	jig'a (a as in about)	One billion times
1 000 000 = 10^6	mega	M**	as in *mega*phone	One million times
1 000 = 10^3	kilo	k**	as in *kilo*watt	One thousand times
100 = 10^2	hecto	h	heck'toe	One hundred times
10 = 10^1	deka	da	deck'a (a as in about)	Ten times
Base unit 1 = 10^0		**		
0.1 = 10^{-1}	deci	d	as in *deci*mal	One tenth of
0.01 = 10^{-2}	centi	c**	as in *centi*pede	One hundredth of
0.001 = 10^{-3}	milli	m**	as in military	One thousandth of
0.000 001 = 10^{-6}	micro	μ**	as in microphone	One millionth of
0.000 000 001 = 10^{-9}	nano	n**	nan'oh (an as in ant)	One billionth of

*The first syllable of every prefix is accented to make sure that the prefix will keep its identity. For example, the preferred pronunciation of kilometre places the accent on the first syllable, not the second.

**Most commonly used and preferred prefixes. Centimetre is used mainly for measuring the body, clothing, sporting goods, and some household articles.

Approximate Customary—Metric Conversions

When you know:		You can find:	If you multiply by:
LENGTH	inches	millimetres	25.0
	feet	millimetres	300.0
	yards	metres	0.9
	miles	kilometres	1.6
	millimetres	inches	0.04
	metres	yards	1.1
	kilometres	miles	0.6
AREA	square inches	square centimetres	6.5
	square feet	square metres	0.09
	square yards	square metres	0.8
	square miles	square kilometres	2.6
	acres	square hectometres (hectares)	0.4
	square centimetres	square inches	0.16
	square metres	square yards	1.2
	square kilometres	square miles	0.4
	hectares	acres	2.5
MASS	ounces	grams	28.0
	pounds	kilograms	0.45
	tons	metric tons	0.9
	grams	ounces	0.04
	kilograms	pounds	2.2
	metric tons	tons	1.1
LIQUID VOLUME	ounces	millilitres	30.0
	pints	litres	0.47
	quarts	litres	0.95
	gallons	litres	3.8
	millilitres	ounces	0.03
	litres	pints	2.1
	litres	quarts	1.06
	litres	gallons	0.26
TEMPERATURE	degrees Fahrenheit	degrees Celsius	0.6 (after subtracting 32)
	degrees Celsius	degrees Fahrenheit	1.8 (then add 32)
POWER	horsepower	kilowatts (kw)	0.75
	kilowatts	horsepower	1.34
PRESSURE	pounds per square inch (psi)	kilopascals (kPa)	6.9
	kPa	psi	0.15
VELOCITY (SPEED)	miles per hour (mph)	kilometres per hour	1.6
	km/h	mph	0.6

3-5. Use this chart to convert from customary to metric units or from metric to customary units.

whether used with the gram or the metre or any other unit. For example, the prefix *kilo* means "1000." Thus a kilogram is 1000 grams; a kilometre is 1000 metres. For everyday measurements the prefixes *kilo, centi,* and *milli* are used most. Other information on the metric system is found in Fig. 3-5 and in the Appendix.

Unit 3: Measurement

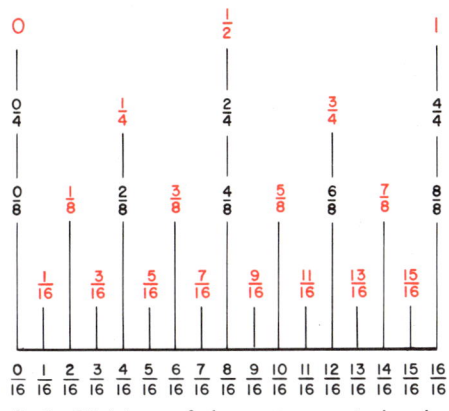

3-6. *Divisions of the customary-inch rule.*

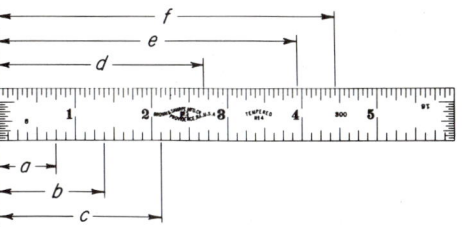

3-7. *Measure the lengths of the lettered lines on this six-inch rule.*

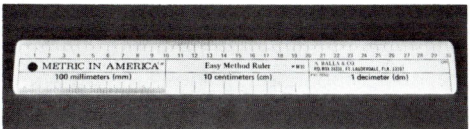

3-8. *Divisions of the metric rule. This rule is marked in centimetres. Others are marked in millimetres.*

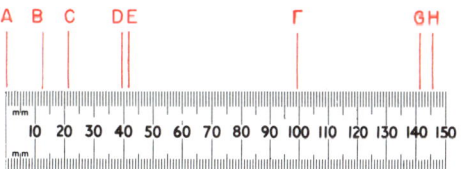

3-9. *Measure these metric lengths.*

MEASURING DEVICES

In order to measure simply and accurately, instruments are needed. There are many devices for measuring. Here are some examples.

Linear Measurement

The rule (often called a "scale") is used to make linear measurements such as length, width, or height. Most customary rules are divided fractionally. In woodworking, the bench rule is accurate to $1/16''$, the metalworker's rule to $1/64''$. Note the divisions on the one-inch rule shown in Fig. 3-6. The longest line between the 0 and the 1 is the $1/2''$ mark. The next longest lines are the $1/4''$ marks. The shortest lines are the $1/16''$ marks. Note that $8/16$ equals $4/8$ or $2/4$ or $1/2$.

To measure a line exactly you can count the number of sixteenths. In Fig. 3-7 line d is eleven sixteenths past the 2'' mark; it is $2 \, 11/16''$ long. Read the other measurements in Fig. 3-7.

Metric rules are also read by counting the divisions. These rules usually come in metre, half-metre, 300 millimetre and 150 millimetre lengths. Longer metric tape measures are also available. Remember that a metre is divided into 100 centimetres and 1000 millimetres. The rule is usually marked in one of two ways: centimetre (cm) divisions (1, 2, 3, 4, 5, etc.) or millimetre (mm) divisions (10, 20, 30, 40, 50, etc.). Remember that 10 mm equal 1 cm, and that each of the divisions between centimetres equals one millimetre. Fig. 3-8. Note that one inch equals 25.4 millimetres (or about 25 millimetres). Two inches equal 50.8 millimetres (or about 50 millimetres).

To read the metric rule in Fig. 3-9 look at distance AB. Notice that it is 2 mm spaces or divisions past the 10 mark. This means that line AB is 12 mm long. Always give the measurement as "12 mm," not "2 cm, 2 mm." Measure the other lines to make sure you know how to read the metric scale. Remember that in the metric system, shop measurements are usually given in millimetres.

Weight Measurement

When we weigh something, we balance it against standard units of weight. Actually, what we are doing is comparing the mass of the object with the mass of

31

Part I: General Industry

the standard unit. You can use an ordinary weighing scale to weigh yourself. Other kinds of scales are used for technical and scientific purposes. Fig. 3-10.

Customary scales weigh in ounces and pounds; metric scales weigh in grams and kilograms.

Temperature Measurement

A thermometer is used to measure temperature. The U.S. customary temperature unit is the degree Fahrenheit (°F). The metric unit is the degree Celsius (°C). A comparison of these temperature units is shown in Fig. 3-11. Other metric temperatures are shown elsewhere in this book.

ACCURACY

It is hard to get exact measurements of objects. For example, you could measure the diameter of a steel rod with a woodworker's rule and get one figure. You could measure it with calipers and a steel rule and get a more accurate figure. Finally you could use a micrometer and get a more accurate measure still. In industry there are also electronic measuring instruments which precisely measure complex shapes. Fig. 3-12.

With precision instruments, measurements can be made with remarkable accuracy. The micrometer is an example of such an instrument. It can make measurements finer than $\frac{1}{20}$ the thickness of this page.

Study the micrometer in Fig. 3-13. Each vertical line on the sleeve (or hub) is equal to 0.025″ (25 thousandths of an inch). Every fourth vertical line is numbered, indicating 0.100″ (100 thousandths, or $\frac{1}{10}$ of an inch). The scale on the thimble is divided into 25 equal parts, each representing 0.001″ (one thousandth of an inch). To use the micrometer, place the object to be measured between the anvil and the spindle and gently draw the measuring surfaces together by rotating the thimble. Do not force the thimble.

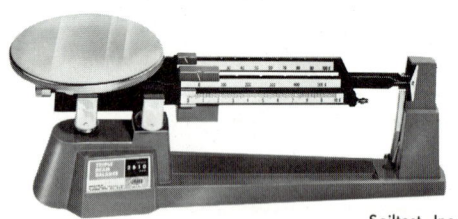

Soiltest, Inc.

3-10. This balance is used in school science and industrial arts laboratories. It weighs accurately in grams.

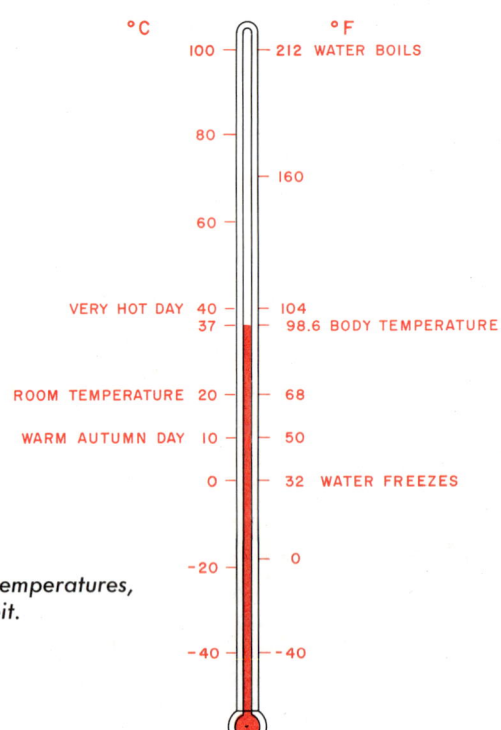

3-11. Comparative everyday temperatures, Celsius and Fahrenheit.

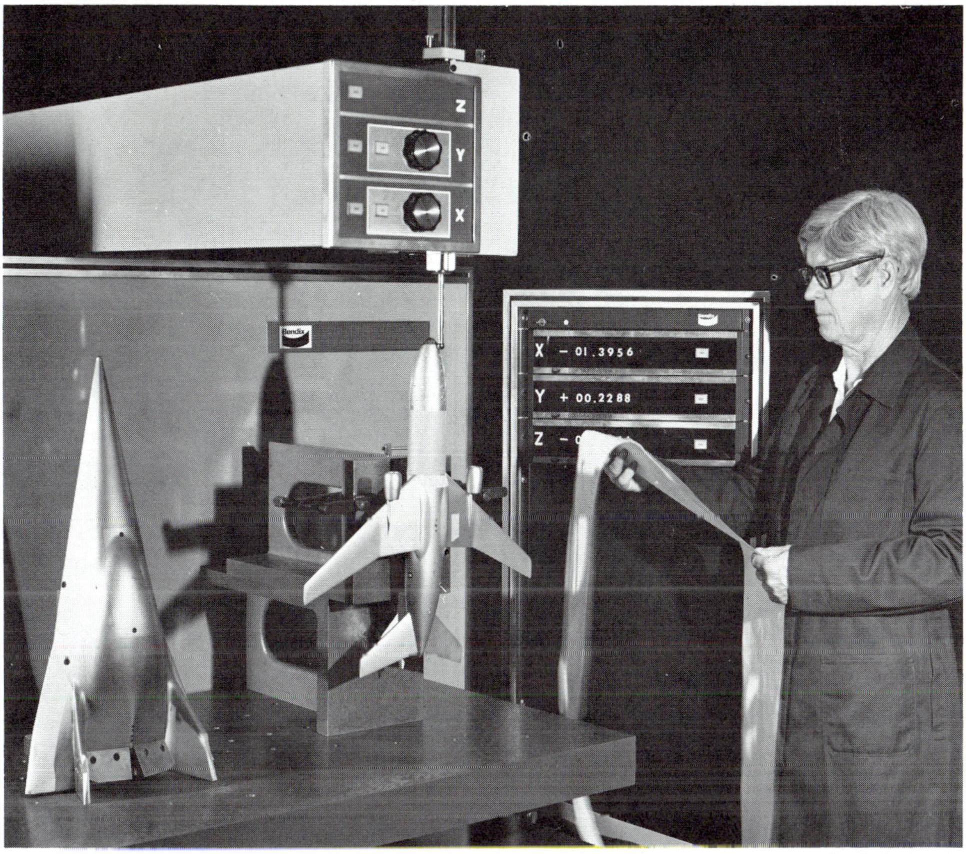

Unit 3: Measurement

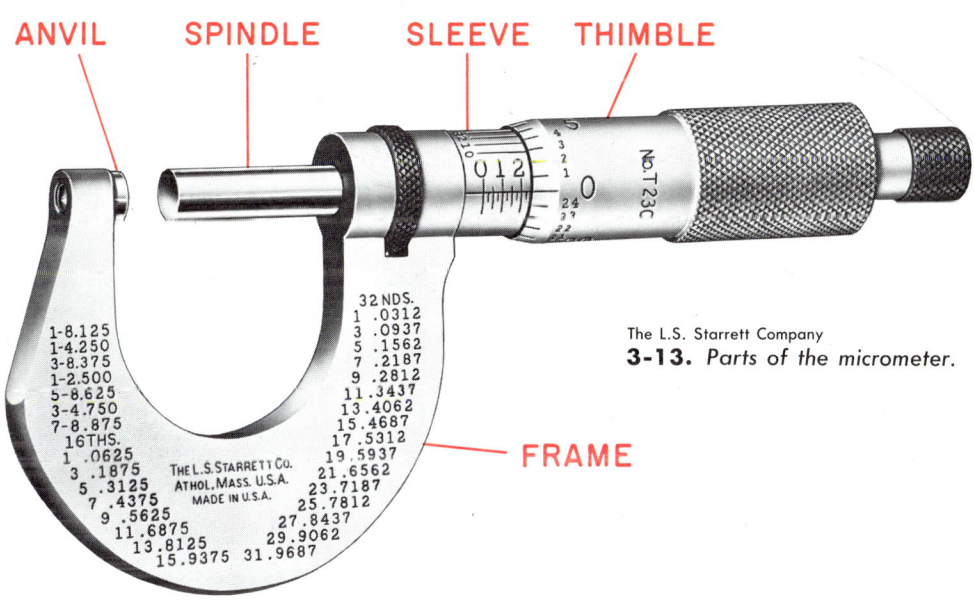

Bendix Corporation
3-12. Free curve shapes of wind tunnel models are accurately measured on this 3-axis machine.

The L.S. Starrett Company
3-13. Parts of the micrometer.

33

Part I: General Industry

The following example will show you how to read a micrometer. (Refer to Fig. 3-14.)

1. The number 1 line on the sleeve is visible, and it equals 0.100″.

2. Three additional lines on the sleeve are visible, each representing 0.025″; 3 x 0.025″ equals 0.075″.

3. Line 3 on the thimble is lined up with the horizontal line on the sleeve. Each line represents 0.001″; 3 x 0.001″ equals 0.003″.

4. The total reading is 0.178″ (0.100 + 0.075 + 0.003).

To read a metric micrometer (Fig. 3-15) do the following:

1. The number 5 line on the sleeve is visible and equals 5 mm.

2. One short line past the number 5 line is visible. This equals 0.5 mm.

3. Line 28 on the thimble is lined up with the horizontal line on the sleeve. Each line represents 0.010 mm; and 28 x 0.010 = 0.28 mm.

4. The total reading is 5.78 mm (5 + 0.5 + 0.28).

The uses of other measuring instruments, both customary and metric, are covered elsewhere in this book.

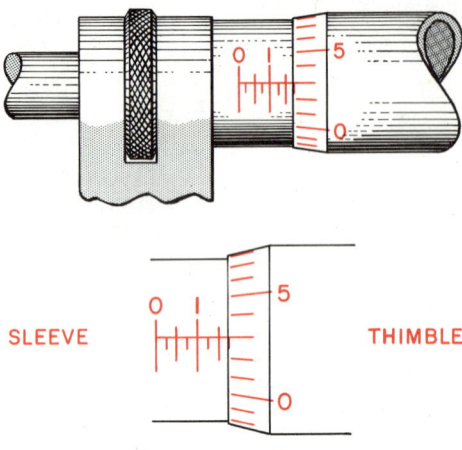

SLEEVE   THIMBLE

READING: 00.178″

3-14. *Reading a customary micrometer.*

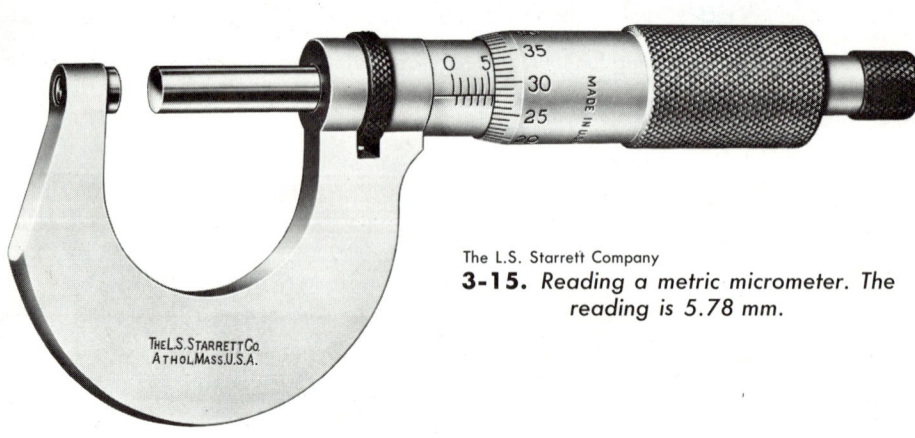

The L.S. Starrett Company
3-15. *Reading a metric micrometer. The reading is 5.78 mm.*

UNIT 4

Planning Procedures

After you have designed a product and completed the drawings, you must decide how you are going to make the product. Fig. 4-1. This is necessary to avoid mistakes and waste of materials. Industry does this through very careful tooling and control procedures in production. You must do this in the shop by preparing a plan of procedure for your work. There are four main parts to this plan.

1. Bill of materials. List all of the items that will actually be part of the project. Be sure to use their right names. Look at the supply catalogs and materials lists in your shop to find these correct terms.

2. List of tools and machines. All of the necessary tools, machines, and other equipment should be listed. This can save you time later if you discover that you don't have a needed tool or machine in the shop.

3. Outline of steps to follow in making the project. To make your outline, first study the individual parts of the project. Next, think of what you must do to make each part. Then think about the assembly and finishing of the project. Listing all of these operations or tasks in proper order will give you the outline. Have your teacher check your list. Steps 1, 2, and 3 are usually placed on a planning sheet, shown in Fig. 4-2.

4. Working drawing. This drawing is necessary for you to learn the sizes and shapes of the project's parts. Both detail and assembly drawings are generally used. Figs. 4-3 and 4-4.

The plan of procedure shown in Fig. 4-2 would be used to make one of the bookracks discussed in Unit 2. Study the differences between these steps and those in Unit 109, "Mass Production In the School," where a project has been planned for mass production.

4-1. *Both school projects and industrial products must have a plan of procedure.*

Georg Jensen Silversmiths, Ltd.
Copenhagen, Denmark

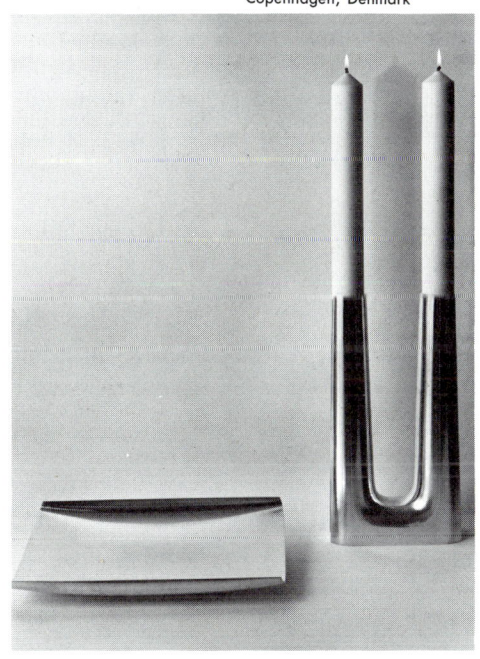

35

Part I: General Industry

Planning Sheet

Name.. Grade..............

............Bookrack..
(Name of project)   (Date started)   (Date completed)

Bill of Materials:

No.	Size T	Size W	Size L	Name of part	Material	Unit cost	Total cost
1	5/8	6	8	Headpiece	Walnut		
1	5/8	1 3/4	5 1/2	Footpiece	Walnut		
1	5/16 D	—	15	Long Rod	CRS		
1	5/16 D	—	14	Short Rod	CRS		
4	5/16 D			Felt Dots			

Tools and Machines: Bench rule, pencil, awl, back saw, band saw, plane, disc sander, sandpaper, drill press, hacksaw, file, bending jig, steel wool, wipe-on finish, lacquer, lacquer thinner, brushes, die, diestock, felt dots.

Outline of Procedure or Steps:
1. Layout and cut wooden parts to shape.
2. Sand surfaces and edges of wooden parts.
3. Drill holes in wooden parts.
4. Apply finish to wooden parts.
5. Cut metal rods to length; remove burrs.
6. Make 90-degree bends in metal rods.
7. Cut threads in metal rods.
8. Clean rods with steel wool and thinner.
9. Apply lacquer to metal rods.
10. Assemble headpiece, footpiece, and metal rods.
11. Place felt dots in position.

4-2. A sample planning sheet.

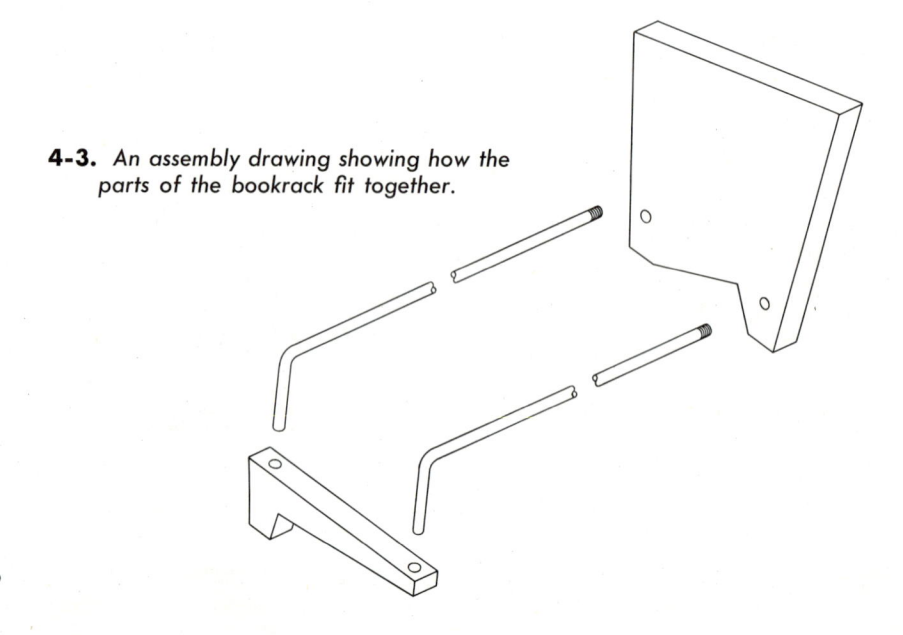

4-3. An assembly drawing showing how the parts of the bookrack fit together.

Unit 4: Planning Procedures

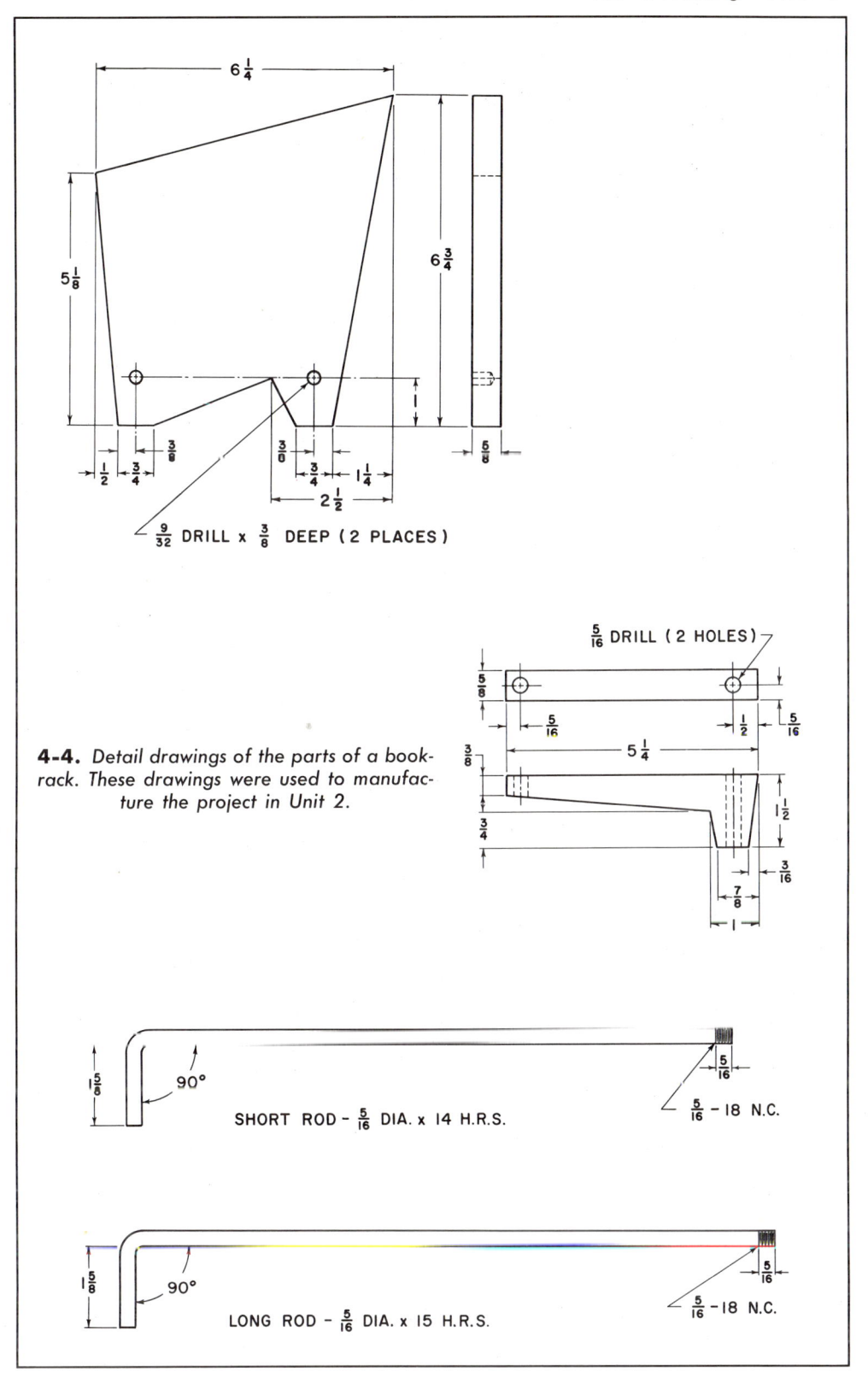

4-4. Detail drawings of the parts of a bookrack. These drawings were used to manufacture the project in Unit 2.

$\frac{9}{32}$ DRILL x $\frac{3}{8}$ DEEP (2 PLACES)

$\frac{5}{16}$ DRILL (2 HOLES)

SHORT ROD - $\frac{5}{16}$ DIA. x 14 H.R.S.
$\frac{5}{16}$ - 18 N.C.

LONG ROD - $\frac{5}{16}$ DIA. x 15 H.R.S.
$\frac{5}{16}$ - 18 N.C.

UNIT 5

Safety

Safety in the school shop, at home, and in industry is important because it protects people. If people become careless about safety, they can lose eyes, fingers—or lives.

This is why industry is so concerned about safety. Fig. 5-1. Every three minutes there are over 350 industrial accidents in this country, some of them fatal. Many hours of work are lost, and some workers are crippled for life. Safety programs are a part of every industry, and workers are reminded to develop safe work habits. Fig. 5-2. People in all industries must practice safety. Fig. 5-3.

As a part of your work in this course, you too must learn to work safely. A careless act can cause you to lose an eye or a finger. Observe all safety rules in the school shop, and be sure you have received proper instructions before operating a machine or using a tool. Remember the ABCs of safety—ALWAYS BE CAREFUL. Here is a list of general safety rules for you to follow. Special safety precautions are listed in other sections of this book.

1. Wear the right clothes for the job. Ties and jewelry should be removed and sleeves rolled up. An apron and approved safety glasses must be worn. Fig. 5-4. Wear special protective clothing when working with hot metals or acids.

2. Know your tools and equipment before you use them. Use the proper tool for each job. Always follow instructions for tool use, and when in doubt, ask your teacher. Fig. 5-5.

3. Don't run or act foolishly in the shop. Practical jokes and pranks often lead to accidents; so avoid them.

4. Keep your shop and work area clean. An orderly shop is a safe one. Pick up tools and scraps of material, which might cause falls. Wipe up water or oil spills. Report broken or unsafe tools to your teacher.

5-1. *People in industry must practice safety in order to protect employees. This technician works with high-pressure gases. Notice how well protected he is.*
NASA

Unit 5: Safety

5-2. Safety posters are a constant reminder to develop safe work habits. Read and remember the safety posters you see in your shop.

Part I: General Industry

5-3. Pilots wear protective clothing and practice safety in their flying.

NASA

5-4. Wear approved safety glasses at all times when you are working in the shop. The lenses must be at least 3.0 mm thick and be specially hardened. The frames must also be of special design and strength.

Jackson Products Company

5-5. Know your equipment before you use it.

Rockwell-Delta Company

Unit 5: Safety

Eagle Manufacturing Company
5-6. Container for oily wastes.

Eagle Manufacturing Company
5-7a. Lab can.

Eagle Manufacturing Company
5-7b. Liquid disposal can.

5. Place oily rags and other materials which can easily catch fire in special containers. These should be emptied daily. Fig. 5-6. Store flammable liquids in small safety lab cans. Fig. 5-7a. Do not store these dangerous liquids in large, five-gallon cans. All flammable liquid waste should be placed in safety disposal cans. Fig. 5-7b. Never pour such liquids down a sink drain.

6. Use common sense when working in the shop. Carry tools safely, and use them so that a slip of a tool won't injure you or your neighbor. If you have an accident, no matter how small, report it right away so that you can get first aid. Most accidents can be prevented if you think about what you are doing.

In 1970 Congress passed the Occupational Safety and Health Act. The purpose of this act is to make sure that people will have safe and healthful working conditions. Safety and health standards have been set up. These must be obeyed by all employees and employers.

The standards cover all types of safety, from safety glasses and ear protection to the height of railings on factory stairways. Fig. 5-8. School shops are also affected by OSHA standards. A typical OSHA safety checklist is shown in Fig. 5-9. How does your school shop measure up?

5-8. Wear ear protection when working near noisy equipment.

Jackson Products Company

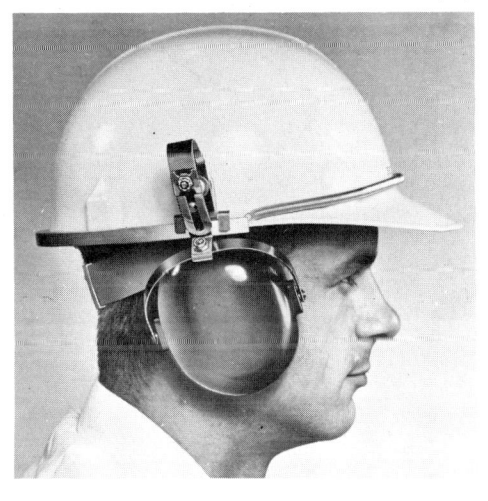

41

Part I: General Industry

OSHA Safety Checklist

Hand and Portable Power Tools

1. All hand and portable power tools are in good operating condition: no defects in wiring; equipped with ground wires. — Yes / No
2. All portable equipment is equipped with necessary guarding devices. — Yes / No
3. All compressed air equipment used for cleaning operations is regulated at 30 psi or less; chip guarding and personal protective equipment are provided. — Yes / No

Machine Guarding and Mechanical Safety

1. Every production machine has been inspected as to the following items, all found to be in satisfactory operating condition:
   a) Cleanliness of machine and area — Yes / No
   b) Securely attached to floor — Yes / No
   c) Operations guarded — Yes / No
   d) Illumination — Yes / No
   e) Effective cutoff devices — Yes / No
   f) Noise level — Yes / No
   g) Adjustment — Yes / No
   h) Material flow — Yes / No

Material Hazards

1. All hazardous gases, liquids, and other materials are properly labeled and stored. — Yes / No
2. Areas where hazardous materials are in use are fire-safe and restricted to authorized employees. — Yes / No
3. Where X-ray is used, the area is properly shielded and dosimeters are used and processed for all authorized employees. — Yes / No
4. Protective clothing is worn by employees when oxidizing agents are being used. — Yes / No
5. All hazard areas are posted with NO SMOKING signs. — Yes / No
6. All areas where caustics or corrosives are used have been provided adequately with eye fountains and deluge showers. — Yes / No

5-9. Checklists like this one are used to find out if OSHA safety rules are being followed.

DISCUSSION TOPICS AND ACTIVITIES

Part 1—General Industry
Unit 1
　1. List four objectives for a general industry course.
Unit 2
　1. What are the three design requirements?
　2. List the four design elements.
　3. Make a bulletin board display illustrating one or more of the principles of design.
　4. Design some simple project using the design-analysis method.
Unit 3
　1. What is measurement?
　2. Select four small pieces of wood. Measure these in inches *and* in millimetres.
　3. What is the smallest inch division on a woodworker's rule? On a metalworker's rule?

Units 1-5: Discussion Topics and Activities

    4. What are the seven base units of the metric system?
    5. Approximately how many millimetres are in an inch?

Unit 4
    1. List the four parts of a plan of procedure.

Unit 5
    1. What is the ABC of safety?
    2. List six important general safety rules.
    3. What does OSHA stand for?

PART II
Graphic Communications

Section 1–Drawing

Unit 6   Introduction to Drawing

Unit 7   Tools and Instruments

Unit 8   Lines, Symbols, and Geometry

Unit 9   Sketching

Unit 10   Lettering

Unit 11   Multiview Drawings

Unit 12   Sectional and Auxiliary Views

Unit 13   Pictorial Drawings

Unit 14   Dimensioning

Unit 15   Metric Dimensioning

Unit 16   Detail and Assembly Drawings

Unit 17   Building Construction Drawing

Unit 18   Printmaking

Discussion Topics and Activities

UNIT 6

Introduction to Drawing

There are about 12 000 parts in the average car. Just think how hard it would be if the people who design and build cars had to use words alone to describe the size and shape of these parts.

No product, be it motor car or missile, could be made without accurate drawings. And the more complex the product, the more drawings are needed—about 14 000 of them to build a car. Some of these are body drawings, which picture sheet metal surfaces. Others are mechanical drawings, which show the size and shape of mechanical parts and assemblies. There are also drawings which show the tools needed to make the various parts. The process of making these drawings is called *drafting*.

In a sense, drafting is a *language*. As a matter of fact, you might call it picture writing. You can see many examples of this in everyday life. One example of picture writing is the international traffic symbol. This kind of symbol gives directions to the motorist without having to use words. In this way you can read the signs in any country of the world without having to know the country's language. Fig. 6-1. Pictures or symbols are just as important in drawings. You will learn about many symbols that are used to make drawings accurate and easy to understand.

6-1. *International traffic signs use no words, just symbols, to give directions. Here the meaning of each symbol is given.*

45

Part II: Graphic Communications

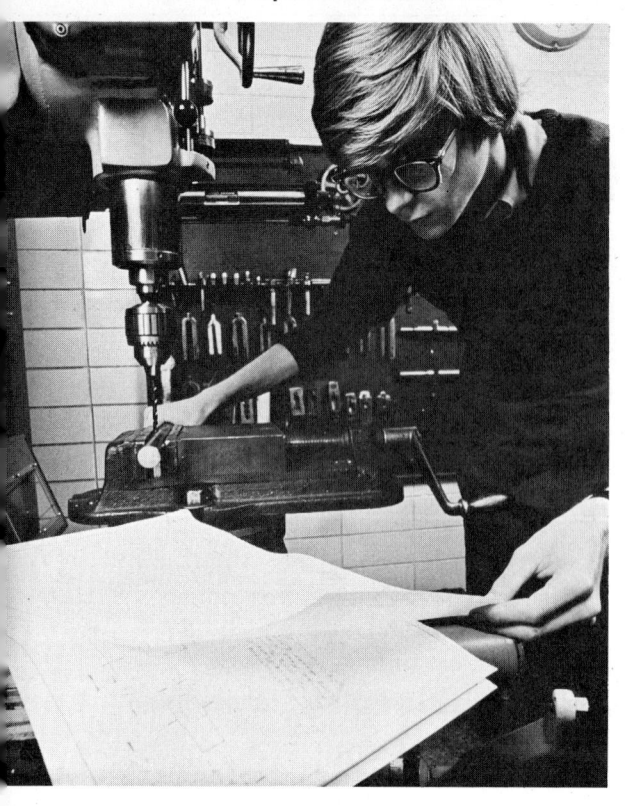

Teledyne Post, Des Plaines, IL
6-2. *This machine shop student is checking his drawing before drilling a hole in a metal part.*

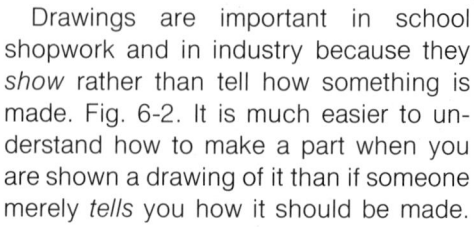

Drawings are important in school shopwork and in industry because they *show* rather than tell how something is made. Fig. 6-2. It is much easier to understand how to make a part when you are shown a drawing of it than if someone merely *tells* you how it should be made.

Drawings show the *shape* and the *size* of the object to be made. The lines of a drawing show the shape, and the size is shown by numbers on the drawing. These numbers are called *dimensions.* Fig. 6-3.

In this section you will learn how to make and read many different kinds of drawings. They include pictorials, sections, and multiview and architectural drawings. You will learn how to use instruments and to make blueprints. Fig. 6-4.

Neatness and accuracy are important if you are to make good drawings. The drawing class you take in school may lead you to a career as a drafter. Fig. 6-5. See Unit 110 for more information on careers in drafting.

Teledyne Post, Des Plaines, IL
6-3. *This architectural drawing shows the shape and size of a house by using lines and dimensions.*

Unit 6: Introduction to Drawing

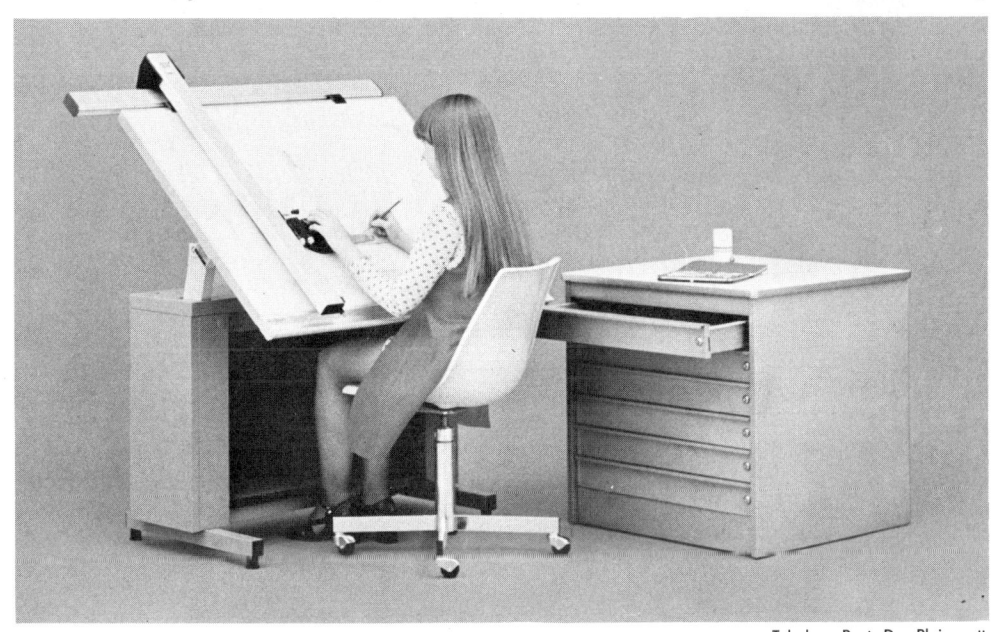

Teledyne Post, Des Plaines, IL
6-4. You will learn how to use drafting machines and other instruments in your study of drawing.

Teledyne Post, Des Plaines, IL
6-5. Your course in drawing may lead to a career in drafting.

47

UNIT 7

Tools and Instruments

Drawing is putting ideas on paper in a graphic or picture form. This unit shows and describes some of the equipment needed to do this.

Drawing boards, Fig. 7-1, provide a flat, smooth surface for drawing. They are made of wood, such as pine or bass, with straight working edges. Some boards have special metal inserts in the working edges to keep them true (square). Sometimes a drawing table becomes the drawing surface. See Fig. 6-4. Drawing boards should be kept free of nicks, dents, and gouges for good drawing quality.

T squares are used for drawing straight horizontal lines. They are also used as guides for holding other instruments, such as triangles. T squares have two

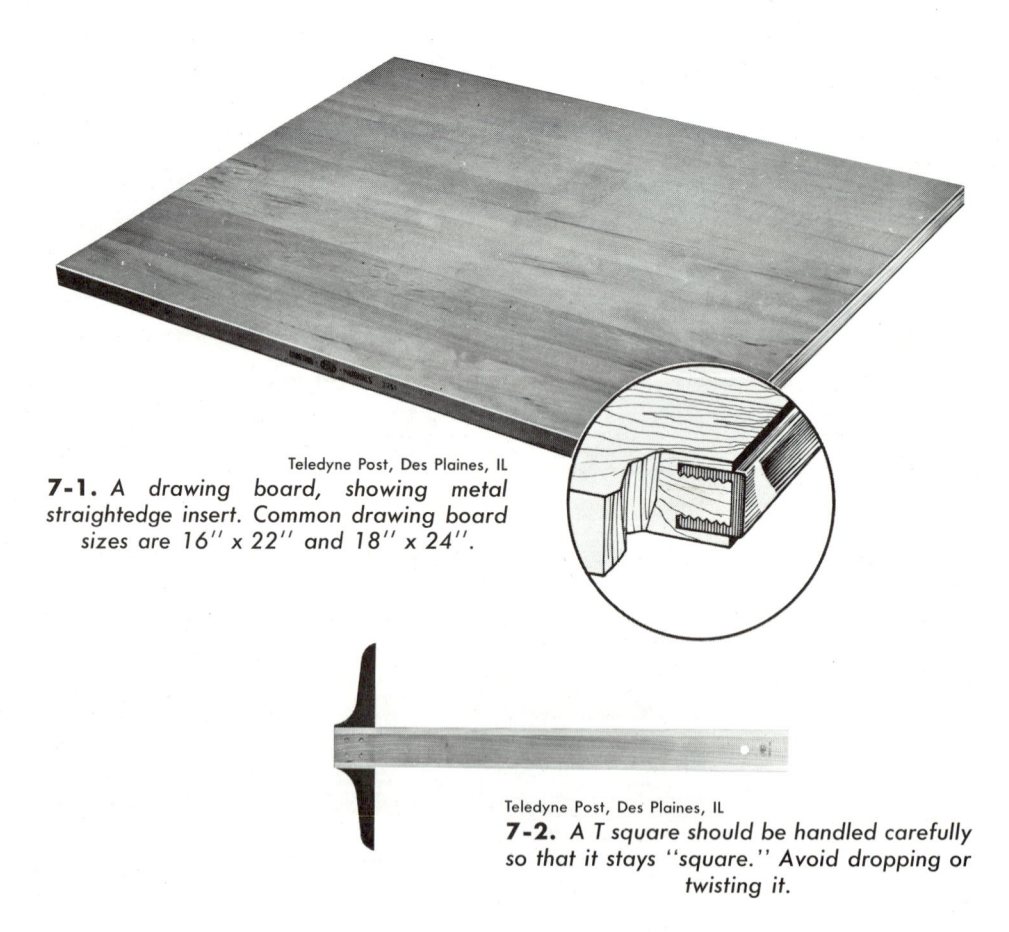

Teledyne Post, Des Plaines, IL
7-1. *A drawing board, showing metal straightedge insert. Common drawing board sizes are 16" x 22" and 18" x 24".*

Teledyne Post, Des Plaines, IL
7-2. *A T square should be handled carefully so that it stays "square." Avoid dropping or twisting it.*

48

Unit 7: Tools and Instruments

parts, the head and the blade. These are firmly fastened at right angles and are made of wood. Better quality T squares have a blade with plastic edges which resist nicks and provide a truer drawing edge. Fig. 7-2.

Triangles are used to draw vertical and inclined (oblique) lines. The two main types of triangles are the 30° x 60° and the 45°. Fig. 7-3. The 30° x 60° triangle has a 90° angle, a 30° angle, and a 60° angle. The 45° triangle has one 90° angle and two 45° angles. These can be used in combination to form angles of 15° and 75°. Fig. 7-4. To form angles of other sizes, use the protractor and combination triangle. Fig. 7-5.

Irregular curves are used to draw curved shapes which cannot be drawn with other instruments. These tools are

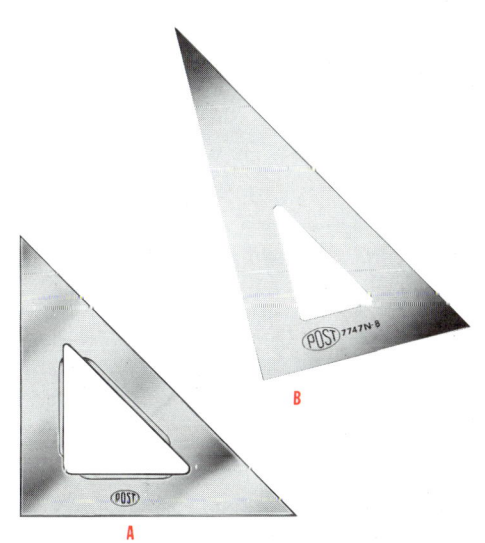

Teledyne Post, Des Plaines, IL
7-3. *Triangles: (A) 45° (B) 30° x 60°. Can you identify all of the angles?*

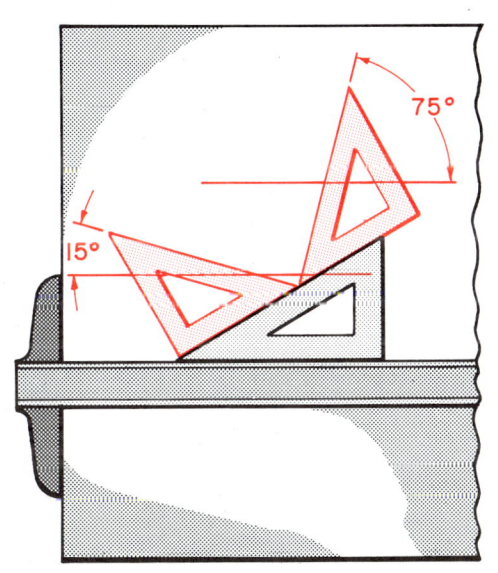

7-4. *Using the triangles to lay out 15° and 75° angles.*

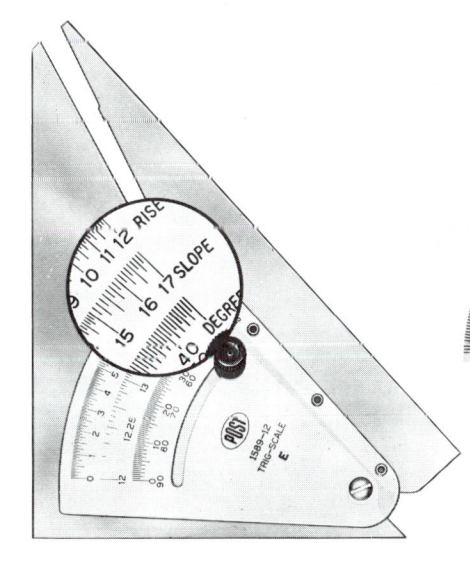

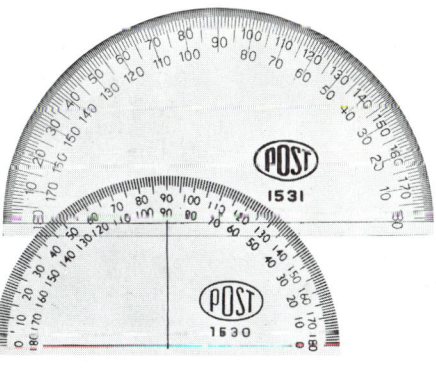

Teledyne Post, Des Plaines, IL
7-5. *The protractor and the combination triangle are used to lay out angles which cannot be formed by triangles.*

49

Part II: Graphic Communications

made of plastic or wood and are available in many styles and sizes. Fig. 7-6. The instrument is used to connect points which have been laid out in a curve. Lay the instrument over at least three of the points and draw the line. Continue until the curve is complete. Fig. 7-7.

Drafting scales are important tools for the drafter. They are used for laying out distances and dimensions on drawings. These scales are made in flat or triangular shapes with many different markings, or *graduations*. These graduations are different for each of the three main types of drafting scales: the architect's, the civil engineer's, and the mechanical engi-

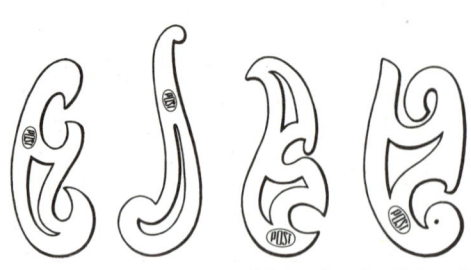

Teledyne Post, Des Plaines, IL
7-6. *Irregular, or French, curves.*

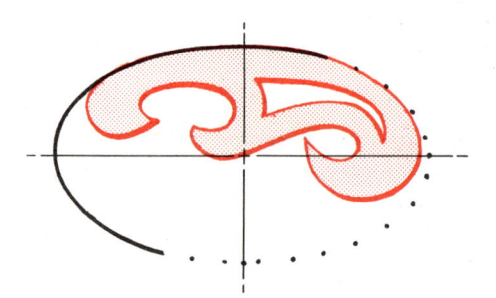

7-7. *Using the irregular curve.*

Architect's Scales

Scale	Meaning	
16	1' = 1'0''	full size
3	3'' = 1'0''	¼ size
1½	1½'' = 1'0''	⅛ size
1	1'' = 1'0''	1/12 size
¾	¾'' = 1'0''	1/16 size
½	½'' = 1'0''	1/24 size
⅜	⅜'' = 1'0''	1/32 size
¼	¼'' = 1'0''	1/48 size
3/16	3/16'' = 1'0''	1/64 size
⅛	⅛'' = 1'0''	1/96 size
3/32	3/32'' = 1'0''	1/128 size

7-9. *This chart shows the various architectural scales.*

7-8. *Drafting scales are available in many sizes and shapes. The architect's scale, commonly used in the school shop, is shown here.*

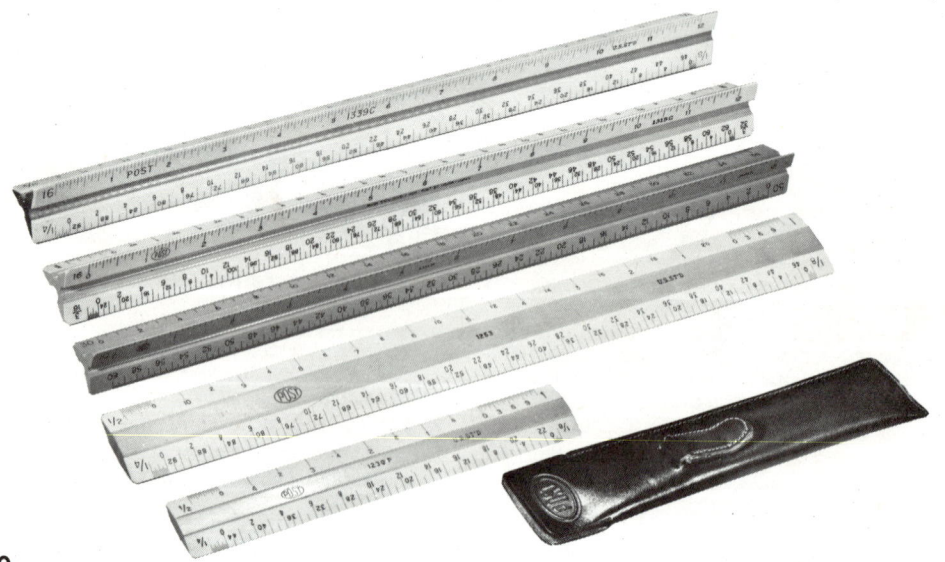

Teledyne Post, Des Plaines, IL

Unit 7: Tools and Instruments

neer's. The wood or plastic triangle shaped architect's scale is commonly used in the school. The architect's scale is used to make working drawings of buildings and machine parts. Fig. 7-8. All scales on this tool are based upon the foot. For example, a ¾ scale means that ¾″ = 1′0″, giving a ¹⁄₁₆ size drawing. Note that it does not mean ¾ size. A scale of ¾″ = 1″ means ¾ size. Other scales on this instrument are shown in Fig. 7-9.

To use this instrument, study the drawing in Fig. 7-10. The distance to the left of the zero mark represents one foot. The numbered divisions to the right of the zero also represent one foot. To measure 2′6″, you must pick up distances on both sides of the zero mark, as shown in the drawing. Fig. 7-10 shows a ¾ scale. For drawing buildings and house plans, the ¼ or ⅛ scales are often used.

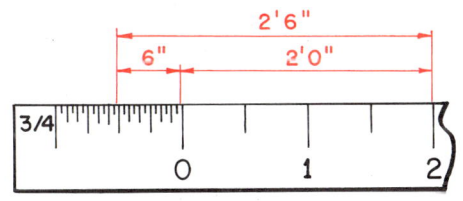

Metric scales will be very important as the United States becomes a metric nation. These scales are used exactly as one would use a customary-inch scale. Fig. 7-11. The metric scale ratios are in some cases identical to the customary. In other cases, they are close. For example, ½″ = 1′ scale means a ratio of 1:24 (1″ = 24″). The metric replacement scale is 1:25 (1 mm = 25 mm). The common customary-inch scales are shown with their metric replacements in Fig. 7-12.

Pencils used for drawing are usually the common wood type, but mechanical models are also used. Fig. 7-13. Pencil

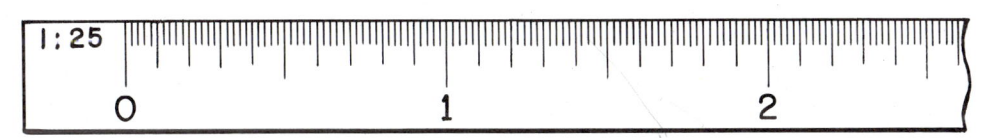

7-10. Reading the architect's scale. Note that you must pick up distances on both sides of the zero mark.

7-11. A metric drafting scale.

7-12. Common customary-inch scales and their metric replacements.

Customary and Metric Scales

Customary Scale (inch/inch)	Means	Metric Scale (mm/mm)
12:12	12″ = 1′0″ full size	1:1
6:12	6″ = 1′0″ half size	1:2
		1:3*
3:12	3″ = 1′0″ quarter size	1:5
1:12	1″ = 1′0″	1:10
¾:12	¾″ = 1′0″	1:20
½:12	½″ = 1′0″	1:25
¼:12	¼″ = 1′0″	1:50
⅛:12	⅛″ = 1′0″	1:100
¹⁄₁₆:12	¹⁄₁₆″ = 1′0″	1:200
¹⁄₃₂:12	¹⁄₃₂″ = 1′0″	1:500

*Available, but not preferred.

Part II: Graphic Communications

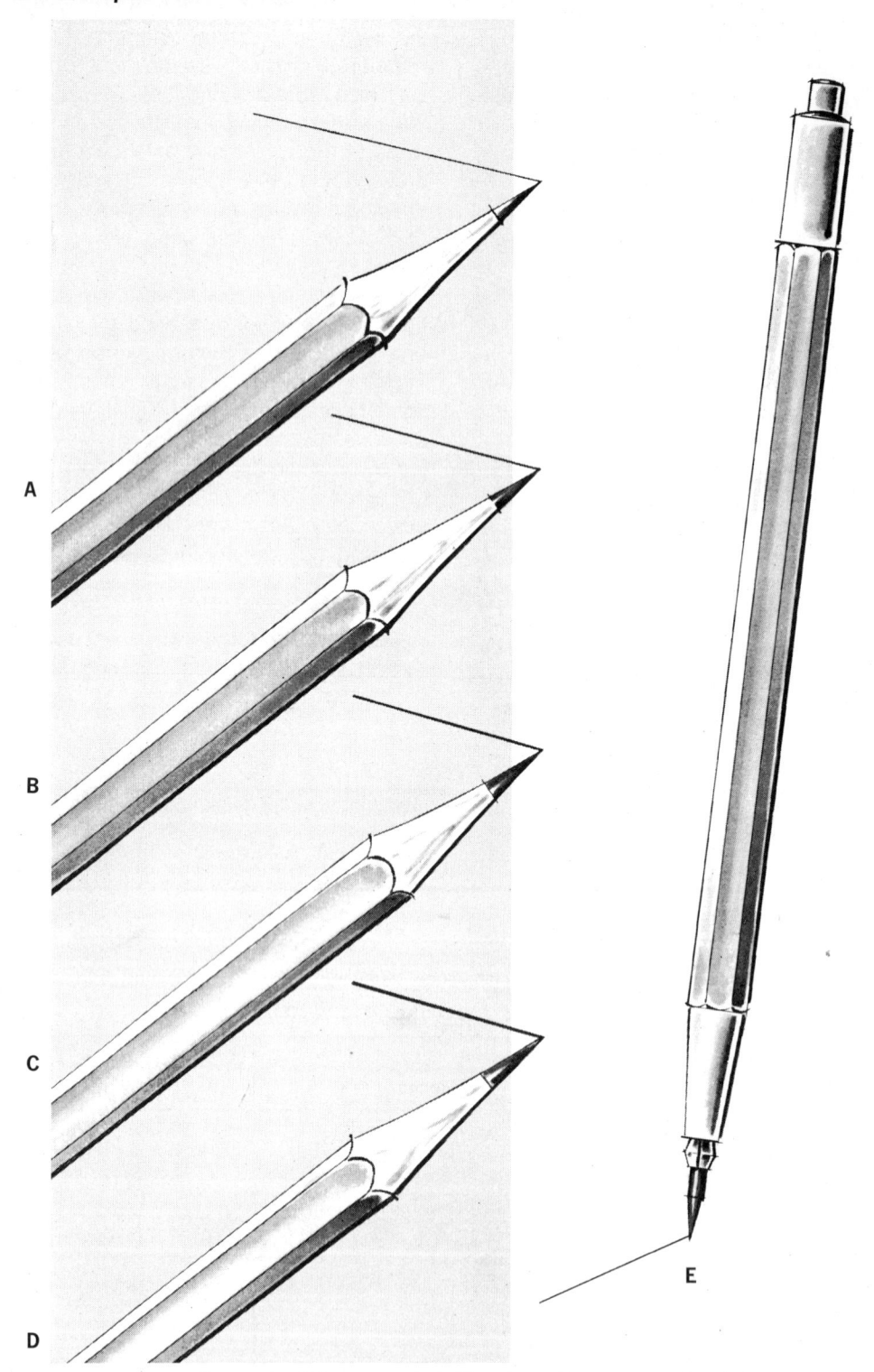

7-13. Drawing pencils come in different grades of hardness. Four common hardnesses are shown here: (A) 4H, (B) 2H, (C) H, (D) HB. A mechanical drawing pencil is also shown (E).

Unit 7: Tools and Instruments

7-14. A sanding pod. 
Teledyne Post, Des Plaines, IL

7-15. Mechanical pencil pointer.
Teledyne Post, Des Plaines, IL

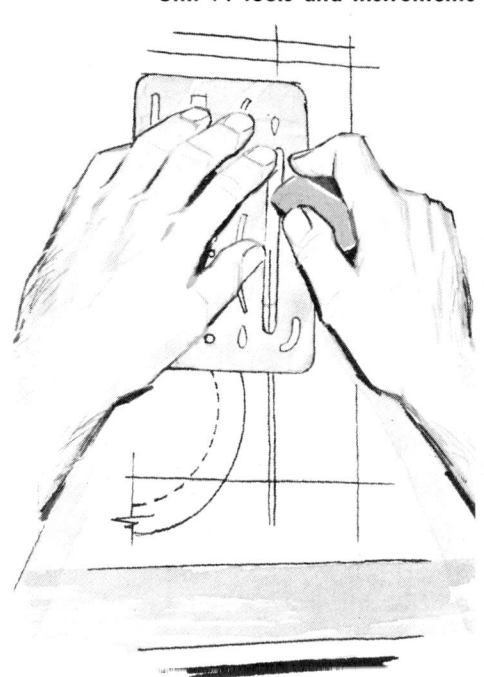

7-16. Using the erasing shield. Position an opening over the line to be erased. Rub gently with the eraser.

leads come in different grades of hardness from 6B, the softest, through grades 5B, 4B, 3B, 2B, B, HB, F, H, 2H, 3H, 4H, 5H, 6H, 7H, 8H, to 9H, which is the hardest. A 3H or 4H pencil is used for making light construction lines. A 2H or H pencil is used for drawing object or finish lines, and the F or HB is used for sketching and shading.

Pencils must have sharp points for good drawing. Use a pencil sharpener, or if you need a strong tip, use a knife. Dress the point with a sandpaper pod Fig. 7-14. Mechanical pointers are also used. Fig. 7-15.

When erasing, an *erasing shield* is used to protect the lines you wish to keep. This tool is usually made of metal. Fig. 7-16. A good gum eraser should be used. Keep it clean for best results.

Drawing instruments have many uses. Fig. 7-17. With them drafters scribe circles, measure distances, and make inked lines. These are precision instruments.

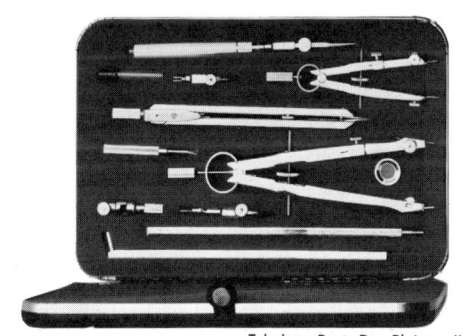

7-17. Drawing instruments shown in their case. These are precision tools. Handle them carefully and use them properly.
Teledyne Post, Des Plaines, IL

They can be used with great accuracy if they are cared for and used properly. Some common instruments are shown in Fig. 7-18. The large pencil spring box compass (A) is used for drawing large circles and arcs. The straight pencil compass (B) is also used for this purpose, but can be less accurate unless used with

53

Part II: Graphic Communications

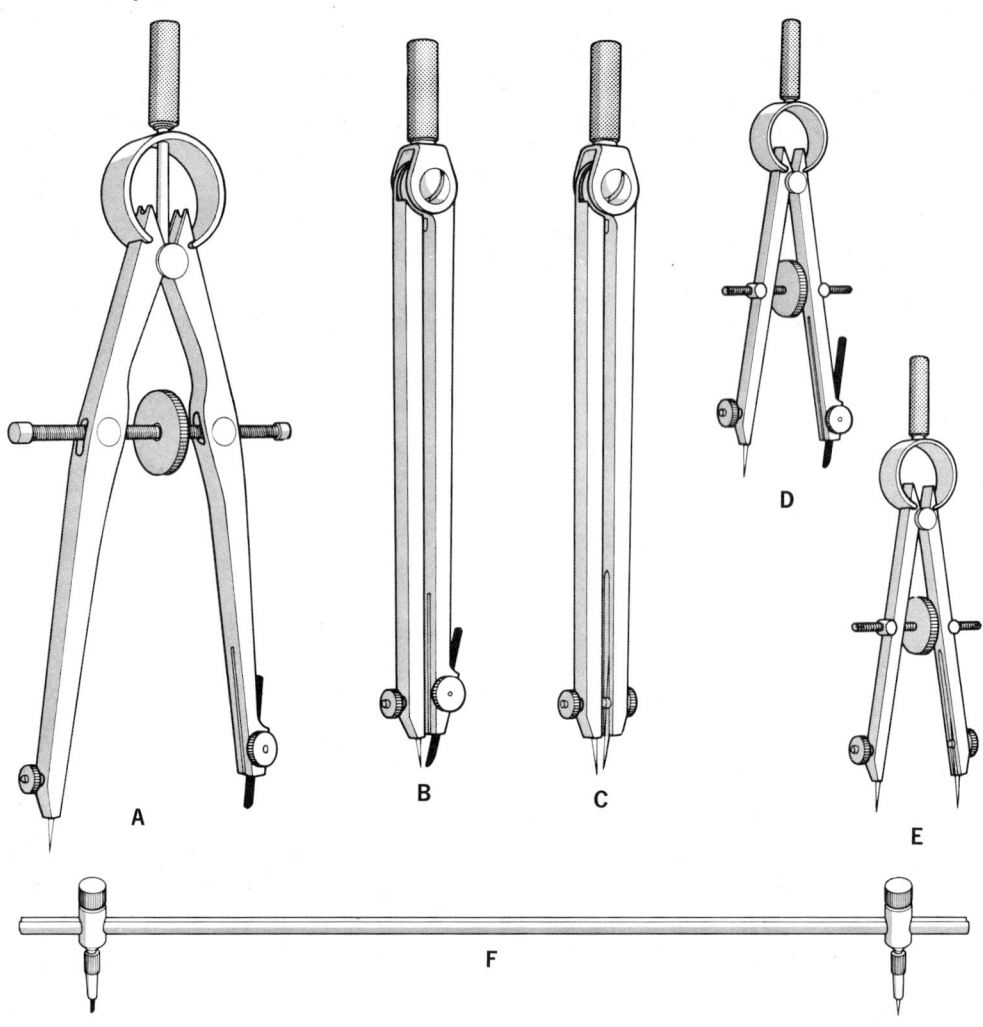

7-18. Drawing instruments: (A) Large pencil spring bow compass (B) Straight pencil compass (C) Straight divider (D) Small pencil spring bow compass (E) Spring bow divider (F) Beam compass.

7-19. A typical drafting machine setup.

care. The small pencil spring bow (D) is used to draw smaller circles and arcs. Dividers (C & E) are used to transfer distances from the drafting scale to the paper. Distances between views can also be laid out with this tool. Beam compasses (F) are used, much like trammel points in metalworking, to draw very large circles and arcs.

The pencil points in compasses should be of the same degree of hardness as the point on the pencil being used. Keep these sharp, and be careful of the needle

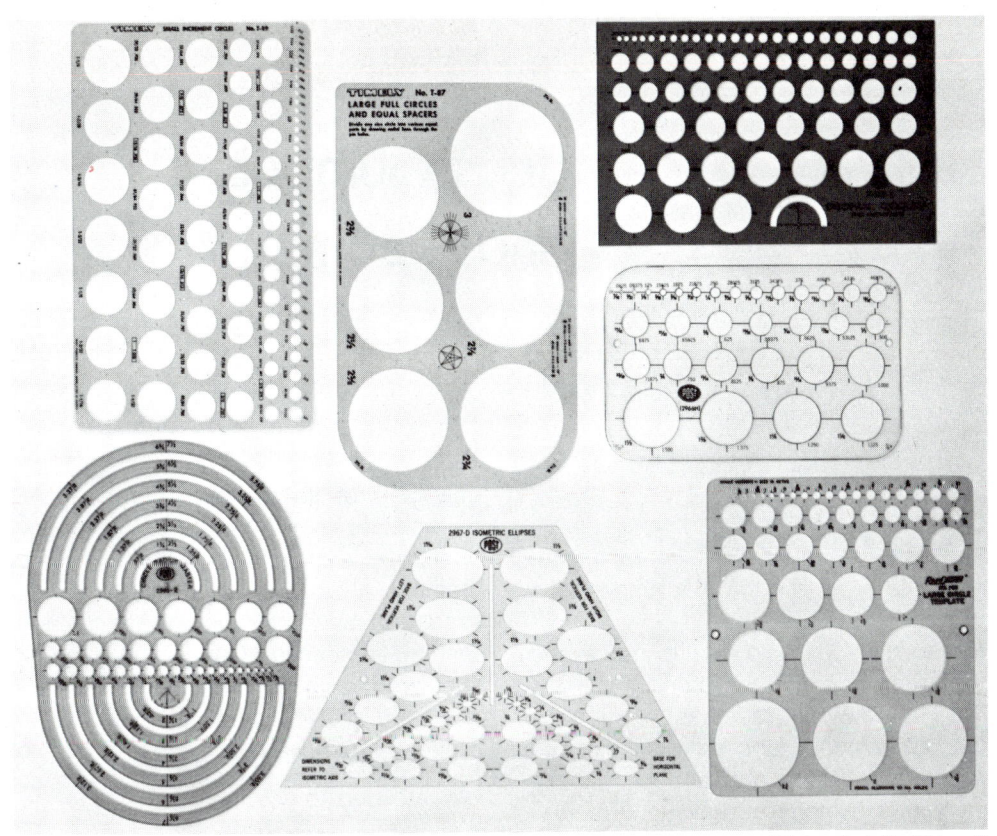

7-20. Drafting templates composed of circles, arcs, and ellipses.

points on instruments. Inking attachments are also available for drawing instruments. Ruling or inking pens may also be used.

Drafting machines combine the scale, protractor, T square, and triangle in one unit. Fig. 7-19. Drafting machines are easy and convenient to use.

Drafting templates are plastic patterns that speed the process of drawing certain shapes. Fig. 7-20. There are many styles available for drawing circles, arcs, squares, bolt heads, nuts, screws, and so forth.

Drawing paper comes in many sizes, weights, and colors. The paper generally used in the school shop is 8½" x 11" white or manila (buff-colored). It is heavy with a hard finish for good line quality. It also erases easily without smudging. Several grades of tracing paper or vellum are also used. The chart in Fig. 7-21

Comparative Sizes of Drawing Paper

Customary (inches)	Metric (millimetres)
A (8½ x 11)	A4 (210 x 297)
B (11 x 17)	A3 (297 x 420)
C (17 x 22)	A2 (420 x 594)
D (22 x 34)	A1 (594 x 841)
E (34 x 44)	A0 (841 x 1189)

7-21. Chart of customary-inch and metric paper sizes.

shows standard inch-dimension paper with metric replacement sizes.

Drawing paper is fastened to a drawing board or table with a special masking tape. Thumbtacks may also be used, but they leave marks on the paper and the drawing board.

UNIT 8

Lines, Symbols, and Geometry

ALPHABET OF LINES

In the language of drawing and sketching, different lines have different meanings. It is important that you understand what these various lines stand for. Studying Fig. 8-1 will help you to make and read drawings and sketches correctly. The lines which represent outline or shape are heavy and solid. These are called *object lines* and are the darkest lines in a sketch or drawing. Fig. 8-2 shows how these lines are used.

SYMBOLS

A drawing in which every screw thread, plumbing fixture, or electric outlet is drawn exactly as it appears would be cluttered and crowded. Such a drawing would also take a long time to make. To simplify drawings so that they are easier to make and to read, drafters use many symbols. There are symbols for building materials, plumbing fixtures, electricity, and home appliances. Some of them are shown in Fig. 8-3. Study these symbols to understand how time is saved by using them in drawing.

Symbols are also used to show threaded fasteners and tapped holes. Study Fig. 8-4. See how difficult it is to draw screw threads. Compare this with the two methods for simplifying thread drawings by using symbols. Tapped holes can also be shown with symbols.

If an object is too long to fit on a piece of drawing paper, the drafter will draw only part of the object. There are set methods for showing where an object has been broken off in such cases. These set methods are called "conventions." This simply means that they are accepted drafting practices. Conventional break lines are shown in Fig. 8-5. Drawing symbols and conventions are important to drafters. Learn what they are and how to use them.

DRAWING PRACTICE

A good way to learn how to use drawing instruments is to practice geometry exercises. These exercises require you to use scales, triangles, T squares, dividers, and compasses.

Drawing Geometric Patterns

The patterns in Fig. 8-6 require a very accurate use of instruments. To draw the tangent arc pattern (A) draw a circle four inches in diameter. Divide the circumference into five equal parts with dividers. Through these points draw radial lines. Divide each line into four equal parts with dividers. With these points as centers, draw the semicircles as shown.

To draw the circles (B) construct an equilateral triangle with a four-inch base using the 60° triangle. Bisect (divide in half) the angles with a 30° triangle, and extend the bisecting line to the opposite side. Using the points on the side as centers and with a radius equal to half the length of the side, draw arcs to cut the

Unit 8: Lines, Symbols, and Geometry

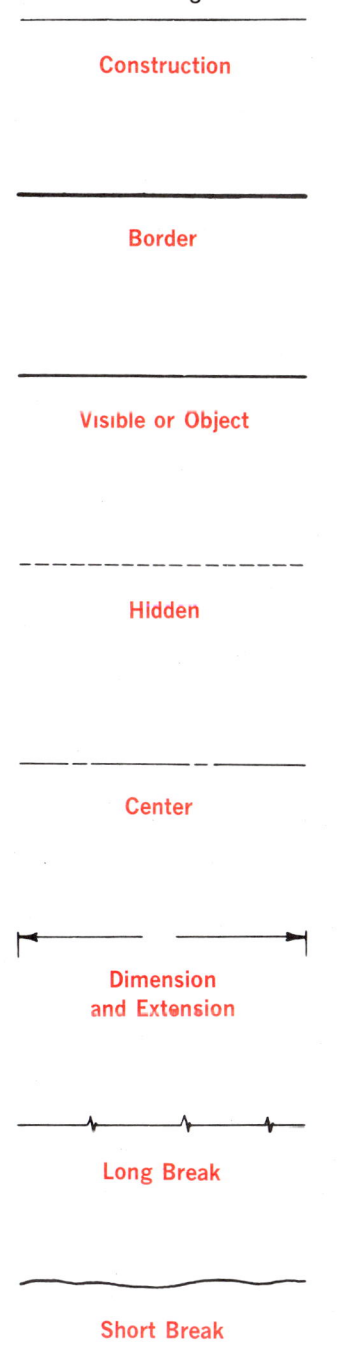

To make the arc cross (C) draw a four-inch square and divide each of the four sides in half. With a radius equal to half the length of one side, use the compass to draw the circles as indicated. Use the four corners and midpoints on the side as centers. Erase parts of the curve not needed, and retrace the figure as shown. Use the T square and 45° triangle, crosshatching as indicated.

The basket weave is made by first drawing a four-inch square. Divide the left and lower side into five equal parts with the dividers. Draw dotted horizontal and vertical lines through these points. Then draw a line 45 degrees through them and erase parts not needed. Retrace the outline of the basket weave with a heavy line.

bisecting lines. Where these arcs meet the bisector, locate the centers to inscribe the circles.

8-1. *The alphabet of lines. As you can see, each kind of line has a different use and meaning.*

Construction

Border

Visible or Object

Hidden

Center

Dimension and Extension

Long Break

Short Break

Dividing a Straight Line into Any Number of Equal Parts

See Fig. 8-7. Let AB be a line that is to be divided into seven equal parts. Draw a line AC at any angle from A. Make the line

8-2. *The alphabet of lines as applied in an instrument drawing. Learn what the various lines mean:* (a) *Object line* (b) *Hidden line* (c) *Centerline* (d) *Dimension line* (e) *Extension line.*

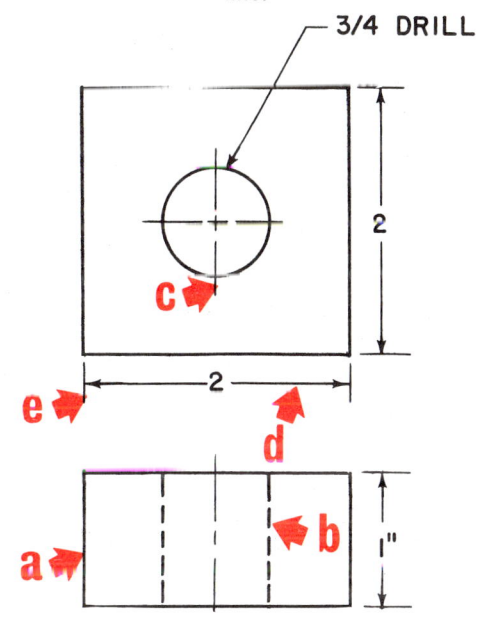

57

Part II: Graphic Communications

CAST IRON

ELECTRIC INSULATION

RUBBER

STEEL

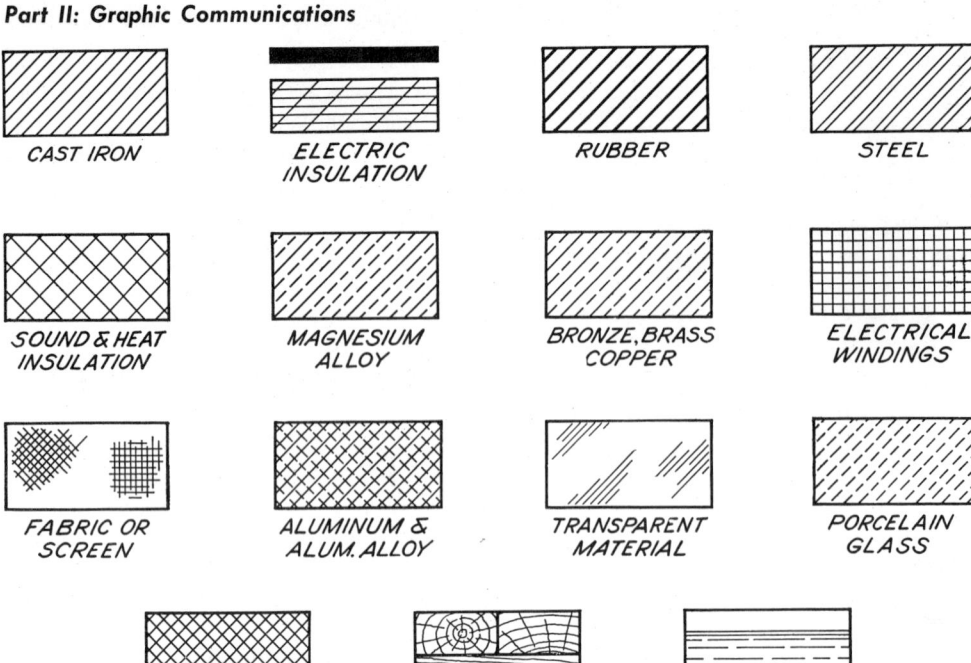

SOUND & HEAT INSULATION

MAGNESIUM ALLOY

BRONZE, BRASS COPPER

ELECTRICAL WINDINGS

FABRIC OR SCREEN

ALUMINUM & ALUM. ALLOY

TRANSPARENT MATERIAL

PORCELAIN GLASS

ZINC, LEAD BABBITT

WOOD

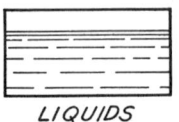

LIQUIDS

General Outlets

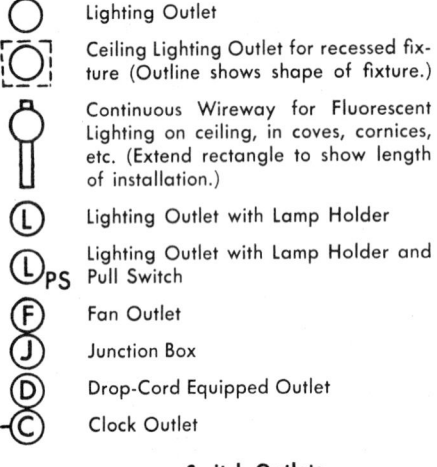

○ Lighting Outlet

Ceiling Lighting Outlet for recessed fixture (Outline shows shape of fixture.)

Continuous Wireway for Fluorescent Lighting on ceiling, in coves, cornices, etc. (Extend rectangle to show length of installation.)

Ⓛ Lighting Outlet with Lamp Holder

Ⓛ$_{PS}$ Lighting Outlet with Lamp Holder and Pull Switch

Ⓕ Fan Outlet

Ⓙ Junction Box

Ⓓ Drop-Cord Equipped Outlet

Ⓒ Clock Outlet

Switch Outlets

S   Single-Pole Switch
S$_3$ Three-Way Switch
S$_4$ Four-Way Switch

Miscellaneous

Service Panel

Distribution Panel

— — — Switch Leg Indication. Connects outlets with control points.

Convenience Outlets

Duplex Convenience Outlet

Triplex Convenience Outlet (Substitute other numbers for other variations in number of plug positions.)

Duplex Convenience Outlet — Split Wired

Duplex Convenience Outlet for Grounding-Type Plugs

Weatherproof Convenience Outlet

Multi-Outlet Assembly (Extend arrows to limits of installation. Use appropriate symbol to indicate type of outlet. Also indicate spacing of outlets as X inches.)

Combination Switch and Convenience Outlet

Combination Radio and Convenience Outlet

Floor Outlet

Range Outlet

Special-Purpose Outlet. Use subscript letters to indicate function. DW-Dishwasher, CD-Clothes Dryer, etc.

8-3. Selected symbols for materials and electricity.

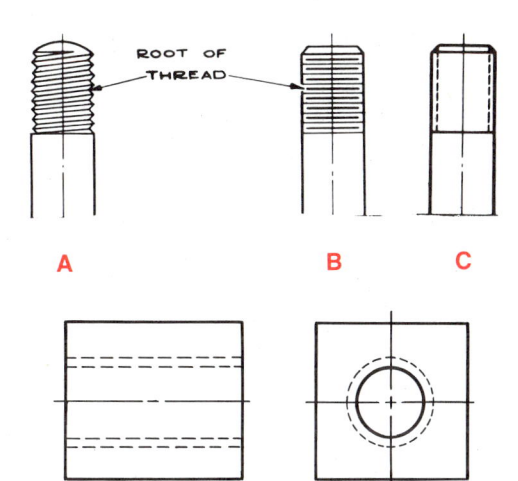

Unit 8: Lines, Symbols, and Geometry

8-4. The three ways of drawing an external thread: (A) Conventional method (B) Regular thread symbol (C) Simplified thread symbol. The symbols for internal threads (front and side views) are shown at D.

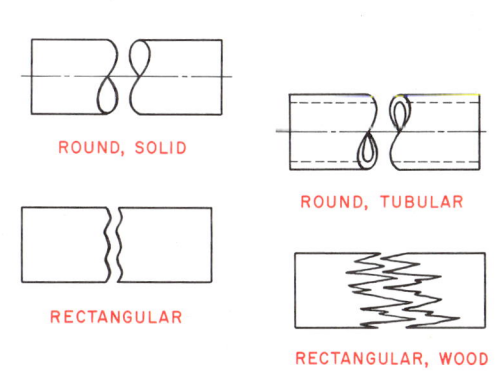

8-5. Conventional breaks used to fit long objects on a drawing sheet.

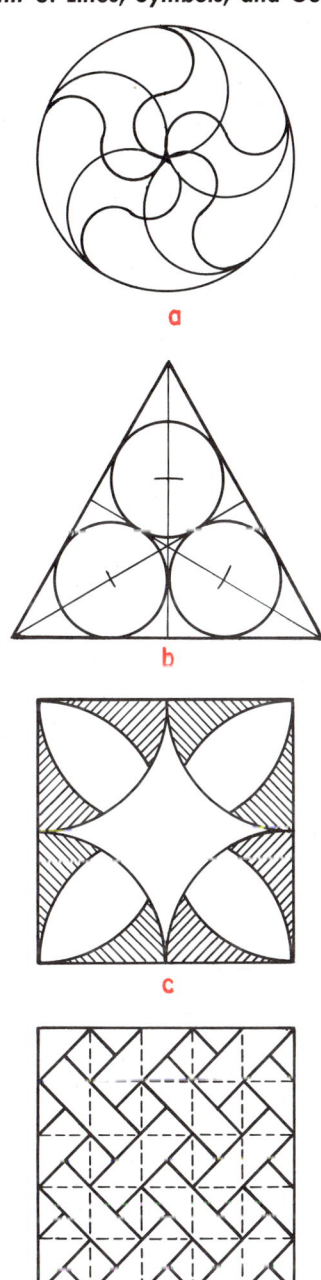

8-6. Geometric patterns: (a) Tangent arcs (b) Inscribed circles (c) Arc cross (d) Basket weave. When you draw these, use colored pencils for an interesting pattern.

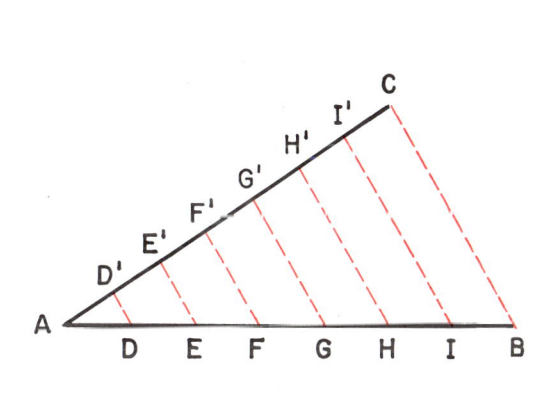

8-7. Dividing a straight line into equal parts.

59

Part II: Graphic Communications

long enough so that it can be easily divided by seven. Divide line AC into seven equal parts with the dividers or scale and label the points D', E', etc. Join the end of the last space on line AC to point B to make line BC. Now, using triangles, draw lines parallel to line BC, through points I', H', etc. In this way you can divide line AB into the required number of equal parts.

Bisecting a Given Angle

See Fig. 8-8. With O as the center at the intersection of the two legs of angle BOA and with any convenient radius, draw the arc LM. This cuts the two legs of the angle at the points L and M. Use the intersections L and M as centers. Set your compass at any radius greater than half the arc LM, and draw the arcs cutting each other at I. Draw a line from O through the intersections of the arcs at I. The line OJ divides the angle into two equal parts.

Finding the Center of a Triangle

See Fig. 8-9. In triangle ABC bisect the three angles with the lines AD, BE and CF. (These angles are bisected as shown in Fig. 8-7.) The three bisecting lines should intersect at a common point O, which is the center of the triangle.

Constructing a Hexagon in a Given Circle

See Fig. 8-10. Through the given circle draw the diameter JOG. Using J and G as centers and with a radius S equal to the radius R, cut the circumference at H, L, I, and K. Draw GH, HI, IJ, JK, KL, and LG to

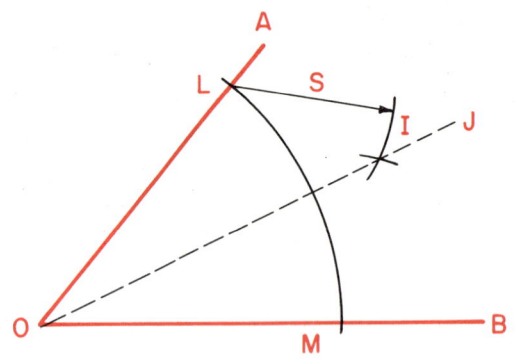

8-8. *Bisecting a given angle. Bisect means to divide into two equal parts.*

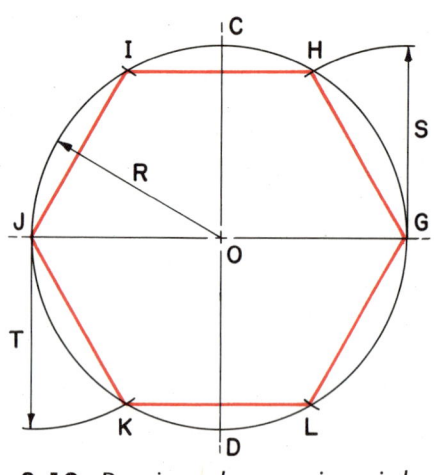

8-9. *Finding the center of a triangle.*

8-10. *Drawing a hexagon in a circle.*

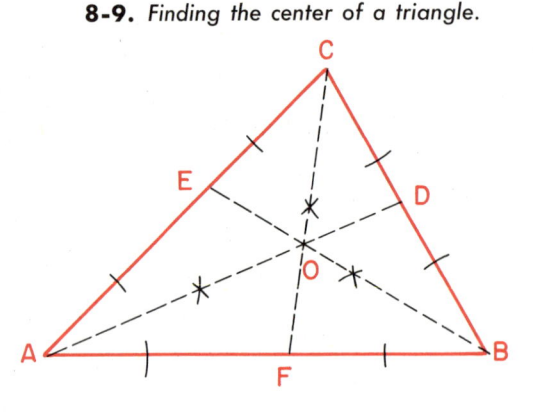

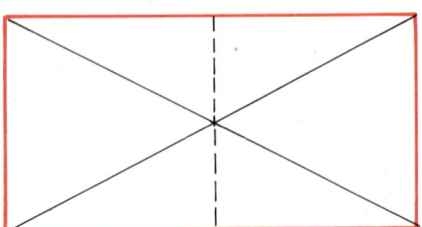

8-11. *Dividing a rectangle.*

form the hexagon. The radius of the circle is equal to the side of the hexagon. Therefore the points H, I, etc. may also be found by stepping the radius six times around the circle.

Dividing a Rectangle into Halves or Quarters

See Fig. 8-11. If you wish to divide a rectangle into two equal parts, draw the diagonals from corner to corner as shown. Draw a vertical line through the point where the two diagonals cross, using a triangle and T square. This will give you two equal divisions.

To divide the rectangle into four equal parts, divide the shape in half as shown in Fig. 8-11. Then divide the two halves into two equal parts each. This gives you a rectangle of four equal parts.

UNIT 9

Sketching

In designing it is necessary to draw pictures which show the ideas you may have for a product. Freehand sketches are better for this than instrument drawings made with T squares and triangles because they are easier and quicker to make. The purpose of this unit is to explain and show how to sketch quickly and accurately. These techniques are not difficult for a beginner. You don't have to be an artist to learn to sketch well. All you need is an understanding of the technique, and a lot of practice. Fig. 9-1.

TOOLS FOR SKETCHING

Sketching tools are very simple; pencil and paper are all you need. Any good, tough paper that you can erase on cleanly can be used. Paper covered with $\frac{1}{4}''$ squares is convenient for making simple sketches. Fig. 9-2a. Isometric grid paper can be used for pictorial sketches. Fig. 9-2b. An HB grade drawing pencil is ideal for sketching because of its soft, black lead. Light or dark lines can be made by changing the pressure. Ordinary writing pencils, Nos. 2 and $2\frac{1}{2}$, are also good. Don't use ball-point pens. Their lines can't be erased, and minor corrections are difficult to make.

9-1. With practice and patience you can learn to make good sketches of many objects, such as this airplane.

61

Part II: Graphic Communications

SKETCHING TECHNIQUES

There are no rules about how you should hold the sketching pencil. Hold it whatever way is easiest and most comfortable for you. The main thing to remember is to make free, easy lines and curves, without forcing them. Free arm movement is essential for sketching smooth, neat horizontal lines. Finger and wrist movement should be avoided. The heaviness of the line can be regulated by changing the amount of pressure on the pencil. Straight lines should always be drawn between two points. One point is used as a starting place and the other is used as a guide for keeping the line straight. The pencil should be placed firmly on the left-hand point, then pulled slowly to the right-hand point. Avoid any jerky, ragged, or curvy lines. Fig. 9-3.

A good way to learn sketching is to practice making "wiggly" lines. This will help you to sketch straighter, more accurate lines and shapes. Exaggerate the wiggles at first and then make them tighter. Leave short breaks in the lines if you wish. Any technique is all right as long as it helps you to produce a good sketch. Fig. 9-4.

Lines

A vertical line should be started at the top of the sheet and sketched downward, using a free arm movement. It is poor practice to turn the paper so that vertical lines can be drawn as horizontal ones, or

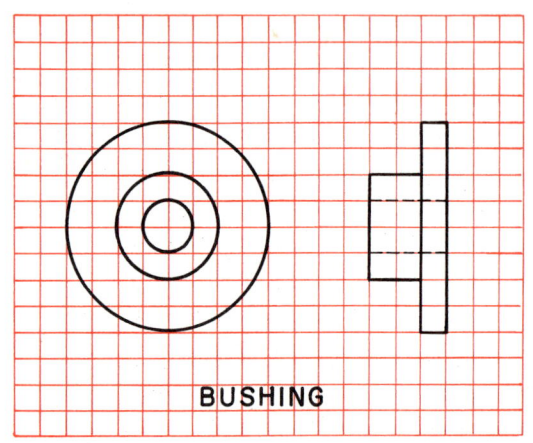

9-2a. *Grid papers are helpful in making good sketches.*

9-2b. *Isometric grid paper.*

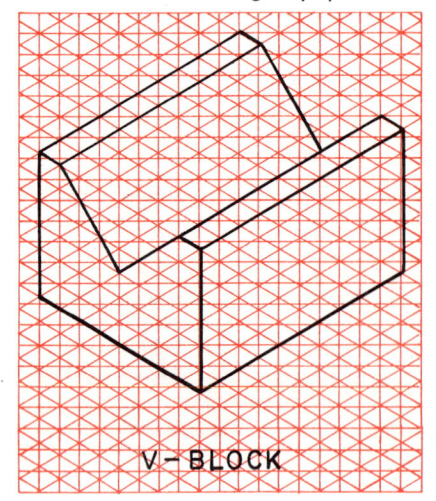

9-3. *Sketch lines properly. Avoid the incorrect lines shown here.*

CORRECT LINES

A SERIES OF SHORT, STRAIGHT LINES.

A SOLID STRAIGHT LINE.

WIGGLY LINE, CONTINUOUS, OR A SERIES OF SHORT LINES.

INCORRECT LINES

FEATHERED LINES IN A SERIES.

RAGGED LINE.

CURVED LINE, DUE TO SWING OF THE ARM.

Unit 9: Sketching

to sketch vertical lines by using the little finger or the paper edge as a guide.

Oblique or angular lines are sketched much the same as horizontal lines. Circles and arcs can be sketched with a quick arm or wrist movement as one becomes more skilled. The beginner should use guide lines to make accurate circles and shapes. This is described in the following paragraphs.

Sketching Objects

To begin pictorial sketching, first form a box of light construction or guide lines, using the same scale as will be used to sketch the object. Next sketch in the top, front, and side views in their proper positions. Then study the object and darken the object lines. Fig. 9-5.

An orthographic sketch is a drawing which shows an object from several views, usually the front, top, and right side. It is made by lightly sketching or blocking in the views in their correct positions and then darkening the object lines.

Fig. 9-6. See Units 11 and 13 for information on orthographic and pictorial theory.

With practice you can acquire the skill to sketch more difficult objects such as the tote box and the boat. Fig. 9-7. For a

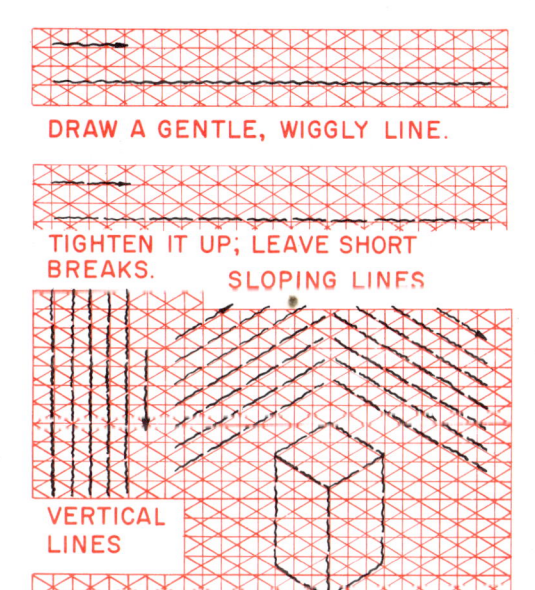

DRAW A GENTLE, WIGGLY LINE.

TIGHTEN IT UP; LEAVE SHORT BREAKS. SLOPING LINES

VERTICAL LINES

PRACTICE SHAPES

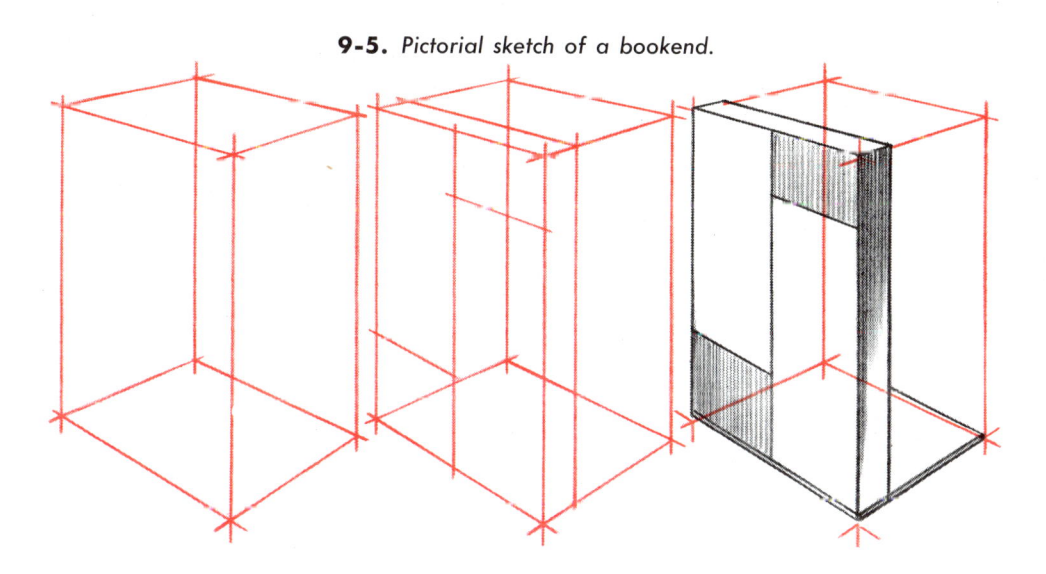

9-4. *Practice making short, wiggly lines as you begin sketching. Arrows show direction of lines for a right-handed person. Use opposite direction if you are left-handed.*

9-5. *Pictorial sketch of a bookend.*

63

Part II: Graphic Communications

more professional-looking sketch, try shading the surfaces as shown on the box.

Pictorial circles are usually drawn as ellipses or ovals. Fig. 9-8. Make these with a quick, easy movement of the pencil. Orthographic circles are sketched more easily if they are first laid out with points marking the circle diameter. Fig. 9-9.

With practice and patience, you can become a skillful sketcher. Fig. 9-10.

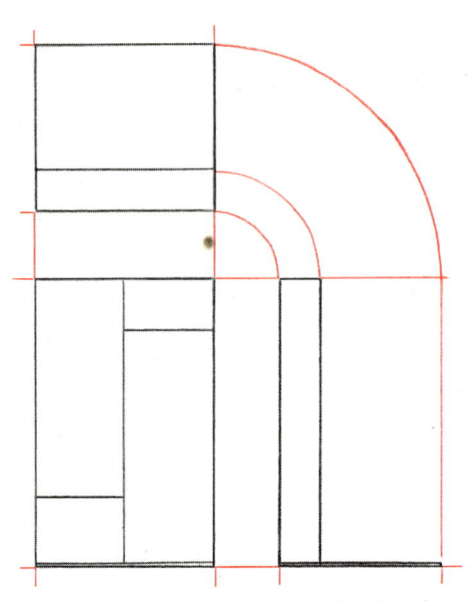

9-6. Three-view sketch of a bookend.

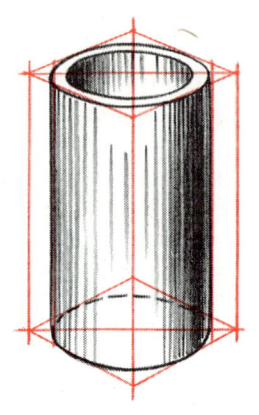

9-7. Pictorial sketches of a tote box and a boat.

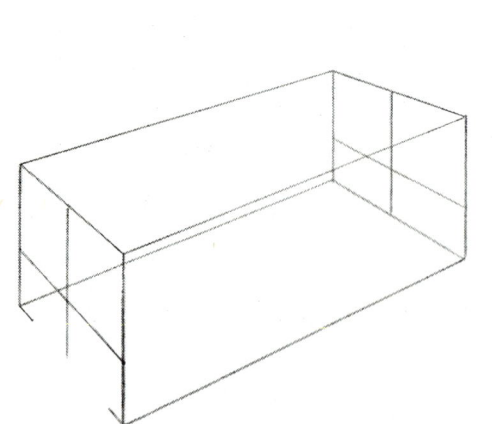

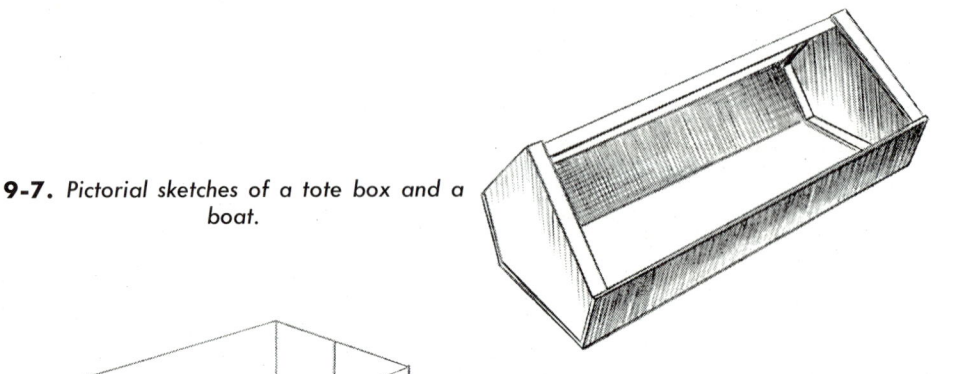

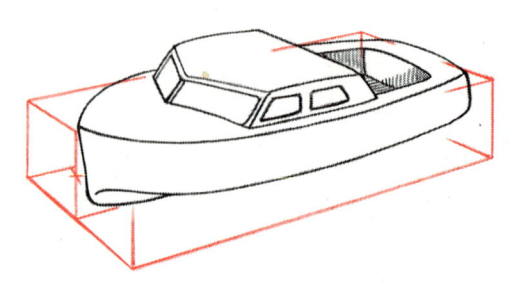

9-8. This sketch of a pencil box is made from two ovals or ellipses and two straight lines. The line shading makes it look more realistic.

64

Unit 10: Lettering

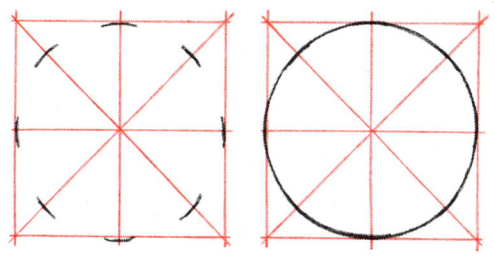

9-9. Circles are made more easily if you use guidelines.

9-10. With practice, you can make simple but accurate sketches. This furniture piece is even more attractive because of the shading and shadowing.

UNIT 10

Lettering

The lines on a drawing describe the shape of an object. However, this is only part of the information needed. The dimensions must be put on a drawing. The title and other special notes must also be given. Adding the necessary numbers and notes to a drawing is called *lettering*.

The style of lettering generally used is *single stroke Gothic*. Each letter is separate; that is, it is not connected to another letter as in script handwriting. This separation makes it unnecessary to trace back on the strokes of each letter. Therefore each stroke of a letter is a single line. Fig. 10-1. Letters can be either lower case or upper case (small or capital). Upper case letters are most often used.

10-1. Single stroke Gothic slant letters. Use guidelines for neat lettering. The letters are slanted at about 68°.

A E F H K L M N T V
W X Y Z .
B C D G J O Ø (major axis) *P Q*
R S U .
1 2 3 4 5 6 7 8 9 0

65

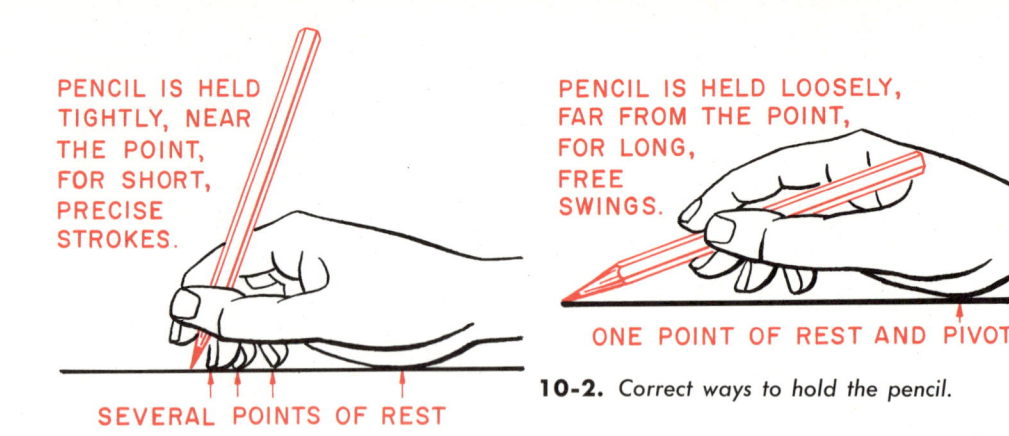

PENCIL IS HELD TIGHTLY, NEAR THE POINT, FOR SHORT, PRECISE STROKES.

PENCIL IS HELD LOOSELY, FAR FROM THE POINT, FOR LONG, FREE SWINGS.

ONE POINT OF REST AND PIVOT

SEVERAL POINTS OF REST

10-2. Correct ways to hold the pencil.

10-3. Forming single stroke Gothic vertical letters. This style of lettering is most often used in mechanical drawings.

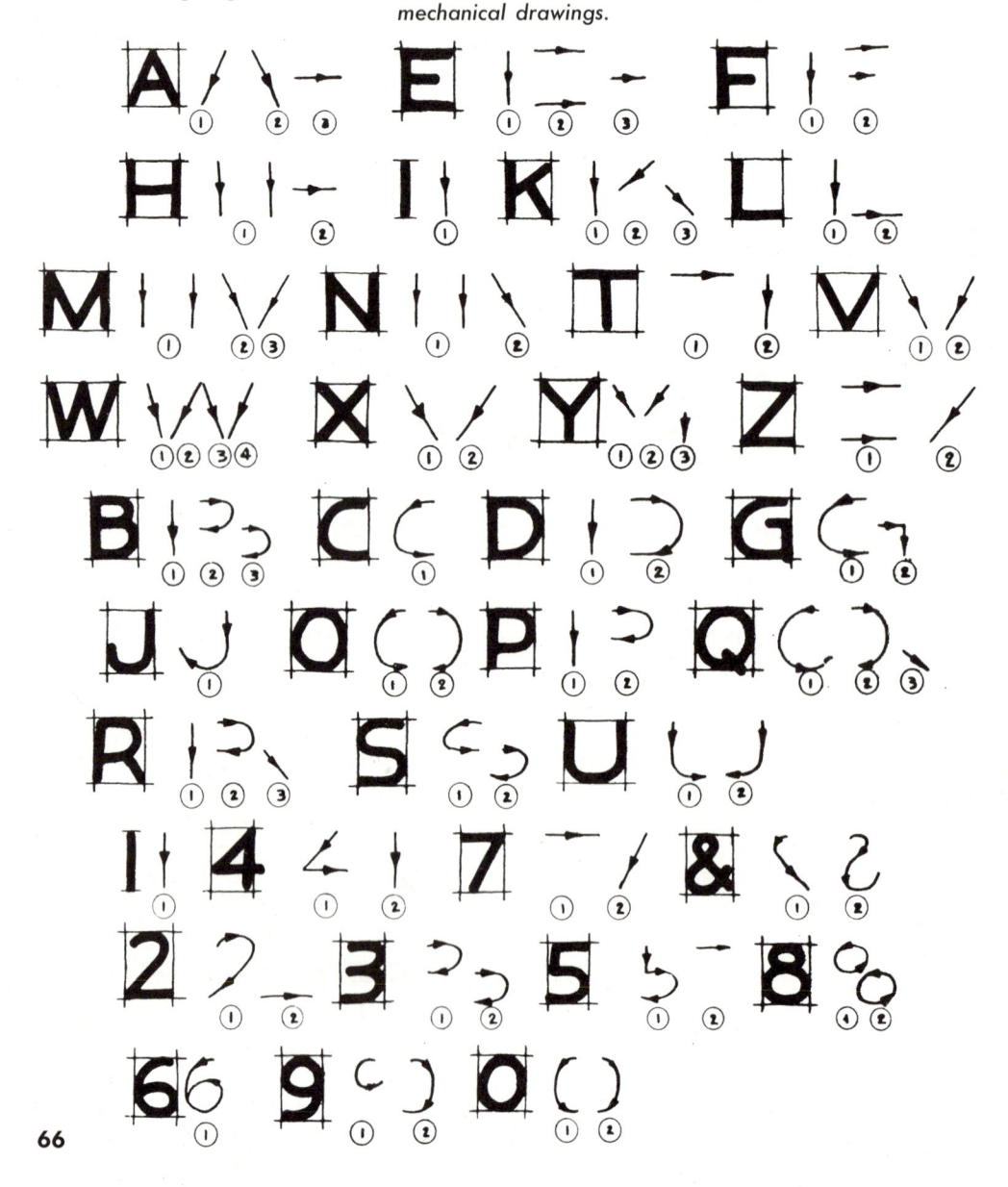

66

Unit 10: Lettering

SELF CHECK YOUR LETTERING AND LINE WORK. PRACTICE IS

10-4. *Use correct spacing when lettering.*

$3\frac{7}{8}$ } TWICE THE HEIGHT OF THE WHOLE NUMBER

$7\frac{5}{16}$ — division line in line with center of whole number. fractional numbers do not touch the line.

10-5. *Notes for forming fractions.*

Lettering should be done with a medium hardness pencil such as an H or 2H. Hold the pencil comfortably but firmly without tiring the hand. Fig. 10-2. Keep the point sharp and rotate the pencil after forming a few letters. This will prevent the point from flattening and the strokes from getting too wide.

Study Fig. 10-3 to learn how to form letters. Note that some letters are wider than others, the *M* and *W* for example. Draw some horizontal guidelines on a piece of paper about 1/4" apart. Practice forming letters. Make firm, straight strokes and regular curves. Continue to practice those letters which give you trouble.

Because of the common use of slant in everyday writing, it is natural to form letters in this way. Slant letters and numbers can be made with ease and speed. In slant lettering all vertical lines slant at 68°. Circles are made as ellipses with the major axis at 68°. See Fig. 10-1. The direction of the strokes and the order in which each is made are similar to that given for vertical upper case lettering.

The spacing between letters is about one-fourth the width of any normal letter. The spacing between words is equal to the width of a normal letter, and the spacing between sentences is twice the height of a letter. Spacing between lines is equal to the height of a letter. Fig. 10-4. When lettering fractions, follow the suggestions shown in Fig. 10-5.

UNIT 11

Multiview Drawings

There are several ways to show the shape of an object with drawings. One way is described in this unit. For example, Fig. 11-1 shows the top, front, and end views of a coffee table. This type of drawing is called a *multiview* or an *orthographic projection*. *Orthographic* means placing the views at right angles to one another. *Projection* means to show the parts of an object on flat surfaces, or planes. To make an orthographic projection you must place the views of an object on planes lying at right angles to one another.

Every object has six views: a top and a bottom, a front and a back, a right side and a left side. Where these come together, they form right angles. To make a multiview drawing of most objects it is necessary to show only three views—usually the front, top, and right side. The front view is generally the most important or most descriptive view.

It is easy to see how orthographic projection works if you imagine that the object is inside a glass box. If you were to look straight into the front of the box and trace what you saw with a wax pencil, you would have sketched the front view. Then if you did the same for the top and right-side views, you would have sketches of all three views. Fig. 11-2. Next, if you could fold the top and right-side views forward, you would have an orthographic projec-

11-1. *Three views are needed to describe the shape of this coffee table. Such a drawing is called an orthographic drawing or a multiview.*

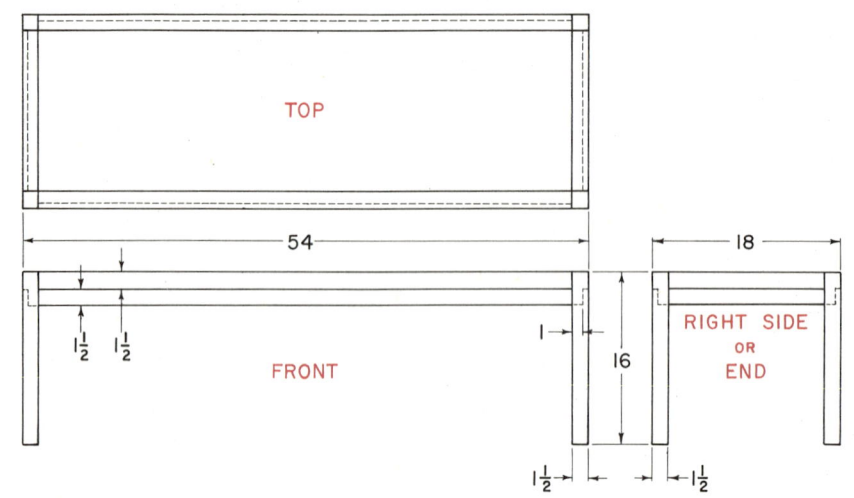

tion showing three views of the object. Fig. 11-3. Orthographic projection is as simple as that.

Not all objects need three views. For example, cylindrical shapes such as a hockey puck or an oil can need only two. The layout of a softball diamond requires only one view (called a *plan view*) to describe its shape. Fig. 11-4. Maps are also examples of one-view drawings. Fig. 11-5.

LAYING OUT A THREE-VIEW DRAWING

You must carefully study the object to be drawn before you can begin. For example, look at Fig. 11-6a. You should select those views of the object which best describe it. It is important to select

11-2. Imagine an object enclosed in a clear box. Tracing what you see would transfer the views onto the planes (surfaces) of the box. T indicates top, F is front, and RS, right side.

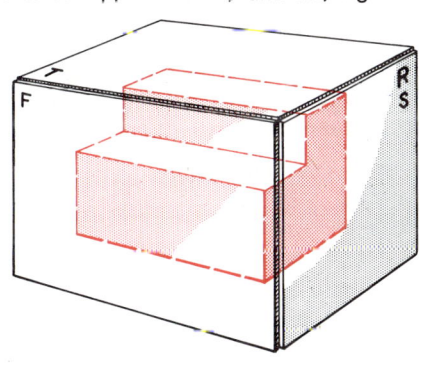

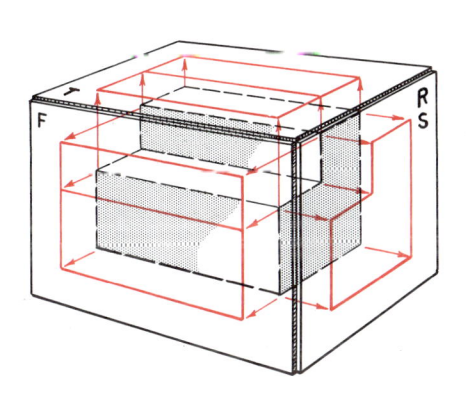

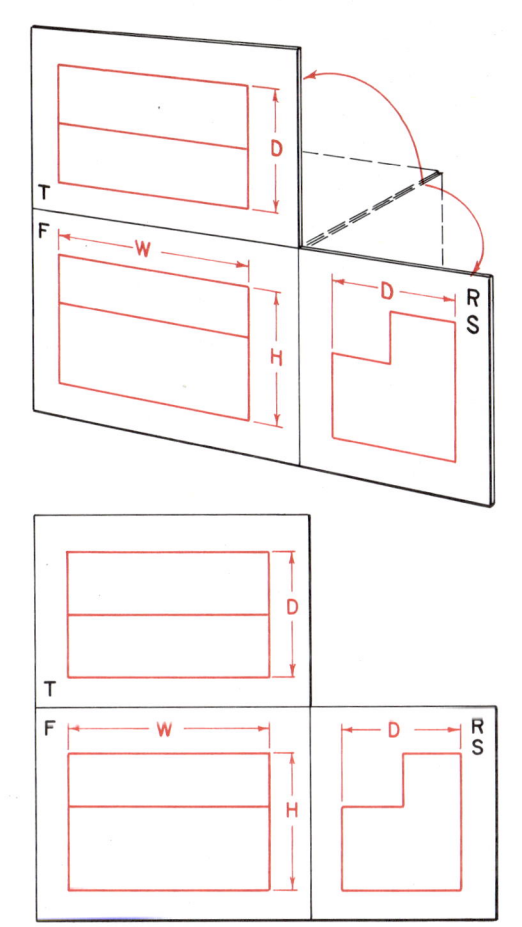

11-3. When you unfold the box, you have an orthographic drawing of the object showing its three main dimensions—height, width, and depth.

11-4. Simple layouts such as this softball field can be made with one view.

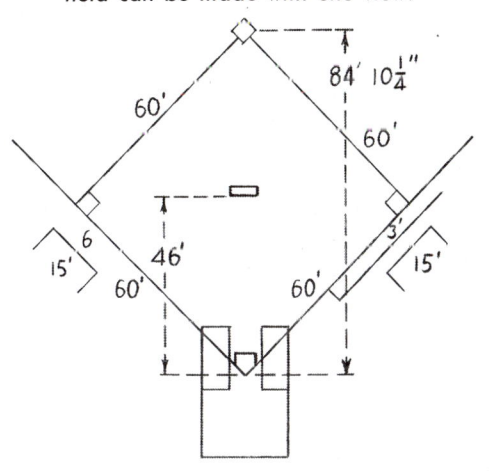

69

Part II: Graphic Communications

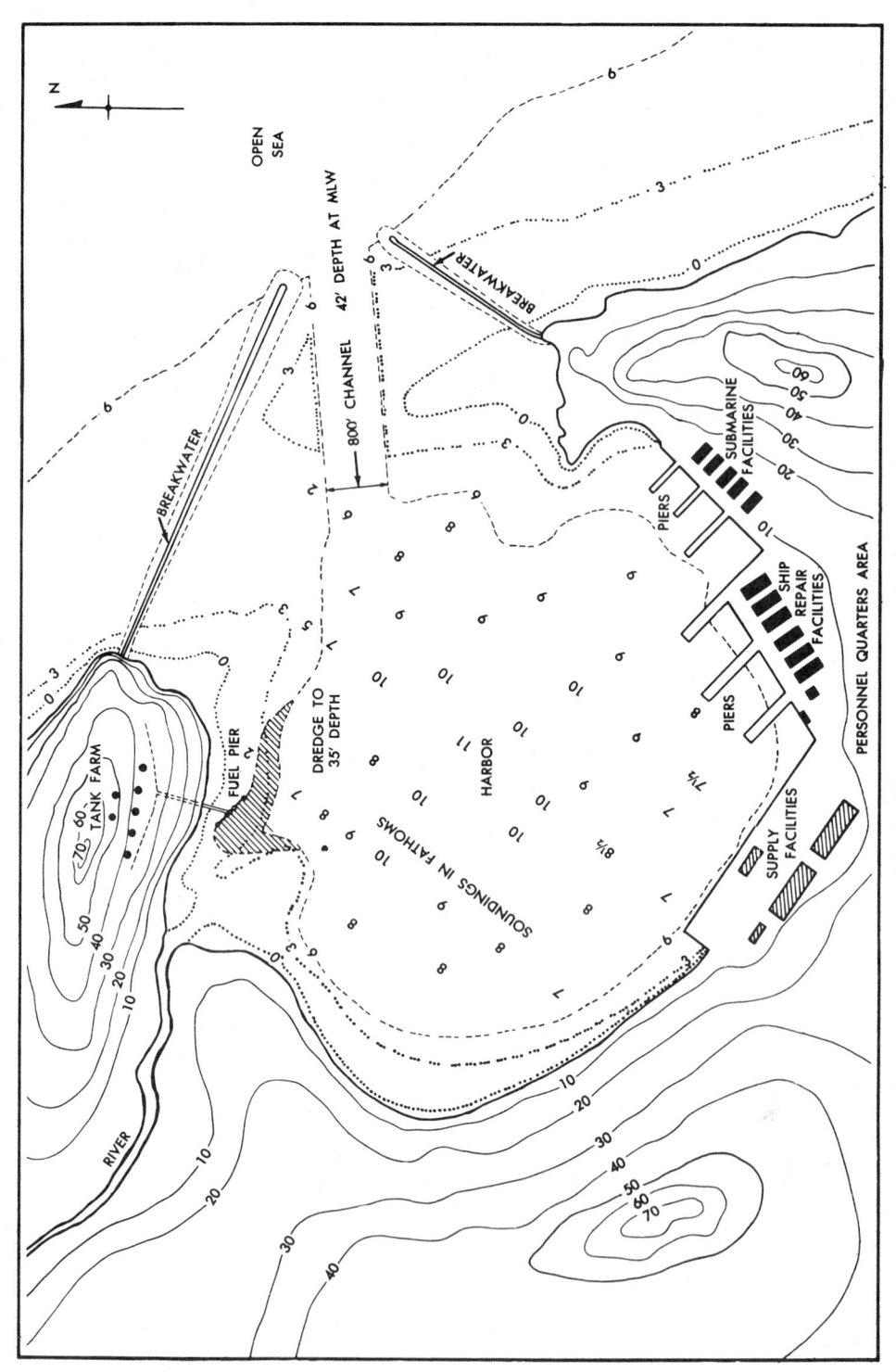

11-5. Maps are one-view drawings.

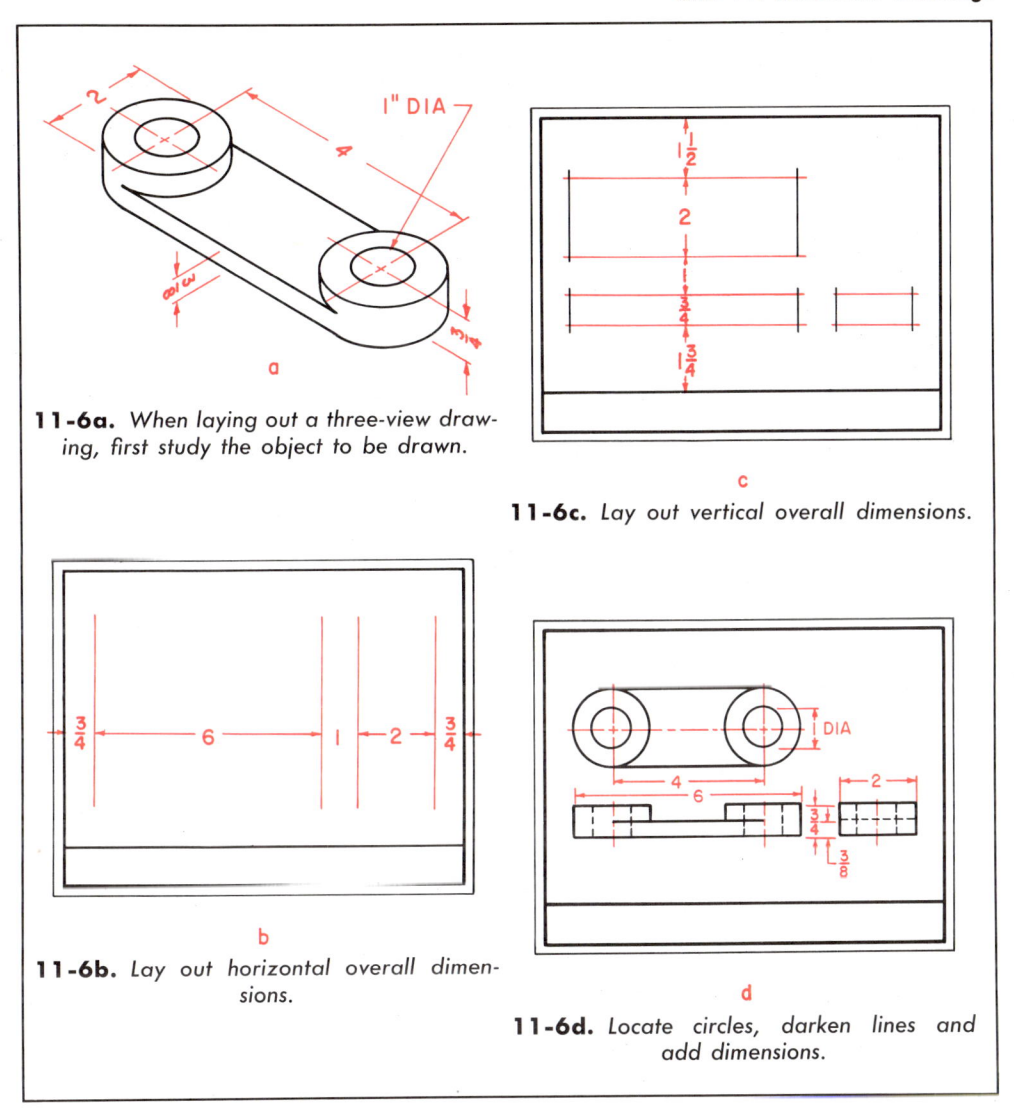

11-6a. When laying out a three-view drawing, first study the object to be drawn.

11-6c. Lay out vertical overall dimensions.

11-6b. Lay out horizontal overall dimensions.

11-6d. Locate circles, darken lines and add dimensions.

those views which show the object in its natural position. For example, it would be wrong to show a drawing of an automobile upside down.

To draw the object in Fig. 11-6a block out the views with construction lines. Figs. 11-6b & c. Notice how the width and depth dimensions are added together to determine the scale and paper size. Leave enough space around and between the views for dimensions and notes.

Add details such as holes. The arcs and circles should be drawn in first with object lines. It is easier to join two arcs with a line than to add two arcs to a line. Try it.

Draw all other object lines. Add dimensions and notes to complete the drawing. Fig. 11-6d. Follow the same procedures for one- and two-view drawings.

UNIT 12

Sectional and Auxiliary Views

It is very important that multiview drawings be as clear and understandable as possible. Sometimes special views, such as *sections* and *auxiliaries,* can help to make them clearer. Sectional views show interior or hidden details of objects. Fig. 12-1. For example, it would be difficult to make an automobile carburetor without knowing what the inside looked like. The method of showing interior views in a drawing is seen in Fig. 12-2. Note how the cutting plane marks the place for the sectional view.

Auxiliary views show true views of surfaces which are set at angles to the planes of the transparent box. Fig. 12-3. Orthographic views of these inclined or angular surfaces appear foreshortened. An auxiliary drawing provides a view which is true in size and shape. Fig. 12-4.

Whirlpool Corporation
12-1. *This cutaway model of a refrigerator compressor shows the interior of the part. A sectional view is a drawing used to show such hidden detail.*

Unit 12: Sectional and Auxiliary Views

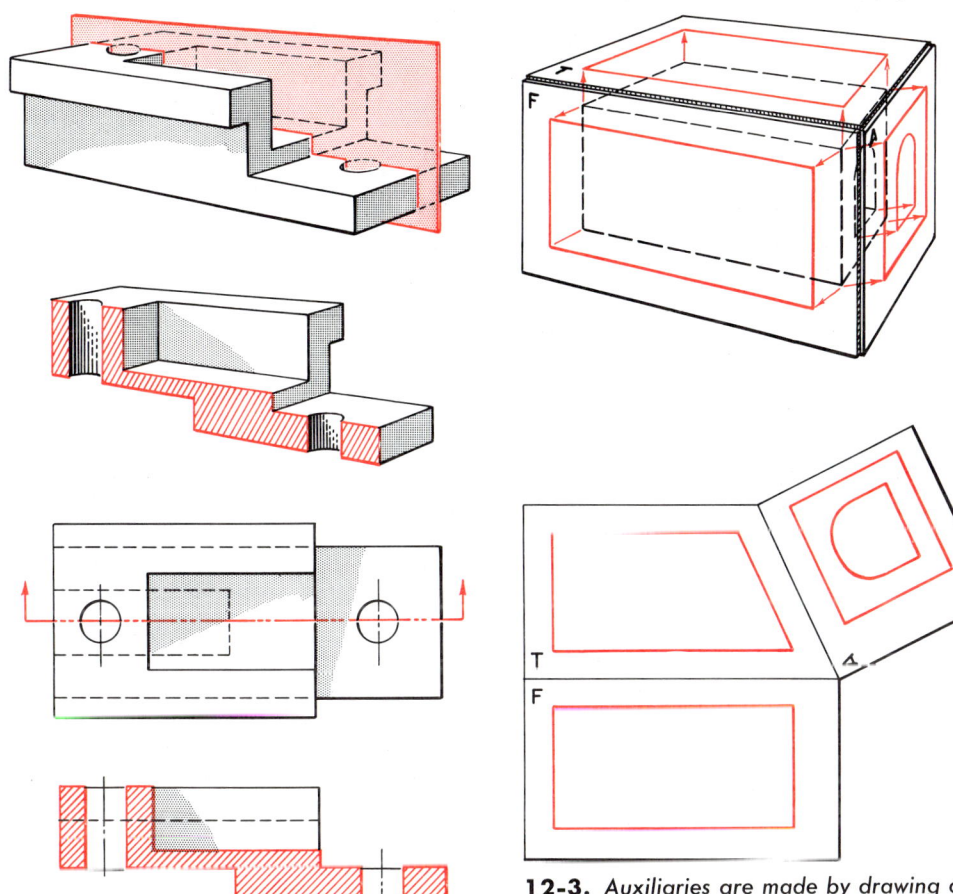

12-2. Sections are made by passing an imaginary cutting plane (A) through an object. By "removing" the front half of the object you see an interior or sectional view of the object. Cutting plane lines (B) should be indicated on the drawing.

12-3. Auxiliaries are made by drawing one side of the transparent box parallel with the oblique (angled) surface of the object. Folding out the sides of the box produces an auxiliary view (A) of the oblique surface. T indicates top and F front. Auxiliary views show the true shape and size of an oblique view.

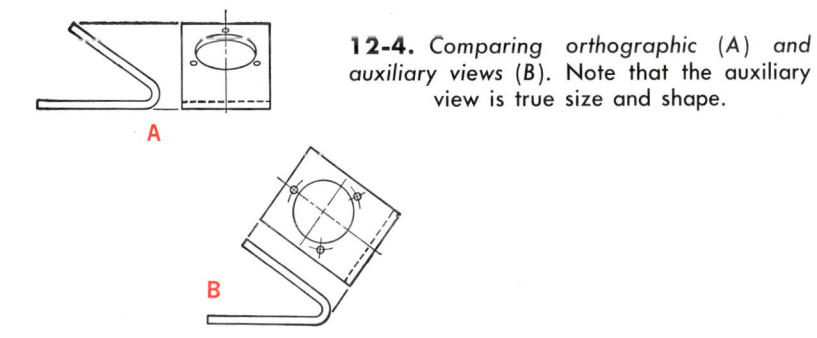

12-4. Comparing orthographic (A) and auxiliary views (B). Note that the auxiliary view is true size and shape.

73

UNIT 13

Pictorial Drawings

When you hold a tackle or tool box in front of you, what you see is a perspective view of it. If you were to make a drawing of what you saw, you would have a perspective drawing of the box. A, Fig. 13-1. Note how it resembles a photograph of the box. Such drawings are called *pictorials* because they are much like a picture. Objects are drawn the way they appear to the eye. Besides the perspective, two other forms of pictorial drawings are used to describe the shapes of objects. These are the isometric and oblique drawings. B & C, Fig. 13-1.

PERSPECTIVE DRAWING

When you look down a railroad track or a long, straight highway, the track or road seems to get narrower and come together at some distant point on the horizon. In

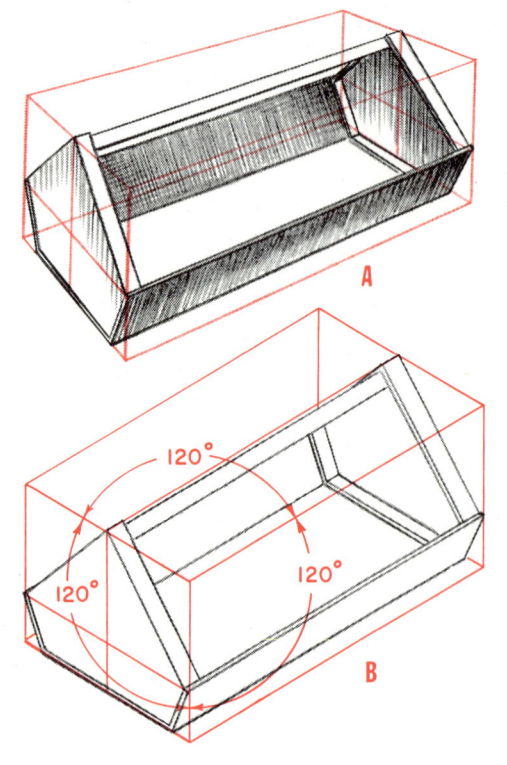

13-1. *Pictorial study of a tool box: (A) Perspective (B) Isometric (C) Oblique. The isometric or oblique pictorials are generally used in the shop.*

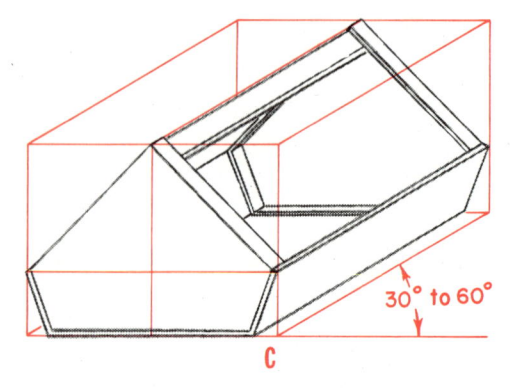

Unit 13: Pictorial Drawings

perspective drawings, lines also meet at a point on the horizon. This horizon point is called a vanishing point. A one-point or parallel perspective drawing has one vanishing point. Fig. 13-2. The two-point or angular perspective drawing has two vanishing points. Fig. 13-3. Architects and designers often use a perspective to show realistic houses or furniture. Fig. 13-4.

ISOMETRIC DRAWING

Isometric drawings are so called because they contain three views or planes with axes that lie 120 degrees apart. Fig. 13-5. *Isometric* means "equal measure." To make an isometric view, first draw a box the same size as the view you plan to make. This box must also be isometric. Note that the base lines are made with the 30° triangle. A, Fig. 13-5. Then take the dimensions of the object you are drawing, transfer them to the proper view, and connect the lines. B, Fig. 13-5. All lines parallel to the 120-degree axes are called isometric lines and are true length. Lines not parallel to these axes are called non-isometric lines.

Circles drawn in isometric are ellipses. Fig. 13-6. To draw an isometric circle, locate e, f, g, and h at the midpoints of the sides of the isometric square ABCD. Next, draw light construction lines to connect opposite corners with opposite sides as shown in Fig. 13-6. Set your compass with the radii shown and draw the arcs. The isometric drawing is much like a perspective and is even easier to make.

OBLIQUE DRAWING

The oblique drawing is made from the front view (plane) of an object, with the top and side views lying back at angles of

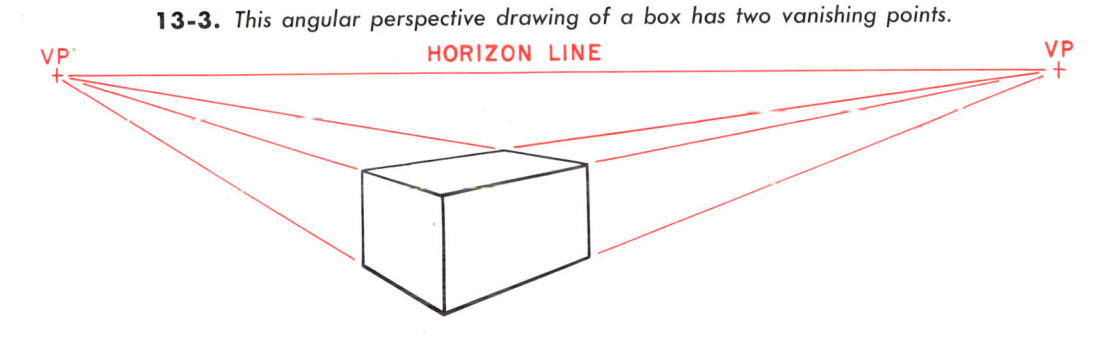

13-2. *This parallel perspective drawing of a book holder has only one vanishing point.*

13-3. *This angular perspective drawing of a box has two vanishing points.*

Part II: Graphic Communications

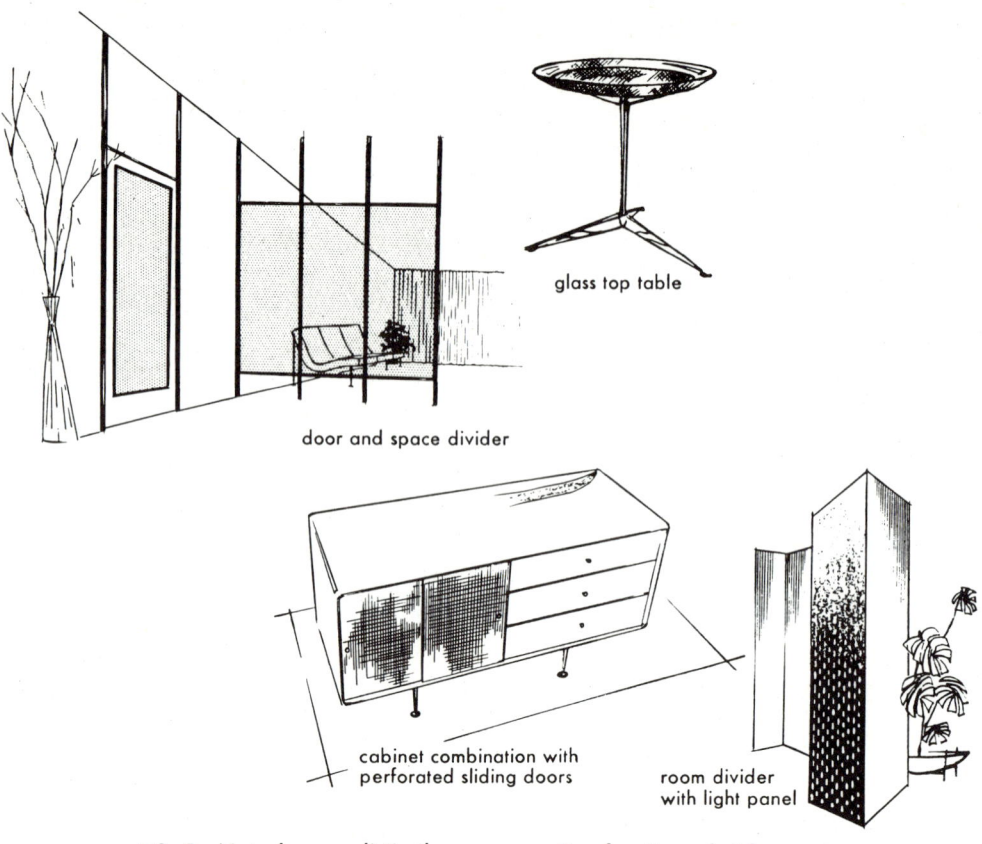

glass top table

door and space divider

cabinet combination with perforated sliding doors

room divider with light panel

13-4. Note how realistic these perspective furniture sketches are.

13-5. An isometric drawing is constructed around three lines drawn 120° apart (A). The completed view, with dimensions, is shown at B.

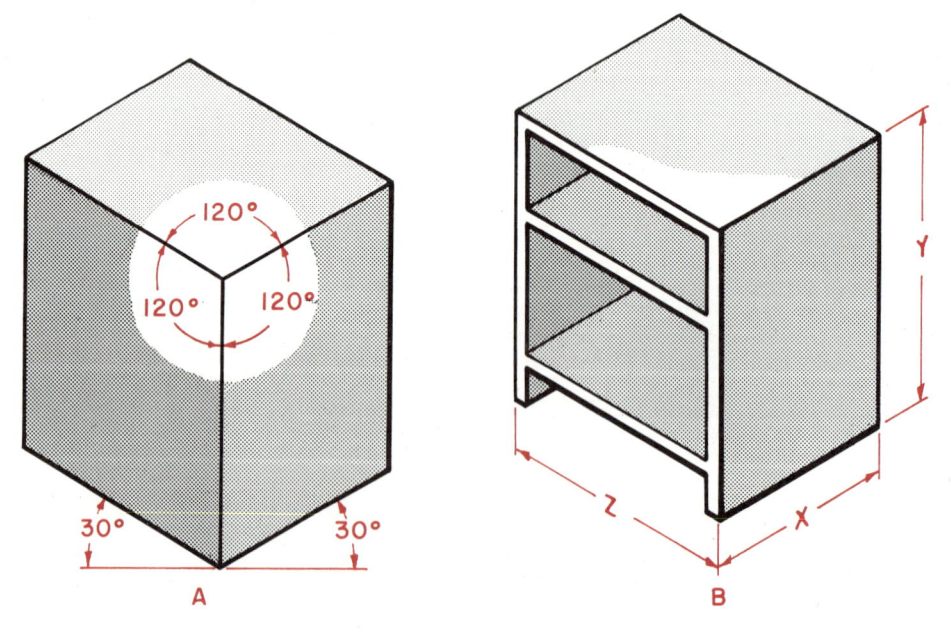

76

Unit 13: Pictorial Drawings

30 degrees or 45 degrees. Fig. 13-7. It is the easiest of the three pictorial methods to use and make. Its most important advantage is that the front view is of a true shape. This is helpful if that view contains many arcs and curves, because arcs and curves in isometric or perspective are more difficult to draw.

There are two kinds of oblique drawings: cavalier and cabinet. In cavalier oblique, the side and top of the object are drawn their true lengths. This makes the object look distorted. A, Fig. 13-8. In a cabinet drawing, the depth is shortened so that it won't look out of proportion. B, Fig. 13-8.

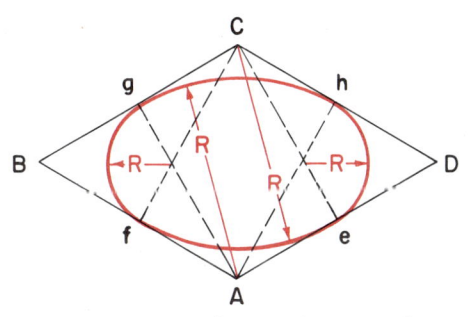

13-6. Isometric circles are drawn as ellipses.

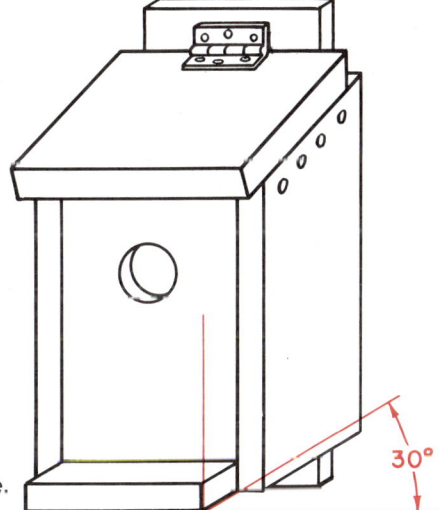

13-7. An oblique drawing of a birdhouse.

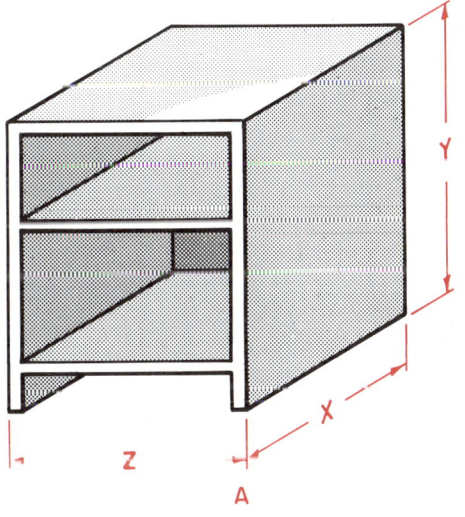

13-8. The cavalier oblique (A) and the cabinet oblique (B) drawings.

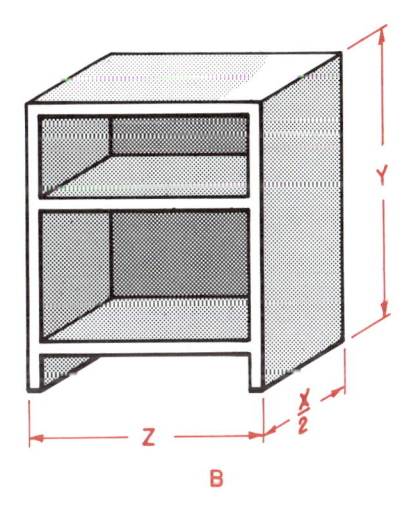

77

UNIT 14

Dimensioning

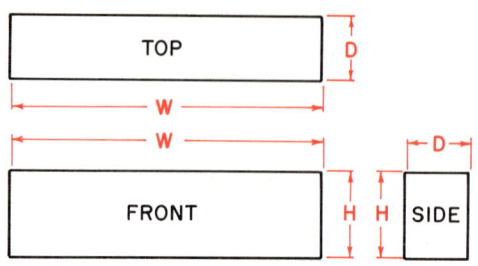

14-1. Drawing of block showing the placement of width, height, and depth dimensions.

The units dealing with multiviews, pictorials, sections, and auxiliaries explain ways of shape description. Shape description is one important part of drawing, but it is not enough to only describe the shape of an object. The drawing must also show its size. Size description involves placing numbers on the drawing which show the object's width, height, depth, size of holes, and similar informa-

14-2. Drawing of a snack tray, showing the shape and size. Dimensions and lettering are shown neatly and accurately.

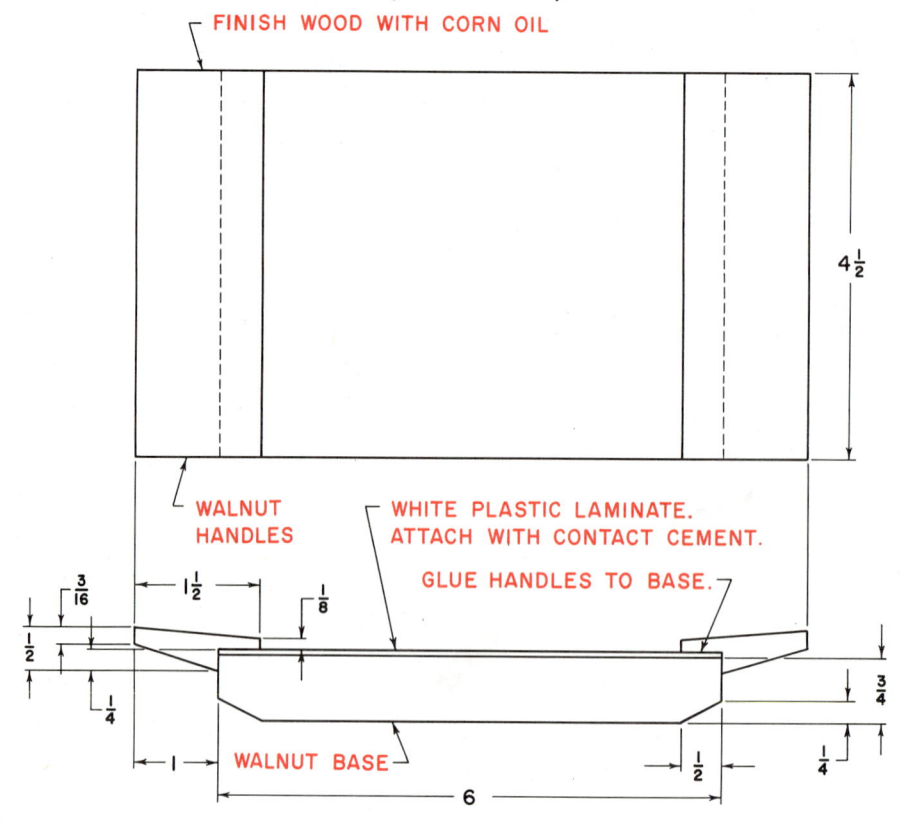

FINISH WOOD WITH CORN OIL

$4\frac{1}{2}$

WALNUT HANDLES

WHITE PLASTIC LAMINATE. ATTACH WITH CONTACT CEMENT.

GLUE HANDLES TO BASE.

$\frac{3}{16}$ $1\frac{1}{2}$ $\frac{1}{8}$

$\frac{1}{2}$

$\frac{1}{4}$

$\frac{3}{4}$

1   WALNUT BASE $\frac{1}{2}$ $\frac{1}{4}$

6

Unit 14: Dimensioning

tion. Fig. 14-1. These numbers are called dimensions. Fig. 14-2 shows a dimensioned drawing. It is complete because it accurately describes the shape and size of the snack tray. This drawing, as well as others in this book, shows how dimensions are properly placed on a drawing.

There are many things to learn about dimensioning so that you can describe the size of an object properly. Some of these important facts are listed below.

1. There are two systems for placing dimensions on a drawing. They can be placed so as to be read from the bottom and right side. This is the aligned system. Fig. 14-3. In the unidirectional system, all numbers are placed so that they can be read from the bottom of the page. Fig. 14-4. Select either of these systems. Do not mix them on the same drawing.

2. Some dimensions are used to show the overall size of an object. These are called *size* dimensions. *Location* dimensions are used to locate holes, slots, etc. Fig. 14-5. In this drawing note the difference between extension and dimension lines. Extension lines should not touch the object. The arrowheads on dimension lines should just touch the extension lines.

Arrowheads should be neat and narrow and should end in a sharp point. They should be about $\frac{1}{8}''$ long. The width should be about $\frac{1}{3}$ of the length. Do not measure each arrowhead. Practice making them until you can do so quickly and neatly.

3. There are a number of ways to dimension narrow spaces, arcs, circles, and angles. The method you use depends upon how much space you have. Do not crowd dimensions. They should be accurately placed, neat, and easy to read. Fig. 14-6.

4. Study an object carefully before you dimension it. There may be a better way of dimensioning to make it less cluttered

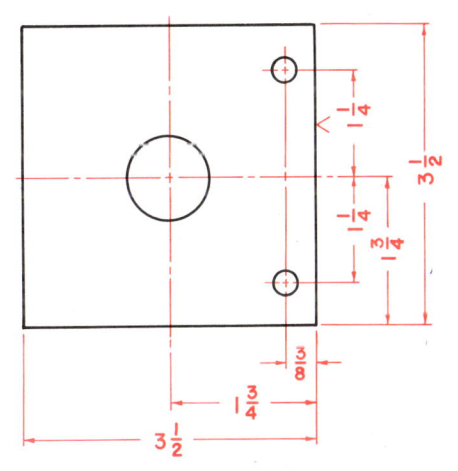

14-3. *Aligned dimensions.*

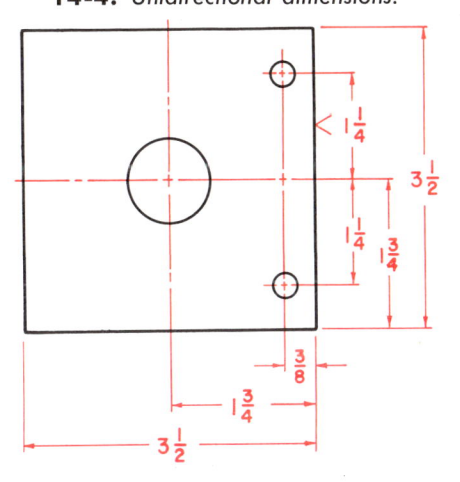

14-4. *Unidirectional dimensions.*

14-5. *Sample drawing showing:* (A) *Extension line* (B) *Dimension line* (C) *Size dimension* (D) *Location dimension.*

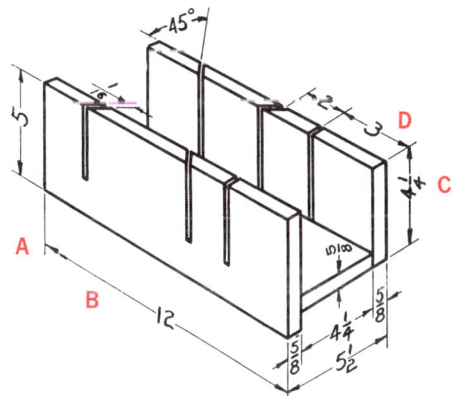

Part II: Graphic Communications

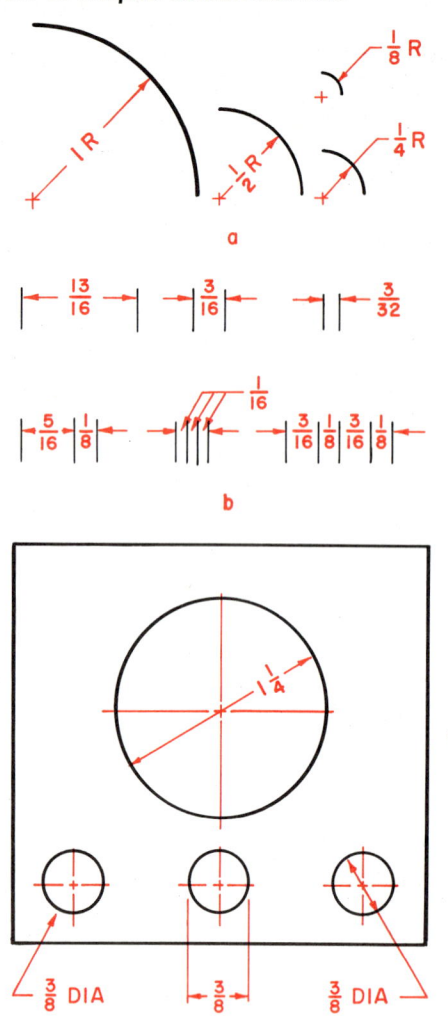

14-6. Methods for measuring (a) arcs, (b) narrow spaces, (c) holes, and (d) angles.

14-7. Crowded dimensions are difficult to read.

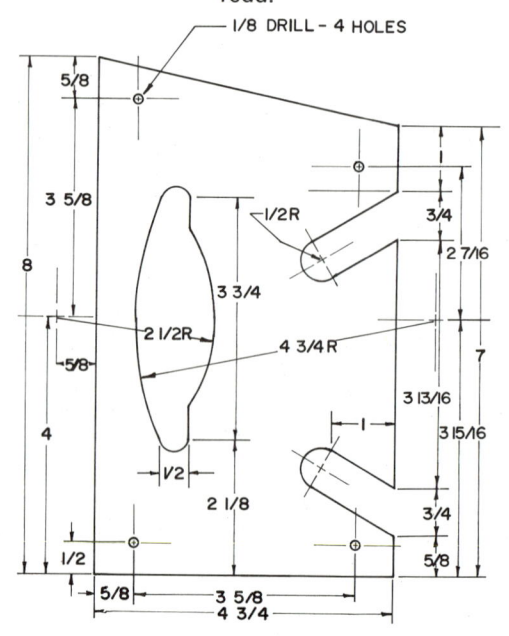

and easier to read. Study the two drawings in Figs. 14-7 & 14-8. Which of the two is easier to read?

5. Do not place dimensions on the views; place them between views whenever possible. Stagger dimensions so that they can be easily read.

6. Dimension in inches up to and including 72 inches. Use feet and inches above this size. (See Unit 15 for metric dimensioning.)

7. Lettering sets or instruments are often used to make neat, clear letters and numbers. These are precision instruments and must be used carefully. Fig. 14-9.

Unit 14: **Dimensioning**

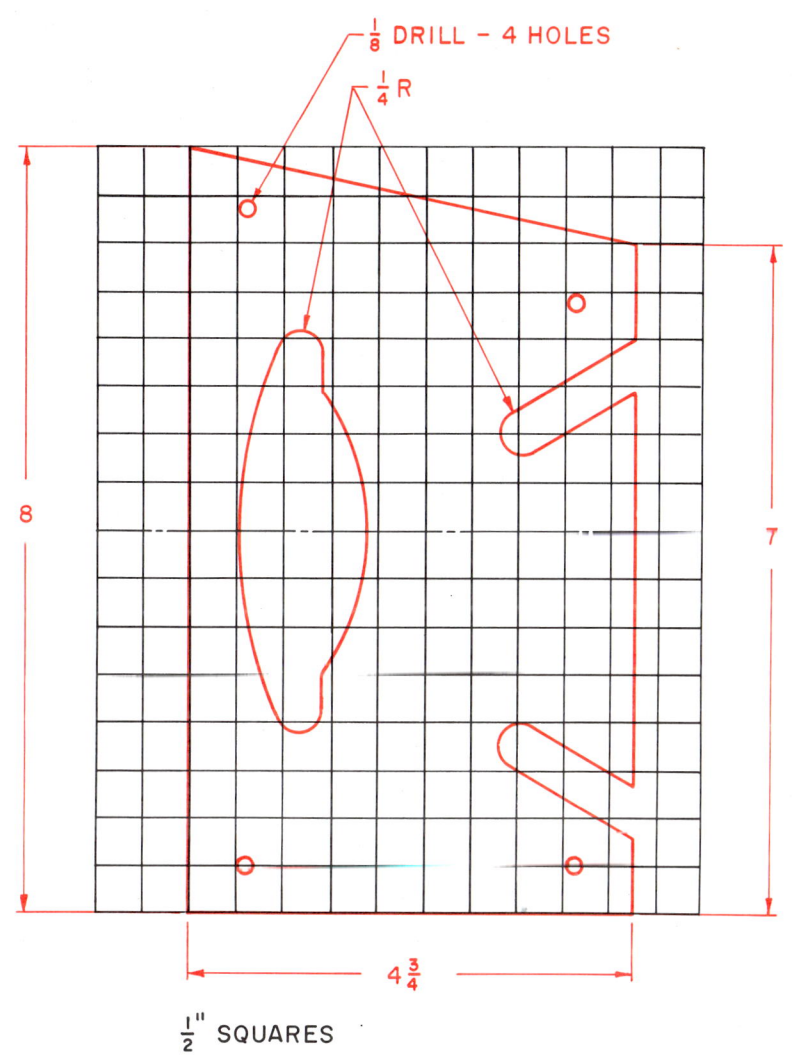

$\frac{1}{8}$ DRILL – 4 HOLES

$\frac{1}{4}$ R

8

7

$4\frac{3}{4}$

$\frac{1}{2}''$ SQUARES

14-8. This is Fig. 14-7 drawn on grid paper. See how much easier it is to read.

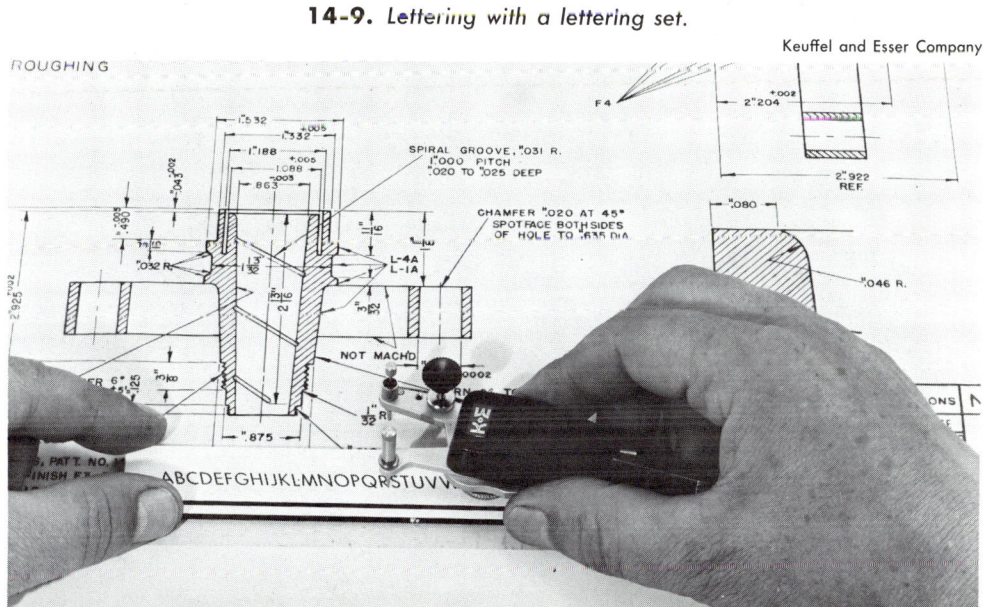

14-9. Lettering with a lettering set.

Keuffel and Esser Company

81

UNIT 15

Metric Dimensioning

There are a number of things to consider in the change from customary to metric drafting. The most important of these are drawing scales and metric dimensioning. Metric scales were discussed in Unit 7. Metric dimensioning, information on rounding off numbers, and designing in metrics are covered in the paragraphs below.

METRIC DIMENSIONS METHODS

Craftsmen have to know how to read and work with metric drawings. Drafters must know how to make metric drawings. As the United States goes metric, drawings will be made and used which show both metric and customary dimensions. Fig. 15-1. This makes it possible to read a

15-1. *An industrial drawing of a metal part showing the use of dual dimensions.*

General Motors Corporation

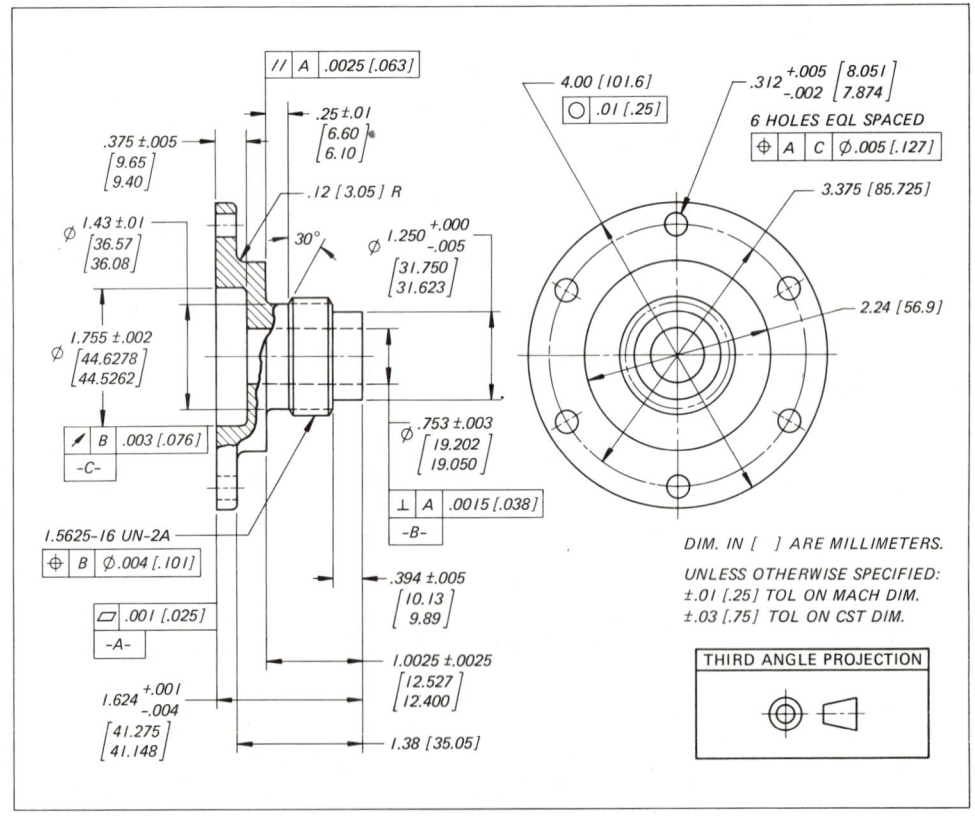

Unit 15: Metric Dimensioning

drawing of a part in metrics, but still use customary tools and machines to make the part. Or the drawing can be read with customary dimensions, but the part made with metric tools and machines. The practice of showing both customary and metric dimensions in the same drawing is called dual dimensioning. In such combination dimensioning systems, all inch-millimetre conversions are done by the engineers and drafters. This makes it unnecessary for others who use the drawing to have to make these conversions or calculations, and possibly make mistakes.

There are three common dual dimensioning methods:
- The bracket method.
- The position method.
- The conversion or equivalency chart method.

While there are others, these are the three used most frequently.

The *bracket* method is a size description system in which inch or millimetre equivalents are shown in brackets next to each dimension. (To obtain a metric equivalent, multiply the inch dimensions by 25.4, one inch equals exactly 25.4 millimetres. To convert millimetres to inches, divide by 25.4.)

Shown in Fig. 15-2 is a drawing of a cold chisel. Note that the dimensions are both metric and customary inch. The mm dimensions are placed on the dimension line and the equivalent inch dimensions are placed next to them in brackets. Of course, you can also put the inch dimensions first and the millimetre equivalents in brackets. It depends on who designed the project or part and in which country the drawing will be used. In order to avoid any confusion, always add this note to the drawing: "dim. in [ ] are millimetres"; or "dim. in [ ] are inches."

The *position* method is shown in Fig. 15-3. The millimetre dimensions are placed above the dimension line and the equivalent inch dimensions are placed below it. You can also put the inch dimensions above the line and the millimetre equivalents below it, depending upon which is the primary dimension. A note should also be added to this drawing to avoid confusion: $\frac{mm}{inch}$; or $\frac{inch}{mm}$.

The *conversion chart* dimensioning method is shown in Fig. 15-4, which is a metric drawing of the cold chisel. In one corner of the drawing is a conversion chart which gives inch equivalents for each of the millimetre sizes. This results in a much neater, less cluttered drawing, especially if the drawing has many dimensions and notes. This also makes it possible to use a computer to figure the equivalencies. The computer printout can be attached to the drawing, eliminating much hand lettering. These chart dimensions should be placed in ascending or descending order (from smallest to larg-

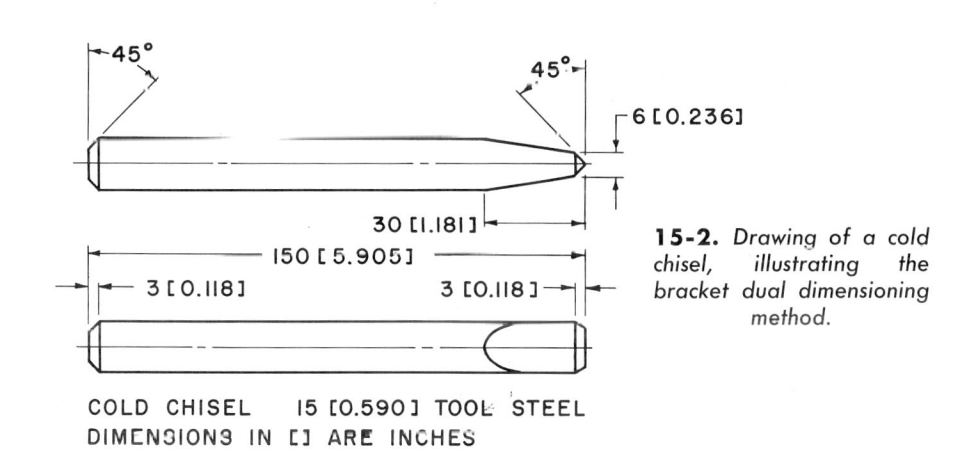

15-2. Drawing of a cold chisel, illustrating the bracket dual dimensioning method.

COLD CHISEL 15 [0.590] TOOL STEEL
DIMENSIONS IN [ ] ARE INCHES

83

Part II: Graphic Communications

est or vice versa) in order to make the chart easier to use. The ordering can be done automatically with a computer. These drawings should also carry the note "dim. in mm" to call attention to the metric dimensions. This type of drawing is becoming very popular in industry because of its convenient application to the computer.

METRIC DIMENSIONING RULES

All drawings showing both customary and metric dimensions must also indicate which angle of projection is used. The United States and Canada use the familiar third-angle projection in making multiview drawings. Most other nations use the first angle of projection. In order to avoid con-

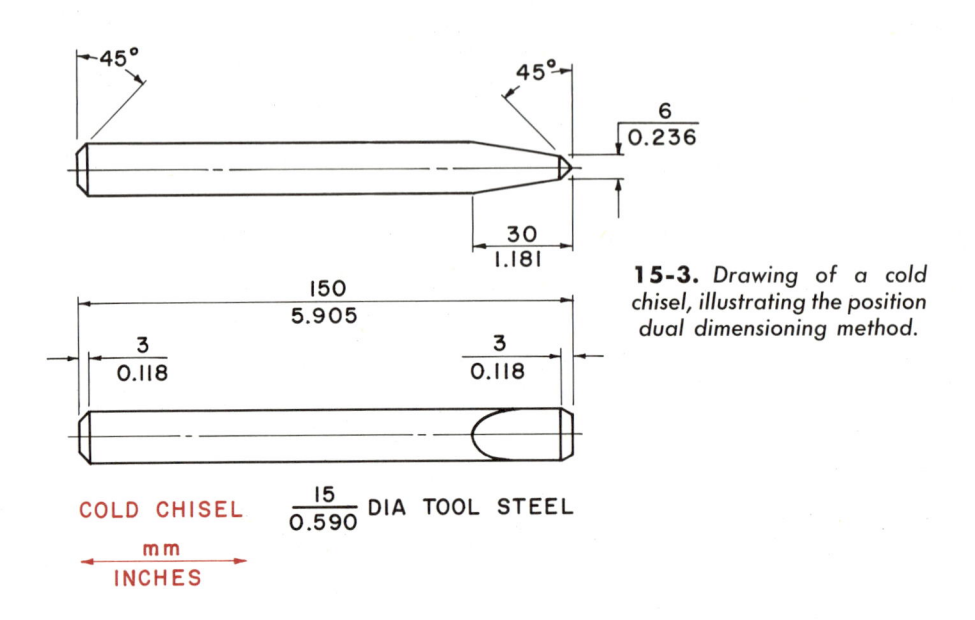

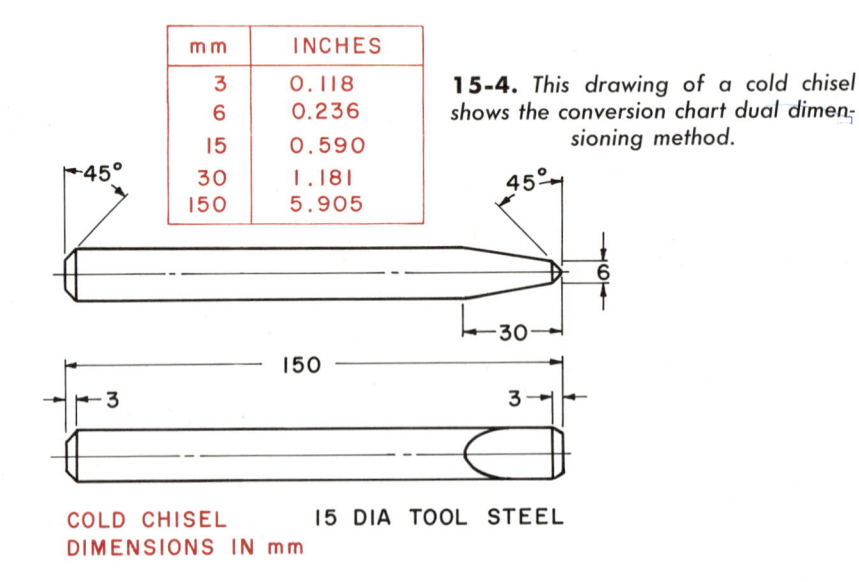

15-3. *Drawing of a cold chisel, illustrating the position dual dimensioning method.*

mm	INCHES
3	0.118
6	0.236
15	0.590
30	1.181
150	5.905

15-4. *This drawing of a cold chisel shows the conversion chart dual dimensioning method.*

COLD CHISEL
DIMENSIONS IN mm

15 DIA TOOL STEEL

84

Unit 15: Metric Dimensioning

fusion among the users of drawings, the angle of projection must be shown by one of the symbols in Fig. 15-5 on all drawings to be used in foreign countries. Procedures for making drawings according to the first angle of projection can be found in any advanced drafting textbook.

To further avoid mistakes and confusion, paper with the word METRIC printed in large letters can be used for drawings. If this paper is not available, the word *metric* can be shown in the title block or the words "all dim. in mm" lettered on the drawing. The important point here is that the person who is making a part from the drawing must know what the dimensions mean in order to know whether to use customary or metric measuring instruments.

In metric drawings, all dimensions will be in millimetres or metres except for maps, where the kilometre is used. On engineering drawings surface roughness is given in micrometres. Centimetres and decimetres should not be used, in order to avoid confusion among metric units. The mm and m are related by 1000 (1000 mm equal 1 m). The important point here is not to mix units on a drawing. It is best and clearest if a drawing contains either mm or m dimensions, not both.

In fact, most drawings will be in mm. Even building construction drawings can be easily understood if they are so dimensioned. For example, a wall that is 15 900 mm long can easily be read as 15.900 m, and the craftsman will use a 30 m measuring tape to lay it out. The use of metres on a drawing is usually limited to projects such as very large construction, shipbuilding, etc. In these cases, dimensions in metres and decimal parts of metres are used. For example, the dimension 15 m and 900 mm is shown as 15.000 m.

In dimensioning, remember that the size of a millimetre is very small:

1 mm = $\frac{1}{25.4}$ inch or 0.039 370, about forty-thousandths (0.040) inch

0.1 mm = 0.0039, less than four-thousandths inch

0.01 mm = 0.000 39, less than four-tenths of one-thousandth inch

You can see that dimensions to more than two decimal places in millimetres are generally not needed.

Rounding Off

When the third digit after the decimal is greater than 5, the second digit is increased by one. Example: 11.346 is rounded off to 11.35. When the third digit is less than 5, the second digit remains as it is. Example: 21.234 99 is rounded off to 21.23.

When the third digit is 5, look at the numbers following. If they are greater than 0, round off to the next highest number. Example: 16.235 3 is rounded off to 16.24. If the 5 is followed only by zeros, the second digit is left unchanged if it is even, and increased by one if it is odd. Example: 3.045 00 is left unchanged as 3.04, and 3.035 00 becomes 3.04 also.

DESIGNING IN METRICS

Good drawing practice includes designing in metric units and not just con-

15-5. *First or third angle projection symbols should be placed on all drawings to be used in foreign countries.*

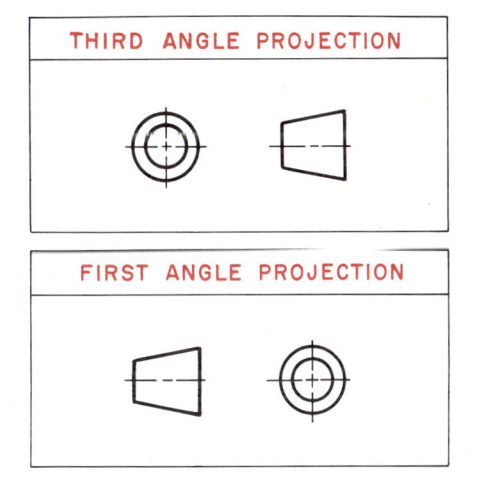

85

Part II: Graphic Communications

verting inch values to millimetres. Fig. 15-6. In this drawing of a serving tray, the millimetre is the original unit of measurement.

If you study the plans for the putty knife in Fig. 15-7, you will see that you can use either inch or millimetre rules to measure the parts as you make the knife. You will recall that this is an example of bracket dual dimensioning. But look carefully at the metric measurements. Notice that they are set at the nearest tenth of a millimetre. Now take a metric rule or scale in hand and study it. You can see that a millimetre is approximately the thickness of a dime. While it is easy to locate full millimetre dimensions, it is harder to find a decimal fraction such as 25.4 mm. Wouldn't it be easier to find a size of 25 mm? This is what designing in metrics is all about—making it simpler to make projects or products based on metric dimensions.

To make metric measuring simpler you can round off numbers to the nearest whole metric size. Avoid using decimal fractions of millimetres when designing a project or a part unless the accuracy of the piece demands it.

Now study the drawing in Fig. 15-8. It too is a putty knife, but it is drawn in millimetres only. It is about the same size as the one in Fig. 15-7, but some important changes have been made. For example, the length of the handle is 100 mm instead of 4 inches. Note that 4 inches converts to 101.6 mm exactly. Obviously, the 101.6 mm can be rounded to 100 mm to simplify the dimension so that the handle is easier to make. Use this kind of logic as you design in metrics. Also, remember the standard material sizes, such as 1" lumber as 25 mm and ½" lumber as 12 mm. A chart of preferred numbers is shown in Fig. 15-9.

To summarize, conveniently rounded-off numbers should always be used as a *first* choice unless other considerations make it impossible. For example, use 65 millimetres or 70 millimetres in preference to 67. Chosen sizes should always be consistent with the available sizes of raw materials, fasteners, etc. Study the units in this book dealing with wood, metal, and plastic materials for metric sizes. You will soon learn to design metric projects which are much simpler and more logical to draw and make.

15-6. *Metric drawing of a wooden serving tray.*

WOODEN TRAY
MATERIAL – WALNUT
GLUE AND NAIL.

ALL DIMENSIONS IN mm.

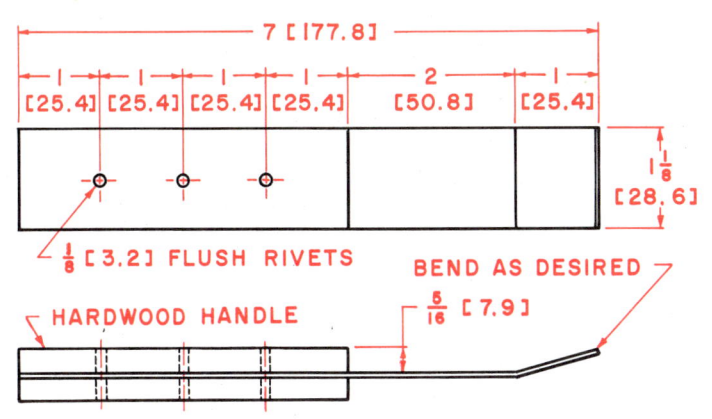

Unit 15: Metric Dimensioning

15-7. Dual dimension drawing of a putty knife.

PUTTY KNIFE
0.020 [0.50] STAINLESS STEEL BLADE
DIMENSIONS IN [ ] ARE millimetres

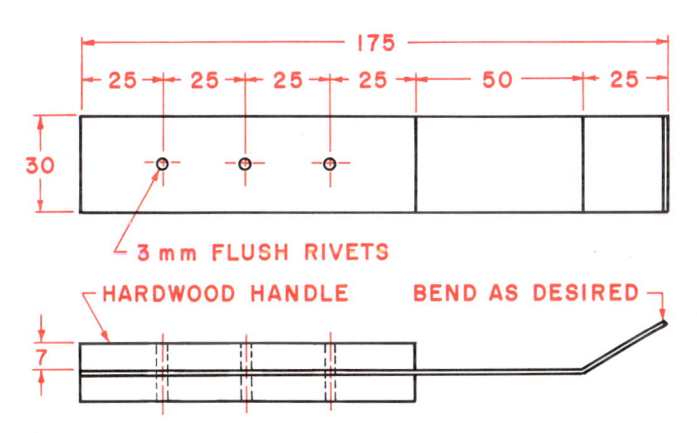

15-8. A metric drawing of a putty knife.

PUTTY KNIFE
0.50 STAINLESS STEEL BLADE
DIMENSIONS IN millimetres

15.9 Table of first choice numbers used in designing metric projects.

First Choice Sizes

	Rising by 5	Rising by 10	Rising by 20	Rising by 50	Then
1 5	20 55	80 150	200	300 650	800 3 000
1.2 6	25 60	90 160	220	350 700	900 4 000
1.6 8	30 65	100 170	240	400 750	1 000
2 10	35 70	110 180	260	450 800	1 200
2.5 12	40 75	120 190	280	500	1 500
3 16	45 80	130 200	300	550	2 000
4 20	50	140		600	2 500

87

UNIT 16

Detail and Assembly Drawings

It has already been stated that drawings must contain all the information needed to construct a product. Such drawings are called *working drawings*. A working drawing for a wooden rocking chair is shown in Fig. 16-1. This drawing shows all the dimensions and notes necessary to make the chair. No other information is needed. The drawing also shows how the parts are assembled, or fit together. This is a common type of working drawing you will make and use in the shop.

There are other types of working drawings used in industry. A product such as an engine carburetor is made up of many parts. Each part is made separately, and for each part one must have a *detail drawing*. Still another drawing is needed to show how the parts fit together. This is called an *assembly drawing*.

Detail drawings are used to show how each part is made. It is necessary to make separate drawings of these parts because, in mass production, different people make different parts of the product. Such drawings include all dimensions, notes, kind of material, and finishing information. A typical shop detail drawing of a C-clamp is shown in Fig. 16-2. Note the information given in this drawing. All these parts are grouped together on one sheet for easy study. In industry each part would be drawn on a separate sheet.

Assembly drawings show how the various parts fit together for the final product. Fig. 16-3 shows the assembly of the parts or details shown in Fig. 16-2.

Industry also uses exploded assembly drawings of numbered parts. Fig. 16-4. You use similar drawings to repair your bicycle or adjust a lawnmower.

Here are some instructions to follow when preparing detail and assembly drawings.

1. Use only the views that are necessary. Sometimes two views are enough. Some objects require three views.

2. Select the views which show the object best.

3. For simple objects with few parts, place both the detail and assembly drawings on one sheet. More complex objects require separate drawings.

4. Make certain that the drawing contains all the information necessary to make the object.

Stanley Tools
16-1. (Page 89) *A working drawing of a rocking chair. All dimensions and notes necessary to build the chair are included on this drawing.*

Unit 16: Detail and Assembly Drawings

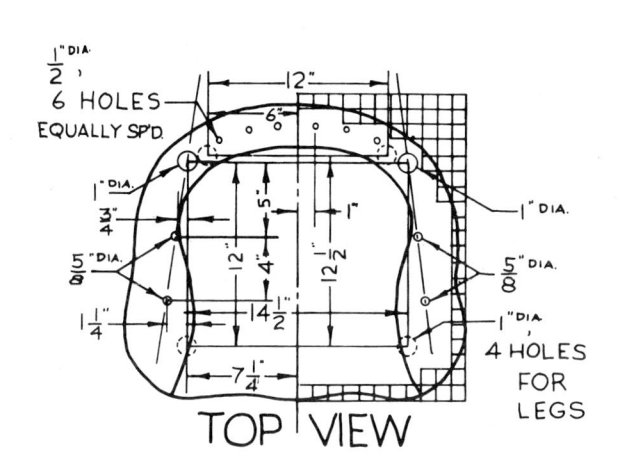

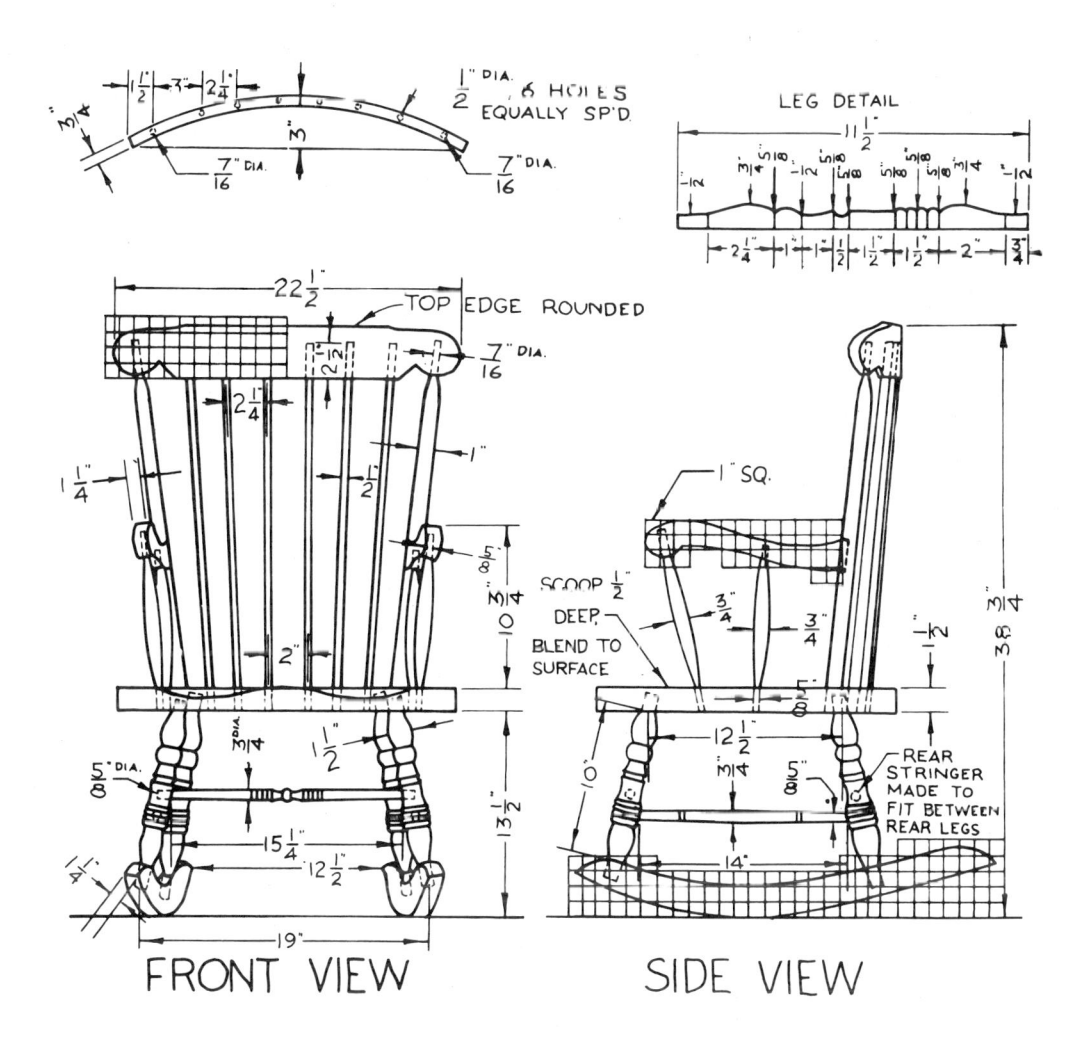

89

Part II: Graphic Communications

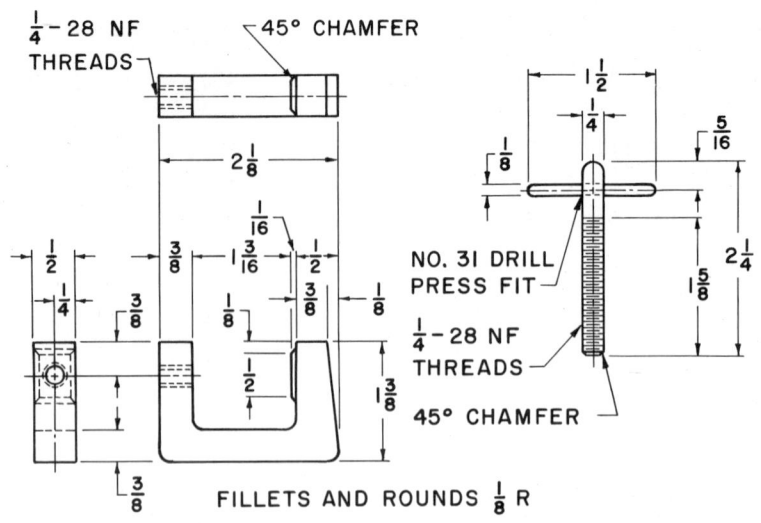

16-2. Detail drawings of the parts of a C-clamp.

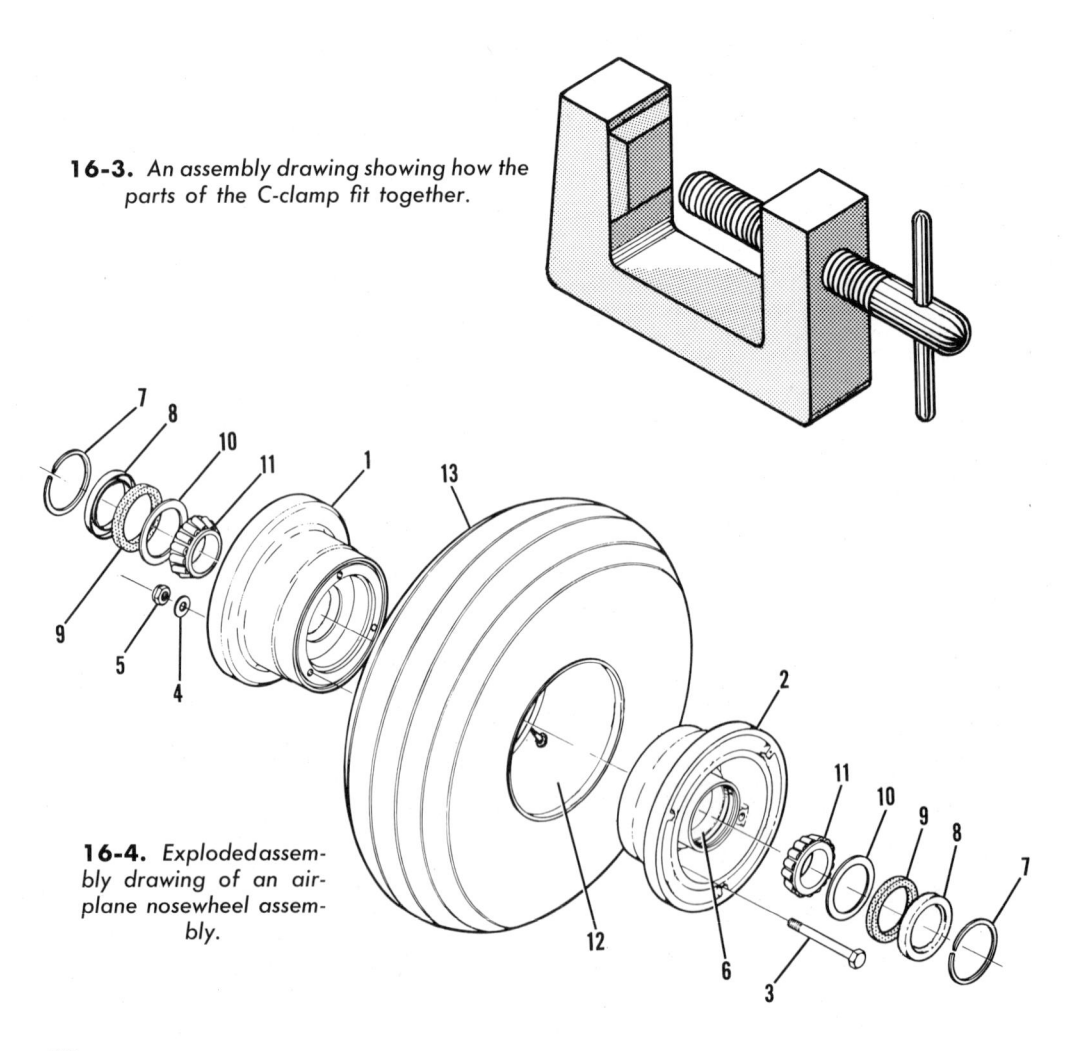

16-3. An assembly drawing showing how the parts of the C-clamp fit together.

16-4. Exploded assembly drawing of an airplane nosewheel assembly.

90

UNIT 17

Building Construction Drawing

Homes, offices, schools, and other buildings require complete plans before they are built. These plans or drawings contain all the information needed by the builders to finish the construction. This type of drawing is called "building construction" or "architectural" drawing. Fig. 17-1.

People who design homes and commercial buildings and draw plans for them are called architects. Architects often have architectural drafters working for them to help in drawing plans. When an architect designs a house, he or she often makes pictorial sketches first to show what the completed structure might look like. Fig. 17-2. The architect also prepares plans to show what interiors will look like. Fig. 17-3. As a student architectural drafter, you would have experiences in drawing house plans or plans for other kinds of buildings. Fig. 17-4.

PLANNING A BUILDING

Designing a home or other building requires much thought and planning before the drawings can be made. In home design, the designer must know the family and how it lives in order to make the home suit the family's wants and needs. How large is the family? What activities do they enjoy? Should there be spaces for hobbies, playing musical instruments, and for study and reading? Where is the home to be built? How can the designer take advantage of the natural surroundings? These and many other questions must be answered. Whether designing a

17-1. Many types of building construction drawings are needed by all craftsmen in the construction industry. This is a drawing of plans for a school.

Teledyne Post, Des Plaines, IL

Part II: Graphic Communications

house or a hardware store, the designer must know how the building is to be used.

As ideas for rooms begin to appear, the designer sketches plans for room spaces and layouts. For example, he or she may think about the shapes of kitchens and how the work areas can be planned. Fig. 17-5. In this way the house begins to take shape.

STEPS IN DRAWING HOUSE PLANS

House plans are prepared in a number of steps. Fig. 17-6. The drafter lays out the basic shape and size of the house. Next, the living, working, playing, sleeping, and eating areas are grouped together. These interior details are studied and refined. Changes and improvements

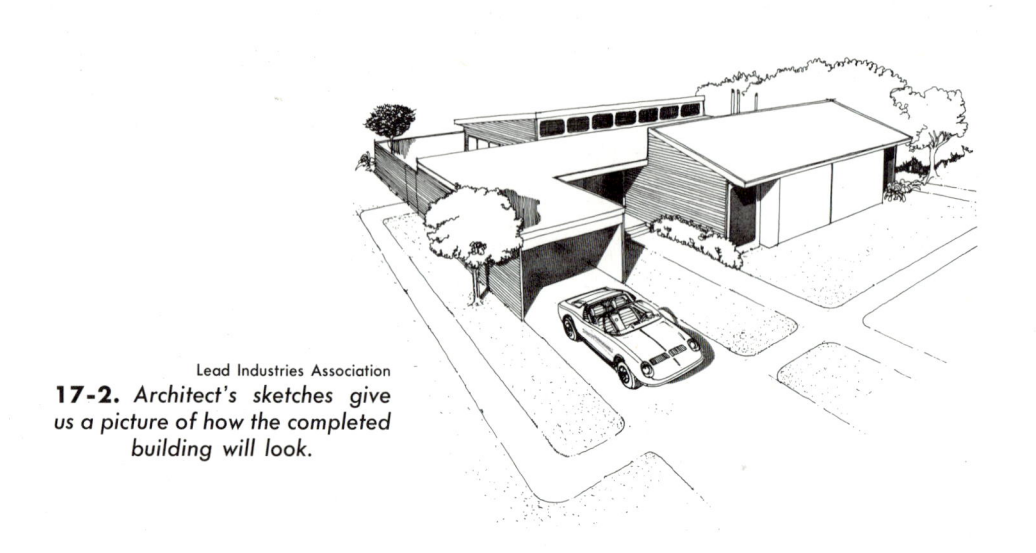

Lead Industries Association
17-2. Architect's sketches give us a picture of how the completed building will look.

17-3. Floor plans show how the interior of a building will look.

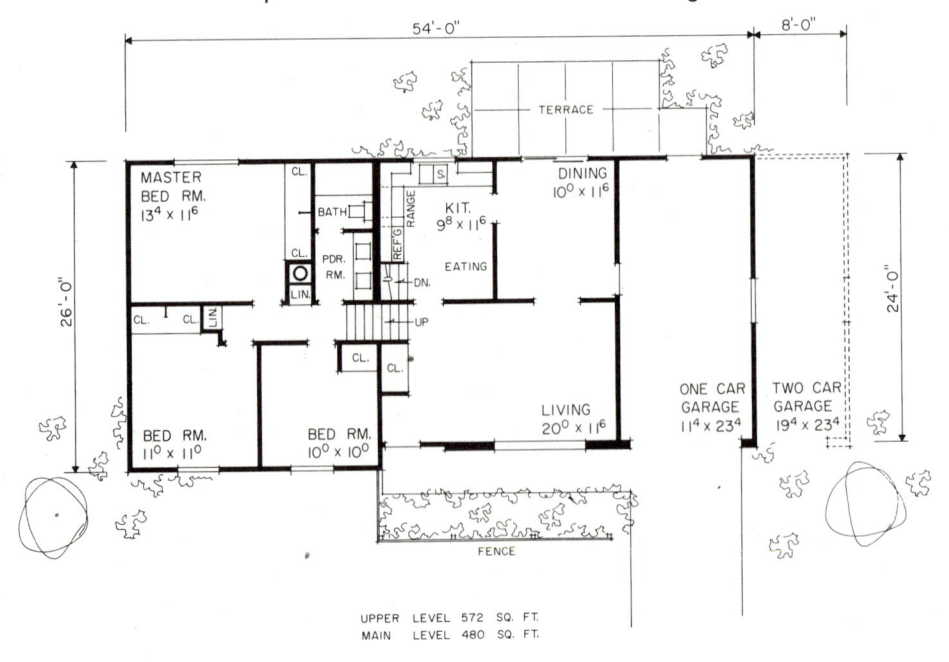

Unit 17: Building Construction Drawing

Teledyne Post, Des Plaines, IL
17-4. Architectural drawing is an important part of the drafting profession. This student is lettering a drawing.

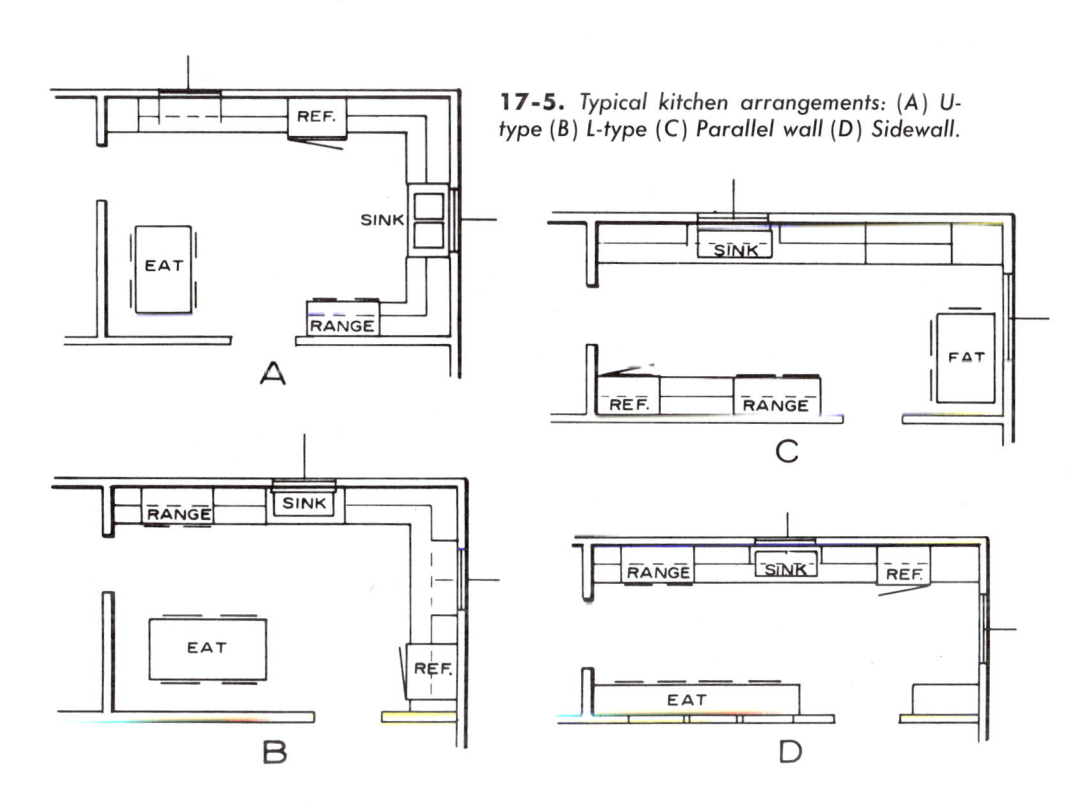

17-5. Typical kitchen arrangements: (A) U-type (B) L-type (C) Parallel wall (D) Sidewall.

93

Part II: Graphic Communications

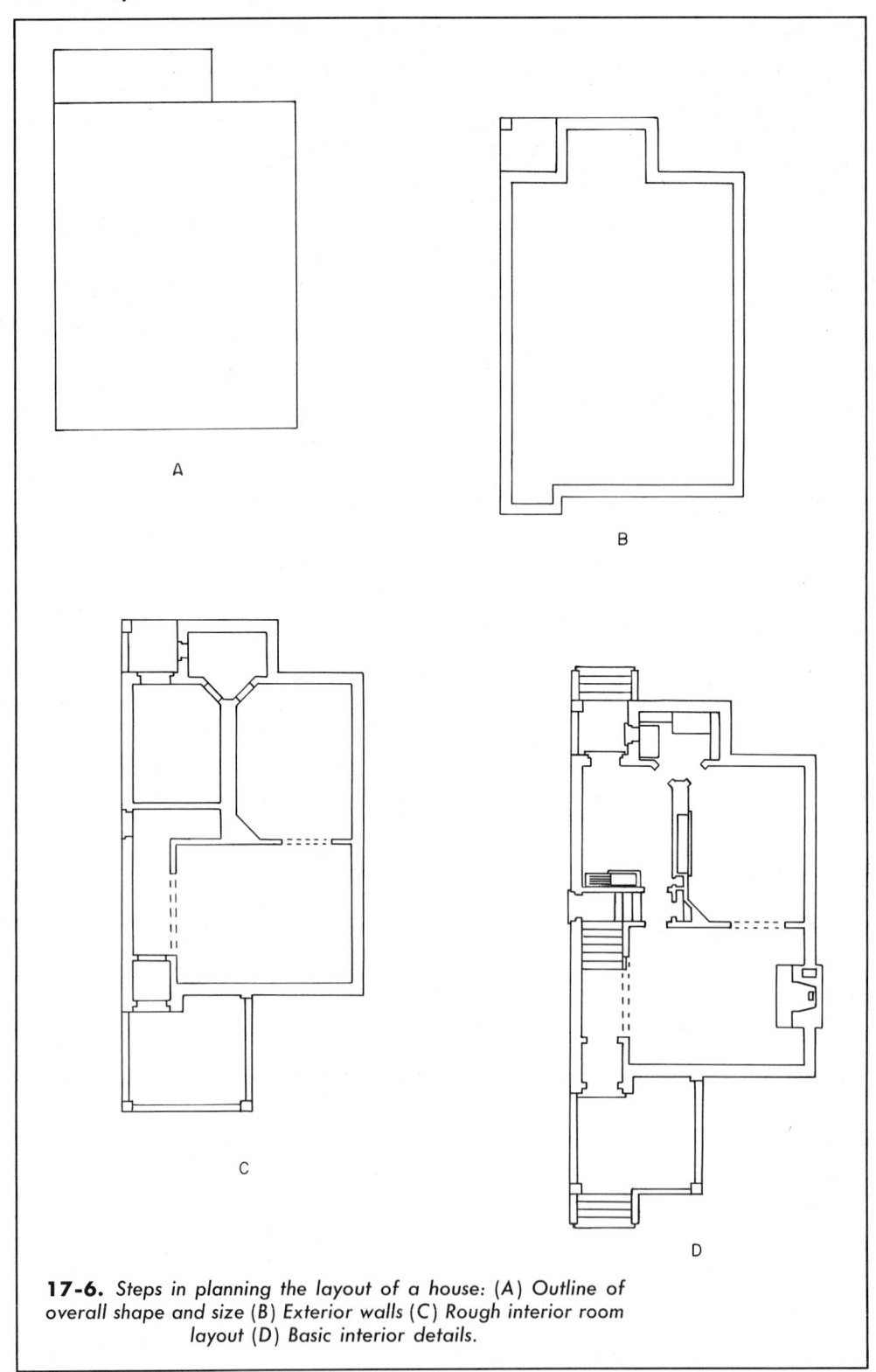

17-6. Steps in planning the layout of a house: (A) Outline of overall shape and size (B) Exterior walls (C) Rough interior room layout (D) Basic interior details.

Unit 17: Building Construction Drawing

are made. There are many problems to be solved: where to locate the chimney and fireplace, how to group plumbing fixtures, how to provide enough storage, where to place stairways and hallways, and where to locate doors and windows. As these problems are solved, the final floor plan takes shape. Fig. 17-7.

The final floor plan includes basic information for the builder. Fig. 17-8. Other plans are often drawn with information on plumbing, heating, and electricity. Sometimes all this information is put on one plan, if it will not look too cluttered.

In addition to the floor plans, others are needed. These are foundation plans, elevations, and construction details. Elevations are views of the outside of the building. Fig. 17-9. There are generally four elevations, one for each side of the house.

When drawing house and building plans, select the proper scales so that the plans will fit on the paper. Plans and elevations are often drawn to a scale of $\frac{1}{4}'' = 1'\ 0''$. Construction details are usually to a scale of $\frac{3}{4}'' = 1'\ 0''$. More information on drawing and using house plans can be found in Part 4, *Building Construction*.

Remember to use architectural symbols to make drawings easier to read. Some examples are shown in Fig. 17-10. Others can be found in Unit 8.

An example of a metric house plan appears in Fig. 17-11. Note that the measurements are in millimetres. Otherwise it looks like a customary house drawing.

As you begin your building construction drawing activities, remember to start with something small and simple. A backyard clubhouse, a small cabin, or an outdoor tool storage shed are some good projects for the beginner.

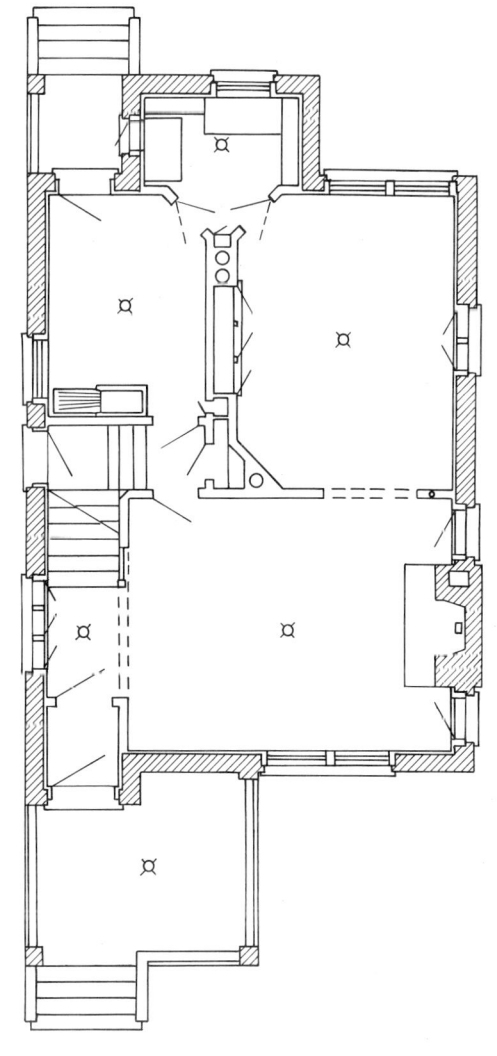

17-7. Complete the interior layout before adding dimensions. This will permit you to make design changes.

Part II: Graphic Communications

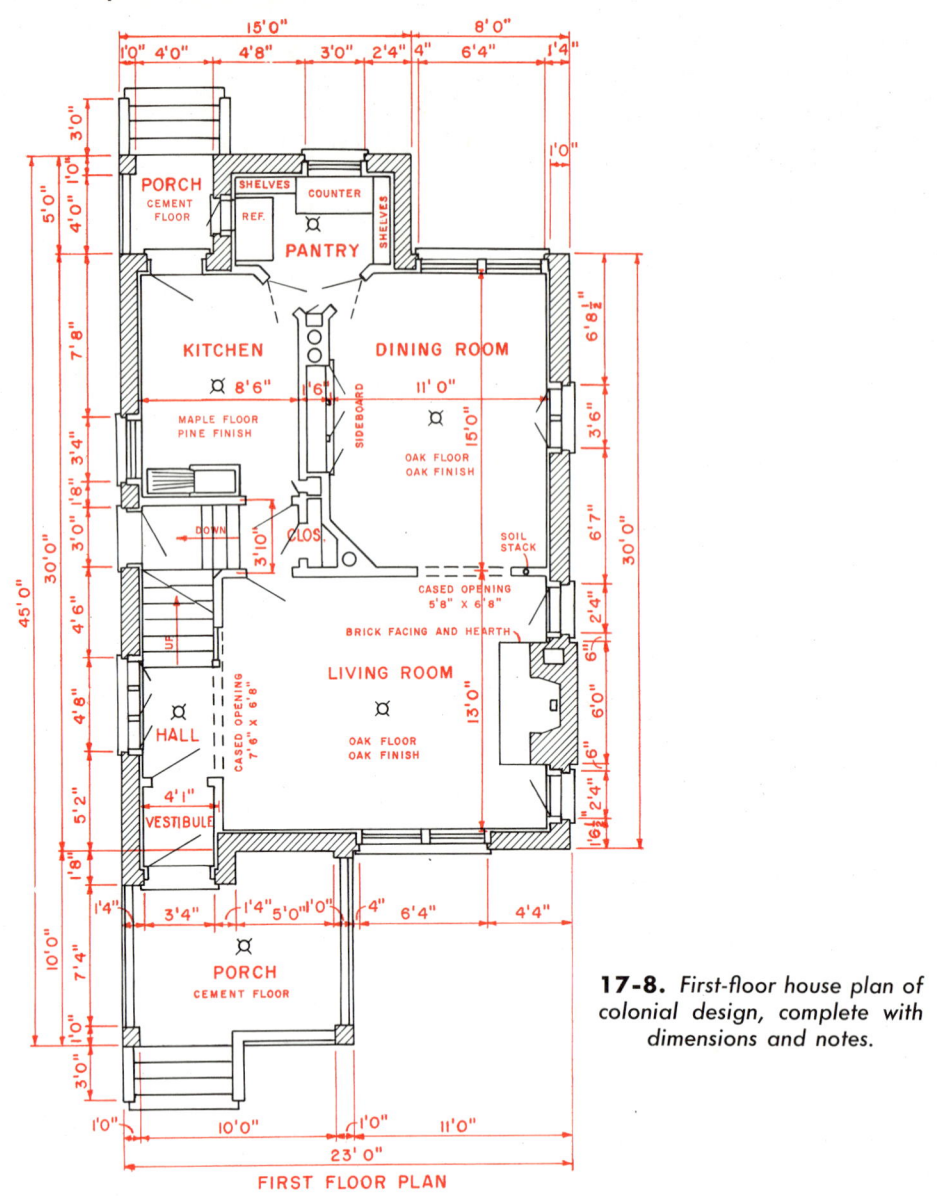

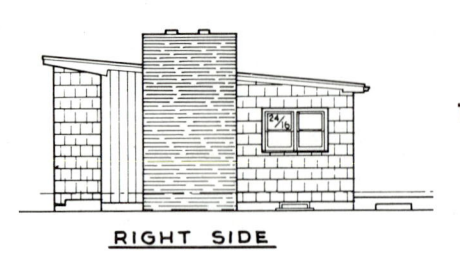

17-8. First-floor house plan of colonial design, complete with dimensions and notes.

17-9. Right side elevation.

96

Unit 17: Building Construction Drawing

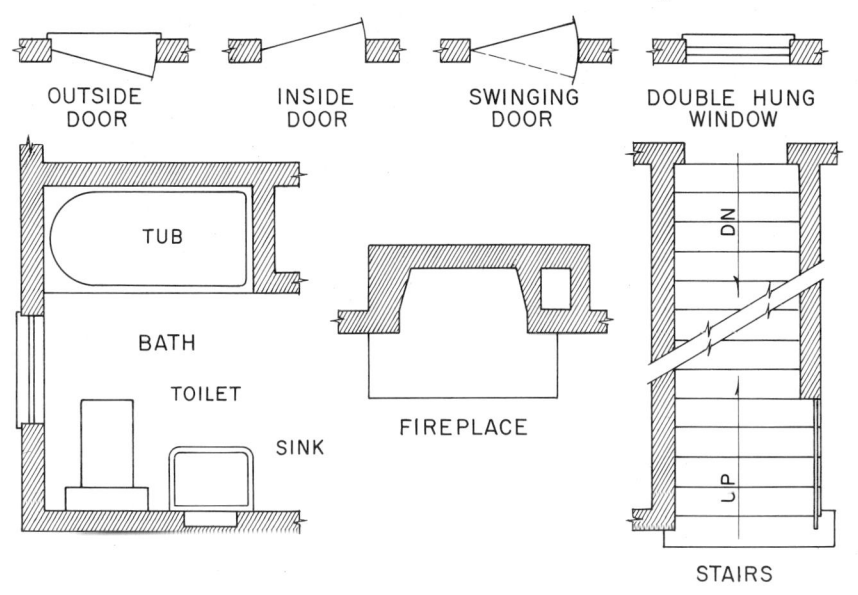

17-10. Some symbols used in architectural drawing.

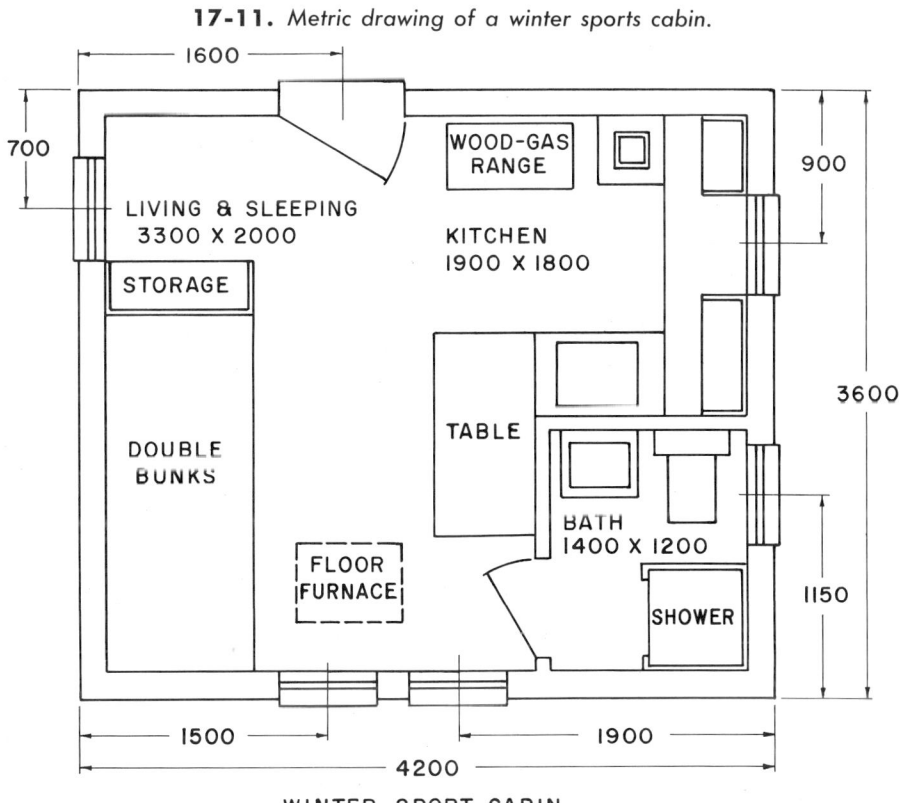

17-11. Metric drawing of a winter sports cabin.

WINTER SPORT CABIN
ALL DIMENSIONS IN mm

97

UNIT 18

Printmaking

Many shop drawings are made on ordinary opaque drawing paper. However, in industry and construction, many different people may use a drawing. To provide enough drawings for everyone, and to keep the original from becoming soiled and torn, copies are made. These copies are called "blueprints," or just "prints." To make a print, you must first make a tracing of a drawing. This is done by fastening a sheet of thin paper over a drawing and then tracing all lines and lettering. Drawings are often made directly on tracing paper to avoid having to make a separate tracing.

The tracing is then used to make a print, much as you would make a photographic print from a negative. There are

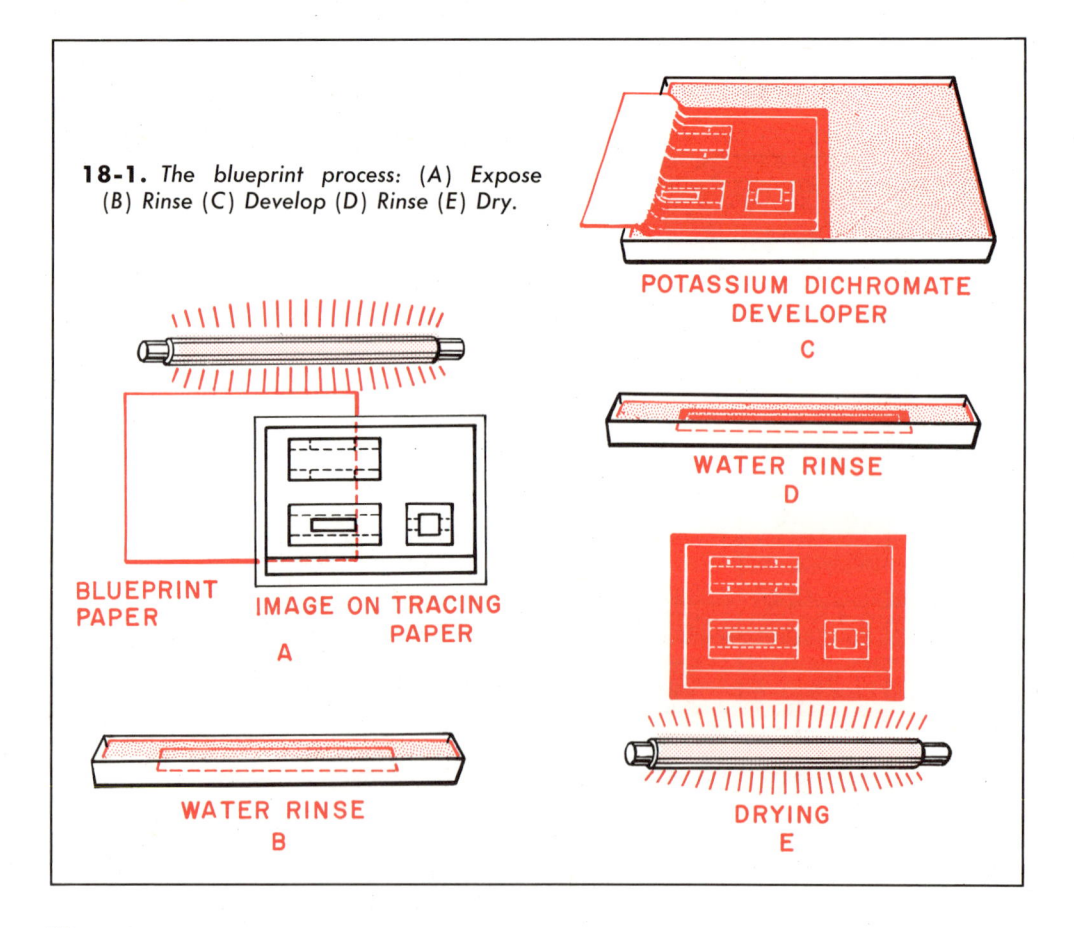

18-1. The blueprint process: (A) Expose (B) Rinse (C) Develop (D) Rinse (E) Dry.

BLUEPRINT PAPER
IMAGE ON TRACING PAPER
A

POTASSIUM DICHROMATE DEVELOPER
C

WATER RINSE
D

WATER RINSE
B

DRYING
E

98

Unit 18: Printmaking

three types of prints generally used in shops and industry.

Blueprints are white-line prints on a dark blue paper. These are often used because they do not fade in sunlight. A blueprint diagram is shown in Fig. 18-1. Blueprints can be made with simple equipment. However, automatic blueprint machines are also used.

Dry-diazo prints have black or blue lines on a white background. The process is explained in Fig. 18-2. The dry-diazo process is convenient because no messy liquids are used. It is often called the Ozalid process.

The *moist-diazo* process is much like the dry-diazo process. The difference is that while the dry-diazo uses an ammonia fume developer, the moist-diazo uses a liquid developer applied with a roller. Fig. 18-3. This is also a fast, convenient printing method, often called the Bruning process. Fig. 18-4. In both diazo processes, the color of the lines depends upon the type of paper used.

18-2. *The dry-diazo or Ozalid process: (A) Expose (B) Develop (C) Finished print.*

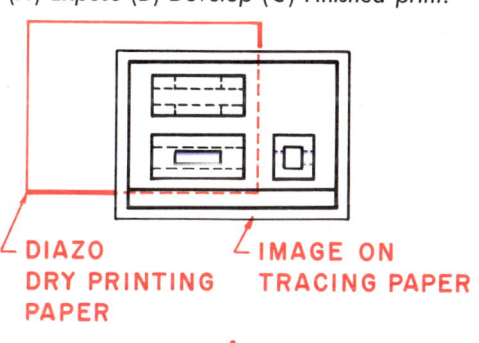

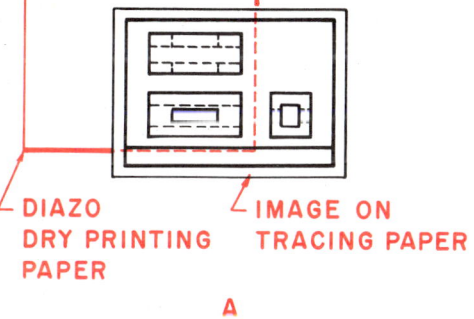

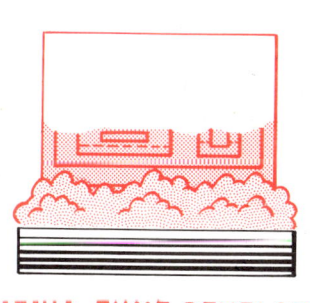

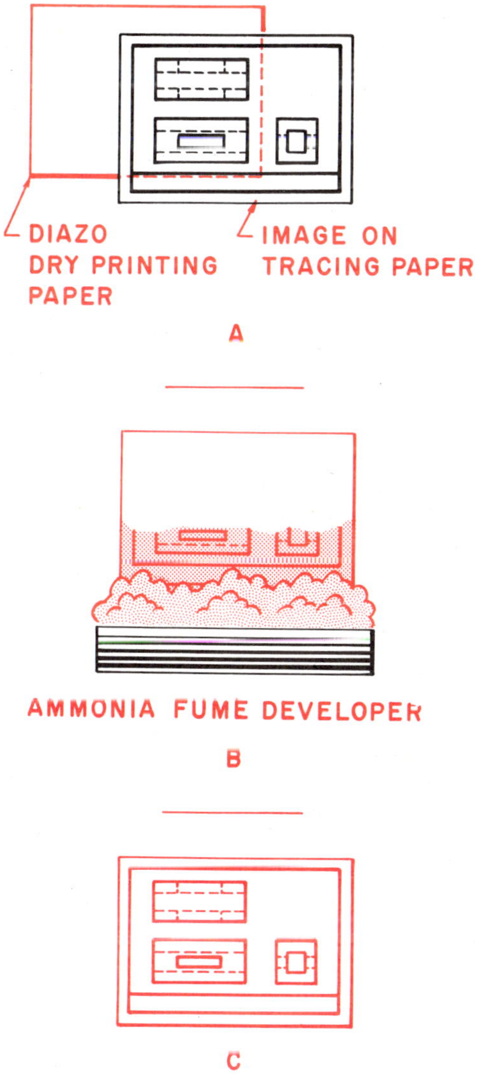

18-3. *The moist-diazo or Bruning process: (A) Expose (B) Develop (C) Finished print.*

99

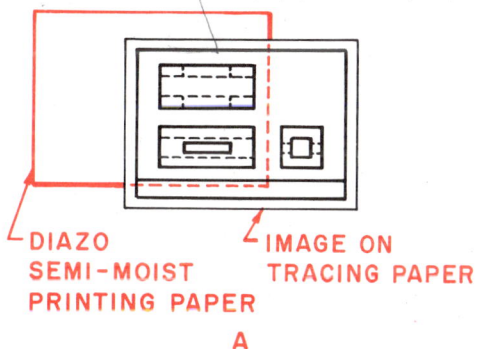

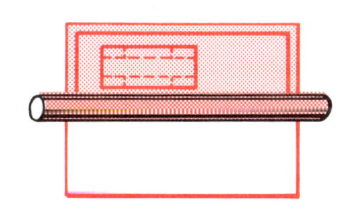

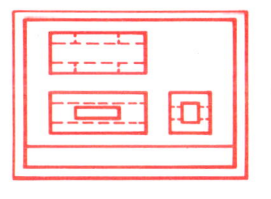

Part II: Graphic Communications

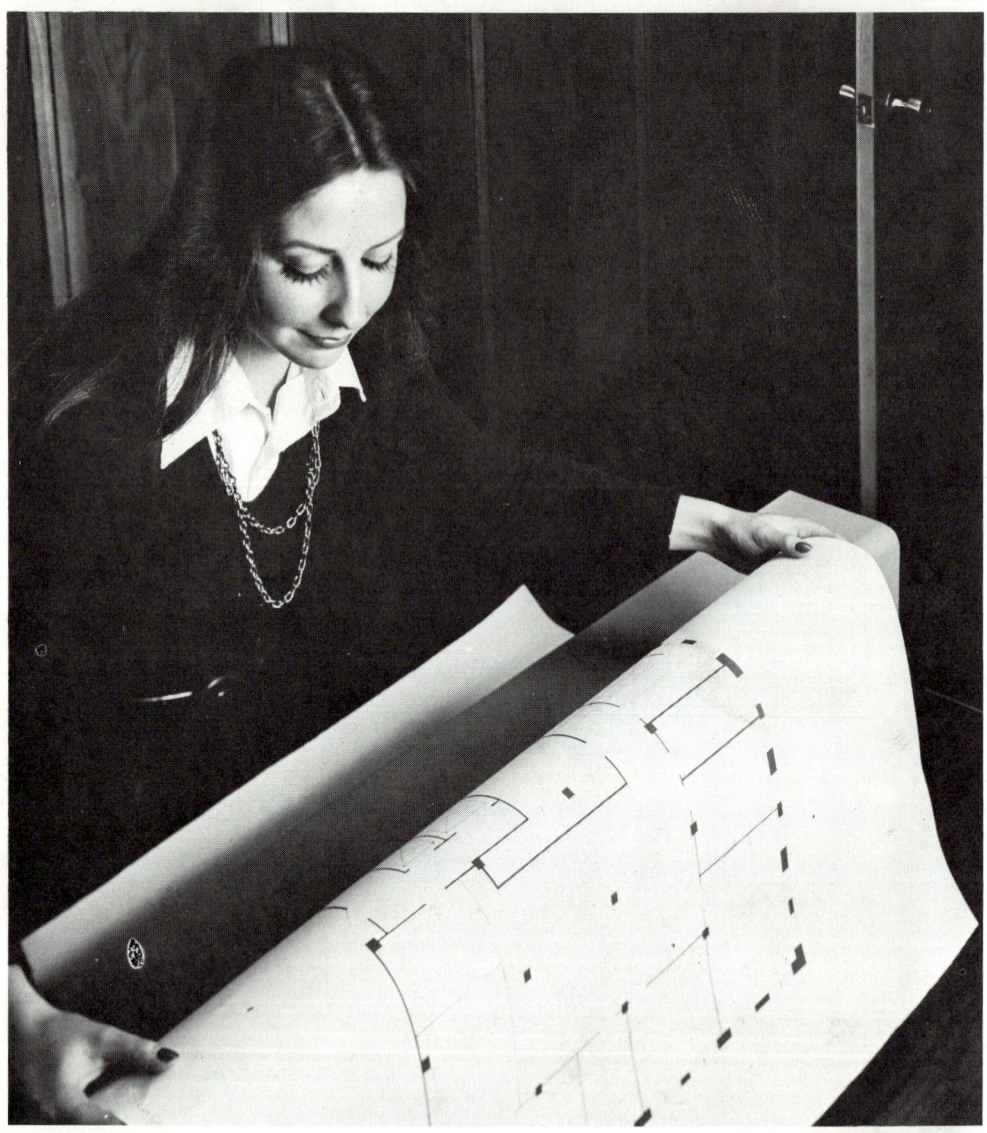

Bruning Division, Addressograph-Multigraph Corporation

18-4. *Using the moist-diazo machine.*

DISCUSSION TOPICS AND ACTIVITIES

Part 2—Graphic Communications
Section 1—Drawing
Unit 6
    1. About how many drawings are needed to build the average automobile?
    2. Why is drafting called a "language"?
Unit 7
    1. List two main types of triangles used in drawings.

Units 6–18: Discussion Topics and Activities

2. What grades of pencils are used for making light construction lines? For drawing finish or object lines? For sketching and shading?

3. What instrument is used for drawing large circles and arcs?

Unit 8

1. List five important kinds of lines in the alphabet of lines.

2. Sketch three different symbols for each of the following: A. Building materials. B. Plumbing fixtures. C. Electricity. D. Small appliances.

3. Select one of the geometric patterns shown in your book and draw it, using instruments.

Unit 9

1. Make sketches of three or four items found around the home such as a glass jar, a toy, a model car, or a hand tool.

Unit 10

1. Get a piece of paper that has $\frac{1}{4}''$ spaced lines on it. Use this as a practice sheet and begin to practice lettering. Follow the examples in the textbook to learn proper techniques.

Unit 11

1. How many views does every object have?

2. Sketch some objects that need only one or two views to describe their shape.

Unit 12

1. What is the purpose of a sectional view of an object?

2. What is the purpose of an auxiliary view of an object? Sketch an example of this.

Unit 13

1. List three types of pictorial drawings.

2. What type of pictorial drawing uses vanishing points?

3. What type of drawing contains views with axes that lie 120° apart?

4. What type of pictorial drawing uses cavalier and cabinet styles?

Unit 14

1. List the two systems used for placing dimensions on a drawing.

2. What is the difference between a size dimension and a location dimension?

3. Get a clean sheet of paper and practice making arrowheads. Follow the examples in the textbook for proper techniques.

Unit 15

1. List three types of common metric dual dimensioning methods.

2. Round off the following numbers to two decimal places. Follow the rules shown in the textbook: A. 12.345 B. 42.3249

3. Sketch a simple object such as an eraser or a pencil. Dual dimension it according to one of the methods described in this book.

Unit 16

1 What is the difference between detail drawing and assembly drawing?

2. List four important instructions to follow in preparing detail and assembly drawings.

Unit 17

1. What is an elevation drawing? How many are needed for a building such as a house?

2. What scale is generally used for plans and elevations? For construction details?

3. Draw a floor plan for a winter sports cottage or a summer beach cottage.

Unit 18

1. List the three types of prints generally used in shop and industry, and write a brief explanation of each.

PART II
Graphic Communications

Section 2–Graphic Arts

Unit 19 Introduction to Graphic Arts

Unit 20 Printing Processes and Materials

Unit 21 Composing Type

Unit 22 Printing by Letterpress

Unit 23 Offset Lithography

Unit 24 Silk-Screen Printing

Unit 25 Taking and Developing Pictures

Unit 26 Printing Pictures

Unit 27 Office Duplicating

Discussion Topics

Metric Fact Sheet*
— Graphic Arts —

- Paper sizes are in mm.
- Paper standards include:
  - —The A series for general use.
  - —The B series for posters, charts, and maps.
  - —The C series for envelopes.
- The basic A sheet has an area of one m² and measures 841 x 1189 mm.
  - —The ratio of length and width dimensions are: $1:\sqrt{2}$.
  - —Get smaller A sizes by dividing the longer side by 2. (See drawing.)
- Basic paper weights are measured in grams per square metre (g/m²) instead of pounds per ream. Forty-pound book paper has a metric equivalent of 60 g/m².
- Liquid volumes are in litres; temperatures are in degrees Celsius (°C).

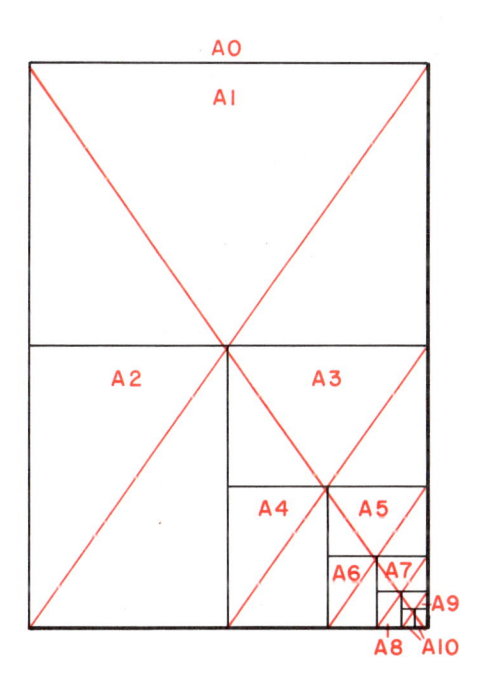

*You will find other information on metrics in the Appendix.

103

UNIT 19

Introduction to Graphic Arts

"Graphic arts" deals with the placing of printed images onto a solid material. This solid material is usually paper. However, other solid materials such as cloth, metal, glass, or plastic may also have designs printed on them by one of the graphic arts processes. What we call the graphic arts industry also includes papermaking, ink making and bookbinding, as well as the actual printing. The graphic arts industry is one of the largest in the country. Almost one million men and women are employed at some occupation connected with the graphic arts.

The purpose of the graphic arts is to communicate. The purposes of printed

19-1. A press used for printing newspapers. It can print as many as 70 000 newspapers an hour.

Graphic Systems Group, Rockwell International

Unit 19: Introduction to Graphic Arts

communication vary from advertising to educating, from making people laugh to making them cry. We look at road maps to check our location during a trip. We read the comics in the Sunday paper to be amused and entertained, and we read the newspaper to be informed. Every day products of the graphic arts industry influence our lives in some way.

Graphic arts is a very old craft. The Chinese printed from wooden blocks long before the birth of Christ. The ancient Koreans printed from type made from porcelain. However, these inventions did not find their way to Europe, so for hundreds of years all books were copied by hand. Therefore they were scarce and costly. This began to change when movable type was invented. Johann Gutenberg first used movable type in Europe about 1445. After this date, reading material was no longer a luxury only the rich could afford.

Fig. 19-1 shows a press used for printing newspapers. Two other things are needed to complete the printing process. These are paper and ink.

PAPER

The art of papermaking is many centuries old. A material similar to the paper we use was invented in China about 105 A.D. The earliest paperlike material was developed in Egypt. This material, called "papyrus," was made from reeds which grew along the Nile River. Today most of the paper is made from wood pulp. Fig. 19-2 shows a diagram of the papermaking process. Fig. 19-3 shows a papermaking machine.

INK

The other material needed for the printing process is ink. Printing inks are similar to paint. Both ink and paint contain *pigment* for color, *vehicle* to carry the pig-

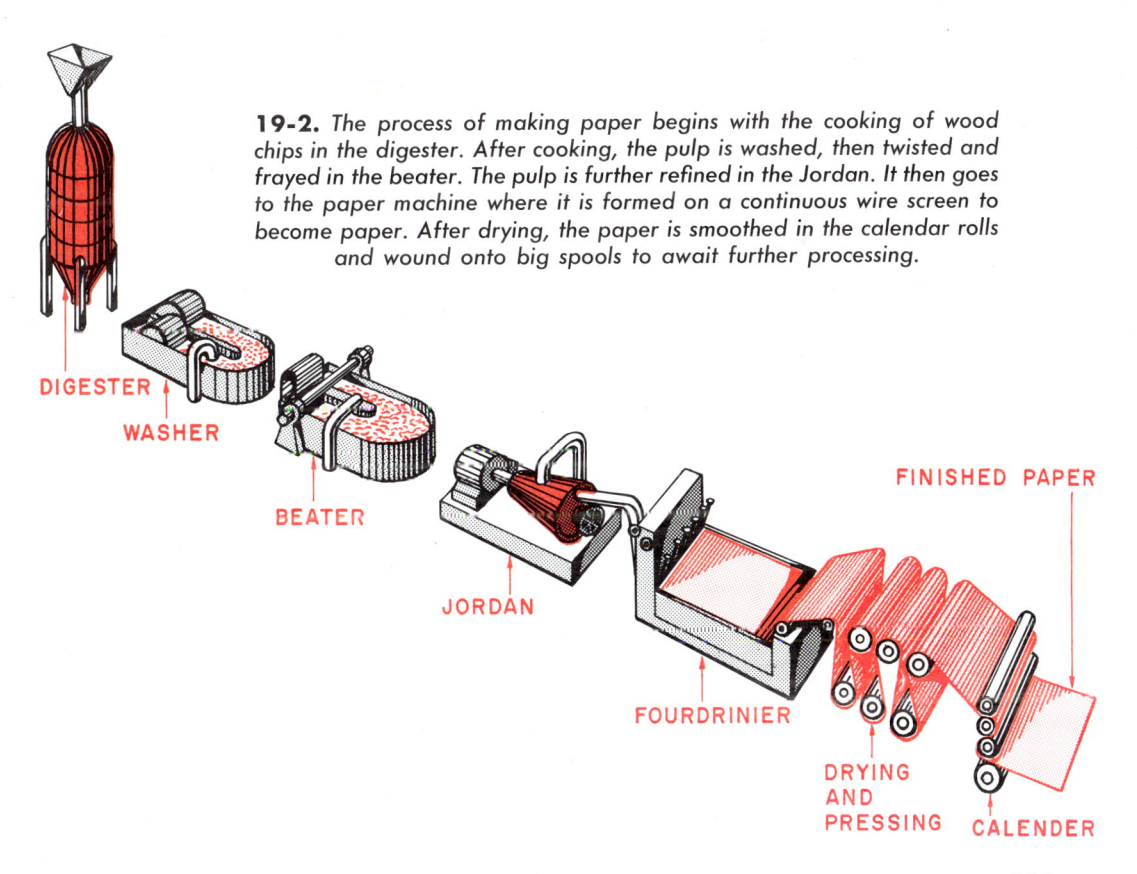

19-2. The process of making paper begins with the cooking of wood chips in the digester. After cooking, the pulp is washed, then twisted and frayed in the beater. The pulp is further refined in the Jordan. It then goes to the paper machine where it is formed on a continuous wire screen to become paper. After drying, the paper is smoothed in the calendar rolls and wound onto big spools to await further processing.

DIGESTER
WASHER
BEATER
JORDAN
FOURDRINIER
DRYING AND PRESSING
CALENDER
FINISHED PAPER

105

Part II: Graphic Communications

19-3. View of the full length of a paper machine. This is one of the largest single pieces of equipment in any industry.

The Beloit Corporation

ment, and *dryer* to help the vehicle to dry. Fig. 19-4 shows an ink mill where the pigment and vehicle are thoroughly mixed together.

Originally, in the time of Gutenberg, printing ink was made from lampblack and linseed oil. Today printing inks are made in a variety of colors and for many special purposes. Many tons of ink are needed each year to print newspapers, magazines, books, and advertisements.

California Ink Co.
19-4. Several ink mills in operation.

106

UNIT 20

Printing Processes and Materials

There are several methods by which an image is placed on material, but most printing is done on paper by one of four major processes:
- Relief printing.
- Lithography.
- Gravure.
- Stencil.

RELIEF PRINTING

Relief printing is done from raised surfaces such as pieces of type, linoleum blocks, or various kinds of printing plates. Ink is applied to the raised portion of the surface, then transferred to the paper. This is the oldest form of printing. Probably the most familiar example is printing with a rubber stamp. Fig. 20-1 shows the principle of relief printing.

Letterpress printing, a very important form of relief printing, is usually done with one of three kinds of presses. These are the platen press, the cylinder press, and the rotary press. You might wonder why all letterpress printing cannot be done with one kind of press. Think of all the products that are printed. Printed jobs range in size from small labels for medicine bottles to thousand-page telephone directories. Each kind of press has been designed for a certain type of work.

If you have a hand-lever press in your shop, you have a form of *platen press*. It brings the type and paper together to make a print. Fig. 20-2. Platen presses

20-1. *Relief printing is done from raised surfaces like this piece of type.*

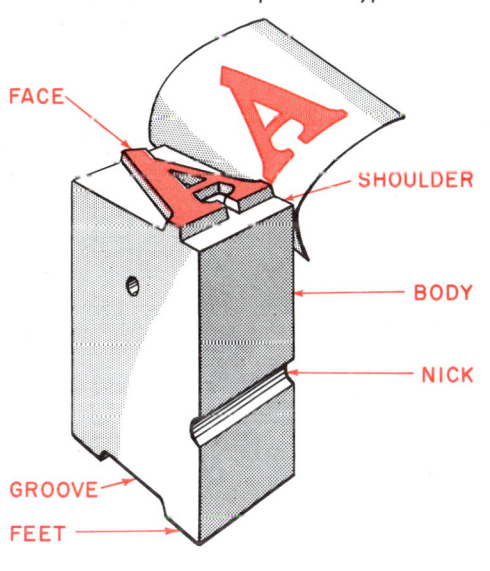

20-2. *The platen press. Many small printing jobs are done on this kind of press.*

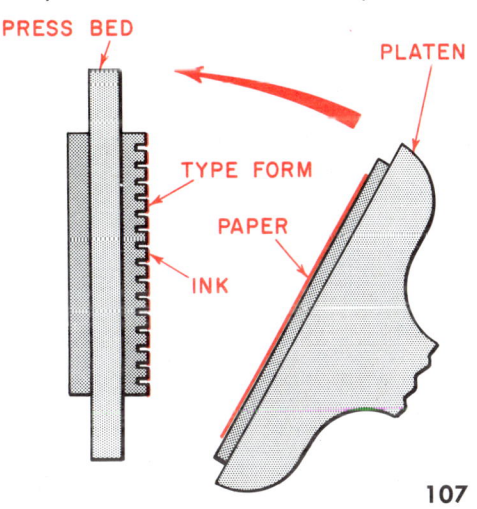

107

Part II: Graphic Communications

used in industry are usually run by electric motors. They may be either automatic or fed by hand. Such presses are used for printing business cards, stationery, tickets, and similar items.

The *cylinder press* uses type and flat printing plates. The paper is wrapped around a cylinder and rolled over the type to transfer the ink as shown in Fig. 20-3. The form moves horizontally back and forth and the paper revolves over it. This kind of press is used for printing such things as booklets, folders, catalogs, and labels. Some cylinder presses have two printing units so that more than one color may be printed as the sheet of paper moves through the press.

The *rotary press* is the fastest press for relief printing. The type material for this press is made into curved plates that fit on a cylinder. The paper goes between the curved plates and another cylinder, called the *impression cylinder*. Fig. 20-4. The most familiar use of rotary presses is for printing newspapers and magazines from rolls of paper. Many high-speed rotary presses can print and fold thousands of newspapers every hour. Some rotary presses print sheets rather than rolls of paper.

OFFSET LITHOGRAPHY

In lithography the printing is done from a flat surface, not a raised one as in letterpress. Lithography is based on the principle that grease and water do not mix. The image areas on the lithographic plate—that is, the parts which are to print—are covered with a greasy substance that will repel water. The plate is then coated with a water solution which sticks to the plate where there is no grease. In the areas where the greasy image has been applied, the water does not stick, but the oil-base printing ink does.

The image can be transferred directly from the plate to the paper. However, in *offset lithography* the image is transferred (or "offset") from the plate to a rubber-covered cylinder, called a blanket, then from this cylinder to the paper. Fig. 20-5 shows the principle of this process.

Originally, stones were used for the lithographic process. The images were placed on the stone by drawing with a grease pencil or wax crayon. This process is still used by artists for making lithographic prints. Industry uses a much faster and more precise method called *photo-offset lithography*. In this process the material to be printed is photographed with a special camera. This produces a negative which is placed on top of a sensitized metal lithographic plate. Then the image is transferred to the plate in much the same way as a photographic print is made. The areas to be printed attract ink but repel water just as if the image had been placed on the plate with a wax crayon.

Offset lithography has become a very important process. Many items that used to be printed by the letterpress process

20-3. *The cylinder press prints from flat plates or type. The paper is printed as it rolls over the type.*

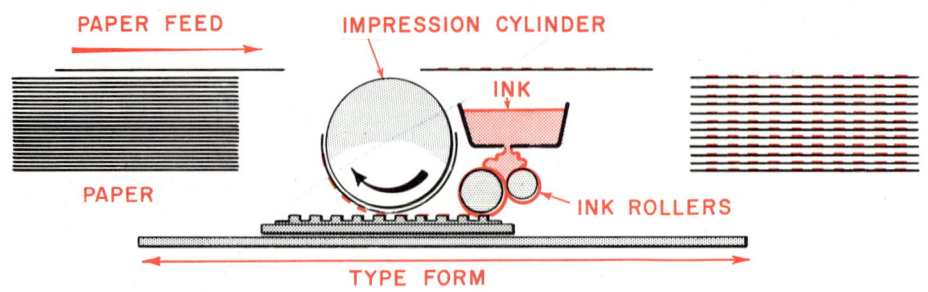

Unit 20: Printing Processes and Materials

are now printed by lithography. Many large mail order catalogs are printed by this process. So are many bulletins, bank checks, stock certificates, and some decals. Large printing firms commonly have complete offset-lithographic departments.

GRAVURE PRINTING

Gravure printing is similar to engraving. The printing is done from recessed or sunken images. Fig. 20-6. This process is the exact opposite of relief printing, in which the printing surfaces are raised. In the *rotogravure* process the printing is done by transferring ink to the paper from *cells*. These are holes of varying depths etched into a copper cylinder.

The first step in the process is to photograph the original material to be printed. Film positives are then made. These are

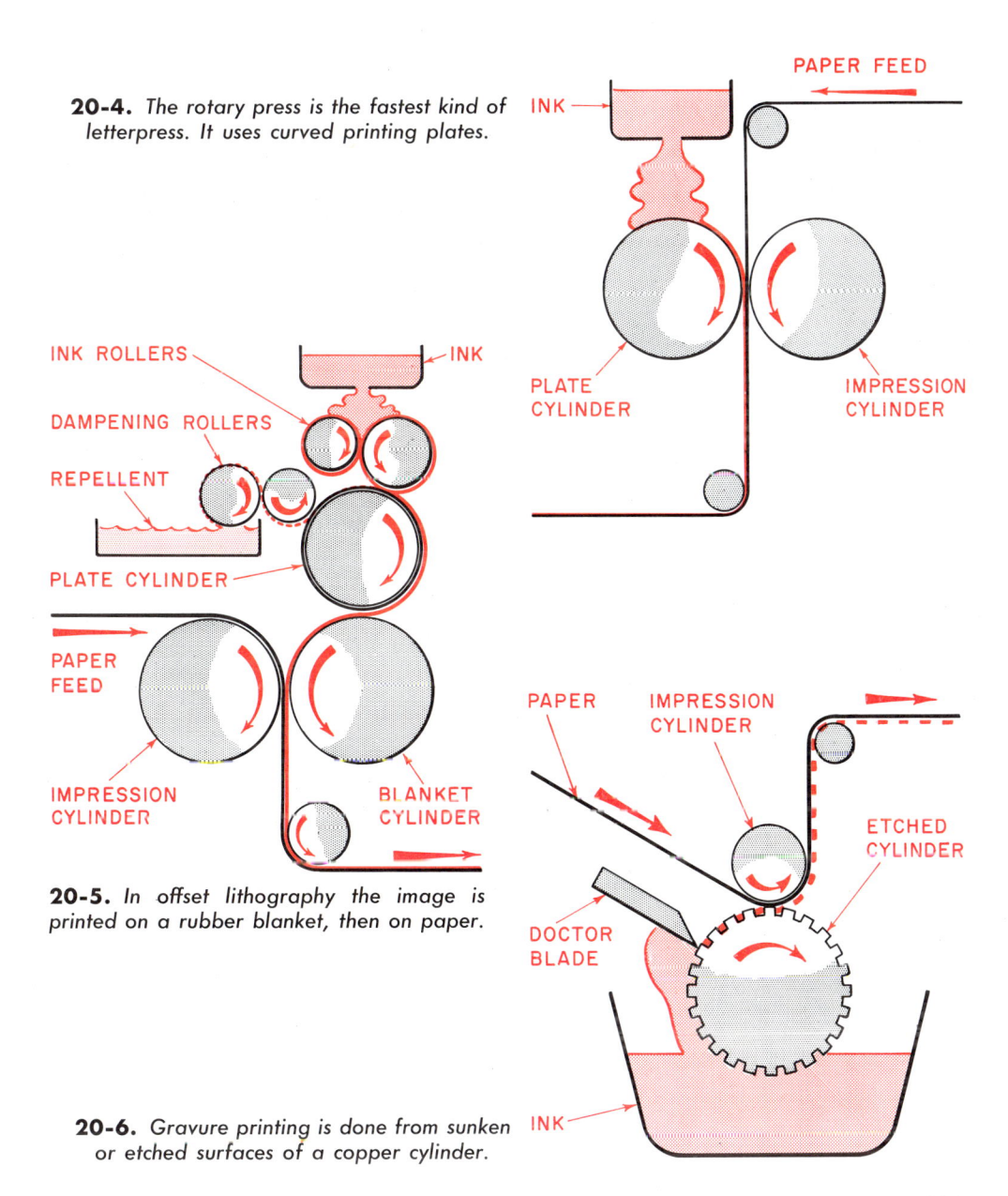

20-4. *The rotary press is the fastest kind of letterpress. It uses curved printing plates.*

20-5. *In offset lithography the image is printed on a rubber blanket, then on paper.*

20-6. *Gravure printing is done from sunken or etched surfaces of a copper cylinder.*

109

Part II: Graphic Communications

used to transfer the design to the copper cylinder, with the help of a special carbon tissue material. When the carbon tissue is applied to the copper cylinder and developed with warm water, an image of the copy is left on the cylinder. The entire cylinder is then etched with acid, forming the cells in the shape of the image.

The copper cylinder is placed on a gravure press for printing. The cylinder turns in a trough of ink and the image cells are filled. The rest of the cylinder is inked too, so it is wiped off with a *doctor blade*. When the paper comes in contact with the cylinder, the ink in the cells is transferred to the paper.

Modern high-speed rotogravure presses can print continuous sheets of paper as wide as eight or nine feet. The copper cylinders can print millions of copies before wearing out.

The gravure process is used for printing such items as paper money, wallpaper, wrapping paper, box labels, packaging materials, and postage stamps.

SILK-SCREEN PRINTING

Silk-screen printing is really stencil printing. A stencil is simply a pattern with certain parts cut out. It is placed over the surface to be printed. Ink or paint is brushed through the cutout areas, forming words or a design on the surface beneath.

In the silk-screen process the stencil is attached to a screen. The type of screen used depends on the design being printed. A coarse mesh is used for large, heavy designs. For detailed work, a fine mesh is used. A squeegee forces paint through the stencil and the screen, onto the object being printed. Fig. 20-7.

20-7. *The squeegee forces paint through the screen onto the paper in silk-screen printing.*

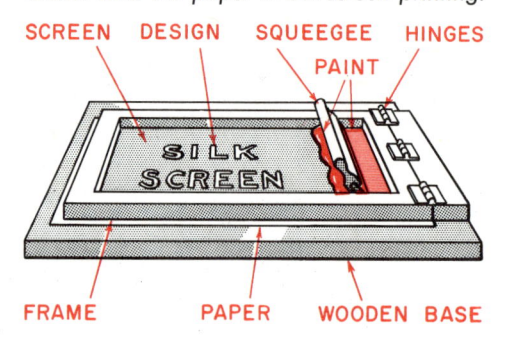

SCREEN   DESIGN   SQUEEGEE   HINGES
PAINT
FRAME   PAPER   WOODEN BASE

UNIT 21

Composing Type

For many years after the invention of movable type, all type was set (assembled) by hand. Today much of the printed material is set by machine. Hand-set type is used for small jobs like business cards, wedding invitations, envelopes, and some advertising. The hand-set type, called *foundry type,* is made of an alloy of lead, tin, and antimony. The type characters look like Fig. 21-1.

Note that each part of a piece of type has a name. Type is one of the most important materials of a printer. You should learn the various kinds of type available in your shop.

Printers use a special measuring system in their work. It is called the point system. The standard unit of the point system is the pica, which equals about $\frac{1}{6}$ of an inch. The pica is divided into twelve equal parts called points. A point is equal to about $\frac{1}{72}$ of an inch.

The printer's measuring tool is called a *line gauge.* Fig. 21-2. It is divided into

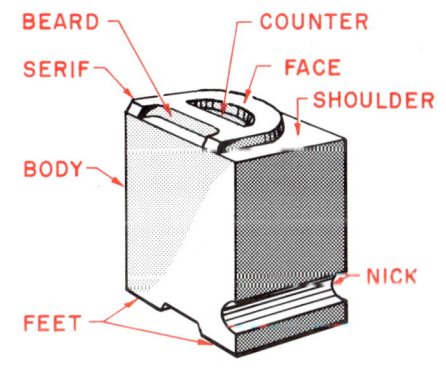

21-1. Parts of a piece of foundry type.

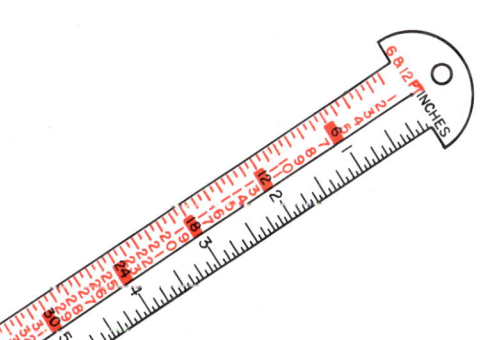

21-2. A line gauge.

Part II: Graphic Communications

inches and picas. Type is measured in points with the line gauge. For example, the type in Fig. 21-3 is 24 points.

Type is stored in drawers which are divided into compartments for each letter, number, and space. This drawer is called a *type case*. The type case most often used is the *California job case*. Fig. 21-4.

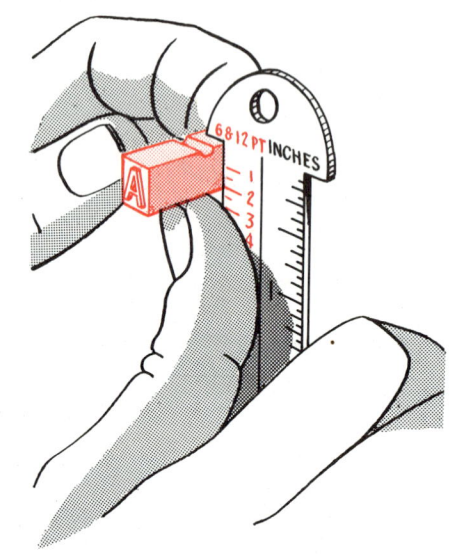

Type cases are stored in a cabinet called a *type bank*. Fig. 21-5. Type banks also provide room to store spacing material and a top surface to hold the type case when type is being set.

To make spaces between lines, *leads* and *slugs* are used. These are 2 points and 6 points thick. Fig. 21-6. To provide space at the beginning of paragraphs and between words, several sizes of spaces are needed. The basic space is the *em quad,* which is one em high and one em wide. (One em is equal to one pica.) The most common space used between words is the 3 em space. A 3 em space is $\frac{1}{3}$ the width of an em quad. Fig. 21-7 shows size relationships.

HAND-SETTING TYPE

Type is set, or composed, in a *composing stick*. Fig. 21-8. To set type the composing stick must first be set to the desired length of line. Raise the clamp and slide the knee to the desired setting. Press the clamp back down to lock the knee. Insert a piece of line spacing material in the composing stick. Usually a slug is used at the beginning of a job.

Select the type you wish to use and place the case on top of the type bank.

21-3. *Measuring the size of a piece of type using a line gauge.*

21-4. *The California job case.*

21-5. Type is stored in a type bank. This type bank also stores leads and slugs.

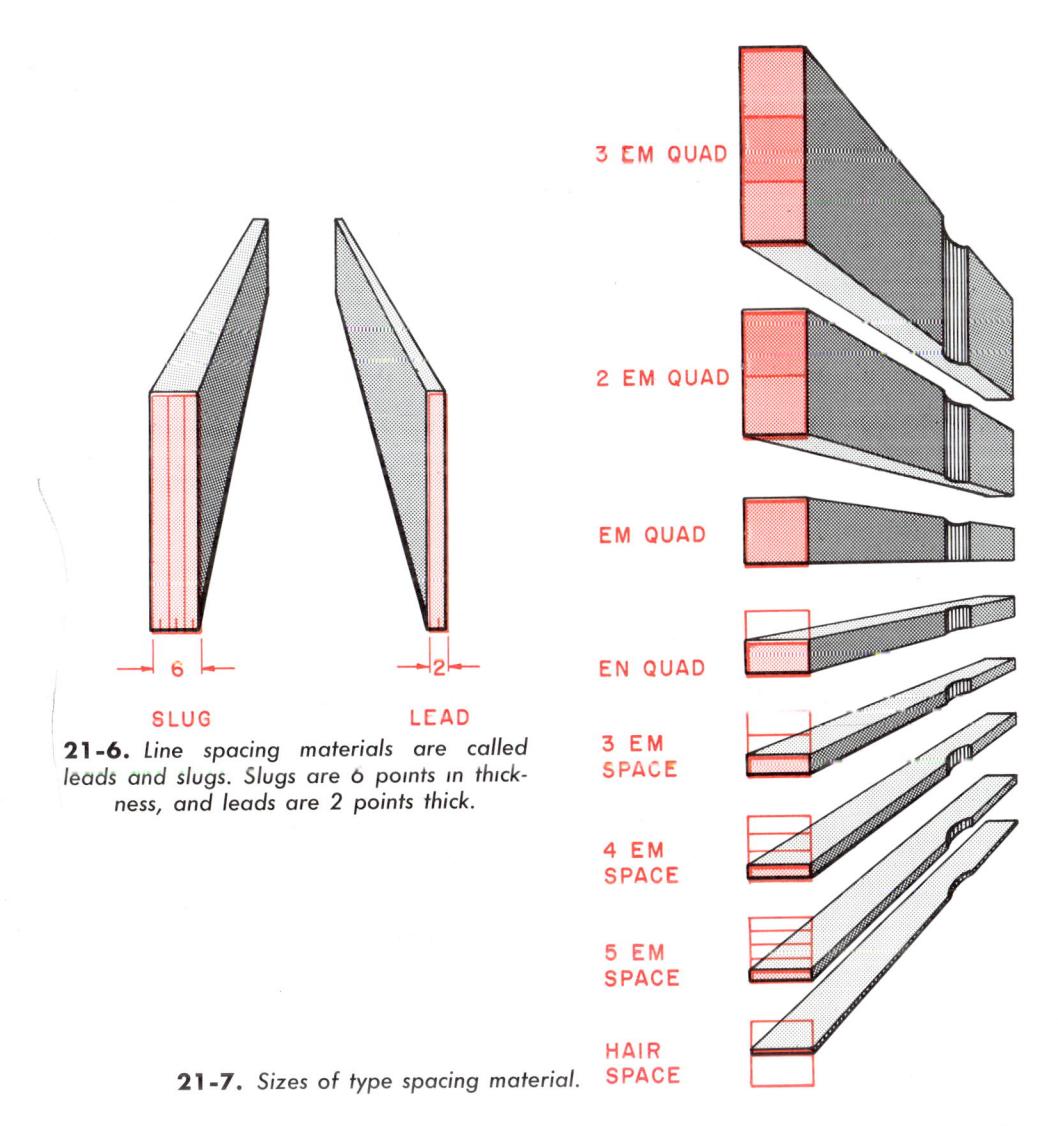

SLUG　　LEAD

21-6. Line spacing materials are called leads and slugs. Slugs are 6 points in thickness, and leads are 2 points thick.

3 EM QUAD
2 EM QUAD
EM QUAD
EN QUAD
3 EM SPACE
4 EM SPACE
5 EM SPACE
HAIR SPACE

21-7. Sizes of type spacing material.

113

21-8. Composing stick.

CAUTION: Be sure to grasp the case firmly to avoid spilling. Stand in front of the type case and hold the composing stick in the left hand as shown in Fig. 21-9. Hold the stick at a slight angle with the thumb against the type. This keeps the type from falling over. Pick up the pieces of type one at a time and place them in the composing stick from left to right with the nick on the letter toward the open side of the stick. You can read the words you are setting from left to right, but the letters are upside down and backwards. CAUTION: Type metal contains lead. *Never place type in your mouth.*

21-9. *Correct way to hold the composing stick. Note how the thumb holds the type in the stick.*

After the line is set, it must be spaced out to the proper length. This is called *justification.* The spaces and quads shown in Fig. 21-7 are used for this purpose.

When the stick is $\frac{1}{2}$ to $\frac{3}{4}$ full, it should be transferred to a three-sided flat metal tray called a *galley.* With the open end of the galley to your left, place the composing stick into the galley. Grip the typeform as shown in Fig. 21-10 and slide the form onto the galley. Place the type in the lower left-hand corner of the galley with the nicks toward the open end. CAUTION: Be sure to slide the typeform. Do not pick up the type.

Cut a piece of string that is long enough to go around the form four or five times. Start the string at one corner and go around the form clockwise. The string should overlap the start so that it may be pulled tight. Wind the string around the form several times, then tuck the end of the string under the windings. Fig. 21-11. This will hold the type tightly together.

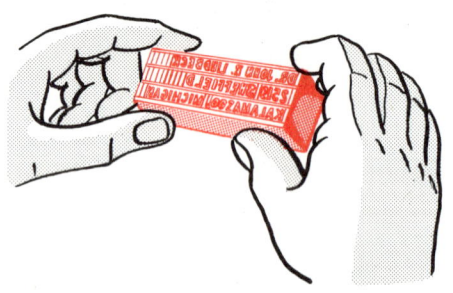

21-10. *Transferring type from the composing stick to the galley. Be sure to hold the type tightly.*

21-11. *Use the makeup rule to tuck under the end of the string.*

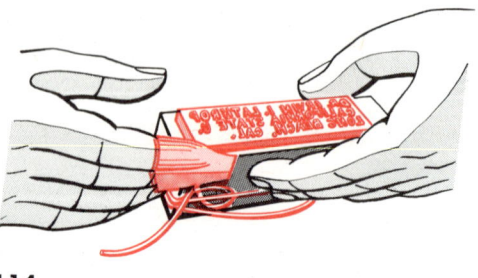

UNIT 22
Printing by Letterpress

MAKING THE PROOF

After the form is in the galley and tied, a proof (sample copy) must be made. The proof is used to check the typeform against the layout and to check for misspelled words as well as broken type. Fig. 22-1 shows one type of press used for proofing.

To pull a proof, place the galley on the bed of the proof press. The open end of the galley should be toward the cylinder. Be sure the ends of the string are not under the form.

Place a small amount of ink on the ink plate. Distribute the ink evenly over the plate using a brayer. Then ink the typeform by rolling the brayer lightly over the form as shown in Fig. 22-2.

Place a sheet of paper carefully on the typeform. Roll the cylinder over the form to transfer the ink to the paper. Do not roll the cylinder more than once over the form because the print may be blurred.

Before removing the galley from the proof press, use a cloth and solvent to clean the ink from the face of the type.

22-1. *One type of proof press.*

Vandercook Co.

115

Part II: Graphic Communications

CAUTION: Be sure to place the used cloth in a safety can.

Remove the galley with the form and place it back on the type bank. Read the proof and replace wrong or damaged type. Most corrections can be made directly on the galley after untying the typeform. Sometimes one or more lines of type have to be removed and returned to the composing stick for corrections.

Tie up the form and make another proof. If it is clean (no mistakes or broken type), the typeform is made ready for the press. This process is called *imposing* the form. During the imposing process, the form is *locked up* in a *chase,* a metal frame which holds the type on the press.

LOCKING UP THE FORM

To lock up a form for the press, follow these steps:

1. Clean the top of the *imposing surface* (a smooth metal or stone top table).
2. Slide the typeform from the galley to the imposing surface.
3. Place the chase over the typeform.
4. Move the form to the proper position within the chase. The long side of the form should be parallel with the long side of the chase. The head of the form should be to the bottom or left of the chase. Fig. 22-3.
5. Place *furniture* around the form. Furniture is the larger pieces of spacing material, made of wood. Each piece of furniture should overlap, or "chase," the other piece around the form. Fig. 22-4.
6. Place *quoins* at the top and right of the form. Quoins are blocks that can be expanded with a key. Fig. 22-5.
7. Fill in the rest of the chase with enough furniture to hold the form. Fig. 22-6. Fill spaces which are too small for wood furniture with *reglets.* Reglets

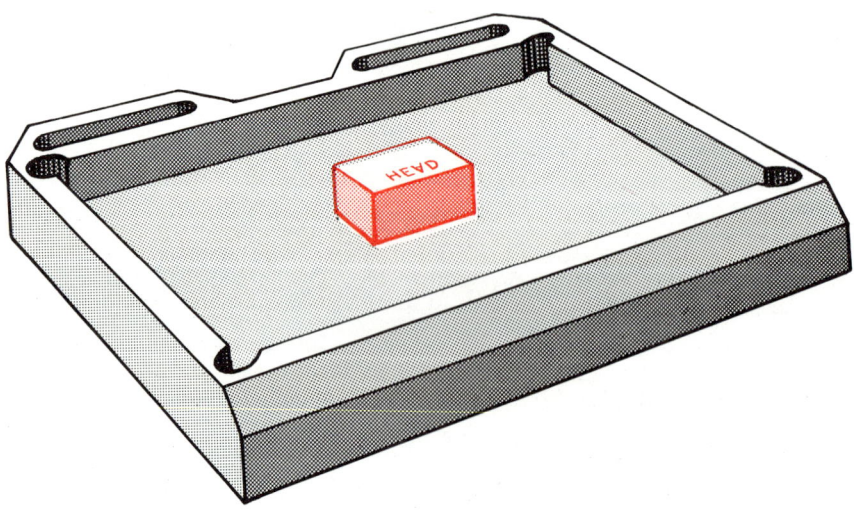

22-2. Inking the typeform with a brayer.

22-3. Position of the type in the chase. The head is at the wide end. Therefore it is placed towards the bottom of the chase.

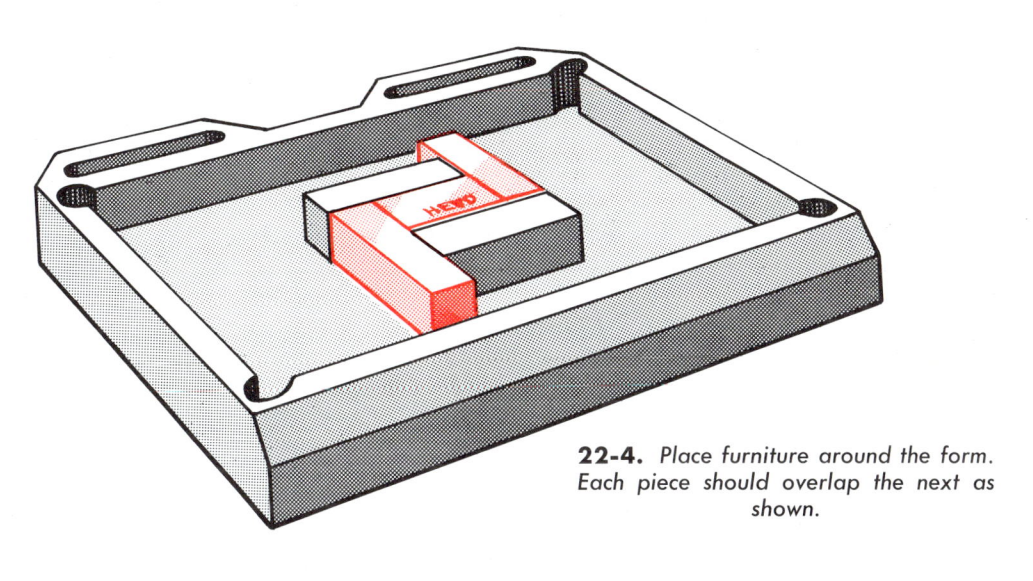

22-4. Place furniture around the form. Each piece should overlap the next as shown.

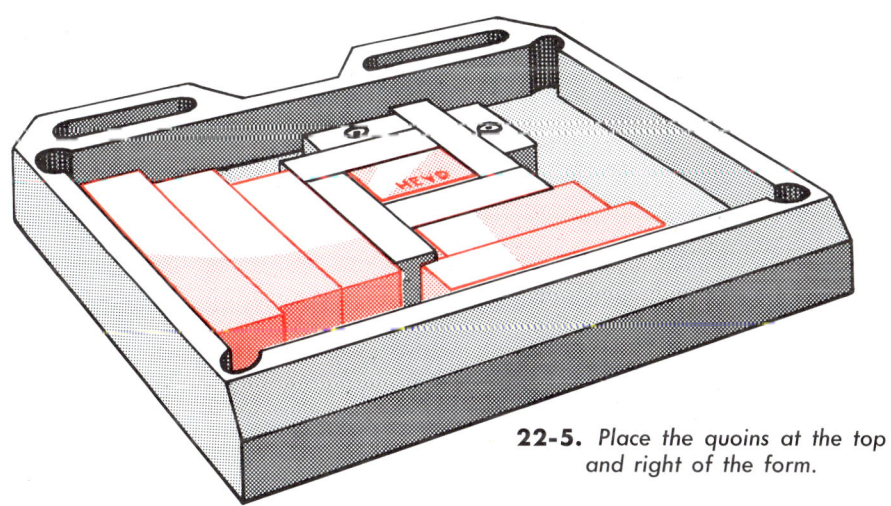

22-5. Place the quoins at the top and right of the form.

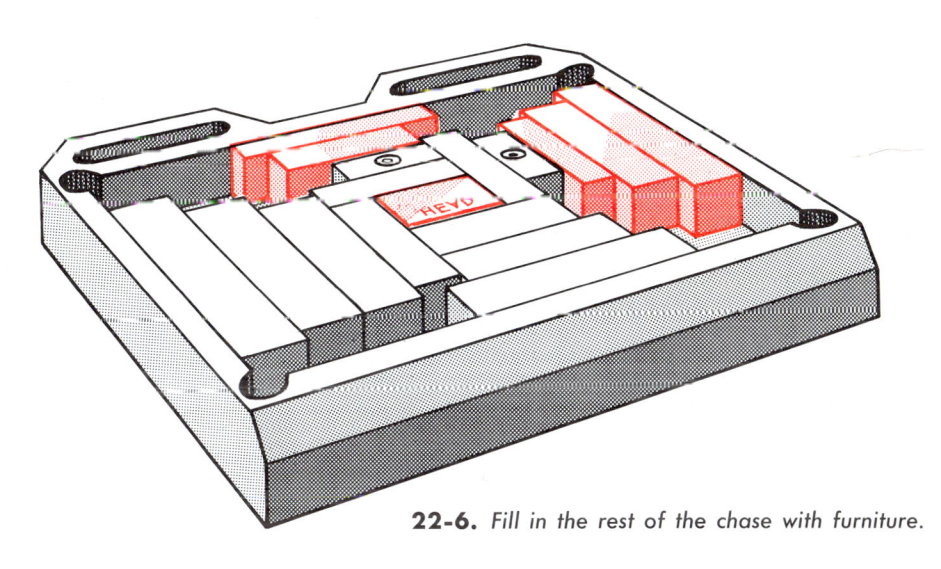

22-6. Fill in the rest of the chase with furniture.

Part II: Graphic Communications

are wood spacing material 6 points or 12 points thick.

8. Remove the string from the form.
9. Lightly tighten the quoins.
10. Plane the typeform so that all printing surfaces will be even. This is done by using a block of wood and a mallet to level the type. Fig. 22-7. CAUTION: Be sure to tap lightly.
11. Tighten the quoins. Lift the chase slightly and tap the type with your fingers. If there is no loose type, the locked form is ready for the press.

PREPARING THE PRESS

As you remember from Unit 20, letterpress printing is done from raised surfaces like the typeform you are now ready to print. The platen press is one kind of press for printing typeforms. It is the kind of press most often found in school shops.

There are two types of platen presses: the hand lever, Fig. 22-8, and the power, Fig. 22-9. Some power platen presses have automatic feeders which feed the printing paper to the press.

The first step in printing your typeform is to dress the platen. This is the operation of covering and packing the platen with tympan paper, a tough, oily paper of uniform thickness.

22-7. *Place the typeform with a wooden block and a mallet.*

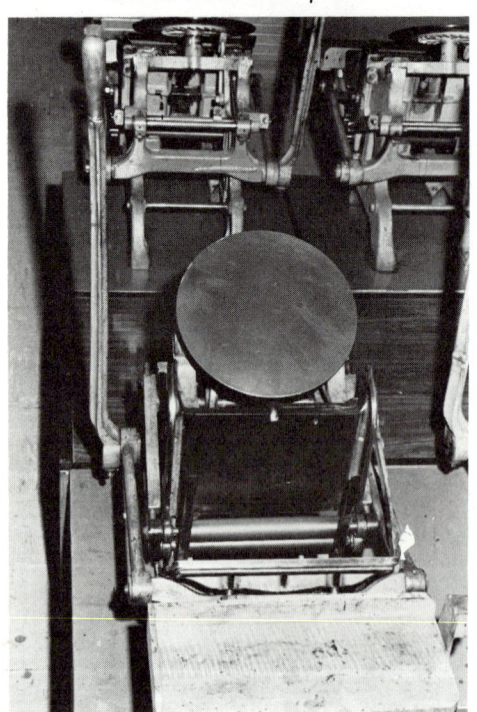

22-8. *Hand lever press.*

22-9. *Power platen press.*

Unit 22: Printing by Letterpress

First, remove the old packing, which is held on the platen by two *bales*, one at the top and the other at the bottom of the platen. Next, dress the platen with one tympan sheet, two sheets of book paper, and one pressboard. The amount of packing will vary from press to press; so check with your instructor about how much packing should be used. Clamp the lower bale over the tympan sheet. Pull the tympan tight and clamp the upper bale. Fig. 22-10. Be sure the pressboard is not clamped under the bale.

Next, ink the press. This is done by placing a small amount of the desired color ink on the left side of the ink disc. Turn the press and allow the ink to distribute evenly. CAUTION: If the form is placed on the press before the ink is well distributed, the letters will fill up with ink.

After the press is inked, lift the chase with the typeform into the bed of the press. The quoins should be up and to the right. Fig. 22-11. Let the ink rollers go over the form a few times to ink it.

Make sure the grippers are to the edge of the platen. Take a trial impression on the tympan. Using a line gauge, measure and mark where the gauge pins are to be placed. Place two gauge pins at the bottom of the sheet and one on the left side. Fig. 22-12. Be sure the gauge pins' points come back through the tympan.

Now place a piece of paper against the gauge pins. Turn the press and print a copy. Check the position of the gauge pins by measuring the print on the sheet. Fig. 22-13. If necessary, move the gauge pins until the printing is in the proper position on the sheet.

PRINTING

Before starting production, some final adjustments in the packing may be nec-

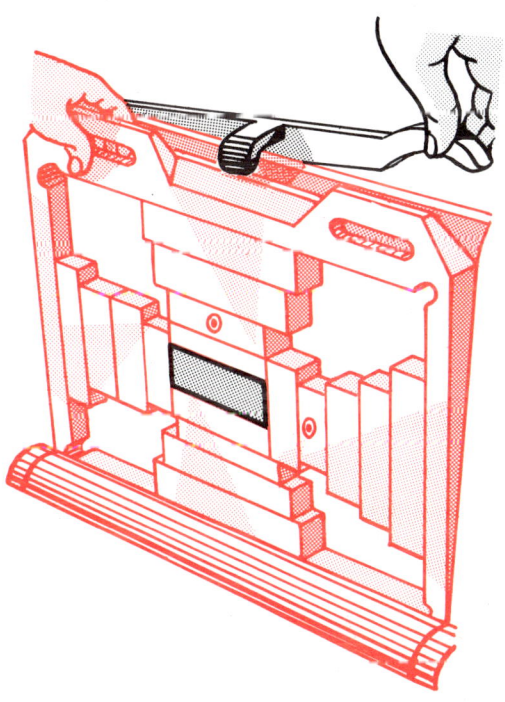

22-10. *Pull the tympan tight and clamp the upper bale.*

22-11. *Placing the chase in the press. Lift the chase up and over the ink roller. Be sure the chase is clamped tightly.*

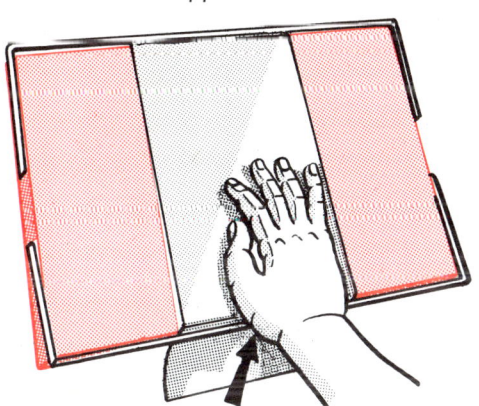

22-12. *Place two gauge pins at the bottom and one at the left side. Insert the gauge pins to the line.*

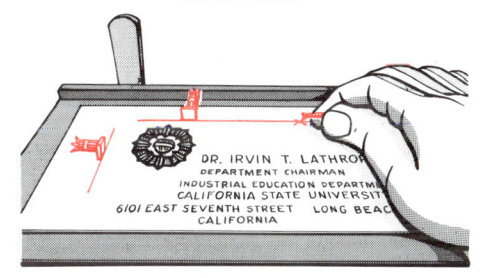

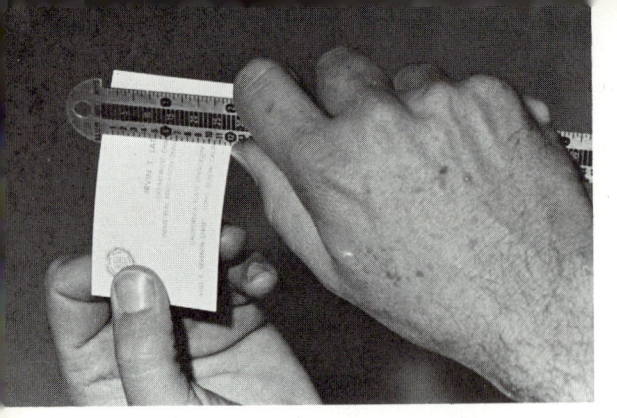

22-13. Checking with a line gauge to make sure the printing is straight.

essary to make the entire impression even. This process is called *makeready*. Make an impression on a sheet of paper to be printed. Check the printing for low places. If the impression is too light, additional packing may be required. If the impression is too heavy, remove some packing. Also check the amount of ink. Too much ink means an easily smudged print. Once all the makeready is completed, the job is ready to run. Now the desired number of copies may be printed. Follow your teacher's instruction for operating the press.

After the copies have been printed, remove the chase from the press and clean the ink from the type. Clean the press by first cleaning the ink disc. Next, clean the ink from the rollers. Unlock the typeform and return all lock-up material to the proper place. Now sort the type back into the proper case. Be sure all tools and materials are returned to their storage places.

22-14. Tracing the design taped over the linoleum block.

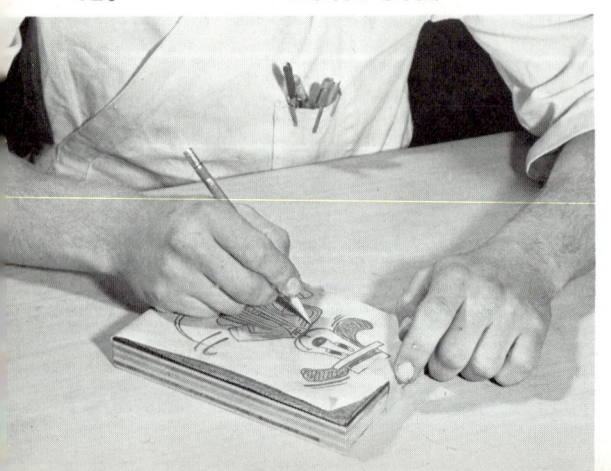

LINOLEUM BLOCK PRINTING

Another form of letterpress printing uses linoleum block in place of type. With the linoleum block printing process, you can make interesting designs on paper or cloth. The first step is to make a *layout*—a drawing of the design to be carved in the block. Since this is a relief printing process, the design on the linoleum block must be drawn in reverse. To do this, draw the layout on tracing paper. This way the design can be seen from the back of the paper.

To transfer the design to the block, first tape a piece of carbon paper to the face of the block. Then tape the layout face down on the carbon paper. Now trace around the design; the carbon will transfer to the block. Fig. 22-14. The designs for linoleum blocks should not have fine lines because these break easily and are hard to carve.

Remove the layout and the carbon. The block is ready to carve. Fig. 22-15. Place the block in a bench hook. Be sure to keep your fingers behind the block when carving. With the V-shaped block-cutting tool, outline the design. After the design has been outlined, use the larger tool—the gouge—to remove the unwanted linoleum.

To print, place paper over the inked block and apply pressure. The best way is to place the block in a platen press and apply pressure. Another way is to apply the ink, place the block on a piece of paper on the floor, and stand on the block. Still another way is to place the inked block on a piece of paper and press with a rolling pin.

22-15. Cutting a linoleum block.

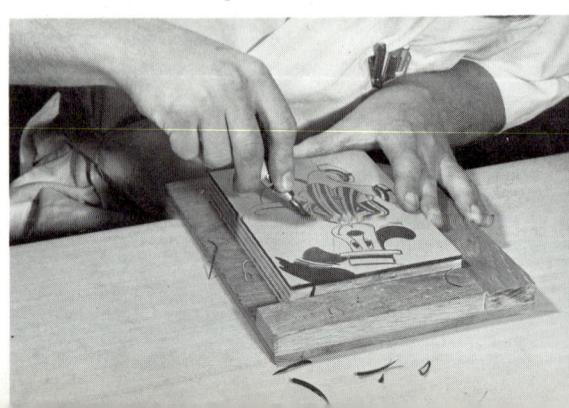

UNIT 23

Offset Lithography

As you remember, lithography is printing from a flat surface rather than a raised one. In offset lithography, the image is transferred from a plate to a rubber blanket on a cylinder and then to the paper. The image is placed on the plate in much the same way a photograph is made. Before the image can be put on the plate, a negative must be prepared.

PREPARING COPY FOR PHOTOGRAPHY

There are two kinds of copy: *line copy* and *continuous tone* copy. Line copy is made up of solid lines. It includes type, line drawings, and lettering done by hand. Continuous tone copy includes photographs, paintings, and shaded drawings. The two types of copy must be prepared separately for offset printing.

Line Copy

There are several ways to prepare line copy for offset printing. The line illustrations may be drawn or cut out of previously printed material. One way to prepare the type is to hand set it, take a proof (called a *reproduction proof*), and then photograph the proof. Another method is to set type with a typesetting machine such as a Linotype, proof it, and then photograph that.

By far the most copy is set for offset printing by methods that do not use metal type characters. These methods of setting type are called *cold composition*. Cold composition may include copy made by using hand lettering, preprinted type, or a typewriter. The IBM Selectric® in Fig. 23-1 is a typewriter which might be used for setting copy. Typefaces can be changed by changing the typing element. There are also machines which produce many sizes and kinds of type. These include the Photo-Typositor and the Photon. Fig. 23-2.

After the copy has been set, it is laid out into the desired design. For this a *light table* is often used. A light table usually consists of a large piece of frosted glass with a light underneath. The light table provides a smooth, flat surface on which to work.

Continuous Tone Copy

If you look closely at a picture in a newspaper, you will see that it is made up of many small dots. The dots are closer together in the darker parts of the picture and further apart in the lighter areas. These dots are produced by a screen which is placed between the film in the camera and the copy.

All continuous tone copy must be screened. Otherwise, it would not reproduce well in print. Copy which is screened is called a *halftone*. Because continuous tone copy is screened, it is photographed separately from line copy.

After negatives of line copy and continuous tone copy have been made, the two kinds of negatives are put together in making the flat. Making a flat will be explained in the following section.

23-1. *Selectric® typewriter composing unit.*

PHOTOGRAPHING COPY

Photographs of line or continuous tone copy are made with a process camera. This camera has special lenses for photographing flat copy to make sharp negatives. By using this camera, the image may also be either enlarged or reduced to the desired size. Fig. 23-3.

23-2. *Photon photo-typesetting system.*

The negatives are positioned and taped onto a special sheet of paper on a light table. After the negatives have been taped in place, the paper is turned over and cut so as to leave the printing area of the negative clear. This process is called *stripping*. Fig. 23-4. All other areas remain covered by the paper. No light must go through any place but the image area. Unwanted holes and scratches are blacked out with opaquing solution. Fig. 23-4. The flat (negative and stripping paper) is now ready to use for making the offset plate.

PREPARING THE OFFSET PLATE

The offset plate is a metal plate that has been made sensitive to light. The flat is placed on the plate, usually in a vacuum frame, and exposed to a bright light. After the plate has been exposed, it is developed using the proper solution for the plate being used. Fig. 23-5. Most offset solutions include an *etch* and a *developer*. If the plate is not to be used right

23-3. Process camera used for making offset negatives. This picture shows the lights and the copyboard (the board onto which material to be photographed is mounted).

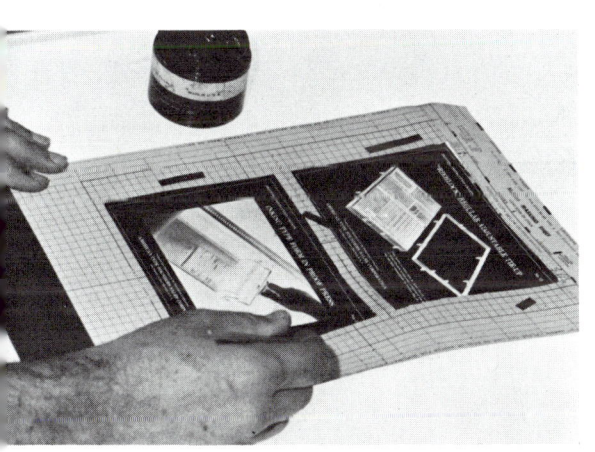

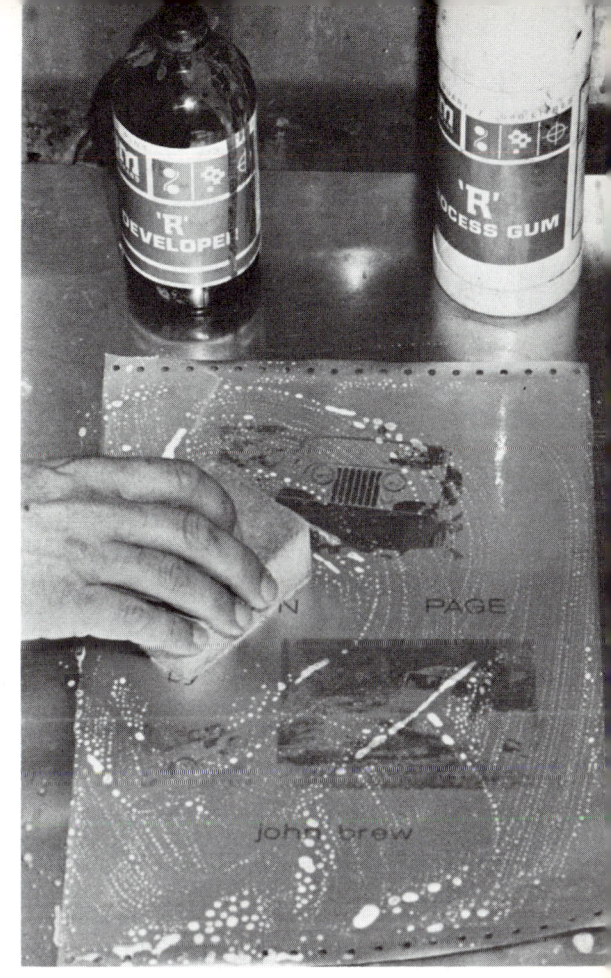

23-5. Developing an offset plate.

23-6. One type of offset press.

23-4. Stripping negatives onto masking sheet. Note the bottle of opaquing fluid.

away, it is covered with a solution of gum arabic to protect it.

PRINTING

The actual printing procedure may vary somewhat depending on the press that is used. Fig. 23-6. Here are the general steps to be followed:

1. Place ink into the ink fountain.
2. Put fountain solution in the water reservoir. At this point you might run the

123

Part II: Graphic Communications

23-7. Paper in paper feeder in proper position for printing.
Addressograph-Multigraph

23-8. Attach the lead edge of the plate to the plate clamps. Turn hand wheel to roll plate around cylinder.
Addressograph-Multigraph

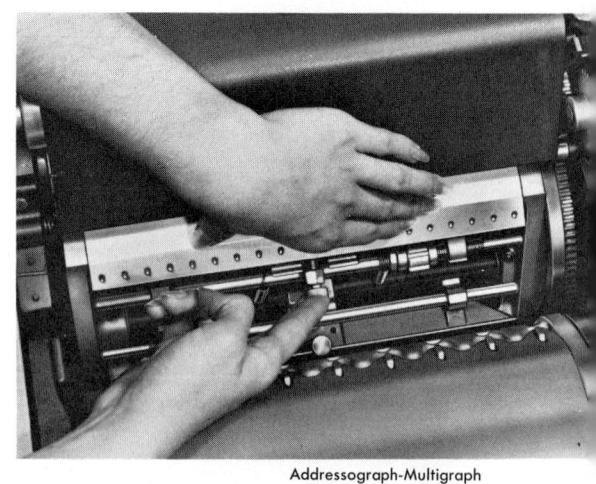

23-9. Fasten the tail of the plate with the plate clamp tightening screw.
Addressograph-Multigraph

press to distribute the ink on the ink rollers and to moisten the fountain rollers.

3. Place paper in the paper feeders and adjust. Fig. 23-7 shows the paper feeder adjusted for $8\frac{1}{2}$ x 11 inch paper. Adjust the feeder so that the paper feeds properly into the press.

4. Fasten the plate to the press. Begin by attaching the lead edge of the plate to the clamp and turning the press by hand. Fig. 23-8.

Fasten the tail of the plate to the clamp, as shown in Fig. 23-9. Tighten the clamp until the plate is held tightly. Do not tighten too much, or the holes in the plate may be torn.

Remove the gum arabic from the plate with a small sponge that has been moistened with fountain solution.

5. Adjust the delivery end of the press so that the paper comes out of the press and stacks neatly.

6. Proceed to print the desired number of copies. After all of the copies have been printed, the plate must be removed and the press cleaned. Both the ink rollers and the fountain should be cleaned, following the directions for the press being used.

If the plate is to be stored for use again, it should be coated with gum arabic to preserve the surface.

UNIT 24

Silk-Screen Printing

As you remember from Unit 20, silk-screen printing is really printing by forcing paint through a stencil which is attached to a screen that has been stretched over a wooden frame. The equipment needed for screen printing is not expensive. In fact, with a little skill in woodworking, much of it can be homemade. There are also supply houses which furnish complete kits ready for printing.

EQUIPMENT

Printing Frame

The printing frame may be made in the school shop or at home, or it may be bought. The size of the frame depends on the size of the designs to be printed. Most schools and commercial shops have many sizes of frames for printing many different designs. If you build a frame, it should be about six to eight inches larger than the largest stencil to be used. The extra space is needed as a reservoir for the ink when printing. For a school, the 8" x 10" and 10" x 15" frames would probably be best. These would be large enough to print posters, but not so large as to waste stencil material or ink. Some schools have one or two very large frames for making large posters and many smaller frames for student use.

The printing frame consists of four pieces of wood joined together at the corners. These form an open rectangle over which the screen is stretched. Usually the frame is made of pine or basswood strips about $1\frac{1}{2}$ inches wide. Whatever wood is used, the frame must be rigid and strong enough to withstand the stretching of the screen. The frame is attached with hinges to a flat base.

Screen

Although silk is most often used, the screen may also be made of organdy, nylon, or a metal such as stainless steel. The mesh openings vary in size, and the size used depends on the design being printed. Coarse screens are used for large, heavy designs. Fine screens are used for designs that are small and detailed.

To attach a screen to the frame, remove the frame from the base and turn the frame over on a table. Spread a piece of silk (or other material) over the frame so that the threads run parallel to the sides of the frame. Cut the silk so that it is about one inch larger than the frame on all four sides.

There are two common ways to fasten the screen to the frame. One way is to use tacks or staples. If the frame has a groove around it, the silk may be attached with a cord wedged into the groove over the silk. Lay the silk on the frame and start forcing one end of the cord into the groove with your fingers. Start at a corner. Pull the silk fairly tight as you force the cord into the groove. When the cord is in the groove on all four sides of the screen, force it further down into the groove with a mallet and a

Part II: Graphic Communications

blunt wooden wedge. This method will hold the silk tighter than the tacks. Fig. 24-1.

After the screen is fastened to the frame, it should be washed in warm water with a detergent to remove any sizing it may contain. The frame is then attached again to the base.

Squeegee

A squeegee is used to push the ink through the open mesh of the screen onto the printing surface. It has a rubber blade and a wooden handle. It should be about two inches shorter than the inside width of the frame. Squeegees can be bought at art supply stores.

STENCIL

Stencils for silk-screen printing may be made from many materials. The easiest and least expensive is paper. A simple stencil may be made from a good grade of bond paper.

The stencil paper should be large enough to cover the entire screen. Trace the design onto the paper from the layout. With this type of stencil material, designs with loose pieces—for instance, the letter *O*—should be avoided.

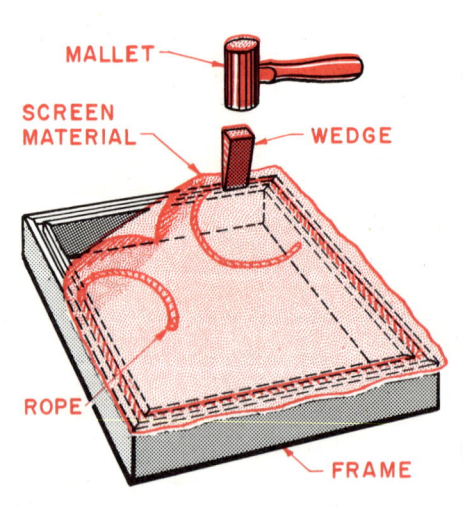

Cut the design in the paper, using a sharp knife. Be sure to use a piece of cardboard or other material under the stencil to avoid cutting the tabletop. Cut all the way through the stencil material. Be careful not to cut yourself. Fig. 24-2.

There are other ways to make stencils. In schools hand-cut lacquer film is often used rather than paper. There are also photographic methods of making stencils.

MAKING A SILK-SCREEN PRINT

After the stencil is prepared, it is attached to the bottom of the screen. This is done with water-soluble glue or with tape. Fig. 24-3. If the stencil material is not large enough to cover the entire screen, the areas around the stencil are covered with a blockout material such as glue or masking paper. This stops the paint from going through the screen at any place but the design.

To print the design, place a sheet of paper on the base of the frame. Put a small amount of ink into the screen frame and pull the squeegee across the screen. Fig. 24-4. This forces the ink through the cut-out parts of the stencil and onto the paper.

Screen process printing has several advantages. First, a fairly heavy layer of ink is pushed through the screen. This means a light color can be printed over a dark color. Also it is possible to print on almost any material or object that can be placed directly under the screen. The silk-screen process is used for printing on such things as bottles, sweat shirts, and T-shirts and for printing panel markings for radios and automobiles, posters, drinking glasses, and decals. It is a small but important part of the graphic arts.

24-1. *One way to attach the screen to the frame is with a cord (rope).*

Unit 24: Silk-Screen Printing

24-2. Cutting a paper stencil for the silk-screen process.

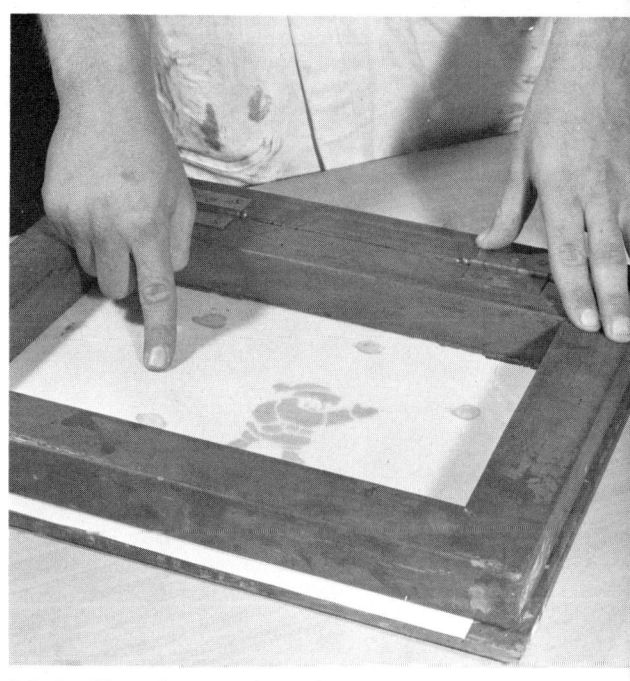

24-3. Glue the stencil to the screen with water-soluble glue.

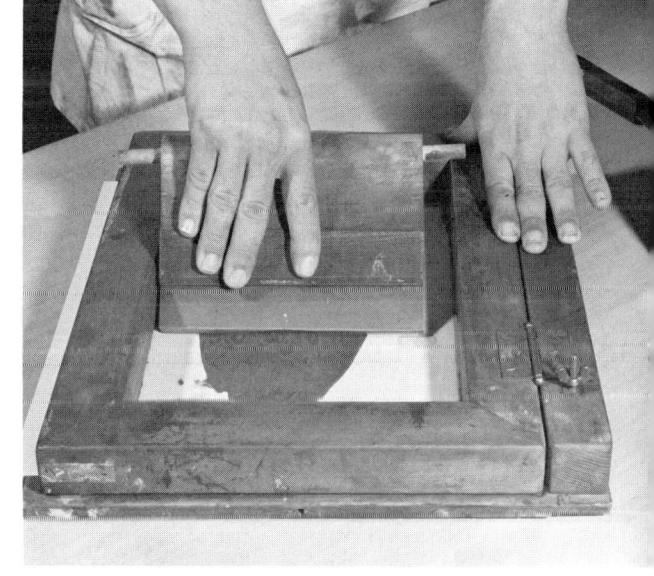

24-4. To print, pull the squeegee across the screen at about a 15 degree angle.

127

UNIT 25
Taking and Developing Pictures

Photographs are made by the reflection of light from the subject to a light-sensitive film. Light areas reflect more light than dark areas. The film is therefore exposed in direct relation to the amount of light. The camera which holds the film is basically a lightproof box with a small, glass-covered opening to admit light and a shutter to close the opening after the film has been exposed.

TYPES OF CAMERAS

There are many types of cameras in common use today. The simplest is the box camera. The box camera does not have a way to control exposure or change focus. The shutter speed is slow, but under the right conditions the box camera will take acceptable pictures. The highly popular pocket-size cameras are examples of modern box cameras. Fig. 25-1.

Two other cameras in popular use today are the 35 mm and the twin lens reflex camera. Thirty-five millimetre cameras are popular because of their small size and great depth of field. (Objects will be in focus from close up to far away.) Thirty-five millimetre cameras are basically of two types, the kind with a range finder and the single lens reflex. Those cameras with a separate range finder use separate lens systems for viewing and for taking the picture. Fig. 25-2. The single lens reflex camera is commonly called the SLR. This camera uses a mirror and lens system so that the viewing is done through the same lens that the picture is taken with. Fig. 25-3. The mirror moves out of the way during exposure. Thus you cannot see the subject you are photographing during the actual exposure time.

The twin lens reflex camera uses a film size slightly larger than the 35 mm film. This camera has two lens systems, one to take the picture and one to view the picture through. When the image is sharp in the viewfinder, it will be just as sharp on the film. An example of a twin lens reflex camera is shown in Fig. 25-4.

TAKING PICTURES

No matter how expensive or complex a camera is, certain procedures must always be followed. The most expensive camera in the world will not give you a good picture unless the camera is held steady. To avoid light streaks and fogged negatives, the camera must be correctly loaded away from bright light. Each type of camera loads differently; so be sure to read and follow the directions for the camera you are using.

There is no substitute for a correctly exposed negative. On very simple cameras, the exposure controls are preset at the factory. Pictures can be taken only in fairly bright light. On more complex cameras, it is possible to set the exposure for existing light conditions.

The *f-stop* and the *shutter speed* control exposure. The f-stop refers to the size of the lens opening. Most of the more complex cameras have an f-stop range of 16, 11, 8, 5.6, 4, 2.8, 2, and 1.4. The higher the number, the smaller the lens opening.

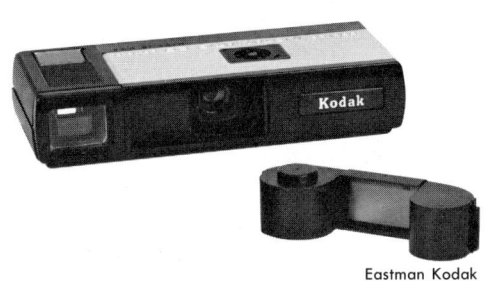

25-1. A pocket-size camera.
Eastman Kodak

25-2. Example of a 35 mm camera with a separate range finder.
GAF

25-3. Common 35 mm SLR camera.

25-4. A twin lens reflex camera.
Honeywell Photographic Products

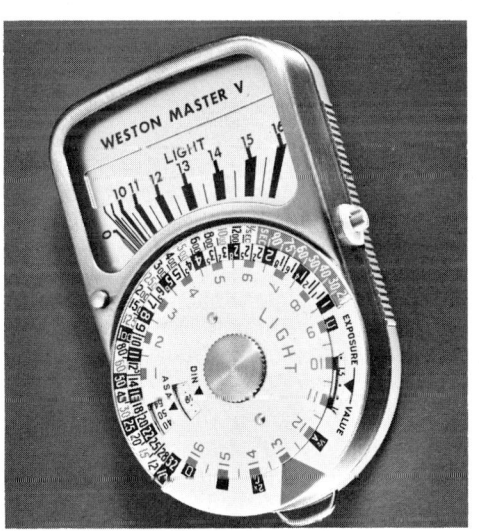

25-5. A light meter for determining exposure.
Weston Instruments

The shutter speed is the amount of time that light is allowed to pass through the lens and strike the film. The shutter speed range on most cameras is $1/1000$, $1/500$, $1/250$, $1/125$, $1/60$, $1/30$, $1/15$, $1/8$, $1/4$, $1/2$, and 1 second.

The combination of f-stop and shutter speed that will be used depends on the amount of light that is reflected from the subject being photographed and on the ASA rating of the film being used. The ASA rating is the film sensitivity rating as set by the American Standard Association. The higher the ASA rating, the more sensitive the film is to light. A light meter is used to help determine the exposure. Fig. 25-5.

129

Part II: Graphic Communications

25-6. Common type of development tank.

Another factor to consider when taking a picture is focusing. Focusing is the process of selecting the correct subject-to-camera distance. On some cameras the focus is preset at about 15 feet. On more expensive cameras there are ways to adjust the subject-to-camera distance.

There are three basic types of view or range finders. The *split image* range finder splits the image in half. When the focusing ring is turned, the top and the bottom halves may be moved into alignment, or focus. The *coincidental* range finder uses a superimposed image. When the subject is out of focus, the same image appears twice. When the subject is in focus, only one image appears. Reflex cameras use a *ground glass screen* range finder. This type of range finder uses a pattern of concentric rings. When the subject is out of focus, it will appear as many small dots in the prism center area. When the subject is in focus, it will appear sharp and clear in the prism.

DEVELOPING FILM

After you have exposed a roll of film in your camera, what is known as a *latent image* has been formed on the film. The image is not visible. The film must be processed, or *developed,* to make the image appear.

The most common method of developing film in homes and schools is the tank method. The tank method is popular because once the film is in the tank the rest of the procedure may be done under ordinary room light. Fig. 25-6 shows a development tank. There are three types of tanks in common use today. These are the plastic apron, the plastic reel, and the metal reel. The plastic reel is the easiest to load and the metal reel the most difficult. Whichever type of tank you intend to use, practice loading unexposed film in the light before trying to load your film in the darkroom. Fig. 25-7.

In addition to correct exposure, correct development is a must for obtaining a usable negative. The time and temperature requirements vary with the type of film and the developer. Be sure to follow the manufacturer's instructions, listed on most film packages.

Even after the film has been developed and the image is visible, it is not permanent until the unexposed and undeveloped silver salts have been removed from the film. This is done with an acid fix solution. However, because the developer is alkaline and the fixer is acid, the film must first be washed in a solution called a stop bath. Otherwise, the fixer would be contaminated with developer.

After the film has been fixed, all of the chemicals must be washed from the film with running water. The film should be washed for about 20 minutes. To avoid water spots, the film is dipped in a wetting agent, then hung up to dry in a dust-free place. After the film is dry, it should be stored in a protective cover such as a glassine envelope.

The following step-by-step procedure is recommended for developing film by the tank method.

1. Place the reel, the tank, and the lid in a convenient position.
2. Turn the room light off.

Unit 25: Taking and Developing Pictures

25-7a. Loading for a plastic apron development tank.

25-7b. Loading a plastic reel.

25-7c. Loading a metal reel.

3. Carefully remove the paper backing from the film. Be sure to touch the film only by the edges. There is also about one inch at the beginning and at the end of the film which may be safely handled without danger of touching the image area.

4. After the reel is loaded, place it in the tank and put the light-tight cover on the tank.

5. Turn on the room lights.

6. Select the correct developer and check its temperature. With certain types of tanks it might be best to fill the tank with cool tap water. This prewets the film and helps to reduce air bubbles, called "air bells," which may cause spots on the negative. If a rapid developer is to be used, prewetting the film will increase the density. This means a slight reduction in development time.

The temperatures of all three solutions—developer, rinse, and fixer—should be within a few degrees of each other. Refer to a time and temperature chart for the film being developed to find the correct temperature. Make sure you have more than enough developer to fill the tank completely.

Part II: Graphic Communications

25-8. Pouring developer into a tank. Fill the tank as quickly as possible.

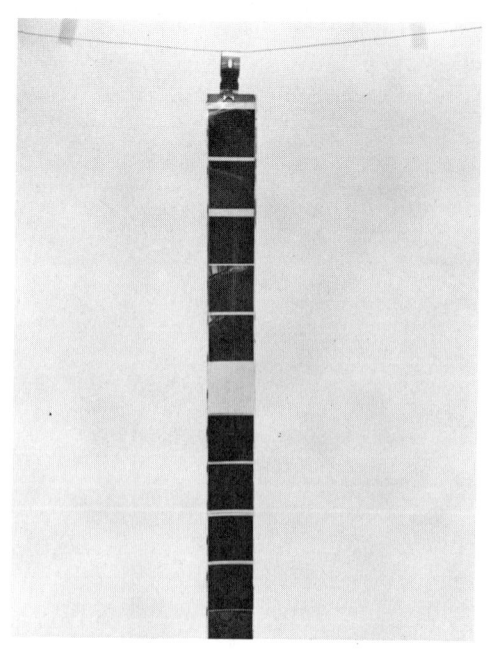

25-9. One way to hang negatives for drying. Be sure to place a weight on the bottom to keep the negatives from curling.

7. Set the timer to the correct development time as given by the time and temperature chart.

8. Pour the water from the tank.

9. Pour the developer into the tank as fast as possible. Fig. 25-8. Start the timer as soon as the tank is full.

10. As soon as the timer has been started, rap the tank smartly against the bottom of the sink in order to dislodge any air bells. Agitate (shake) the tank according to the film manufacturer's directions. Improper agitation will cause air bells and streaked negatives.

11. When development is complete, pour out all of the developer. Be sure to pour the developer back into the right container. If at any time you think you may have contaminated a solution, throw it away. Or, if you used a developer in a diluted form, be sure to discard it.

12. Pour enough stop bath into the tank to completely cover the film. If you do not have stop bath, use a tap water rinse for 60 seconds after the development. Be sure to agitate while the film is in the stop bath.

13. Pour out the stop bath or rinse water and pour in enough fixing solution to completely cover the film. Again, it is important to shake the tank, especially for the first few seconds. The film should then be agitated at least once every 90 seconds. It should stay in a normal acid fixing solution from 7 to 10 minutes. Then return the fixer to the proper container.

14. Wash the film in the tank for at least 20 minutes using running tap water. After the film has been washed, it should be immersed for at least one minute in a wetting agent. This helps to eliminate water spots and streaks during drying.

15. Hang the film in a dust-free room to dry. Place a weighted clip on the bottom of the film to prevent it from curling. One typical drying arrangement is shown in Fig. 25-9.

16. When the negatives are dry, place them in protective envelopes.

UNIT 26

Printing Pictures

In photography, printing is the term used to describe the process by which positive images are made from negatives. The most familiar example of this is the print made on a paper base. This print is made by passing light through a negative onto a piece of sensitized paper by either the *contact* or *projection* printing method. By either of these methods, any number of copies can be made from one negative.

Contact printing produces positives of the same size as the negative. Projection printing allows you to choose the size of the print. Some projection prints are large enough to cover a wall. These are called "photomurals."

CONTACT PRINTING

A contact print is made by placing a piece of light-sensitive material, usually a printing paper, and a negative in direct contact with each other, emulsion to emulsion. The printing papers come with different kinds of light-sensitive emulsions (coatings). The type of emulsion to choose depends on the method of printing that will be used.

To make a contact print, a device to hold the negative and the printing paper tightly together is required so that a sharp image will be produced. One such device is the printing frame shown in Fig. 26-1. In this frame, the negative and the paper

26-1. *Contact printing frame. The printing paper and the negative are placed in the frame and exposed to light.*

Part II: Graphic Communications

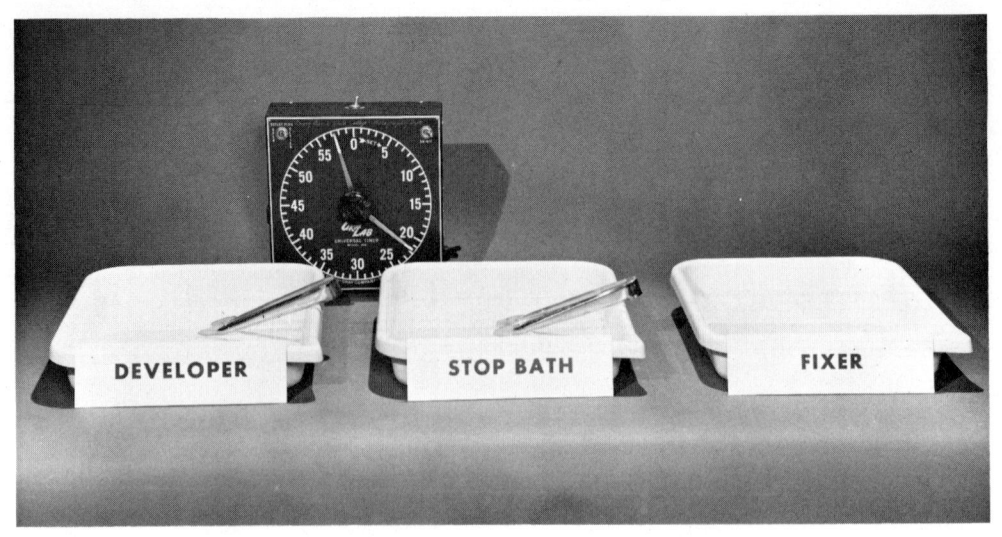

26-2. *Arrangement of solution trays for print processing.*

are kept tightly together between a glass plate and a spring-loaded back. The negative is placed emulsion side upward on the printing glass. Then the paper is placed emulsion side downward on the negative, and the back is locked securely in place. The paper is exposed to white light (room light) for a set time. After exposure, the paper is processed using developer, stop bath, fixer, and a water rinse.

Making contact prints is quite simple. First set up three trays, as shown in Fig. 26-2.

1. Dust the negative carefully on both sides with a negative brush. Place the negative on the printer glass with the emulsion side up. Slide the border mask into position over the edges of the negative if white borders are desired on the print. Be sure that the printer glass is clean and free of lint and dust.

2. Turn on the safelight and turn off the room lights. (A safelight is a lamp with a filter to screen out rays that would harm the light-sensitive paper.)

3. Grade 2, normal contrast paper must be used. With clean, dry hands, open the package of paper and take out one sheet. Cut this sheet into test strips about one inch wide. Then return all test strips but one to the envelope.

4. Place one of the test strips diagonally across the negative with the emulsion side down.

5. Close the cover of the printer and expose the test strip. The exposure time will depend on the density of the negative and the wattage of the bulb in the printer. There is no standard printing time, but a good starting point is to expose the paper for ten seconds.

6. Slide the test strip into the tray of developer. Agitate the developer by rocking the tray constantly during the development time. Develop the test strip for a full two minutes. This will assure you of the fullest range of tones that the paper can produce.

7. When the two minutes are over, pick the test strip up with tongs and drop it into the stop bath. *Do not put the tongs from the developer into the stop bath.* Agitate the test strip for at least thirty seconds.

8. Using a second set of tongs, remove the test strip from the stop bath and place it in the fixer. Agitate the print constantly for at least the first ten seconds and periodically after that. After two minutes the test strip may be inspected under white

134

Unit 26: Printing Pictures

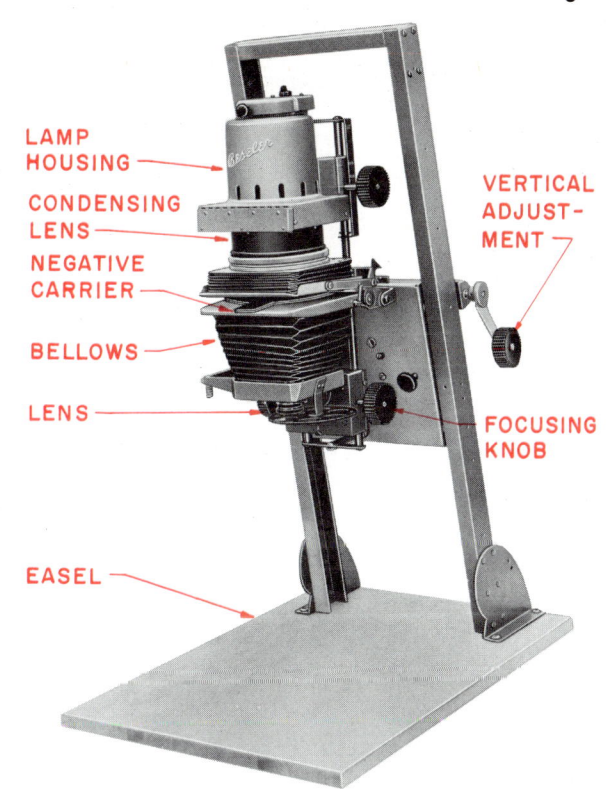

26-3. Typical enlarger.

Labels on figure: LAMP HOUSING, CONDENSING LENS, NEGATIVE CARRIER, BELLOWS, LENS, VERTICAL ADJUSTMENT, FOCUSING KNOB, EASEL

light. If the strip appears too light or too dark, the printing time (exposure time) will have to be lengthened or shortened. A longer printing time makes the print darker; less printing time will lighten the print. Prints should be left in the fixer for eight to ten minutes. If prints are left in fresh fixer longer than ten minutes, they will tend to bleach.

9. Repeat the printing process with a full sheet of printing paper. Expose it for the amount of time determined from inspecting the test strip. Process the print in the same manner as the test strip.

10. After the prints have been fixed for the proper time, they must be washed to remove all traces of the processing chemicals, particularly the fixer. All prints should be washed in running water for about one hour. For this, some form of print washer or a tray siphon is recommended to make sure that the prints are thoroughly washed. Hypo clearing agent may be used to shorten the washing time if desired. Follow the manufacturer's instructions for using hypo clearing agents.

11. Air dry the prints on a photo blotter.

PROJECTION PRINTING

One of the greatest thrills in photography is making a large print from a small negative. Here you have a chance to be creative in the use of light and materials. A print made by projection allows you to change the tone relationships of the finished print. By using the many print control methods available, you can create unique and pleasing pictures. Only after you have practiced with the various projection printing control methods will you fully realize the potential of the enlarging process. Fig. 26-3.

Procedure for making projection prints:

1. Set up the three trays for printing as you did for contact printing. The chemical

135

Part II: Graphic Communications

26-4. Sample test strip.

mixing and temperature requirements are also the same.

2. Carefully dust the negative to be enlarged and place it in the negative carrier (Fig. 26-3) emulsion side down. When placing or removing negatives in the carrier, do not pull the negative between the pressure plates, or it will be scratched.

3. If you are using an adjustable easel, set the masking guides for the desired border size.

4. Turn on the safelight and turn off the room light.

5. Turn on the enlarger light.

6. Focus the enlarger with the lens wide open until the image is sharp.

7. If the image on the easel is too small, raise the enlarger head and refocus. If the image is too large, lower the enlarger head and refocus.

8. After adjusting the image to the correct size, make sure that you have the sharpest possible focus with the lens wide open.

9. Close the lens down until the fine detail just begins to disappear, but is still plainly visible.

10. Select a sheet of No. 2 paper or place the No. 2 filter in the enlarger. (Remember, a No. 2 paper or No. 2 filter must be used with a normal negative.) Take a sheet of paper from the package and cut it into one-inch test strips and return all but one of these strips to the package.

11. Place one of the test strips on the easel, emulsion side up, in a position to sample the widest possible changes in tone.

12. Cover three-fourths of the test strip with a piece of cardboard. Expose the strip for five seconds. Move the cardboard cover so that about one-half of the test strip is uncovered. Expose it for five seconds. Move the cardboard again to uncover three-fourths of the test strip and expose for five seconds. Uncover the entire test strip and expose for another five seconds. This will fill a strip with expo-

Unit 26: *Printing Pictures*

26-5. *Typical finished print.*

sures of 5, 10, 15, and 20 seconds. Fig. 26-4.

13. Process this test strip in exactly the same way as outlined for contact printing.

14. Inspect the test strip under white light and select the length of exposure which produced the best result. You may find that a time between two of the blocks would yield the best print. If this is the case, make another test strip, exposing for the time that will produce the best print. When you have a satisfactory strip, you are ready to make a full-size print. If the contrast is not satisfactory, a harder or softer grade of paper or another filter should be used.

15. Place a full sheet of paper in the easel and expose for the proper time. NOTE: Before handling any paper, make sure your hands are clean and dry. Process in the same way used for processing the test sheet. Fig. 26-5.

16. The prints may be washed and dried as outlined for contact printing.

UNIT 27

Office Duplicating

Many offices need copies of letters and memos quickly and inexpensively. Many schools need rapid, inexpensive ways to duplicate lessons and tests. Office duplicating processes and machines fulfill these needs. The most commonly used methods of duplicating are:
- Electrostatic.
- Spirit.
- Stencil, or mimeograph.

ELECTROSTATIC DUPLICATING

Electrostatic duplicating makes copies directly from the original. It uses an electrostatic charge and a dry powder called "toner." The process is often called *xerography*. An example of a xerographic copying machine—the Xerox® 3000—is shown in Fig. 27-1. This machine will also reduce the size of the original.

To make a copy, the original is placed face down on a curved glass called a platen. Fig. 27-2, #1. Reflected light from the original is measured by a photocell which signals the lens (#2) to open or close depending upon the light. The oscillating mirror (#3) scans the original and reflects the image through the lens to the fixed mirror (#4). The fixed mirror reflects the image to the selenium drum (#5) which receives a positive charge from the corotron (#6).

The positive charge on the drum is in the same pattern as the reflected image. In other words, the positive charge is held on the dark areas of the image, but not on the light areas. Toner (#7), which is negatively charged, is then poured between the drum and the electrode (#8). Because opposite charges attract, the

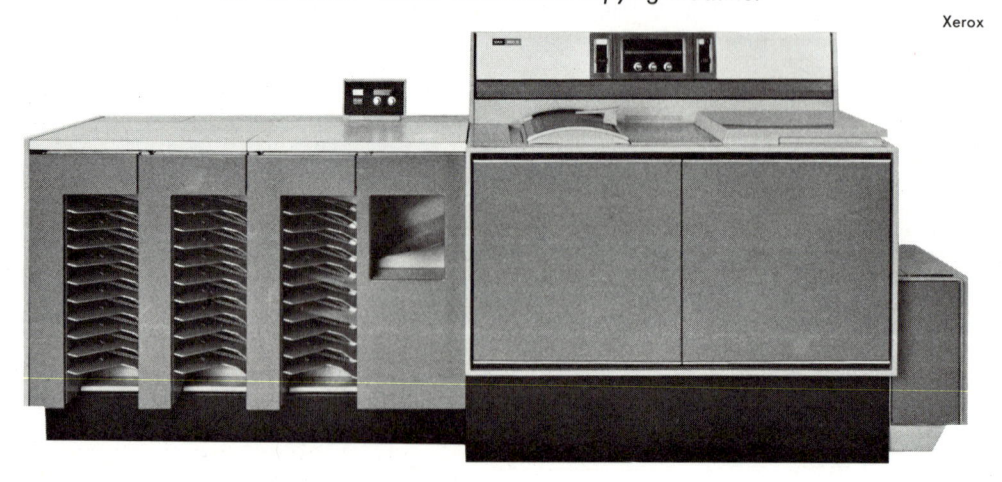

27-1. *Xerox® 3000 electrostatic copying machine.*

Xerox

Unit 27: Office Duplicating

toner is drawn to the positively charged image areas on the drum. The darker the image, the more toner clings to it.

The paper input unit (#9) stores the copy paper, which is always kept at the proper feed level by an automatic elevator. As the positively charged copy paper passes under the drum, the toner is drawn to it. Thus the image is transferred from the drum to the paper (#10). The paper is then moved to the fusing lamp (#11) where the toner is heated and fused to the paper. Any excess toner is brushed away by the copy brush (#12). Finished copies are stacked in the output tray (#13).

SPIRIT DUPLICATING

In spirit duplicating, a master which has a carbon image is placed on a cylinder. As paper is fed into the machine, it is moistened by duplicating fluid. When the moistened paper comes in contact with the master, a small amount of carbon is transferred to the paper. Fig. 27-3.

The master may be drawn, handwritten, or typed. To prepare a master, first remove the tissue paper sheet which separates the master paper from the carbon paper. The carbon side of the carbon paper will contact the back of the master sheet. Thus, whatever is drawn, written, or typed on the front of the sheet will show up in reverse on the back of the sheet. One master may be used to reproduce several colors at one time by using different colors of carbon paper while preparing the master.

To correct a mistake, use a razor blade or sharp knife to scrape away the carbon

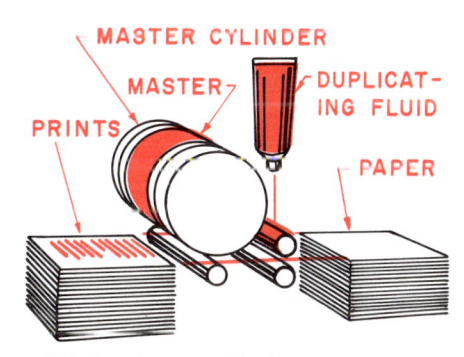

27-3. *The spirit duplicating process.*

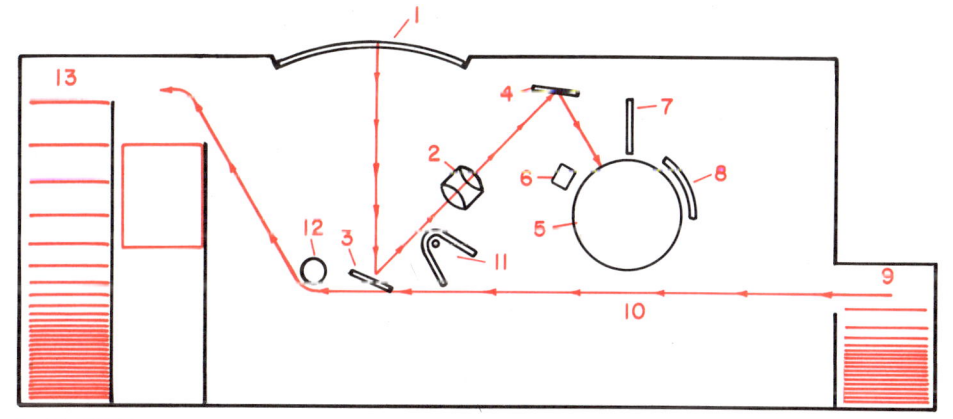

27-2. *Path of paper through a Xerox machine.*

1 PLATEN	5 DRUM	10 IMAGE TRANSFER
2 PHOTOCELL LENS	6 CHARGED COROTRON	11 FUSING LAMP AND REFLECTOR
3 OSCILLATING MIRROR	7 TONER	
4 FIXED MIRROR	8 ELECTRODE	12 COPY BRUSH
	9 PAPER INPUT UNIT	13 OUTPUT TRAY

Part II: Graphic Communications

on the master. Put a piece of unused carbon paper over the place where the mistake was and make the correction.

When the master is completed, it is placed on a spirit duplicator such as the one in Fig. 27-4. When preparing a duplicator for printing, first check the duplicator fluid level and prime the wick. Allow the machine to operate a few revolutions with the fluid turned on.

Load paper into the feed tray. Adjust the side guides for the size paper you are using. Position the paper feed wheels about one inch from each side of the sheet. Attach the spirit master by raising the master clamp and inserting the master *carbon side up* under the clamp so that the printing area is in the proper position on the paper. CAUTION: The master must lie flat, or it will wrinkle and not print properly. Adjust the receiving tray so that the paper will stack properly after it is printed.

Adjust the pressure control so that the master will print. To print the most copies from a master, begin with a low pressure and gradually increase it as the copies are being printed. After the copies have been run, turn off the pressure and remove the master. Be sure to turn off the fluid if the machine is not to be used again soon. The master may be kept for future runs by placing the tissue or a clean sheet of paper against the carbon to preserve it.

MIMEOGRAPH

The mimeograph process uses a stencil through which ink is forced onto paper. The stencil is placed on the outside of the mimeograph cylinder. As paper is fed through the machine, the impression roller presses it against the stencil on the cylinder. The ink, which is stored inside

Bell & Howell
27-4. Example of a spirit duplicator.

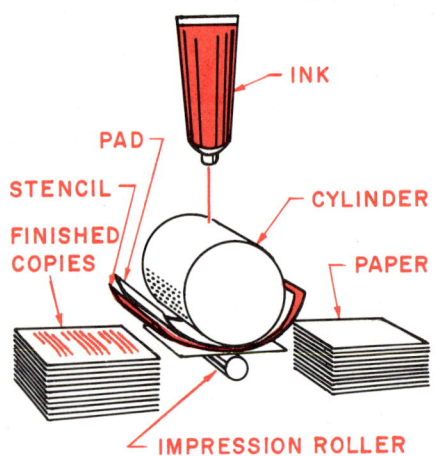

27-5. The stencil duplicating process.

27-6. Mimeograph stencil master.

Unit 27: Office Duplicating

the cylinder, flows through the openings in the stencil to make the image impression on the paper. Fig. 27-5.

Mimeograph stencils may be typed, handwritten, or drawn. They have a fibrous base tissue which is coated on both sides. When the image is prepared on the stencil sheet, the coating is pushed aside by the pressure of typewriter keys or stylus, leaving the fibrous base tissue exposed. During the duplicating process, the ink passes through the fibrous tissue wherever the coating has been pushed aside.

A stencil master consists of three parts: the stencil, a cushion sheet, and a backing sheet. Fig. 27-6. The cushion, between the stencil sheet and the backing, softens the pressure of the typeface when the image is prepared by typing. The hard, smooth surface of the backing provides a uniform base on which to prepare the stencil.

When a stencil is prepared on a typewriter, a typing film is placed over the stencil to protect the typewriter keys from becoming gummed with the wax coating. The ribbon must be moved out of the way so that the keys will not strike it. If a mistake is made, correction fluid is applied to the area and allowed to dry for a minute. Then the letter or word is retyped.

When a stencil is to be prepared by hand, a stylus or ball point pen is used to draw the image. This pushes the coating aside in the same manner as the typewriter key. When drawing on a stencil, a writing plate must be inserted between the cushion and the backing. For tracing, a stencil may be placed over the original copy on a light table. Be sure to draw slowly and with even pressure, or the stencil may tear.

When the stencil is completed, it is printed on a duplicating machine like the one in Fig. 27-7. Remove the ink pad cover from the cylinder. Hold the tail end of the stencil and attach the head of the stencil and backing sheet to the head clamp. Fig. 27-8. Close the clamp and pull the stencil smoothly over the ink pad. Tear off the backing sheet and fasten the tail of the stencil under the tail clamp.

Load paper into the feed tray and position feed rollers. Set the receiving tray to receive the paper. Run several sheets of paper through the machine and check for placement on the page. To move the printing from side to side, move the paper in the feed tray. To move the image up or down, adjust the raise/lower knob on the hand wheel. When the position is correct, print the desired number of copies.

After the desired number of copies has been run, remove the stencil (tail end

27-7. *Mimeograph stencil duplicator.*
A B Dick Co.

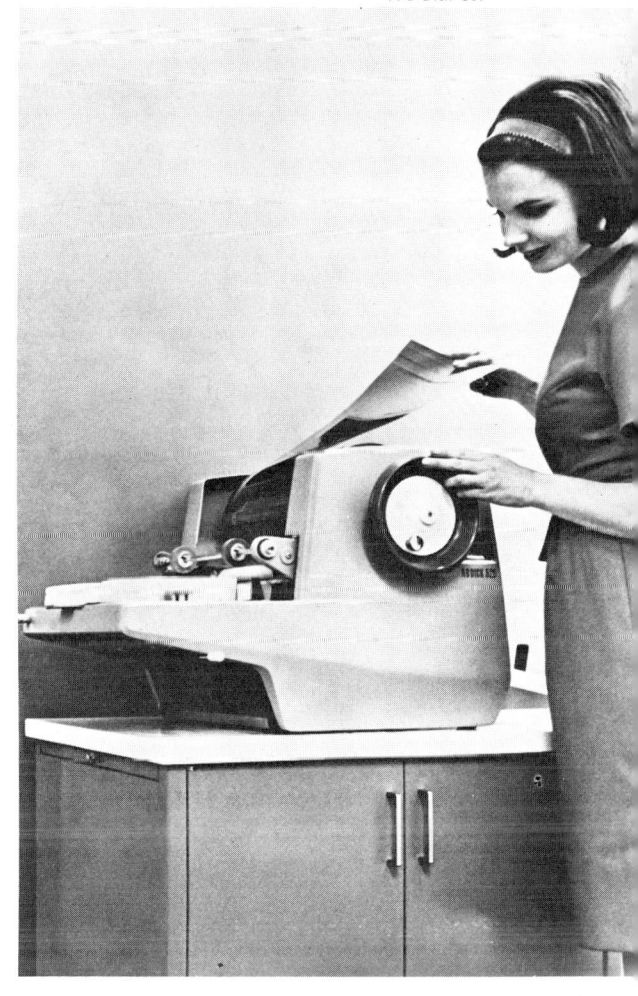

141

Part II: Graphic Communications

first) and place it inside a folder, ink side up. Close the folder and rub the surface. The file folder will absorb the ink and clean the stencil. Before filing, open the folder and turn the stencil over.

To protect the ink pad, place a cover on the cylinder using the same procedure as for attaching a stencil. The ink pad cover should be smoothly positioned over the cylinder before the tail clamp is closed. Run about five sheets of paper through the duplicator to seal the cover.

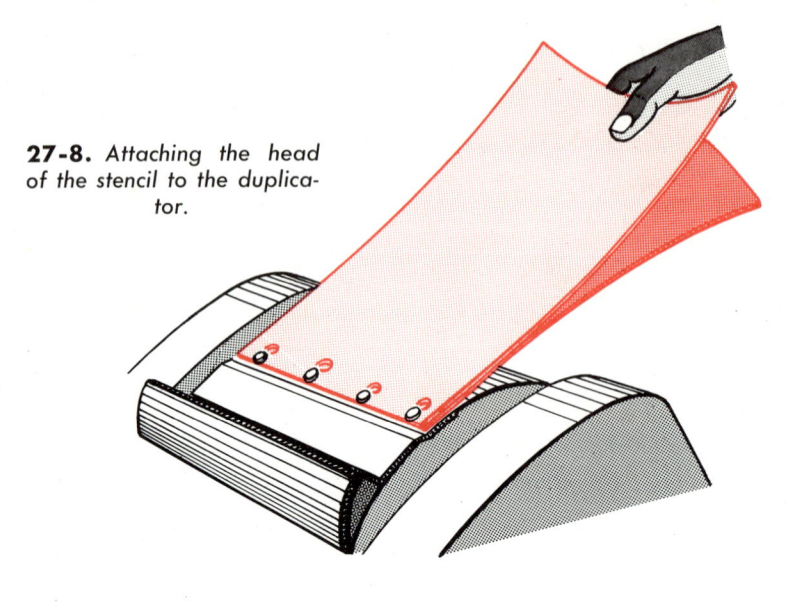

27-8. *Attaching the head of the stencil to the duplicator.*

DISCUSSION TOPICS

Part 2—Graphic Communications
Section 2—Graphic Arts
Unit 19
   1. What is the purpose of graphic arts?
   2. When did Johann Gutenberg first use movable type?
   3. Why were books once a luxury which only the wealthy could afford?
Unit 20
   1. Printing from raised surfaces is known by what name?
   2. What method of printing is based on the principle that grease and water do not mix?
   3. What printing process uses recessed surfaces in a copper cylinder?
   4. Printing done by pushing paint through a screen is known as what process?
   5. Name and briefly describe three types of presses used in the letterpress process.
Unit 21
   1. Of what metals is foundry type made?
   2. What is a line gauge?
   3. Briefly describe how to use a composing stick.

Units 19-27: Discussion Topics

Unit 22
1. Why are galley proofs made?
2. What is meant by "locking up a form" for the press?
3. What is the makeready process?
4. Briefly describe how to do linoleum block printing.

Unit 23
1. What is line copy? What is continuous tone copy?
2. What is cold composition?
3. Why must continuous tone copy be photographed separately from line copy?
4. What type of camera is used to make offset negatives?
5. Describe how an offset plate is prepared.

Unit 24
1. Must the screen for silk-screen printing be made of silk?
2. What are the two common ways of attaching the screen to the printing frame?
3. Name two advantages of silk-screen printing.

Unit 25
1. Name three types of cameras in popular use today.
2. What two factors control the exposure of the negative?
3. What is a latent image?
4. Describe how a negative is developed by the tank method.

Unit 26
1. What are the two ways of printing pictures from negatives?
2. Why are test exposures made?
3. Can pictures be enlarged with the contact printing method?

Unit 27
1. Name three commonly used methods of duplicating.
2. When preparing a master for spirit duplicating, how are mistakes corrected?
3. Briefly describe the mimeograph process.

PART III
Manufacturing—Principles, Materials, and Processes

Section 1–Metalworking

Unit 28 Introduction to Metalworking

Unit 29 Mining and Refining Metals

Unit 30 Metal Materials

Unit 31 Metal Layout and Pattern Development

Unit 32 Modern Metalworking

Unit 33 Metal Cutting Principles

Unit 34 Sawing Metal

Unit 35 Shearing Metal

Unit 36 Abrading Metal

Unit 37 Shaping Metal

Unit 38 Drilling Metal

Unit 39 Milling and Filing Metal

Unit 40 Turning Metal

Unit 41 Etching and Flame Cutting of Metal

Unit 42 Metal Forming Principles

Unit 43 Bending Metal

Unit 44 Casting Metal

Unit 45 Forging and Heat-Treating Metal

Unit 46 Pressing Metal

Unit 47 Drawing Metal

Unit 48 Extruding Metal

Unit 49 Rolling Metal

Unit 50 Metal Fastening Principles

Unit 51 Mechanical Fastening of Metal

Unit 52 Adhesive Fastening of Metal

Unit 53 Cohesive Fastening of Metal

Unit 54 Metal Finishing Principles

Unit 55 Coat Finishing of Metal

Unit 56 Remove Finishing of Metal

Unit 57 Displacement Finishing of Metal

Unit 58 Color Finishing of Metal

Discussion Topics and Activities

Part III: Manufacturing—Principles, Materials, and Processes

Metric Fact Sheet*

— Metalworking —

- Millimetre (mm) and metre (m) are the important linear measurement units.
- Drawings are in mm.
- Common measuring tools are the steel rule in 150 and 300 mm lengths; metre rule and steel tape used for longer measurements.
- Precision measurements are made with the micrometer, vernier caliper, and dial indicator reading in mm.
- Welding tank pressure gauges read in kilopascals (kPa). Some gauges show dual pressure readings in both psi and kPa.
- Temperatures for foundry, forging, and heat treating will be shown in degrees Celsius (°C). A typical melting point: aluminum melts at 1218 °F or 659 °C.
- Material standards change—specification in mm, lengths in m.
- A typical metric screw thread designation is shown in Fig. 51-8.

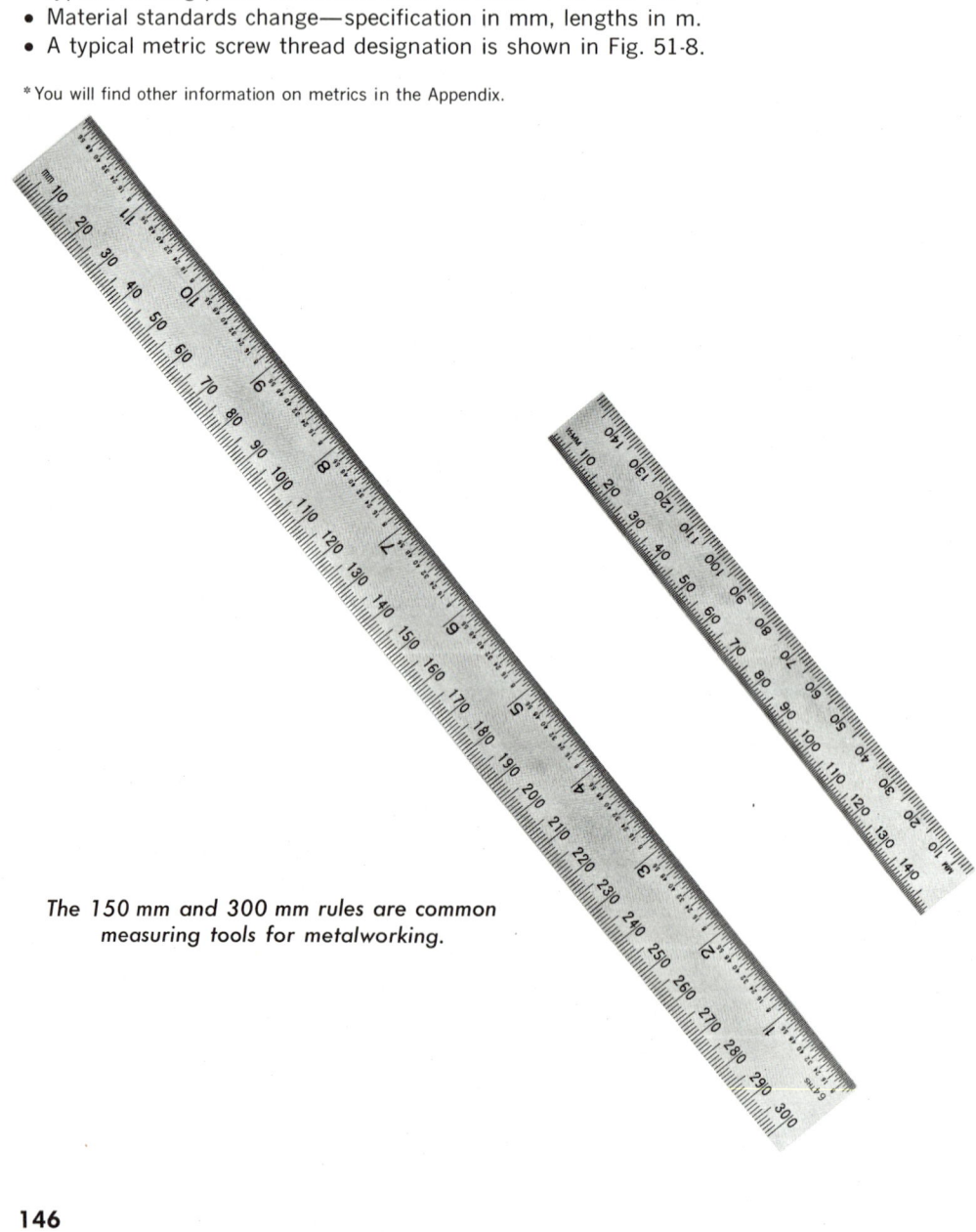

*You will find other information on metrics in the Appendix.

The 150 mm and 300 mm rules are common measuring tools for metalworking.

UNIT 28

Introduction to Metalworking

The metalworking industries make metals from raw ores and then build usable products from the metals. These industries use various mechanical means of doing this, such as turning, milling, extruding, drawing, and casting. Important processes of the metals industries will be explained in the following units.

In a broader sense, metalworking may be said to include any method of changing the shape, size, and physical form of metals, such as casting, powder metallurgy, and heat treatment.

It is almost impossible to think of any object that does not contain metal, or that does not require metal for its manufacture or production. Fig. 28-1. Tools and machines from typewriters to gasoline engines are made chiefly of metals. All forms of transportation—automobiles,

28-1. *Hundreds of things are used each day that are made of metal. Because metal is strong and easily shaped, it is an ideal material for this bicycle.*

Murray Ohio Manufacturing Company

147

Part III: Manufacturing—Principles, Materials, and Processes

ships, aircraft, trains—are moving masses of metal and metal parts. Almost everything depends on metal, from the modern skyscraper to the production and distribution of electricity. With these facts in mind, it is not difficult to see that the metalworking industry is important to every other industry—farming, transportation, manufacturing, construction, and power being among the major ones. As a necessity for life and a wealth producer, metalworking is second only to farming.

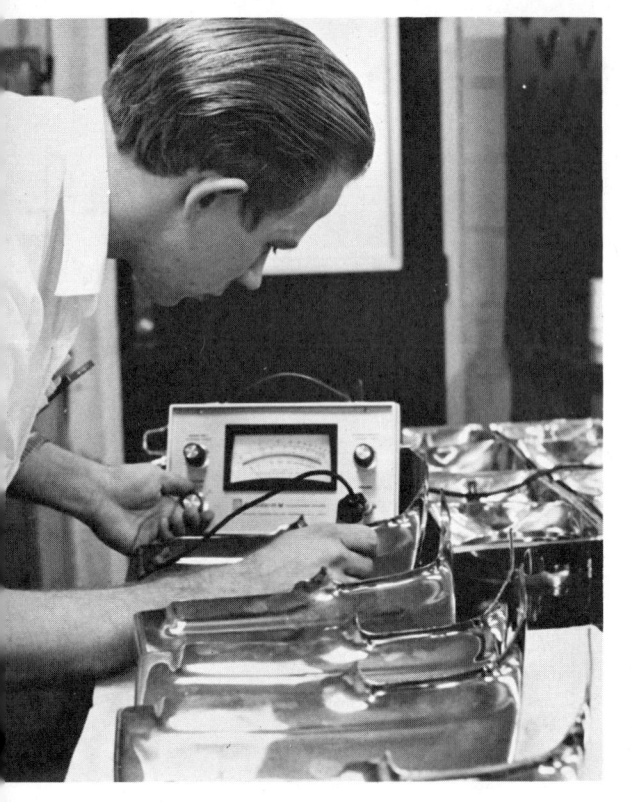

Metalworking has a great deal to offer as a vocation. The field is so broad, and includes so many types of activities and materials, that the opportunity is practically limitless. Fig. 28-2. The growth of the industry and the constant demand for improved materials leads to employment possibilities equal to or better than most other fields.

The chart in Fig. 28-3 shows the breadth and structure of the metalworking industries.

General Motors Corporation
28-2. *There are many career opportunities in the modern metals industries. This technician is testing thickness of the metal plating on automobile bumpers.*

28-3. *Metals are used by many industries in the production of goods, as shown in this chart. There are great opportunities for employment in the metals industries.*

METALWORKING INDUSTRIES

- TOY
- SHEET METAL
- METAL CONTAINER
- FURNITURE
- CONSTRUCTION
- HOME APPLIANCE
- HEAVY EQUIPMENT
- MINING
- REFINING
- FABRICATING
- RAW MATERIALS
- AUTOMOBILE
- RAILROAD
- HARDWARE
- MARINE
- MACHINE TOOL
- SPORTING GOODS
- METALCRAFT
- AIR CRAFT

148

UNIT 29

Mining and Refining Metals

Our supply of metals comes from the earth in the form of metal *ores*. That is, the metals are combined with other materials, such as rock. The ores are refined and then made into forms usable by the manufacturing industry. Many kinds of metal—steel, copper, nickel, lead, aluminum, gold, silver, and others—are used to make the products we need. In this unit the processing methods for three of these metals—steel, aluminum, and copper—will be discussed.

STEEL

Steel is one of our most important metals. It is tough, durable, plentiful, and is used in every industry. Well over 500 000 people in this country are involved in the mining, refining and fabricating of steel.

Shown in Fig. 29-1 is a chart of the steelmaking process. Note that the first important step is to take out the iron from the ore in the blast furnace. Coke, iron ore, and limestone make up the charge for the furnace. The coke supplies the heat (about 3500 degrees F), and the limestone serves as a flux to draw off the impurities. Fig. 29-2. The iron is then made into steel by one of three processes: open-hearth furnace, electric furnace, or basic-oxygen furnace.

The open-hearth furnace produces about 125 tons of steel in 12 hours. Roughly 30 percent of the steel in this country is produced by this process. The electric furnace system accounts for about 20 percent of this country's steel production. About 25 tons can be produced in one furnace charge, requiring 4 to 6 hours. The basic-oxygen furnace speeds up the steelmaking process by forcing blasts of oxygen into the combustion chamber. About one hour is needed to produce 82 tons. Fifty percent of our steel is now made this way, but in the future most steelmakers will probably use this method. Fig. 29-3.

In each of these three systems, raw iron, which is fairly soft, is made into steel by adding other metals and chemicals to it to form *alloys*. The alloys are varied to make special steels for drawing into pipe, for casting, for machining, and for many other uses.

After the steel is made, it is poured into ingot molds. Later it is milled into bars, sheets, plates, and other forms to be used by industries.

Instead of reheating ingots and rolling them into blooms, slabs or billets, these three shapes of steel can also be made by a new process called *continuous casting*. Fig. 29-4. Molten steel is poured continuously into a water-cooled mold that is open at the top and bottom. A starting bar temporarily closes the bottom. The steel gradually cools and begins to become solid in the mold. Then the starting bar is slowly pulled downward, drawing the steel with it.

The rate at which molten steel is poured in at the top is matched with the rate at which the solid steel is pulled out at the bottom. In this way, a long continuous piece is formed. It can then be cut into lengths as desired. Different shapes

Part III: Manufacturing—Principles, Materials, and Processes

of molds are used, depending upon whether blooms, slabs, or billets are being made.

The great iron ore producing areas in this country are in Minnesota, Michigan, and Wisconsin. In these areas there are also large amounts of taconite, a lower grade ore which is balled into pellets rather than shipped as raw ore. The steel-making centers are in Indiana, Ohio, and Pennsylvania.

ALUMINUM

This wonder metal is remarkably light. Though soft, it can be made strong by adding copper or zinc. Large deposits of aluminum ore (bauxite) are found in Arkansas. Other mining areas are in Africa, Australia, Brazil, and the U.S.S.R.

Aluminum alloys are used for bridges, airplanes, house siding, kitchen utensils, and many other products. The chart in Fig. 29-5 shows the flow of raw material

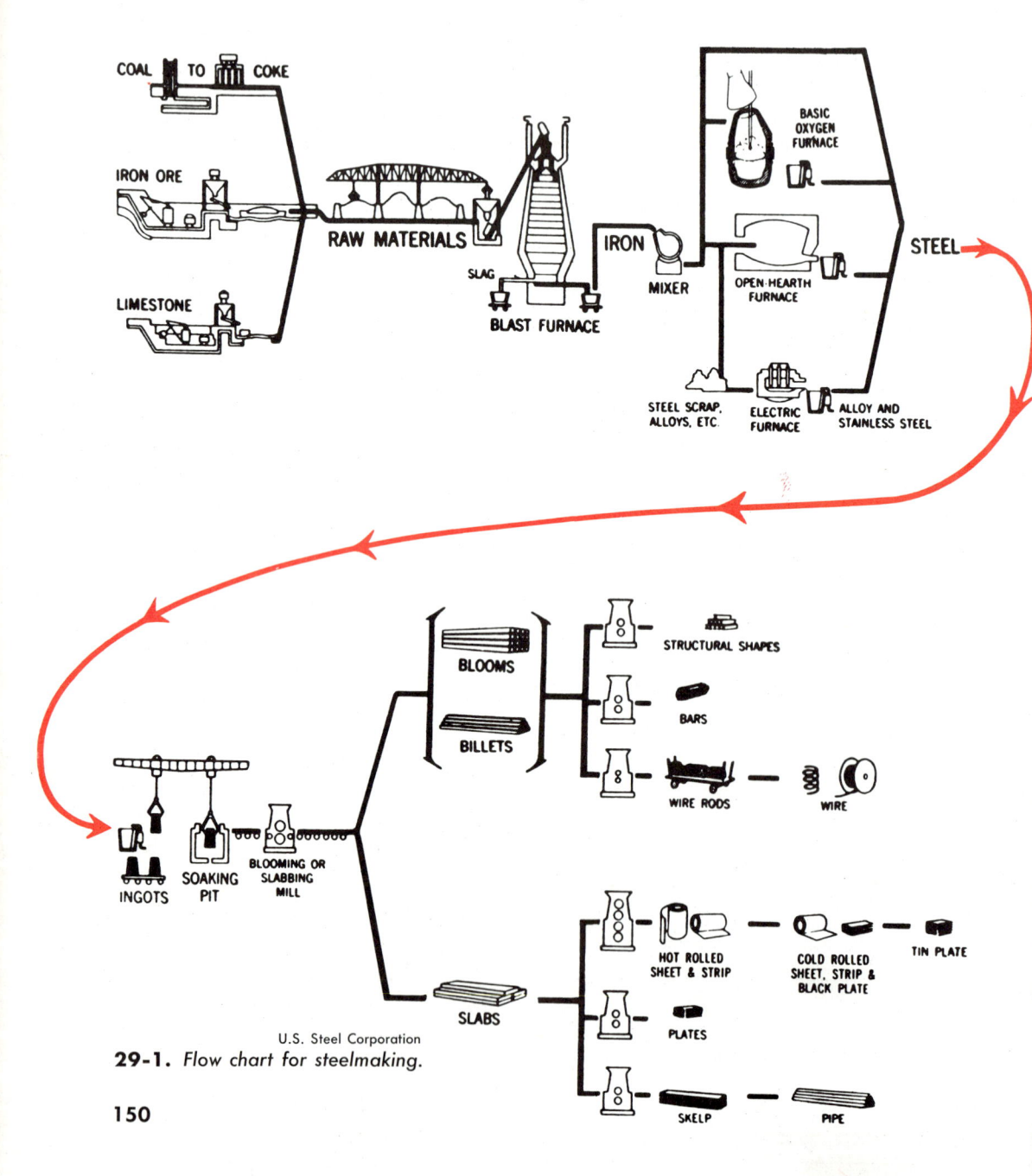

29-1. *Flow chart for steelmaking.*

U.S. Steel Corporation

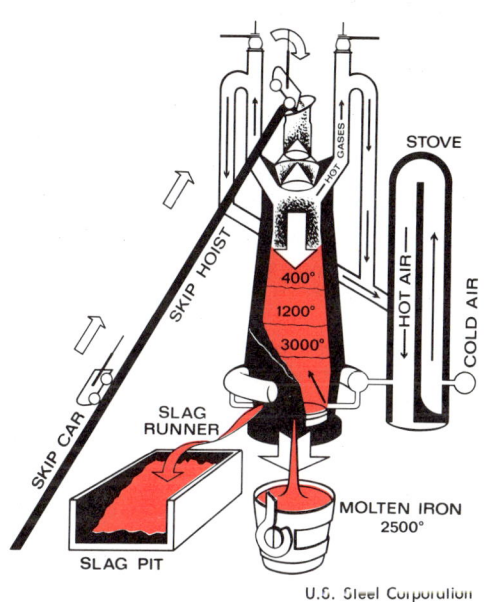

29-2. The blast furnace is the first step in the steelmaking process. In the blast furnace, iron is extracted from the iron ore.

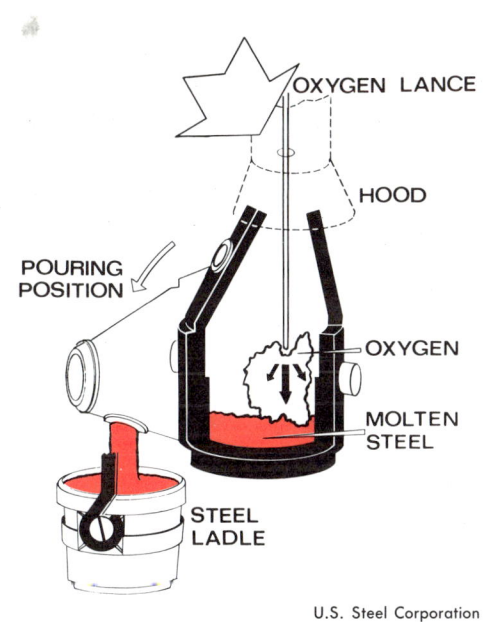

29-3. Blasts of oxygen speed up the steelmaking process in the basic-oxygen furnace.

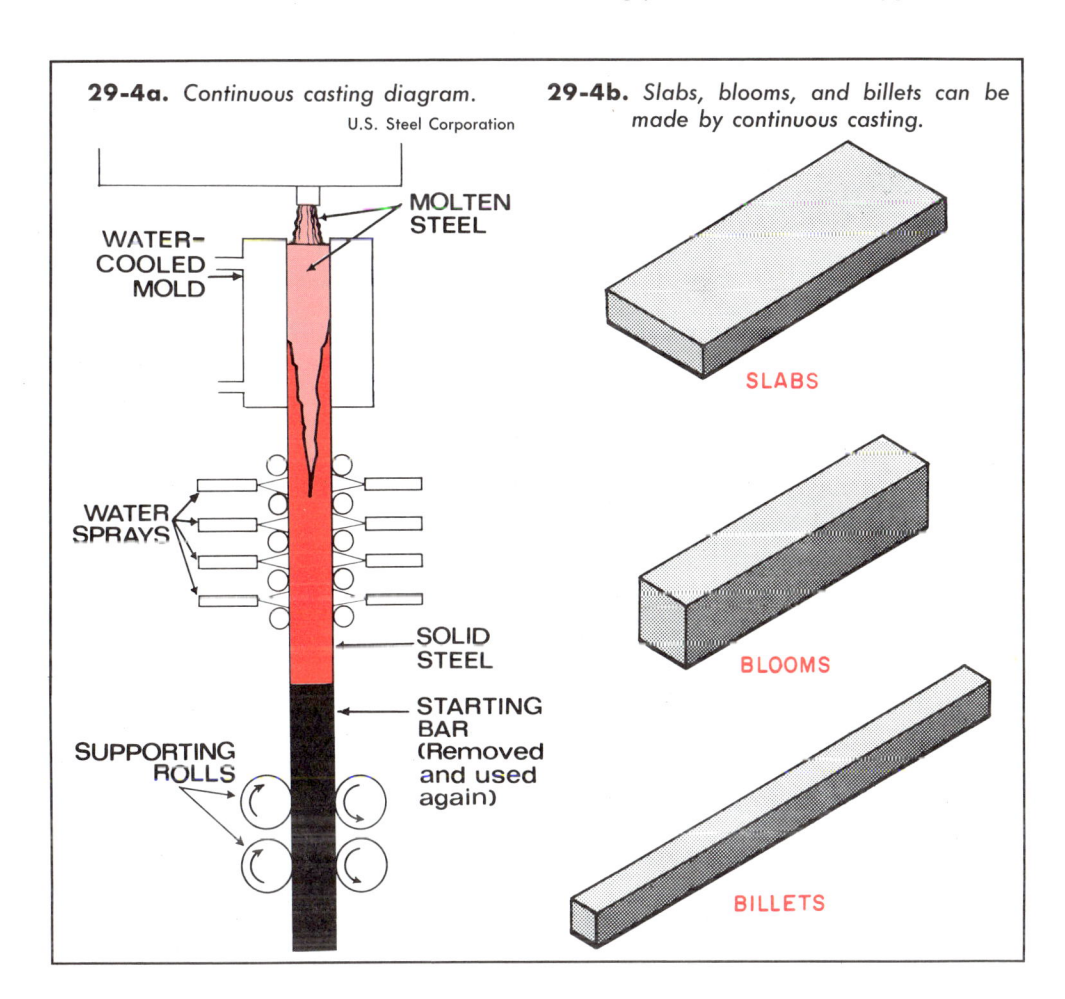

29-4a. Continuous casting diagram.

29-4b. Slabs, blooms, and billets can be made by continuous casting.

151

Part III: Manufacturing—Principles, Materials, and Processes

to finished aluminum. Fig. 29-6 shows a typical pouring operation at the smelter.

COPPER

Copper is perhaps best known for its uses in the electrical industry. It is a good conductor of electricity. Copper is also used for working utensils, roofing and as an alloy for other metals. The chart in Fig. 29-7 describes the process of making copper. Large copper deposits are found in Chile, Canada, and the United States. Some of the mining centers in this country are in Montana, Arizona, and Utah.

MINING
Bauxite is mined, crushed, washed, and dried. The miner in the drawing is drilling a blasting hole.

SMELTING
Alumina is reduced to metallic aluminum in carbon-lined pots. Electric current passes through the molten alumina to free the metal which is then siphoned off into pig molds.

REFINING
Processed bauxite is converted to aluminum hydrate crystals. These crystals are roasted to produce a white powder called alumina. The drawing shows a converter.

FABRICATING
Ingots are formed into bars, sheets, wires, and tubes for industrial use.

29-5. Flow chart for aluminum production.

29-6. Molten aluminum is siphoned from smelting pots and poured into pig molds. Pig is either sold as such or remelted and alloyed for use as ingot.

Kaiser Aluminum

Unit 29: Mining and Refining Metals

BASIC STEPS—COPPER ORE TO FINISHED PRODUCT

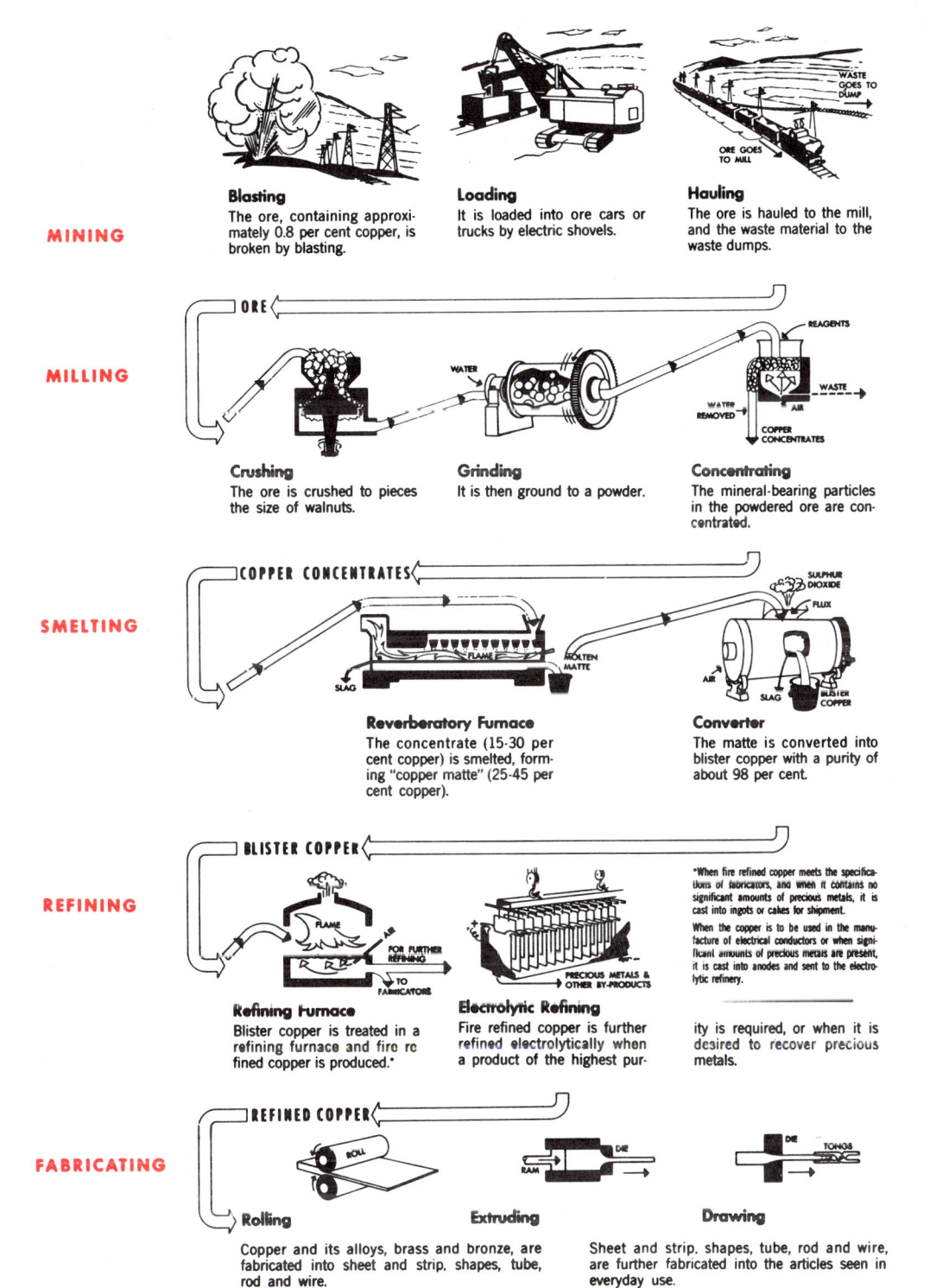

MINING

Blasting
The ore, containing approximately 0.8 per cent copper, is broken by blasting.

Loading
It is loaded into ore cars or trucks by electric shovels.

Hauling
The ore is hauled to the mill, and the waste material to the waste dumps.

MILLING

Crushing
The ore is crushed to pieces the size of walnuts.

Grinding
It is then ground to a powder.

Concentrating
The mineral-bearing particles in the powdered ore are concentrated.

SMELTING

Reverberatory Furnace
The concentrate (15-30 per cent copper) is smelted, forming "copper matte" (25-45 per cent copper).

Converter
The matte is converted into blister copper with a purity of about 98 per cent.

REFINING

Refining Furnace
Blister copper is treated in a refining furnace and fire refined copper is produced.*

Electrolytic Refining
Fire refined copper is further refined electrolytically when a product of the highest purity is required, or when it is desired to recover precious metals.

*When fire refined copper meets the specifications of fabricators, and when it contains no significant amounts of precious metals, it is cast into ingots or cakes for shipment.

When the copper is to be used in the manufacture of electrical conductors or when significant amounts of precious metals are present, it is cast into anodes and sent to the electrolytic refinery.

FABRICATING

Rolling

Extruding

Drawing

Copper and its alloys, brass and bronze, are fabricated into sheet and strip, shapes, tube, rod and wire.

Sheet and strip, shapes, tube, rod and wire, are further fabricated into the articles seen in everyday use.

Kennecott Copper Corporation

29-7. *Flow chart for copper production.*

UNIT 30

Metal Materials

Metals are among the most widely used materials. They are useful to us for so many purposes mainly because of their physical and mechanical properties, which are very different from those of other materials such as wood, concrete, and plastic. For instance, metals are strong enough to withstand high loads at high temperatures, yet flexible enough to be worked easily. Fig. 30-1. The properties of metals are due to their structure, that is, the special way their atoms are grouped together to make up a solid metallic material. Pure metals have simple structures. Alloys have more complex structures.

30-1. *This attractive "melon pot" was formed from sterling silver sheet. Metal is strong, yet it is easy to work.*

Sally Dickson Associates

ALLOYS

Most metals used in product manufacturing are alloys, not pure metals. Pure metals are seldom used except in the laboratory. Alloys contain several metals as well as small amounts of nonmetallic

30-2. *This metallurgist is using an electron microscope to examine metal samples magnified 200 000 times.*

Carpenter Technology Corporation

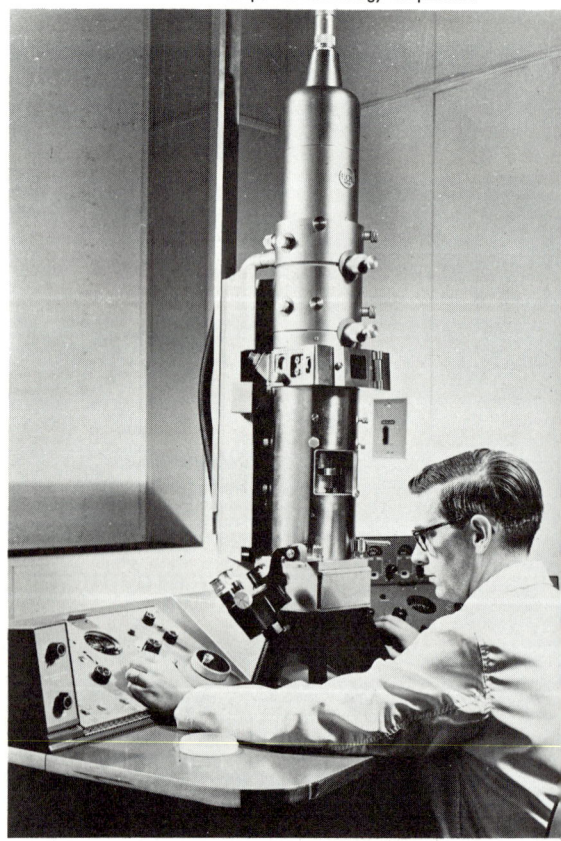

Unit 30: Metal Materials

elements. By careful alloying, new metals with desirable properties are created. Some of the results are surprising. For example, nickel can be combined with copper to produce an alloy that is stronger than either nickel or copper. A great number of alloys can and have been made because of the ease with which metal atoms combine with other atoms.

Many scientists and engineers are concerned with metals. Chemists are interested in how metals behave in certain environments and how they form alloys. Physicists are interested in their electrical and atomic structure. Mechanical engineers are concerned with their fabrication. Electrical engineers are concerned with their electrical and magnetic properties, and chemical engineers with their specialized applications. The metallurgist works in all these areas. Fig. 30-2.

Metallurgy involves making metals and alloys for practical use. For thousands of years it was an art where results came from hard experience and little understanding. Now it is a science using the basic principles of the microstructure (microscopic structure) of metals and alloys and how that structure affects their behavior and properties. Many of the most important advances, such as those made possible by the development of the electron microscope, have come only in recent years. Scientists continue to experiment with metals, to create the new and improve the old.

PROPERTIES OF METALS

The many kinds of metals used in schools and industry have different characteristics. Some are described as very hard. This means they resist scratching. Others are strong, yet tough and ductile. Metals are also good conductors of electricity and heat. These characteristics are called metal "properties." Because of the many properties of the various kinds of metals, almost every product need can be met. The chart in Fig. 30-3 describes some of the most important and useful properties and the way these are tested. The test most commonly used in the

30-3. *Metal properties chart. Metals are selected according to the products to be made from them.*

Metal Properties

Property	Description	Test
Hardness	Resists penetration, wear, and scratching; difficult to form and machine	Brinell, Rockwell—a metal ball or diamond point is pressed against a test specimen
Tensile strength	Resists stretching (or strain) and breaking	A test specimen is pulled under a tension load to break it in two
Ductility	Easy to form without tearing or rupturing	A test specimen is stretched without breaking
Toughness	Resists shock and impact; tough materials are not brittle	Charpy or Izod impact tests—a notched specimen is struck to fracture it
Elasticity	Resists bending, returns to original shape after bending; springy metal	A test of stiffness or springiness—a deflection or vibration test where the load is applied and then removed

Part III: Manufacturing—Principles, Materials, and Processes

30-4. A Rockwell hardness tester.
Wilson Mechanical Instrument Division

school shop is the hardness test. Fig. 30-4. This test is described in Fig. 30-5.

METAL SHAPES AND SIZES

The metal materials used in school and industry are available in a number of different shapes and sizes. Fig. 30-6. Bars, tubing, angles, etc., are available in lengths from 10 to 20 feet. Sheet metals are sold by weight or by the square foot.

The thickness of sheet metal is indicated by a gauge number.* A disc-type gauge is used to make this measurement. Fig. 30-7. Ferrous metals—those which contain a high percentage of iron—are measured with a United States Standard gauge. Galvanized iron and tin plate are ferrous metals. The Brown and Sharpe, or American Standard gauge, is used for most nonferrous metals—metals contain-

---

*Gauge is sometimes spelled gage. Either spelling is acceptable.

156

ing little or no iron. Copper, aluminum, and brass are nonferrous metals. Fig. 30-8.

Other methods of measuring sheets are also used. Aluminum is measured in decimal units. Copper is sometimes measured by the weight per square foot. For example, 20-gauge copper weighs 24 ounces per square foot. The charts in Fig. 30-9 (Pages 160, 161) describe the common sizes of metal bar materials.

KINDS OF METALS

The following paragraphs describe metals you will probably find in the shop. Learn something about them so that you will be able to select wisely for any projects you make. Ferrous metals are mostly iron in content. Nonferrous metals contain little or no iron. The common kinds of metals used in school and industry are described here.

Ferrous Metals

The main materials in this group are iron and steel. Iron is one of the basic elements used in making cast iron, wrought iron, and steel. Steel is actually an alloy of iron and carbon. The chart in Fig. 30-10 (Page 162) describes some of the more common ferrous metals and their uses.

The carbon content of a metal is shown as a percentage or as "points." One percent (1.00%) carbon is called 100 carbon, 100 point carbon, or point 100 carbon.

Some steels are hot rolled (squeezed between rollers while red hot). Such metals have a bluish scale on the surface and are called hot-rolled steel (HRS). Cold-rolled steels (CRS) are smoother and have a clean shiny surface finish.

You can tell the difference among steels by grinding a piece and studying the sparks. High-carbon steel gives off a bomblike cluster, while low-carbon steel

30-5. (P. 157) *Three kinds of hardness tests.*

Hardness Testing

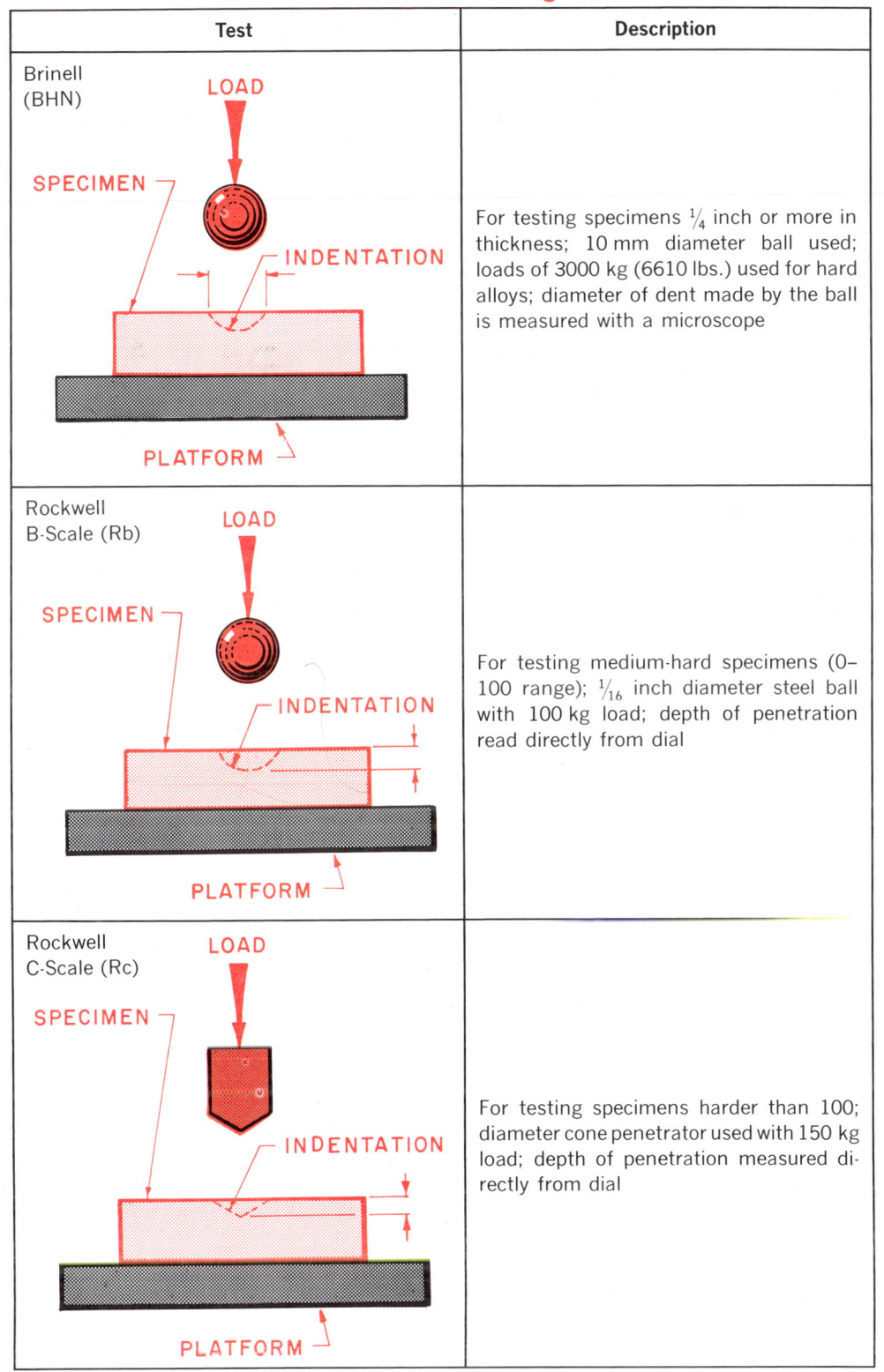

Test	Description
Brinell (BHN)	For testing specimens $\frac{1}{4}$ inch or more in thickness; 10 mm diameter ball used; loads of 3000 kg (6610 lbs.) used for hard alloys; diameter of dent made by the ball is measured with a microscope
Rockwell B-Scale (Rb)	For testing medium-hard specimens (0–100 range); $\frac{1}{16}$ inch diameter steel ball with 100 kg load; depth of penetration read directly from dial
Rockwell C-Scale (Rc)	For testing specimens harder than 100; diameter cone penetrator used with 150 kg load; depth of penetration measured directly from dial

Part III: Manufacturing—Principles, Materials, and Processes

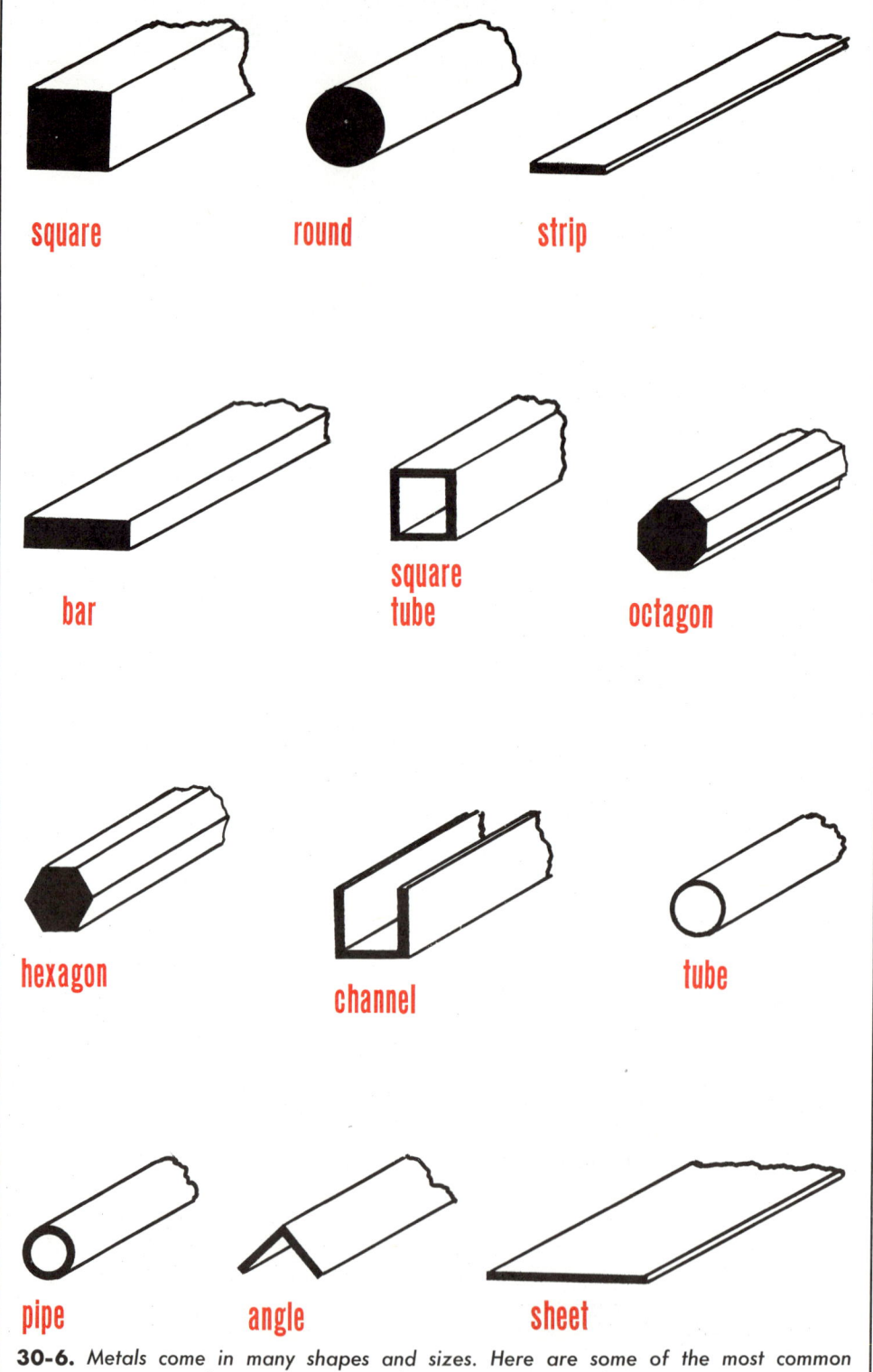

square   round   strip

bar   square tube   octagon

hexagon   channel   tube

pipe   angle   sheet

30-6. Metals come in many shapes and sizes. Here are some of the most common shapes, those generally found in the school shop.

Unit 30: Metal Materials

30-7. Disc-type sheet and wire gauge. Place the metal sheet into several openings to find the one that fits correctly. This will be the smallest one into which the metal fits easily. The number stamped near the opening tells the gauge of the metal.

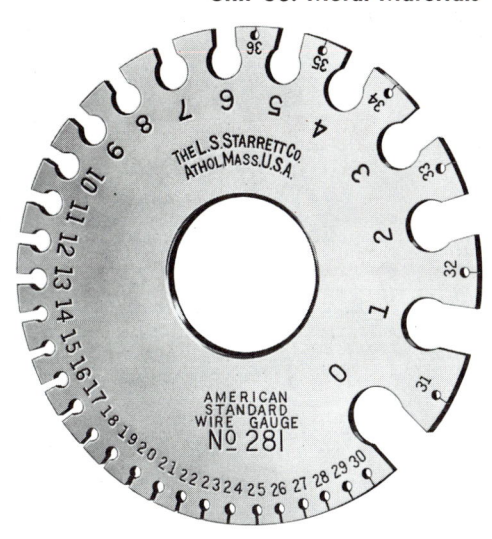

Metal Sheet Thicknesses

Gauge number	Brown & Sharpe or American Standard for nonferrous wire and sheet metals (inches)	United States Standard for ferrous sheet metals (inches)	ISO metric replacement sizes* (mm)
16	0.0508	0.0625	1.25
18	0.0403 (32 oz.)	0.0500	1.00
20	0.0320 (24 oz.)	0.0375	0.80
22	0.0253 (20 oz.)	0.0313	0.63
24	0.0201 (16 oz.)	0.0250	0.50
26	0.0159	0.0188	0.40
28	0.0126	0.0156	0.315
30	0.0100	0.0125	0.250
32	0.0079	—	0.200

*Based on ISO R 388, not yet adopted in USA. Gauge numbers will not be used; use mm sizes only.

30-8. This chart gives the inch and millimetre equivalents of various gauge numbers.

gives off a long, spread pattern. Fig. 30-11 (Page 163).

Nonferrous Metals

These metals contain little or no iron and are soft, easily worked, good conductors of heat and electricity, and are generally more durable than iron and steel. Here are some common examples.

COPPER

Copper is reddish brown and can be bought as sheets, tubes, or rods in a variety of sizes. It is easily worked into bowls, but hammering makes it harder. (This is known as work hardening.) To soften the copper, it must be heated red hot and plunged into water. Copper is second only to silver as a conductor of

159

Flat Metal Bars Common Sizes

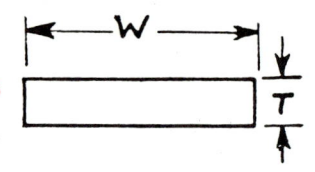

Thickness	
inch	mm*
1/16	1.6
1/8	3
3/16	5
1/4	6
5/16	8
3/8	10
7/16	11
1/2	12
9/16	14
5/8	16
11/16	18
3/4	20
7/8	22
1	25
1 1/8	28
1 1/4	30
1 15/16	32
1 3/8	35
1 1/2	40
1 3/4	45
2	50

Width	
inch	mm*
3/8	10
1/2	12
5/8	16
3/4	20
1	25
1 1/4	30
1 1/2	40
1 3/4	45
2	50

*Metric replacement sizes based upon ANSI B32.3-1974

Round, Square and Hexagon Metal Bars Common Sizes

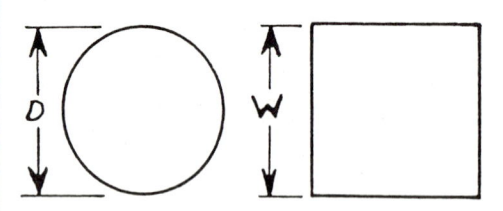

Diameters or Across Flats Distances

inch	mm*
1/8	3
1/4	6
3/8	10
1/2	12
5/8	16
3/4	20
1	25
1 1/4	30
1 1/2	40
1 3/4	45
2	50

*Metric replacement sizes based upon ANSI B32.4-1974

Common Steel Angle Sizes

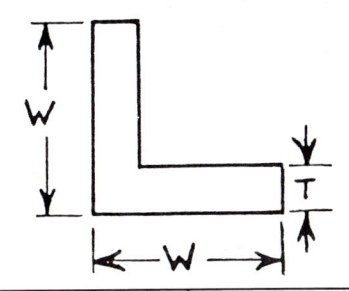

Customary Inch		Probable ISO Metric Replacement Size (mm)*	
Width	Thickness	Width	Thickness
3/4	1/16, 1/8, 3/16	20	3, 4, 5
1	1/8, 3/16, 1/4	25	3, 4, 5
1 1/4	1/8, 3/16, 1/4	30	3, 4, 5
—	—	35	3, 4, 5
1 1/2	1/8, 3/16, 1/4	40	3, 4, 5, 6
1 3/4	1/8, 3/16, 1/4	45	3, 4, 5, 6
2	1/8, 3/16, 1/4, 5/16, 3/8	50	3, 4, 5, 6, 7, 8

*Based on sizes recommended in ISO R657/1, not yet adopted in USA.

30-9. *These charts include probable ISO metric replacement sizes, not yet adopted in USA.*

electricity. Copper tarnishes easily and does not machine easily.

BRASS, BRONZE, AND PEWTER

Brass is an alloy of copper (90 percent) and zinc (10 percent). It is yellow-gold and more brittle than copper. Brass comes in forms similar to copper. Bronze resembles brass in both color and working properties. It is an alloy of about 90 percent copper and 10 percent tin, with small amounts of nickel or aluminum. Pewter is also an alloy containing about 10 percent copper and 90 percent tin. It is an excellent material for making bowls and vases because it is so easily formed.

STERLING SILVER

This lovely, warm, lustrous metal is used for jewelry and fine tableware. An article marked "sterling" must contain not less than 0.925 parts of silver with 0.075 parts of copper or some other alloying metal added for hardness.

ALUMINUM

Aluminum, which is silver-white, is easily worked. It work-hardens quickly and must be softened as follows: Cover the metal with chalk, heat until the chalk turns brown, and allow the metal to air-cool. It too is available in sheets, tubes, rods, and bars. Commercially pure aluminum is designated as No. 1100. Other alloy numbers go up to 7072 to indicate hardness and workability. Aluminum is very light, corrosion-resistant, and an excellent conductor of electricity.

NICKEL SILVER (GERMAN SILVER)

This is not silver at all but an alloy of copper, nickel, and zinc. It is widely used in metalcraft work and as a substitute for silver. It is light and silvery in color and takes silver plating well.

Common Ferrous Metals

Name	Characteristics	Uses
Cast iron	2–6 percent carbon; white and gray types are very brittle; malleable cast has been annealed	Main material used in iron castings
Wrought iron	Almost pure iron; little or no carbon in it; easily worked	Ornamental work
Low-carbon steel	Known as mild or machine steel; 10 to 30 point carbon; cannot be hardened; easily welded, machined, and formed; cold-rolled steel	Rivets, chains, machine parts, forged work, school projects
Medium-carbon steel	Stronger than low-carbon steel; 30 to 60 point carbon; can be hardened	Machine parts; bolts, shafts, axles, hammer heads
High-carbon steel	Known as tool steel; 60 to 130 point carbon; best steel for heat-treating and hardening; hard to cut and bend	Tools such as drills, taps, chisels, etc.
Alloy steel	Alloying elements are added to steels to produce steels with special properties: *nickel* increases strength and corrosion resistance; *chromium* adds toughness and resistance to wear; *tungsten* adds strength and heat resistance; *vanadium* adds shock resistance	wire cables, rails gears, axles, bearings cutting tools, armor springs, gears, splines
Sheet steels	Hot- or cold-rolled sheets, generally coated for protection: a *zinc* coat gives a rustproof finish (galvanized sheet); a *tin* coat gives a bright, corrosion-proof finish suitable for food tins (tinplate)	Sheet metal products, heating and air conditioning ducts, automobile bodies

30-10. *This chart lists the more common ferrous metals and their uses.*

Unit 31: Metal Layout and Pattern Development

SPARK IDENTIFICATION PATTERNS
– STEEL –

STAINLESS

LOW CARBON

HIGH CARBON

30-11. *Steel can be identified by the spark pattern given off when grinding.*

UNIT 31
Metal Layout and Pattern Development

Measuring and laying out stock (the materials) is a key step in making a project. Accuracy is important. Study your project plans carefully before laying out your patterns. Selection of proper materials is also important, and so is care to avoid waste.

LAYOUT TOOLS

You will soon become familiar with the tools used in layout work. They must be used constantly to check proper sizes and squareness. The basic tools you will use are shown in Fig. 31-1.

The *ball-peen hammer* is used for general pounding and straightening. It is also used with center and prick punches to produce marks on metal. Ball-peen hammers range in size from four ounces to two pounds. A one-pound hammer is satisfactory for layout work. Smaller layout hammers are also used.

Center punches are used to mark the centers of holes before drilling. If you don't indent the metal slightly, the drill will skip around and mar the surface. The point of this punch is ground at 90 degrees.

Prick punches are similar to center punches, except that they are ground to a 30 degree point. They are used for making light indentations as location points

Part III: Manufacturing—Principles, Materials, and Processes

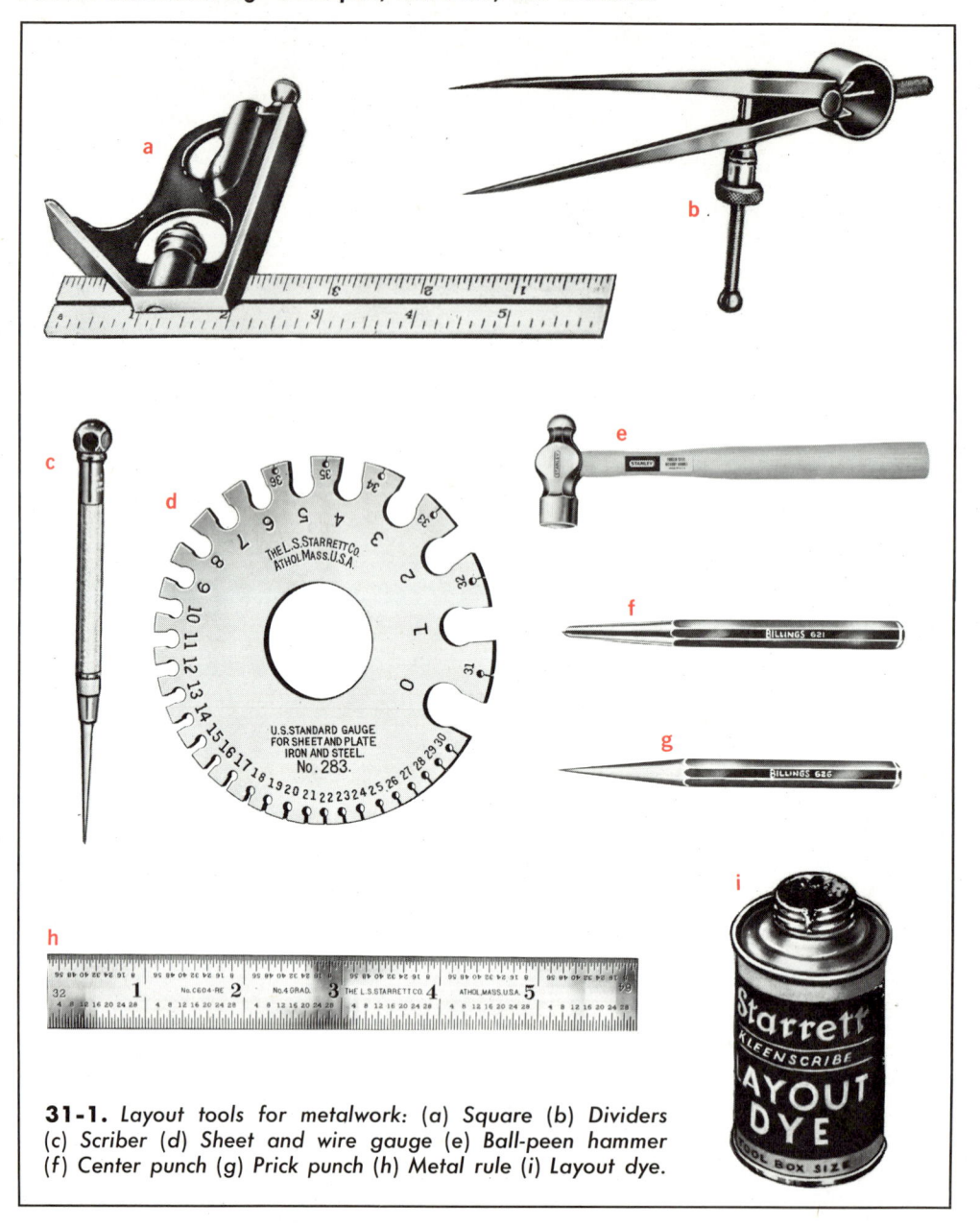

31-1. Layout tools for metalwork: (a) Square (b) Dividers (c) Scriber (d) Sheet and wire gauge (e) Ball-peen hammer (f) Center punch (g) Prick punch (h) Metal rule (i) Layout dye.

for scribing straight lines, or for centers of circles to be made with dividers. Fig. 31-2.

The *sheet and wire gauge* is used to measure the thickness of metal sheets and the diameter of wire.

Metal rules are important measuring and layout instruments. Be careful not to dent or knick their edges. Rules come in many lengths; common shop sizes are 6″, 12″, and 36″. See Unit 3 for information on reading the rule. Steel tapes are frequently used for measuring long pieces.

Layout dye makes it possible to see layout lines clearly. This fluid can be re-

164

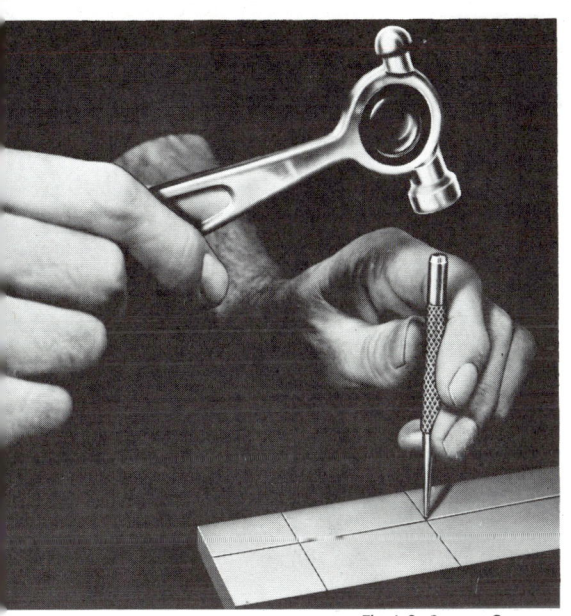

Unit 31: Metal Layout and Pattern Development

31-2. Locating points for scribing circles. A prick punch and layout hammer are used. 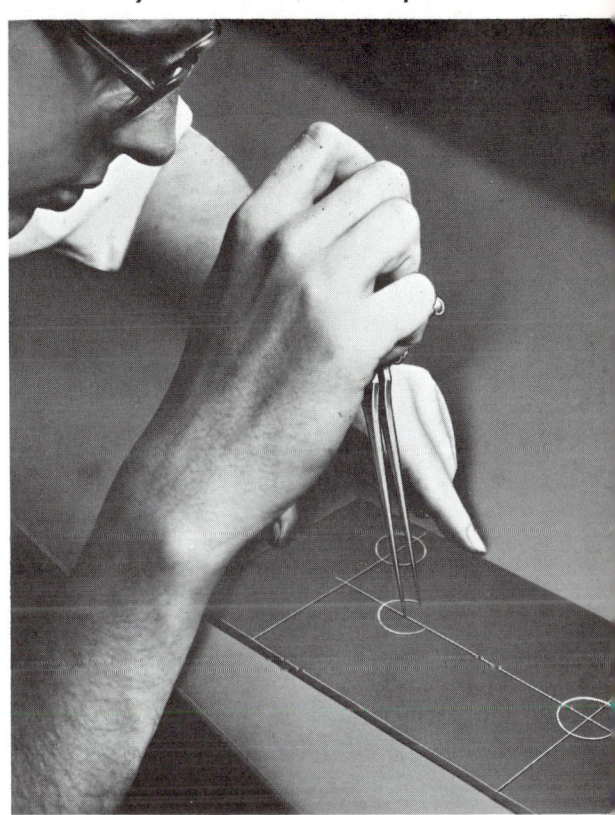
The L.S. Starrett Company

31-3. The dividers are used to scribe circles on metal.
The L.S. Starrett Company

31-4. To scribe lines, hold the square in place and pull the scriber firmly along the edge of the blade.
The L.S. Starrett Company

moved with turpentine or paint thinner. Common chalk may also be used in layout work.

The *scriber* is the metalworker's pencil. Its sharpened point produces a clean line on metal. This tool is also called a scratch awl.

Circles are scribed in metal with *dividers*. These tools are also used for accurately marking out and transferring distances. Fig. 31-3.

Squares are available in several sizes and styles. Solid or adjustable heads with 6" or 12" blades are most common. Fig. 31-4. They are necessary for laying out rectangles and checking the squareness of stock. The *combination set* is a familiar and important tool in the shop. Figs. 31-5 & 31-6.

Another valuable tool is the *hermaphrodite caliper*. Fig. 31-7. It is used to scribe parallel lines along a metal edge.

MEASURING HEAVY STOCK

Metal bars, tubes, rods, and angles must be accurately measured before they

165

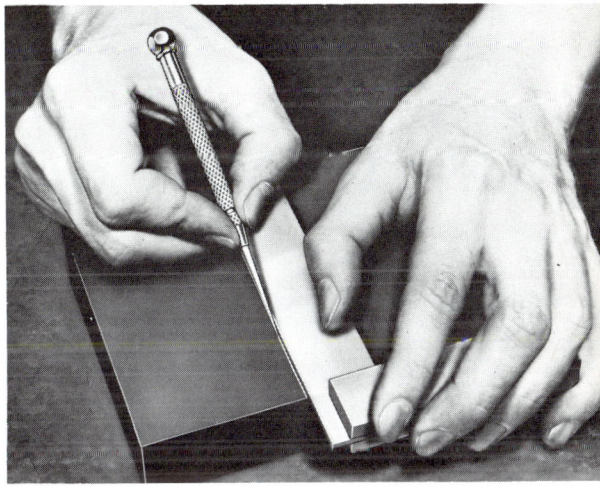

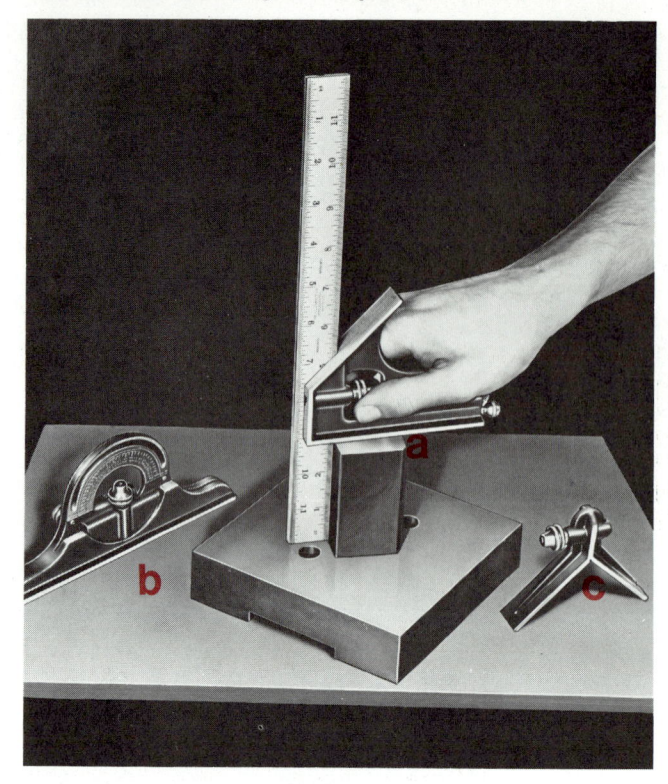

Part III: Manufacturing—Principles, Materials, and Processes

The L.S. Starrett Company

31-5. The combination set. The squaring head (a) is used for general-purpose measuring and scribing of lines at 90 degrees and 45 degrees. The protractor head (b) produces accurate lines at any angle from 0 to 180 degrees. The centering head (c) is used for marking the centers of circles and rods.

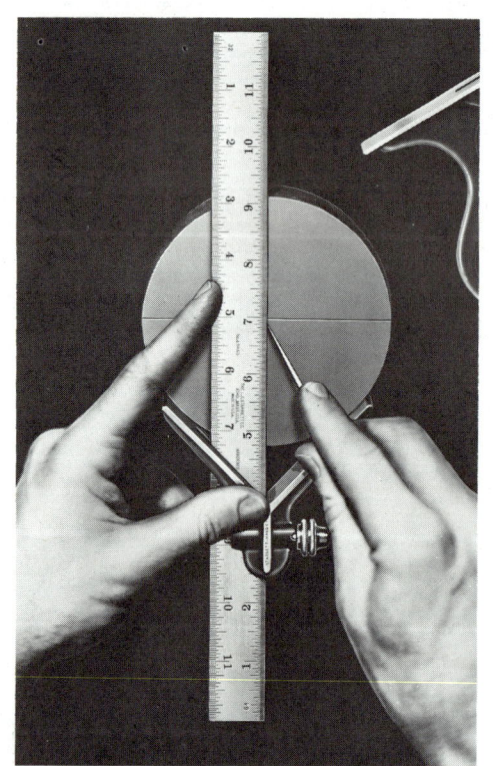

The L.S. Starrett Company
31-6. Using the centering head.

31-7. Using the hermaphrodite calipers.
The L.S. Starrett Company

166

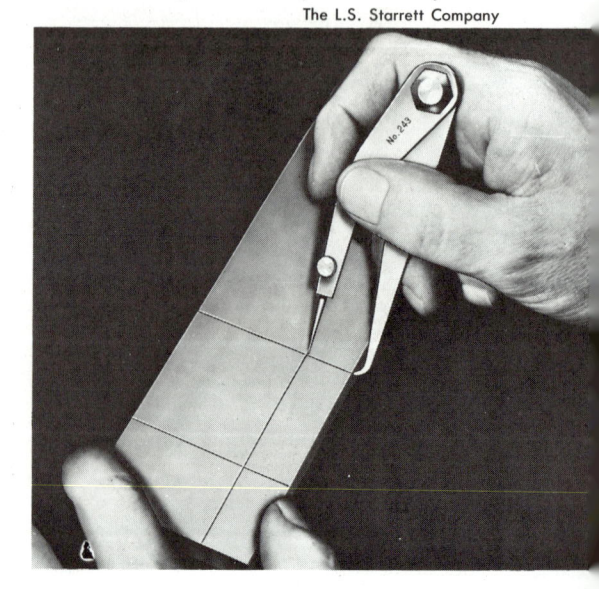

Unit 31: Metal Layout and Pattern Development

are cut to length. The steel tape or metal rule is generally used for this measuring. Hold the end of the rule directly over the end of the stock and make a scriber mark at the desired length. Holes to be drilled are located in a similar manner and then marked with the center punch.

DEVELOPING SHEET METAL PATTERNS

Before sheet metal objects can be cut and formed, a pattern, or stretchout, of the project must be made. In Fig. 31-8 are shown four methods of pattern development. Patterns can be made on paper or on the metal.

Instructions for preparing these patterns, and uses of the various kinds of patterns, are described in the following paragraphs.

Angular Developments

Angular developments are used for boxes, trays, and other rectangular items. Fig. 31-9 is a layout for a utility box. This was made by drawing a rectangle equal to the size of the box bottom and adding the end and side pieces in position. Material for hems and lap seams was added next. For most small boxes, $\frac{1}{4}''$ or $\frac{3}{8}''$ hems and $\frac{5}{16}''$ lap seams are adequate. Note that notches are laid out on the

31-8. *Four methods of developing sheet metal patterns: (a) Angular (b) Cylindrical (c) Conical (d) Triangulation. The huge metal duct was made from cylindrical and triangulation developments.*

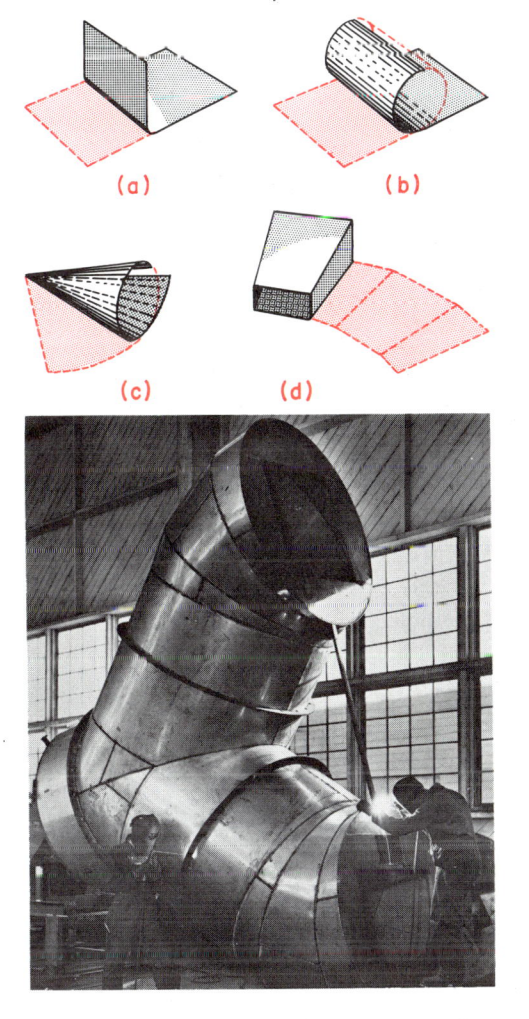

31-9. *A sheet metal utility box laid out by angular development method. Note the notch cuts made to remove unneeded material.*

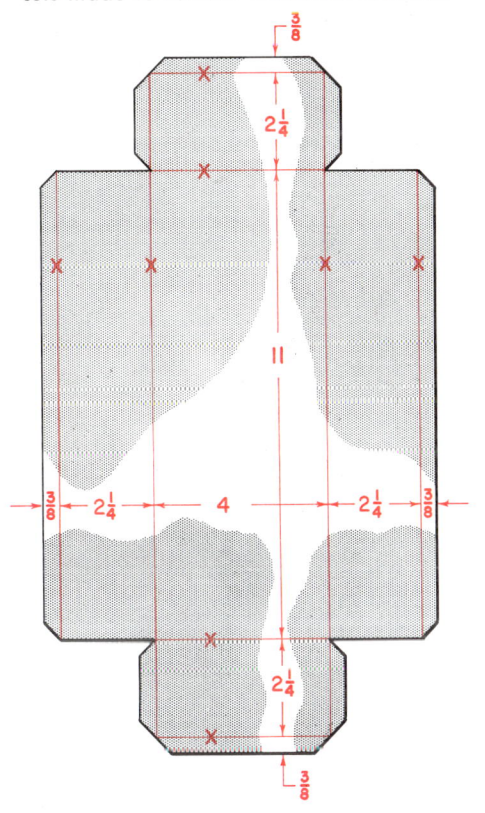

167

Part III: Manufacturing—Principles, Materials, and Processes

pattern to provide for a better fit of the bends by eliminating excess material. A notch is cut at 45 degrees across the corners of the lap seams. Notch cuts ranging from 30 to 45 degrees may be used for single and double hems.

Cylindrical Developments

Cylindrical, or parallel-line, developments are used for cans or other cylindrical containers with vertical sides. Fig. 31-10 is an example of this kind of pattern. This is made by drawing a top and side view of the bird feeder, and dividing the top view into equal parts. These numbered points are then dropped down (projected) into the side view.

A stretchout line (line H in Fig. 31-10) is drawn next to the side view. On this line, step off the number of spaces shown on the top view. In this case, there are twelve equal spaces. Number these points and drop perpendicular lines from them.

Next, extend the numbered points of the side view over to the stretchout. Where like-numbered lines intersect, make a mark. Connect these marks with heavy lines to get the outline of the stretchout. Don't forget to add material for the grooved seam (three times the width of the seam—see Unit 51).

Cylinders without the slanted line in the front view may be laid out by merely finding the circumference of the cylinder. The

31-10. *This bird feeder hopper was made from a parallel-line development. Make certain that all points are projected properly.*

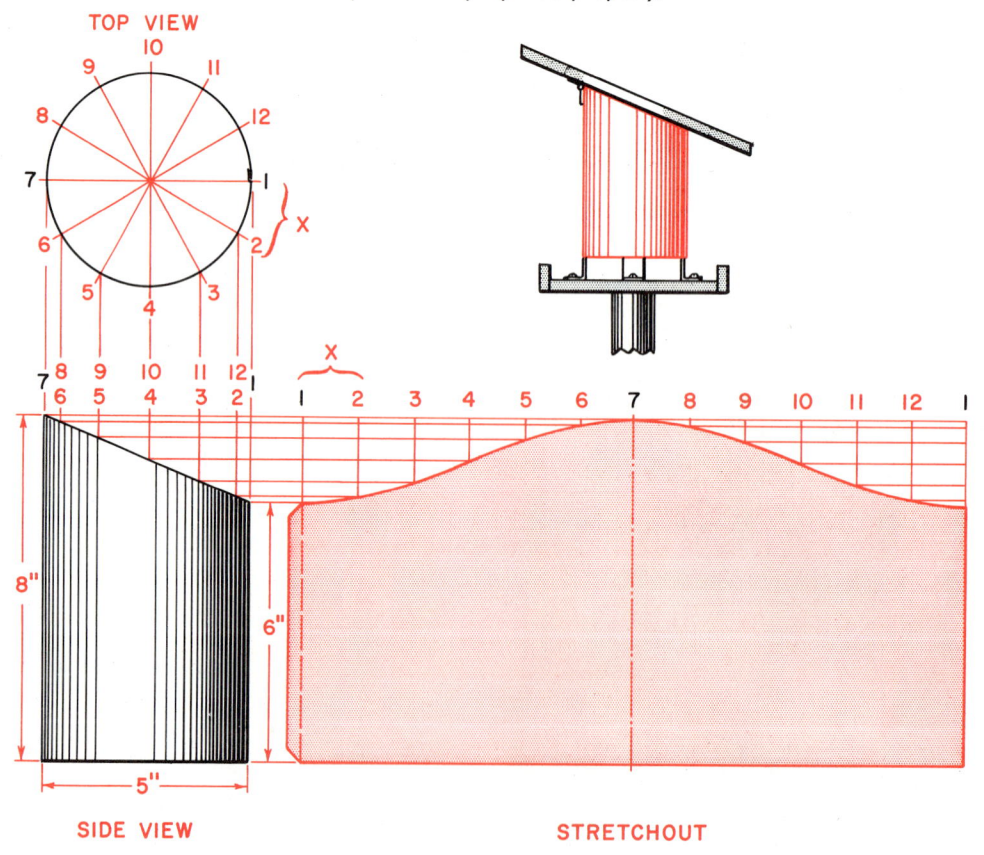

Unit 31: Metal Layout and Pattern Development

formula for this is diameter times 3.1416 (*pi*). A circumference rule may also be used.

Conical Developments

Conical, or radial-line, developments are used for making cone-shaped objects such as funnels, pails, covers, and shades. The patio-lamp shade is a good example of this. Fig. 31-11. Cone patterns are made by drawing a full-size front view of the object. Extend the taper lines until they intersect at point "a." Draw semicircle "bc" and divide into an even number of equal parts. Number these divisions. Draw arc "bg" with radius "ab." Use the same center and draw arc "df" with radius "ad." On arc "bg" mark off twice the number of equal divisions found on the semicircle. Draw a line from the last division point (in Fig. 31-11 this is point 12) to "a" to form the layout "dbgf." Add ¼" for a plain lap, riveted seam.

Triangulation

Triangulation is used to develop transition pieces in sheet metal ductwork. Examples of this are square-to-round pieces, or, as shown in Fig. 31-8, a large rectangle to a smaller rectangle. Very few triangulation pieces are made in the school shop.

ENLARGING PATTERNS

Sometimes you may want to develop a pattern from a picture or print in a book or magazine. These are often too small, but can be enlarged by the use of grid systems. Fig. 31-12. Directly over the print draw a grid system with small squares.

31-11. A radial-line (or conical) development was used to lay out this patio-lamp shade. Funnels are also made this way.

MAJOR DIAM. = 7 1/2
MINOR DIAM. = 2 1/4
HEIGHT = 6 1/4

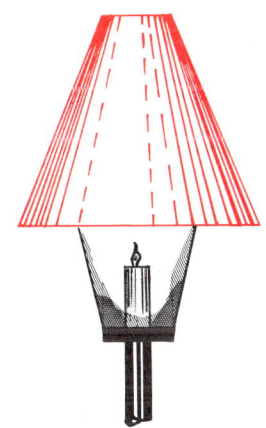

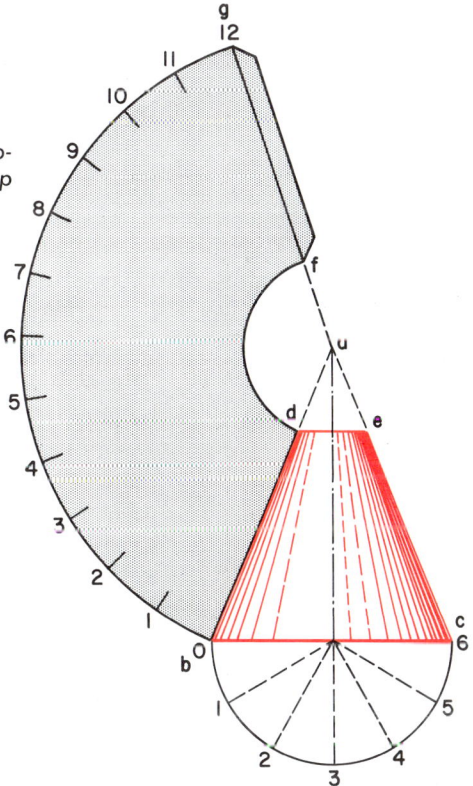

Part III: Manufacturing—Principles, Materials, and Processes

Letter the vertical lines and number the horizontal ones, as shown in the top part of Fig. 31-12.

Perhaps you are planning to triple the size of the pattern. If so, make another grid system with squares three times as large. Letter and number the lines as before. If a line on the pattern crosses the grid system where lines H and 4 come together, make a small dot at point H4 on the large grid. Transfer enough of these points to show the outline of the pattern. Connect the points with lines to complete the pattern.

31-12. *Enlarging a pattern by using a grid system. Patterns may be reduced in a similar manner.*

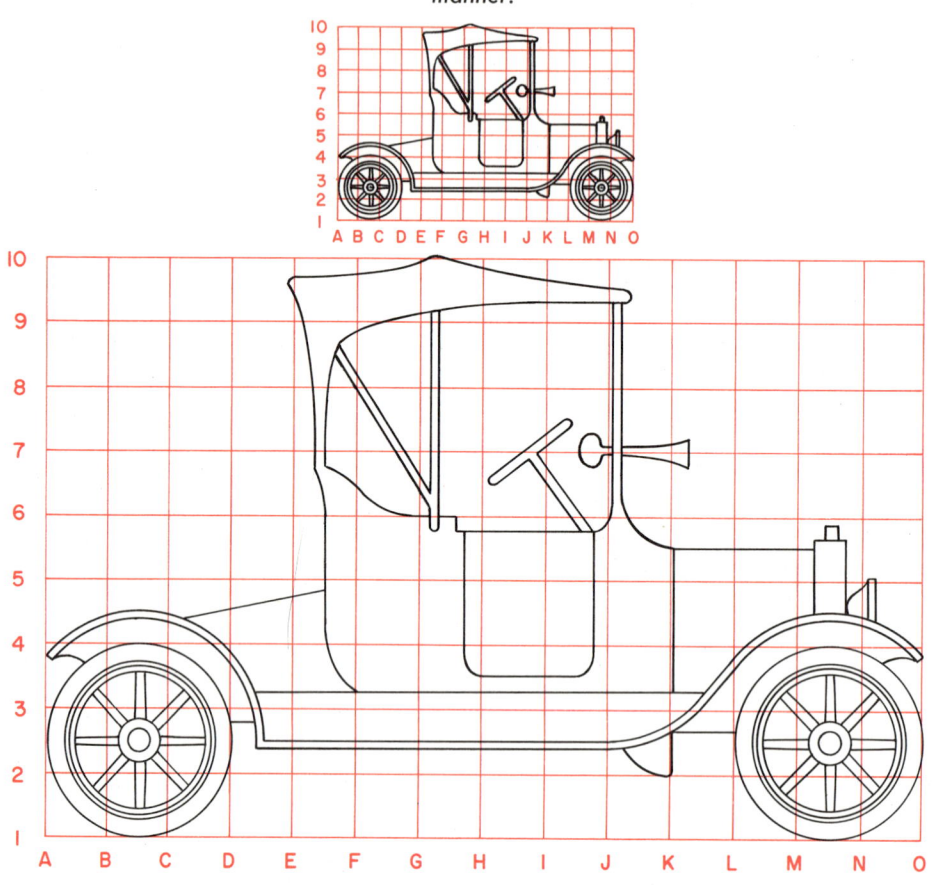

UNIT 32

Modern Metalworking

The needs of modern technology and the aerospace industry have made it necessary to invent new ways of working metals. The ordinary methods of cutting, forming, fastening, and finishing metals may not meet some modern requirements for accuracy and finish. A number of these developments are described and illustrated in this unit.

METAL CUTTING— ULTRASONIC MACHINING

Ultrasonic machining, Fig. 32-1, is a way of cutting hard materials quickly, economically, and accurately. The machine used consists of three major units: a frame with an adjustable table; a power and frequency generator; and a pump for circulating a liquid (called a *slurry*) which contains abrasive particles.

The pump circulates the slurry between the face of the tool and the workpiece.

The power unit causes the tool to move up and down about 20 000 times per second. Under these conditions the tool drives against the workpiece with great force. The impact of the abrasives on the workpiece does the actual cutting (cavitation) by chipping away small pieces of the material. Typical ultrasonic-machining operations include drilling, shaving, slicing, and cutting unusual punch and die shapes. Other materials besides metal can be machined ultrasonically. These include ceramics, glass, and plastics.

METAL CUTTING— ELECTRICAL DISCHARGE MACHINING

Electrical discharge machining (EDM) is the removal of metal by the energy of an electric spark that arcs between a tool and a workpiece. Fig. 32-2. The tool and the workpiece are immersed in a dielec-

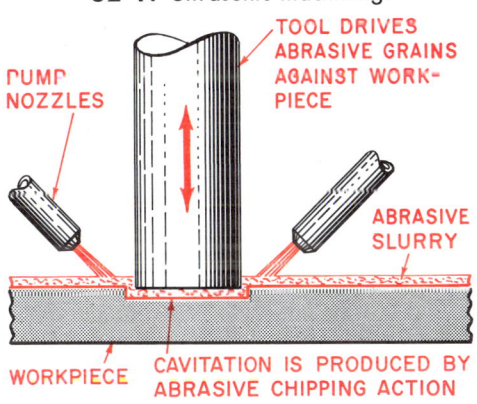

32-1. *Ultrasonic machining.*

32-2. *Electrical discharge machining.*

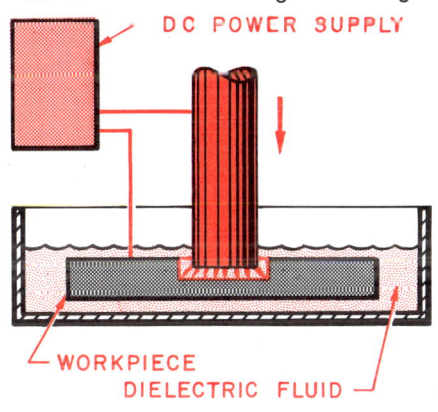

171

Part III: Manufacturing—Principles, Materials, and Processes

tric fluid such as oil. *Dielectric* means that the fluid will not conduct direct electric current. The tool is placed at a slight distance from the workpiece to be machined. Rapid pulses of electricity are delivered to the tool, causing sparks to jump from the tool to the workpiece. The heat from each spark melts away a small amount of metal. As the metal is removed, it is cooled and flushed away by the fluid being circulated through the spark gap. The spark also removes material from the tool, so the tool is slowly consumed as machining progresses. Because the tool is destroyed, complex shapes are not often produced by EDM. The greatest use of the process is to produce holes or cavities.

OTHER CUTTING DEVELOPMENTS

New materials and new requirements for accuracy in products for the space age have led to other ways of cutting metals. Some of these new methods are *chemical milling,* a kind of etching; *laser cutting,* a process that uses a concentrated light beam; and *ultra-high-speed machining,* or machining at speeds much faster than normal.

METAL FORMING— EXPLOSIVE FORMING

Explosive forming, Fig. 32-3, is much like exploding a firecracker under a tin can, causing the sides of the can to expand outward. Needed for explosive forming are a tank of water, a die, a blank of metal to be formed, and some explosives. The metal is clamped over the die cavity and the air is removed from the cavity through a vacuum tube. The metal and the die are lowered into the water. The charge of explosive sets off a powerful wave traveling from 250 to 500 feet per second with a force of five to six million pounds per square inch. This deforms the metal so fast it doesn't have a chance to break. Huge pieces of metal can be formed this way. Typical explosive-formed items are jet engine covers, railroad tank cars, and radar reflectors.

METAL FORMING— HYDROSPINNING

Hydrospinning is a forming process in which a workpiece is forced to take the shape of a hardened, rotating mandrel, or pattern. The workpiece turns with the mandrel and is shaped by one or two hardened, polished rollers which stretch

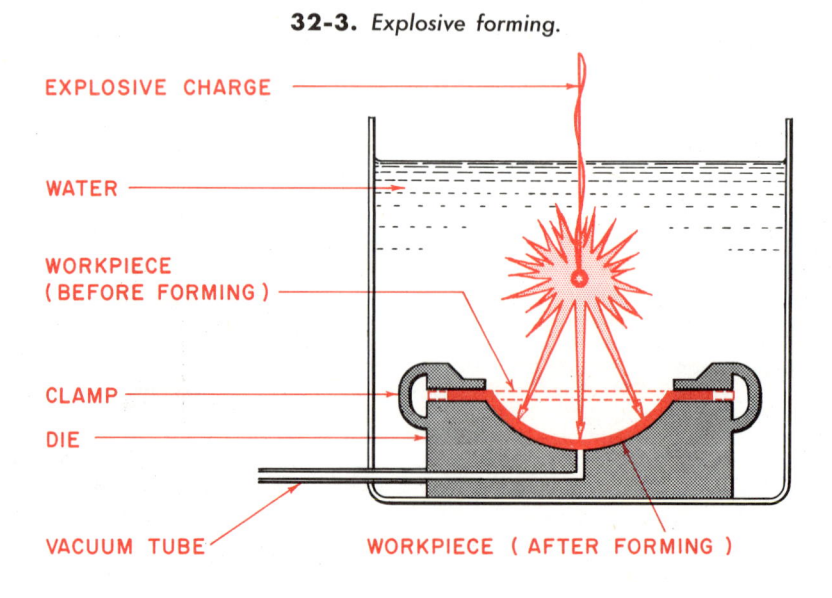

32-3. *Explosive forming.*

Unit 32: Modern Metalworking

and form the workpiece around the rotating mandrel as the rollers move along the mandrel's length. Fig. 32-4.

During hydrospinning, the metal being formed undergoes a deformation where the grain structure of the metal is stretched. This deformation is usually done cold and results in considerable work hardening. The work hardening is accompanied by an increase in tensile strength. A hydrospun part has high fatigue resistance—the surface of the part has no small ruptures or tears in it.

Hydrospun parts are stronger than forgings. During machining or forging, the grain structure of the part is changed very little. During hydrospinning, however, the grain structure is "stretched out" to follow the shape of the part, making the part even stronger. The hydrospun part will have a finish comparable to a good commercial grind finish. The part will be made from a much simpler workpiece using about $\frac{1}{4}$ as much material as for ordinary machining. And, the hydrospun part will be produced more quickly and at less cost.

OTHER FORMING DEVELOPMENTS

Newer methods of forming are being used more and more by industry. *Gas forming* uses gases under high pressure to force metal into a die. *Magnetic forming* uses a strong electric field to do the same thing. In *powder metallurgy,* metal powders are forced into a die and then sintered (or welded) together with heat.

METAL FASTENING— EXPLOSIVE BONDING

This metal fastening method uses explosive energy to join two or more pieces of metal together permanently, without using fluxes, rods, or heat. The technique was developed and patented by duPont; the trade name "Detaclad" is used for the products thus produced. The prime metal, or clad, is placed above the backer metal at a carefully controlled standoff distance, or spacing. Fig. 32-5. The explosive (fastened to the clad) is then fired, causing the clad and the backer to collide and form a metallic jet. This jet is trapped between the clad and backer and solidifies into a wavy bond joint. Some applications for this bonding method are clad plates for the fabrication of chemical pressure tanks, heat exchangers for nu-

32-4. *Hydrospinning.*

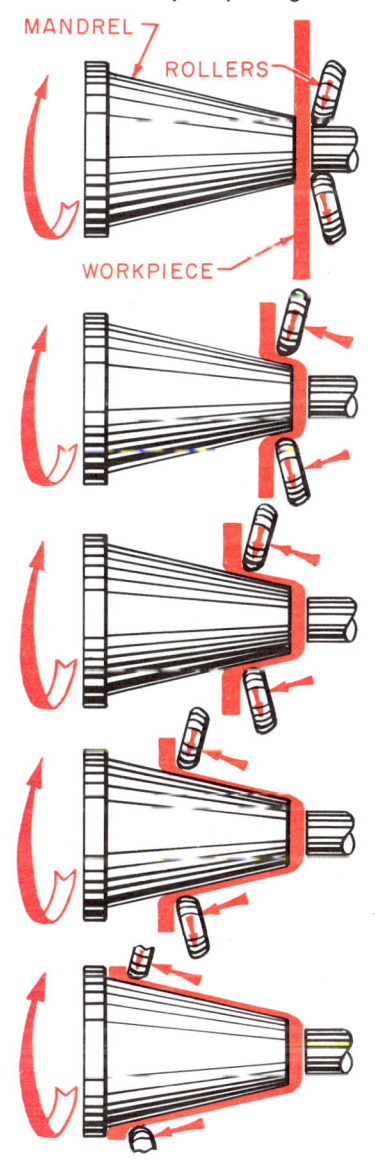

Part III: Manufacturing—Principles, Materials, and Processes

clear power plants, and heat-sealing jaws for plastic film packaging machines.

OTHER FASTENING DEVELOPMENTS

Research in metal fastening has changed some of the theories that were accepted for a long time. Explosive bonding has made it possible to weld dissimilar metals together. With *special adhesives,* metal can be "glued" to almost any surface. *Low-temperature* brazing and soldering fluxes and rods now provide a practical means for joining materials such as aluminum. *Ultrasonic* soldering and welding techniques are used to make strong, durable joints automatically. Continuing experimentation with joining methods will result in newer and better fastenings for metals.

METAL FINISHING— ELECTROSTATIC SPRAYING

This process is a special method of coating products with paint or other finishing solution by giving the finish an electrical charge. The product to be coated is grounded, so that the electrically charged solution particles are attracted to the product. When the particles strike the metal product, they lose their charge and stick to its surfaces. The spraying unit consists of a grounded conveyor, an atomizer gun, a paint pump, and an electrostatic voltage supply. Fig. 32-6. The development of this process has made it possible for industries to reduce the amount of paint used by 30 to 80 percent, and to produce finishes of higher quality.

OTHER FINISHING DEVELOPMENTS

Many new weather-resistant, durable paints and lacquers are available today. Plastic coatings such as vinyls are also used. With the *vinyl-dip* process, a tough, acid-resistant coating is deposited on metals. Another new method is *pressure-curtain* coating, in which an article passes through a flowing curtain of paint and gets a smooth, even finish.

32-5. *Explosive bonding.*

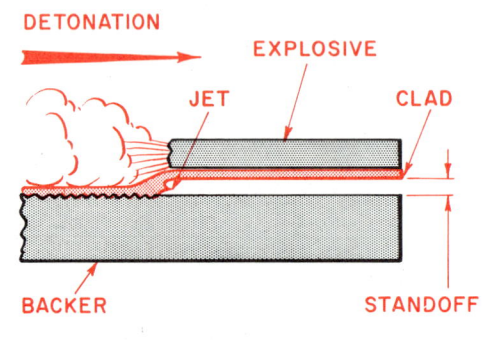

32-6. *Electrostatic spraying.*

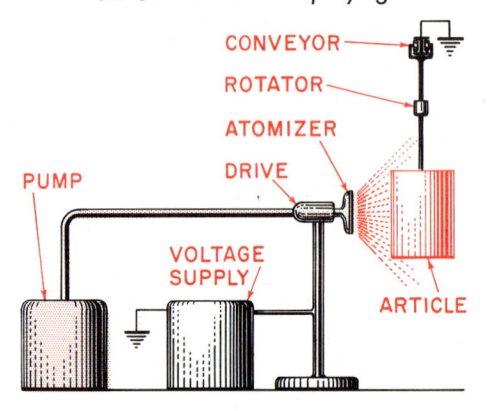

UNIT 33

Metal Cutting Principles

Cutting is very important in metalwork. Metal which is to be worked by the other three methods—forming, fastening, and finishing—must first be cut. For example, a tool box could not be formed until the sheet had been cut to size.

To many people the term "cutting" means work done with a knife or shears. However, the metalworker knows that cutting is done in a variety of ways, some of which do not make use of any tool with a blade or cutting edge.

Cutting is done for two main purposes: separating and removing. When a large piece of metal is cut into two or more smaller pieces, as with shears, this is *separating*. When small bits of metal are cut away, as with a file, this is *removing*.

Drilling, turning, milling, shaping, and grinding (abrading) are commonly called the basic metal machining processes, both for school and industrial purposes. Fig. 33-1. Sawing, shearing, and electro-chemical cutting are other important kinds of cutting. These eight methods are illustrated and described in the cutting chart, Fig. 33-2. Tools and machines listed are the ones you will probably see or use in school and industry.

Science and technology have developed many new ways of cutting metal such as by electric discharge machining, chemical milling, and numerical control. These newer cutting methods are, for the most part, merely refinements of the eight basic kinds listed in the chart. Chemical milling, for instance, is nothing more than a highly specialized process of etching.

As you read on in this section, you will find further descriptions and examples of each of the eight basic cutting methods. You will see some of the common tools used and learn how to use them, and will learn what these can do. It will be helpful for you to refer back to this cutting chart frequently. You can see then how these cutting systems differ, and also how much they are alike.

33-1. *Shaping is one of the five basic ways of machining metal. Here you see it being done on a piece of modern industrial equipment. This process is more fully described in Unit 37.*

175

Part III: Manufacturing—Principles, Materials, and Processes

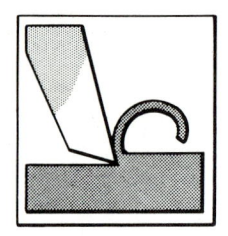

Cutting

Cutting is the process of removing or separating pieces of material from a base material.

KIND OF CUTTING	DEFINITION	EXAMPLES
Sawing	Cutting with a tool having pointed teeth equally spaced along the edge of a blade.	Cutting with a hacksaw, metal band saw, jeweler's saw.
Shearing	Cutting, usually between two cutting edges crossing one another, or by forcing a single cutting edge through a workpiece.	Cutting with tin snips, bench shears, squaring shears, hollow punch, solid punch, cold chisel.
Abrading	Cutting by wearing away material, usually by the action of mineral particles.	Grinding, polishing, buffing, and operations using a sharpening stone or abrasive papers.
Shaping	Cutting by moving a single-edge tool across a fixed workpiece in a straight-line cutting path.	Operations on the metal shaper.

Unit 33: Metal Cutting Principles

KIND OF CUTTING	DEFINITION	EXAMPLES
Drilling	Cutting with a cylindrical tool usually having two spiral cutting edges.	Operations using the hand drill, electric hand drill, drill press, twist drill.
Milling	Cutting with a tool having sharpened teeth equally spaced around a cylinder or along a flat surface.	Operations using the horizontal milling machine, vertical milling machine, hand file, needle file.
Turning	Cutting by revolving a workpiece against a fixed single-edge tool.	Operations on the metal lathe.
Cutting Electro-Chemical	Cutting with heat or acids.	Etching; oxyacetylene and carbon-arc cutting.

33-2. *The eight basic cutting methods. These will be discussed in the following units.*

UNIT 34

Sawing Metal

Sawing is a way of separating material (such as cutting a short piece of stock from a longer piece). Chips are produced in sawing, but not in shearing. Common metal sawing tools are the hacksaw, the metal-cutting band saw, and the jeweler's saw.

HACKSAWS

Hacksaws are used to cut metal sheets, rods, bars, and pipes. There are two parts to a hacksaw: the frame and the blade. Common hacksaws have either an adjustable or solid frame. Fig. 34-1. Adjustable frames can be made to hold blades from 8 to 16 inches long, while those with solid frames take only the length blade for which they are made.

Hacksaw blades are made of high-grade tool steel, hardened and tempered. These blades are about one-half inch wide, have from 14 to 32 teeth per inch,

34-1. *Parts of the hacksaw: (A) Frame (B) Blade.*

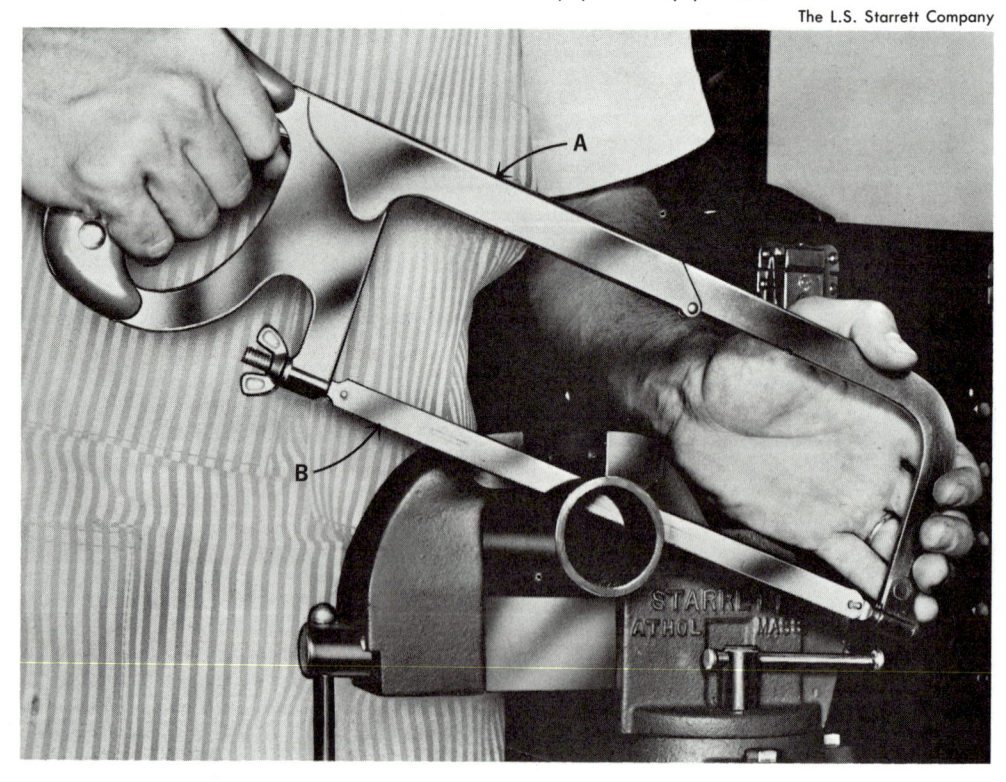

The L.S. Starrett Company

Unit 34: Sawing Metal

and are from 8 to 16 inches long. The blades have a hole at each end, which hooks to a pin in the frame.

The *set* in a saw refers to how much the teeth are pushed out in opposite directions from the sides of the blade. Three kinds of sets are "alternate set," "raker set," and "wave set." Fig. 34-2.

The set in a blade helps to prevent the blade from binding or jamming as it cuts through metal. A few drops of machine oil on the blade will also make the cutting easier.

Using the Hacksaw

Good work with a hacksaw depends not only upon the proper use of the saw, but also upon the proper selection of the blades for the work to be done. Fig. 34-3 shows which blade to use. Coarse blades with fewer teeth per inch cut faster and do not clog up with chips. However, the finer blades with more teeth per inch are necessary when thin sections are being cut.

To use the saw, first install the blade in the hacksaw frame so that the teeth point away from the handle of the hacksaw. Fig. 34-4, top. Hand hacksaws cut on the forward stroke. Turn the wing nut so that the blade is tight. Fig. 34-4, bottom. This helps make straight cuts.

Place the material to be cut in a vise or hold it with clamps. Protect the workpiece by covering the vise jaws with pieces of copper sheet. The proper method of holding the hacksaw is shown in Fig. 34-5. Grasp the saw firmly with both hands as shown. When cutting, let your body sway ahead and back with each stroke. Apply pressure on the forward stroke, which is the cutting stroke. From 40 to 50 strokes per minute is the usual speed. Long, slow, steady strokes are preferred.

ALTERNATE SET

RAKER SET

WAVE SET

34-2. *Three types of "set" for hacksaw blades. The blade set helps to prevent binding while cutting.*

34-3. *Blade section chart shows the blades recommended for use on different metals and metal shapes.*

14 Tooth - Soft materials, larger cross sections

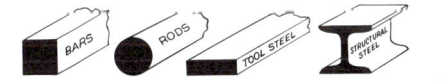

MILD STEEL, COPPER, LEAD, ALUMINUM

18 Tooth - General use, same blade on several jobs

BARS, RODS, TOOL STEEL, STRUCTURAL STEEL

24 Tooth - Cross sections 1/16" to 1/4"

DRILL ROD, PIPE, ANGLE IRON, STEEL PLATE

32 Tooth - Cross sections 1/16" or less

TUBING, BX CABLE, CONDUIT, SHEET STOCK

34-4. *Installing a hacksaw blade. The blade teeth should point away from the handle.*

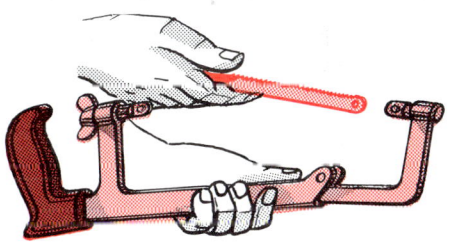

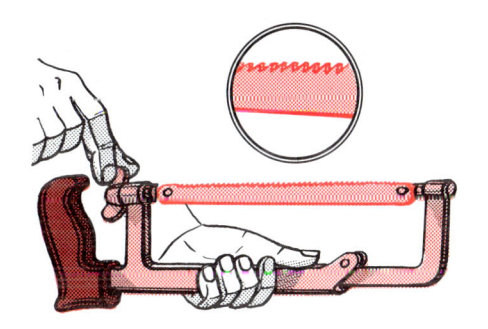

179

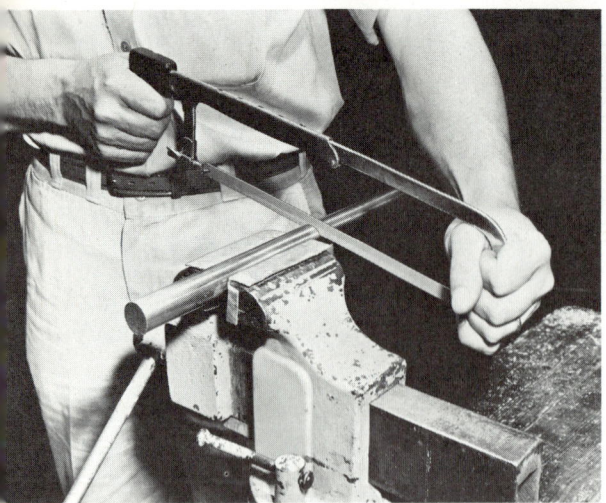

Part III: Manufacturing—Principles, Materials, and Processes

The L.S. Starrett Company

34-5. *Cutting with the hacksaw. Apply pressure on the forward stroke. Note that the vise jaws are covered with copper sheet metal to protect the work.*

For deep cuts rotate the blade in the frame so that the length of the cut is not limited by the depth of the frame. Fig. 34-6. Hold the work with the layout line close to the vise jaws, raising the work in the vise as the sawing proceeds.

Metal which is too thin to be held without bending can be placed between blocks of wood and tightened in the vise.

Hacksaw Safety

The main danger in using hacksaws is injury to your hand if the blade breaks.

34-6. *Making a deep cut by turning the blade position in the frame.*

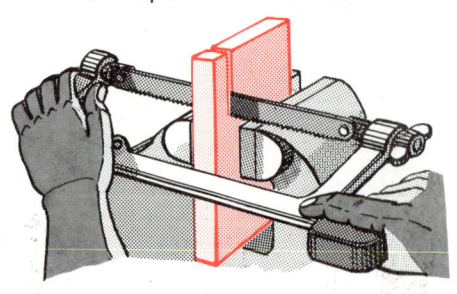

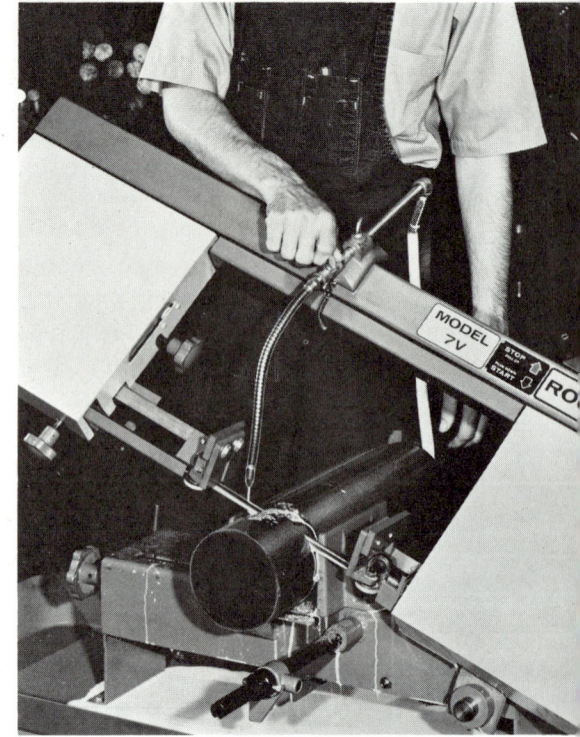

Rockwell-Delta Company

34-7. *Cutting a piece of pipe on a metal-cutting band saw.*

The blade will break if too much pressure is applied when the saw is twisted, when cutting too fast, or when the blade becomes loose in the frame. If the work is not tight in the vise, it will sometimes slip, twisting the blade enough to break it. Be careful when using the hacksaw.

METAL-CUTTING BAND SAW

The metal-cutting band saw cuts as a hacksaw when in the down position. Fig. 34-7. It can also be used in an upright position as a conventional band saw for cutting arcs and circles. Make sure that the workpiece is securely fastened in the vise. Use cutting oil to lubricate and cool the blade.

The hole saw, Fig. 34-8, can be mounted in a drill press and used to cut holes in metal. The sizes range from $3/4''$

180

Unit 34: Sawing Metal

34-8. The hole saw (inset) and the saw in use cutting holes in 1/4" metal.
The L.S. Starrett Company

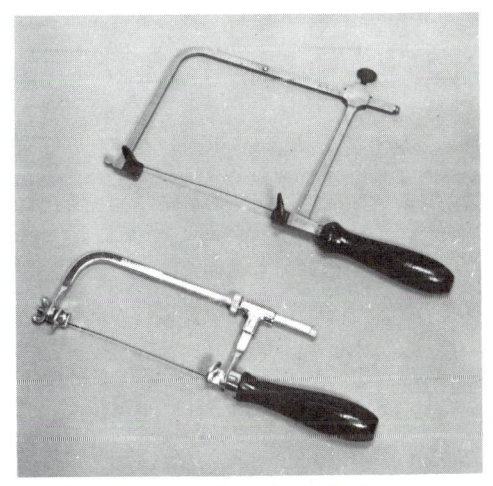

34-9. Two styles of jeweler's saws.

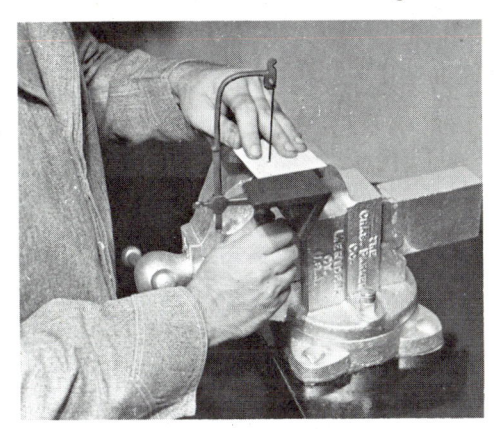

34-10. Using the jeweler's saw.

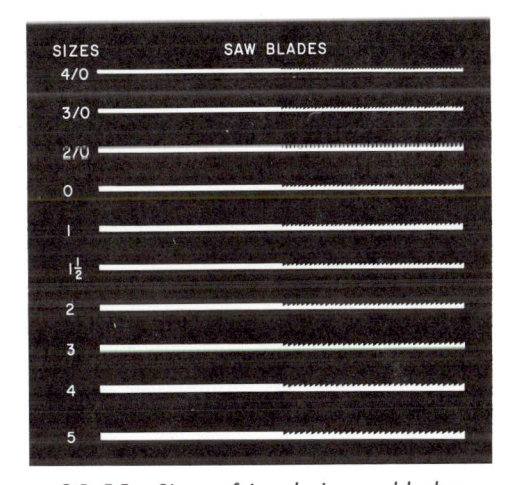

34-11. Sizes of jeweler's saw blades.

to 2" or 3". Be sure your instructor has demonstrated this tool before you use it.

JEWELER'S SAW

The jeweler's saw makes internal cuts by a method called *piercing*. Fig. 34-9. Workpieces to be pierced are held over a V-block fastened in a vise. Fig. 34-10. A hole must first be drilled in the metal workpiece, and the blade fed through the hole. The teeth should face toward the handle. Cut carefully on the down stroke so as not to break the fragile blades. These come in sizes ranging from No. 610 (thinner than a thread) to No. 14 (about 1/8" wide). Common sizes for jeweler's saw blades are shown in Fig. 34-11.

Sawing is a quick way to cut metal. Be careful to file off all the sharp burrs which remain on the cut pieces.

181

UNIT 35

Shearing Metal

Almost all cutting can be viewed as shearing. Even tearing a piece of paper in your hands is a kind of shearing. However, when people in industry speak of shearing, they usually have a certain kind of cutting in mind. Do you remember how the chart in Unit 33 defined the term? It said that shearing is cutting between two edges that cross one another or cutting by forcing a single cutting edge through a workpiece.

Shearing is done chiefly for separating. It produces no chips; so it is different from sawing. Shearing is a fast, clean, accurate way to cut light and heavy metals. It is widely done in industry. Industrial shears are generally power driven and can cut metals up to $\frac{1}{2}''$ thick. Following are descriptions of shearing tools commonly found in the shop.

TIN SNIPS

Sheet metals of gauge 20 or lighter are easily sheared with tin snips. These tools are also called hand snips or hand shears, and come in three common styles. Fig. 35-1.

The *straight snips* are for making straight cuts and range in size from 6'' to 14''. Fig. 35-2. To make straight cuts on larger pieces, place the sheet metal on a bench with the scribed guideline over the edge of the bench. Hold the sheet down with one hand. Be careful of sharp edges. With the other hand hold the snips so that the flat sides of the blades are at right angles to the surface of the work. If the blades are not at right angles to the surface of the work, the edges of the cut will

35-1. *Tin snips are used for light shearing: (A) Aviation snips (B) Straight snips (C) Trojan snips.*

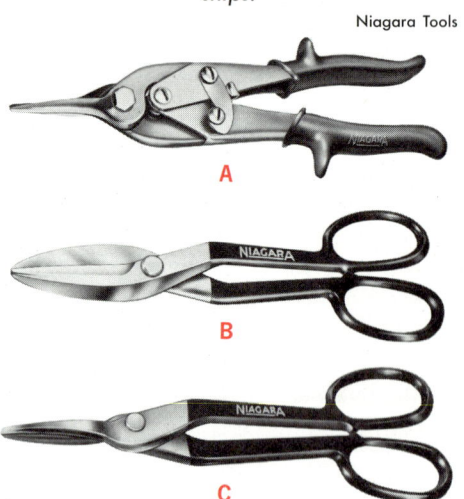

Niagara Tools

35-2. *Using the straight snips.*

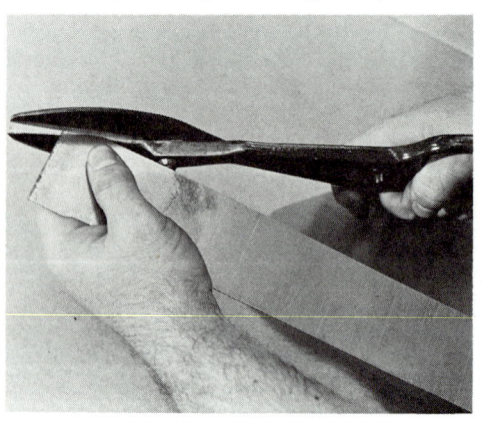

Unit 35: Shearing Metal

be slightly bent and burred. Any of the hand snips may be used for straight cuts. When notches are too narrow to be cut out with a pair of snips, make the side cuts with the snips and cut the base of the notch with a cold chisel.

Aviation snips are double hinged for easier cutting. They are designed for right-hand or left-hand irregular cuts or for straight cutting. Fig. 35-3. *Trojan shears* are for curved cuts.

To cut large holes in sheet metal, start the cut by punching a hole in the center of the area to be cut out. With aviation snips or some other narrow-bladed snips, make a spiral cut from the starting hole out toward the scribed circle and continue cutting until the scrap falls away.

SQUARING SHEARS

The squaring shears, Fig. 35-4, are for straight shearing of large pieces of metal up to 18 gauge. (The gauge capacity is stamped on the machine. Do not exceed this.) The shears come in bench and floor models and in several sizes to take various widths of metal. Do not use this machine to cut rods or bars as these will damage the blade. Never permit anyone to stand near the squaring shears while you are using them. Be sure to keep your hands and feet away from the treadle and blade when shearing. Fig. 35-5.

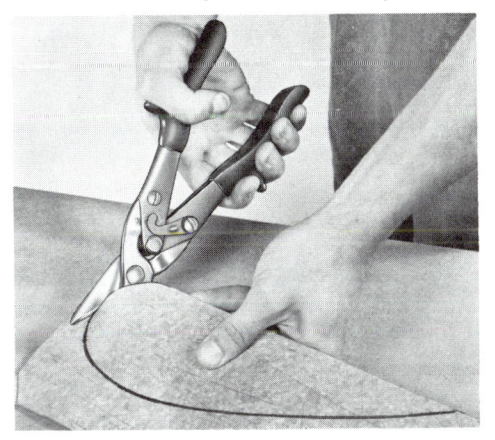

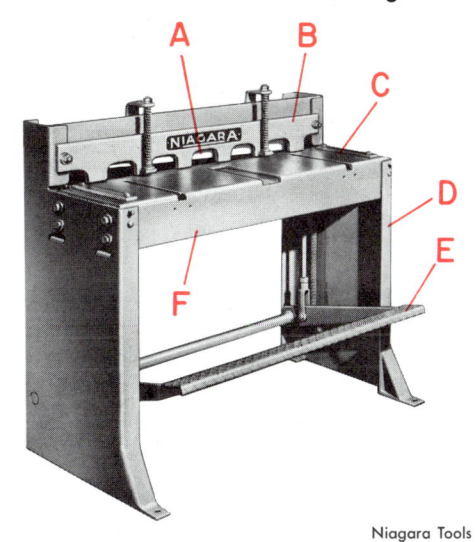

Niagara Tools

35-4. The foot-operated squaring shears: (A) Blade (B) Safety guard (C) Slide gauge (D) Housing (E) Foot treadle (F) Bed. Remember to keep your feet out from under the treadle and fingers away from the safety guard. Rods and wire should not be cut on this machine.

35-5. Using the squaring shears. This is a hand-operated bench model.

35-3. *Using the aviation snips.*

183

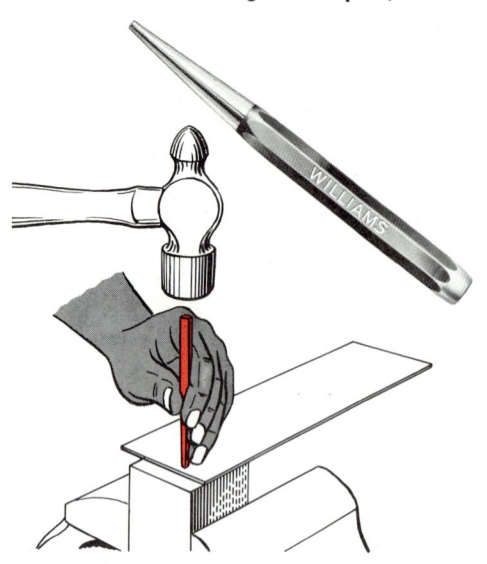

Part III: Manufacturing—Principles, Materials, and Processes

PUNCHES

Holes are punched in light metals with the solid (hand) and hollow punches. Fig. 35-6. To use them, place the metal over a block of wood and strike the punch sharply with a ball-peen hammer. Fig. 35-7.

CHISELS

Chisels are tools that can be used for chipping or cutting metal that is softer than the materials of which they are made. Cold chisels (chisels made for chipping or cutting cold metal are classified according to the shape of their points, and the width of the cutting edge denotes their size. The most common shapes of chisels are flat, cape, round nose, and diamond point. Fig. 35-8.

35-6. *The solid punch comes in several sizes for punching holes up to $7/16''$ in diameter.*

35-7. *The punch is especially useful for making rivet holes. The hollow punch is used for larger holes, from $1/4''$ to $2''$ in diameter.*

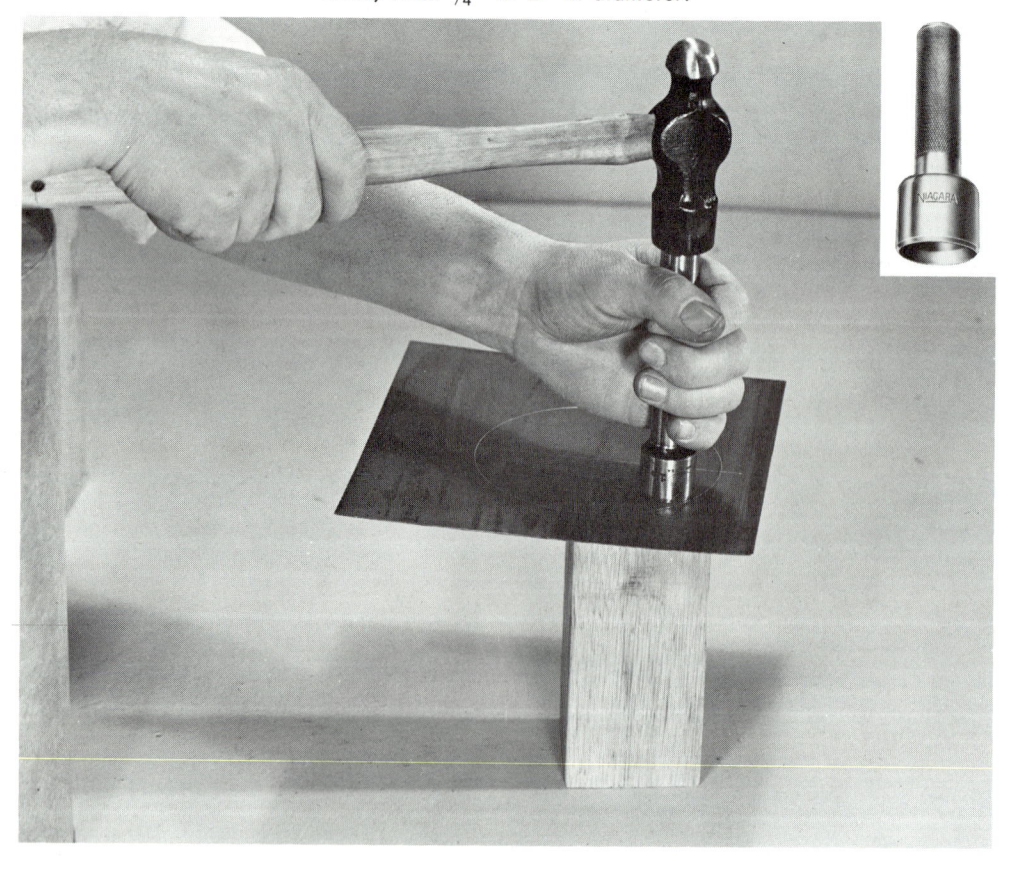

184

Unit 35: Shearing Metal

The type of chisel most commonly used is the flat cold chisel, which serves to cut rivets and thin metal sheets, split nuts, and chip castings. Fig. 35-9. The cape chisel is used for special jobs like cutting keyways, narrow grooves, and square corners. Round-nose chisels make circular grooves and chip inside corners with a fillet. Finally, the diamond-point is used for cutting V-grooves and sharp corners.

Using a Chisel

As with other tools, there is a correct technique for using a chisel. Select a chisel that is large enough for the job. Be sure to use a hammer that matches the chisel; that is, the larger the chisel, the heavier the hammer.

As a general rule, hold the chisel in the left hand with the thumb and first finger about 1 inch from the top. It should be held steadily but not tightly. The finger muscles should be relaxed, so if the hammer strikes the hand it will permit the hand to slide down the tool and lessen the effect of the blow. Keep the eyes on the cutting edge of the chisel, not on the hand, and swing the hammer in the same plane as the body of the chisel. When using a chisel, always wear goggles to protect your eyes.

BENCH SHEARS

Another method of cutting heavy metal is to use the slitting shears, also called

35-8. Types of cold chisels.

COLD CHISEL

CAPE CHISEL

HALF ROUND CHISEL

DIAMOND POINT CHISEL

ROUND NOSE CHISEL

35-9. *Using the cold chisel. Hold the chisel firmly in the fist and strike its head squarely with a hammer. When the chisel head "mushrooms" over enough to be dangerous, dress it on the grinder. The chisel's cutting edge should be ground to an angle of 60 degrees.*

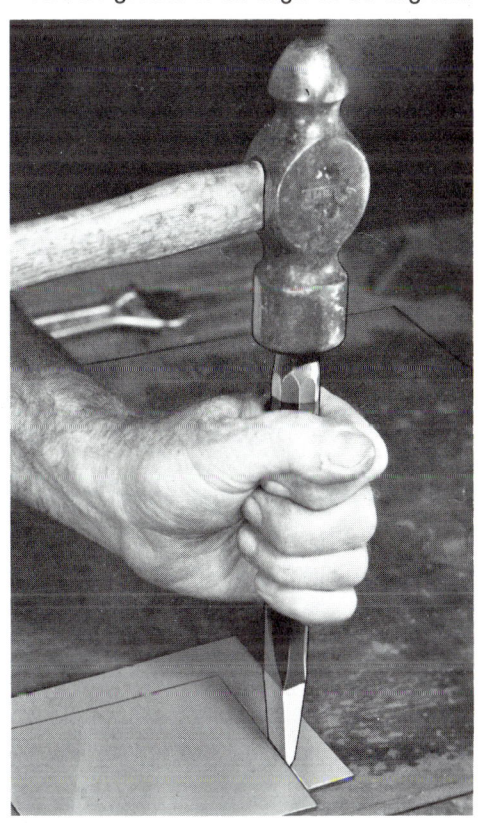

185

Part III: Manufacturing—Principles, Materials, and Processes

bench shears. Fig. 35-10. This tool comes in many sizes and capacities. The capacity is stamped on the machine. A common shear can cut $\frac{1}{4}''$ x 2'' bar stock and $\frac{5}{8}''$ rod. Hold the workpiece firmly and keep your fingers away from the blade. For large pieces, have a friend help you hold the workpiece.

A similar machine is the throatless shears. Fig. 35-11. It is used for making irregular cuts on wider pieces of stock. Never cut rod or wire on this machine, for they can nick the blade.

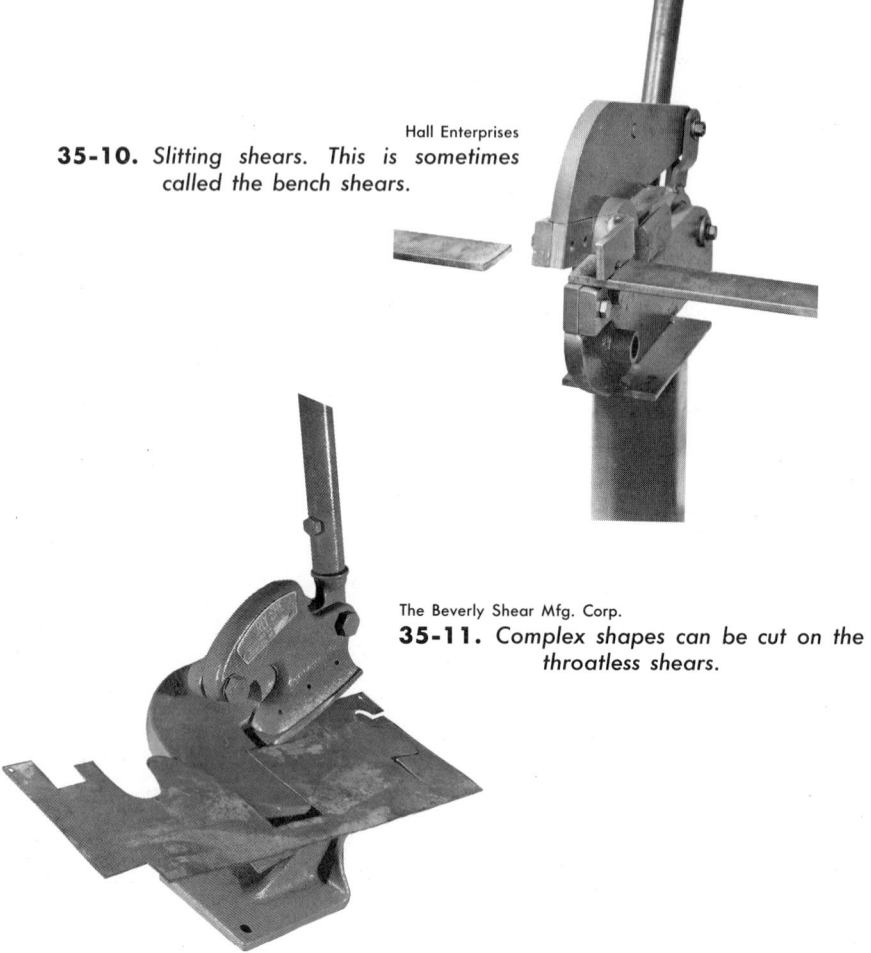

Hall Enterprises
35-10. Slitting shears. This is sometimes called the bench shears.

The Beverly Shear Mfg. Corp.
35-11. Complex shapes can be cut on the throatless shears.

UNIT 36

Abrading Metal

Abrading is a form of removal cutting; small mineral grains wear away the surface of the metal until the desired size or effect is achieved. Grinding, polishing, and buffing metal are types of abrading. *Grinding* is the process of removing large amounts of material or fine finishing a metal surface by precision methods. *Polishing* is the process of removing burrs, deep scratches, and nicks from metal. Coated abrasives are used for this. *Buffing* is the process of final finishing a metal piece to improve its appearance. Buffing wheels and stick abrasives are used. In this unit you will learn about metal grinding and heavy polishing and the kinds of abrasives used on all materials. Light polishing and buffing are a part of metal finishing and will be covered in Unit 56.

KINDS OF ABRASIVES

Abrasives are hard substances used to wear away softer materials. Whether you are grinding metal or sanding wood or plastic, you are abrading, and the cutting action is the same. The tiny particles of abrasive act as chisels to cut material. The kinds of abrasives are many. Here are some important ones.

Emery

Although many people call all abrasive papers emery papers, actually very little emery is used today except for polishing. Emery is a natural abrasive; it is used as it is mined from the earth. It is dull black and rocklike.

Flint

Flint is another natural abrasive. It is whitish and is not as good as garnet or emery. It is used primarily in woodworking.

Garnet

This is a red, very sharp and hard natural abrasive used in woodworking. It is more durable than flint. All the natural abrasives are used mainly for abrasive papers.

Aluminum Oxide

This gray-brown abrasive is artificial. It is made from bauxite, a mineral from which aluminum is also made. A very tough, durable abrasive, it is made into grinding wheels and coated abrasives for working steel and other hard materials.

Silicon Carbide

Another artificial abrasive, this shiny black material is used on aluminum, copper, and other soft materials, including wood. It is made from coke, sand, and salt.

GRADING ABRASIVES

To grade abrasives means to separate them according to size. This size is called the "grit number" and is determined by the number of holes in a sifting screen.

Part III: Manufacturing—Principles, Materials, and Processes

For example, abrasive grains that will sift through a screen having 60 openings per square inch are said to have a grit size of 60. These grit numbers range from very fine (No. 600) to very coarse (No. 12). Fig. 36-1.

USING ABRASIVES

Abrasives are made into grinding wheels, coated papers of many shapes, sharpening stones, and polishing grains. The uses of these abrasives in metalworking are described here.

Polishing

To remove scratches, nicks, and burrs from metal, coated abrasives are used. These are made by coating sheet materials with abrasive grains. Fig. 36-2. Some are waterproof. To use them in hand methods, wrap a small piece around a block or a file, add a few drops of light machine oil, and rub back and forth gently.

Machine polishing is done on machines such as those shown in Figs. 36-3 and 36-4. Aluminum oxide belts, discs, and drums are used. Do not use machines reserved for sanding wood or plastic. The metal workpiece will ruin the belts or discs. Be careful that the machine does not tear the workpiece from your hands. Hold it securely. The workpiece should be held near the bottom of the moving belt. Fig. 36-4. Use gloves if necessary, and be sure to wear safety glasses.

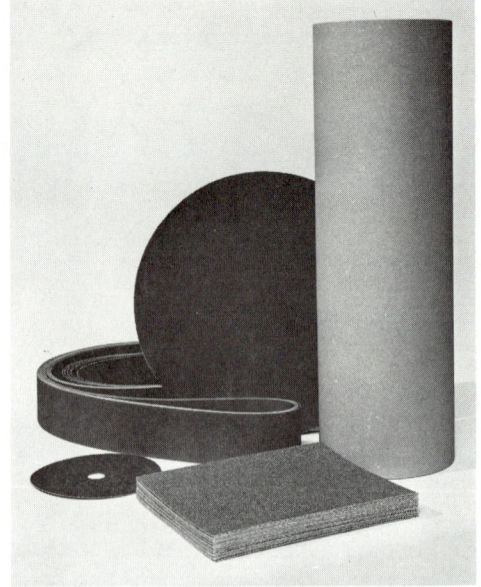

Norton Company

36-2. *Coated abrasives are made by glueing abrasive grains to backing materials such as paper, cloth, or fiber. They come in many forms such as discs, belts, sleeves, and sheets.*

Grinding

Hand grinding is a quick way to rough-shape metal and to sharpen tools. The floor grinder, Fig. 36-5, is used in the shop. Grinding wheels are made of abrasive grains bonded (stuck) together with resin, rubber, shellac, or ceramics. Make sure the wheels are free of cracks or nicks before using. These wheels are available in many shapes and sizes. For hard and brittle metals, use grit numbers

36-1. *Comparative abrasive grit numbers. Emery and flint papers are not generally sold according to grit size. Instead, use the terms very coarse, coarse, etc.*

Abrasive Grit Numbers

	Very Coarse	Coarse	Medium	Fine	Very Fine
ALUMINUM OXIDE & SILICON CARBIDE	12 16 20 24 30	36 40	50 60 80 100	120 150 180	220 240 280 320 360 400 500 600
GARNET	3 2½	2 1½	1 ½ 0 2/0	3/0 4/0 5/0	6/0 7/0 8/0

Unit 36: Abrading Metal

36-3. Belt and disc sanders, with aluminum oxide abrasives, are used for metal polishing.
Rockwell-Delta Company

36-4. Hold the workpiece securely when machine polishing. Wear safety glasses.
Baldor Electric

60 or 80. For softer metals, use numbers 36 or 46.

"Off-hand" grinding is so called because the workpiece is held by hand. Fig. 36-6. To do off-hand grinding, the tool rest should be locked tightly in position 1/16″ or 1/8″ away from the wheel. Hold the work tightly, wear safety glasses, and be certain to tuck in loose clothing. The water pot is used to cool the metal while grinding. If the wheel becomes loaded or clogged with metal, clean it with the wheel dresser. A clean wheel cuts faster.

Wheel dressers are used to free wheels which have become loaded with metal chips. Dressing also removes gouges from the wheel surface. Mechanical disc

36-5. Parts of the floor grinder. Bench models of this machine are also available.
Baldor Electric

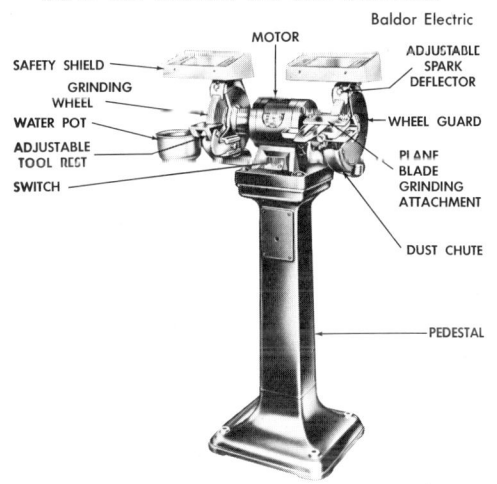

Labels: SAFETY SHIELD, MOTOR, ADJUSTABLE SPARK DEFLECTOR, GRINDING WHEEL, WATER POT, ADJUSTABLE TOOL REST, SWITCH, WHEEL GUARD, PLANE BLADE GRINDING ATTACHMENT, DUST CHUTE, PEDESTAL

189

Part III: Manufacturing—Principles, Materials, and Processes

Rockwell-Delta Company

36-6. Hold the workpiece firmly when grinding. Press gently against the face of the wheel. Pressing against the sides of the wheel may damage it.

Rockwell-Delta Company

36-8. Sharpening a cold chisel on a grinder. This special clamping device produces a type ground at the correct angle.

36-7. A diamond tip wheel dresser. This one is locked in a special clamp. Move the clamp back and forth slowly with the machine running. Move the dresser forward into the wheel as needed. Wear safety glasses.

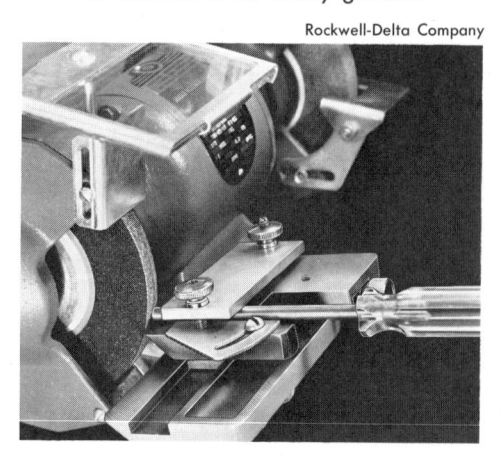

Rockwell-Delta Company

36-9. Sharpening a lathe tool. Be careful not to overheat the tool.

190

36-10. Surface grinding diagram.

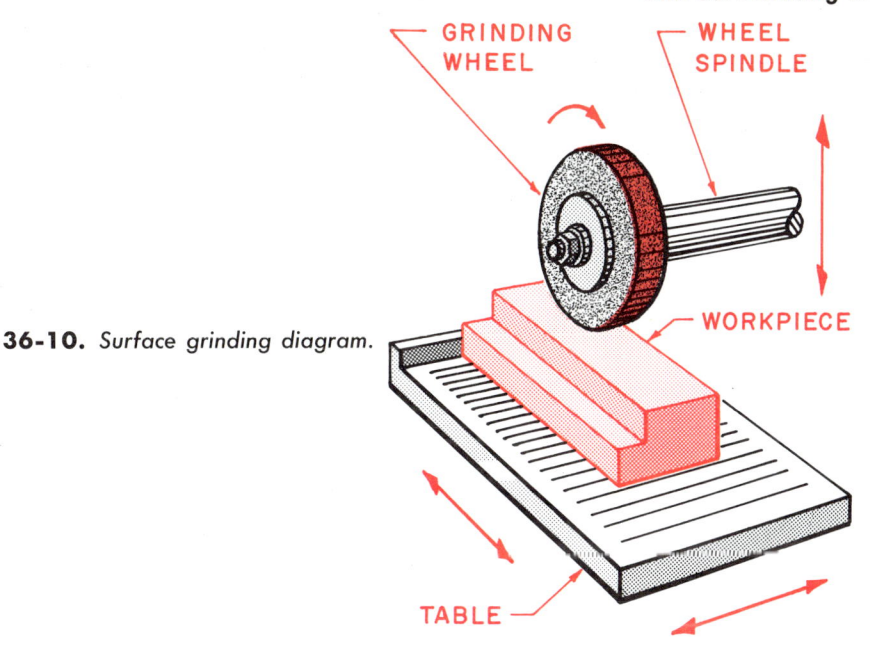

dressers are used, as are diamond tip dressers. Fig. 36-7.

Sharpening Tools

Edge-cutting tools such as cold chisels, punches, drills, tool bits, and scribers should be regularly sharpened on a grinder. Use a fine wheel and be certain that you do not overheat the tools as this will soften them. Use the water pot frequently for cooling. There are special clamps available for sharpening chisels and drills. Fig. 36-8. These hold the tools at the proper angle for grinding. If such a clamp is not available, hold the tools carefully at the proper angle and press lightly against the wheel. Lathe tool bits are also sharpened on grinders. This process is shown in Fig. 36-9.

Precision Grinding

This is an industrial finishing method. It produces a workpiece finished to a tolerance as close as 0.0002 inch. Some of the types of industrial precision grinding are cylindrical, internal, centerless, and surface. Surface grinding is the type generally used in schools.

Surface grinding produces a flat, accurate surface on a metal workpiece. The most common type has a horizontal spindle and wheel and a reciprocating table. (That is, the table moves back and forth.) Fig. 36-10. The wheel can be raised or lowered to grind various sizes of workpieces.

The table (and the workpiece) move back and forth under the wheel. In school shopwork, some hand-feed tables are used. However, in industrial production, the table feeds are automatic. The workpiece can be fastened to the table with clamps. Most steel workpieces are held in place on magnetic tables called chucks. The parts of a surface grinder are shown in Fig. 36-11. Be sure to tuck in loose clothing and wear safety glasses when using this machine.

191

Part III: Manufacturing—Principles, Materials, and Processes

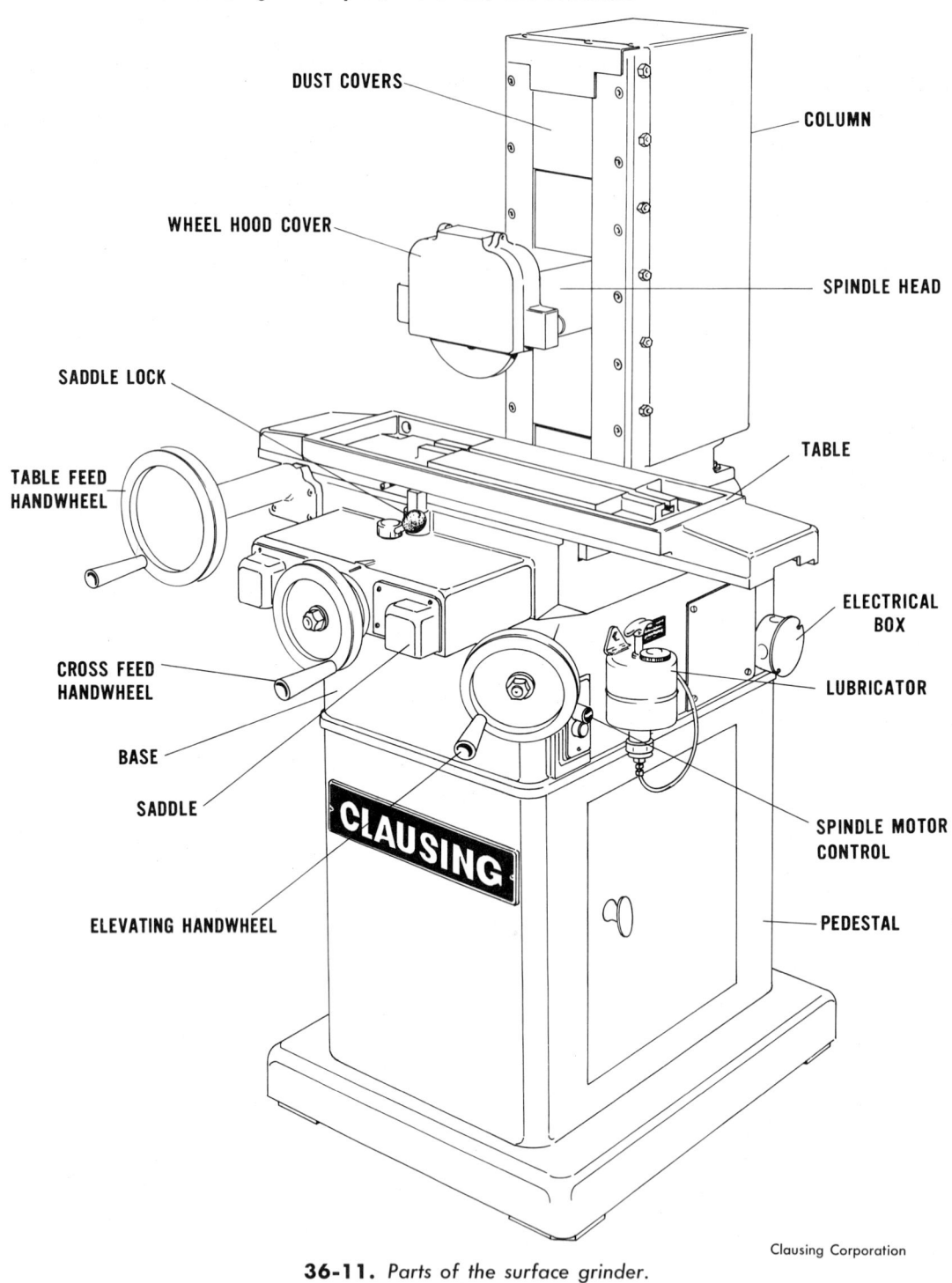

36-11. Parts of the surface grinder.

UNIT 37

Shaping Metal

Shaping is a removal cutting process used to smooth rough surfaces and to cut grooves in metal. For example, some rough foundry castings are smoothed by shaping. The metal shaper, Fig. 37-1, has a tool which moves back and forth through a stationary workpiece.

Metal planing is similar to shaping, except that in planing the workpiece moves through a stationary tool.

Shaping and planing are important ways of producing smooth and accurate surfaces on metal parts in the school shop. Industry now does most shaping operations on a milling machine.

37-1. *The metal shaper. With this metal removing machine, the tool (a) moves through the workpiece (b).*

UNIT 38

Drilling Metal

Drilling is the cutting of round holes in material. It is an important first step in preparing pieces to be bolted or riveted together, in tapping (threading holes), and reaming (making holes smooth and accurate). Industry uses many kinds of hand and automatic drilling machinery. Fig. 38-1.

DRILLING TOOLS

The common drilling tools which are found in the shop are shown in Fig. 38-2. *Hand drills,* both manual and electric models, will generally take straight shank twist drills up to $\frac{1}{4}''$ in diameter. Larger models of hand drills are available for heavier work.

38-1. *Industry uses many types of automatic drilling machines.*

Rockwell-Delta Company

194

Unit 38: Drilling Metal

Twist drills are generally made of high-speed steel. (That is the meaning of the marking HSS or HS found on many of these drills.) The drill size is also marked on the shank of the drill. The sizes are shown as whole numbers, letters, or fractions. Sizes shown by whole numbers range from the largest, No. 1, to the smallest, No. 80. In lettered drills, Z is the largest, A the smallest. Fractional drills are most commonly used; they range from 1/64" upwards by 64ths.

It is necessary to understand all three size systems because the drill you need may be available in only one of them. For example, if you need a drill with 0.368" diameter, you will not find it in the fractional system, which skips from 23/64" (0.359) to 3/8" (0.375). However, letter size "U" is exactly 0.368" in diameter. A drill chart, including metric sizes, is found in the Appendix. Attention to such tiny differences in size is important, especially in tapping and reaming.

Drill gauges are used to check the sizes of number, letter, and fractional twist drills. Use the *center punch* to mark holes to be drilled. Fig. 38-3.

A *countersink* is used to enlarge one end of a drilled hole to a cone shape, to accommodate a flathead rivet or machine screw.

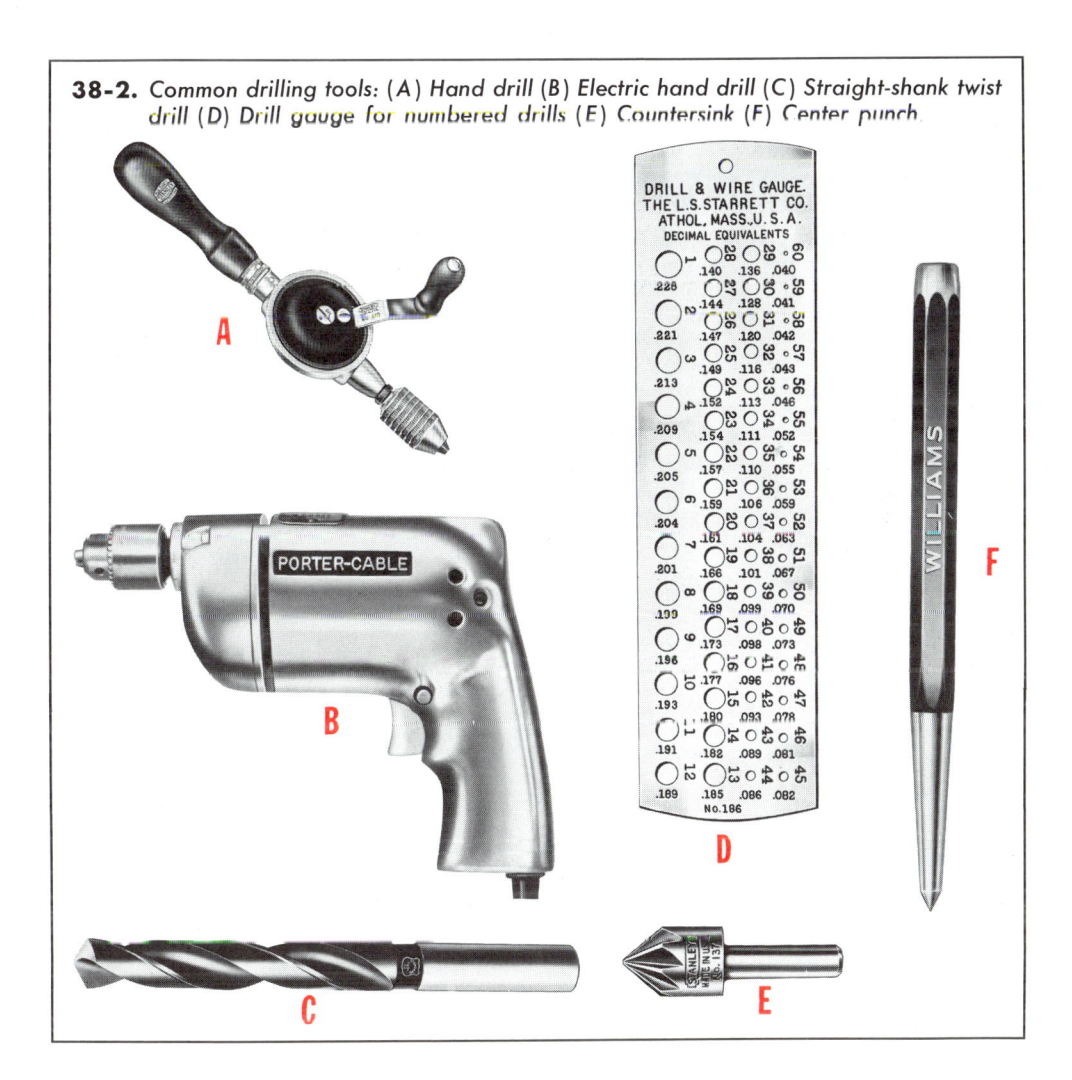

38-2. Common drilling tools: (A) Hand drill (B) Electric hand drill (C) Straight-shank twist drill (D) Drill gauge for numbered drills (E) Countersink (F) Center punch.

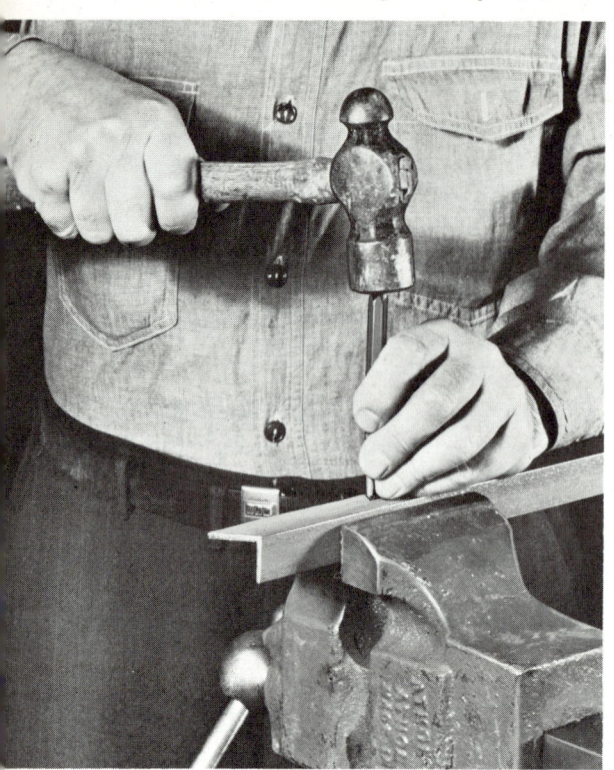

Part III: Manufacturing—Principles, Materials, and Processes

38-3. *Mark the hole to be drilled with a center punch and ball peen hammer.*

DRILLING HOLES

Both the hand drill and the electric hand drill should be operated carefully to reduce drill breakage. Hold the tools firmly and straight. Remember to locate holes with the center punch.

38-4. *Using the hand drill.*

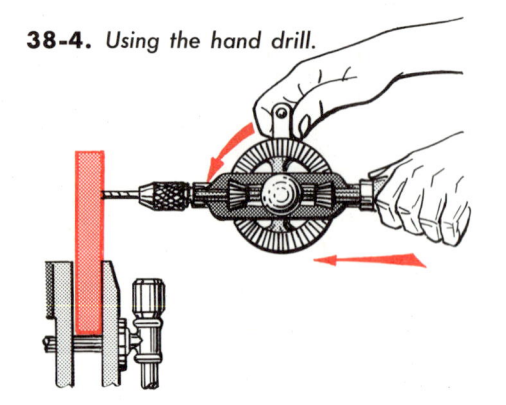

To use the hand drill, fasten the workpiece firmly in the vise. Hold the tool straight and place the drill point in the center punch hole. Turn the handle slowly, being careful not to force the drill. A drop or two of cutting oil will making drilling easier. Fig. 38-4.

The drill press is used for heavy drilling. Fig. 38-5. To operate the drill press, fasten the twist drill in the chuck and make sure it runs true. Fig. 38-6. Wear safety glasses. Tuck in loose clothing. Hold the workpiece securely in a drill press vise or with pliers or fasten it to the table with a clamp. Fig. 38-7. The drilling speed varies with the diameter of the twist drill and the kind of material to be drilled. For example, a $\frac{1}{4}''$ hole in aluminum or brass shuld be drilled at about 4500 RPM (revolutions per minute); in mild steel, 1500 RPM. For a $\frac{1}{2}''$ hole in aluminum, operate at 2200 RPM; in mild steel, 700 RPM. In other words, use fast speeds for small diameter drills and soft materials and slow speeds for large drills and hard materials.

With the power on, apply enough pressure to produce chips. A cutting oil will improve the cutting action of the drill. Fig. 38-8.

SHARPENING DRILLS

A dull, worn, or bent drill is dangerous to use. Inspect it before using. If the drill needs sharpening, dress it carefully with a grinder. Be careful not to overheat the drill. Use the waterpot often. Check the drill with a gauge frequently to be sure it is being ground at the proper angle. Fig. 38-9.

REAMING

Reamers are used to enlarge holes and make them true. A drilled hole is usually slightly oversize, which is all right for rivets and bolts. When greater accuracy is required, the hole is first drilled undersize and reamed to the proper size. Reaming is done with a reamer held in a tap wrench. Fig. 38-10.

Unit 38: Drilling Metal

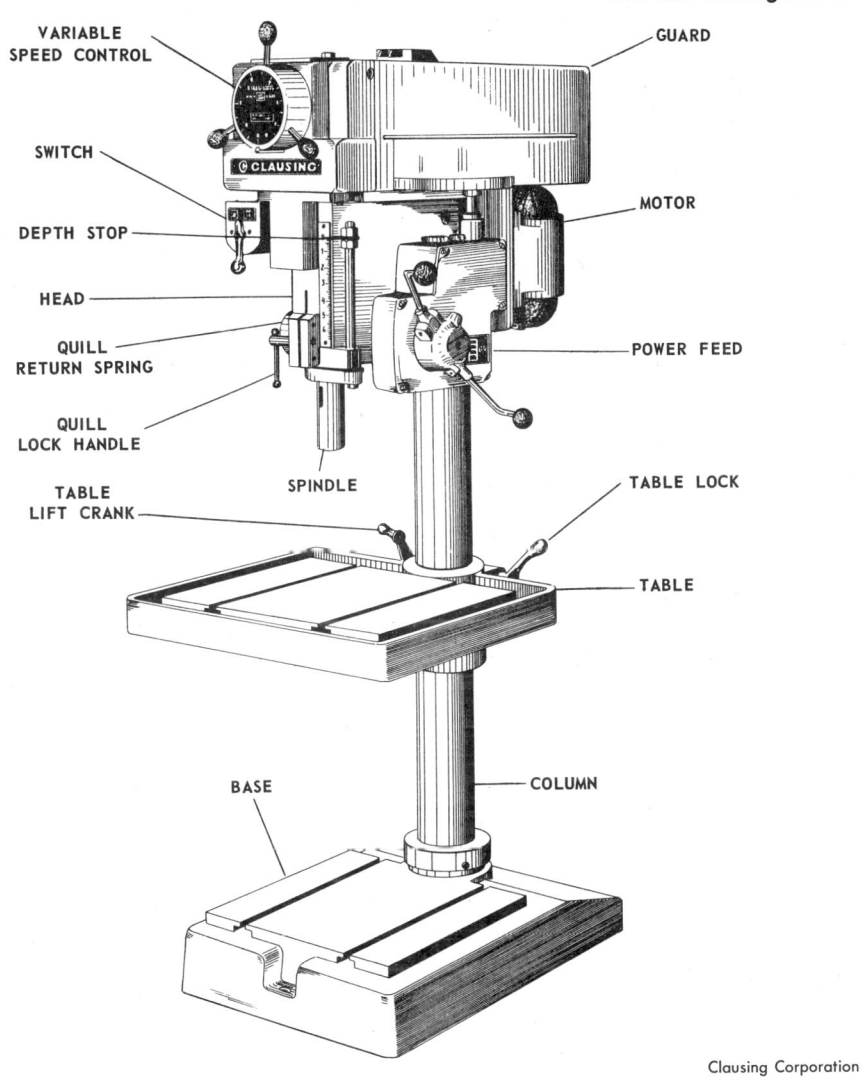

38-5. Parts of the drill press. This machine drills accurate holes quickly and easily.

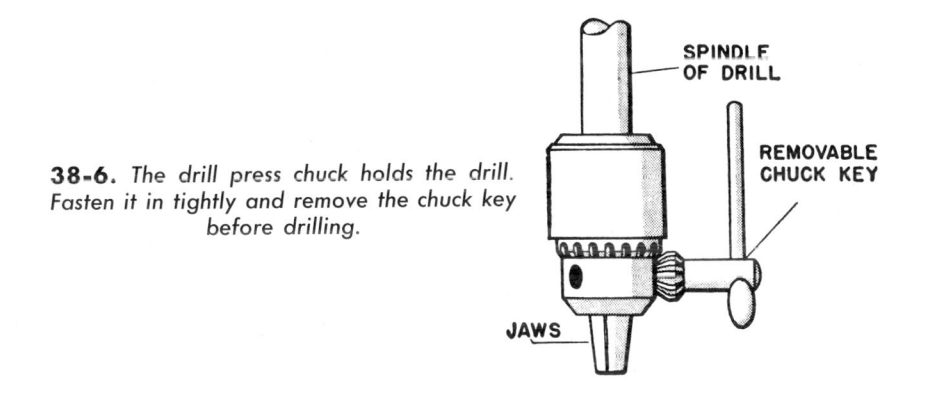

Clausing Corporation

38-6. The drill press chuck holds the drill. Fasten it in tightly and remove the chuck key before drilling.

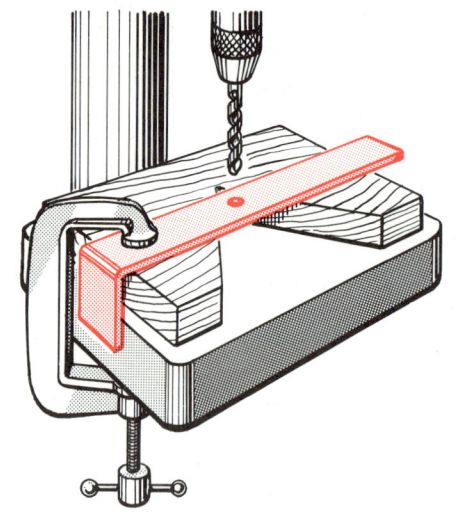

Part III: Manufacturing—Principles, Materials, and Processes

38-7a. The workpiece can be clamped to the table for drilling.

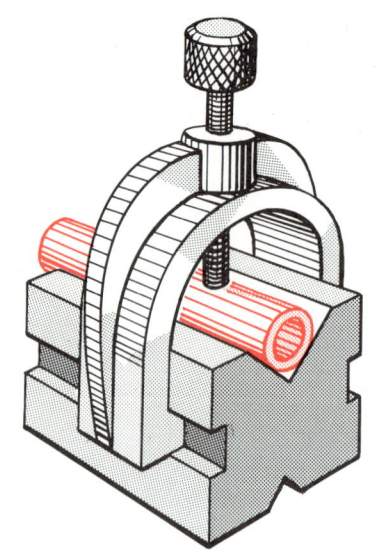

38-7b. Round workpieces are held in a V-clamp.

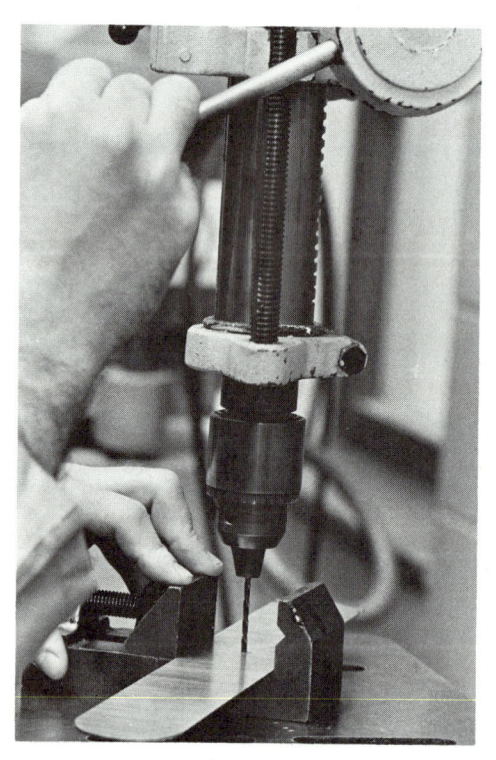

38-8. Using the drill press. This workpiece is held in a drill press view.

198

Unit 38: Drilling Metal

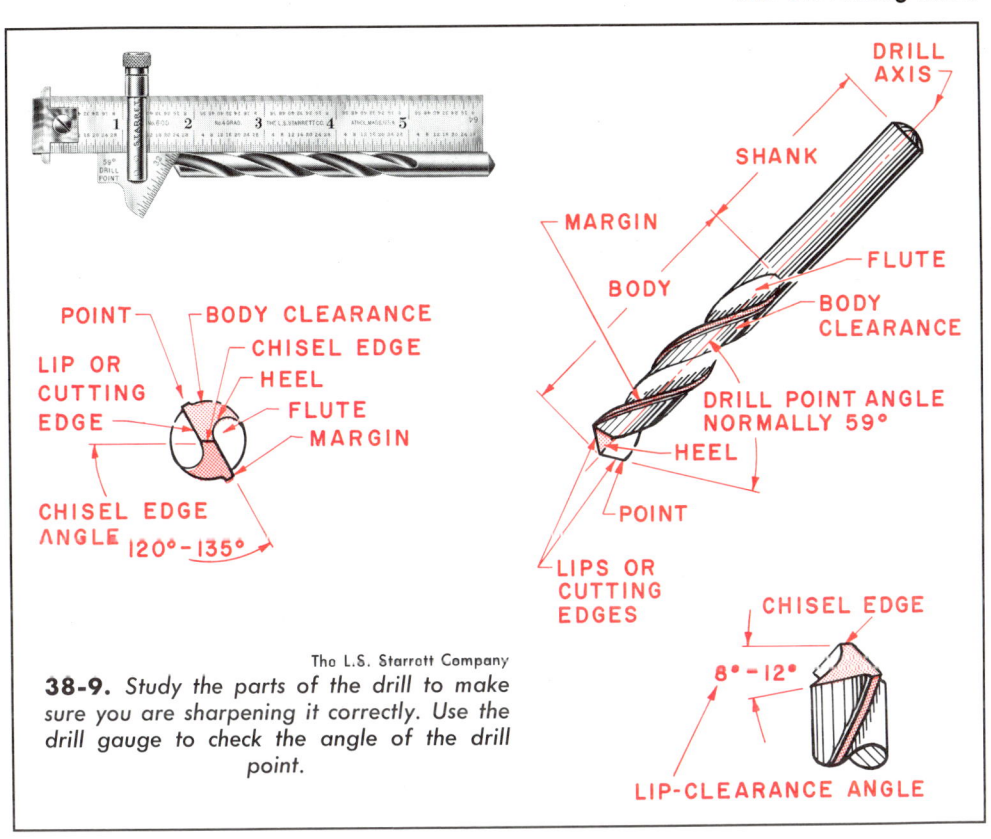

38-9. Study the parts of the drill to make sure you are sharpening it correctly. Use the drill gauge to check the angle of the drill point.

The L.S. Starrett Company

38-10. Using the reamer to enlarge and true a hole. Spiral and straight flute reamers are also shown.

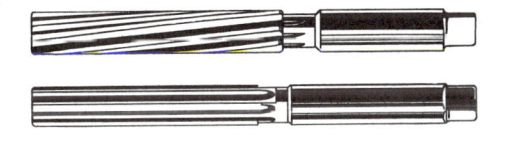

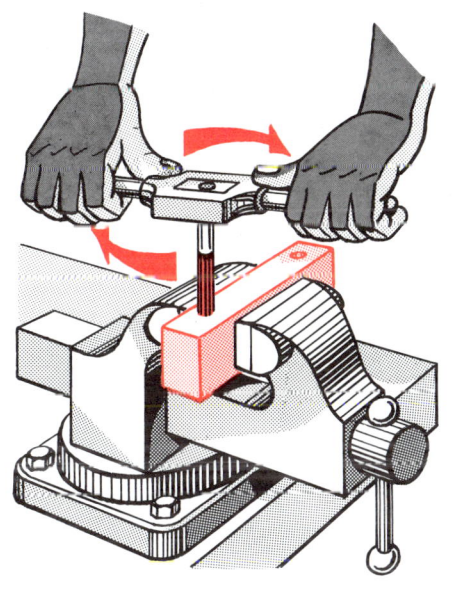

199

UNIT 39

Milling and Filing Metal

Milling metal is a removal cutting process in which a wide cutter revolves against a workpiece. The machine in Fig. 39-1 is called a horizontal mill, because of the position of the tool. The vertical mill works like a drill press and can mill surfaces or true holes at many angles. Fig. 39-2. Both are accurate machines for producing smooth surfaces and for cutting grooves and slots.

39-1a. *The horizontal milling machine removes metal quickly and accurately. The metal workpiece (A) moves slowly against the revolving cutter (B).*

Clausing Corporation

FILING

Filing is a common hand milling operation which is widely used in the shop. A file works much like the mill. If you took a milling cutter and stretched the teeth out on a flat surface, you would have a file. Fig. 39-3.

Files are classified according to length, shape, type of tooth (cut), and coarseness (number of teeth in relationship to the file length). Files range in length from 3" to 20". An 8" or 10" file is best for general use. Some common shapes are shown in Fig. 39-4. Files are made with various types of teeth for different kinds of cutting. A double-cut file has two rows of teeth which cut in opposite directions. There are also single-cut files. Rasp-cut files are for woods and very soft metals, as are curved-tooth files. File coarseness

39-1b. *The cutting action of the milling machine.*

Clausing Corporation

Unit 39: Milling and Filing Metal

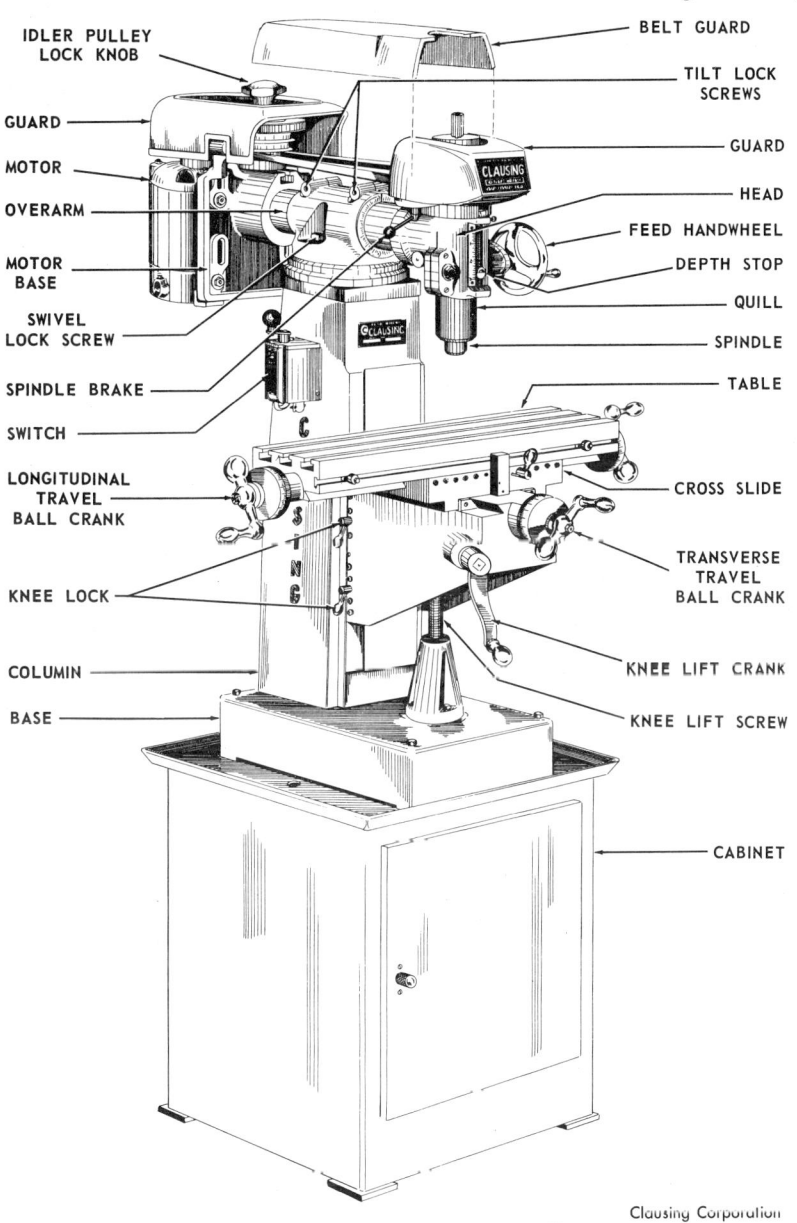

39-2. Parts of the vertical mill.

39-3. The cutting action of the file. This tool is like a stretched-out milling cutter.

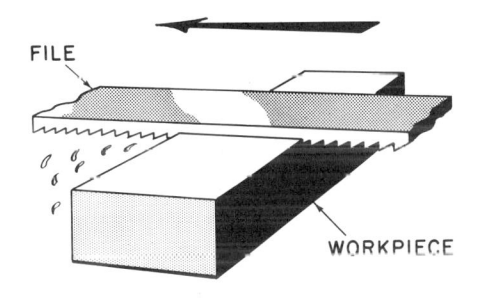

201

Part III: Manufacturing—Principles, Materials, and Processes

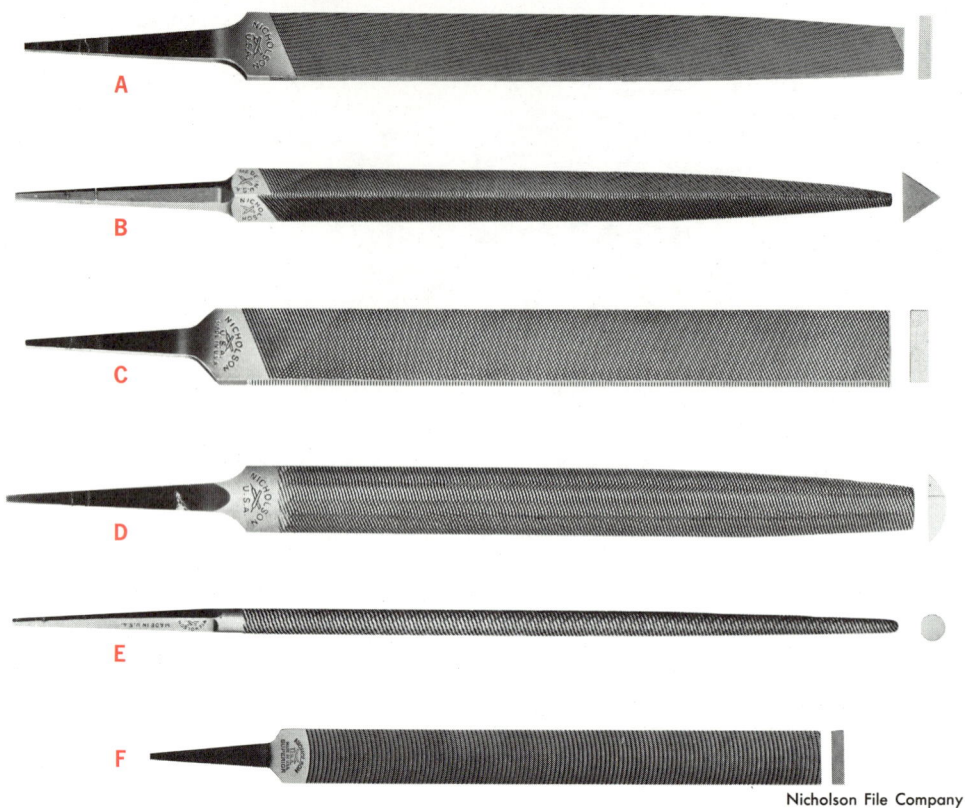

39-4. Common shapes of files: (A) Mill (B) Triangular (C) Hand (D) Half round (E) Round (F) Curved tooth.

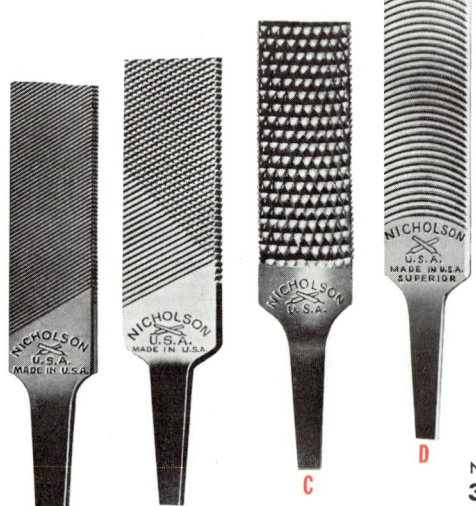

Nicholson File Company

grades range from rough to dead smooth. Fig. 39-5.

Files are used to remove scratches and nicks from metal, to remove burrs, to shape material, and to sharpen tools.

Use mill files for general-purpose work. Fig. 39-6. Needle files are used for fine filing on jewelry, or in special die work. Figs. 39-7 and 39-8.

Nicholson File Company

39-5. The cut of the file shows how the teeth are cut on the file face. (A) Single cut (B) Double cut (C) Rasp cut (D) Curved cut.

202

Unit 39: Milling and Filing Metal

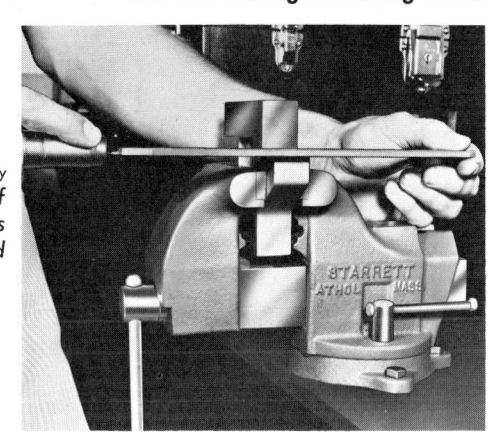

The L.S. Starrett Company

39-6. Using the mill file. This file is one of the most common tools used in the shop. It is rectangular in shape with single-cut teeth and is slightly tapered in width and thickness.

39-7. Types of jeweler's files.

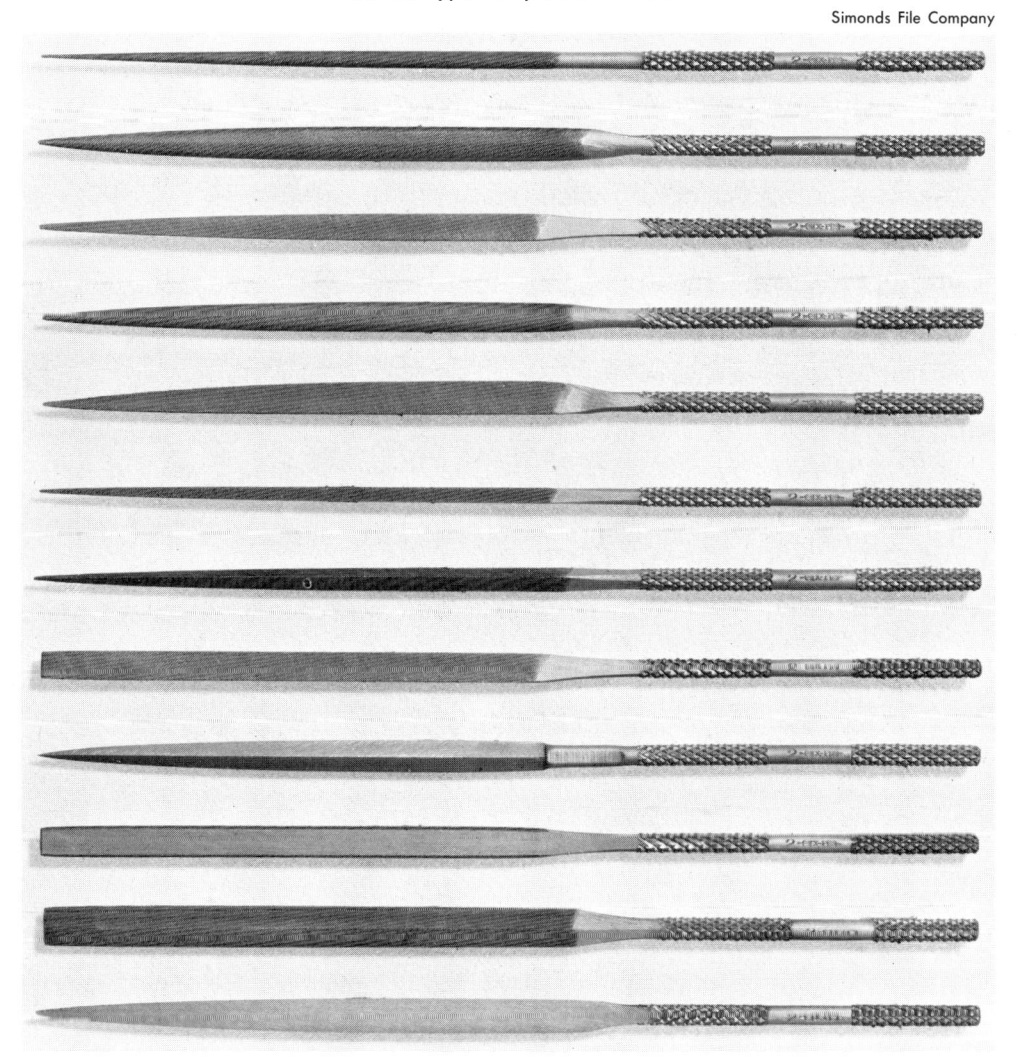

Simonds File Company

203

Part III: Manufacturing—Principles, Materials, and Processes

Before using the file, make certain it is clean and free of oil and grease. Use a file card to clean any metal clogging the teeth. Check to see that the handle is tight. Never use a file without a handle. The workpiece should be fastened securely in a vise. Grasp the file by the handle and the tip, and press gently against the workpiece. The file cuts on the forward stroke. Draw filing is another way of rapidly removing metal from a workpiece. Fig. 39-9.

39-8. Using the jeweler's file. The file cuts on the forward stroke.

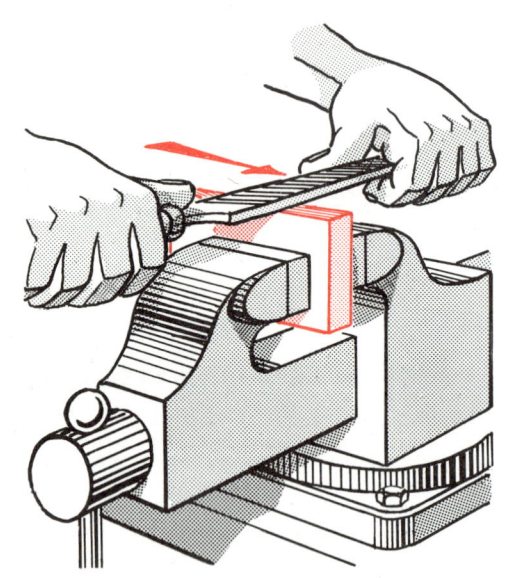

39-9. Draw filing produces a smooth, true surface on a workpiece.

UNIT 40

Turning Metal

The metal-cutting lathe is a machine which removes metal by a process called *turning*. In this process the tool is stationary, or fixed, and the workpiece revolves. Fig. 40-1. This machine is used for many kinds of cutting. For example, it can be used for accurate turning to precise dimensions, for cutting threads on shafts, for cutting tapers, and for drilling holes.

Fig. 40-2 shows the parts of the lathe. The size of the lathe is determined by the swing—that is, the largest diameter which can be turned on it—and by the length of the bed.

The lathe is so basic in metalworking that it is sometimes called the father of all machine tools. Industry uses several kinds of complicated lathes for produc-

40-1. *Removing metal by turning is a process done on a metal-cutting or engine lathe.*
Clausing Corporation

205

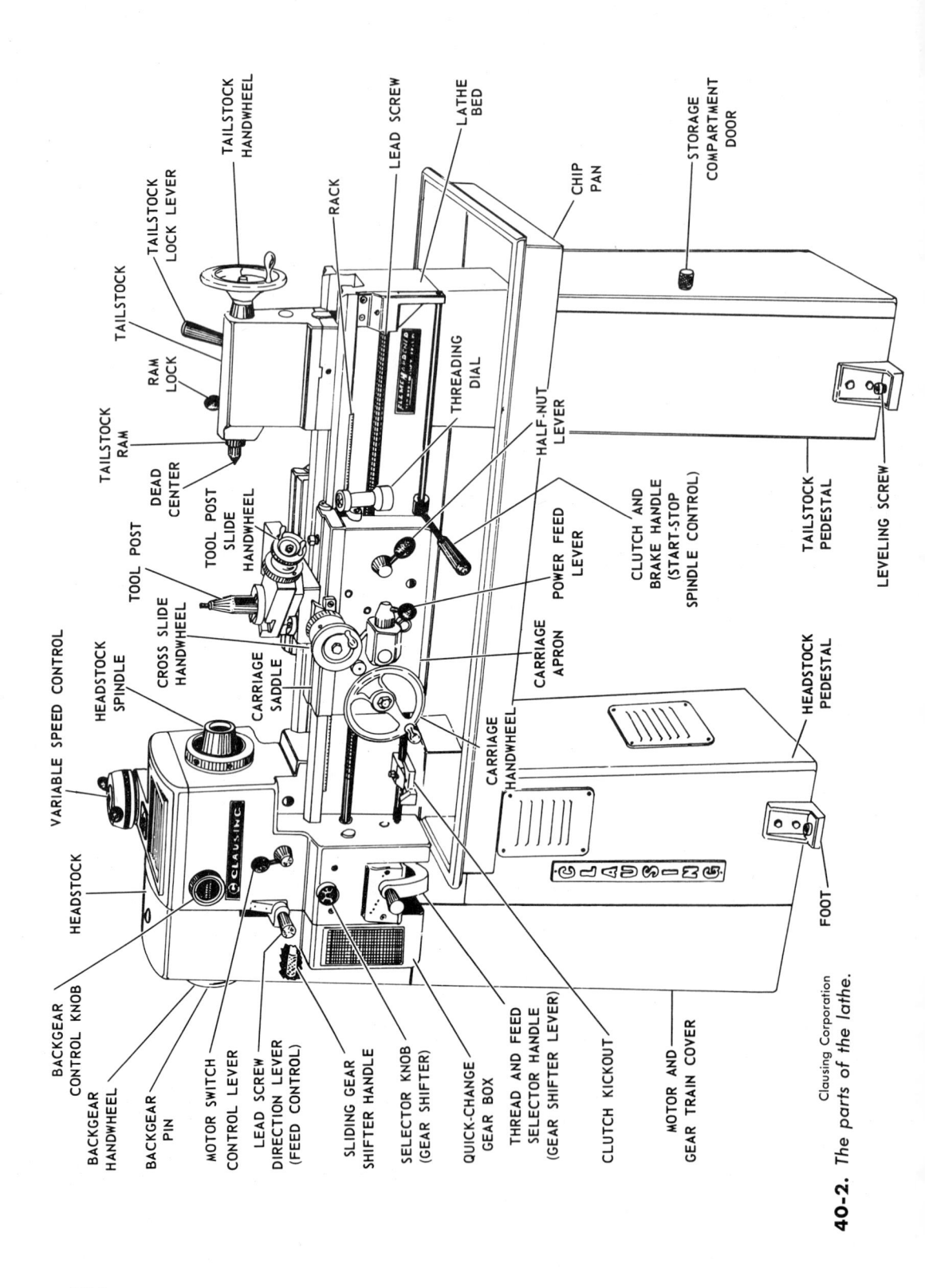

Part III: Manufacturing—Principles, Materials, and Processes

40-2. The parts of the lathe.

Clausing Corporation

206

Unit 40: Turning Metal

40-3. Lathe turning is an important machining operation in school shops.
Clausing Corporation

40-5a. Face plates.

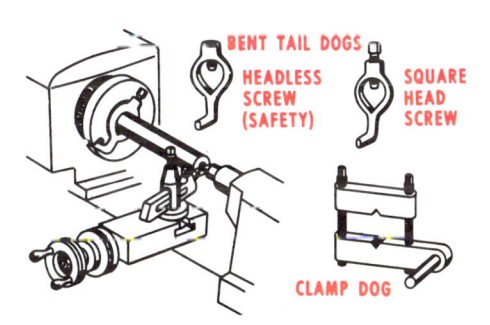

40-4. Types of lathe dogs.

40-5b. The universal three-jaw chuck (top) and the independent four-jaw chuck (bottom).

tion work, including the turret lathe, the automatic screw machine, and the tracer lathe. The operation of the type of lathe generally used in the school shop is described here. Fig. 40-3.

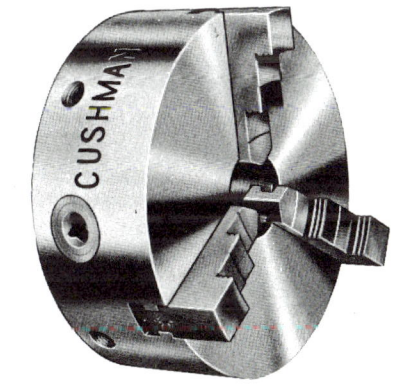

LATHE ACCESSORIES

1. *Lathe dogs* are used to hold workpieces when turning between centers. The three types of lathe dogs are shown in Fig. 40-4.

2. The *faceplate* fastens to the headstock spindle and holds the lathe dog in place. Fig. 40-5a.

3. *Chucks* are used to hold workpieces for chuck-turning, drilling, reaming, and tapping. The two types of chucks are shown in Fig. 40-5b.

207

Part III: Manufacturing—Principles, Materials, and Processes

4. *Tool bits* are small rectangular pieces of hard, high-speed steel. They are of several shapes for different types of cutting. Fig. 40-6.

5. *Toolholders* hold tool bits and are in turn held in the *tool post.* There are several types of toolholders, as shown in Fig. 40-7.

6. The *knurling tool,* Fig. 40-8, is used to produce a cross-hatched design in metal. This is used on tool handles to give the tool a better grip.

MEASURING TOOLS

There are a number of different measuring tools used in machine shop work. A steel rule (see Unit 31) has many uses, as do the inside and outside calipers. Typical uses of these tools are shown in Figs. 40-9 and 40-10. One very important precision tool is the micrometer. Fig. 40-11. Besides the common micrometer shown in Fig. 40-12, there are the tube, inside, thread, and hub measuring types. Both customary-inch and metric models are available, Fig. 40-13.

USING THE LATHE

Common lathe operations include turning between centers and chuck turning.

40-6. *Types of lathe cutting tools: (A) Right-hand turning (B) Left-hand turning (C) Round-nose (D) Cut-off (E) Thread-cutting (F) Left-hand facing (G) Right-hand facing.*

40-7. *Types of toolholders: (A) Straight (B) Right-hand (C) Cut-off (D) Boring (E) Left-hand.*

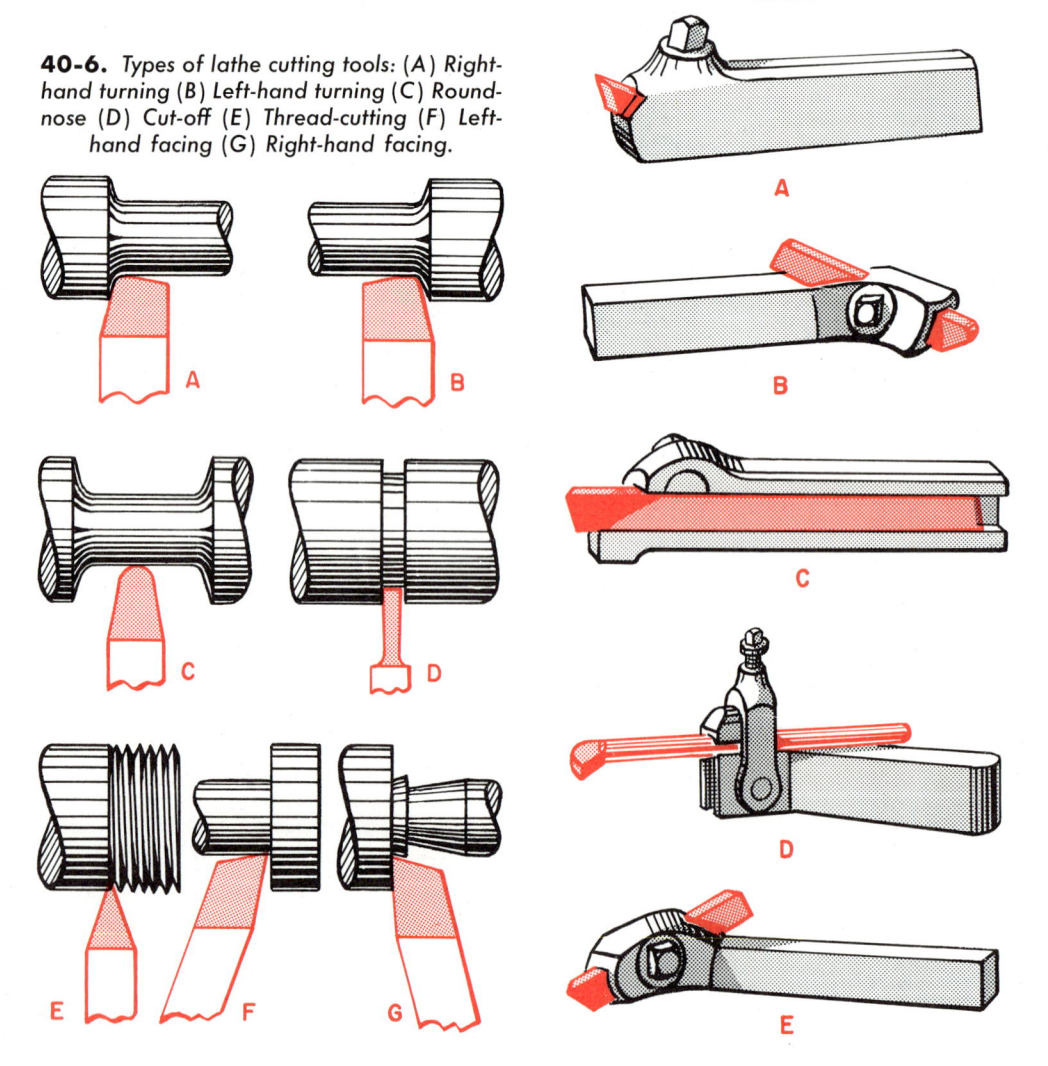

Unit 40: Turning Metal

The workpiece should be about 1" longer and $\frac{1}{8}$" larger in diameter than the finished size. Be careful when using the lathe. Tuck in loose clothing and wear safety goggles.

Work Held between Centers

1. The main way of holding work in a lathe is to mount it between centers. To do this, drill countersunk holes in the

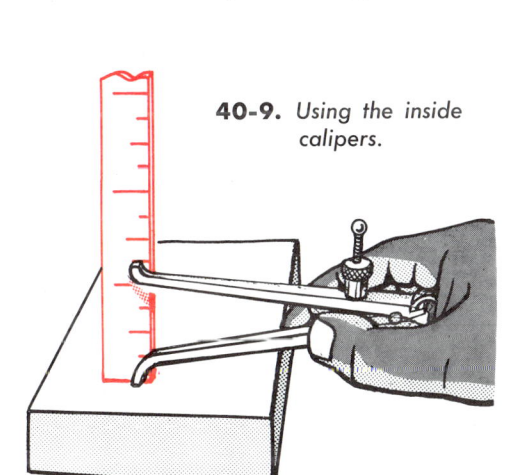

40-8. Using the knurling tool.
Clausing Corporation

40-9. Using the inside calipers.

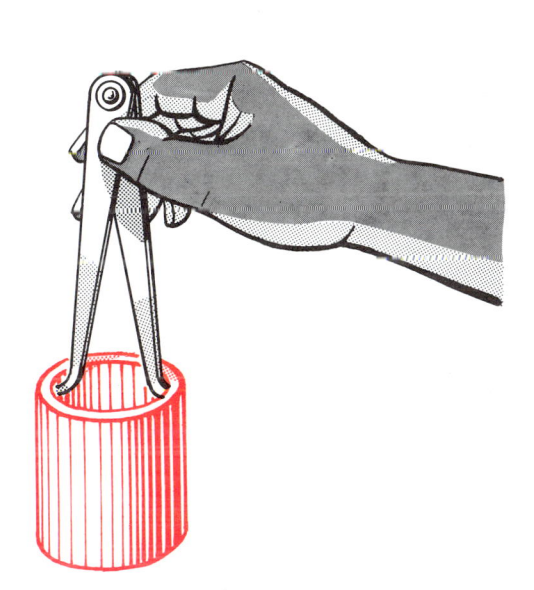

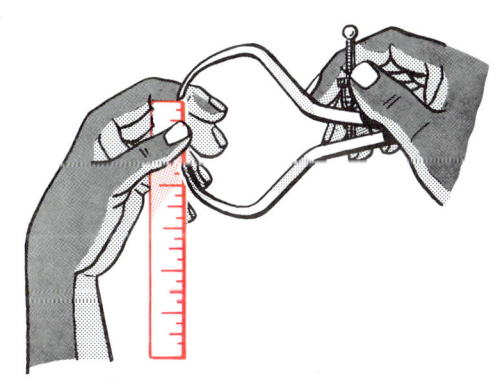

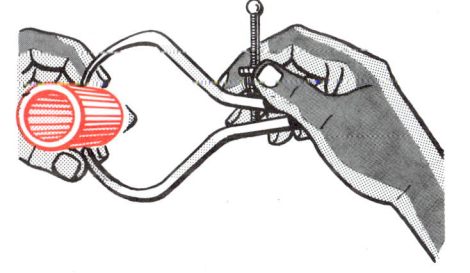

40-10. Using the outside calipers.

40-11. The micrometer is an important precision tool for machine shop work. It must be used carefully. Tighten the barrel against the workpiece lightly. Do not force it, or you will damage the tool.

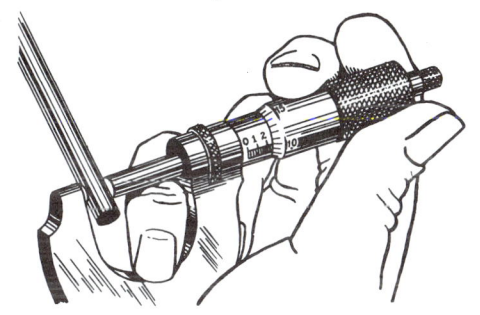

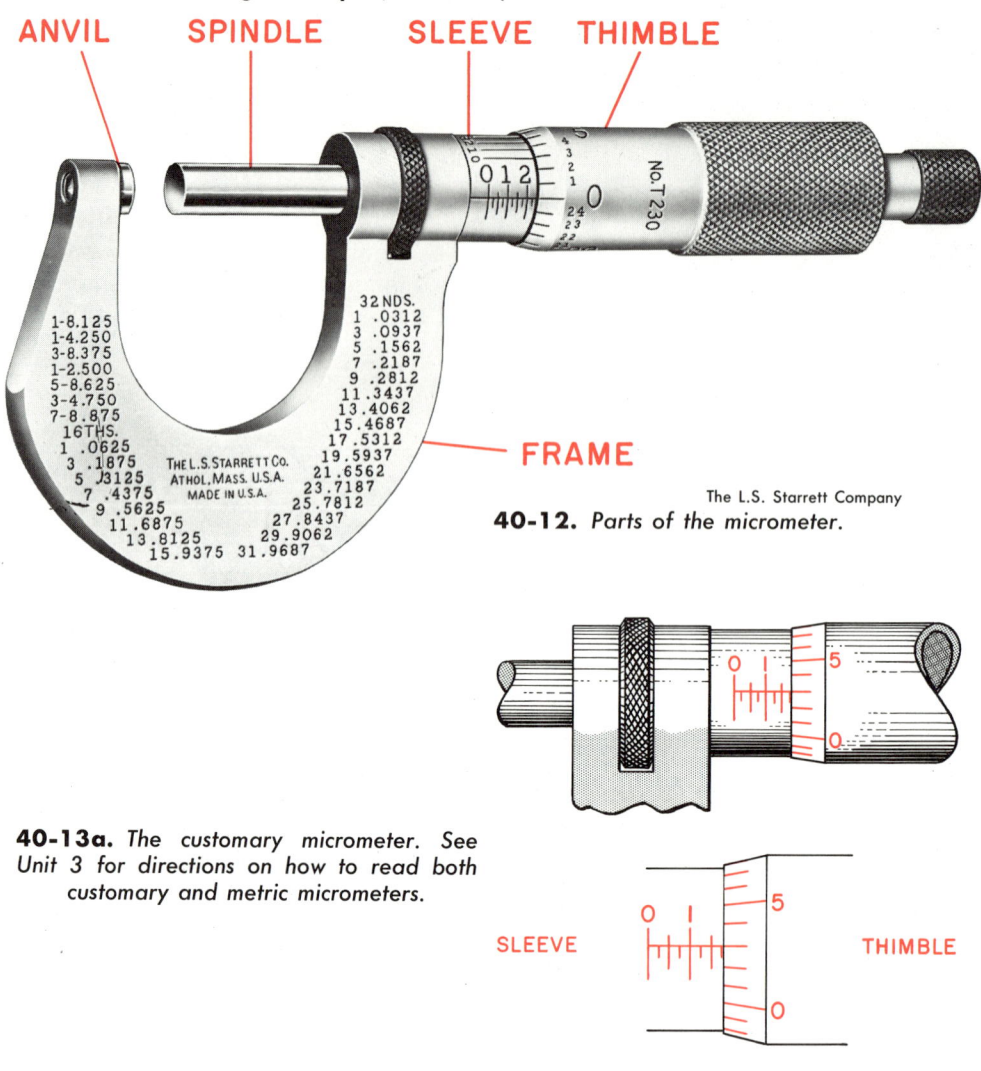

Part III: Manufacturing—Principles, Materials, and Processes

40-12. Parts of the micrometer.

The L.S. Starrett Company

40-13a. The customary micrometer. See Unit 3 for directions on how to read both customary and metric micrometers.

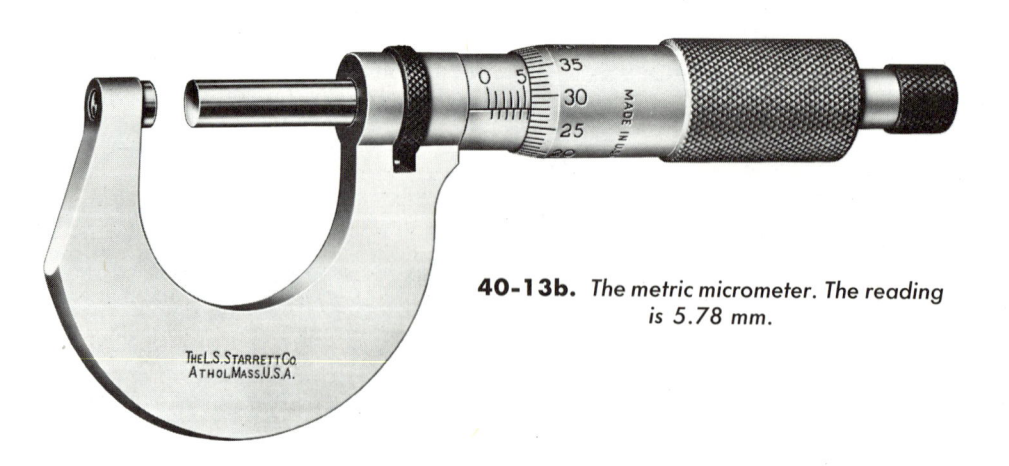

READING: 0.178"

40-13b. The metric micrometer. The reading is 5.78 mm.

210

Unit 40: Turning Metal

ends of the work. Locate these as shown in Fig. 40-14. Drilling methods are illustrated in Fig. 40-15.

2. Clamp a lathe dog on the drive end of the work so that the tail of the dog will fit in a slot in the faceplate. Place the hole in the workpiece against the center in the lathe spindle and turn the tailstock handwheel until the dead center meets the center hole of the free end of the workpiece. This center should fit the countersunk hole just loosely enough so the work will revolve, but not so loose that it will wobble. Place a little lubricant on the dead center to reduce friction. A mixture of white lead and oil can be used.

3. Place a sharpened tool bit in the toolholder. Fig. 40-16. Lock this in the tool post. Set the cutting edge of the tool so that it is slightly above the centerline of the workpiece. The tool should be turned slightly away from the headstock.

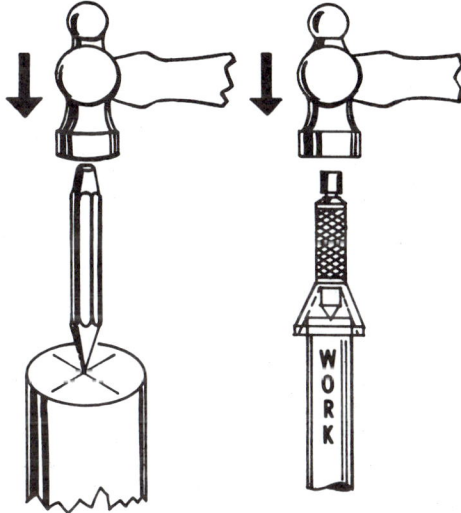

40-14. Locating the marking centers: (A) Using the centering head and scriber (B) Marking the center with a center punch (C) Using the bell punch.

A — SCRIBER
B — PUNCHING THE CENTER
C — BELL CENTER PUNCH METHOD

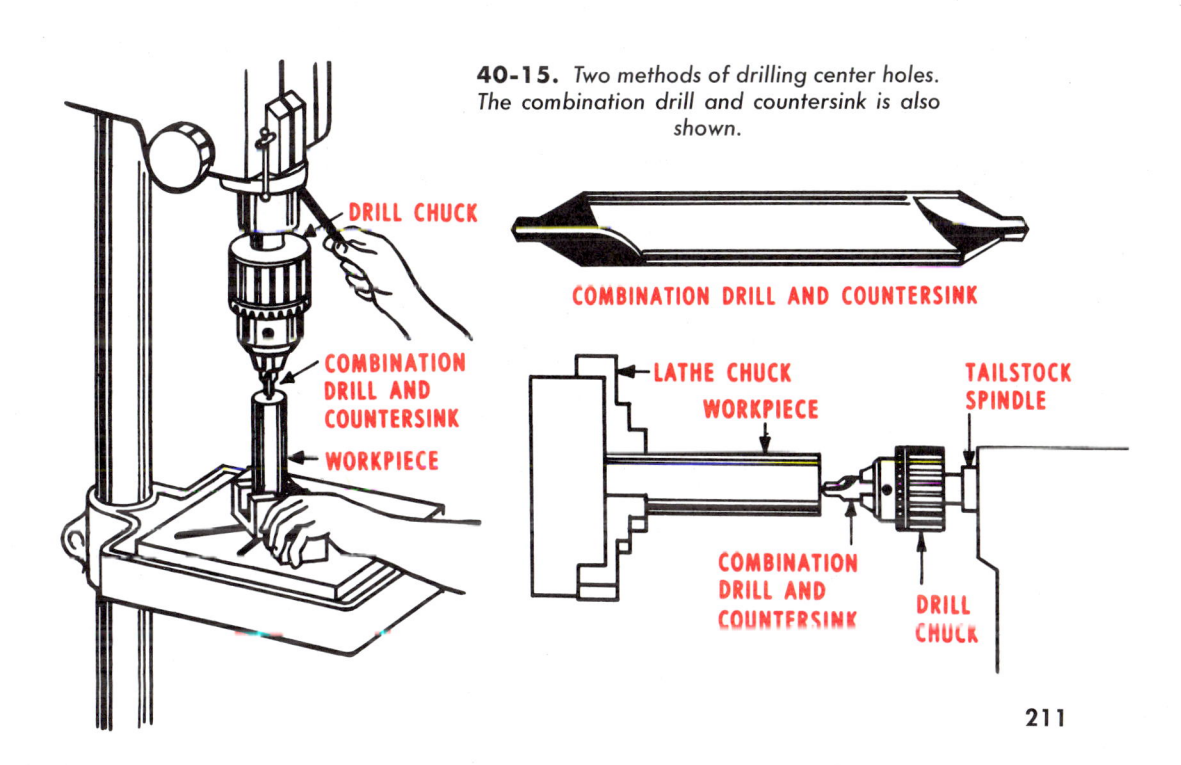

40-15. Two methods of drilling center holes. The combination drill and countersink is also shown.

COMBINATION DRILL AND COUNTERSINK

DRILL CHUCK
COMBINATION DRILL AND COUNTERSINK
WORKPIECE

LATHE CHUCK
WORKPIECE
TAILSTOCK SPINDLE
COMBINATION DRILL AND COUNTERSINK
DRILL CHUCK

211

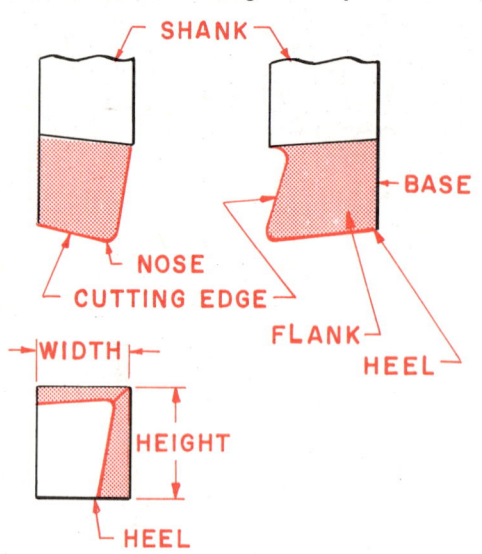

Part III: Manufacturing—Principles, Materials, and Processes

40-16. Tool sharpening diagram.

40-17. Turning between centers on the metal lathe. What type of lathe dog is being used?

Clausing Corporation

4. Adjust the speed so that it is correct for the kind of metal and the diameter of the workpiece.

5. Move the carriage back and forth by turning the carriage handwheel. The point of the tool should clear the right end of the workpiece, and it should not touch the lathe dog. The carriage should move from the tailstock to the headstock when the power is on.

6. The outside calipers should be set about $\frac{1}{16}$" larger than the finished diameter.

7. For rough cutting (turning the workpiece to "roughly" the finished size) move the carriage over until the tool point clears the right end of the workpiece. Start the lathe. Turn the cross slide handwheel in and the carriage handwheel toward the headstock until the tool begins to remove a small chip. Continue to feed the carriage handwheel by hand for a short distance. Stop the lathe and check the trial cut with the calipers to make sure you have left enough stock for the finishing cut—usually about $\frac{1}{32}$". If the diameter is satisfactory, restart the lathe and engage the power (longitudinal or lengthwise) feed lever. Continue the cut until over half the length of the stock has been cut. At the end of the cut, turn the cross feed out and release the power feed lever at the same time.

8. Return the carriage to the right-hand starting position. Repeat the rough cutting operation if more material must be removed.

9. If the full length of the workpiece is to be turned, move the workpiece and turn it end for end. Rough cut the remaining length. Resharpen the tool bit, and set the lathe for a higher speed and finer feed. Finish turning the workpiece, checking carefully with the caliper now set for the finished diameter. After the finish cut, again turn the workpiece end for end and finish cut the second half. Fig. 40-17.

Work Held in a Chuck

Holding the workpiece in a chuck makes it possible to turn short pieces without using the tailstock for support. This method also permits drilling, boring, reaming, tapping, and cutoff operations.

1. Mount a three- or four-jaw chuck on the lathe. Mount the workpiece in the chuck. Make sure it is seated properly, then tighten with the chuck wrench.

Unit 40: Turning Metal

40-18. Here the workpiece is being held in a universal three-jaw chuck.

40-19. Drilling on a lathe with the workpiece held in a universal three-jaw chuck. Reaming and tapping are done in a manner similar to this.

40-20. Using the collet chuck.

2. To face the end of the workpiece, place a left-hand facing tool in the tool post. Set the point of the tool at the center of the workpiece. Move the carriage so that the tool clears the workpiece. Turn the lathe on. The rough cutting should start at the outside of the workpiece and move into the center. For the finish cut, start at the center and move outwards.

Remember to lock the carriage by turning the carriage lock screw. The tool is fed by hand for most cutting. For large diameters, use the power cross feed.

3. Turning the chuck-held workpiece to diameter is done as you would when working between centers. Fig. 40-18. Be careful not to run the tool into the chuck jaws.

4. Drilling is done as shown in Fig. 40-19. Set the lathe for the proper drilling speed and feed the drill slowly. Clear chips from drill frequently and use cutting oil.

5. The collet chuck is shown in Fig. 40-20. This is a special chuck available in a number of diameters. It speeds the chuck turning operation.

213

Part III: Manufacturing—Principles, Materials, and Processes

FILING AND POLISHING

Both chuck-held and lathe dog-held workpieces can be filed and polished on a lathe. Fig. 40-21. Choose a smooth file, clean and free of nicks. Set the lathe for a faster speed and slowly press the file along the surface of the workpiece. Be very careful. Make certain your arm clears the machine. Roll up your sleeves and wear goggles.

Use a file card to clean the file frequently. Polishing is done with strips of abrasive cloth and machine oil.

Clausing Corporation
40-21. *Filing on the lathe. This is a dangerous operation. Be sure your sleeves are rolled up. Hold your arm out of the way of the revolving lathe dog.*

UNIT 41 — Etching and Flame Cutting of Metal

Not all metal cutting involves the use of sharpened tools. Chemicals and heat are also used in both separating and removing metal. For example, acids are used to etch (or eat away) metal surfaces. Chemical milling (see Unit 32) is a modern method of cutting away metal from thin sections.

Thermal cutting is the melting of a narrow section of a metal workpiece to separate it into two parts. It is closely related to welding. The main difference is that, in cutting, the molten metal is removed from the workpiece. In welding, the molten metal remains to join two workpieces together. Industry uses flame, carbon arc, powder, and laser thermal cutting processes. Flame cutting is commonly used in school shopwork. In flame cutting, metal is heated and oxygen is played on the hot spot to melt the metal away.

ETCHING

Etching in the shop is a process for decorating the surface of metal. In this process, the metal article to be etched is

Unit 41: Etching and Flame Cutting of Metal

41-1. *The process of etching. The etching solution will not attack those areas covered by the resist.*

placed in an etching solution. Metal is removed or eaten away by the action of the solution. Those parts of the surface which are not to be etched are covered by a *resist*. This material prevents the etching solution from eating away the metal. Fig. 41-1.

The following steps describe how etching is done:

1. The article to be etched should be polished, buffed, and cleaned. Clean it by wiping with a soft cloth dipped in lacquer thinner. Once the article has been etched, it should not be buffed again, as this will destroy the effect of the etching.

2. Carefully transfer the design you want to the metal, using carbon paper and a firm pencil.

3. Apply asphaltum varnish resist with a fine brush. Flow the material on so that everything is covered except the areas to be etched. Allow this to dry for 24 hours. Beeswax, plastic self-adhering wallpaper, and masking tape may also be used as resist materials.

4. Dip the article into the etching solution. For copper and brass, mix one part nitric acid with one part water. For aluminum, use one part muriatic (hydrochloric) acid and one part water.

CAUTION: Always pour the acid into the water. Pouring water into acid is dangerous. There are safer etching solutions called *mordants*. Mordants are available for etching most metals and should be used whenever possible in the shop. Wear goggles, gloves, and a rubber apron when working with acids or mordants.

5. When the etching is deep enough, remove the article from the solution with plastic or wooden tongs. Rinse with water and remove the resist. Asphaltum varnish can be removed with paint thinner, lac-

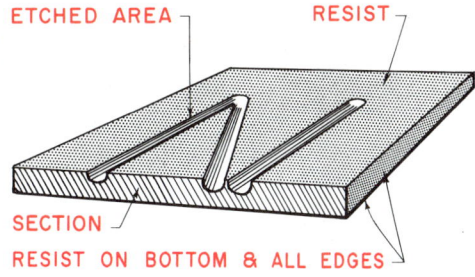

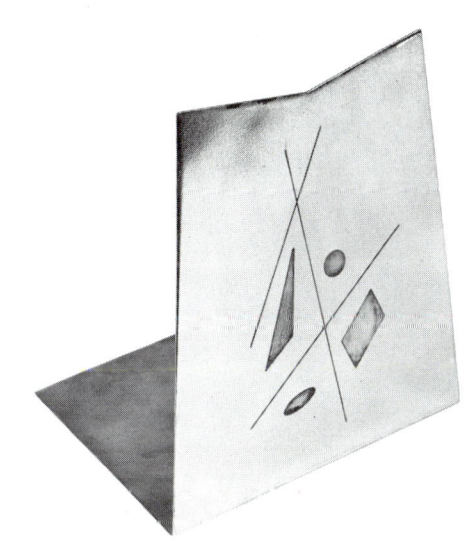

41-2. *A decoration etched on a metal bookend. A deep etch requires that the piece be left in the solution longer.*

quer thinner, or turpentine. Gently rub the surface dry with a soft cloth. Fig. 41-2.

FLAME CUTTING

This cutting is done with an oxyacetylene torch. See Unit 53 for information on this torch. To use the cutting torch, Fig. 41-3, mark the metal to be cut with a piece of white chalk. Start the cut by getting the metal red hot. Next, press the oxygen lever on the torch. This will cause pure oxygen to be fed to the tip of the torch to produce the cut. Be sure to keep the tip out of the molten pool. Wear safety clothing—goggles, gloves, and apron.

Flame cutting can also be done with carbon arc cutting torches. Fig. 41-4.

Part III: Manufacturing—Principles, Materials, and Processes

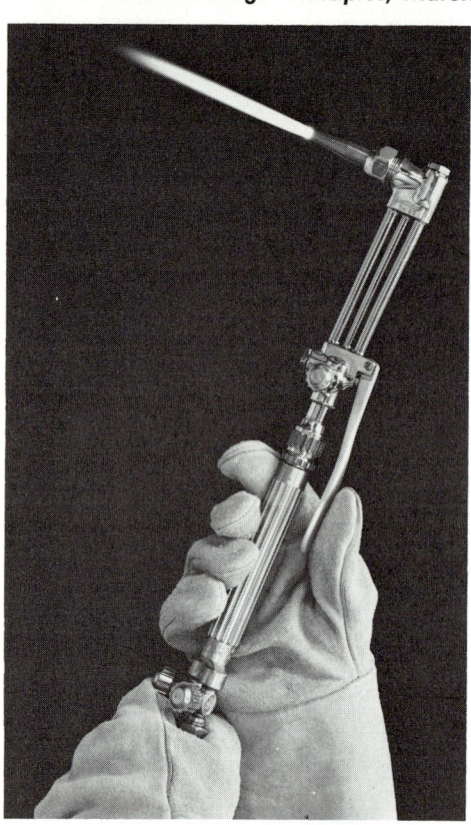

41-3. *Using the cutting torch. This process is used for the removal cutting of heavy material such as steel plate and pipe.*

41-4. *A carbon arc cutting torch. The torch melts metal, and a blast of air blows it away from the cutting path.*
Jackson Products Company

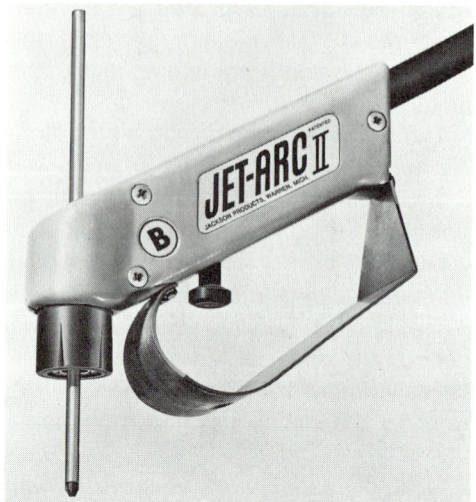

UNIT 42 — Metal Forming Principles

Very simply, metal forming is giving a shape to a piece of metal without adding or removing any of the material. You can also give shape to metal by turning it on a lathe, but you would have to remove some metal. For example, a bar of metal 2" square and 1' long could be turned and drilled on the lathe to make a piece of pipe 1' long. However, a better way of producing the pipe is to *form* it by extrusion. The difference between these two ways of producing pipe illustrates the effectiveness of the forming process. The pipe is formed quickly without any metal removal or waste.

The first four basic processes shown in the forming chart in Fig. 42-1 are commonly done in the shop. They are used in

Unit 42: Metal Forming Principles

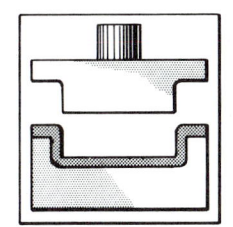

Fig. 42-1

Forming

Forming is the process of shaping a material without adding to or removing any of the material.

KINDS OF FORMING	DEFINITION	EXAMPLES
Bending	Forming by uniformly straining metal around a straight axis.	Operations on the bar folder, sheet metal brake, box and pan brake, bender, forming rolls.
Casting	Forming by pouring molten metal into a hollow cavity and allowing it to harden.	Operations such as die casting, sand casting, investment casting, powdered metal sintering (special form of casting).
Forging	Forming by applying blows or steady pressure to a heavy workpiece, forcing it to take the shape of a die.	Operations such as hand forging, drop forging, automatic closed die forging.

217

Part III: Manufacturing—Principles, Materials, and Processes

Fig. 42-1 (Continued)

KINDS OF FORMING	DEFINITION	EXAMPLES
Pressing	Forming by forcing sheet material between two dies.	Operations such as stamping, embossing, hand raising and sinking, spinning, metal tooling.
Drawing	Forming by pulling a metal rod or ribbon through a die to reduce it to a wire or form a tube.	Tube and wire drawing operations.
Extruding	Forming by forcing metal through an opening (or die) which controls its cross-sectional area.	Molding and channel extrusion operations.
Rolling	Forming by passing metal between rollers which change its cross-sectional area.	Metal sheet and bar rolling operations.

42-1. *This chart illustrates the kinds of forming that will be discussed in the following units.*

product manufacture. Drawing, extruding, and rolling are mainly metal fabrication processes used to produce raw materials for industry.

Forging in the shop is mainly done by hand. For instance, you might flatten the end of a piece of rod to form a screwdriver. In this case the anvil becomes a

Unit 42: Metal Forming Principles

42-2. When this large shaft becomes red-hot it will be in a softened (or plastic) condition. It can then be formed to the desired shape by forging. Unit 45 will tell you more about this important industrial process.

kind of die which controls the shape of the metal. In industry, forging is done by machines. Fig. 42-2.

Industrial pressing is done with huge machinery to form such items as pots and pans and automobile fenders. In the shop, typical pressing operations might involve sinking a copper ashtray into a wooden form by hammer blows, or tooling a piece of aluminum foil with a modeling tool.

As you read the following units on metal forming, try to learn something about how industry might do these same kinds of forming, but under mass production conditions.

UNIT 43

Bending Metal

There are many ways of bending metal. Machines used to bend light sheet metals are different from those used for heavy rods or bars. There are also many hand tools which are used in bending. But the purpose of all bending is the same—to change the form of the metal so that it can be made into usable products. Metal formed by this process is bent in one direction only. This unit shows some ways of changing the form of light and heavy metals.

BENDING LIGHT METALS

Simple hand bends can be made by forcing sheet metal around stakes made for this purpose. Mallets and hammers can be used to work the metal on these stakes. Fig. 43-1. The metal can also be clamped on a bench or between blocks of wood in a vise and folded over by beating.

Sheet metal stakes come in a variety of shapes and styles. Fig. 43-2. They are

43-1. *Hammers for bending light metals: (A) Plastic-tipped hammer (B) Fiber mallet (C) Wooden mallet. The mallets shown here will not mar or nick the surface of the metal.*

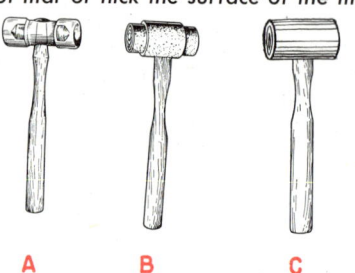

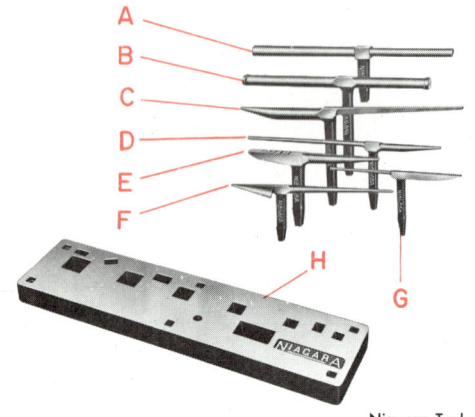

43-2. *Metal bending stakes are used for light- and heavy-gauge metals: (A) Conductor (B) Double seaming (C) Beak-horn (D) Candle mold (E) Creasing (F) Blowhorn (G) Needlecase (H) Stake holder.*

43-3. *Making a curved bend on a conductor stake. Do not use metal hammers on stakes.*

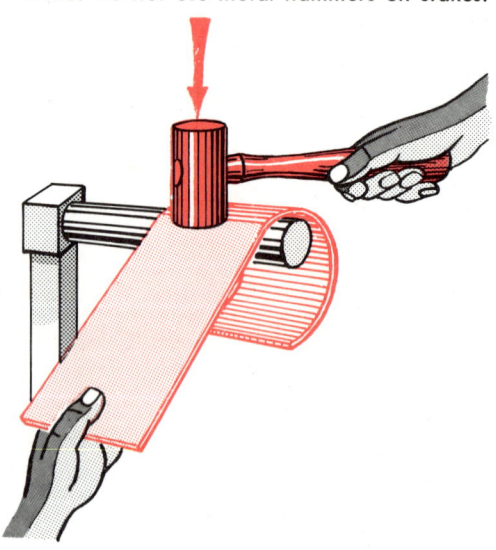

Unit 43: Bending Metal

43-4. Bending sheet metal on the vise. The metal can also be clamped in the vise jaws to make sharp bends.

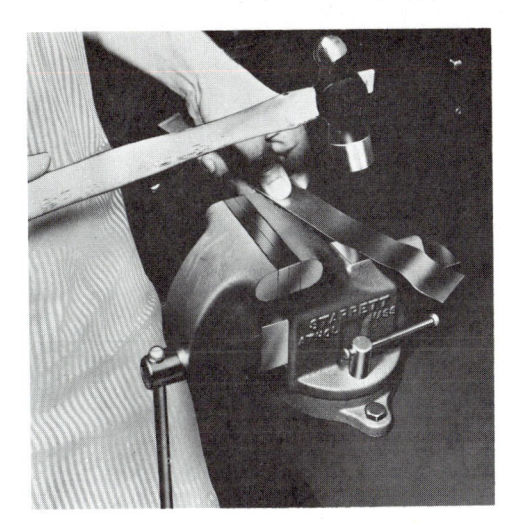

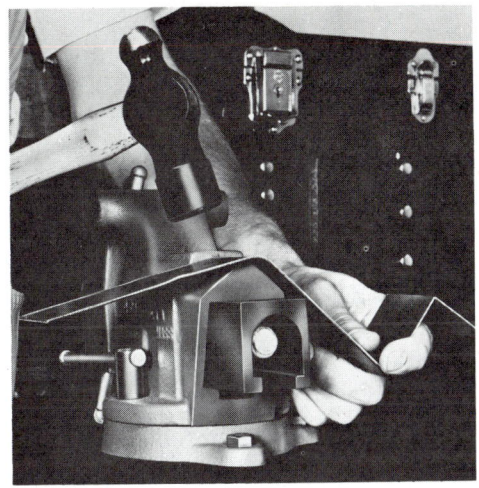

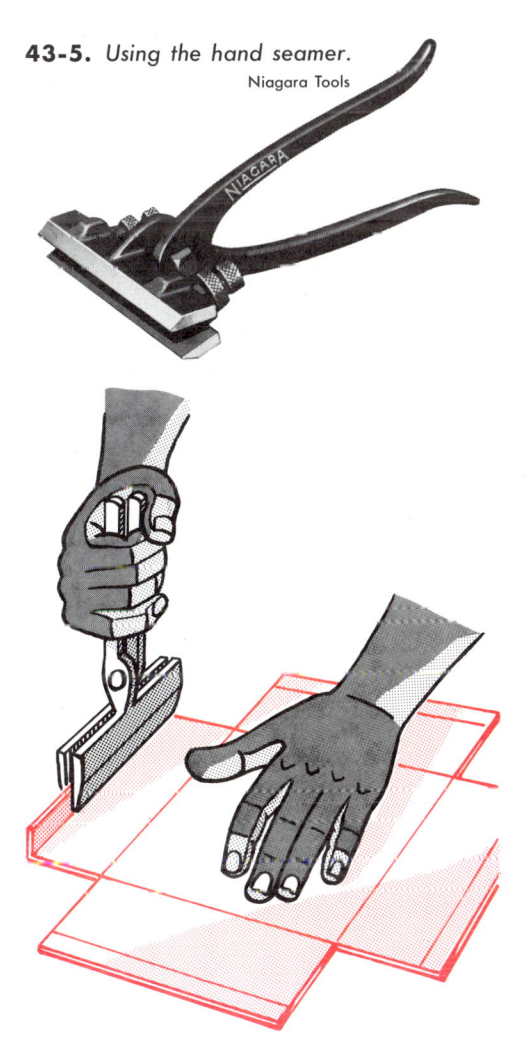

The L.S. Starrett Company

43-5. Using the hand seamer.
Niagara Tools

used for making sharp and round bends of many kinds. Do not use metal hammers for sheet metal stake bending. They will mar and dent the stake. Fig. 43-3.

The *metal vise* can be used for many kinds of bends. Curved bends are made on the special vise surfaces. Fig. 43-4. Sharp bends are made by clamping the workpiece between the jaws of the vise and striking with a hammer.

The *hand seamer* is used to make straight, shallow bends in light-gauge sheet metals. Fig. 43-5.

Bar folders work much like the hand seamer except that they can make longer bends in heavier sheet metals. The parts of this machine are shown in Fig. 43-6. Shop models of this machine usually are 30" wide. They can make bends from 1/8" to 1" wide in metals up to 22 gauge. Bends, hems, and open folds for grooved seams or wired edges can be made on this machine. Fig. 43-7.

To use the bar folder, set the depth adjusting gauge to the size of bend desired. Set the wing adjusting lever for a sharp or rounded bend, as needed. Set the 45° or 90° stop, if necessary. Carefully place the workpiece in the opening, hold it firmly, and pull the handle to make

221

Part III: Manufacturing—Principles, Materials, and Processes

the bend. Caution: Handle the metal with care to avoid painful cuts.

The *box and pan brake,* Fig. 43-8, is used for deeper bends in sheet metals. It is used much like the bar folder and comes in lengths up to eight feet. The machine can make many kinds of bends for a variety of product applications. It has removable fingers, which permit the bending of boxes and trays. Figs. 43-9 and 43-10. Larger machines of this type are called cornice brakes and do not have removable fingers.

To use the box and pan brake, lift the clamping bar handle and insert the metal in the brake. Tighten the clamping bar handle with the layout line marking the bend directly under the clamping bar. Lift the bending wing until the bend is made. It is a good idea to bend a little past the desired bend angle to allow for springback in the metal. If you are bending the ends of a box, remove the necessary clamping bar fingers. Fig. 43-11.

Cylinders are formed on the *slip roll forming machine.* Fig. 43-12. To use the machine, adjust the bottom roll to the thickness of the metal workpiece. The metal should just slip between the top and bottom rolls. The back, or idler, roll is adjusted to the diameter of the cylinder to be formed. Insert the metal and crank it through to form the cylinder. Several passes may have to be made. Readjust the back roll as needed. Trip the release

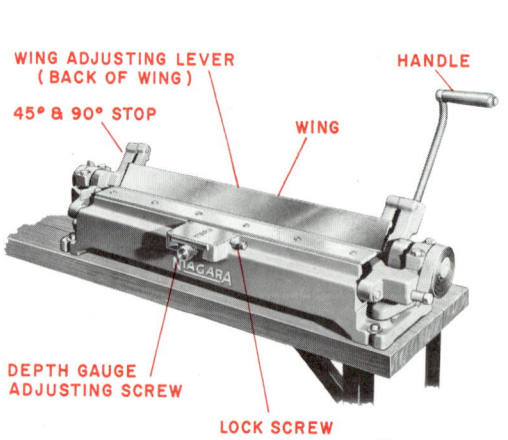

43-6. Parts of the bar folder.

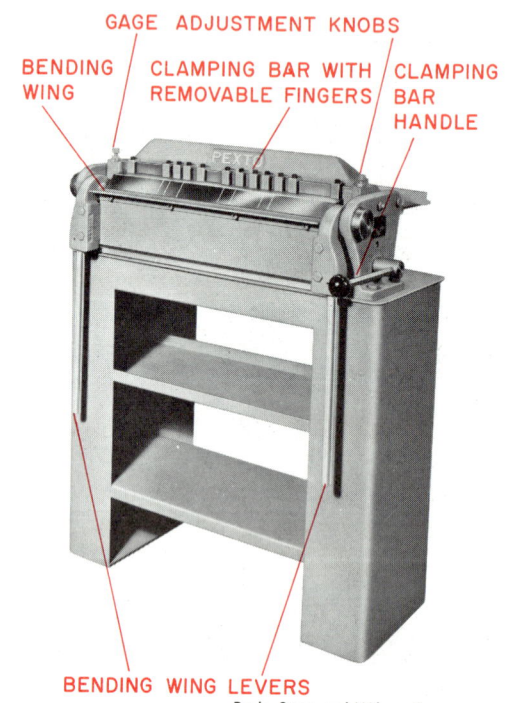

43-8. Parts of the box and pan brake.

43-7. Some typical bends made on the bar folder: (A) 90 degree bend (B) Single hem (C) Double hem. Hems are used to strengthen the edges of sheet metal.

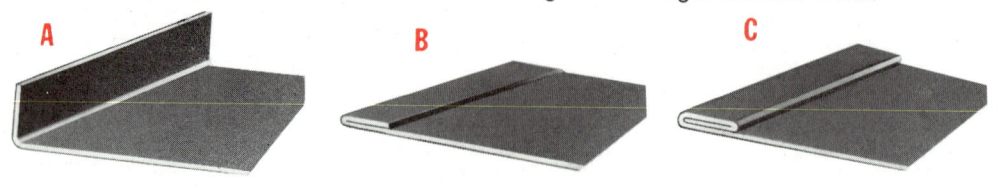

Unit 43: Bending Metal

43-9. The box and pan brake has removable fingers which permit the forming of boxes and trays.

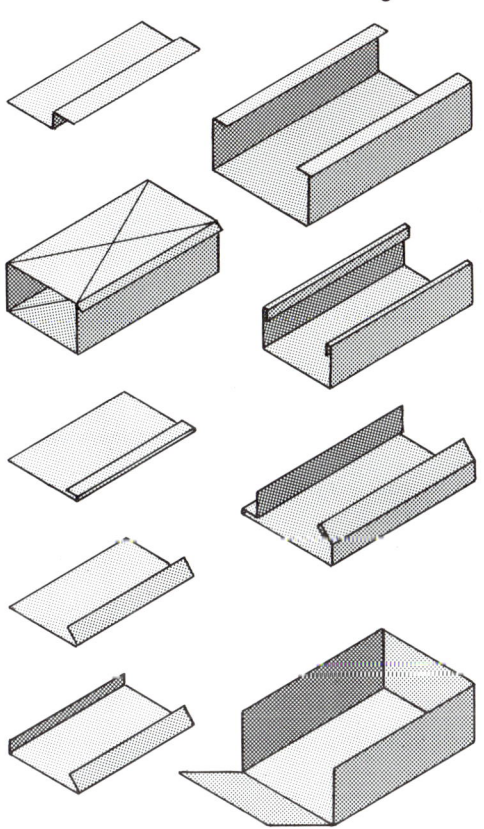

43-10. Typical bends made on a box and pan brake.

43-11. This putty knife bend is made on the box and pan brake.

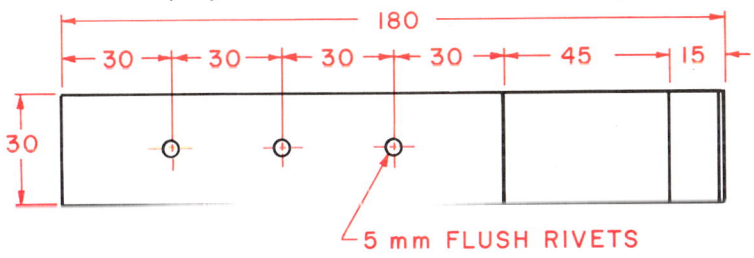

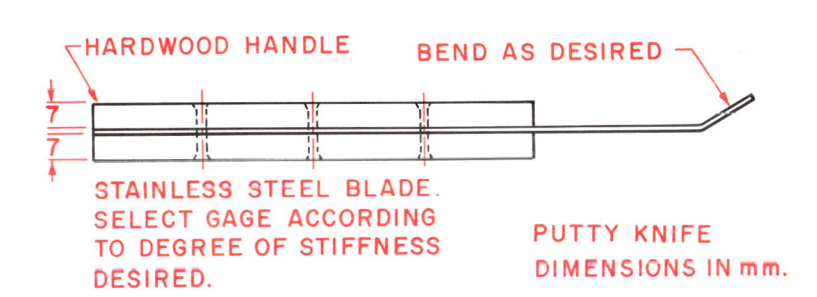

5 mm FLUSH RIVETS

HARDWOOD HANDLE

BEND AS DESIRED

STAINLESS STEEL BLADE. SELECT GAGE ACCORDING TO DEGREE OF STIFFNESS DESIRED.

PUTTY KNIFE
DIMENSIONS IN mm.

223

Part III: Manufacturing—Principles, Materials, and Processes

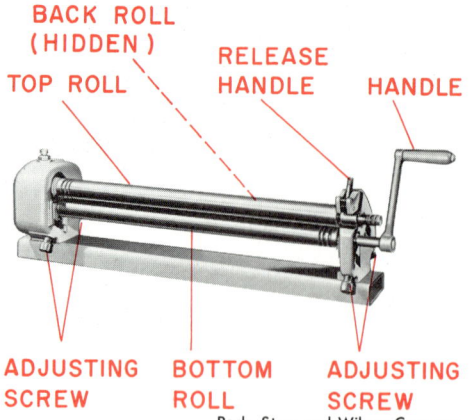

43-12. The slip roll forming machine is used for rolling metal into cylinders or cones.

43-13. Using the slip roll forming machine. The rolls are adjusted for thickness of metal and diameter of bend: (A) Top roll (B) Bottom roll (C) Back roll.

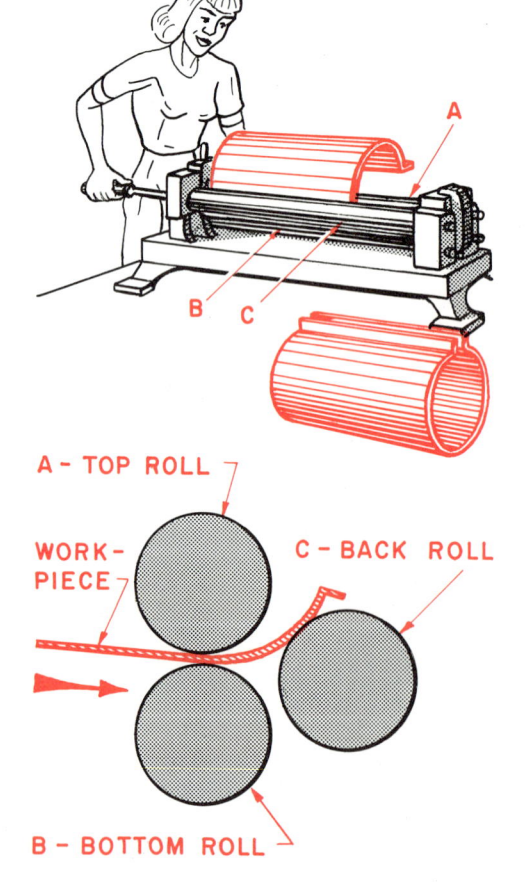

handle to remove the formed workpiece. Fig. 43-13.

BENDING HEAVY METALS

Sharp bends can be produced in heavy metals by placing the material in a sturdy vise and striking it with a ball peen hammer. To prevent the vise jaws from marring the metal, use vise jaw protectors. Metal can also be twisted in the vise by turning the workpiece with an adjustable wrench. Fig. 43-14. (To prevent the twist from becoming crooked, slip a piece of pipe over the workpiece.) Round bends can be made by hammering the metal over a piece of heavy pipe or by using the bending fork. Fig. 43-15. The fork is also used for forming scrolls.

MACHINES FOR BENDING

Metal bars, rods, and tubes are easily and accurately bent with special *bending machines.* All bending machines merely provide a way to apply power, either manually or mechanically, for the bending operation. They also supply mountings for the bending tools. Fig. 43-16. These tools are a form or radius collar having the same shape as the desired bend, a clamping block or locking pin that securely grips the material during the bending operation, and a forming roller or follow block which moves around the bending form.

When bending materials such as tubing, channel, or angle, the bending form

43-14. Metal can be twisted as shown here.

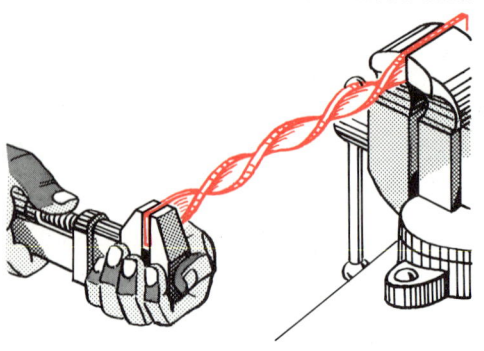

Unit 43: Bending Metal

should exactly fit the contour of the metal to provide support during the forming operation. This is also true of the clamping block and forming roller. Only by completely confining the metal can a perfect bend be made. As with any metal operation, the results obtained will be in direct proportion to the care taken in properly tooling the machine for the job to be done.

Making a circle is a typical bending operation. Fig. 43-17. Although a circle can be easily formed with benders, you must remember that most materials "spring back" after they have been formed. To allow for this, you must use a radius collar having a smaller diameter than that of the circle to be made. Actual size can best be determined by experiment, as the "springback" varies in different materials. Material should be precut to exact length before forming.

A complete circle can also be formed in one operation by clamping the material at one end and revolving the operating arm 360°. However, this method produces longer unformed lengths of material where the ends meet than when using the two-operation method shown in Fig. 43-17. Study the manual included with each machine to find out what other shapes can be formed.

Another type of bending machine is shown in Fig. 43-18. This machine is

43-15. *Use the bending fork for forming scrolls and rounded bends.*

43-16. *The parts of the bending machine. Several styles and models of these machines are available, both power and manually operated.*

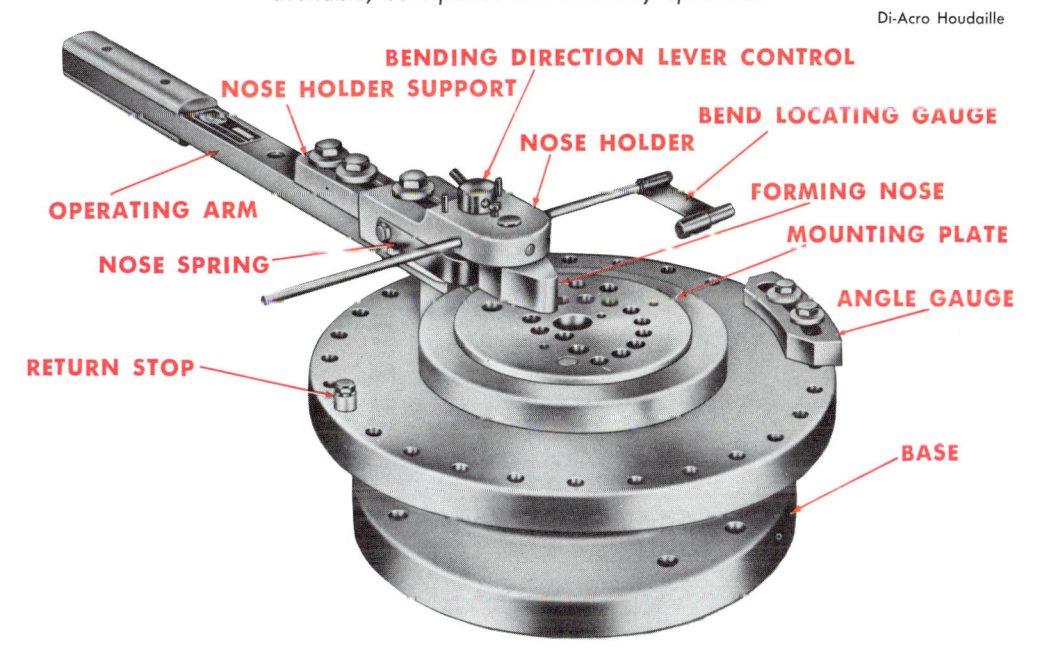

Di-Acro Houdaille

BENDING DIRECTION LEVER CONTROL
NOSE HOLDER SUPPORT
BEND LOCATING GAUGE
NOSE HOLDER
OPERATING ARM
FORMING NOSE
MOUNTING PLATE
NOSE SPRING
ANGLE GAUGE
RETURN STOP
BASE

225

Part III: Manufacturing—Principles, Materials, and Processes

used much like the one already described.

Industry uses metal-forming machines similar to those described in this unit. These machines are power operated and can form metals as much as one inch thick. One typical machine is shown in Fig. 43-19.

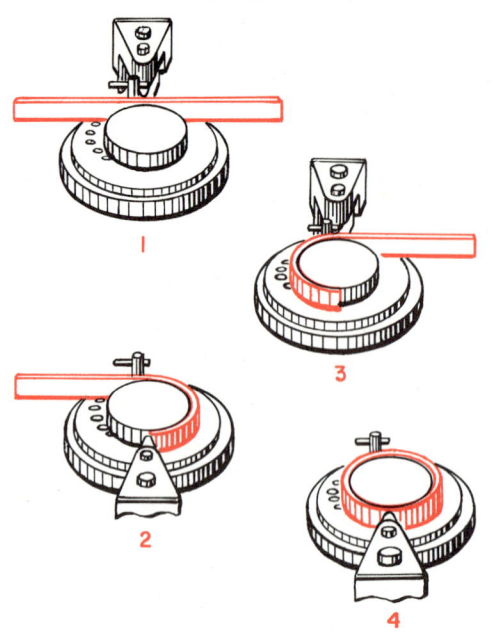

Di-Acro Houdaille

43-17. Forming a circle on a bending machine: (1) Set forming nose against material and clamp material against radius collar with locking pin. (2) Advance operating arm until forming nose reaches extreme end of material. (3) Relocate material and clamp with locking pin at a point where radius is already formed. (4) Advance operating arm until forming nose again reaches extreme end of material.

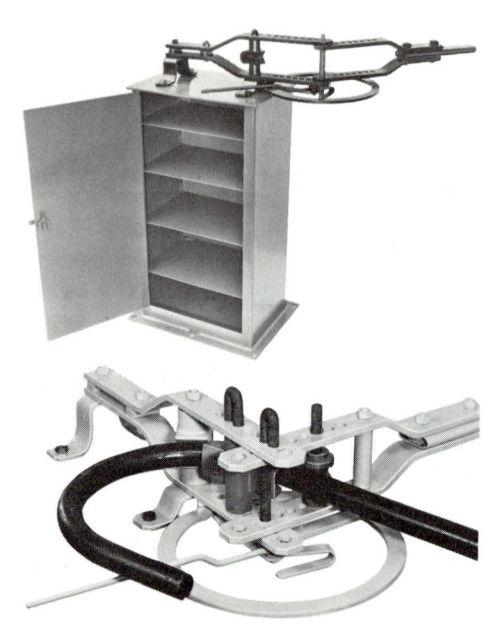

Hossfeld Manufacturing Company
43-18. A universal bending machine.

Niagara Tools
43-19. This mechanical press brake used in industry can bend metal plate 1" thick.

226

UNIT 44

Casting Metal

If you dig a hole in the ground, fill it with cement, and then remove the cement piece after it has hardened, you have made a casting. This is basically all there is to the process. Many kinds of castings are used in industry: investment casting (the kind used by dentists to make a gold filling for your tooth), shell molding, die casting, and sand casting. Sand casting is commonly done in the school to produce interesting projects. Fig. 44-1. This process is explained in this unit.

SAND CASTING

The engine block of an automobile is one product made by this method of casting. Wooden or plastic patterns of the object to be cast are first made. You may also use plastic, ceramic, or metal objects purchased in stores as patterns. Simple one-piece patterns can be made of pine, then waxed so that the sand doesn't stick to them. The sides should be tapered slightly to make the pattern easier to remove. (The taper is called *draft*.) More complex objects are made of two-piece or split patterns. Patterns can also be made of styrofoam plastic. These can be left in the sand, as the molten metal will melt them away. After the casting hardens, the gate, riser, and sprue must be machined off and the edges smoothed.

44-1. *These attractive projects were made by sand casting.*

Genevro Machine Company

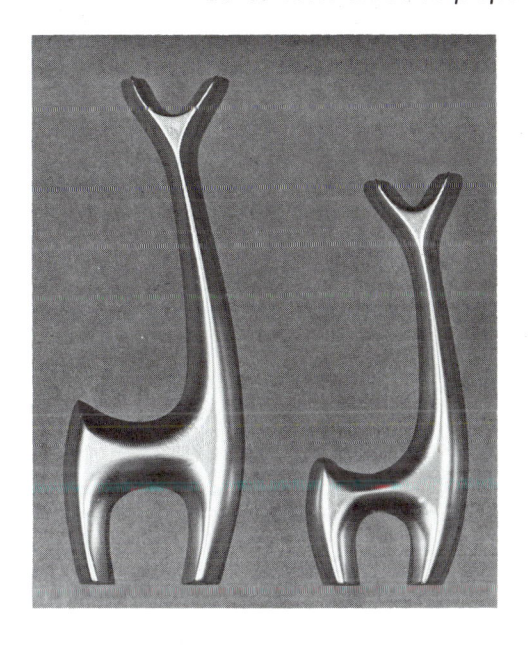

227

Part III: Manufacturing—Principles, Materials, and Processes

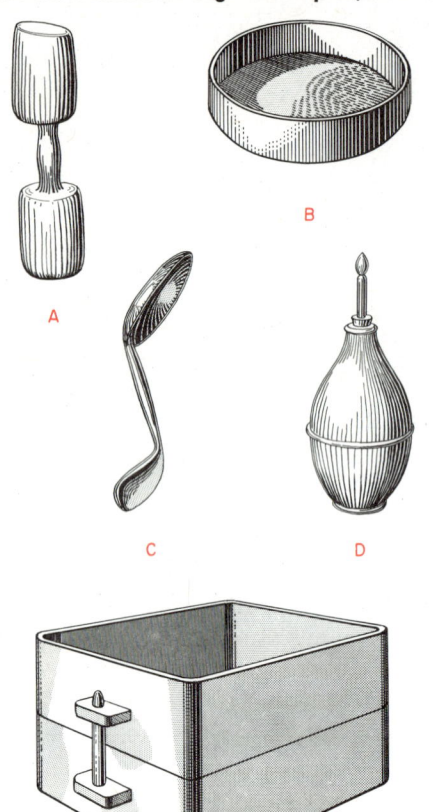

Some of the common casting tools are shown in Fig. 44-2.

Instructions and illustrations showing how to make a simple mold are shown in Figs. 44-3 through 44-11. Study these carefully to learn proper procedures.

The metal to be poured is melted in a foundry furnace. Fig. 44-12. When the metal is molten, it must be carefully poured into the cavity. Wear safety glasses or a mask and asbestos leggings, apron, and gloves. Fig. 44-13. Melting temperatures of some common metals are shown in Fig. 44-14.

After the mold has cooled, remove the casting and cut off the sprue, riser, and gates with a hacksaw. Grind and clean the cast piece as needed.

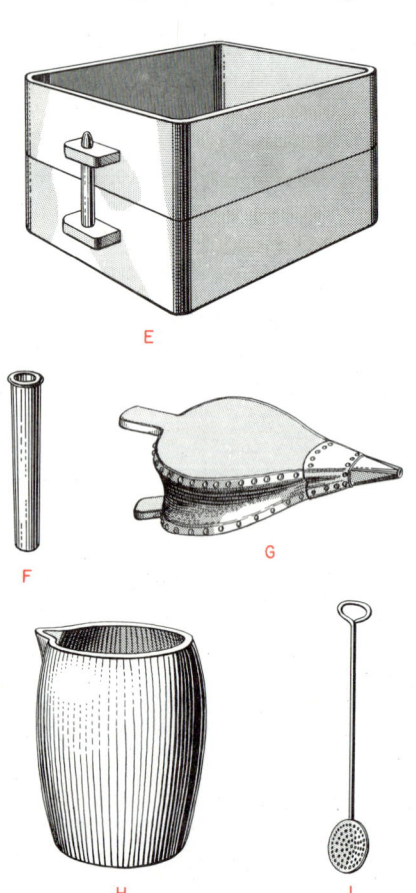

44-2. Common casting tools: (A) Rammer (B) Riddle (C) Spoon slick (D) Bulb (E) Flask (F) Sprue pin (G) Bellows (H) Crucible (I) Skimmer.

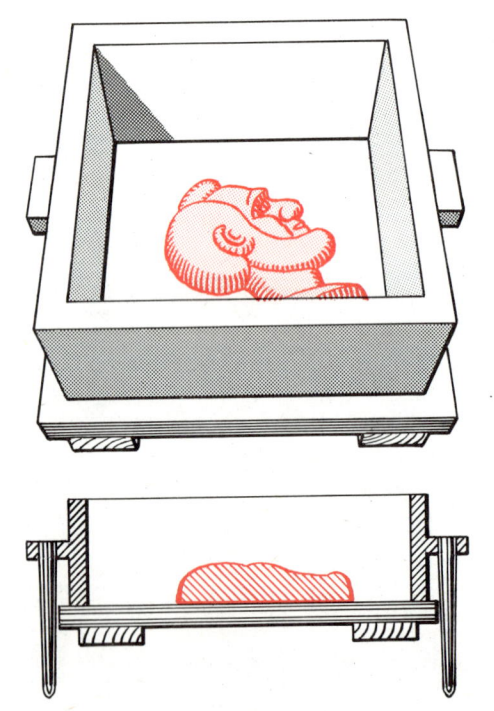

44-3. Place drag (bottom half of flask) on moldboard, pins down. Center pattern on moldboard. Dust pattern lightly with parting dust and blow off excess with bellows.

Unit 44: Casting Metal

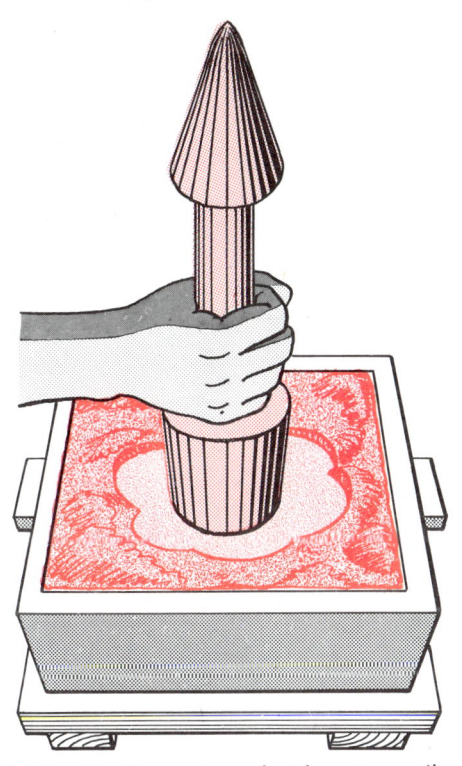

44-5. Strike off excess sand with steel bar.

44-4. Mix (temper) sand with water until a handful squeezed will break cleanly. Shovel sand into riddle and shake until pattern is covered. Fill drag with sand and ram firmly.

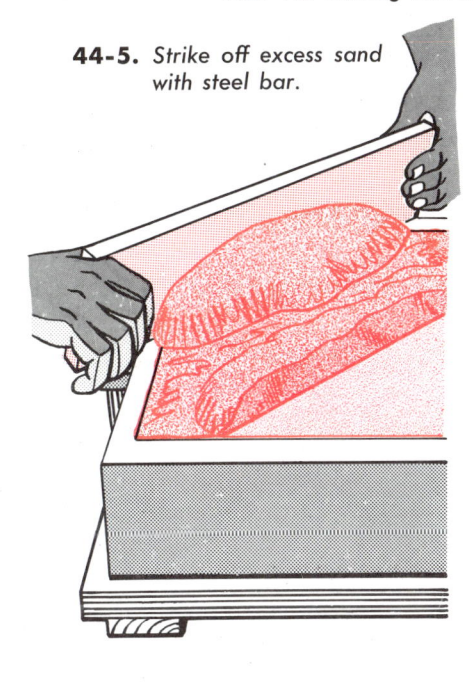

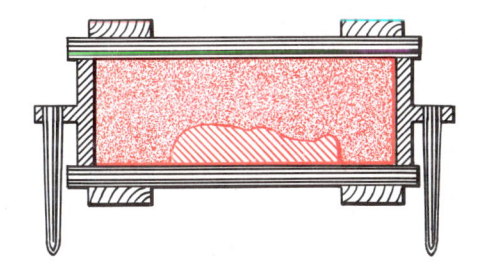

DRAG READY TO BE TURNED OVER

44-6. Place a second moldboard over drag, and turn top and bottom moldboards and the drag over.

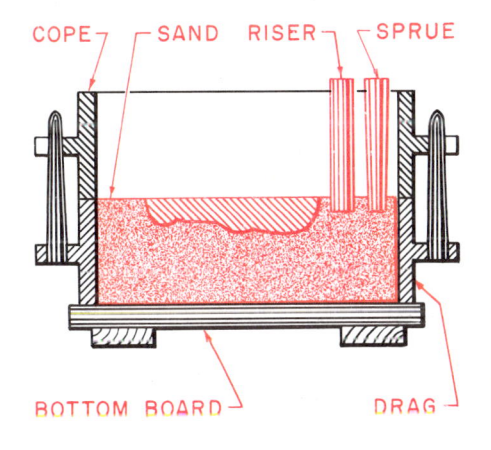

COPE — SAND — RISER — SPRUE

BOTTOM BOARD — DRAG

44-7. Remove board now on top and place cope (top half of flask) in position. Dust with parting dust. Place sprue and riser in position. Riddle sand over pattern, fill cope with sand, ram, and strike off excess. Vent pattern with piece of wire. Vent holes should not touch pattern. Remove sprue and riser pins.

229

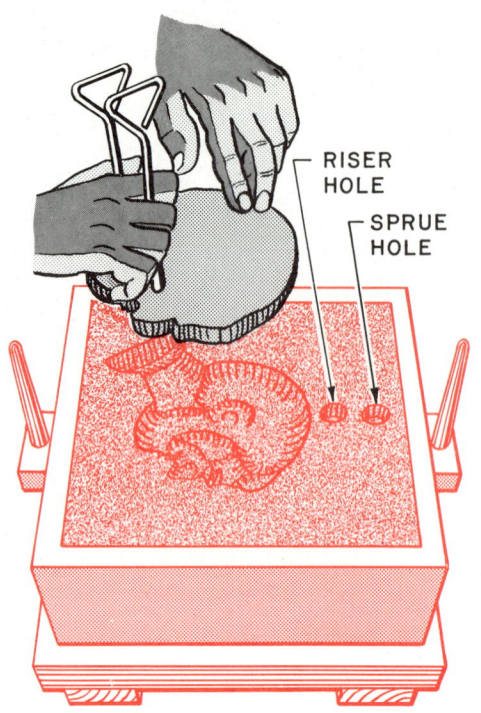

Part III: Manufacturing—Principles, Materials, and Processes

44-8. Carefully remove cope and set aside on edge. Use a wire lifter to remove pattern.

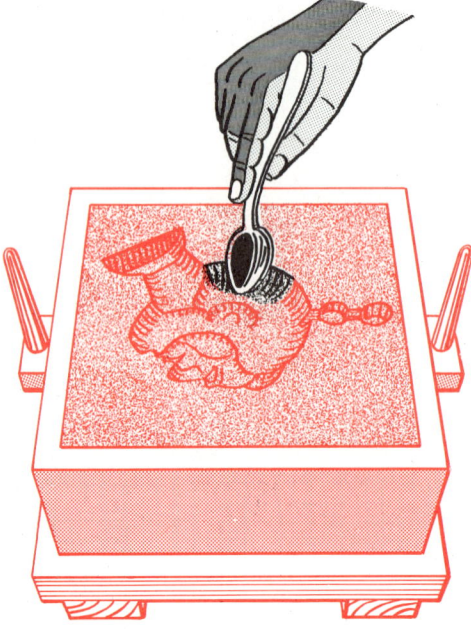

44-9. Cut gate with piece of sheet bent to a V shape. The molten metal will run down the sprue and through the gate into the cavity left by removing the pattern.

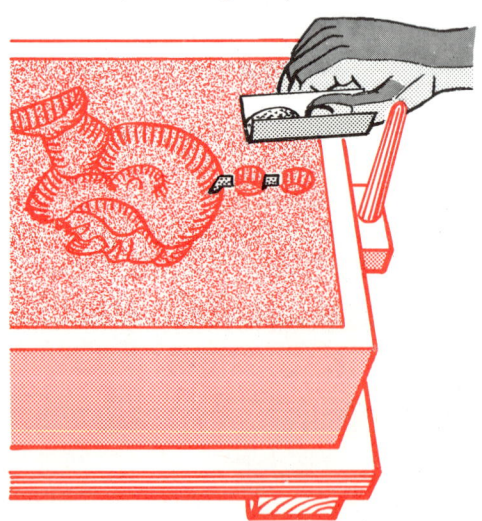

44-10. Make any repairs to mold with bulb sponge and spoon slick. Clean mold by blowing gently with bellows.

44-11. Drawing shows flask assembled. The mold is ready to pour.

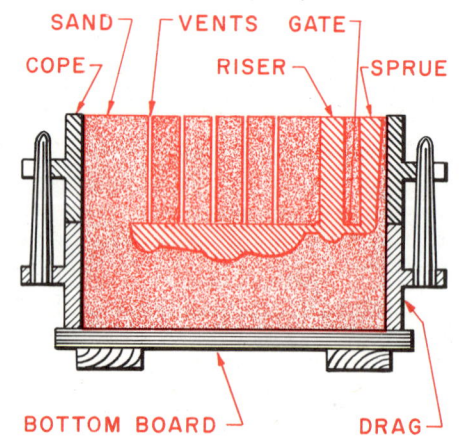

Unit 44: Casting Metal

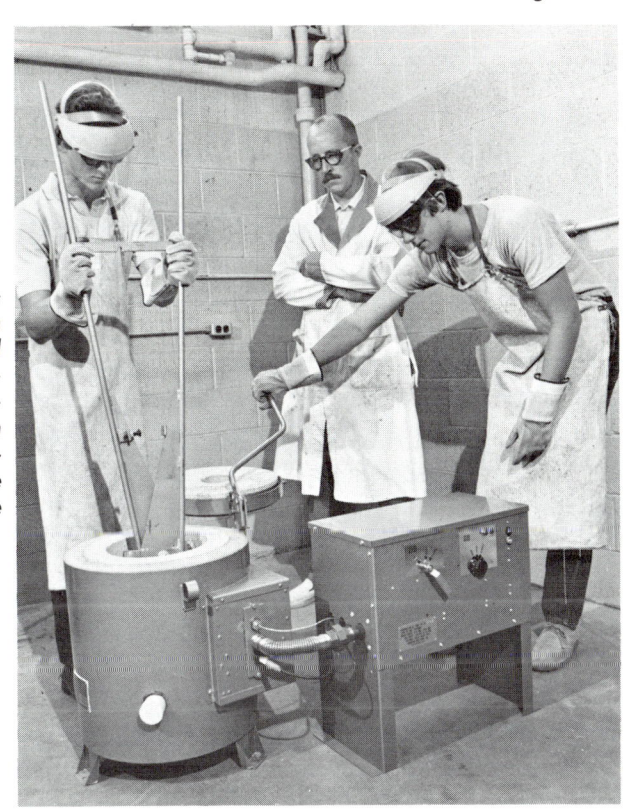

Johnson Gas Appliance Company
44-12. The crucible of molten metal must be carefully removed from the furnace with tongs. Before pouring, sprinkle some powdered casting flux into the molten metal. This will cause the impurities in the metal to collect on the surface. Remove these with the metal skimmer.

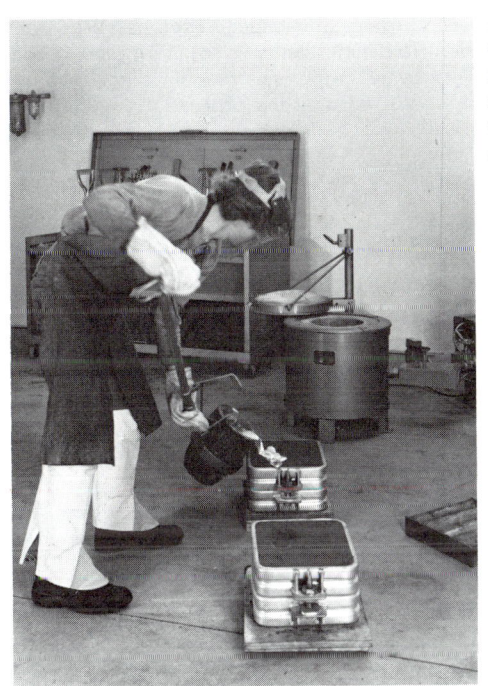

McEnglevan Heat Treating and Manufacturing Company
44-13. Pouring molten metal into a mold to make a casting. Pour the metal slowly to avoid spills. The metal will take the exact shape of the mold into which it is poured. This is one of the forming processes used in metalworking.

44-14. Melting temperatures of various metals, in Fahrenheit and Celsius.

Melting Temperatures of Common Metals

Metal	°F	°C
Lead	621	328
Aluminum	1218	659
Bronze	1675	914
Brass	1700	927
Copper	1981	1082
Cast Iron	2200	1204

231

UNIT 45

Forging and Heat-Treating Metal

In industrial forging, huge drop, steam, or trip hammers are dropped automatically on hot (or sometimes cold) workpieces to form tools, automobile crankshafts, airplane propellers, and many other metal parts. Fig. 45-1. Both open and closed dies are used in forging operations. Forging increases the strength of the metal by changing its grain structure. No metal is removed, and the pieces gain strength in the process. Fig. 45-2.

Forging in the shop is limited to the hot forming of screwdrivers, chisels, and other small items and to the hot bending of metal rings and other shapes. Drawing may also be done, as when you change the shape of a metal rod or decrease its diameter.

Although heat treating is not a forging process, the two are closely related because many tools must be strengthened by heat treatment after forging. For this reason both processes are included in this unit.

FORGING

The tools needed for shop forging are shown in Fig. 45-3. Forging should be

45-1. *Forging aluminum airplane propeller blades. The huge hammer (a) beats the blade (b) into a die shape. The forging diagram illustrates the process.*

U.S. Steel Corporation

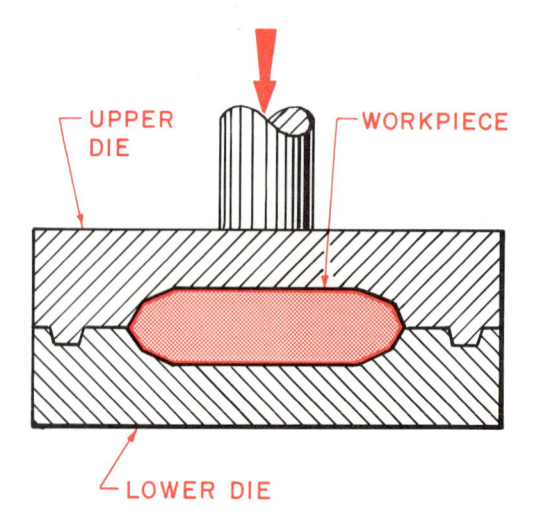

Unit 45: Forging and Heat-Treating Metal

45-2. *Flow lines in forged and machined parts. The forged part is stronger because the flow lines follow the contour of the part.*

done on the anvil and not on sheet metal stakes. The anvil hardy (a, Fig. 45-3) fits into the hardy hole on the anvil. It is used for cutting metal bars and rods. Tongs are used to hold the metal while forging.

Heavy hammers work the metal more easily than light ones. Remember to wear safety glasses, gloves, and an apron when forging metal.

When forging mild steel, heat it in the forge until it is cherry red. Fig. 45-4. Work it before it begins to cool. Fig. 45-5. Tool steel requires slightly less heat. In addition to drawing and bending, metal may also be "upset." This involves striking the ends of metal rods to increase their thickness (the opposite of drawing).

HEAT-TREATING

In the forging process, the metal becomes soft when you heat it and hard and brittle when you work it. In order to make chisels and other tools usable, they must be hardened and tempered. This is called

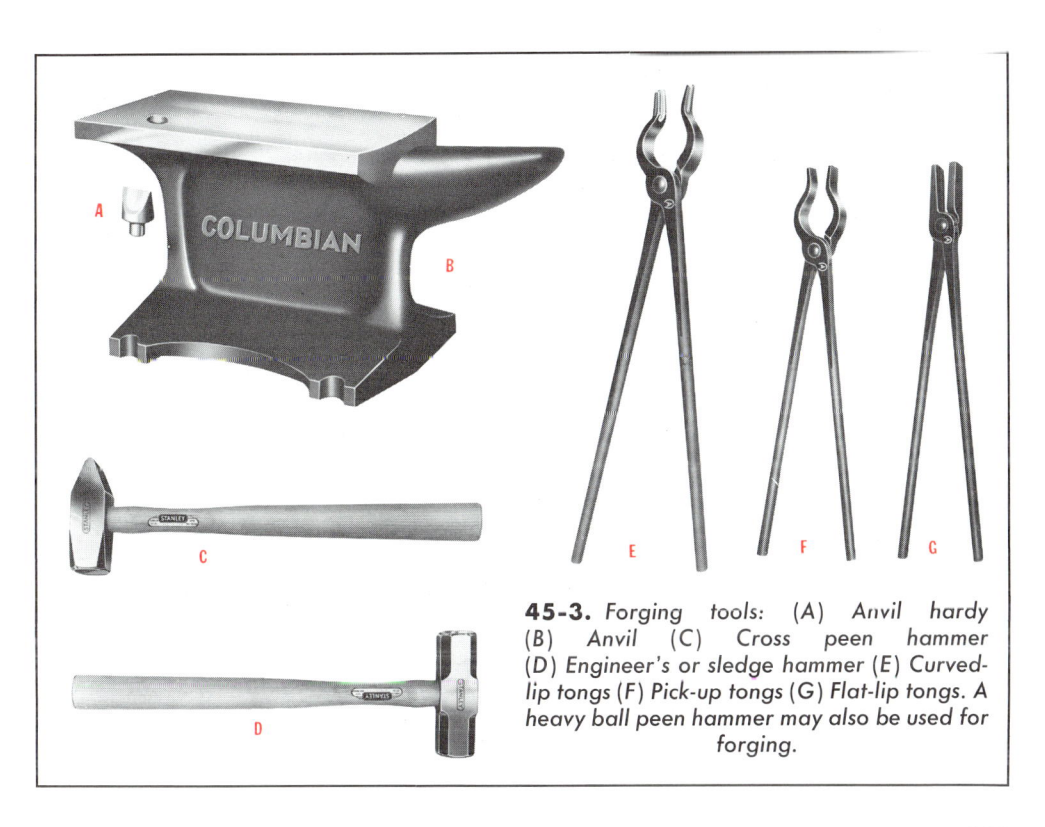

45-3. *Forging tools: (A) Anvil hardy (B) Anvil (C) Cross peen hammer (D) Engineer's or sledge hammer (E) Curved-lip tongs (F) Pick-up tongs (G) Flat-lip tongs. A heavy ball peen hammer may also be used for forging.*

233

Part III: Manufacturing—Principles, Materials, and Processes

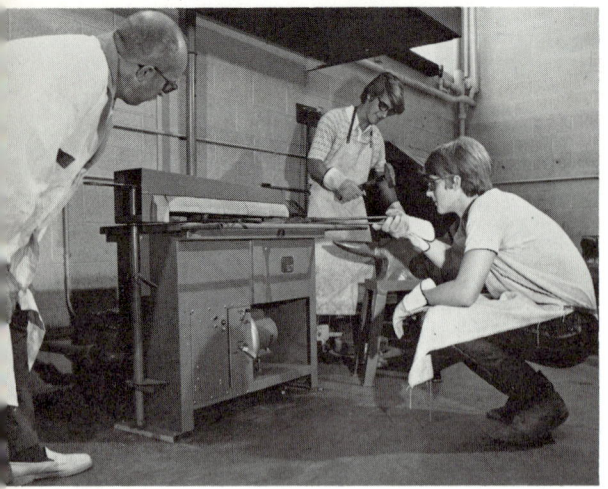

Johnson Gas Appliance Company

45-4. Using the forge. Caution should be used in lighting the gas forge. Ask your instructor to show you how to do this. Heated metal should be carefully moved to the anvil for working to avoid burning someone.

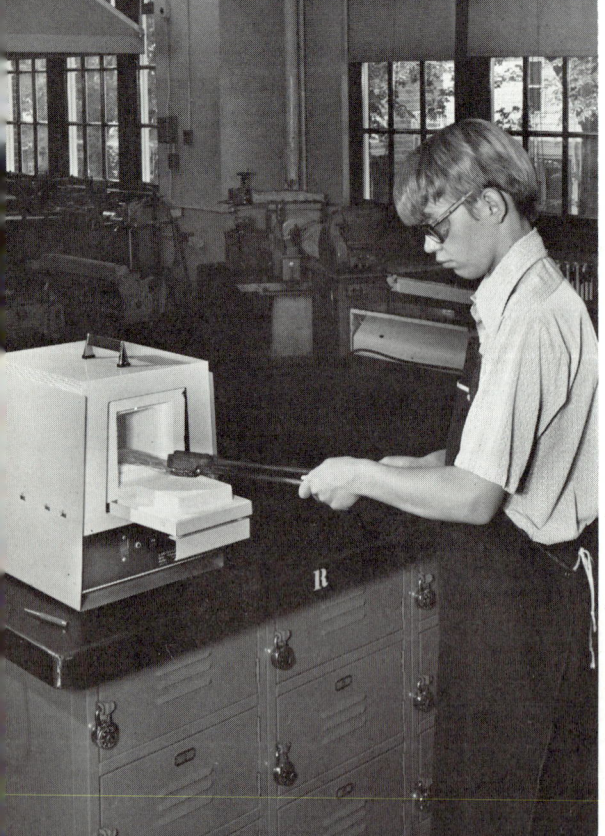

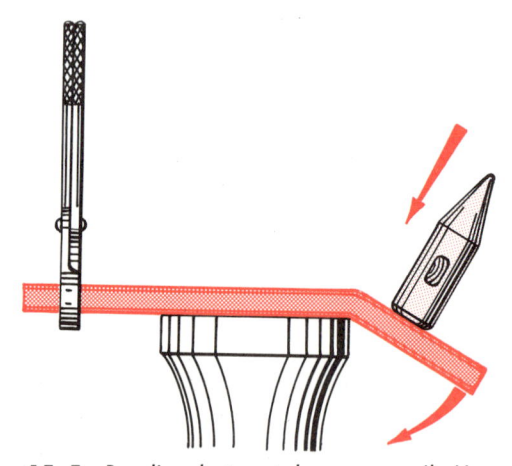

45-5. Bending hot metal on an anvil. Use tongs to hold the metal workpiece.

Lindberg Company

45-6. The heat-treating furnace is used for annealing and hardening steel. This model is used for small workpieces. Larger furnaces are also available.

234

Unit 45: Forging and Heat-Treating Metal

heat-treating, and it is usually done in a heat-treating furnace. Fig. 45-6. (It can also be done in a forge, but less conveniently.) Here, for example, are the steps in heat-treating a screwdriver made of tool steel.

First, *anneal* the workpiece by heating until cherry red, then cooling in air. This process, called *normalizing,* softens the metal and relieves the strains of forging.

Fig. 45-7. File smooth and polish with abrasive cloth and oil.

Next, *harden* by reheating about 3/4" of the screwdriver tip until it is cherry red. This is called the critical temperature. Plunge the metal quickly into water, moving it with a circular motion. Test its hardness with a file. If the file nicks the screwdriver, anneal and harden again.

Finally, *temper* the metal by polishing the tip with abrasive cloth and applying heat about 1" above the tip. When the temper color (purple in this case) reaches the tip, plunge the tool into water. Temper colors for other tools are shown in Fig. 45-8. Tempering reduces the brittleness of the piece.

Mild steel is heat-treated by a process called *case hardening.* This is done by adding a special carbon hardening powder to the surface of a metal workpiece, and then hardening this outer case. To case harden metal, heat the workpiece to a bright red. Remove any scale with a wire brush. Dip, roll, or sprinkle the powder on the workpiece. The powder will melt and adhere to the surface, forming a shell around the work. Reheat to bright red, holding at this temperature for a few minutes and quench in clean, cold water. This will give the workpiece a completely hard outer surface, or case.

Steel Temperature Chart

Color	Temperature °F	Temperature °C
White	2200	1205
Lemon	1825	997
Orange	1725	940
Bright red	1650	874
Cherry red	1325	718
Dark red	1175	635
Faint red	900	482
Pale blue	590	310

45-7. *The temperature of steel as it is heated can be accurately estimated by observing its color.*

45-8. *Temper colors and temperatures for common shop tools.*

Tempering Chart

Tools	Color	Temperature °F	Temperature °C
Scribers	Pale yellow	430–450	220–230
Center punches	Full yellow	470	243
Cold chisels	Brown	490–510	255–265
Screwdrivers	Purple	530	275

UNIT 46

Pressing Metal

Pressing is a process whereby sheet metals are forced to take the shape of dies (forms) by hand or machine methods. Huge machines form automobile hoods by pressing the metal between dies. Fig. 46-1. Smaller pieces such as kitchen utensils are also formed this way. Fig. 46-2.

Many kinds of pressing operations are done in the school shop. The most common are sinking, raising, tooling, stamping, chasing, and spinning. These forming methods are a part of art metalwork.

SINKING

Sinking, or low raising, is a method of forming shallow dishes or trays by beating down sheet metal into a wooden form. Fig. 46-3 shows typical projects made by sinking. Sinking is done by nailing a piece of sheet copper, brass, or aluminum to a wooden form which has been hollowed out to the desired shape of the dish. Metal forms may also be used. Fig. 46-4. Small bowls are made from 24- or 22-gauge metal. Use 20 or 18 gauge for large trays, pans, etc. A form for sinking can be made by turning on a wood lathe or by cutting a hole in a piece of $3/4''$ plywood and nailing this to a base board.

The metal is beaten down by striking it with a wooden forming hammer. Fig. 46-5. Work the metal down near the edges of the form first. Then move to the

46-1a. *This huge press is forming automobile hoods from metal sheets.*

General Motors Corporation

Unit 46: Pressing Metal

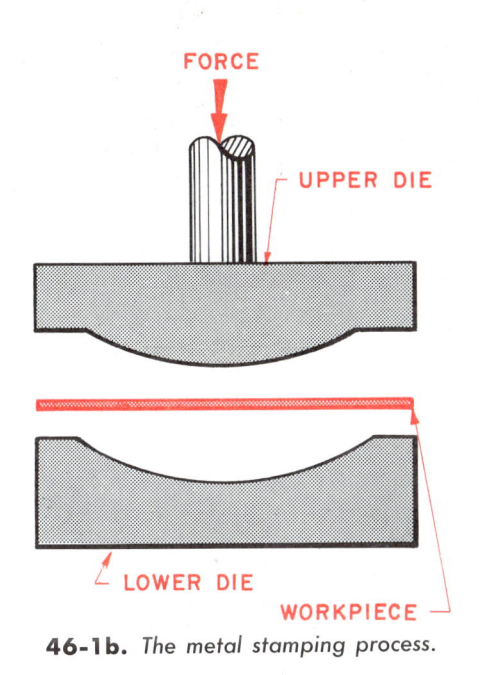

46-1b. The metal stamping process.

46-2. This metal dish and the cap on the salt shaker were industrially produced by pressing. This kind of pressing is called "deep drawing" because it stretches the metal considerably.

46-3. Shallow nut dishes made by sinking.

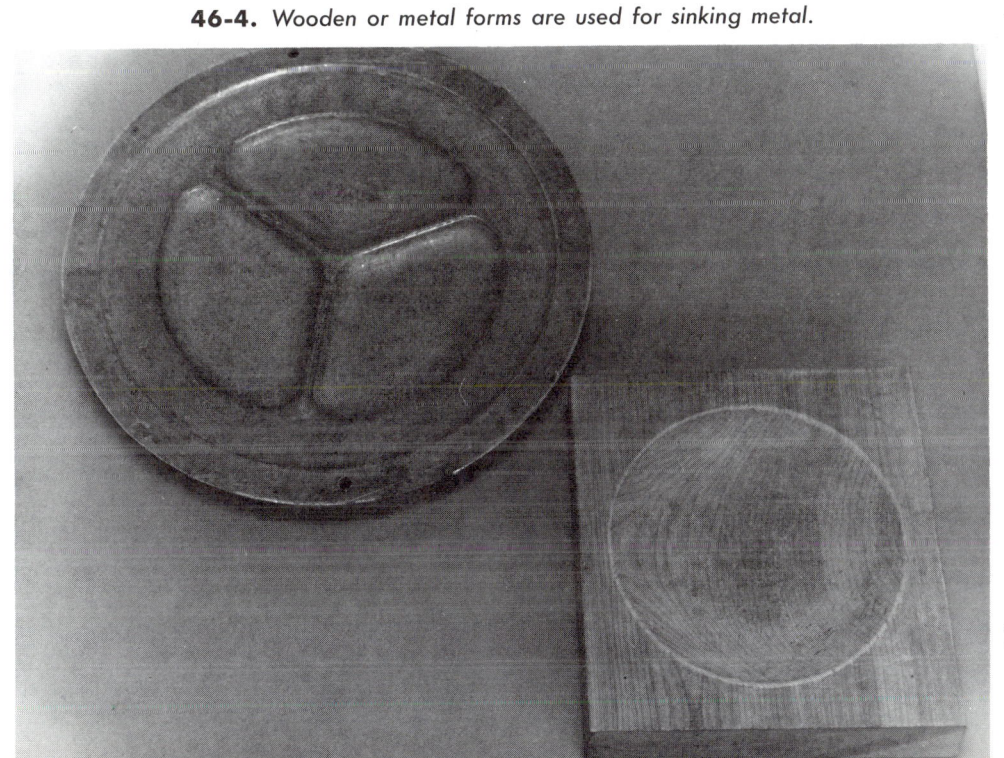

46-4. Wooden or metal forms are used for sinking metal.

237

Part III: Manufacturing—Principles, Materials, and Processes

center and work back toward the edges. Fig. 46-6. After sinking, the piece is removed and trimmed with tin snips. Any dents or imperfections can be removed by planishing. (Planishing is a way of finishing metal by hammering it lightly. See Unit 57 for details.)

When metal is pounded or bent, it *work hardens.* That is, it becomes stiff and brittle. It must be softened before you can continue to work it. To soften the metal you must *anneal* it. To anneal copper, brass, or nickel-silver, heat it to a faint red color in a soldering furnace or use a torch. Avoid overheating. Allow the metal to cool in air. To anneal aluminum, rub the surface with cutting oil and heat until smoke appears. Cool the metal in air.

When copper is heated, it becomes tarnished and scaly. It can be cleaned by pickling in a mild acid. A pickling solution for copper is made by pouring one cup of hydrochloric acid into four cups of water. The solution must be mixed in a ceramic or plastic container. CAUTION: Always pour the *acid* into the *water.* Pouring water into acid causes dangerous splattering.

Copper can be annealed and pickled at the same time. To do this, heat the copper to a faint red color, remove from heat, and plunge it into the pickling solution. Rinse in cold water and wipe dry.

RAISING

Raising is a method of forming deeper dishes. Fig. 46-7. A piece of 20- or 18-gauge brass or copper is cut to a desired shape, then beaten into a small round depression in a wooden stake. A sandbag can also be used. The metal workpiece, Fig. 46-8, is moved back and forth as the metal is beaten. Metal raising hammers

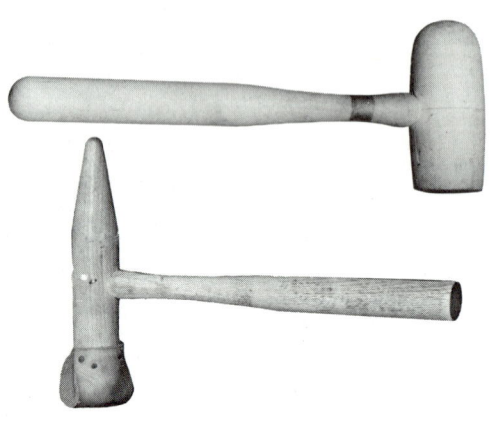

46-5. *Wooden forming hammers are generally used for sinking, although metal hammers may also be used. The hammers should be smooth and free of dents. Sand them if necessary. They may also be capped with leather to prevent marring the metal. The blunt end is used for truing the bottoms of the trays or flattening their edges.*

46-6. *Sinking is done by beating metal down into a form. If the metal becomes stiff (work hardened), it must be softened by annealing.*

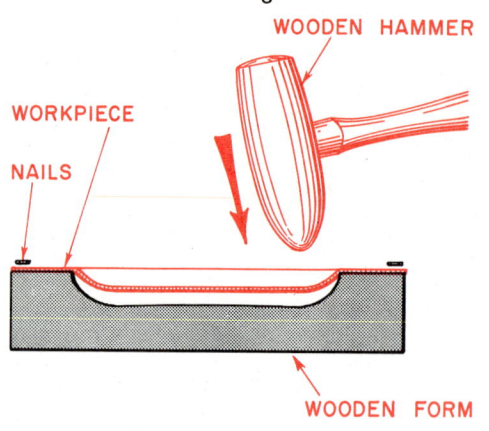

46-7. *Deeper bowls such as these are made by raising. Bowls and deep dishes of many shapes can be formed by using metal raising hammers. Wooden hammers are also used for shallow forms.*

238

Unit 46: Pressing Metal

are used for this. Fig. 46-9. As in sinking, planish to remove imperfections and anneal if the metal becomes stiff.

TOOLING

In metal tooling (or embossing), a design or decoration is raised on a piece of thin metal sheet (about 36 gauge). Fig. 46-10 shows a tooled project and the simple tools used in making it. The steps involved in metal tooling are shown in Figs. 46-11 to 46-15. The finished pieces can be colored and highlighted by dipping in liver of sulfur (see Unit 58) and

46-8. *Metal raising differs from sinking in that the metal is moved by hand while it is being hammered. (The broken-out section is to help you see the inside of the bowl.)*

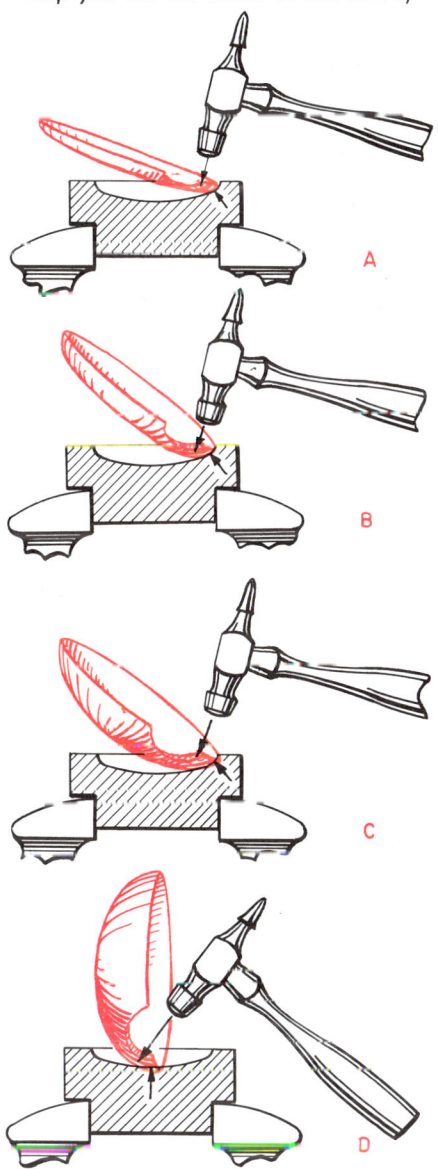

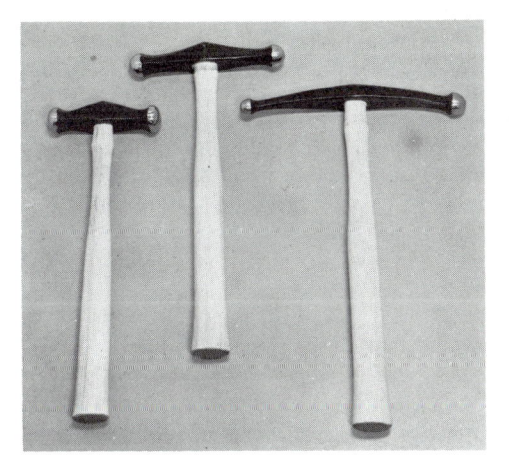

46-9. *Metal raising hammers come in many shapes and sizes.*

46-10. *A tooled-metal wall plaque and the tools used to make it: (A) Hardwood smoothing tool (B) Modeler (C) Hardwood tracing tool.*

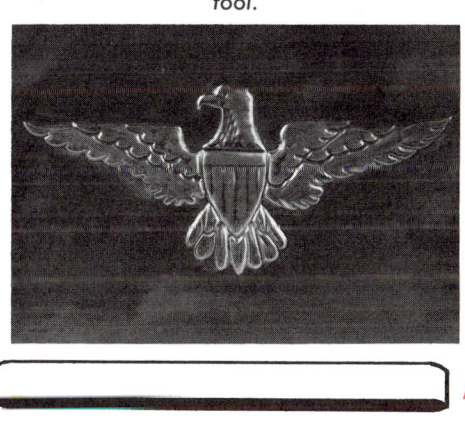

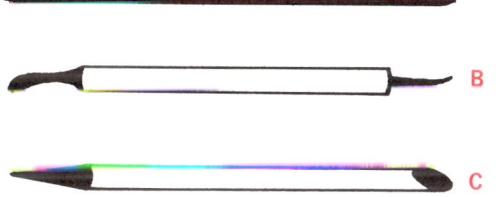

239

Part III: Manufacturing—Principles, Materials, and Processes

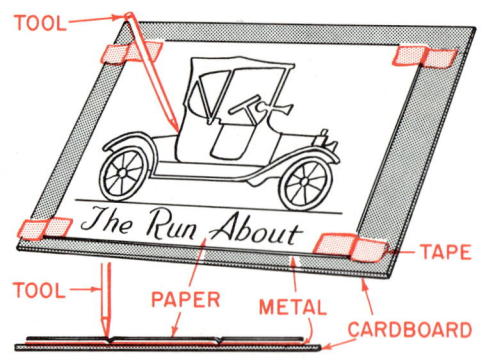

46-11. Transferring the design. Fasten the paper to the metal with masking tape. Place the metal on a piece of cardboard. With the tracing tool, press the lines of the design firmly, thus transferring the design to the metal.

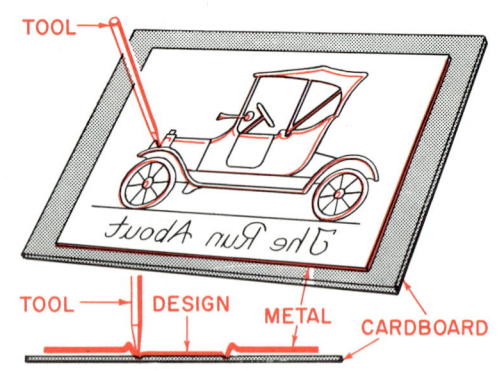

46-13. Interlining the design. Turn the metal over and place it on the cardboard. Use the modeler to interline the design. Be careful to line just inside the original design lines, not on them.

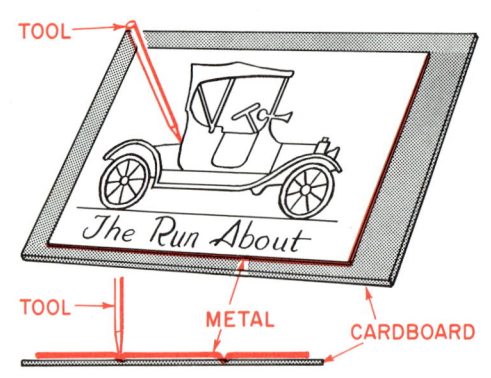

46-12. Deepening the design. Check the back of the metal before removing the design to be sure all lines have been traced. Remove the paper and deepen the traced lines by going over them directly on the metal. Use the tracing tool or modeler.

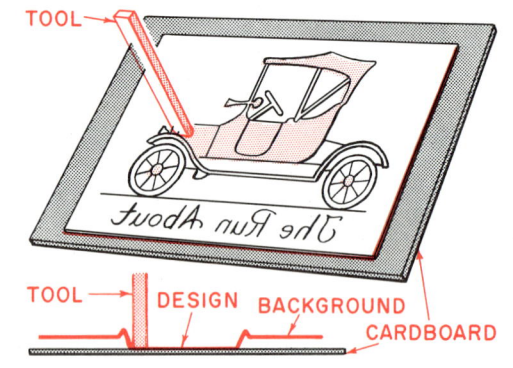

46-14. Raising the design. Using the flat end of the smoothing tool, push the design out from the back. Raising the design in this manner is often called "embossing."

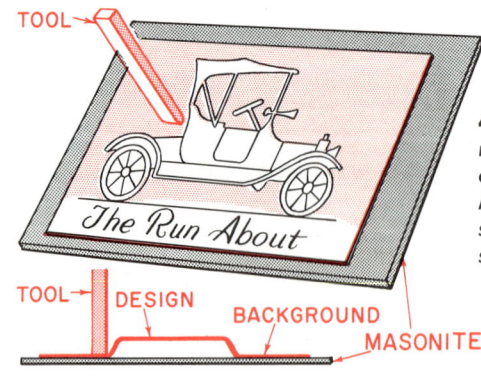

46-15. Flattening the background. Turn the metal so that the front side is up and place it on a smooth hard surface such as glass or Masonite. Using the smoothing tool, carefully smooth down the background. Use even pressure and be careful not to scratch the surface.

Unit 46: Pressing Metal

rubbing with steel wool. Brush or spray on a flat lacquer finish.

The finished tooled workpieces can be mounted on a piece of wood or heavy cardboard and framed. The raised back of the workpieces should be filled with clay, plaster, or some other material to prevent denting the formed piece.

STAMPING

The Indians of the American Southwest make decorative patterns in metal with steel stamping tools, repeating or alternating their markings in rows. Fig. 46-16. The designs depend upon the shapes of the tools and the skill of the craftsman.

Workpieces are usually of 16-gauge sheet copper. Anneal the copper and flatten it with a rawhide mallet on a hardwood block before stamping.

Design a pattern by drawing on a strip of cardboard. Then transfer to the copper by carbon paper tracing. Place the copper strip on a metal plate. Hold the tool perpendicular to the work and give it a sharp blow with a ball peen hammer. The impression should be about $\frac{1}{32}$" deep.

When the stamping is complete, bend to shape (as for a bracelet) over a forming stake. With a rawhide mallet, begin from the ends and work toward the middle. If the bracelet is the closed type, fit the joint, bend it, and solder. Smooth the edges with a file and emery cloth and finish with spray lacquer.

Metal tapping is similar to stamping except that nails, ice picks, pricks, or center punches are used as tapping tools. Lighter, 30-gauge metals are more commonly used.

CHASING

Metal chasing (or repoussé) depresses the heavy-gauge metal on one side to raise it on the opposite side and form a design. It is done with blunt tools of various shapes, much like stamping, but it gives a much greater depth to the design. Fig. 46-17. The work is held in a bowl of pitch or on a block of lead to allow the metal to be pushed into it when chased. Chasing is similar to tooling or embossing

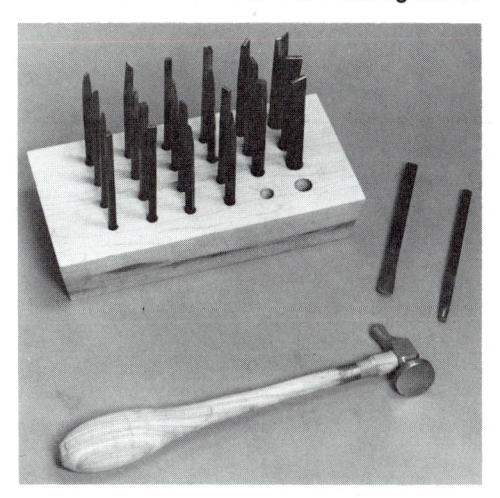

46-17a. Chasing tools and hammer.

46-16. Typical stamped designs.

SUN SYMBOL
HAPPINESS

SUNRAYS
CONSTANCY

HORSE
JOURNEY

THUNDERBIRD
SACRED BEARER OF
HAPPINESS

RAIN CLOUDS
GOOD PROSPECTS

CACTUS FLOWER
COURTSHIP

46-17b. Typical chasing (A) and matting (B) tool shapes.

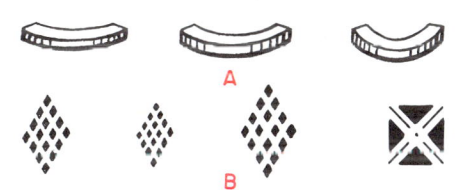

Part III: Manufacturing—Principles, Materials, and Processes

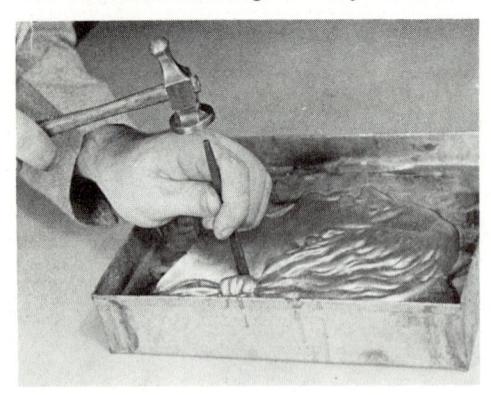

46-18. *Using a chasing tool.*

except that the 24-gauge copper used is so thick that metal tools are needed. Fig. 46-18.

A metal shape such as an ivy leaf or other design is a good beginning chasing project. The stem, veins, or other details are drawn on the copper. A pan at least 1½" deep is filled with chaser's pitch. The pitch surface is gently heated and the copper pressed into the surface. A thin coat of oil on the copper makes removal easier.

The tracing tool has a blunt chisel shape. It travels toward the worker with the top tilted back slightly. With a tracing tool and a chasing hammer, punch along the drawn lines of the design strongly enough to make the line protrude on the opposite surface as a guide.

Remove the work from the pitch, clean it with turpentine, then embed the "reverse" side in the pitch. Choose a tool that approximates the finished curve as nearly as possible. Model the stem, veins, etc., to the desired depth. Remove and clean. Fig. 46-19 shows the steps in forming a design by metal chasing.

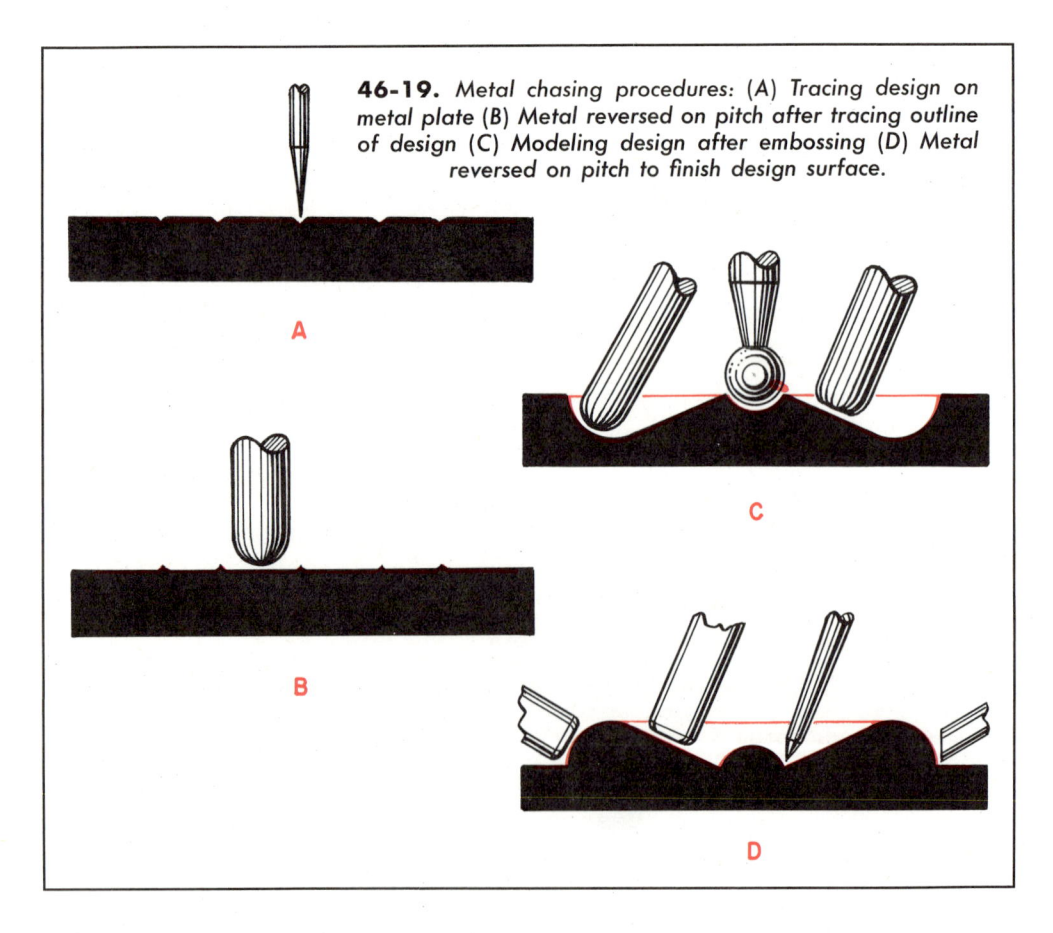

46-19. *Metal chasing procedures: (A) Tracing design on metal plate (B) Metal reversed on pitch after tracing outline of design (C) Modeling design after embossing (D) Metal reversed on pitch to finish design surface.*

Unit 46: Pressing Metal

To shape the leaf, select a polished raising hammer with the curve desired. Rest the work on a lead block. Pound to the desired shape. Anneal whenever necessary for easier working.

SPINNING

Spinning, one of the oldest of the metalworking arts, is still widely used. In this process a circular metal blank or shell is pressed against a chuck rotating at high speed on a lathe. Fig. 46-20. Pressure applied manually or mechanically with forming tools forms the blank to the shape of the chuck. Fig. 46-21.

Typical articles produced by spinning include cooking utensils, water pitchers, bowls, reflectors, kettle shells, ring molds, tapered pans, perforated cones, milk cans, and parts for aircraft and street lights.

Rockwell-Delta Company
46-20. Metal spinning.

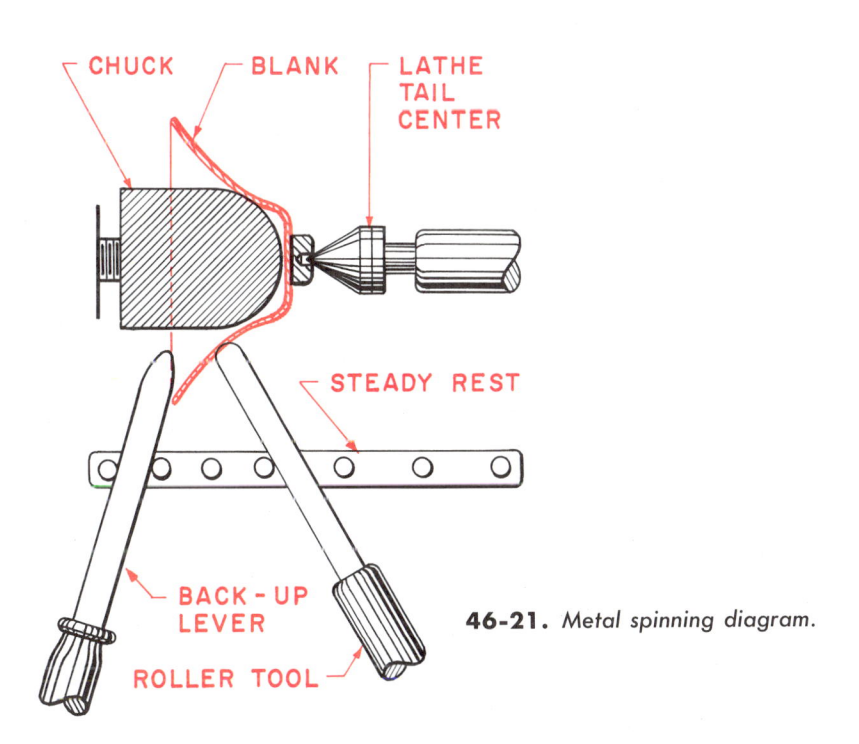

46-21. Metal spinning diagram.

243

UNIT 47

Drawing Metal

Metal products other than sheet and strip are produced by drawing or cold drawing. This is done by pulling a rod, tube, or bar through a hole in a die. The hole is smaller than the starting size of the workpiece. As it is pulled through the die, the workpiece is stretched out and reduced in cross section. Fig. 47-1.

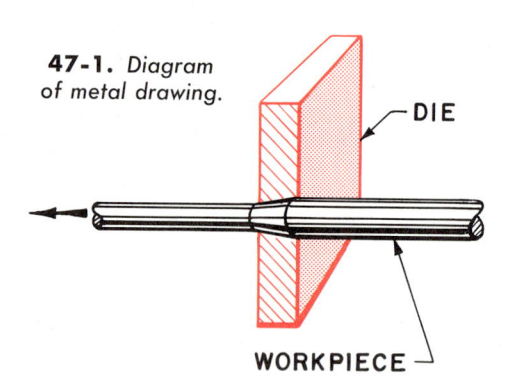

One end of the workpiece is usually pointed by grinding or some other method so that it can be inserted in the die to begin drawing. Grippers grasp the pointed end extending from the die and pull the rest of the piece through. A variety of shapes can be cold-drawn by using different dies. For example, drawn wire of exact diameters, which is used in the making of nails, wire mesh, fencing, and so forth, can be made by this process. Fig. 47-2.

Drawing is an industrial process not usually done in the shop, except sometimes in art metalwork and forging projects.

47-1. *Diagram of metal drawing.*

47-2. *Aluminum wire is being drawn to a smaller diameter through a die (A) on this machine.*
Aluminum Company of America

UNIT 48

Extruding Metal

In the basic metal extrusion process, a ram forces a heated billet (or block) of metal through a die to produce a rod or bar of a given shape. This is much like squeezing toothpaste out of a tube. Industry uses this process to form hundreds of different metal shapes to be used in manufacturing such items as storm and screen windows, frames of many kinds, and decorative moldings. Fig. 48-1 shows an industrial extrusion process for making hollow metal tube and pipe. A diagram explaining this process is shown in Fig. 48-2.

The process is called forward extrusion if the metal flows in the same direction that the punch travels. It is called backward extrusion if metal flow is opposite to the motion of the punch. Other directions of metal flow are possible, depending on the location of the hole in the container. To extrude parts that require metal flow in directions other than straight forward or backward, the container must be made in two pieces so that the workpiece can be removed. Many shapes can be made by these extruding processes. Fig. 48-3.

Very little metal extruding is done in the shop because of the heavy machinery required. Plastics and ceramics can also be formed by extrusion.

48-1. *Aluminum pipe (a) is being extruded from a die (b) on this hydraulic extrusion press.*

Reynolds Aluminum

48-2. *The aluminum pipe in Fig. 48-1 is produced by a hollow forward extrusion process.*

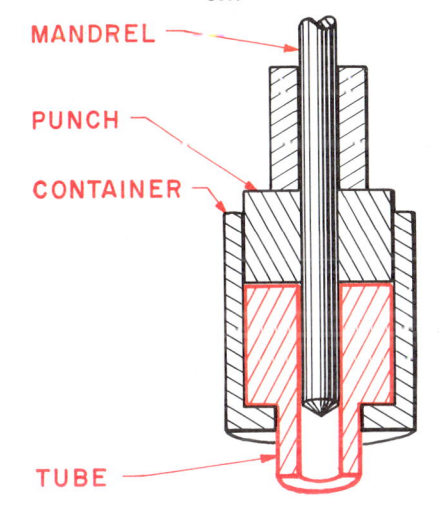

245

Part III: Manufacturing—Principles, Materials, and Processes

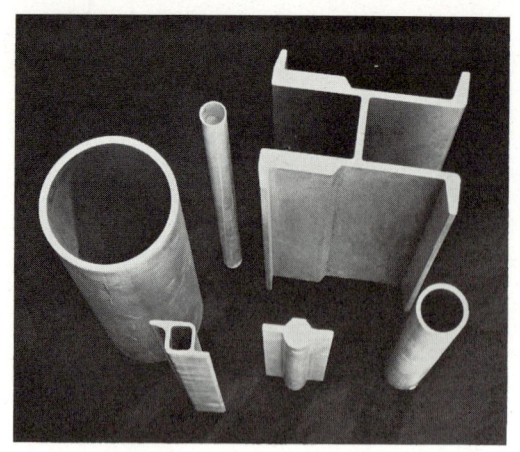

Reynolds Aluminum
48-3. Many complex shapes can be formed by the extrusion process.

UNIT 49

Rolling Metal

Rolling is the process of passing slabs of metal, up to 26" thick, between huge cylinders which reduce them to heavy metal plates or to thin sheets and foils. Fig. 49-1.

49-1. Diagram for rolling metal. Both hot- and cold-rolling operations are used by industry.

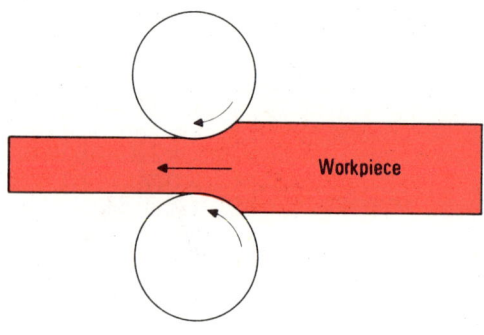

Industry uses both hot and cold metal rolling operations. Hot rolling is mainly a roughing operation. Its chief use is to shape and refine the large cast ingots that come from the first metal production processes. Fig. 49-2. The rolling operation puts the metal in a form that can be further changed by other methods. With grooves in the rolls, rolling mills can produce a variety of shapes. Some of the more common ones are sheet, round rods, flat bars, and angles. Other shapes produced by hot rolling are half-rounds, channels, T-bars, and I-bars. Fig. 49-3.

Cold rolling, however, is usually used to produce thin, flat products such as sheet and strip. Cold-rolling mills usually have smaller rolls than hot-rolling mills. Cold rolling requires much more force, and smaller rolls are required to concen-

Unit 49: Rolling Metal

Reynolds Aluminum
49-2. This heated aluminum ingot is being removed from the soaking pit. It will be taken to the hot-rolling machine.

Aluminum Company of America
49-3. Hot-rolling aluminum. Often weighing over 10 tons, the huge cast blocks are rolled by both hot and high speed cold finishing mills into coils of sheet miles long and only 0.008 to 0.016 inches thick.

trate the force over a smaller area. These rolls also enable thinner material to be rolled. Cold rolling is seldom used to produce finished products. Cold-rolled sheet and strip are made into finished articles by other methods.

Rolling is seldom done in the school shop. However, it is an important process in industry.

247

UNIT 50

Metal Fastening Principles

Fastening methods most commonly used by the metalworker include riveting, soldering, and welding. The decision to use mechanical, adhesive, or cohesive fastening methods depends upon what is needed for the product. For example, the wheels on an automobile are fastened to the drums by screwing nuts onto threaded studs. If they were riveted on or welded, changing a tire would be almost impossible. What is needed for the wheels is a safe, efficient, semipermanent method of fastening them to the drums. The nuts are safe because they can be drawn tight to hold the wheel in place. They are efficient because they make wheel changing an easy task; and they are semipermanent because they can be screwed on and removed, over and over again. By contrast, the heavy beams on bridges need to be permanently fastened. Therefore they are riveted or welded together. Fig. 50-1.

There are many ways of fastening things together, as shown in the chart, Fig. 50-2. Study these and become familiar with them, so that the following units on fastening methods will mean more to you. You will use many of them in your shopwork. Fig. 50-3.

50-1. *Arc welding is an important industrial fastening process. This craftsman is welding sections of pipe for a fuel pipeline.*

The Lincoln Electric Company

Unit 50: Metal Fastening Principles

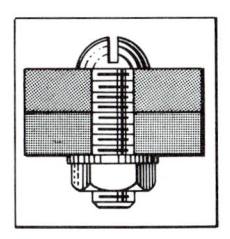

Fastening

Fastening is the process of joining materials together permanently or semipermanently.

KIND OF FASTENING	DEFINITION	EXAMPLES
Mechanical	Permanent or semipermanent fastening with special locking devices.	Threaded fasteners, rivets, sheet metal joints.
Adhesive	Permanent fastening by bonding like or unlike materials together with molten metal or cements.	Soldering, brazing, contact cementing, epoxy cementing.
Cohesive	Permanent fastening by fusing like materials together with molten metal or pressure.	Oxyacetylene welding, arc welding, spot welding.

50-2. This chart illustrates the different kinds of fastening that will be explained in the following units.

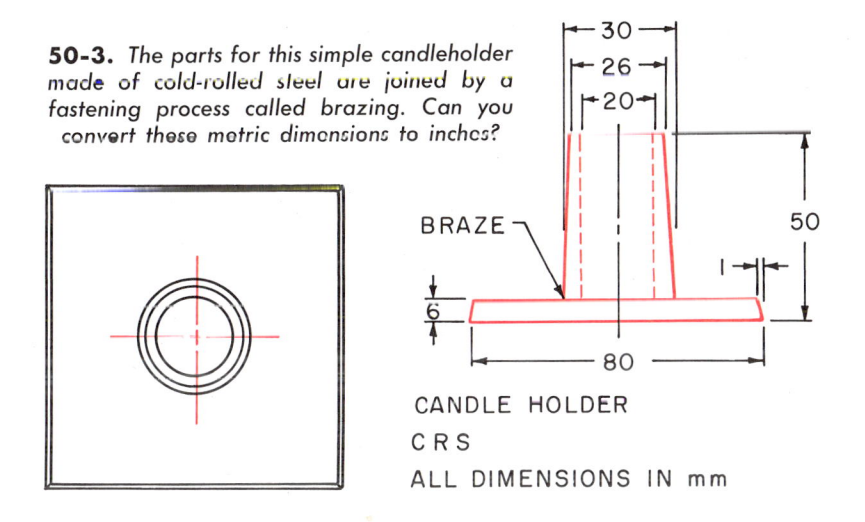

50-3. The parts for this simple candleholder made of cold-rolled steel are joined by a fastening process called brazing. Can you convert these metric dimensions to inches?

CANDLE HOLDER
CRS
ALL DIMENSIONS IN mm

UNIT 51

Mechanical Fastening of Metal

Mechanical fasteners are used to join parts together, either permanently or semipermanently. License plates are fastened to your family car with nuts and machine screws so that they can be removed and replaced each year. In mechanical fastening, threaded fasteners are usually used for semipermanent fastening. Rivets and sheet metal joints are generally of a permanent type so that fastened parts cannot be easily separated.

THREADED FASTENERS

Many kinds of threaded fasteners are used in metalworking. As stated before, they allow machines and appliances to be taken apart and put back together again. Common fasteners are shown in Fig. 51-1. As you can see, they have several head shapes. Hexagon, square, round, oval, and flat are the most common. Fig. 51-2.

Machine bolts and nuts have diameters up to 1" and lengths up to 30". They are often used to fasten machine parts together. They have either square or hexagon heads and are tightened with wrenches.

Machine screws and nuts are used much the same way as machine bolts, but

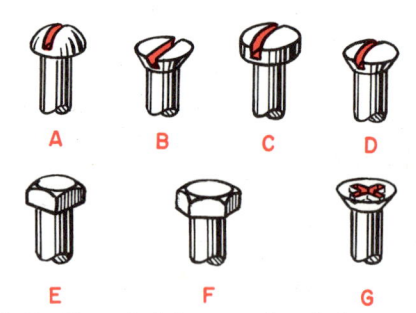

51-2. Threaded fastener head shapes: (A) Round (B) Flat (C) Fillister (D) Oval (E) Square (F) Hexagon (G) Phillips. All screwdriver-shape heads are either standard or Phillips.

51-1. Threaded fasteners: (A) Hexagon-head machine bolt and nut (B) Phillips-head machine screw and nut (C) Hexagon-head cap screw (D) Stud (E) Lock washer (F) Plain flat washer (G) Cone-point socket set screw (H) Flathead self-tapping screw.

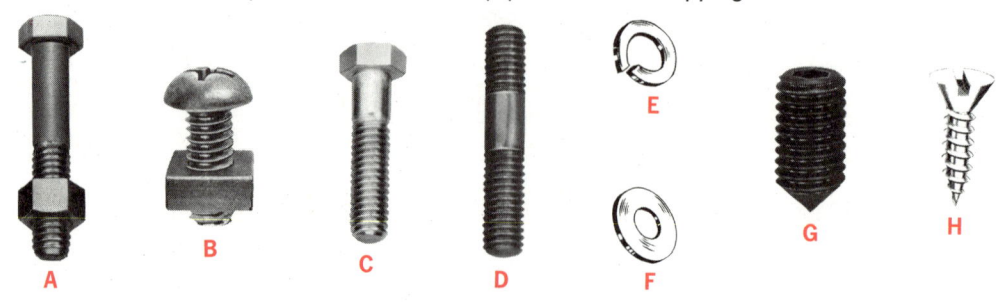

Unit 51: Mechanical Fastening of Metal

generally for lighter work. They come in both fractional and wire gauge diameters up to about ½" and in assorted lengths. They commonly have flat or round heads, worked with standard or Phillips screwdrivers. Machine screws are also used in tapped holes for the assembly of metal parts.

Cap screws are similar to machine bolts except that they are not used with nuts. They hold parts of machinery together by passing through an unthreaded hole in one piece and into a threaded hole in the second piece. The threaded hole acts as the nut. Cap screws are made in lengths up to 6" and diameters up to 1".

Studs are headless fasteners. Their use on automobile wheel drums, mentioned in the previous unit, is typical of the ways they are used. They come in various lengths.

Set screws are available with various head and point styles. Cone, oval, and flat points are most common. These screws are generally used for such purposes as holding pulleys on shafts.

Self-tapping screws cut their own threads in sheet metal pieces to bind them together. Many head, point, and thread styles are available.

Washers are used to protect metal surfaces under the heads of fasteners, or to lock the fasteners in place.

Some common tools used to hold and turn threaded fasteners are shown in Fig. 51-3. Adjustable, open-end, and box wrenches come in various sizes and are used to hold and turn nuts and bolts. Pipe wrenches are used on pipe and rod. Screwdrivers are designed for turning screw heads. DO NOT use them as pry bars or chisels. Pliers are also useful tools in the shop and around the home. There are many types and sizes of pliers. Some examples are shown in Fig. 51-4.

Types of Threads

Industry makes threaded fasteners by cutting or rolling threads on them with automatic machines. In the shop, a die is used to cut threads on a rod (external threads) and a tap is used to thread a hole

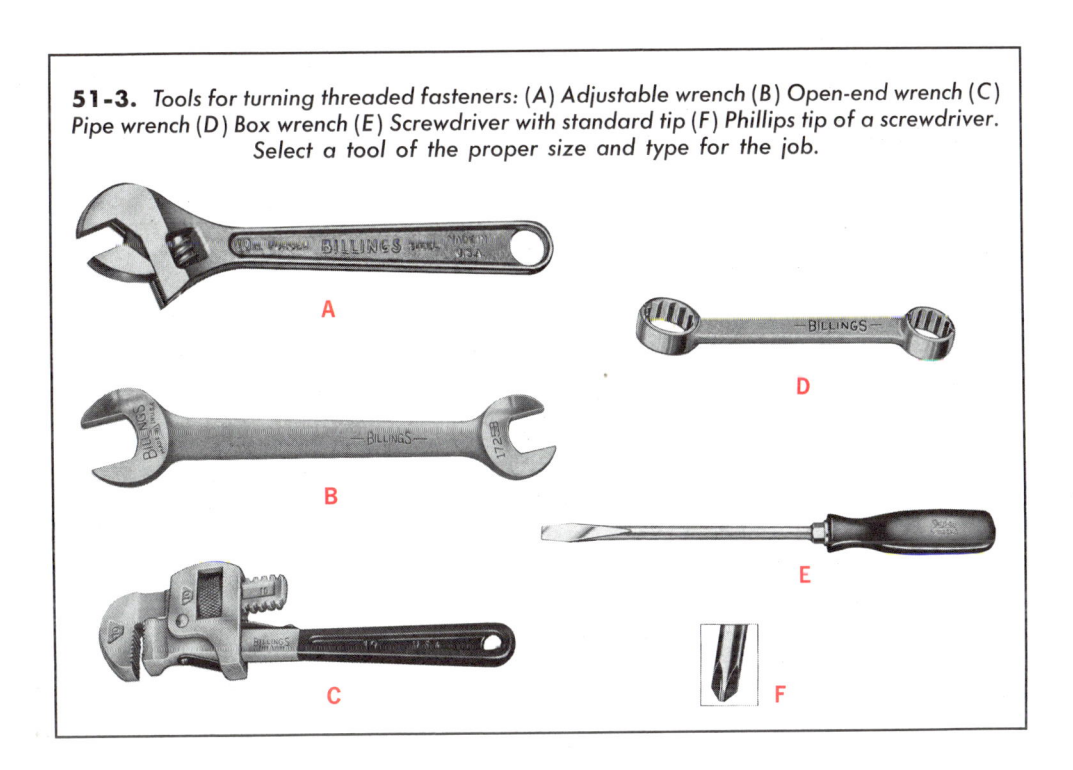

51-3. Tools for turning threaded fasteners: (A) Adjustable wrench (B) Open-end wrench (C) Pipe wrench (D) Box wrench (E) Screwdriver with standard tip (F) Phillips tip of a screwdriver. Select a tool of the proper size and type for the job.

251

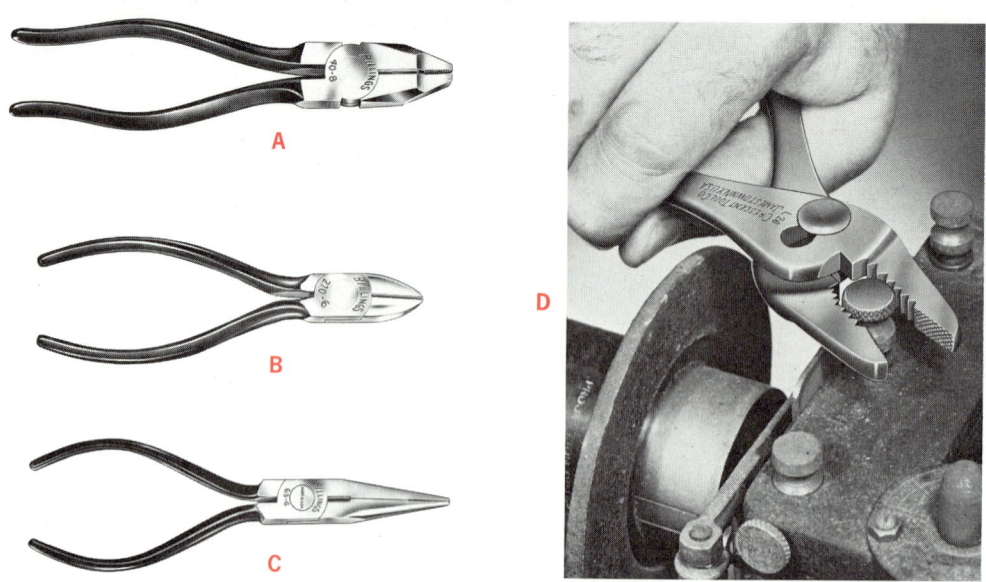

Part III: Manufacturing—Principles, Materials, and Processes

51-4. Pliers are used for cutting, bending, and twisting. They are also used for holding and tightening mechanical fasteners. Types of pliers: (A) Side cutting (B) Diagonal cutting (C) Long-nose (D) Slip-joint.

Billings and Crescent Tools

51-5. Tools for cutting threads: (A) Tap wrench (B) Bottoming tap (C) Taper tap (D) Plug tap (E) Die (F) Die stock. Remember to use a cutting oil when cutting threads. This makes threading easier and prevents tap and die breakage.

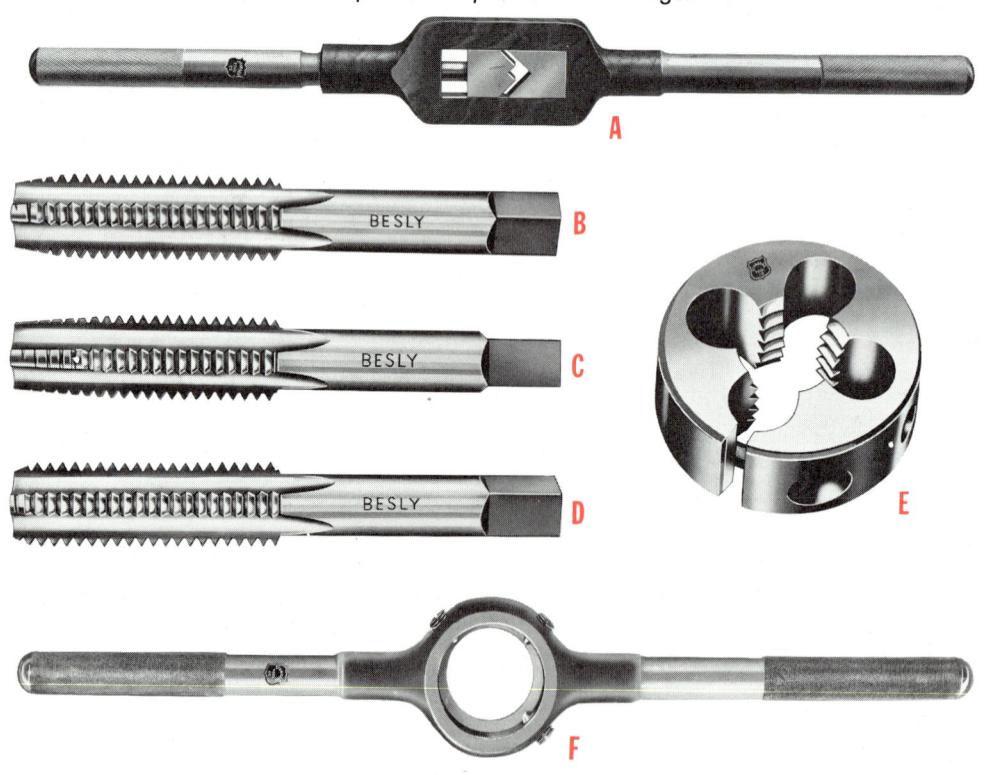

252

Unit 51: Mechanical Fastening of Metal

(internal thread). Fig. 51-5. A bolt has external threads; a nut has internal threads.

The most common kind of thread used in this country is the American National thread, in both the National Coarse (NC) and the National Fine (NF) series. NF bolts have more threads per inch than NC bolts of the same diameter. Fig. 51-6. For example, a ¼" diameter National Fine bolt has 28 threads per inch. The National Coarse bolt has 20 threads to the inch. The designation for this bolt in the NC series would read: ¼-20 NC. Use a screw pitch gauge to check thread sizes.

Below ¼" diameter, wire gauge sizes are generally used to designate the thread. Fig. 51-7. For example, a 10-32 NF bolt is made of #10 wire (measured by the American Screw and Wire gauge) and has 32 threads per inch.

Metric Threads

As the United States becomes a metric nation, we will be using *metric* instead of customary-inch threads. You can't tell these apart by looking at them because

FINE

COARSE

SCREW PITCH GAUGE

51-6. *The difference between coarse and fine threads is shown here. The screw pitch gauge is used to check thread sizes.*

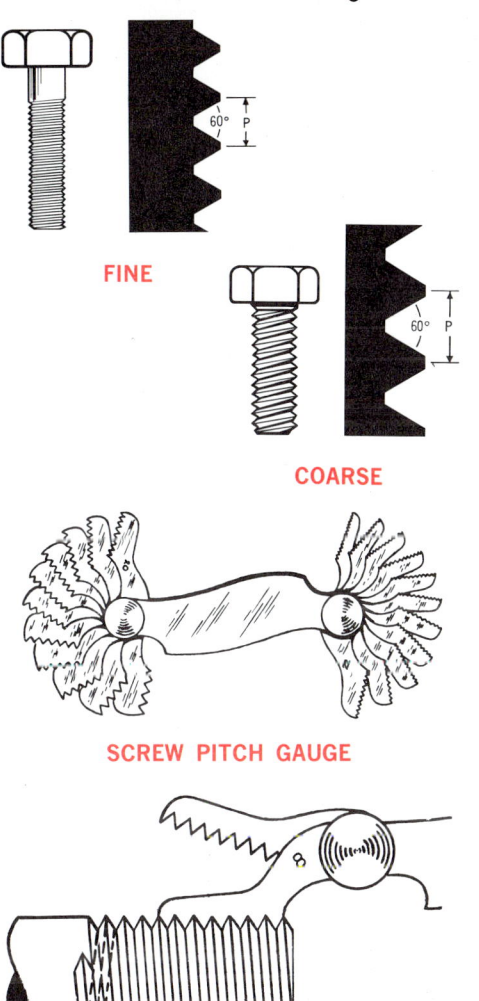

51-7. *This chart tells which tap drill to use for various thread sizes.*

Tap Drill Chart

National Fine		National Coarse	
Size & Thread	Tap Drill	Size & Thread	Tap Drill
4-48	#42(0.0935)	4-40	#44(0.0860)
5-44	37(0.1040)	5-40	39(0.0995)
6-40	34(0.1110)	6-32	36(0.1065)
8-36	29(0.1360)	8-32	29(0.1360)
10-32	22(0.1570)	10-24	26(0.1470)
¼-28	3(0.2130)	¼-20	8(0.1990)
5/16-24	"I"(0.2720)	5/16-18	"F"(0.2570)
3/8-24	"Q"(0.3320)	3/8-16	5/16(0.3125)
7/16-20	"W"(0.3860)	7/16-14	"U"(0.3680)
½-20	29/64(0.4531)	½-13	27/64(0.4219)

Part III: Manufacturing—Principles, Materials, and Processes

they do not look different. A typical thread designation is shown in Fig. 51-8. The thread dimensions are, of course, in millimetres. The metric pitch is the distance from the top of one thread point to the next. In customary threads, the pitch means the number of threads per inch. Metric thread designations also include the class of fit, or tightness. This is a number followed by a small *g* if it is an external thread, as on a bolt, or followed by a capital *H* if the thread is internal, as on a nut. In Fig. 51-8, the class of fit is 6g. This is a medium or general-purpose fit for an external thread.

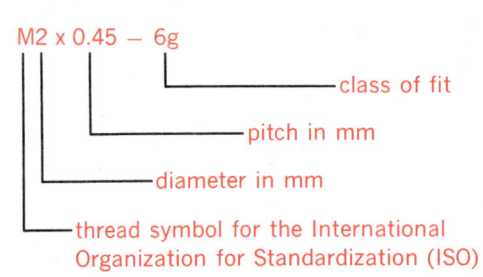

The metric threads which will probably be used in this country are shown in Fig. 51-9. There are about 56 different types of fine and coarse customary-inch threads used today. Note that there are only 25 metric threads (all coarse) which will be used in the United States. Note too how easy it is to get the tap drill size: you just subtract the pitch from the diameter. Metric drills will be used in school shops and in industry. A customary-metric conversion chart for drill sizes is in the Appendix. A set of metric drills can also be made from customary drills. A list of these can be found in the Appendix.

Cutting Threads

To tap a hole, select the proper taper tap and secure it in a tap wrench. Look at a tap drill chart and select the proper tap drill. After the hole has been drilled, start the tap in straight and turn slowly until the thread catches the work. Apply a few drops of cutting oil and give the tap one more turn. Back the tap off slowly to clear the chips and then continue tapping. Back off again occasionally to remove chips. Fig. 51-10.

```
M2 x 0.45 — 6g
 │    │      │
 │    │      └── class of fit
 │    └────────── pitch in mm
 └──────────────── diameter in mm
└─────────────────── thread symbol for the International
                     Organization for Standardization (ISO)
```

51-8. *Typical metric external thread designation.*

51-9. *ISO metric coarse threads. (The ISO is the International Organization for Standardization.)*

ISO Metric Threads*

Diameter mm	Pitch mm	Tap Drill mm	Diameter mm	Pitch mm	Tap Drill mm
M 1.6	0.35	1.25	M 20	2.5	17.50
M 2	0.40	1.60	M 24	3.0	21.00
M 2.5	0.45	2.05	M 30	3.5	26.50
M 3	0.50	2.50	M 36	4.0	32.00
M 3.5	0.60	2.90	M 42	4.5	37.50
M 4	0.70	3.30	M 48	5.0	43.00
M 5	0.80	4.20	M 56	5.5	50.50
M 6.3	1.00	5.30	M 64	6.0	58.00
M 8	1.25	6.75	M 72	6.0	66.00
M 10	1.50	8.50	M 80	6.0	74.00
M 12	1.75	10.25	M 90	6.0	84.00
M 14	2.00	12.00	M 100	6.0	94.00
M 16	2.00	14.00			

*Not yet adopted in the United States.

Unit 51: Mechanical Fastening of Metal

51-10. *Tapping a hole. The tap and the tap wrench are being used to cut internal threads.*

Threading a rod with a die is done in much the same way as tapping. Fig. 51-11. Be especially careful to turn both taps and dies slowly, to lubricate well, and to remove chips frequently. This will produce sharp, clean threads and will prevent tool breakage. The tap and die set generally found in the school shop is the screw plate shown in Fig. 51-11.

RIVETS

Rivets provide a permanent mechanical fastening method for metal parts. Riveting is a simple process; a headed metal pin is placed in a hole through two or more metal pieces. It is then headed at the other end to clinch the pieces together.

Rivets are made of copper, aluminum, and steel in many lengths and diameters. Select a rivet made of the same material as the workpiece to be joined. There are several different head styles. Fig. 51-12. Tinners rivets are very common in sheet metal work. The size of the tinners rivet is indicated by its weight per thousand. Common sizes are 10 ounce, 1 pound, and 2 pound. Others are sold by diameter and length.

The hole for the rivet is punched or drilled in the metal. (See Units 35 and 38.) Holes should be at least two rivet diameters (shank diameters) from the metal joint and three diameters from other rivets for strength and grip. Fig. 51-13.

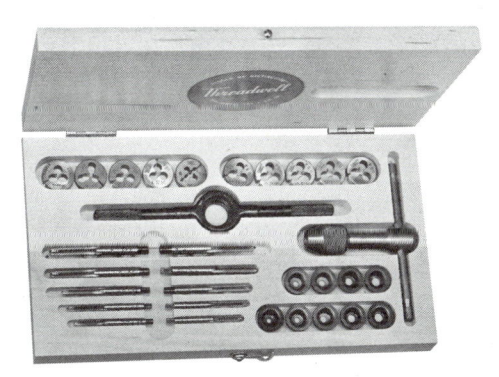

51-11. *Cutting external threads on a rod. A die and a die stock are being used. Hold the die stock square to the work and turn slowly. The screw plate is also shown.*

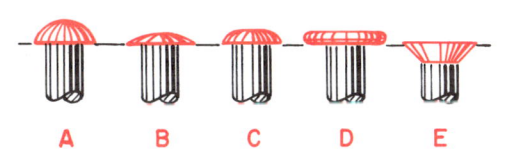

51-12. *Typical solid rivet heads: (A) Button, or round (B) Truss (C) Universal (D) Tinners (E) Flat.*

51-13. *Select rivets of the proper length to make sure the joint will be strong. This is called the "grip" of a rivet.*

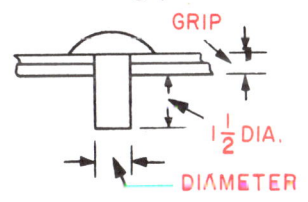

255

Part III: Manufacturing—Principles, Materials, and Processes

On heavy metals, the rivet is inserted and the head formed by striking gently with a ball peen hammer. Fig. 51-14. On sheet metals, the rivet set is used. Fig. 51-15. Place the open hole of the set over the rivet and gently strike with a hammer to draw the pieces of metal together.

Then place the concave part of the rivet set on the end of the rivet and strike with a hammer to form the head. Fig. 51-16. When riveting a seam or long joint, install rivets at both ends. Complete the job by riveting from the center to both ends of the joint.

For blind holes and for general fast riveting, pop or blind rivets can be used. There are several types. One of the most common is shown in Fig. 51-17. These rivets come in several sizes and materials. To use the pop riveter, insert the rivet, attach the riveting tool, and squeeze firmly. The result is a fast, strong joint.

SHEET METAL JOINTS

Common joints are shown in Fig. 51-18. They may be soldered, spot welded, riveted, or, for the grooved seam, clinched to form permanent joints in materials. Semi-permanent joining is pos-

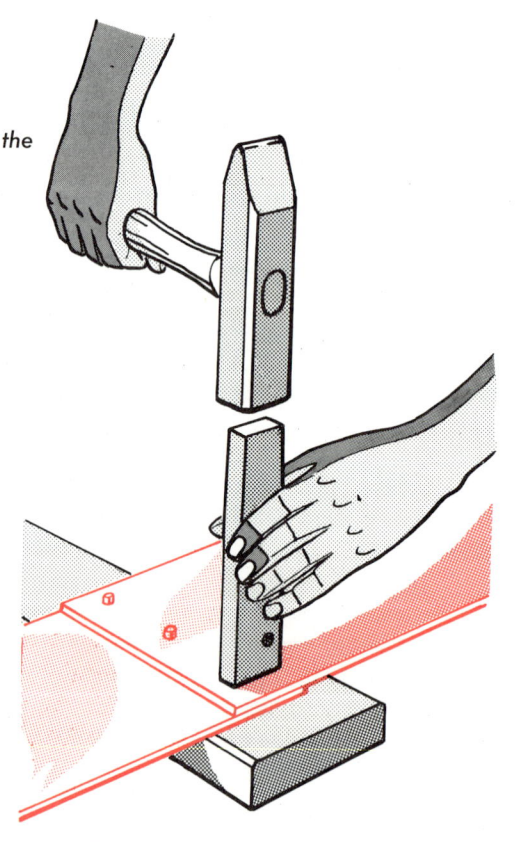

51-14. *For heavy metals, select the proper rivet and form the head with a ball peen hammer.*

51-15. *Using the rivet set. Make sure the hole and the rivet diameter match.*

Unit 51: Mechanical Fastening of Metal

sible in the lap and folded seams by using threaded fasteners.

The grooved seam is formed by making two opposite folds in the metal. Select a hand groover of the proper size. Fig. 51-19. Place the hand groover over the seam and strike firmly to lock. Fig. 51-20. Remember to allow for the folding of the metal by adding three times the width of the grooved seam to the pattern layout.

51-16. Steps in riveting.

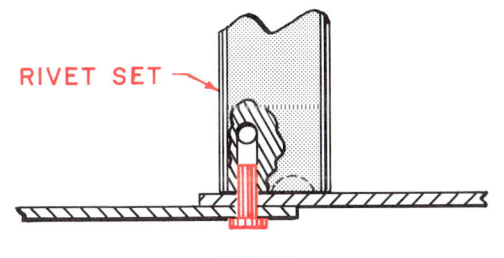

RIVET SET

DRAW

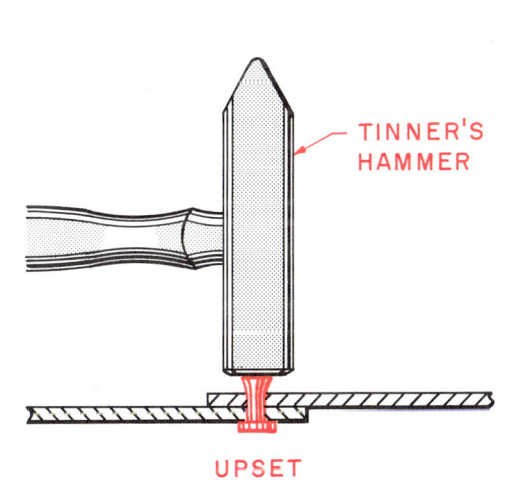

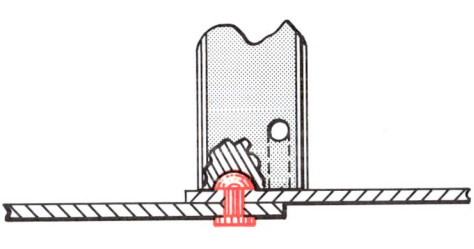

TINNER'S HAMMER

UPSET

HEAD

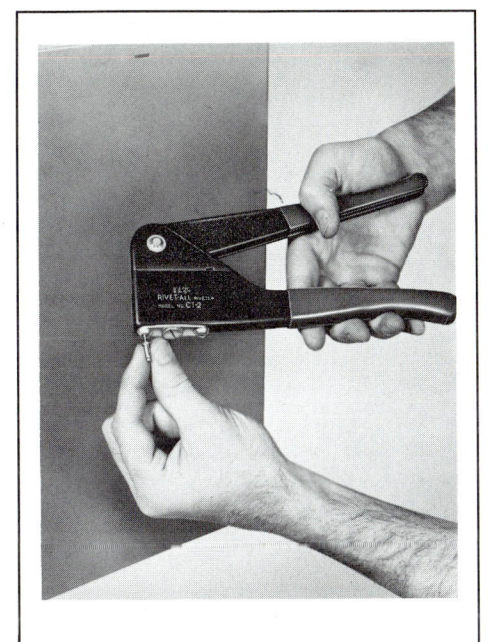

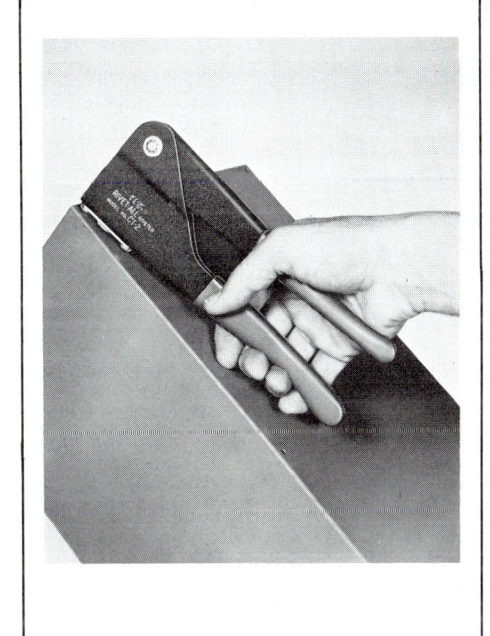

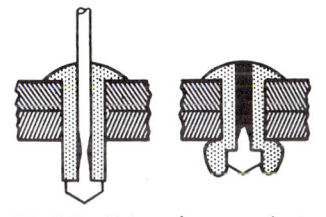

51-17. Using the pop riveter.

257

Part III: Manufacturing—Principles, Materials, and Processes

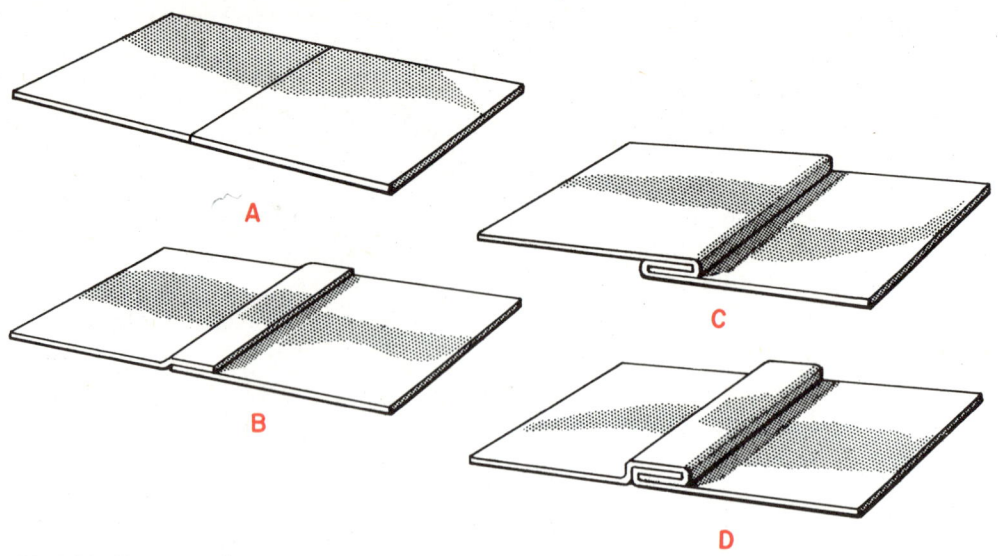

51-18. Sheet metal joints: (A) Butt (B) Lap (C) Folded (D) Grooved. The butt joint is generally soldered. Lap and folded joints can be riveted or soldered. The grooved seam is locked with a hand groover. It can be soldered to make it watertight.

51-19. The hand groover and table of sizes.

Hand Groover Sizes

The small number stamped on the face of the groover indicates the size.

Number	Width of Groove
6	1/8
5	5/32
4	7/32
3	9/32
2	5/16
1	11/32
0	3/8

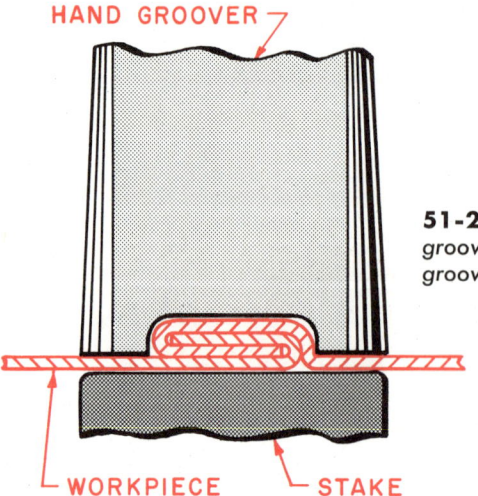

51-20. The hand groover is used to lock a grooved joint or seam together. Hold the groover square with the work to avoid unsightly dents in the work.

258

UNIT 52

Adhesive Fastening of Metal

A good example of fastening by adhesion is gluing two pieces of wood together. In the adhesion process, a layer of bonding material separates the two workpieces to be joined. This layer penetrates the surfaces of the workpieces slightly and causes a tough bond or joint to be formed. (Cohesion forms a different type of joint. See Unit 53.) In both industry and the shop, soldering, brazing, and cementing are common ways of joining materials by adhesion.

SOLDERING

Equipment

Soldering is joining pieces of metal together with a filler metal called solder at temperatures below 800 degrees F. The metal parts to be joined are called the *base metals*. They are not melted; only the solder is. The molten solder dissolves a small amount of the base metal; so a strong bond between the metals is formed upon cooling. Soldering is an inexpensive, efficient way of joining sheet metal or electrical parts. It is widely used in the metalworking and electrical industries.

The heat for soldering is provided by the equipment shown in Fig. 52-1. These devices are usually found in the school shop. They should be used carefully to avoid burns. Wear safety glasses when soldering.

Common soldering materials are shown in Fig. 52-2. Solder is a mixture (alloy) of tin and lead. The 40/60 solder (40 percent tin and 60 percent lead) is most often used and is available in many forms. Acid and rosin fluxes are needed to prevent heated metals from tarnishing (oxidizing) and to help the solder flow easily. Rosin fluxes are noncorrosive. That is, they won't continue to dissolve the metal and weaken the joint. Therefore they are especially good in electrical work.

Procedures

Soldering is not hard if it is done with care. There are four steps to be followed for successful soldering.
1. Clean the workpieces thoroughly.
2. Select the proper flux for the job.
3. Select the correct solder.
4. Apply the proper amount of heat.

To clean the workpieces, rub with steel wool or abrasive paper. Apply flux to the clean surfaces. Place a few drops of solder on a soldering copper and draw it slowly along the fluxed surfaces of the seam or joint. Fig. 52-3. Hold the workpieces with a file or scriber so that they stay in place until the melted solder hardens. Cylinders and other structures should be wired together to hold pieces in place while soldering. Fig. 52-4.

Keep the soldering copper hot. Most poor soldering jobs are the result of insufficient heat. Sweat soldering involves coating each surface of a seam with solder (called tinning), clamping the parts together, and heating them with a propane torch or soldering copper. Fig. 52-5.

The soldering copper should be cleaned and tinned before using. To do this, carefully clamp the heated copper in

Part III: Manufacturing—Principles, Materials, and Processes

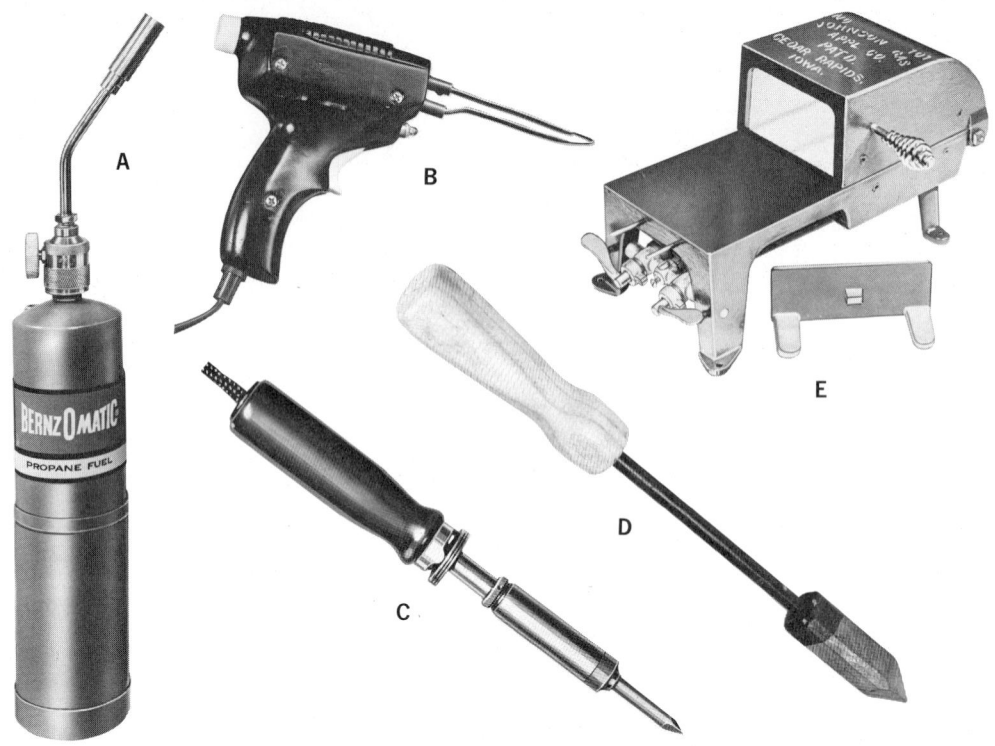

52-1. *Sources of heat for soldering: (A) Propane torch (B) Soldering gun used in electrical work (C) Electric soldering copper (D) Soldering copper (E) Soldering furnace for heating coppers.*

52-2. *Materials for soldering. (A) Solder preforms are widely used in industry. (B) Wire solder is available as solid wire or with a flux core. (C) Cross section of flux core solder. (D) Bar solder.*

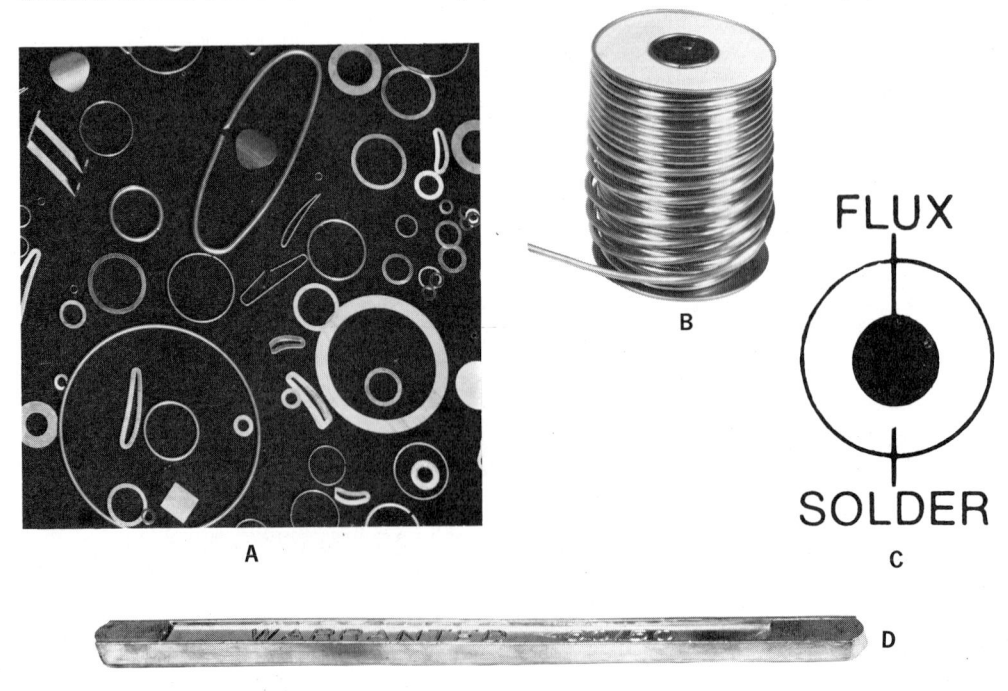

260

52-3. Move the soldering copper slowly along the joint. Hold the workpieces until the solder sets up. Reheat the soldering copper as necessary.

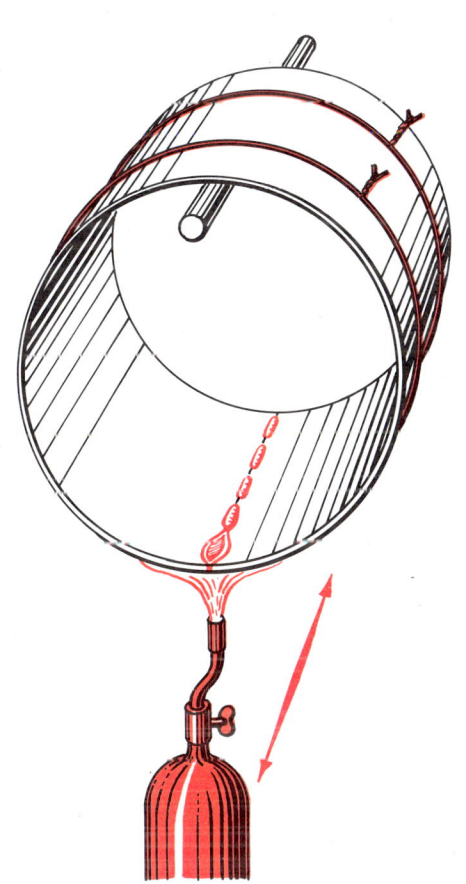

52-4. Soldering a cylinder. Other similar structures should be wired to hold pieces in place while soldering.

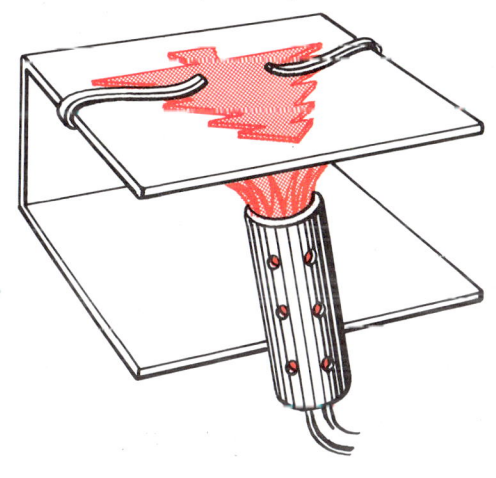

52-5. Sweat soldering. Metal clips hold the workpiece in place.

Part III: Manufacturing—Principles, Materials, and Processes

a vise and file it smooth and flat with a coarse file. Then reheat it (but never allow it to get red hot), melt a few drops of solder on a sal ammoniac block, and rub the copper back and forth.

Make certain that the tip of the copper is covered with a light coating of solder, about $\frac{1}{2}$" up each face. Tinning makes it possible for the solder to stick to the copper when you are soldering. Fig. 52-6.

BRAZING

Brazing is a way of joining metal workpieces by using a filler rod which has a lower melting point than either of the pieces to be joined. The most common filler rods are made of copper alloys such as bronze, or of silver alloys. In this process, the cleaned workpieces are heated cherry red. The filler rod is then touched to the heated area. It melts and begins to flow into the joint. Upon cooling, this leaves a strong bond. Notice that the workpieces are not melted. (In welding they are melted.)

The equipment for brazing is shown in Fig. 52-7. This equipment, if used wrongly, can be very dangerous. Follow instructions carefully. Report to your instructor any equipment which is damaged or not working properly.

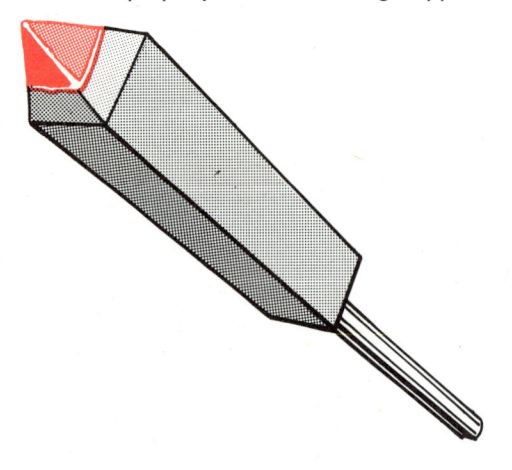

Refer to Fig. 52-7 and follow the directions given here for using the brazing equipment. These instructions are for general brazing of light materials.

1. Check to see that all hose, regulator, and blowpipe connections are tight.

2. Slowly turn the oxygen cylinder valve wide open. Open the acetylene cylinder valve $1\frac{1}{2}$ turns. Do not stand facing the regulators while you are turning the valves. Stand to one side. The valves should be opened as far as they will go.

3. Set the oxygen regulator to 20 lbs. pressure by slowly turning the valve clockwise. In the same manner, set the acetylene regulator to read 5 lbs.

4. To light the blowpipe, first open the acetylene blowpipe valve slightly. Use a sparklighter to ignite the gas. (Never use matches—you might burn your hands.) Be sure to wear gloves. Readjust the regulator pressure if necessary.

5. Open the oxygen blowpipe valve until the flame is *slightly oxidizing*. Fig. 52-8. This flame is identified by a clear, well-defined white inner cone and a short heat envelope. When there is excess oxygen in the burning mixture, the flame is called an *oxidizing flame*. When there is excess acetylene, the flame is called a *carburizing* or *reducing flame*. The *neutral flame* has equal parts of oxygen and acetylene.

6. To extinguish the flame, close the acetylene blowpipe valve, then the oxygen blowpipe valve. Next, close the acetylene and oxygen cylinder valves. Open the acetylene blowpipe valve until the regulator returns to zero. Close the acetylene blowpipe valve, and turn the acetylene regulator valve wide open to release the tension on the regulator. Do the same for the oxygen system.

Metal pieces to be brazed must be clean and must fit together closely for the best joint. Heat the metal until it is cherry red and hold the filler rod on the heated metal until it begins to flow. Fig. 52-9. Keep the torch and the rod moving slowly along the joint. The brazing rod must be

52-6. *A properly tinned soldering copper.*

Unit 52: Adhesive Fastening of Metal

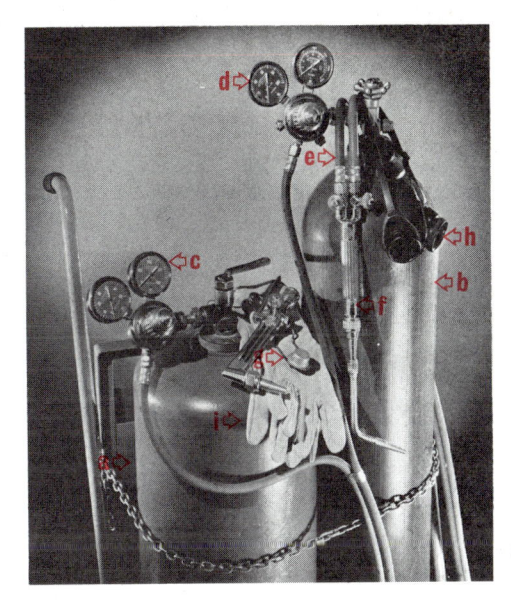

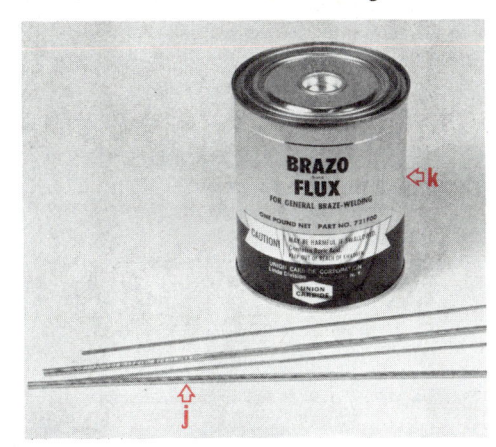

52-7. Equipment for brazing: (a) Acetylene cylinder (b) Oxygen cylinder (c) Acetylene regulator (d) Oxygen regulator (e) Hoses (f) Blowpipe (g) Sparklighter (h) Goggles (i) Gloves (j) Brazing rods (k) Brazing flux.

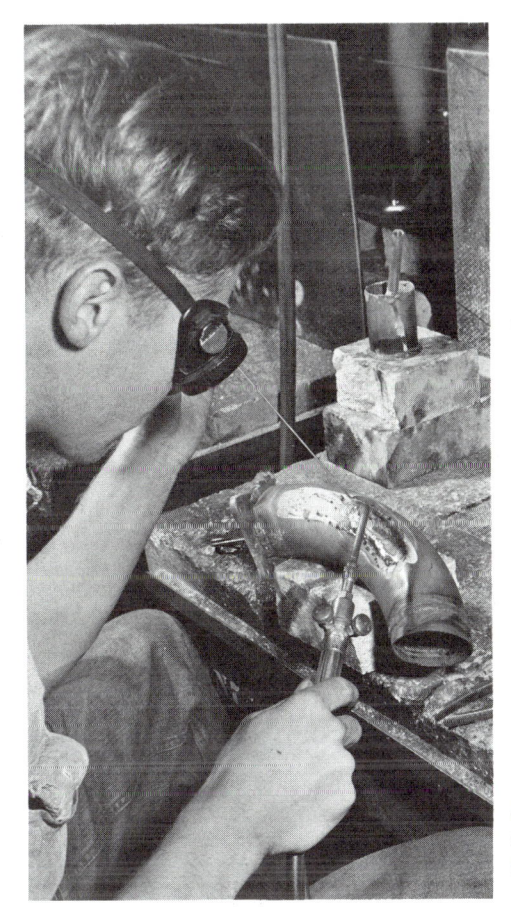

52-8. Oxyacetylene flame patterns: (A) Oxidizing flame used for braze welding with a bronze rod (B) Carburizing flame for hardfacing and welding white metal (C) Neutral flame for welding steel and cast iron. The oxidizing flame is the correct flame for general brazing.

52-9. Using the brazing torch. Hold the rod on the red-hot metal and draw it along slowly. Remember to heat the rod slightly and dip it into the flux before use.

263

Part III: Manufacturing—Principles, Materials, and Processes

dipped in flux before using. This dissolves impurities (oxides) and permits the bronze to penetrate the metal pores. Hold workpieces in place with a clamping device to prevent movement while brazing. Fig. 52-10.

HARD SOLDERING

Hard soldering (sometimes called silver soldering) is much like brazing. It is done at temperatures generally below 1400 °F (750 °C), and the workpieces are not brought to a red heat. Follow the instructions given here to hard solder jewelry and other small metal workpieces. Fig. 52-11.

1. Clean the metal parts thoroughly. File so that they fit together as closely as possible. Hold pieces together with clips.

2. Apply a special borax hard soldering flux.

3. Select a hard solder to match the job; the solders melt at different temperatures. They are available in foil, wire, and powder forms.

4. Cut snippets of hard solder and lay them in place about ½ inch (13 mm) apart.

5. Gently apply heat with a propane torch or bunsen burner. Play the flame over the joint until the solder melts. Do not overheat as the workpiece may melt and ruin the job.

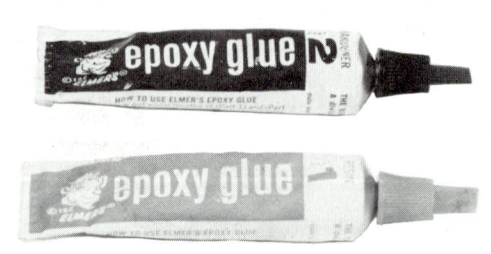

52-10. *Workpieces should be held in place with clips or clamps so that they do not move while brazing. In this illustration, the brass candle cup is being held with an aluminum clip.*

52-12. *Epoxy glues are used for bonding metals to wood, plastic, cloth, and ceramics as well as to other metals.*

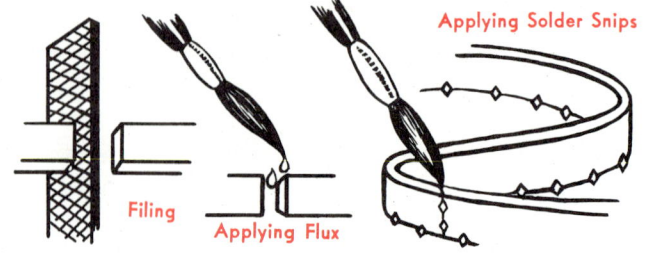

52-11. *Hard soldering operation.*

HARD SOLDERING

Filing — Applying Flux — Applying Solder Snips

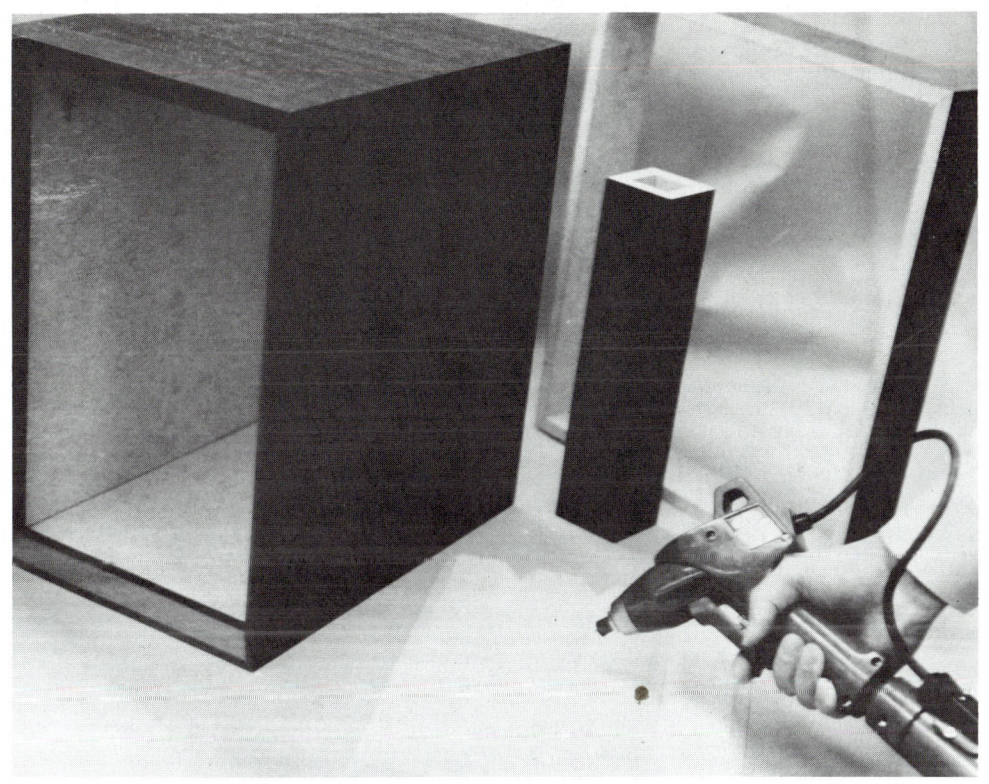

Unit 52: Adhesive Fastening of Metal

52-13. *Assembling a fiber container by the hot melt adhesive process. Metal parts are joined in a similar way.*

6. Allow the workpiece to cool. Clean by dipping in acid (pickling) solution.

CEMENTING

In modern metalworking processes, glues and cements are sometimes used for fastening metal pieces together. Three of the common adhesives used in industry and the shop are contact cement, epoxy glue, and hot melts. Contact cements are used to join pieces of sheet metal. This is done by first cleaning the surfaces of the joint with lacquer thinner and then coating them with the cement. Coat both surfaces and allow them to dry. Then press the pieces together, place a block of wood over the joint and strike with a hammer. (No clamping is necessary.)

When using epoxy glues, Fig. 52-12, the hardener and resin are mixed in equal proportions and applied to the cleaned surfaces. Clamp the surfaces together and allow to cure for about eight hours.

Hot melts are applied with a special gun. Hot melt adhesive sticks are loaded into the gun and allowed to heat to a liquid state. A trigger squirts out a small amount of the hot adhesive onto the joint. The parts are held together for a few seconds until the hot melt cools. Most materials can be joined in this way, including wood, metal, plastic, and ceramics. Fig. 52-13.

UNIT 53

Cohesive Fastening of Metal

In cohesive fastening of metal, the pieces are melted together to form one continuous mass. This process is called welding. Welding is done by heating the metal pieces to their melting temperature, causing them to flow and join together. Metal filler, usually in the form of rods, is sometimes added to the molten pool to make the joint neater and stronger. Pressure or force is sometimes used to help join the workpieces. This is called *pressure welding*. Welding in which no pressure is required is called *fusion welding*. In both cases, the metal is melted to make the joint. This permanent fastening process is used in making small precision parts, toys, automobiles, steel bridges, and many other products. The three most common kinds of welding are gas, arc, and resistance welding.

53-1. *Gas welding is a form of fusion welding. Here oxygen and acetylene are being burned to supply the heat to melt the metal workpieces and the steel filler rod.*

GAS WELDING

A flammable gas can be burned with oxygen to produce the heat needed for welding. Acetylene is the gas most often used for this purpose, and the process is called *oxyacetylene welding.* Hydrogen, propane, and butane can also be used. Gas welding is fusion welding and usually requires a filler rod to help form the joint. Fig. 53-1.

Welding equipment is similar to that used in brazing. (See Unit 52.) Procedures for lighting and using this equipment are also similar. The filler rod, however, must be identical to the material being welded, and no flux is necessary. The neutral flame is used for most welding. Fig. 53-2. (See also Fig. 52-8.) Remember to wear goggles and gloves when welding.

There are five basic types of welding joints. Fig. 53-3. Most welding jobs will involve at least one of these. The edge

53-2. *The neutral flame is used for most welding operations.*

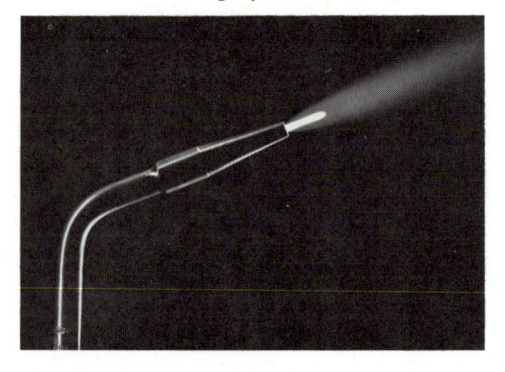

Unit 53: Cohesive Fastening of Metal

weld is a good one to use for welding practice because it does not require the use of a filler rod. Begin by welding a tack at each end. This will prevent the joint from opening while you are welding. Play the flame back and forth in a zigzag pattern. Fig. 53-4. Draw the puddle along, making certain that you leave no openings or voids. Welding can be done by either the backhand or forehand method. Fig. 53-5.

You should next practice welding with a filler rod. The rod should match the material you are welding. Begin the weld by melting a puddle. Pull the puddle along, touching the filler rod to the puddle as needed to insure a full, firm joint.

ARC WELDING

In arc welding, a fusion welding process, the heat for fusing the metal pieces is supplied by an electric arc or spark. The arc is produced by an electric current jumping an air gap between an electrode

53-3. Basic welding joints: (A) Edge (B) Butt (C) Tee (D) Lap (E) Corner.

53-4. Practice welding to develop a good zigzag pattern in your work. This will result in an even, strong welded joint.

53-5. Welding can be done by either of these two methods. Practice them both to see which works better for you.

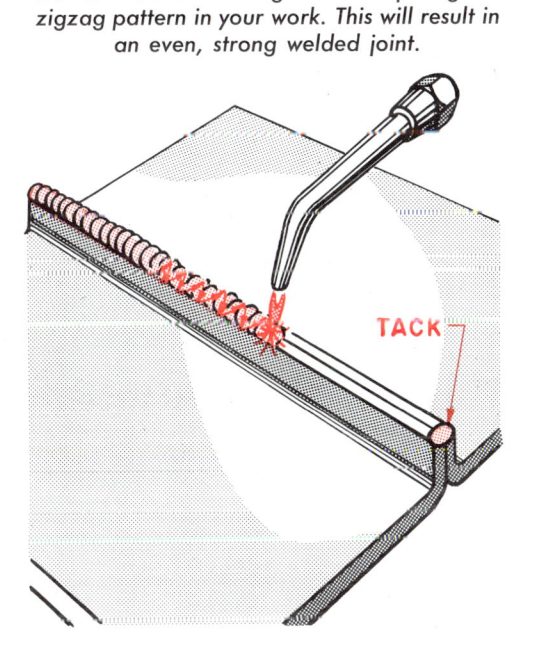

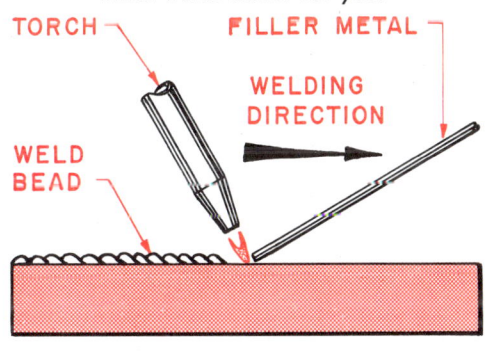

FOREHAND WELDING

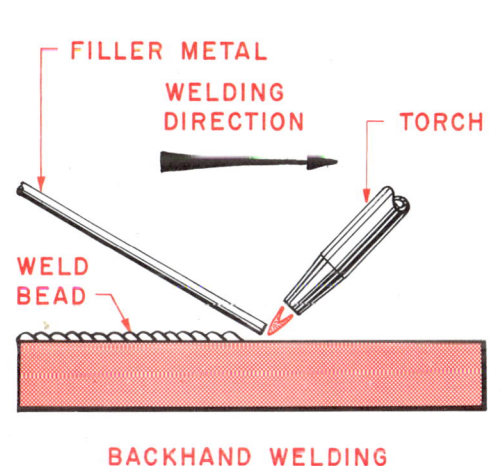

BACKHAND WELDING

Part III: Manufacturing—Principles, Materials, and Processes

(welding rod) and the metal to be welded. Fig. 53-6.

There are many kinds of arc welding, such as metal-arc, carbon-arc, and inert gas. In the metal-arc process, common in the school shop, the electrode itself melts away as a filler material. Fig. 53-7. The carbon-arc method uses a carbon electrode which provides heat but no filler material. The inert gas method provides a shield of argon or helium gas around a tungsten electrode. This shield prevents oxidation in the tungsten inert gas (TIG) process. A similar process is the metal inert gas method (MIG) in which the metal electrode is consumed. (See *Technology Reports,* at the end of this book.)

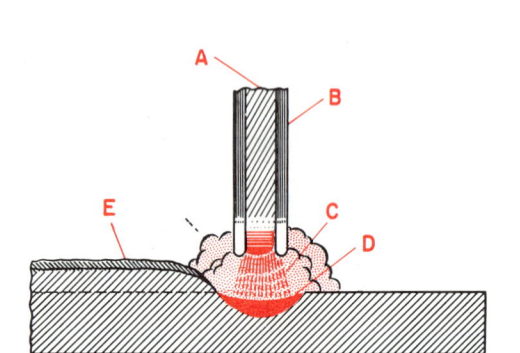

Jackson Products Company

53-6. *In arc welding, the heat is supplied by an electric arc.*

53-7. *Arc welding diagram: (A) Electrode core (B) Electrode coating (C) Arc (D) Molten metal puddle (E) Slag.*

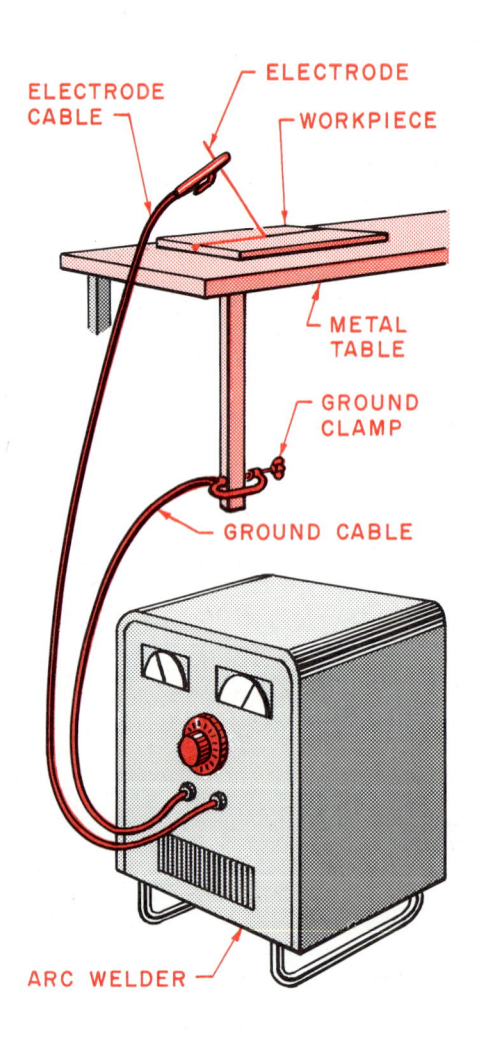

53-8. *Equipment for metal-arc welding. When the electrode touches the workpiece, an arc is struck. The heat produced begins to melt the metal.*

268

Unit 53: Cohesive Fastening of Metal

The equipment for metal-arc welding is shown in Fig. 53-8. Make certain that the ground clamp is securely attached. Fig. 53-9. If it is not, the welding circuit will not be complete and arc welding cannot take place.

To arc weld, place an electrode in the holder. Fig. 53-10. Remember to wear a helmet and protective clothing. Fig. 53-11. An arc is struck by lightly scratching the electrode tip against the workpiece. When the arc starts, move the electrode in a zigzag pattern similar to that of oxyacetylene welding. The electrode is fed to the molten puddle and consumed.

RESISTANCE WELDING

Resistance welding methods use resistance to the flow of electric current to produce the heat for welding. This heat is localized in the weld area, producing a small fused section. Pressure is also used to insure a solid weld. Typical resistance methods are spot and seam welding.

Resistance welding methods are efficient and economical. They can be used in mass production techniques. Resist-

53-10. The two types of electrode holders.
Jackson Products Company

53-11. Wear a protective helmet and gloves when arc welding.
Jackson Products Company

53-9. The ground clamp must be clean and attached securely to a clean surface.
Jackson Products Company

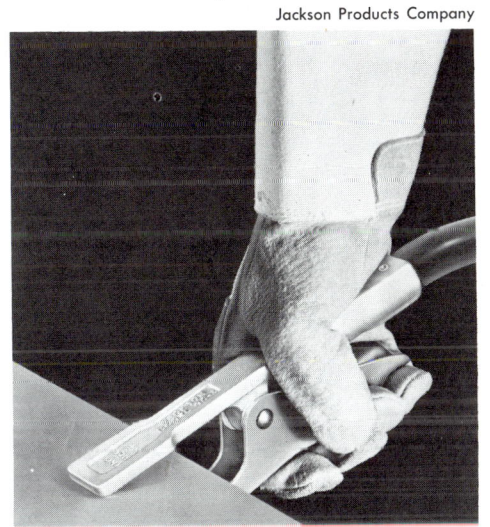

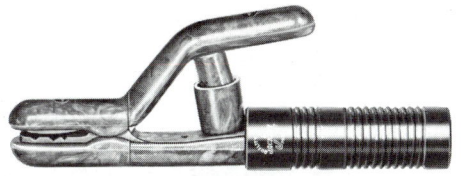

269

Part III: Manufacturing—Principles, Materials, and Processes

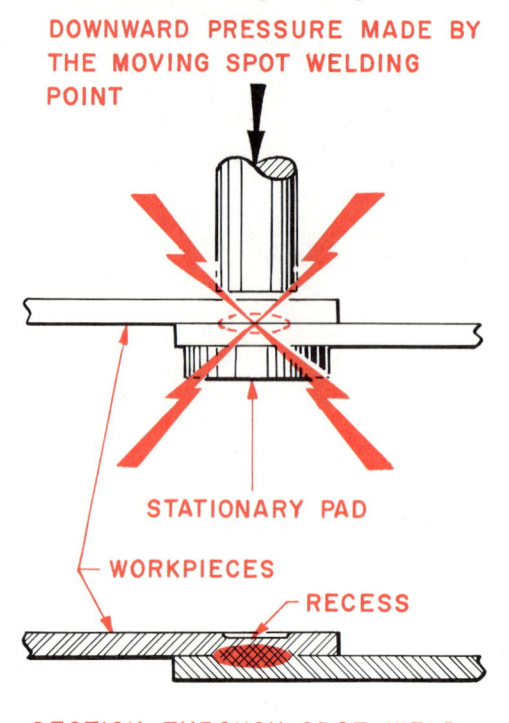

DOWNWARD PRESSURE MADE BY THE MOVING SPOT WELDING POINT

STATIONARY PAD

WORKPIECES

RECESS

SECTION THROUGH SPOT WELD

53-12. *Spot welding diagram. The welded spot joins the two workpieces.*

ance welding produces relatively little heat and does not distort the metal.

A common resistance welding method is spot welding. Fig. 53-12. Thin metal sheets or rods can be spot welded together by placing them between two electrodes made of a copper alloy. The electrodes are pressed together, causing the temperature of the metal sheets to reach their melting point. This in turn causes them to be welded at that spot. Floor and hand-held spot welders are used. A common shop model is shown in Fig. 53-13. Spot welders are often water cooled to prevent warping of the workpieces. A timer usually controls the duration of the weld operation and the amount of heat.

Seam welding is a type of "continuous" spot welding. The welding wheels roll along the joint and produce a series of spot welds. Fig. 53-14. Cylinders and other containers are often welded this way.

53-13. *A floor model spot welder.*

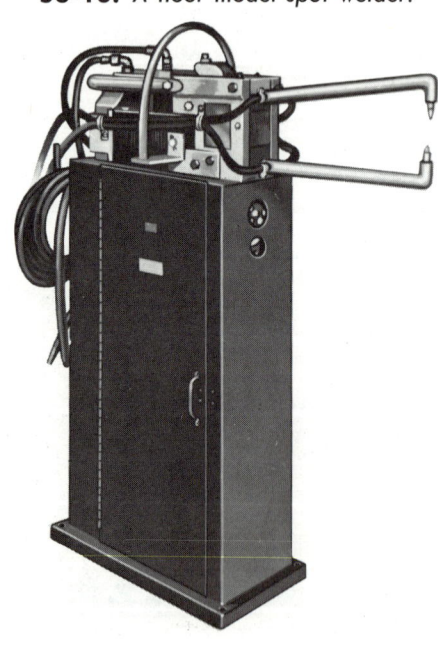

53-14. *Seam welding diagram.*

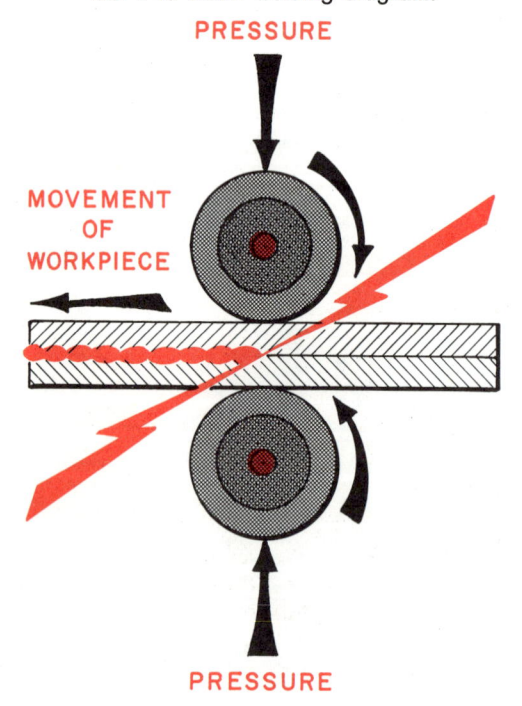

PRESSURE

MOVEMENT OF WORKPIECE

PRESSURE

270

UNIT 54

Metal Finishing Principles

Most materials require some sort of protection if they are to last when exposed to weather, dampness, or similar conditions. Wood will rot and metal will rust if not covered by some protective coating. Such a coating is called a *finish*. But coatings, such as paint and lacquer, are only one kind of finish. Fig. 54-1. The finishing chart, Fig. 54-2, shows three other kinds.

Remove finishing resembles both abrasive and chemical cutting. It is in fact a finishing method which uses a cutting action to produce a desired surface treatment. The buffer and polisher use abrasives, and etching tanks use chemical cutting as a finishing method.

Hammering and peening are examples of the displacement method of finishing. Metal knurling and decorative embossing are other common displacement finishes.

Remove and displacement finishes are often called *mechanical finishing*.

Coloring metal not only changes its appearance but also makes it more durable and serviceable. This is true of both the heat and chemical methods. Gun barrels are blued to prevent rust and to improve the looks of the weapon.

As you can see, many finishes both beautify *and* protect an object. Paint improves appearance and prevents rusting. A scratch finish or satin finish produced by the buffer adds interest to a surface and prevents minor nicks and fingerprints from showing. Peening a surface does the same thing as the satin finish, and the example of gun bluing shows how chemicals beautify and protect.

The tools, materials, and techniques for producing these four major kinds of finishes are discussed in the units which follow. The finishing chart will help you to see the differences and similarities among these surface treatments for metals.

54-1. *Industrial spray painting is one of the common finishing methods.*

271

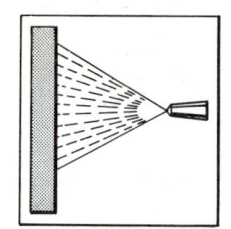

Part III: Manufacturing—Principles, Materials, and Processes

Finishing

Finishing is the process of treating the surface of a material for appearance and/or protection.

KIND OF FINISHING	DEFINITION	EXAMPLES
Coating*	Applying a layer of finishing substance to the surface of a material.	Lacquer, enamel, electroplate, flock, wrinkle finish, plastic dip.
Remove Finishing	Finishing by cutting the surface by abrasive or chemical action.	Grinder, wire brush, sand blaster, etching tanks, polisher, buffer, steel wool, coated abrasives.
Displacement Finishing	Finishing by the movement of surface material to a different position, to form a new appearance.	Hammer, peen, knurl, emboss, planish.
Coloring*	Applying penetrating chemicals or heat to a material to change its color.	Chemical coloring, bluing, tempering.

*Coating could be considered a coloring process, since coating usually does change a product's color. However, it is customary to consider coating and coloring to be separate processes, as defined in the chart above.

54-2. *These metal finishing methods will be discussed in the following units.*

UNIT 55

Coat finishing of Metal

Coating metal involves applying a layer of paint, metal lacquer, wax, metal, or glass to the surface to protect it, improve its appearance, or both. Coat finishes are widely used by industry. For example, metal finishes are sprayed on such items as automobiles and metal furniture. Fig. 55-1.

55-1. *Spray lacquering automobile body parts on a production line. These parts will have a hard, bright, durable finish.*

Du Pont Magazine

LACQUERS

Clear lacquer is generally sprayed or brushed on art metal objects made from copper, brass, or aluminum. Projects must first be cleaned with lacquer thinner and dried with a soft cloth. If brushing, flow the metal lacquer on with a soft, camel's hair brush; use quick, even strokes. Fig. 55-2. Apply two coats, allowing about 20 minutes between coats. Clean the brush with lacquer thinner in a well-ventilated area. Spray cans of clear lacquer are quick and easy to use. The nozzle should be held about 12" away from the project for good coverage. Fig. 55-3. Lacquers adhere best if the project is first warmed in an oven.

Colored lacquers are applied in the same way to projects made of ferrous metals (those containing iron). However, it is wise to apply a prime coat to the

55-2. *Brush lacquer onto a project with quick, even strokes.*

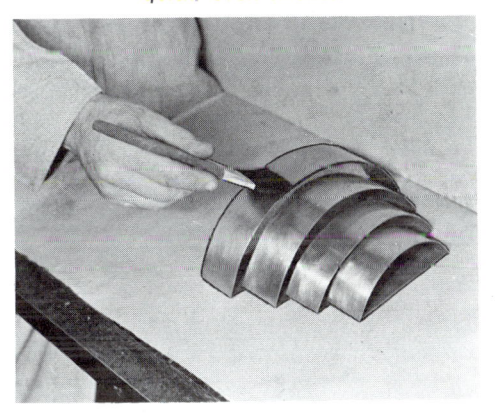

273

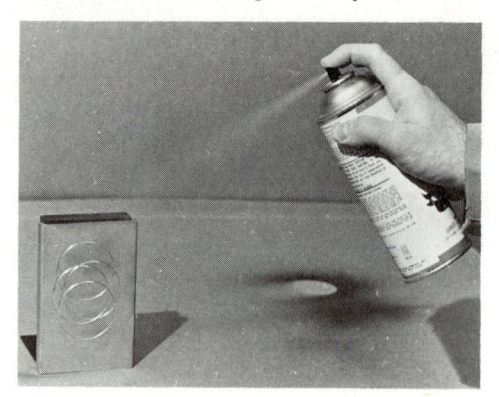

Part III: Manufacturing—Principles, Materials, and Processes

55-3. *Spraying a project. Hold the spray can about twelve inches from the workpiece.*

piece first, followed by two coats of lacquer.

PAINTS

Paints are applied much the same as lacquers are, and for similar purposes. The drying time for paints is generally longer, and brushes should be cleaned in turpentine or paint thinner. Fig. 55-4. Wrinkle finishes are also available for metal applications. These provide a hard, scratch resistant surface for tool boxes and tools. Some wrinkle finishes require oven baking; so be sure to follow the directions printed on the can.

Paint is often called *enamel,* but actually enameling is a method of applying small grains of glass to metal, and fusing them to the surface with high heat. This process is discussed later in this unit.

WAX

A semipermanent finish may be achieved by waxing. A coat of paste or liquid wax is applied with a clean cloth, allowed to dry, and then buffed to a high gloss. This finish will wear off in time and must therefore be reapplied occasionally. Fig. 55-5.

ELECTROPLATING

Using electricity and chemicals to cover a metal object with a thin metal coating is called *electroplating.* This process is widely used in industry to apply chrome plating to automobile bumpers and other parts. It both beautifies and protects metal objects.

In electroplating, the object to be plated becomes the cathode (negative pole) in an electrolytic cell. This cell contains a solution of the salts of the metal to be deposited. The anode (positive pole) is the metal to be deposited. When an electric current passes through the cell, metal particles are separated from the anode and go into the electrolytic solution. They are then separated from the solution and deposited on the cathode.

A simple electroplating device is shown in Fig. 55-6. The tanks must be made of plastic, glass, or ceramic stoneware. The metal to be plated must be thoroughly cleaned in a pickling solution or buffed and cleaned with lacquer thinner. The metal must be absolutely clean, or the plating will not hold properly. Copper, nickel, and cadmium are commonly used as plating (anode) materials.

Assemble the device as shown in Fig. 55-6. Remember that the plating solutions are different, depending on the type of metal anode used. The voltage required is from one to three volts. Adjust the machine properly and continue plating until the proper thickness of plate has been reached. Remove and rinse. CAUTION: Wear safety glasses and protective clothing.

ENAMELING

Enameling is the process of decorating metal by melting a layer of colored glass on the surface. The enamel is crushed and screened to size, then applied to the metal in powder or paste form. The enamels are fused to the metal by heating to about 1500 °F (815 °C). Fig. 55-7. While steels and other metals are enameled industrially, copper is the metal generally used for enameling in the school shop. The simple equipment is shown in Fig. 55-8. Make sure the enameling powders are finely ground and free from dirt.

Unit 55: Coat Finishing of Metal

55-4. Paint brushes are cleaned in turpentine or paint thinner. Lacquer brushes are cleaned in lacquer thinner. Be sure to work in a well-ventilated area.

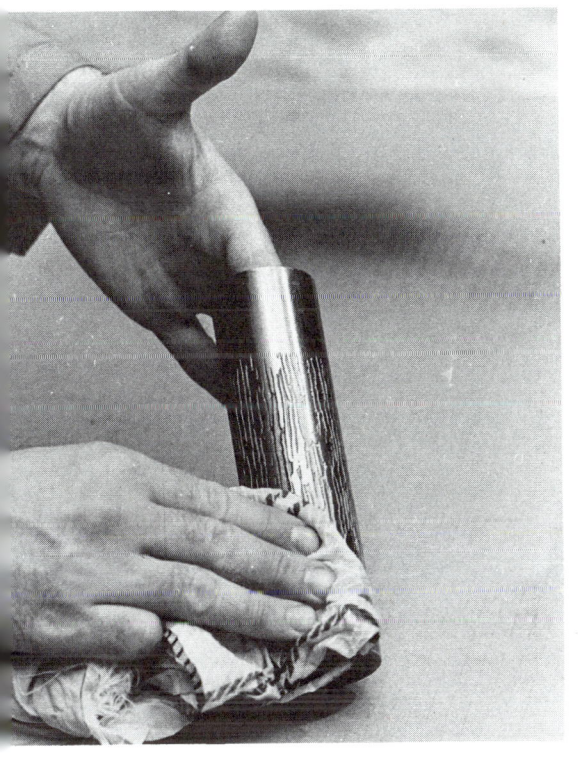

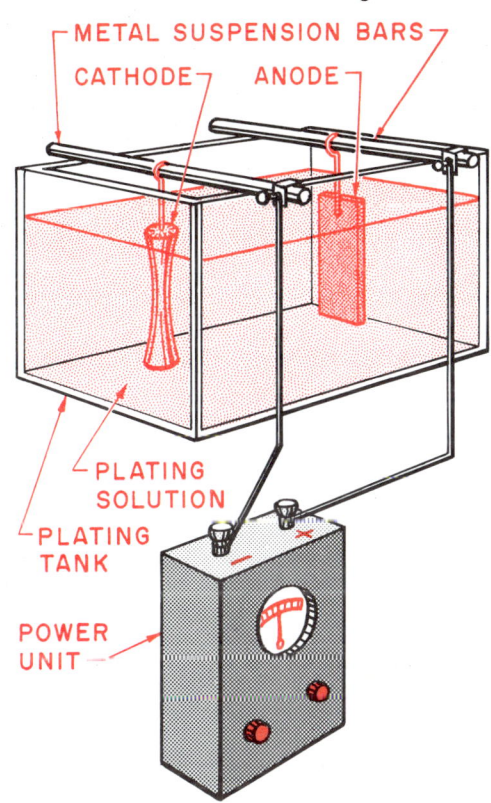

55-5. Wax can be applied to a project as a semipermanent finish.

55-6. The electroplating apparatus. The power unit includes a rheostat, ammeter, and voltmeter. For simple plating jobs a dry cell may be used.

55-7. Copper enameled decorative dishes.
America House

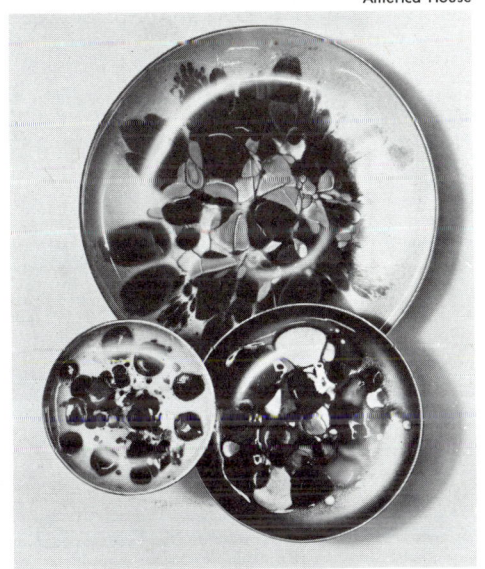

275

Part III: Manufacturing—Principles, Materials, and Processes

The procedures for enameling are few and simple:

1. Select a desired copper shape and clean thoroughly with any good scouring powder and water, or dip in pickling solution. Rinse and dry with a clean, soft cloth.

2. Lay the copper shape on a piece of clean, white paper. Then choose one of the enameling colors and cover the surface by sifting gently until the copper shape is completely covered.

3. With a spatula, very carefully place the copper shape on a trivet in a preheated kiln.

4. In a very few minutes the copper shape will take on a wavy glazed appearance. When this occurs, very carefully remove the copper shape with a spatula and allow to cool for about ten minutes. For additional color and design, repeat the process. Fig. 55-9.

The cooled workpiece should be cleaned of tarnish and scale with abrasive cloth or a file. Attach findings (tie tacks, stickpins, etc.) as needed.

55-8. *Equipment for enameling: (A) Kiln (B) Trivet for large workpiece (C) Trivets for small workpieces (D) Spatula.*

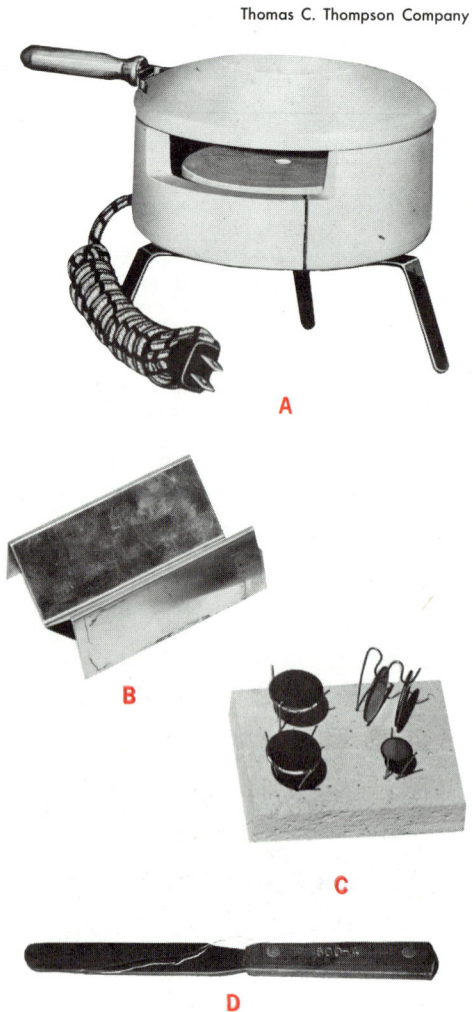

Thomas C. Thompson Company

A

B

C

D

55-9. *Steps in copper enameling.*

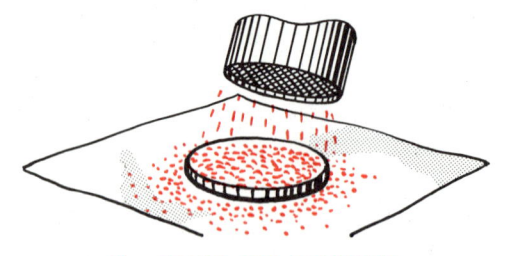

1 PICKLE CLEAN

2 DUST ON POWDER

3 FIRE

276

UNIT 56
Remove Finishing of Metal

Remove finishing methods are used to produce smooth, bright surfaces on metals. Shiny or brushed finishes on brass hardware such as hinges, doorknobs, and drawer pulls are produced this way. Industry uses many automatic polishing and buffing devices. In the shop, this kind of finishing is done by hand or with buffing machines.

POLISHING

Polishing is done with hard, felt wheels coated with abrasive grains. Coated abrasive belts, discs, or sheets are also used. (See Unit 36.) A new polishing method uses wheels made from stiff plastic bristles. These are used for polishing industrial metal parts and for general shopwork. Fig. 56-1.

Polishing removes nicks and scratches left after grinding or filing, and it is often used to remove burrs.

BUFFING

Buffing, which follows polishing, is done mainly to make the metal surface look better. Very little metal is removed in comparison to polishing. The buffing produces bright or satin finishes on metal.

Buffing wheels are made of loose pieces of flannel or cotton stitched together. Fig. 56-2. Buffing compounds are usually bars of fine abrasive grains bonded with grease or wax. Tripoli and rouge are common buffing compounds. Greaseless compounds made with glue binders are also available. These do not clog or dirty the wheels as much as other compounds. Industry also uses liquid spray compounds.

Coat the wheel with the compound by turning off the power and gently pressing the bar to the wheel as the machine is coming to a stop. This prevents the compound from spattering onto your clothes. To buff, hold the metal piece firmly in your hands and press lightly to the wheel. Continue until the piece is buffed to the

56-1. *Removing burrs from a manufactured metal part.*

3M Company

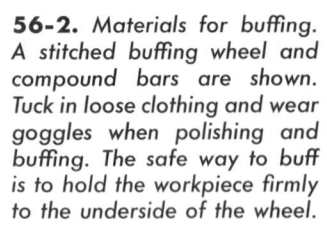

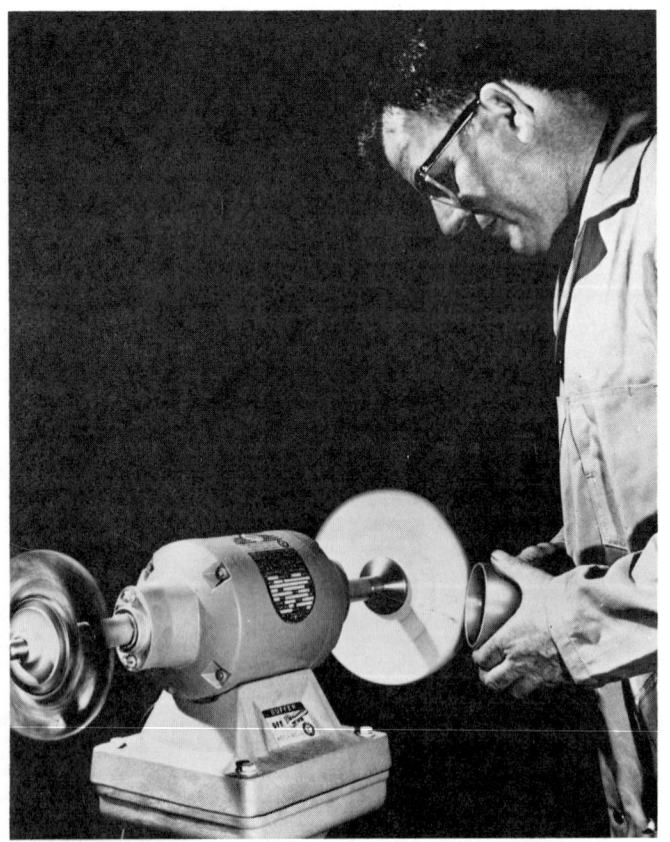

Part III: Manufacturing—Principles, Materials, and Processes

56-2. Materials for buffing. A stitched buffing wheel and compound bars are shown. Tuck in loose clothing and wear goggles when polishing and buffing. The safe way to buff is to hold the workpiece firmly to the underside of the wheel.

Rockwell-Delta Company
56-3. Buffing a metal vase. Be careful that the machine does not tear the workpiece from your hands. Hold it firmly and safely.

278

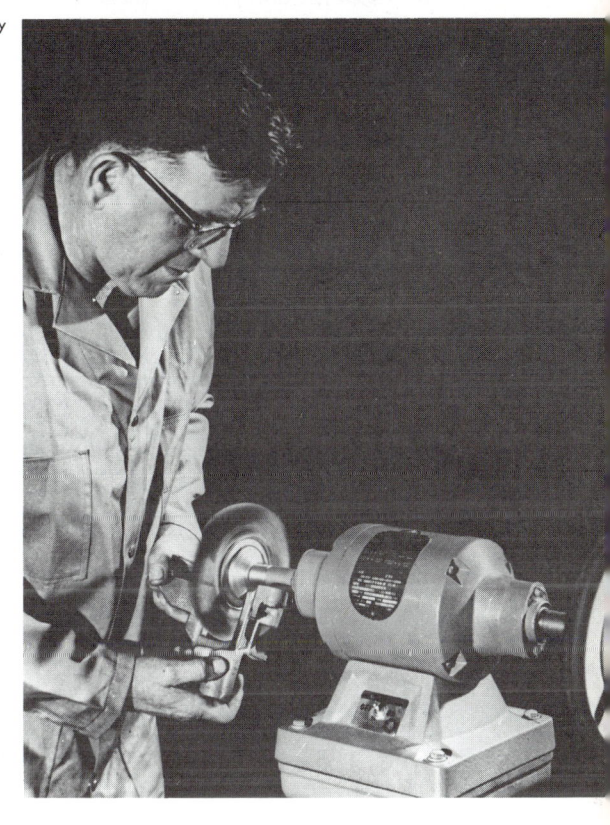

Unit 56: Remove Finishing of Metal

Rockwell-Delta Company
56-4. *Using the wire wheel.*

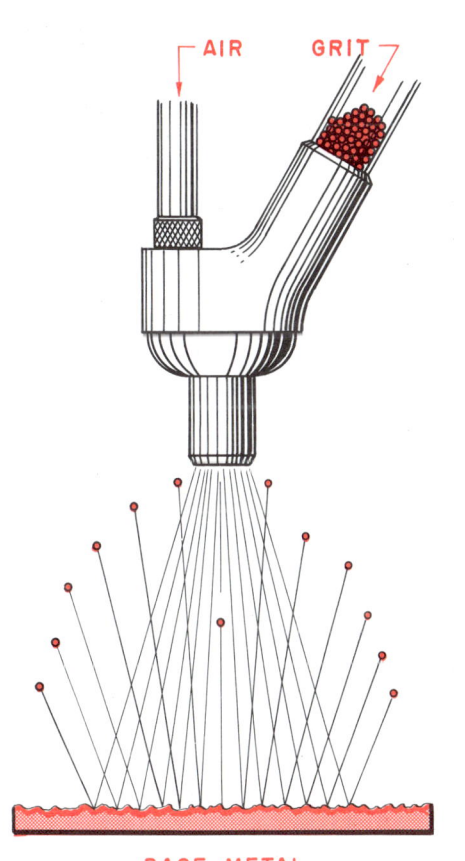

56-5. *Abrasive blasting diagram.*

desired finish. The wheel may have to be coated several times before the buffing is completed. Fig. 56-3.

Satin, or brushed, finishes may be produced by using special satin compounds or a fine wire wheel. When using wire wheels, select a fine wheel for a soft, smooth sheen. Use a coarse wheel for a frosted finish. Fig. 56-4. When buffing has been completed, clean the metal with lacquer thinner and dry with a clean, soft cloth. Apply a preserving finish such as lacquer or wax.

ABRASIVE BLASTING

One of the quickest ways to finish metal is with an abrasive blast. This type of finish uses a blast of air and abrasive particles. It is commonly called sand blasting, although abrasive grains other than sand are generally used. Fig. 56-5. Glass, steel shot, grit, and silica sand are the commonly used abrasives.

For this type of finishing, the workpiece is placed in a special cabinet, which is then shut tightly. The blasting gun is hand-controlled, and the operator must wear protective gloves. Fig. 56-6.

Depending upon the abrasive used, the finish can range in smoothness from a satin-matte to a hammered or pebble-grain effect.

279

Part III: Manufacturing—Principles, Materials, and Processes

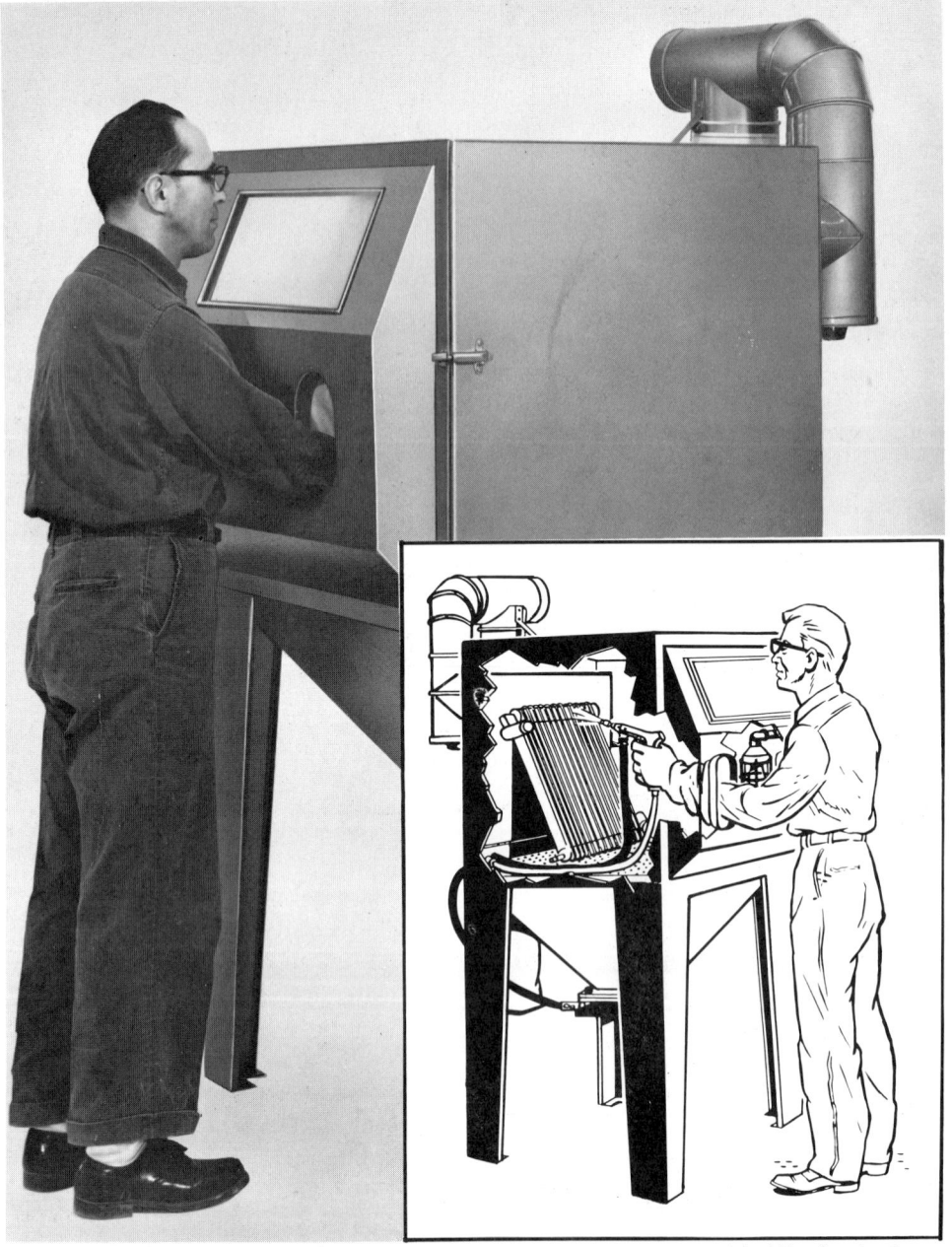

Inland Manufacturing Company

56-6. An abrasive blasting cabinet. The inset shows the interior of the unit.

UNIT 57

Displacement finishing of Metal

Displacement finishing is a metal forming process. The appearance of a metal surface is changed without adding or removing any material. This is also called *mechanical finishing*. The hammered surfaces commonly found on wrought iron hinges or on metal ash trays are good examples of displacement finishes. Industry also embosses decorative patterns on sheet metals and metal tubing. The most common methods of displacement finishing in the shop are peening and planishing.

PEENING

Peening is simply producing a hammered effect on metal by striking it with the ball end of the ball peen hammer. The metal is held on a flat surface and peened gently. By overlapping the peen marks slightly, a better-looking surface can be produced. Fig. 57-1.

PLANISHING

Planishing is smoothing metal which has been formed by sinking or raising. (See Unit 46.) It is similar to peening except that the planish marks are finer and smoother. The planishing tools are shown in Fig. 57-2. Make certain that the hammers are free from nicks before using them.

Planishing is done by placing the metal object over a stake which has a similar shape. For example, the metal bowl, Fig. 57-3, is placed over a round stake. The planishing should be done with gentle, regular blows. Try to overlap the marks,

57-1. *Both planishing and peening hammer marks must overlap slightly for the best appearance.*

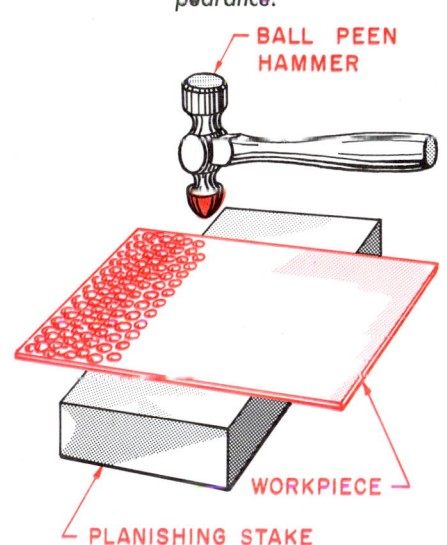

57-2. *Tools for planishing. Hammers and stakes should be clean and free of nicks before using. Remove nicks by grinding on a fine wheel, then buffing.*

Niagara Tools

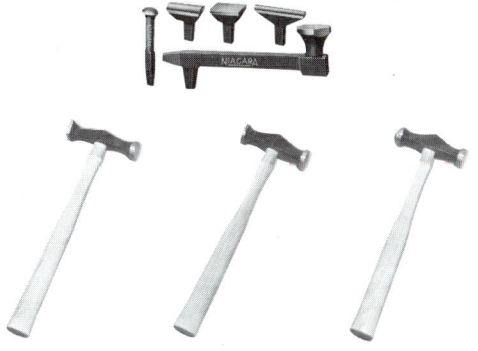

281

Part III: Manufacturing—Principles, Materials, and Processes

as in peening, and work from the center of the bowl toward the edges. The edges of the bowl will become uneven due to the planishing. True them with a file after the planishing is complete. Never buff the piece after planishing, as this will cause the marks to run together and ruin the effect.

57-3. *Planishing a bowl. Work from the center toward the edges with gentle, even hammer blows.*

UNIT 58
Color Finishing of Metal

Metals can be given interesting color treatments by applying chemicals or heat to their surfaces. Shades of brown, red, green, or black can be produced on metals to provide interesting accents and appearances. After coloring, metals should be coated with lacquer to preserve the finish.

CHEMICALS

The metals commonly colored in the shop are steel, copper, and brass. The chart in Fig. 58-1 shows chemical solutions for coloring copper and brass. All metals to be colored chemically must be buffed, then cleaned in pickling solution. Handle metal with wooden or plastic tongs to protect the hands and to prevent contamination of the solution. The solutions must be mixed in acid-proof containers. Slip the clean metal carefully into the solution. When the desired color is obtained, remove the piece, rinse with water, and allow to dry. The metal may be shaded or highlighted by rubbing with steel wool.

Steel may be given a blue or a brown color, such as found on the barrels of rifles and pistols. This is a very desirable finish for many projects you might make. Special equipment and solutions are available for these coloring operations.

HEAT

Cleaned metals are heated with a propane or welding torch. Watch the colors as they appear on the surface. Remove the heat when the desired color is obtained. Most metals can be colored this way.

Unit 58: Color Finishing of Metal

Coloring Solutions

These formulas are given in amounts that are easy to handle. If you need more or less, you may change the amounts of ingredients, provided you keep the same proportions.		
BROWN 4 oz. iron nitrate 4 oz. sodium hypo-sulfite 1 qt. water	**ANTIQUE COPPER** 3 oz. potassium sulfide (liver of sulfur) $\frac{1}{2}$ oz. ammonia 1 gal. water	**GREEN ANTIQUE** 3 qts. water 1 oz. ammonium chloride 2 oz. salt
RED 4 oz. copper sulfate 2 lbs. salt 1 gal. water	**PICKLING AND CLEANING** 1 pint sulfuric acid 1 pint nitric acid 4 pints water	**SATIN DIP** 1 pint hydrofluoric acid 3 pints water

58-1. *Solutions for coloring copper and its alloys.*

SAFETY RULES

The following safety rules should be observed when working with chemicals and heat:

1. Wear protective clothing—safety glasses, gloves, and apron.
2. Always pour acid into water. Pouring water into acid causes spattering.
3. Always work in a well-ventilated area.
4. Use the "buddy" system so that someone will always be ready to help you if necessary.
5. Be careful not to splash acid solutions. If a drop gets onto your skin, rinse with water and tell your instructor.

DISCUSSION TOPICS AND ACTIVITIES

Part 3—Manufacturing—Principles, Materials, and Processes
Section 1—Metalworking
Unit 28
 1. List some of the mechanical methods used to work metal into usable products.
 2. List some of the important metalworking industries.
Unit 29
 1. About how many persons work in the steelmaking industry?
 2. What three materials make up the charge for the blast furnace?
 3. How is limestone used in extracting iron from ore?
 4. What percentage of our steel is made by the open-hearth process? The electric process? The basic-oxygen process?
 5. What is aluminum ore called?
 6. What is alumina?
 7. Where is aluminum ore found in the United States?
 8. Why is copper such an important metal in the electrical industry?
 9. List some places in the world where copper is mined.
Unit 30
 1. Define a ductile metal; a hard metal.
 2. What thickness gauge is used to measure ferrous sheet metals? Nonferrous sheet metals?

Part III: Manufacturing—Principles, Materials, and Processes

   3. What is a ferrous metal?
   4. How many points of carbon are contained in mild steel?
   5. List some common metal shapes.
   6. What is the metric replacement size for ½″ round stock?
   7. What is brass made of? Bronze?
   8. What is an alloy?
   9. Name three tests for metal hardness.

Unit 31
   1. List some of the common layout tools.
   2. Name four methods of pattern development.
   3. What are the three heads of the combination square used for?
   4. What development method is used for laying out funnels? Cylinders?
   5. How much metal must be allowed to form a grooved seam?

Unit 32
   1. How does the ultrasonic cutting machine work?
   2. What is EDM, and how does it work?
   3. Visit an industry which uses one of these new metalworking methods and report to the class what you saw.
   4. Write a research report on one of the new developments in metalworking.
   5. What is hydrospinning?
   6. Describe the explosive forming process.
   7. What kinds of objects can be formed by explosive forming?
   8. Write a short research report on the use of adhesives in industry.

Unit 33
   1. Define metal cutting.
   2. List the eight kinds of metal cutting.

Unit 34
   1. What is sawing?
   2. List some common metal sawing tools.
   3. Hacksaw blades for sawing large, soft pieces of metal should have how many teeth?
   4. Should the teeth on the hacksaw blade point toward or away from the handle?
   5. About how wide is a No. 14 jeweler's saw blade?

Unit 35
   1. What are some differences between sawing and shearing?
   2. Is shearing a metal separation or a metal removal process?
   3. List some tools used for shearing light metals.
   4. List some tools used for shearing heavy metals.
   5. List some safety rules to be followed when using the squaring shears.
   6. Why should wire never be cut on the slitting shears?
   7. Which tin snips should be used for making straight cuts?

Unit 36
   1. What are abrasives?
   2. List five kinds of abrasives.
   3. Which abrasives are best for metalworking?
   4. What does the grit number of an abrasive mean?
   5. List four kinds of abrasive materials used in the school shop.
   6. What are coated abrasives?
   7. List some safety rules to follow when using the grinder.

Units 28-58: Discussion Topics and Activities

Unit 37
1. What are shapers used for?
2. How does the metal shaper work?

Unit 38
1. What is drilling?
2. List the three systems for identifying drill sizes.
3. What size metric drill comes close to the ½" customary size?
4. What is the center punch used for?
5. What tool is used to enlarge a hole for a flathead machine screw?
6. List some rules to follow when using the drill press.
7. At what RPM should a ¼" hole be drilled in aluminum?

Unit 39
1. Why is filing like the milling process?
2. What are two kinds of milling machines?
3. How are files classified?
4. List some common file shapes.
5. What are rasp-cut files used for?
6. What are needle files used for?
7. Does the file cut on the forward or the return stroke?

Unit 40
1. What machine is used for metal turning?
2. Name two operations besides turning that can be performed on the lathe.
3. List three types of lathe dogs.
4. List two types of lathe chucks.
5. What is knurling?

Unit 41
1. What is etching?
2. Is etching a metal removal or metal separation process?
3. What is a resist used for?
4. List some safety rules to follow when etching metal.
5. Describe how the oxyacetylene torch cuts metal.

Unit 42
1. What is metal forming?
2. How do metal forming and metal cutting differ?
3. List the seven basic kinds of metal forming; give an example of each.

Unit 43
1. What is metal bending?
2. List some common tools used in bending light metals.
3. List four kinds of metal bending stakes.
4. What is the bar folder used for?
5. What is the box and pan brake used for?
6. What machine is used to roll sheet metal into cylindrical shapes?
7. What is the bending fork used for?

Unit 44
1. List four kinds of metal casting.
2. What kind of casting is used by dentists to make gold fillings?
3. What are patterns used for?
4. List some of the tools used in sand casting.
5. What is the melting temperature of brass? Aluminum? Bronze?

Part III: Manufacturing—Principles, Materials, and Processes

   6. What safety clothing should be worn when casting?
   7. What are the two parts of the flask?
   8. What is flux used for in metal casting?

Unit 45
   1. What is forging?
   2. Is any metal removal involved in forging?
   3. Is heat-treating a forging process?
   4. List some tools used in forging.
   5. What is "upsetting" in forging?
   6. What safety clothing should be worn while forging?
   7. What is the heat color for forging mild steel?
   8. List the steps in heat-treating a screwdriver.
   9. What is normalizing?
   10. What is the color of steel at 1325 °F? What is this temperature in degrees Celsius?
   11. What is the tempering color for cold chisels?

Unit 46
   1. What is pressing?
   2. What are some common pressing operations which can be done in the school shop?
   3. What is another name for sinking?
   4. Describe how sinking is done.
   5. What kind of hammer is generally used in sinking?
   6. Describe how raising is done.
   7. What kind of hammer is generally used in raising?
   8. What is another name for metal tooling?
   9. Make a chart showing the steps in metal tooling.
   10. How can tooled-metal designs be colored and highlighted?
   11. Make a display of products made by metal spinning.

Unit 47
   1. How is metal drawing done?
   2. List some objects formed by drawing.

Unit 48
   1. Describe the process of extrusion.
   2. List some objects formed by extrusion.

Unit 49
   1. What is metal rolling?
   2. What kinds of metal shapes are formed by rolling?

Unit 50
   1. Define metal fastening.
   2. List the three main metal fastening methods.
   3. In your own words, what is the purpose of metal fastening?

Unit 51
   1. What is mechanical fastening?
   2. List the three main mechanical fastening methods, and give examples of each.
   3. List five kinds of threaded fasteners.
   4. List some tools used in turning and holding threaded fasteners.
   5. Make a display of different kinds of metal fasteners.
   6. What is the hand groover used for?
   7. Sketch three kinds of sheet metal joints.

Units 28–58: Discussion Topics and Activities

Unit 52
1. Define adhesion.
2. What is the main difference between adhesion and cohesion?
3. List the three main adhesion methods.
4. What is the difference between soldering and brazing?
5. What is the purpose of a flux?
6. List three sources of heat for soldering.
7. Describe how a soldering copper is tinned.
8. What are most brazing rods made of?
9. List some safety rules for soldering and brazing.

Unit 53
1. What is cohesion?
2. List the three main kinds of welding.
3. How does welding differ from brazing?
4. Explain how resistance welding works.
5. What two kinds of gas are burned in gas welding?
6. Write a research report on other welding methods. See *Technology Report* No. 1.

Unit 54
1. What are two reasons for finishing metal?
2. List some important methods of metal finishing.

Unit 55
1. What liquid is used to clean lacquer brushes?
2. What liquid is used to clean enamel brushes?
3. What is "true" enamel?
4. Why should metal be heated before it is lacquered?

Unit 56
1. Why is remove finishing a kind of cutting?
2. What is the difference between polishing and buffing?
3. What are buffing wheels made of?
4. What are buffing compounds?
5. What is a greaseless buffing compound?
6. Explain how buffing compound is applied to the wheel.

Unit 57
1. What is planishing?
2. What are planishing stakes used for?
3. Why should peen or planish marks overlap?
4. Should you start peening from the edge or from the center of a bowl? Why?

Unit 58
1. List three safety rules for working with chemicals.
2. Explain how heat coloring is done.
3. What chemicals are used to make copper turn green? Black?
4. Why should the pieces to be colored be handled with wood or plastic tongs?

PART III

Manufacturing—Principles, Materials, and Processes

Section 2–Plastics

Unit 59 Introduction to Plastics

Unit 60 Industrial Processing of Plastics

Unit 61 Forming Plastics in the School Shop

Unit 62 Cutting Plastic

Unit 63 Fastening Plastic

Unit 64 Finishing Plastic

Discussion Topics

UNIT 59
Introduction to Plastics

Plastics has become one of the leading industries in the United States. It is also one of the fastest growing. Today plastics are used in the manufacture of a wide range of products, especially those once made of metal or wood. Fig. 59-1.

Celluloid, developed in 1869, was the first plastic to have commercial success. It was widely used as a substitute for ivory in billiard balls. Motion picture film and automobile windshields were also made of Celluloid.

The greatest development of new plastics and new uses has occurred since the 1940s. Today plastics are used in everything from spaceships to artificial heart valves. Fig. 59-2. They are widely used by the communications industry as insulation for power lines and housing for telephones. Fig. 59-3.

Plastics are also widely used in the furniture industry. They increase comfort and help to simplify household chores. Much furniture including frames, foam cushions, and chair coverings—is made of plastic. Many easy-to-clean floor coverings are also made from plastics.

THE PLASTICS INDUSTRY

Today there are about 6000 companies in the United States that manufacture plastics. These companies produce material worth billions of dollars. Three types

59-1. *This protective dome is constructed of acrylic plastic.*

Rohm and Haas

59-2. *Artificial heart valve. The plastic covering enables the surgeon to attach the valve to the heart muscles.*

Edwards Laboratories

289

Part III: Manufacturing—Principles, Materials, and Processes

59-3. Plastic pellets like these are used to make telephone housings, handsets, and cord insulation.
Western Electric Corporation

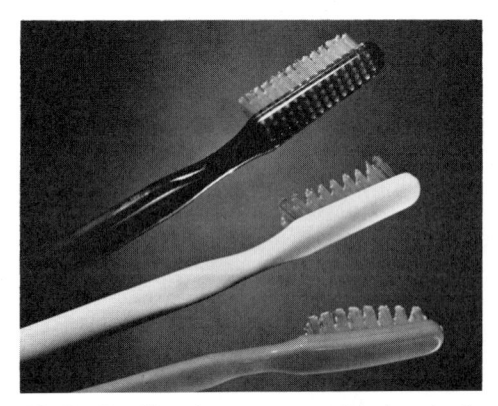

59-4. Toothbrushes are molded plastic products.

of plastic—polyethylene, vinyl, and styrene—exceed two billion pounds annual production. Research continues to develop new plastics and new ways to use them.

The plastics industry has always been in need of skilled people. One of the most important workers is the mold maker. This person must be a highly skilled machinist. Many plastic items such as toothbrushes, are formed in molds. Fig. 59-4. Mold makers design and machine those molds.

Now there is a need for a new type of worker called a plastics or polymeric materials engineer. Such a person usually has some experience in mechanical engineering and schooling in chemistry and plastics. The plastics engineer needs to be experienced in all aspects of plastics production, from mold making to the finishing of the final product. Because there are few schools where a person can acquire this background, many mechanical engineers go into the plastics industry and gain experience on the job.

Other jobs in the plastics industry are like those in other industries. These include jobs for machine operators, quality-control technicians, foremen, and inspectors, to name but a few. The plastics industry will continue to grow, and thus will need many more workers in all job classifications.

Unit 59: Introduction to Plastics

```
                          ┌──────────┐
                          │ PLASTICS │
                          └────┬─────┘
                   ┌───────────┴───────────┐
           ┌───────┴────────┐       ┌──────┴──────┐
           │ THERMOPLASTICS │       │  THERMOSETS │
           └────────────────┘       └─────────────┘
```

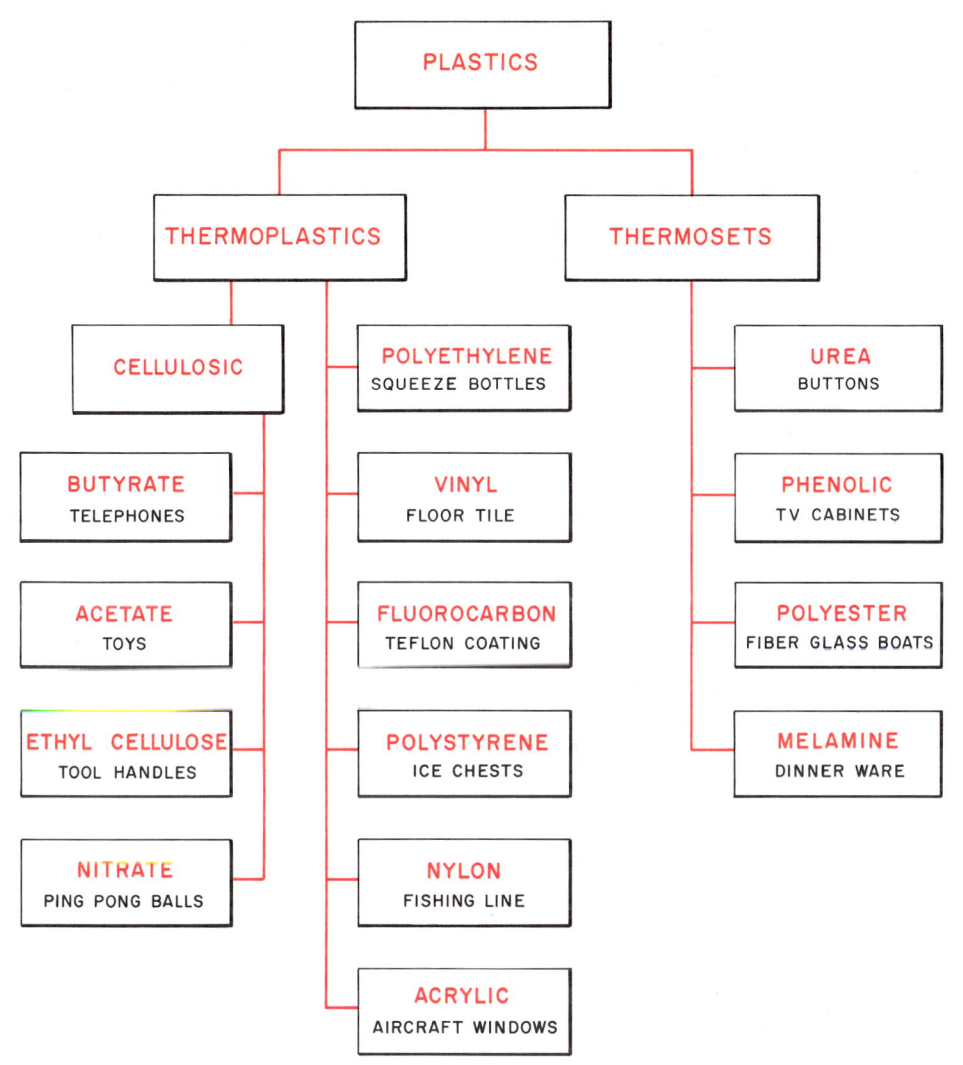

THERMOPLASTICS			THERMOSETS
CELLULOSIC	POLYETHYLENE — SQUEEZE BOTTLES		UREA — BUTTONS
BUTYRATE — TELEPHONES	VINYL — FLOOR TILE		PHENOLIC — TV CABINETS
ACETATE — TOYS	FLUOROCARBON — TEFLON COATING		POLYESTER — FIBER GLASS BOATS
ETHYL CELLULOSE — TOOL HANDLES	POLYSTYRENE — ICE CHESTS		MELAMINE — DINNER WARE
NITRATE — PING PONG BALLS	NYLON — FISHING LINE		
	ACRYLIC — AIRCRAFT WINDOWS		

59-5. *This chart lists common plastics and some of the products made from them.*

THE FAMILY OF PLASTICS

Plastics are *synthetic* materials, unlike wood and metal, which are found in nature. Plastics are usually made from some combination of carbon, oxygen, hydrogen, and nitrogen. Other elements may also be present. The source for many of the raw materials for making plastics is oil or coal.

Plastics are a family of materials. Each branch of the family has certain characteristics. However, whatever the properties or form, all plastics fall into two groups: *thermoplastic* and *thermosetting*.

Thermoplastics soften when heated and harden when cooled. When heated, they may be shaped or molded. They can be reheated and changed to a different shape.

Thermosetting plastics are cured or set into permanent shape by heat. They get soft or burn if reheated, but they cannot be reshaped. Fig. 59-5 shows some common kinds of plastics and typical products made from them.

UNIT 60

Industrial Processing of Plastics

The processing of plastic materials is done in several ways. Some manufacturers use only one technique while others may use several techniques in the same plant. The common industrial processes include:

- Extrusion.
- Calendering.
- Coating.
- Blow molding.
- Compression molding.
- Transfer molding.
- Thermoforming.
- Injection molding.
- Rotational molding.
- Solvent molding.
- Casting.
- High-pressure laminating.
- Reinforcing.
- Foaming.

EXTRUSION

Extrusion molding is used to form thermoplastic materials into continuous sheeting, film, tubes, rods, profile shapes, and filaments, and to coat wires and cables. Fig. 60-1.

Dry plastic material is loaded into a hopper. It is then fed into a long heating chamber through which it is moved by the action of a continuously revolving screw. At the end of the heating chamber the molten plastic is forced out through a *die*. This is a small opening with the shape desired in the finished product. As the plastic is forced through the die, it is fed onto a conveyor belt where it is cooled, most often by blowers or in water.

In the case of wire and cable coating, the thermoplastic is extruded around a continuing length of wire or cable which, like the plastic, passes through the extruder die. The coated wire is wound on drums after cooling.

60-1. *Extrusion molding.*
The Society of the Plastics Industry, Inc.

MOLDING POWDER
FEED HOPPER
EXTRUDED PLASTIC
HEATING UNIT
DIE
STRAINER
MECHANICAL SCREW
CONVEYOR

CALENDERING

Calendering is a process for making plastic into film and sheeting. *Film* is plastic up to and including 10 mils in thickness. (A mil is $\frac{1}{1000}$ of an inch.) *Sheeting* refers to plastic more than 10 mils thick.

In calendering, heated plastic material is squeezed between heated rollers. The space between the rollers determines the thickness of the plastic. Fig. 60-2.

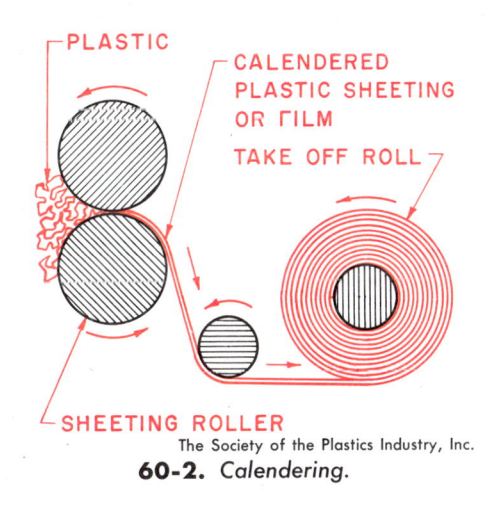

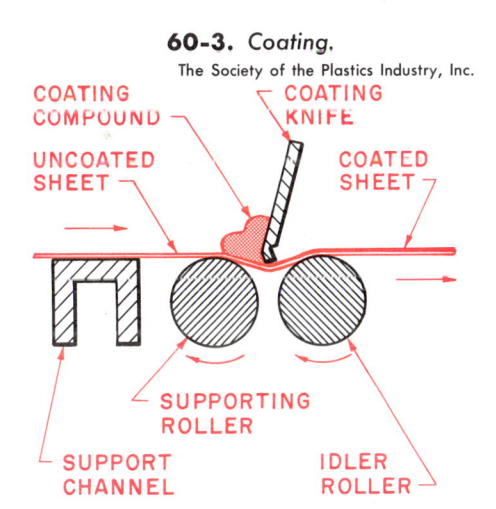

Unit 60: Industrial Processing of Plastics

COATING

Coating is the process of applying plastic material onto a support base such as metal, paper, wood, fabric, glass, ceramic, or other plastics. Coating may be done with a knife, spray, roller, or brush. It can also be done by dipping. Fig. 60-3 shows how calendering can be used to coat a material with plastic. The material can be spread coated as it passes over a roller and under a blade.

BLOW MOLDING

Blow molding stretches a thermoplastic material against a mold and then hardens it. There are two types of blow molding: *direct* and *indirect*.

In the direct method a hot, molten tube, called a *parison*, is placed into a mold. Air is blown into the plastic, like blowing up a balloon. The air forces the plastic against the cold sides of the mold. The plastic is then cooled and hardened. Fig. 60-4.

The indirect method uses a plastic sheet which is heated and clamped be-

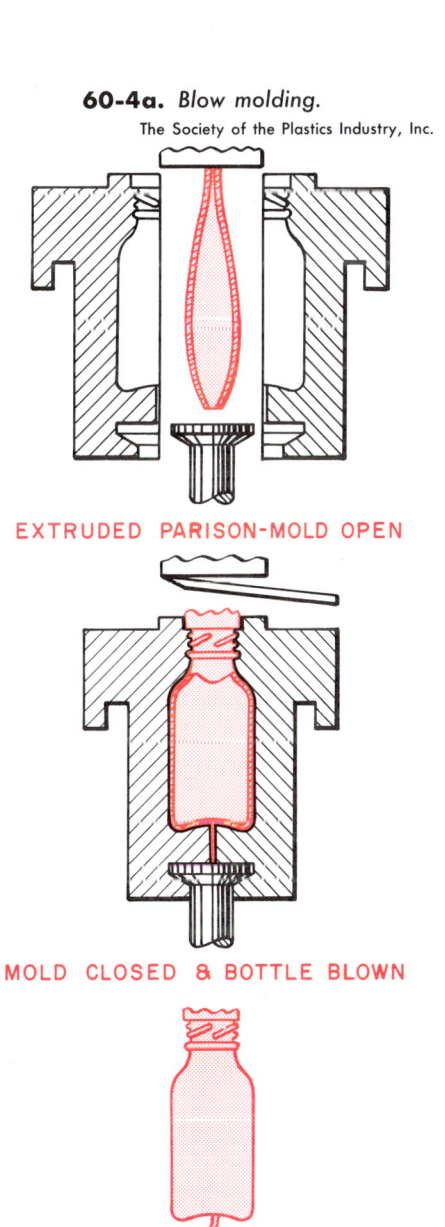

60-2. Calendering.
The Society of the Plastics Industry, Inc.

60-3. Coating.
The Society of the Plastics Industry, Inc.

60-4a. Blow molding.
The Society of the Plastics Industry, Inc.

EXTRUDED PARISON-MOLD OPEN

MOLD CLOSED & BOTTLE BLOWN

FINISHED BOTTLE

293

Part III: Manufacturing—Principles, Materials, and Processes

60-4b. These plastic bottles were blow molded. *Creative Packaging Co.*

60-5b. After molding, plastic parts are cleaned by an abrasive cylinder brush. *3M Company*

tween a die and a cover. Air pressure is used to force the plastic material against the die. The plastic is then cooled and hardened.

COMPRESSION MOLDING

Compression molding is the most common method of forming thermosetting materials. Fig. 60-5a. The plastic material is squeezed into the desired shape by using heat and pressure in a mold.

60-5a. Compression molding. *The Society of the Plastics Industry, Inc.*

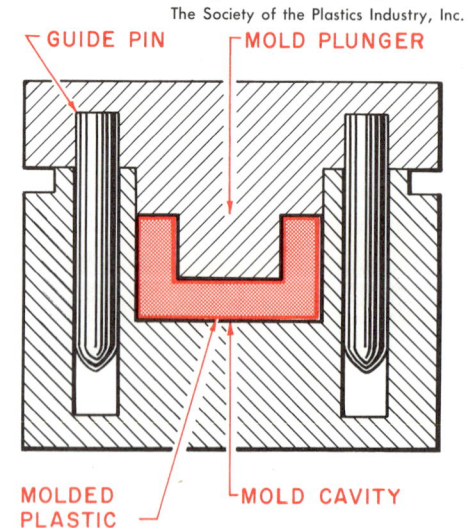

Plastic molding powder is mixed with fillers to add strength or other qualities to the product. This mixture is placed in a heated mold. The mold is closed, causing the plastic to flow to all parts. While the mold is closed, the plastic undergoes a chemical change that permanently sets its shape. After cooling, the mold is opened and the part removed. Fig. 60-5b.

TRANSFER MOLDING

Transfer molding is usually used with thermosetting plastics. This method is like compression molding in that the plastic is cured in a mold under heat and pressure. It differs from compression molding in that the plastic is heated to a formable state before it reaches the mold, and it is forced into a closed mold by a plunger. Fig. 60-6.

Transfer molding was developed as a way of molding parts with small deep holes or numerous metal inserts.

THERMOFORMING

Thermoforming consists of heating a thermoplastic sheet to a formable state and then using air and/or mechanical assists to shape it.

There are many methods of thermoforming. One technique is simple vacuum

Unit 60: Industrial Processing of Plastics

forming. In this process, a plastic sheet is clamped over an airtight box. Electric heaters above the box soften the plastic. Then the air is drawn out of the box, pulling the soft plastic down on a "former" in the box. The plastic thus becomes shaped like the former. Another method uses compressed air to force the plastic into a former. Fig. 60-7.

INJECTION MOLDING

Injection is the most common method of forming thermoplastic materials. In injection molding, plastic material is put into a hopper which feeds into a heating chamber. A plunger pushes the plastic through this long heating chamber where the material is softened to a fluid state. At the end of this chamber there is a nozzle which is placed firmly against the opening to a cool, closed mold. The liquid plastic is forced at high pressure through this nozzle into the cold mold. As soon as the plastic cools and becomes solid, the mold opens and the finished plastic piece is ejected from the press. Fig. 60-8.

ROTATIONAL MOLDING

This method is used to make hollow, one-piece flexible parts. A measured amount of plastic material is placed into a mold which is rotated in an oven. The

60-6. *Transfer molding.*
The Society of the Plastics Industry, Inc.

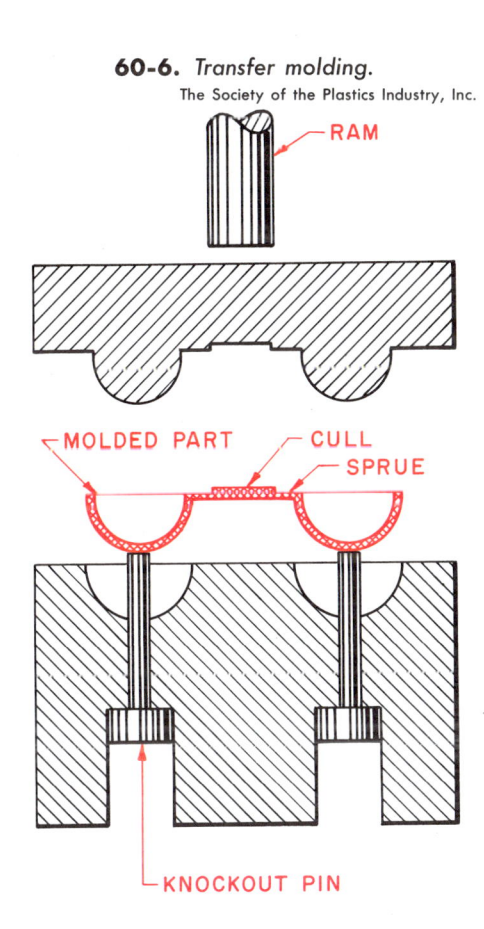

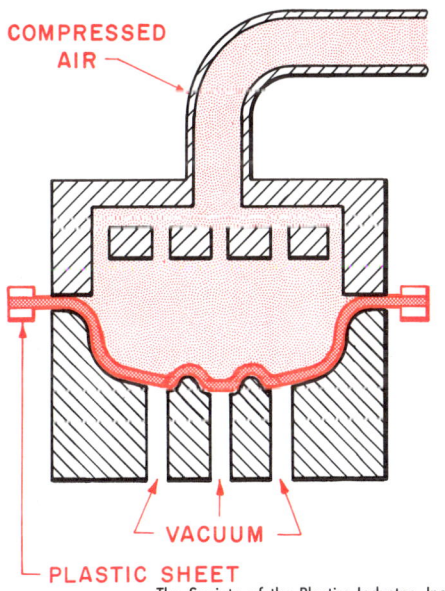

60-7. *A thermoforming mold.*
The Society of the Plastics Industry, Inc.

60-8. *Injection molding.*
The Society of the Plastics Industry, Inc.

295

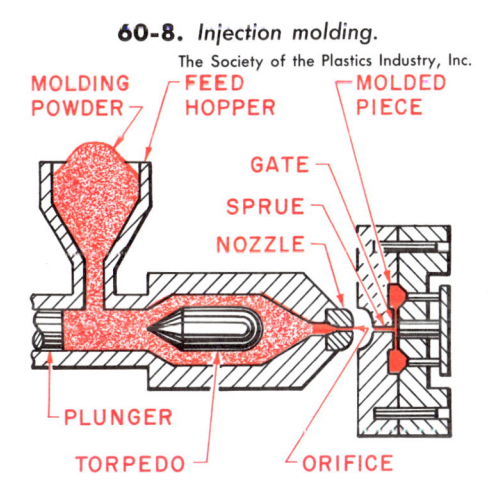

Part III: Manufacturing—Principles, Materials, and Processes

movement spreads the material throughout the inside of the mold. The mold is then cooled to harden the plastic into the shape of the mold.

SOLVENT MOLDING

In solvent molding a mold is dipped into a plastic solution and withdrawn, or filled with a liquid plastic and then emptied. A layer of plastic film sticks to the sides of the mold.

Some items thus formed, like a bathing cap, are removed from the molds. Other solvent moldings remain permanently on the form. Examples are plastic coatings on pliers or wire cutters.

CASTING

In the casting process no pressure is used. Plastic material is poured into molds. After it cures (hardens), it is removed from the mold. Casting may be done with either thermoplastic or thermosetting materials.

HIGH-PRESSURE LAMINATING

Thermosetting plastics are generally used in high-pressure laminating, which is done with high heat and pressure. The plastics are used to hold together the reinforcing materials that make up the body of the finished product. The reinforcing materials may be cloth, paper, wood, or fibers of glass. These materials are soaked in a plastic solution. After drying, layers of these materials are stacked between polished steel plates and subjected to heat and high pressure to bond them permanently together. Fig. 60-9.

The end product of high-pressure laminating may be plain flat sheets; decorative sheets like those used for counter tops; or rods, tubes, or formed shapes.

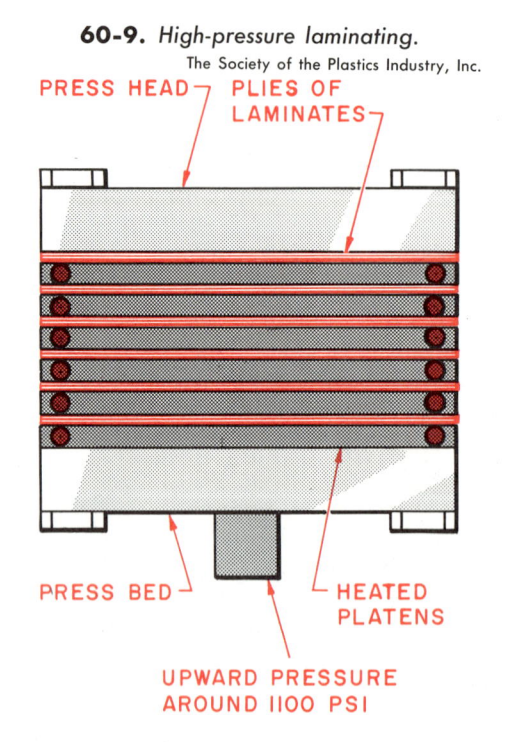

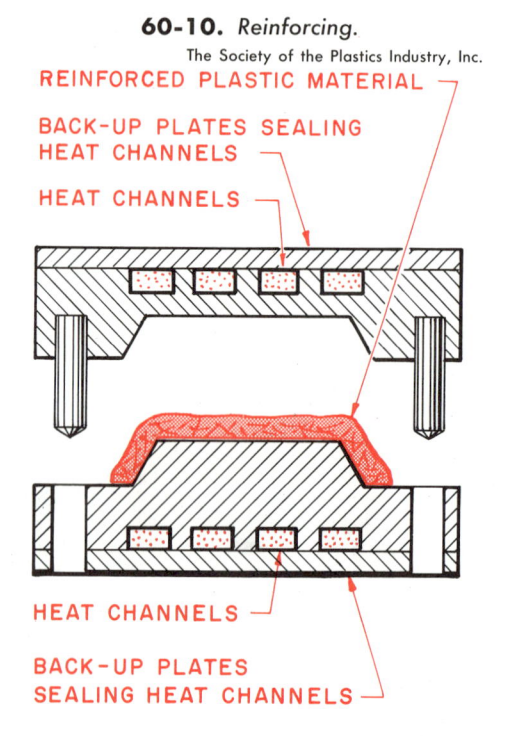

60-9. *High-pressure laminating.*
The Society of the Plastics Industry, Inc.

60-10. *Reinforcing.*
The Society of the Plastics Industry, Inc.

Unit 60: Industrial Processing of Plastics

REINFORCING

Reinforced plastics differ from high-pressure laminates in that the plastics used require very little or no pressure in the processing. Fig. 60-10. In both methods, however, plastics are used to bind together the cloth, paper, or glass fiber reinforcing material used for the body of the product. The reinforcing material may be in sheet or mat form, and the selection depends on the qualities desired in the end product. Reinforced plastics have very high strength, yet are lightweight.

FOAMED PLASTICS

Foamed or expanded plastics are materials made by forming gas bubbles in plastic material while it is in a liquid state. Several processes are used to make the bubbles. In most foamed plastics, the bubbles (cells) are separate from each other. They are connected by partitioned "walls." This makes the foams very good insulating material for heat or cold.

Foamed materials are made in two ways. One way uses beads of thermoplastic or thermosetting material that expand when heated. The heat causes a chemical reaction within the beads and produces a gas. It is this gas which causes the beads to expand and make the cell structure. Fig. 60-11.

Another way to make foam is to blow a gas, such as carbon dioxide, into the foam material while it is in a molten state and being formed. Fig. 60-12.

Plastic foams may be flexible or rigid. They are used in many forms and for a variety of purposes, from decorating to insulating. Some typical products are sponges, seat cushions, padding, insulation, automotive parts, and picnic coolers.

FORMING PLASTICS IN THE SCHOOL SHOP

Many of the forming methods discussed in this unit require expensive, complex equipment. They can be done only in large factories. However, there are some types of plastics forming which can easily be done in the school shop. You will learn about these in the next unit.

60-11. *One method of foaming plastics. The molded articles may be anything from dashboards to airplane parts.*

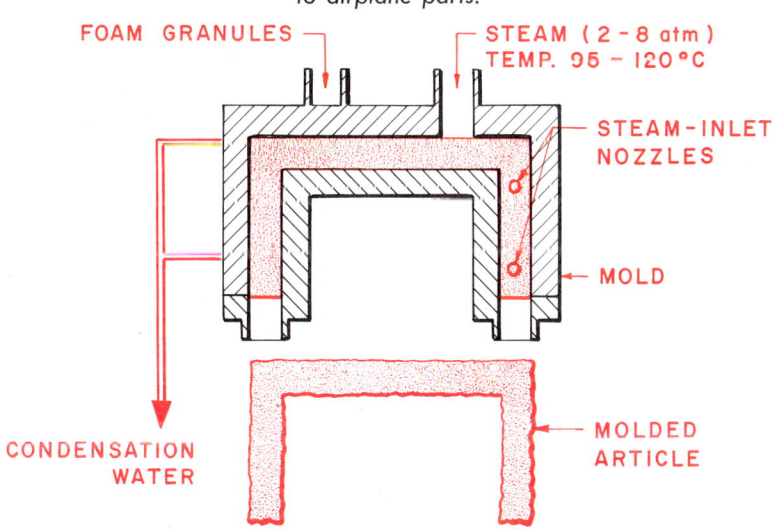

Part III: Manufacturing—Principles, Materials, and Processes

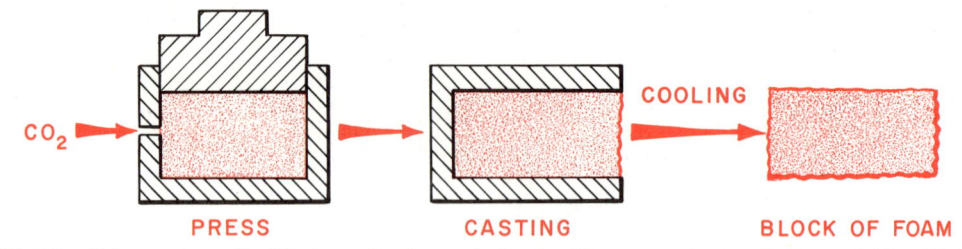

60-12. Using carbon dioxide to make foamed plastics. The press shapes the material in which the expanding gas is dissolved. The casting is then heated. This is called thermal stabilization. The resulting product may be a simple form from which sheets or various shapes are cut, or it may be a molded item.

UNIT 61

Forming Plastics in the School Shop

One of the outstanding characteristics of plastics is that they can be formed in many ways. They can be bent, cast, extruded, pressed, and molded into hundreds of different products. Fig. 61-1.

BENDING

One of the easiest ways to form plastic is by *bending*. When acrylic plastics such as Lucite® or Plexiglas® are heated, they soften. Remember, they are thermoplastics; when soft, they may be made into almost any shape.

Bending of plastic requires just a few tools. You need a device to heat the plastic, such as an electric hot plate or oven. Never use an open flame on plastic. You also need a pair of cotton gloves to handle the hot plastic. If you are going to bend the plastic around a form, make the form before the plastic is heated. The form should be sanded smooth because the hot plastic will pick up any saw marks, and they will appear on the finished piece.

Cut a piece of plastic the desired size. Smooth the edges. Be sure to remove all the masking paper from the plastic before it is heated.

Put the plastic on a piece of asbestos. Place it on a hot plate, or in an oven at about 300 degrees. Heat until the plastic can be bent easily. Remove it from the heat and bend to the desired shape, either by hand or on a form. Be sure to wear gloves. Fig. 61-2.

When the plastic cools, it will retain this shape. If reheated, it will go back to its original form. This is useful if you did not get the desired shape on the first try. Just reheat the piece and bend it again.

In industry, strips of plastic are heated and bent to form letters for signs, or decorations.

298

Unit 61: Forming Plastics in the School Shop

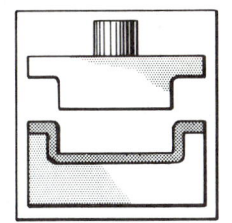

Forming in the Shop

Forming is the process of shaping a material without adding to or removing any of the material.

KINDS OF FORMING	DEFINITION	EXAMPLES
Bending	Forming by stretching heated plastic around a straight axis.	Letter-forming operations for signs and displays; forming heated plastic strips.
Casting	Forming by pouring liquid plastic into a hollow cavity and allowing it to harden.	Die casting and open-mold casting.
Molding	Forming by squeezing a heated plastic between two dies.	Compression molding, injection molding, blow forming and vacuum forming, foam molding.
Extruding	Forming by forcing the heated plastic through an opening (or die) which shapes the plastic.	Plastic molding and tubing extrusion operations.

61-1. This chart shows some of the ways plastics can be formed in the school laboratory.

299

Part III: Manufacturing—Principles, Materials, and Processes

61-2. Bending plastic around a dowel form. The plastic must be heated before it can be bent.

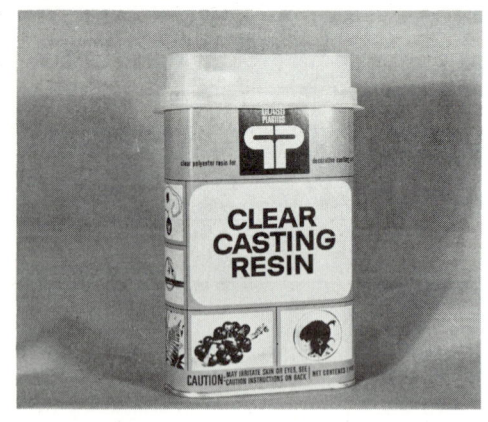

61-3. Clear casting resin can be mixed with dyes to make objects of many colors. The resin must be mixed with a catalyst before using.

CASTING

Plastic casting is generally done by pouring liquid polyester resin into a mold. Fig. 61-3. After the plastic resin has hardened, the finished piece is removed from the mold. Industry casts lenses and jewels by this method. In the school shop, the casting resin is mixed with a catalyst or hardener before pouring. The required amounts of resin and catalyst vary; so read the directions on the container.

The molds to be used must first be coated with a liquid release so that the finished piece can be removed easily. Carefully pour the resin into the mold. Wear gloves and safety goggles, and work in a well-ventilated area. Allow to harden overnight. Fig. 61-4 shows the plastic molds (available from the resin supplier) and the finished pieces.

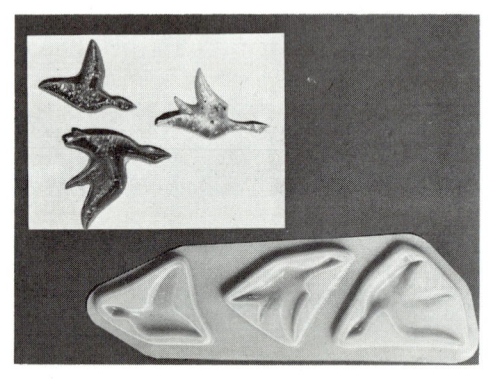

61-4. Plastic molds and finished castings. Molds may be made of wood or metal also.

OTHER FORMING PROCESSES

Industry *compresses* thermosetting plastic granules between dies to form distributor caps, radio cases, knobs, handles, and dishes. Thermoplastic materials are used in *injection molding* to form such things as telephone parts, Fig. 61-5, and appliance parts.

Compression and injection molding may also be done in the school shop. For each of these processes a mold or die is needed, along with the right machine. Fig. 61-6 shows a student using a small injection molder. Fig. 61-7 shows a student forming a part on a compression molding machine.

In industry, polystyrene or styrene sheets are *blow formed* or *vacuum formed* to make battery cases, trays, and assorted food containers. *Foam molding* is used to produce packaging cases, ice chests, and floating devices from expandable polystyrene beads. Foam molding, as well as blow and vacuum forming, is commonly done in the school shop.

300

Unit 61: Forming Plastics in the School Shop

Western Electric Corporation
61-5. These thermoplastic dial wheels for telephones were made by an injection molding process.

61-6. Student using a small injection molding machine for making a project in the school laboratory.

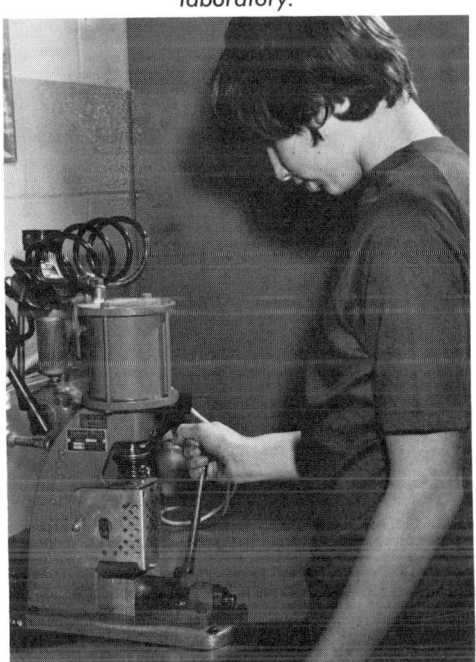

61-7. Student using a compression molding press.

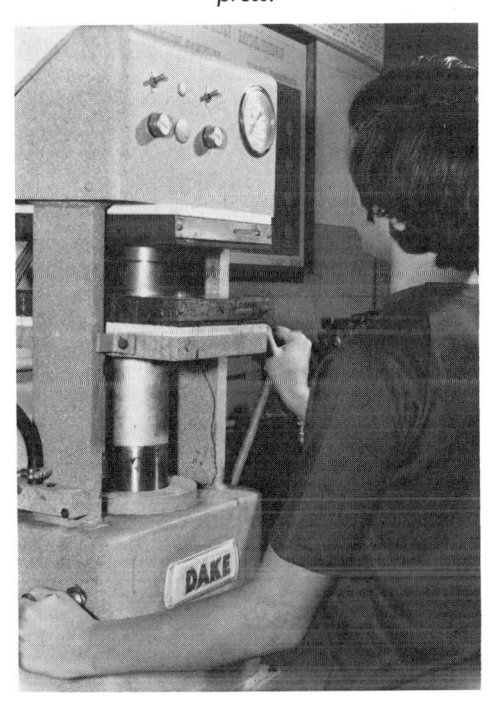

UNIT 62

Cutting Plastic

Plastics used in the shop may be cut in several ways. The tools and methods are similar to those used in woodcutting. *Shearing* may be done on very thin sheets with scissors or tin snips. Thicker sheets, as well as rods and bars, are usually cut with a saw. The cutting tools should be sharp. *Sawing* should be done very carefully and not too fast. If you saw too fast, you will heat the plastic, causing the saw to stick. You may use a hacksaw, a backsaw, a jigsaw, or a band saw for cutting plastic.

A fine-tooth hacksaw is good for cutting rods, tubes, bars, and narrow sheets of plastic. A coping saw or jeweler's saw may be used for cutting curved designs in sheet plastic. Fig. 62-1. When sawing plastic, it is best to clamp the piece securely in a vise or to a sawhorse.

The jigsaw is also used for cutting curved designs and irregular shapes from sheet plastic. Fig. 62-2. The band saw works well for cutting rods and tubing to length. It can also be used for making

62-1. *Cutting plastic with a coping saw. Hold the plastic on a V-block. Note that the protective paper has been left on the plastic.*

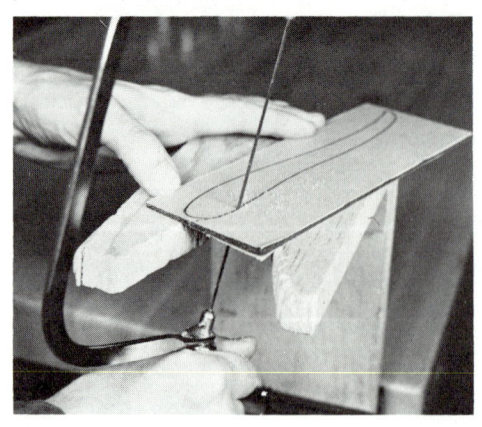

62-2. *Cutting an irregular shape on a jigsaw.*

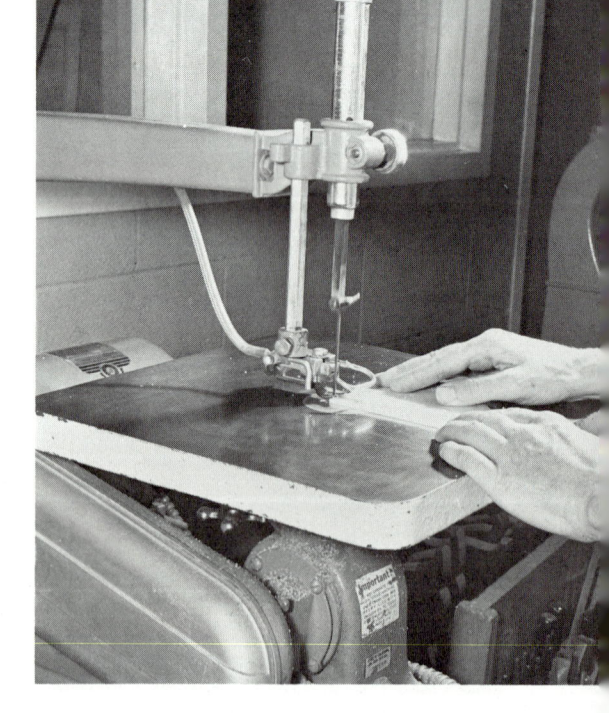

Unit 62: Cutting Plastic

62-3. Plastic may be drilled with ordinary wood and metal drilling equipment. Do not force the tool, as this will cause the plastic to melt.

62-4. Smoothing plastic sheets with a Surform® shaping tool.

straight cuts on sheet plastic when a guide is used. **Always ask the instructor before using any power machinery.**

The circular saw can be used for cutting sheets of thick plastic. It is used for squaring ends and cutting grooves in sheet plastic. Cutting plastic on a circular saw should usually be done by the instructor.

Methods for *abrading,* or sanding, plastic are the same as for woodworking. It is important to remember that the plastic will melt if it is pressed too hard on a sanding machine.

Twist drills used in woodwork or metalwork can also be used for *drilling* holes in plastic. Holes can be drilled with either a hand drill or a drill press. Fig. 62-3. The work must be held securely. With a center punch, indent the place where you want the hole. This will keep the drill from wandering and damaging the surface of the plastic. If you are drilling holes wider than $\frac{1}{4}''$ in thick plastic, drill a $\frac{1}{8}''$ pilot hole first. When drilling holes in plastic, use a slow or medium speed. If you drill too fast, the drill will get hot and stick to the plastic.

Shaping and *smoothing* of plastic is done with files and other shaping tools as in woodworking. The plastic should be held firmly in a vise. Fig. 62-4. Be careful not to bend it, as this will cause crazing or cracking. Plastic can also be *turned* on a lathe. The work must be held carefully in a chuck or between centers. Too much pressure on the cutting tool can cause the plastic to break. This can be very dangerous; so check with your instructor before lathe-turning is attempted.

UNIT 63

Fastening Plastic

Plastic materials can be joined together with glues and cements, and with mechanical fasteners. Permanent fastening is done with cements, and semipermanent joints are made with fasteners such as screws. Fig. 63-1.

MECHANICAL FASTENERS

Plastic parts to be joined with screws or with nuts and bolts must be carefully drilled. Otherwise the plastic will fracture and split. The same techniques used for preparing holes for screws in wood and metal should be followed for plastic. Plastic pieces can also be drilled and tapped.

ADHESION

Adhesives used for wood do not work well for gluing plastics. The two general-purpose glues for plastics are epoxy glue and contact cement. Epoxy glues come in two separate tubes. To use them, take equal amounts of material from each tube, mix them together, and apply the mixture to the surfaces to be joined. The pieces must be held or clamped until the glue sets. Fig. 63-2.

To fasten plastic with contact cement, coat both surfaces with the cement and allow to dry (about 20 minutes). Then bring the two surfaces together *carefully*. Once they touch, they will stick so tight that they cannot be moved. No clamps are needed.

COHESION

Plastics can be fastened together by cohesion—that is, by fusing the two pieces of plastic together. This may be done by solvent cementing or by thermal welding. The most common example of thermal welding is the heat sealing of plastic food bags. Other thermal welding methods involve friction and hot gas. (Thermal welding is not generally done in the school shop.)

Another way of forming a cohesive bond in plastics is by sound waves. Very high frequency sound waves are used to "excite" the molecules of plastic. The movement of the molecules creates friction, which generates heat. The heat causes the materials to bond together. Fig. 63-3.

In school projects, solvent cement is used to fuse plastic. This is done by the following method.

First make sure the plastic is clean, and that the joint fits well. (The solvent will not make up for a poor joint.) Then apply the cement to all surfaces to be joined. This is usually done by soaking the plastic in the solvent or applying with a hypodermic needle. Fig. 63-4. Solvent cement may also be applied to the edges of the plastic from a tube, as in Fig. 63-5. The solvent softens the plastic. The pieces to be fastened are held together with spring clamps until the solvent evaporates. If the pieces are moved before the solvent

Unit 63: Fastening Plastic

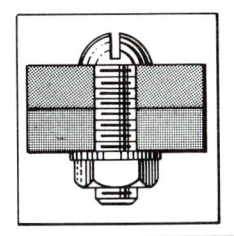

Fastening

Fastening is the process of joining materials together permanently or semipermanently.

KIND OF FASTENING	DEFINITION	EXAMPLES
Mechanical Fastening (Machine screws in tapped holes, plastic parts)	Permanent or semipermanent fastening with special locking devices.	Fastening with screws, bolts and nuts, or drive screws.
Adhesion (Glue, plastic parts)	Permanent fastening by bonding like or unlike materials together with cements.	Epoxy cementing. Contact cementing.
Cohesion (Solvent cement, plastic parts)	Permanent fastening by fusing plastic pieces together with softened or liquid plastic and pressure.	Solvent cementing. Thermal welding. Sonic welding. Plastic resins.

63-1. Various methods of fastening plastics.

63-2. Two pieces of plastic being held by spring clamps until the cement dries.

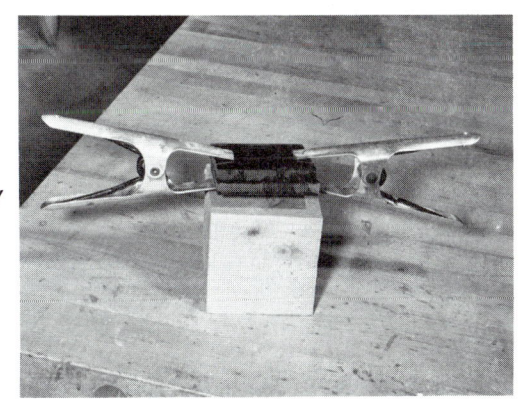

Part III: Manufacturing—Principles, Materials, and Processes

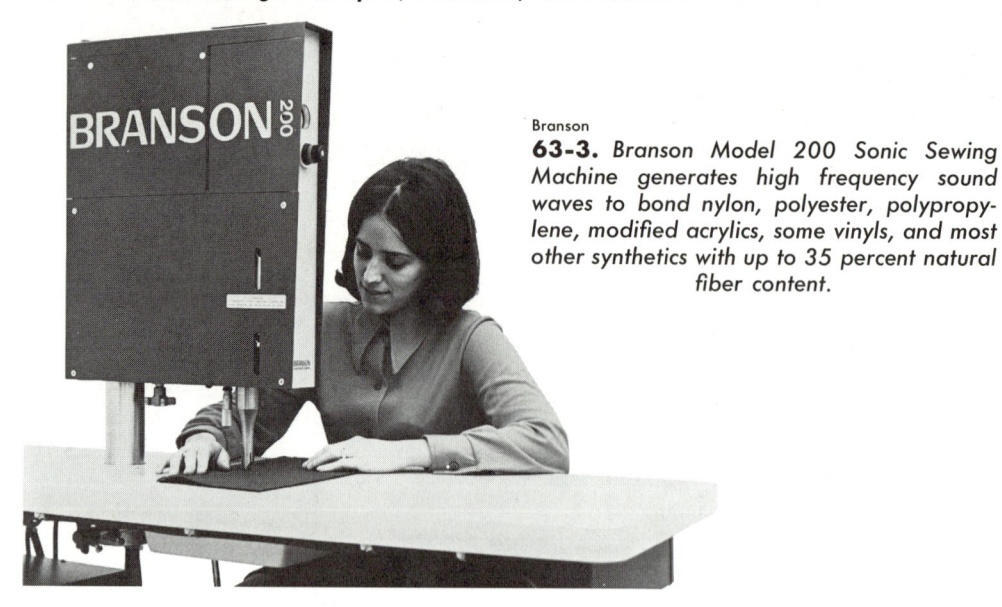

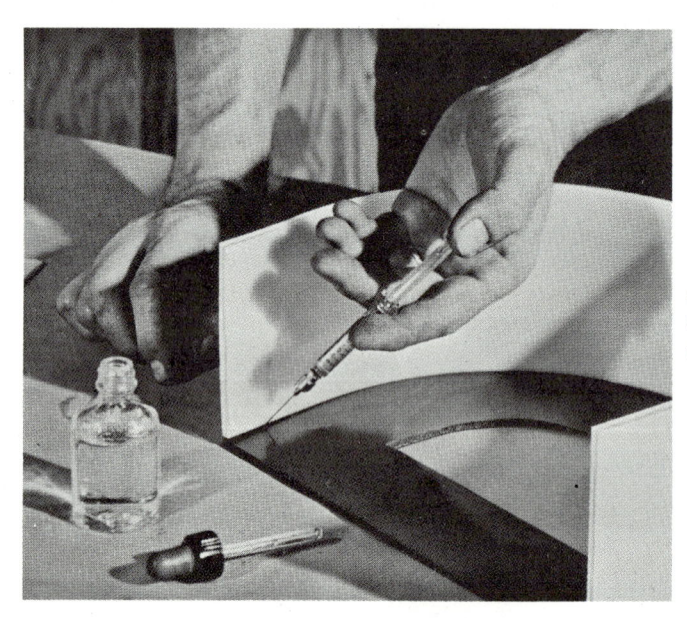

Branson
63-3. Branson Model 200 Sonic Sewing Machine generates high frequency sound waves to bond nylon, polyester, polypropylene, modified acrylics, some vinyls, and most other synthetics with up to 35 percent natural fiber content.

63-4. Solvent cementing can be done by soaking or by flowing cement into the joint.

evaporates, the joint will be broken. As a substitute for clamps, you can make a special fixture for holding the parts. Fig. 63-6.

LAMINATED PLASTICS

Many plastics are laminated commercially. Circuit boards in many transistor radios and television sets are laminated plastics. In the school shop there are two ways plastics may be laminated. Acrylic plastics may be laminated by applying solvent cement to the surface of the pieces and then placing them together. The pieces should be clamped to keep them in close contact until the plastic

Unit 63: Fastening Plastic

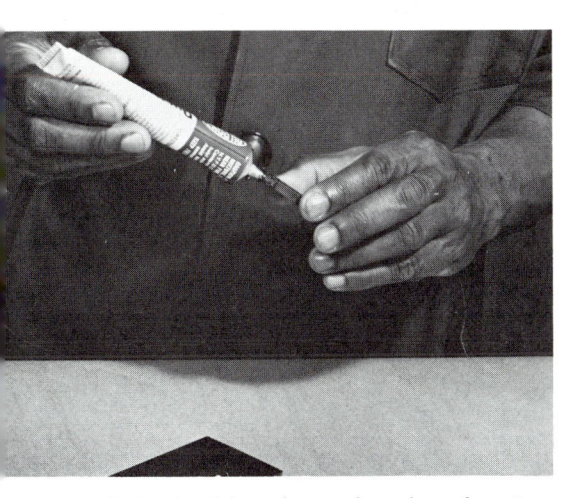

63-5. Applying glue to the edge of a piece of plastic for fastening.

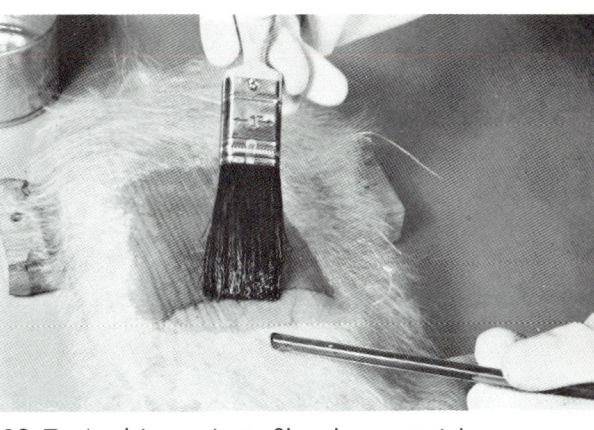

63-7. Applying resin to fiberglass material for a fruit tray. Layers of the glass material are laminated together using the liquid resin. Notice the protective gloves.

hardens. Laminated pieces of different colors can be made by this process.

Another type of plastic laminate that is used a great deal is *fiberglass*. You may be familiar with fiberglass coverings on boats. This material is made from glass fibers laminated or fastened together by means of special resins. The resin and a catalyst are mixed as in plastic casting. Be sure to follow the directions that come with the material. The resin mixture and fiberglass are applied to a mold in alternate layers. Fig. 63-7.

Some familiar commercial laminates are Formica and Panelyte. These have a hard surface and are used for tabletops and counter tops. They can be cut with ordinary woodworking tools and are applied with contact cement. The cement is applied to the back of the laminate and to the surface to be covered. The cement is allowed to dry (about 20 minutes); then the laminate is placed on the surface. It should be pressed down firmly. A rolling pin works well for this. A block of soft wood and a hammer may also be used.

63-6. One method of holding the cemented pieces while drying. Make sure that the parts are held firmly in place.

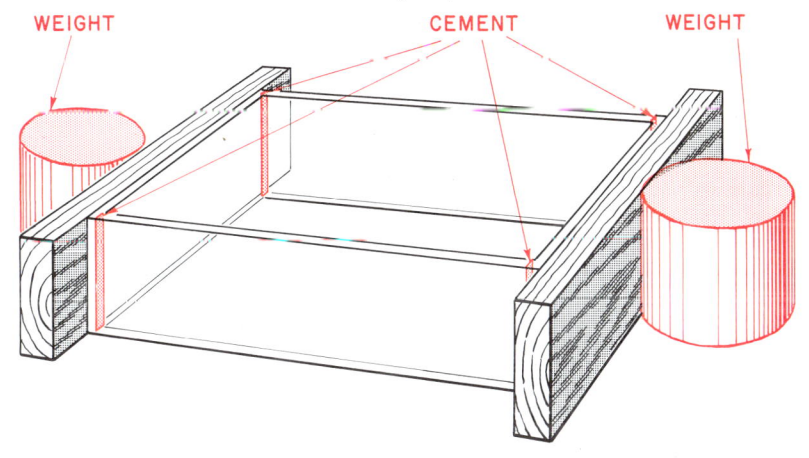

WEIGHT   CEMENT   WEIGHT

307

UNIT 64

finishing Plastic

Among the several unique properties of plastic materials is that they do not need to be protected with a coating of finishing material. Plastic is its own finish. It is waterproof and resists many stains. It is generally smooth and needs little attention after it has been formed into a product. However, if a decorative finish is desired, it may be applied by one of two primary methods—*coloring* and *coating*. Fig. 64-1.

Note: Before plastic is finished, it should be polished and buffed. Remove deep scratches with abrasive paper; then buff to a high lustre on a buffing wheel. Use a light pressure on the wheel, and

64-1. *This chart illustrates methods of finishing plastics.*

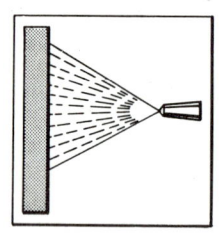

Finishing

Finishing is the process of treating the surface of a material for appearance and/or protection.

KIND OF FINISHING	DEFINITION	EXAMPLES
Coloring* DYE PENETRATES WORKPIECE	Applying penetrating dyes or chemicals to a material to change its color.	Dyeing sheet materials and liquid resins.
Coating* WORKPIECE	Applying a layer of finishing substance to the surface of a material.	Brush and spray lacquering and glazing.

*Coating could be considered a coloring process, since coating usually does change a product's color. However, it is customary to consider coating and coloring to be separate processes, as defined in the chart above.

Unit 64: Finishing Plastic

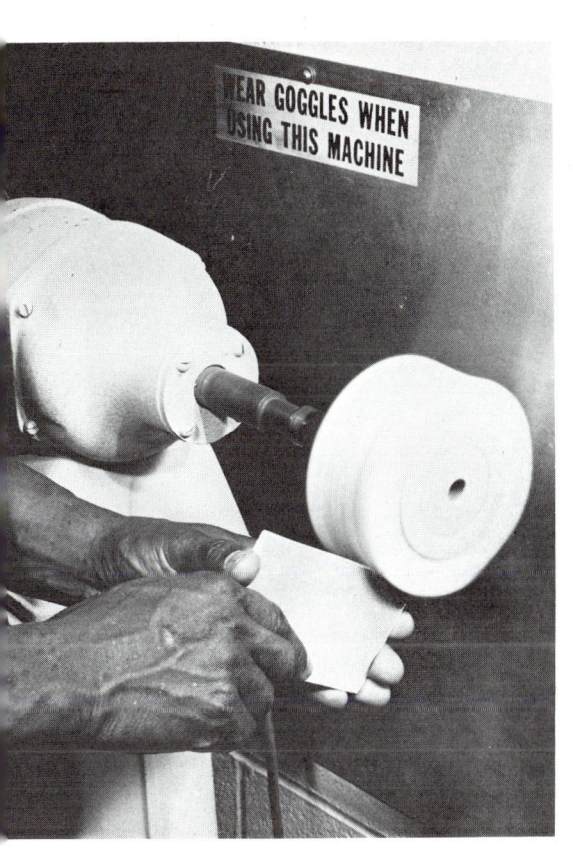

64-2. Buffing plastic on a cloth buffing wheel. Be sure to keep the plastic moving.

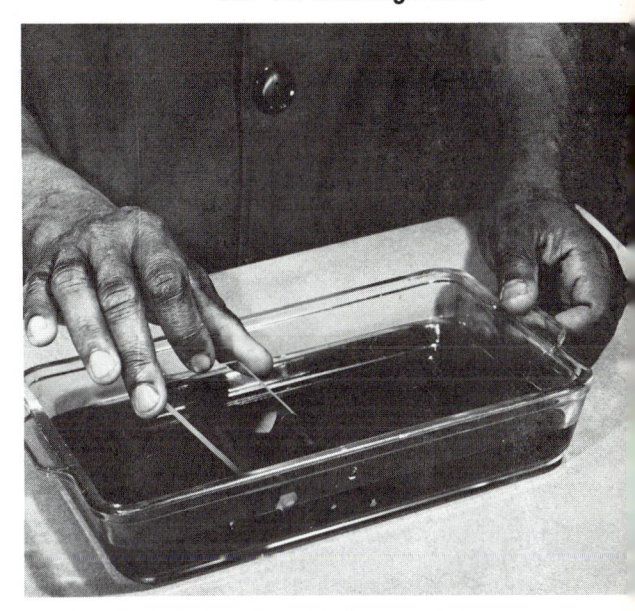

64-3. Plastic being placed in a tray of dye for coloring.

64-4. Dye being inserted into an internally carved flower.

keep the plastic moving to prevent burning. Fig. 64-2. (See Unit 36 for more information on abrasives and buffing.)

COLORING

Most plastic sheet materials (acrylics) can be bought in a variety of colors. Clear plastic can, however, be colored with special dyes. The plastic should be buffed smooth and cleaned with detergent and water. The plastic is placed in a pan or dish of dye and allowed to soak until colored to the desired shade. Fig. 64-3. (The dye is made from plastic coloring powders mixed with warm water.) Remove the plastic and rinse in warm water. Resins for plastic casting and fiberglass laminating can be dyed by adding the colored powder directly to the resin.

Certain plastics can be colored by applying paint to a carved design. The plastic can be carved using a high-speed cutting tool. Flower designs as well as other designs can be carved into plastic this way. The carved design may be colored by using a hypodermic needle and dye as shown in Fig. 64-4. Certain plastics can also be colored by painting the

309

Part III: Manufacturing—Principles, Materials, and Processes

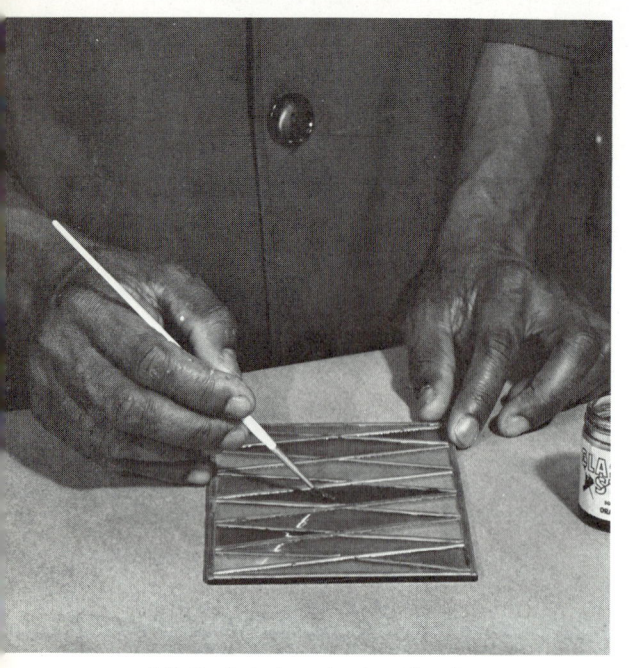

64-5. Painting plastic with coloring material.

64-6. This glazed decorative jar shows interesting crystal formations.

coloring material on the surface with a brush. Fig. 64-5.

COATING

Lacquer or enamel can be sprayed or brushed on plastic. Be sure the surface is clean, dry, and completely free of fingerprints.

Some very interesting effects may be obtained by glazing a plastic surface. Crystal-glazing liquids can be purchased in a wide range of colors and applied with equal success on plastic, glass, and metal. The liquid is brushed or sprayed on a clean, dry surface and allowed to dry. In drying, the beautiful crystals are formed. Fig. 64-6. No further treatment is necessary, other than wiping with a clean cloth. Plastic trays, bowls, wall plaques, and containers can be glazed to add to their beauty.

DISCUSSION TOPICS

Part 3—Manufacturing—Principles, Materials, and Processes
Section 2—Plastics
Unit 59
   1. What was the first plastic to have commercial success? When was it developed?
   2. Are plastics a synthetic or natural material?
   3. What are the two groups into which plastics may be divided?
   4. List some of the plastic products in your home.
Unit 60
   1. Name seven common industrial methods for processing plastics.
   2. Briefly describe blow molding.

Units 59-64: Discussion Topics

  3. What is the most common method of forming thermosetting materials?
  4. How does transfer molding differ from compression molding?
  5. What is the most common method of forming thermoplastic materials?

Unit 61
  1. What tools are needed for bending plastics?
  2. To what temperature should plastic be heated for bending?
  3. What plastic products do industries make by the casting process?
  4. What materials are needed for casting plastics?
  5. What plastic products do industries make by the foam molding process?

Unit 62
  1. What method is commonly used for cutting thin sheets of plastic?
  2. How are plastic rods and bars cut?
  3. What methods may be used for abrading plastic?
  4. What types of drills are used for drilling holes in plastic?
  5. Why should you use slow or medium speeds when drilling plastic?
  6. How may plastic sheets be shaped?

Unit 63
  1. What are three basic ways plastics can be joined?
  2. What types of mechanical fasteners may be used to join plastics?
  3. What is meant by cohesion of plastics?
  4. How may plastics be laminated in the school shop?

Unit 64
  1. Why doesn't plastic need to be protected by a coating of finish?
  2. Name two ways plastics may be colored.
  3. What does glazing of plastics mean?

PART III

Manufacturing—Principles, Materials, and Processes

Section 3–Woodworking

Unit 65 Introduction to Woodworking
Unit 66 Lumbering
Unit 67 Wood Products and Occupations
Unit 68 Estimating and Laying Out Stock
Unit 69 New Developments in Woodworking
Unit 70 Woodcutting Principles
Unit 71 Sawing Wood
Unit 72 Planing and Chiseling Wood
Unit 73 Abrading Wood
Unit 74 Drilling Holes in Wood
Unit 75 Milling, Shaping, and Filing Wood
Unit 76 Wood Turning
Unit 77 Wood Forming Principles
Unit 78 Wood Fastening Principles
Unit 79 Woodworking Joints
Unit 80 Mechanical Fasteners for Wood
Unit 81 Adhesive Fastening of Wood
Unit 82 Wood Finishing Principles

Unit 83 Color Finishing of Wood

Unit 84 Coat Finishing of Wood

Discussion Topics

Part III: Manufacturing—Principles, Materials, and Processes

Metric Fact Sheet*

— Woodworking —

- Important linear measurement units are the millimetre (mm) and the metre (m).
- Common measuring tool sizes: bench rules—300, 450, and 600 mm; steel tapes—2, 3, 5, 7.5, 15, and 30 m; zigzag rules—2 m. Measuring tools available in dual-dimension models.
- Lumber standards: 4' x 8' plywood sheet becomes 1200 x 2400 mm; nominal 2" x 4" becomes 38 x 89 mm.
- Board foot volume measure replaced by m^3.
- Finishing materials available in 0.5, 1, 4, and 20 litre sizes.
- In building construction, stud spacings are 300, 400, and 600 mm.
- Masonry brick and block sizes designed to fit 600 x 600 mm modules, interchangeable.
- Drawings are in mm and m. (See floor plan of tool shed.)

*You will find other information on metrics in the Appendix.

FLOOR PLAN – GARDEN TOOL SHED

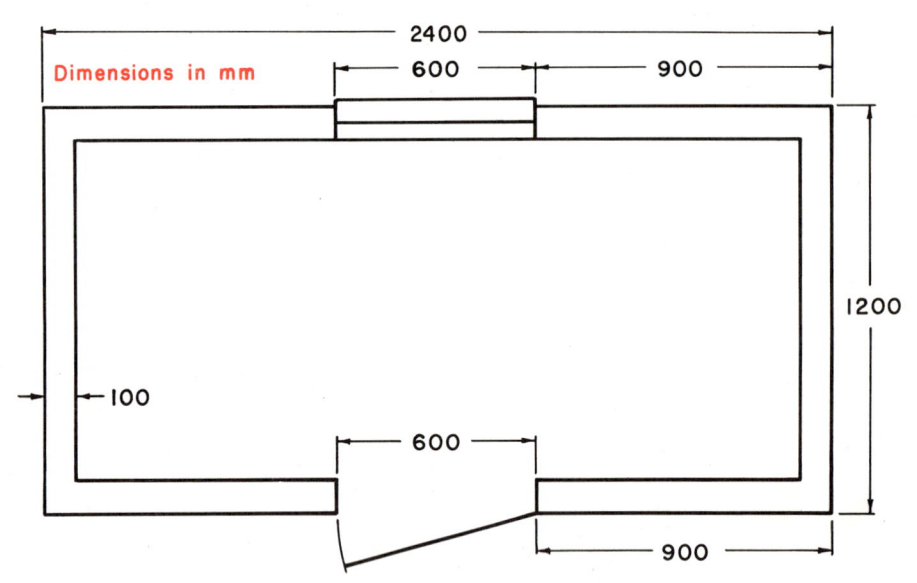

Dimensions in mm

2400
600
900
1200
100
600
900

314

UNIT 65

Introduction to Woodworking

From earliest times wood has always served people in one form or another. In most of the areas of the world, wood has been plentiful and easy to obtain. In the United States wood has always been one of the most plentiful of our raw materials. Fig. 65-1.

Today wood is used for a variety of purposes, from building homes to making fine furniture. The raw material, lumber, is changed to many forms of material for the woodworker. Plywood, particle board, hardboard, and wallboard are all made from the basic material wood. All these give the woodworker a wide range of materials from which to choose for a project. With the materials available a skilled woodworker is limited only by imagination.

What you learn in this section about wood and how to work with it may lead to an interest in one of the many occupations in wood. Understanding of the materials and the tools will also provide you with information and skill you may use around your home. Working with wood is one of the oldest crafts in this country and one of the most interesting.

65-1. *Logging trucks move through a forest toward the sawmill. Each truckload of logs will make enough lumber for a single house. Forests are one of our most important natural resources.*

UNIT 66

Lumbering

Lumbering is one of the oldest industries in America. Working with simple hand tools, the early colonists used trees to make their houses, furniture, wagons, bridges, and many other items in daily use.

The lumber industry grew as the country grew. Today the logger makes use of many machines. Lumbering methods vary depending on the part of the country and the size of the company, but the basic process remains fairly standard. It involves cutting trees, taking the logs to a sawmill, cutting them into lumber, and seasoning or drying the lumber.

LUMBERING PROCESSES

The first step is to select and mark the trees to be cut. The trees are then partially cut, using power saws. Wedges are driven into the cut to make the tree fall in the right direction, then the cut is finished. After the tree is felled, the limbs and branches are trimmed off. The trunk is cut into logs of the desired length. The logs are moved to a loading site and stacked. Today most logs are carried to the sawmill on trucks or railroad cars. In years past, logs were floated to the sawmill in rivers and streams. There are a few places where this is still done.

At the sawmill the logs are stored in a *mill pond*. This keeps them from drying out before they are sawed. It is also easier to sort the logs in the water than to move them on land.

From the pond the logs are towed into the mill. Inside the mill each log is loaded onto a *carriage* which holds it as it is being sawed. Here a worker called a *sawyer* takes over. The sawyer knows how to get the most high grade lumber from each log by controlling the movement of the *head rig,* where logs are cut into boards. In large sawmills the head saw is a band saw. Fig. 66-1. As the carriage moves forward, the log is carried into the saw. When the first cut is finished, the carriage returns to the starting place. The log is moved over and the carriage takes it into the saw again. The process is repeated until the entire log is cut into boards.

Other saws trim the edges and cut the boards to standard sizes. Fig. 66-2. Softwoods such as pine and fir are cut to standard length, thickness, and width. Hardwoods are cut to standard thickness only. They are more expensive and there would be too much waste if they were cut to width and length.

Boards are cut from logs in two common ways. The cheaper way is called *plain-sawing* (or plain-slicing). The log is squared and sawed lengthwise from one side to the other. The more expensive method of cutting is *quarter-sawing* (or quarter-slicing). This method is used for sawing many hardwoods because it shows a better grain. Quarter-sawed lumber warps less than plain-sawed lumber. Fig. 66-3.

A conveyer belt moves the boards into a sorting shed, where trained workers sort and grade each board for quality. Then the lumber is stacked in piles with small

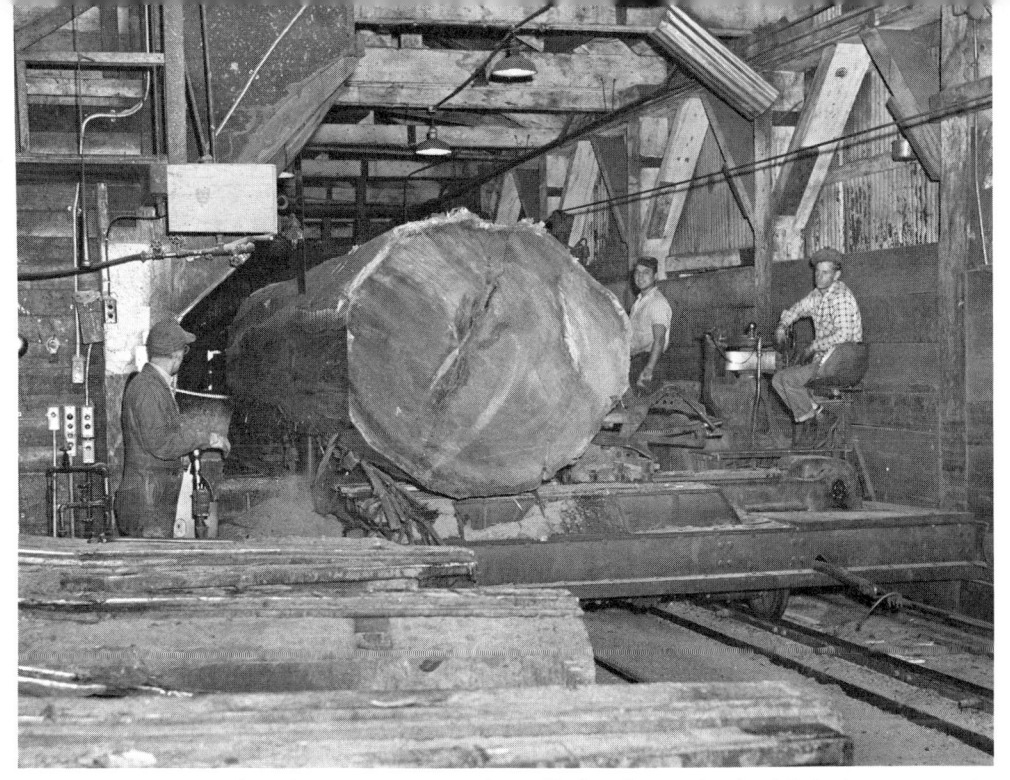

66-1. Logs up to 6' in diameter are sawed on this band saw. At the left is the sawyer, the worker responsible for getting the most lumber from each log.

66-2. After the logs have been cut on the head saw, they go to the edger, which trims the edges.

Part III: Manufacturing—Principles, Materials, and Processes

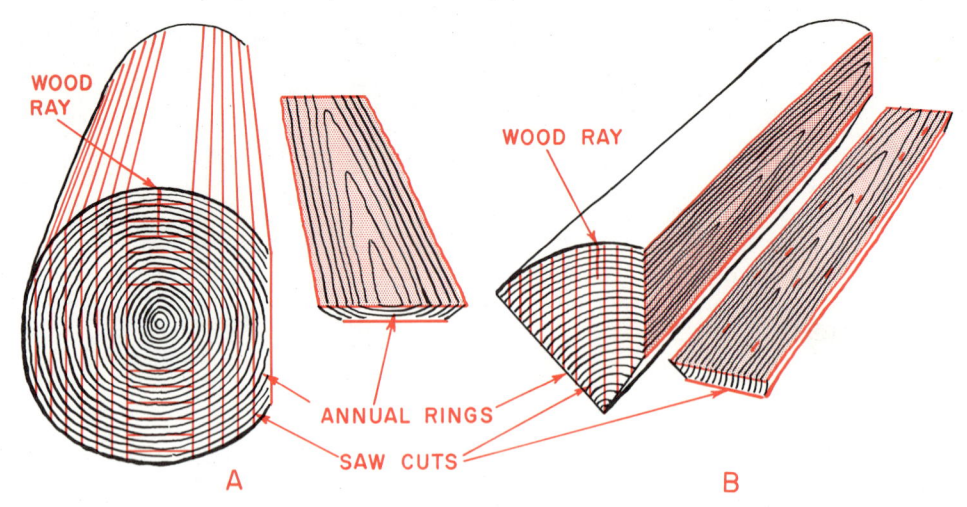

66-3. Two ways of cutting lumber: (A) Plain-sawed (B) Quarter-sawed.

blocks between pieces so that air can move around the wood. Some lumber is stacked in the yard for drying. Fig. 66-4. This is called *airdrying*. It takes several months to dry a stack of lumber this way. Much lumber is dried in *kilns*—large rooms where the heat can be controlled. Lumber dried this way is called *kilndried*. Lumber can be kiln dried in two to eight days. Kiln-dried lumber is better for construction and furniture making than air-dried lumber. This is because the moisture content of the boards has been controlled more accurately.

Wood shrinks as it dries and swells as it absorbs moisture. When a tree is cut, it contains a great deal of moisture. Before the lumber is used, this moisture is removed. As the lumber is dried, it shrinks.

Large sawmills have a *planing mill*. This is where the rough lumber is given a smooth surface by passing through a set of rotating knives. Here boards are also made into flooring, siding, molding, and other kinds of trim. Most softwoods are run through the planing mill. Much hardwood lumber is sold rough or unsurfaced.

WOOD IDENTIFICATION

Each kind of wood has its own color, working qualities, and other properties.

You should select the wood for your projects carefully. To do this you must know something about the more common kinds of wood. Much information is available from the government and from commercial sources to help you in recognizing and choosing woods.

Woods are divided into **softwoods** and **hardwoods**. The names really have little to do with how soft or hard the wood is. Softwoods are obtained from cone-bearing trees that stay green all year. Hardwoods are obtained from trees that have broad leaves which they lose in the winter.

Softwoods

Common softwoods are Douglas fir, ponderosa pine, sugar pine, and redwood. Douglas fir is used for construction lumber and for plywood. It is fairly hard, heavy, and stiff. Ponderosa pine is also used for construction lumber. It is fairly light and soft. Sugar pine is used for making patterns for foundries and for millwork. It is of a light color, soft, and straight grained. It is easy to work. Redwood is used for home construction, fences, and outdoor furniture. It is lightweight and strong. Redwood is very resistant to decay.

Unit 66: Lumbering

66-4. Lumber stacked in a yard for air drying.

Hardwoods

Common hardwoods are basswood, birch, cherry, mahogany, maple, oak, and walnut.

Basswood, one of the softest hardwoods, is white with a few black streaks. It is fuzzy, good for bending, and has almost no grain. Basswood is used for drawing boards. It is also good for burned designs and thin lumber for jigsaw work. It is not good for use outside. Basswood is usually painted.

Birch has fine texture and close grain. It grows in the north central states. It has a fine wavy figure and is used for paneling and some furniture. Birch is a difficult wood to work, but will take almost any type of stain.

Cherry grows in most parts of the United States. Very desirable for furniture, it is a reddish brown, durable wood, and does not dent and mar easily. It is often given a lacquer finish.

Mahogany is a fine cabinet wood. Its color ranges from dark red to brown. True mahogany grows in Honduras, Africa, and South America. Mahogany is tough, strong, and easy to work. It polishes well and has a very distinctive grain pattern. Lauan, while not a true mahogany, is often called Philippine mahogany. It is excellent, inexpensive wood for furniture, cabinetwork, and boats.

Maple is a hard, tough, strong wood that wears well. The grain is usually straight. Maple is used a great deal for flooring and for furniture. A hard wood, it does not work too easily. Maple can be stained or given a natural finish.

Oak trees grow in all parts of the United States. There are almost 300 kinds of oak, but for woodworking only the white oak

Part III: Manufacturing—Principles, Materials, and Processes

and the red oak are important. Oak is used for flooring, furniture, and construction. White oak is a very popular cabinet wood. It is hard to work.

Walnut is one of the most beautiful woods that grow in the United States. A dark brown wood, strong and durable, walnut is used for furniture, cabinetwork, veneers, and gunstocks. Walnut is usually given a natural finish with varnish, lacquer, or oil. Fig. 66-5 shows some common woods and their characteristics.

66-5. *Common woods and their characteristics.*

Common Hardwoods and Softwoods

Kind	Color	Working Qualities	Weight	Strength	Lasting Qualities (Outside Use)
HARDWOODS					
* Ash	Grayish brown	Hard	Heavy	Strong	Poor
Basswood	Lt. cream	Easy	Light	Weak	Poor
Beech	Lt. brown	Hard	Heavy	Medium	Medium
Birch	Lt. brown	Hard	Heavy	Strong	Fair
Cherry	Dk. red	Hard	Medium	Strong	Fair
Gum	Red-brown	Medium	Medium	Medium	Medium
* Mahogany (true)	Gold-brown	Easy	Medium	Medium	Good
* Mahogany (Philippine)	Med. red	Easy	Medium	Medium	Good
Maple, sugar	Red-cream	Hard	Heavy	Strong	Poor
* Oak, red	Flesh-brown	Hard	Heavy	Strong	Fair
* Oak, white	Grey-brown	Hard	Heavy	Strong	Fair
Poplar	Yellow	Easy	Medium	Weak	Fair
* Walnut	Dk. brown	Medium	Heavy	Strong	Good
* Willow	Brown	Easy	Light	Low	Fair
SOFTWOODS					
Fir, Douglas	Orange-brown	Medium	Medium	Medium	Medium
Pine, ponderosa	Orange to red-brown	Easy	Light	Weak	Poor
Pine, sugar	Creamy brown	Easy	Light	Poor	Fair
Redwood	Dk. red-brown	Easy	Light	Medium	Good

Woods marked with (*) are open grain and require a paste filler.

UNIT 67

Wood Products and Occupations

Forests are very valuable, not only as a source of wood but for other reasons as well. They reduce the washing away of soil during heavy rainstorms and melting snows. They help to prevent dust storms, protect wildlife, and provide recreational areas for hiking, fishing, and hunting. Trees also provide shade and protection from the wind.

Lumber is very important, and so are the many by-products of the wood industries. You are familiar with some of the more common uses for lumber, such as for houses and furniture. Fig. 67-1 shows other forest products.

VENEERS AND PLYWOOD

One very important use of wood is for the making of veneers and plywood. Veneer is a thin sheet of wood that is sawed, peeled, or sliced from a log. To make plywood, several sheets of veneer are glued (laminated) together. To make *lumber-core plywood,* the sheets of veneer are glued to lumber. To make *veneer-core plywood,* sheets of veneer are glued to each other. In veneer-core plywood, the veneer sheets in each layer are placed with the grain at right angles to the grain of the sheet above and below. This gives the plywood great strength.

Hardwood plywoods may be either veneer-core or lumber-core. Construction and industrial plywoods (once called softwood plywoods) are always veneer-core.

Veneer is cut in one of three ways: *rotary-cut, plain-sawed* (or *plain-sliced*), and *quarter-sawed* (or *quarter-sliced*). Fig. 67-2. Hardwood veneers are usually plain-sawed or quarter-sawed. Construction and industrial plywood is rotary-cut.

For making veneer for construction and industrial plywood, the logs are first cut into 8', 10', or 12' lengths and the bark is removed. The logs are placed on giant lathes which turn them against a razor-sharp knife. A thin, continuous sheet of wood is peeled off the log. Fig. 67-3.

The veneer is cut into specific widths. It is then sorted for grade. Sheets of green veneer are put through driers to remove the moisture.

Glue is applied to the sheets, or *plies*. Fig. 67-4. Sometimes two plies are glued with their grains parallel to form one layer. Then the layers are stacked with their grains at right angles to each other. The glued sheets are placed in large hydraulic presses in which the glue is set under heat and pressure. When dry, the panels are sanded, cut to certain lengths and widths, and then inspected and sorted.

Plywood is made with an odd number of layers such as three, five, or seven. The number of plies may be three, four, five, six, or seven, since one layer may have two plies. The veneers are held together with glue that is either moisture resistant or moisture proof. For outside use plywood that has been put together with moisture proof glue should be selected.

Part III: Manufacturing—Principles, Materials, and Processes

Plywood has great strength and is fairly light. Because of these properties, plywood is often used for small boats such as the one in Fig. 67-5.

Some plywoods have special decorative faces. They may have a lined surface to give a combed look, a brushed face, or a sandblasted surface.

OTHER WOOD PRODUCTS

Today several types of panels are made from the waste of lumber mills. Two of

67-1. Here are some of the many products that come from trees.

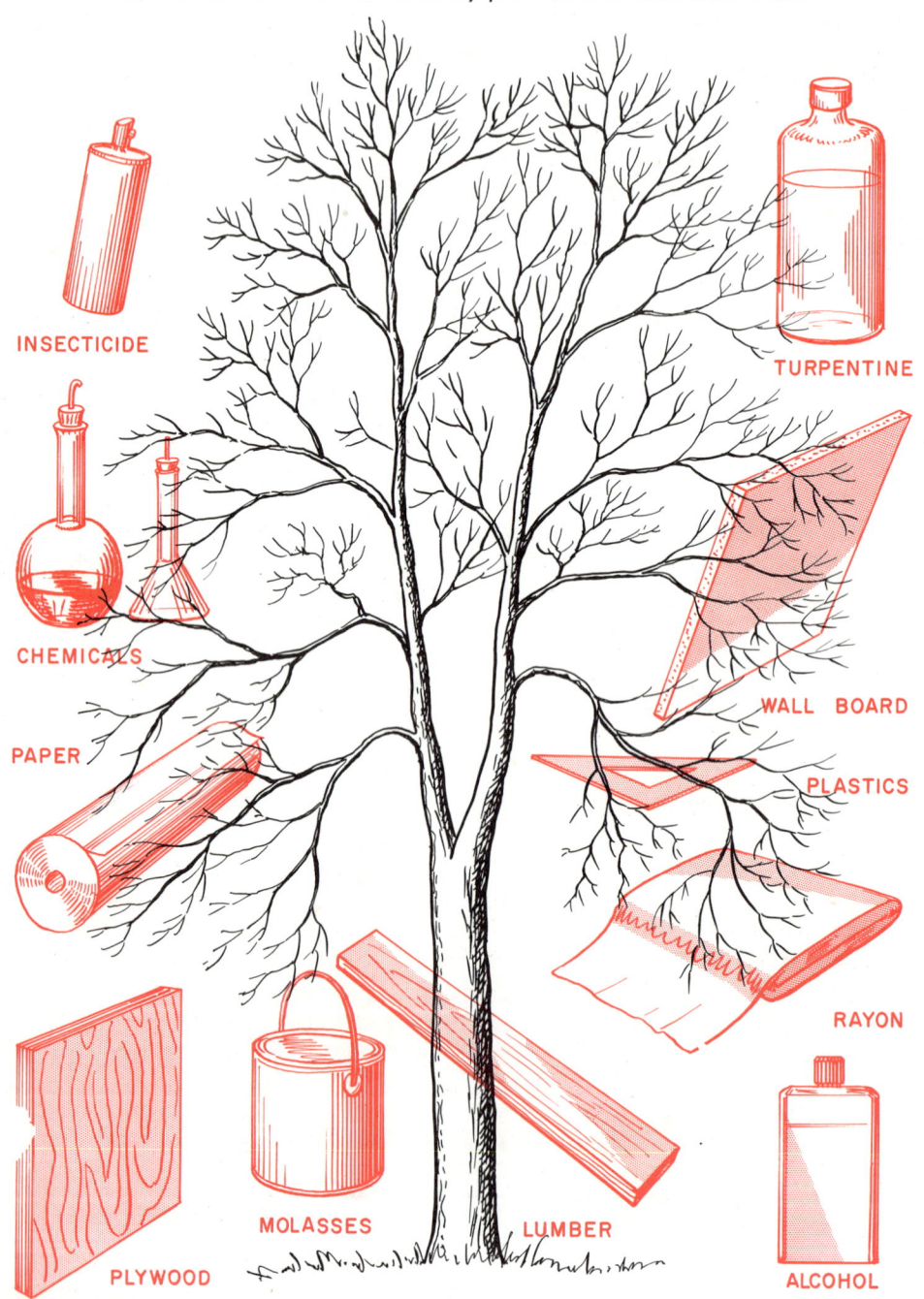

INSECTICIDE
TURPENTINE
CHEMICALS
WALL BOARD
PAPER
PLASTICS
RAYON
PLYWOOD
MOLASSES
LUMBER
ALCOHOL

Unit 67: Wood Products and Occupations

67-2. Veneer is cut in one of three ways—rotary-cut, plain-sliced, or quarter-sliced.

KNIFE — ROTARY

KNIFE — PLAIN SLICING

KNIFE — QUARTER SLICING

67-3. Rotary cutting of veneer to make plywood.

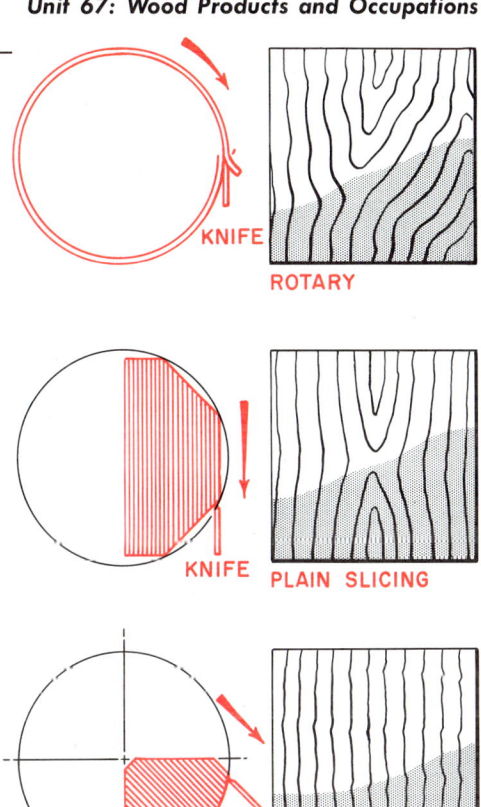

67-4. Applying adhesive to the veneer.

67-5. This 20' cabin cruiser is constructed of fir plywood.

Part III: Manufacturing—Principles, Materials, and Processes

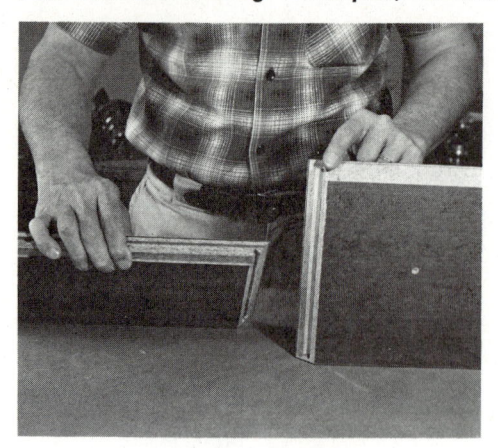

67-6. Particle board panels that have been mitered for a cabinet.

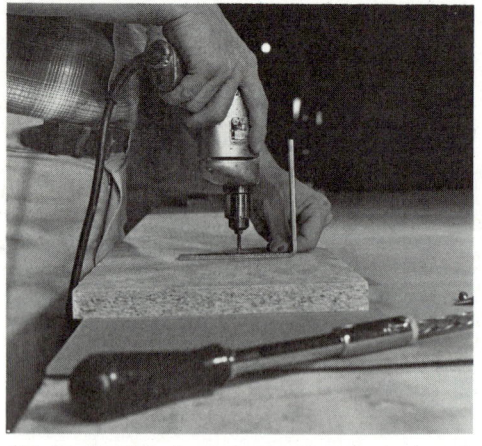

67-7. Particle board may be worked with ordinary woodworking tools.

these products are hardboard and particle board.

Hardboard is made by smashing wood into small chips. These chips are then refined and compressed in heated hydraulic presses. This material has no grain. It will not split, splinter, or crack. It has a very hard surface. Hardboard panels can be worked with ordinary woodworking tools.

Hardboard panels are used for construction. They can be used for walls and ceilings, and also for cabinetwork. Some types of hardboard panels have wood-grained surfaces to make them look like natural wood.

Particle board is made from wood shavings. The shavings are soaked and softened, then spread out on a steel plate. The layer is placed in a hydraulic press where it is heated and squeezed. The thickness of the finished board may be regulated from $\frac{1}{8}''$ to $2''$. The common widths of panels are $3'$ to $8'$, and they may be up to $24'$ in length. After the board is cooled, it is trimmed and sanded.

Particle board is used for furniture, for subflooring, paneling, counters, shelving, and concrete forms. It is also used for toys, Ping-Pong tables, cabinets, truck bodies, and signs. Fig. 67-6. Particle board can be worked with ordinary hand and power woodworking tools. Fig. 67-7.

OCCUPATIONS IN THE WOOD INDUSTRY

There are many jobs in the woodworking industries. Some require years of college education. These include the professional such as the research worker or the teacher of woodworking. Other jobs require less education. Some jobs are around the lumber mills where the trees are cut and made into lumber. Some people work in factories, also called *mills,* where the lumber is made into things such as doors and cabinets. These workers may have to know how to run such woodworking machines as the planer, the jointer, and the circular saw. In these mills there are also maintenance workers who keep the machines running and the saws and cutter knives sharp.

Many people earn their living as carpenters, cabinetmakers, patternmakers, and boat builders. They must be able to use all the hand and power woodworking tools. Each of these skilled crafts requires some training beyond high school, such as vocational school or apprenticeship. Perhaps you will find you have an interest in woodworking and want to take more courses in high school. Your instructor can give you information about jobs in woodworking and the training that is required.

UNIT 68

Estimating and Laying Out Stock

In Units 66 and 67 you studied some important facts about wood. Earlier units covered designing and planning. Now you are ready to start working with wood and tools.

One of the first things to do is to figure out how much wood you need. Plywood is sold by the *square foot,* lumber by the *board foot.* In simplest terms, one board foot is a piece of wood 1″ thick, 12″ wide, and 12″ long. (Thinner boards are usually figured as if they were 1″ thick.)

A simple formula for figuring board feet is:

$$\frac{\text{No. pcs.} \times \text{T (in.)} \times \text{W (in.)} \times \text{L (in.)}}{12 \times 12}$$

To find the board feet of four pieces, each of which is 1″ thick, 6″ wide, and 24″ long, use the formula:

$$\frac{4 \times 1 \times 6 \times 24}{12 \times 12} = 4 \text{ board feet}$$

You can then figure the cost by multiplying the price of one board foot by the number of board feet needed.

Lumber comes rough cut from the sawmill. If you want smooth lumber, order *S2S* or *S4S.* S2S means the lumber has been surfaced (finished or planed) on two sides. S4S means all four sides have been surfaced.

Surfacing lumber makes it smaller. For instance, a piece of hardwood that is 1″ thick before surfacing will be $^{13}/_{16}$″ thick when finished.

After you have the plans and have figured the amount of lumber, you need to measure and lay out the pieces for your project. To lay out you must know how to measure accurately. The tool in Fig. 68-1 shows the common markings for an inch. The common tools for measuring and laying out are the 2′ wooden rule, Fig. 68-1; the try square, Fig. 68-2; the zigzag rule, Fig. 68-3; the T bevel, Fig. 68-4; and

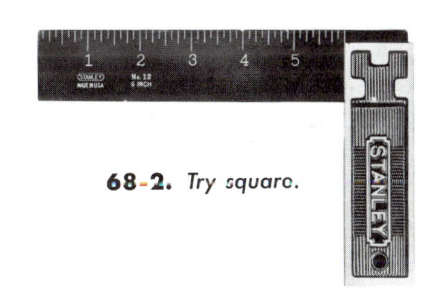

68-2. *Try square.*

68-3. *Zigzag rule. This rule is used mostly by carpenters and cabinetmakers.*

68-1. *Two-foot wooden bench rule. The common markings for this rule are inch, half-inch, quarter-inch, eighth-inch, and sixteenth-inch.*

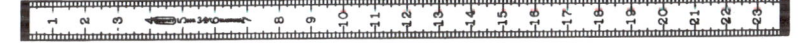

Part III: Manufacturing—Principles, Materials, and Processes

the marking gauge, Fig. 68-5. The framing square may be used for laying out large projects. Fig. 68-6.

USING METRIC MEASUREMENTS

As you remember from Unit 3, the United States is moving toward metric measurement. You may be required to use metric measurements for some of your projects.

Metric measurements in woodworking are rather simple. The important SI base unit for woodwork is the metre. The derived units of area and volume will also be used. Fig. 68-7.

The main measuring tools for the woodworker are the 150, 300, 450, 600, and 1000 millimetre bench rules. These are roughly the same as the present 6, 12, 18, 24, and 36 inch rules. Steel tapes are used for longer measures. Fig. 68-8 shows a 3 metre steel tape. Fig. 68-9 shows a metric framing square.

Metric Standards

Metric lumber sizes (or standards) have not yet been determined for the United States. We are not sure what these metric standards will be. For example, the standard thickness of a 3/4" board may become 20 mm. If you measure a 3/4" board, you will find that it comes closer to 19 mm, but this is an odd metric size. In order to make the dimensions more convenient, we will probably accept a 20 mm size to replace the 3/4" board thickness. A 1/2" piece of lumber may be 12 mm thick, and a 1" thick board will probably be 25 mm.

The standard 4' × 8' sheet of plywood will probably be 1200 × 2400 mm. It is interesting to note that this size will have a

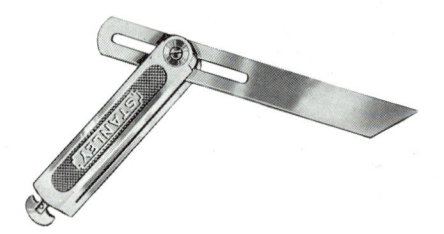

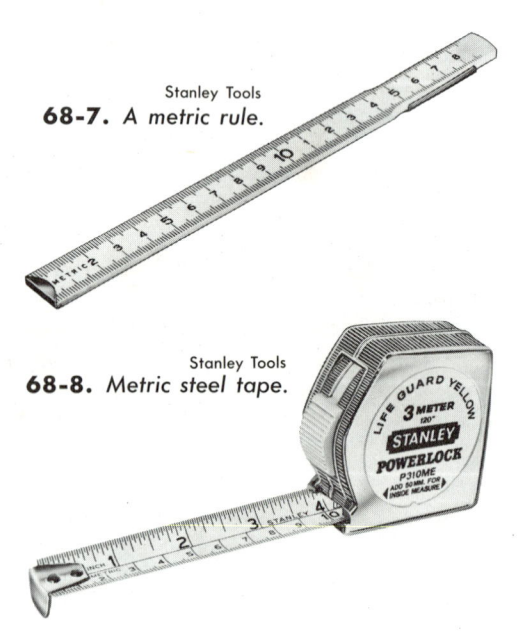

68-4. Sliding T bevel. This tool can be adjusted to any angle.

68-5. Marking gauge.

68-6. Framing square. This tool is used for laying out large projects.

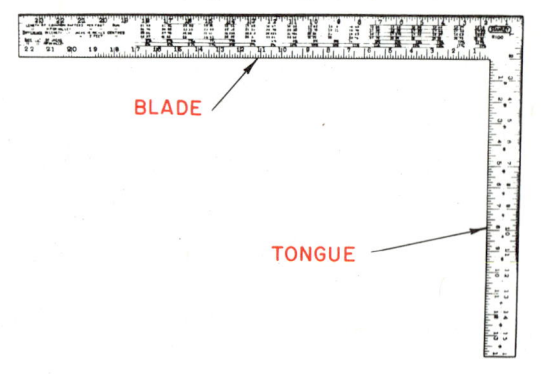

BLADE

TONGUE

Stanley Tools
68-7. A metric rule.

Stanley Tools
68-8. Metric steel tape.

Unit 68: Estimating and Laying Out Stock

bearing on the spacing of the studs and joists in house construction. The standard 4' × 8' (48" × 96") sheets of plywood are sized so that they will join at the center of a stud. Studs are spaced 16" (or sometimes 24"), center to center. A 1200 × 2400 mm sheet of plywood would be 46.8" × 93.6". It could not be used with the present stud spacings. Thus the spacing of the studs, and other framing members, will have to be changed. Plywood sheathing, insulation board, plaster board, and a number of other sheet construction materials will come in this 1200 × 2400 mm size.

MARKING STOCK FOR LENGTH

Place the blade of the try square against the edge of the board and mark a line across the end. Be sure to miss cracks or other imperfections in the end of the board. On wide boards you may use a framing square for this.

Lay out the length with a rule. Mark with a sharp pencil. Square off the length with a square as you did for the first end.

MARKING FOR WIDTH

Measure the desired width with a rule as you did for length. If you need to divide a board into several equal parts this may be done as shown in Fig. 68-10. Place a rule across the board and shift the angle until the inch marks evenly divide the board.

A marking gauge may be used for marking the width or thickness of stock. Set the gauge to the proper width with a rule. Fig. 68-11. Mark the board by pushing the gauge forward with the head held firmly against the edge of the board. Fig. 68-12. Do not mark the board too deeply. The thickness can be marked in the same way.

Angles may be marked with a T bevel. Set the T bevel to the desired angle and tighten the blade. Then hold the handle against the edge of the wood and mark along the edge of the blade with a pencil.

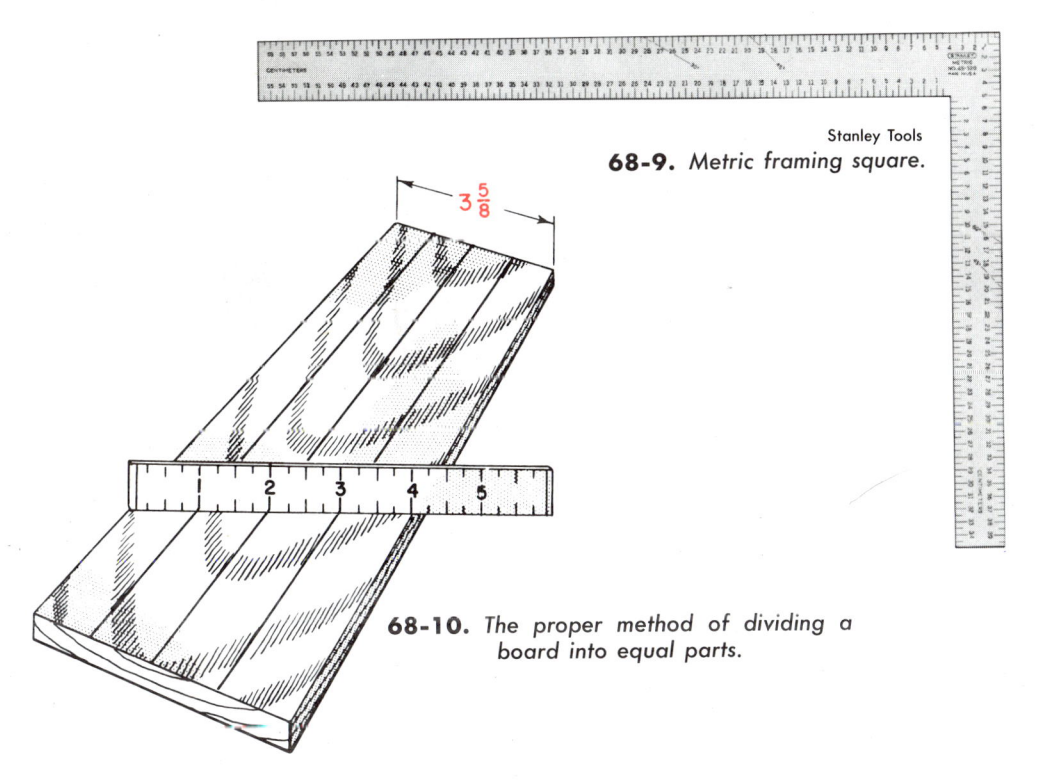

Stanley Tools
68-9. Metric framing square.

68-10. The proper method of dividing a board into equal parts.

327

Part III: Manufacturing—Principles, Materials, and Processes

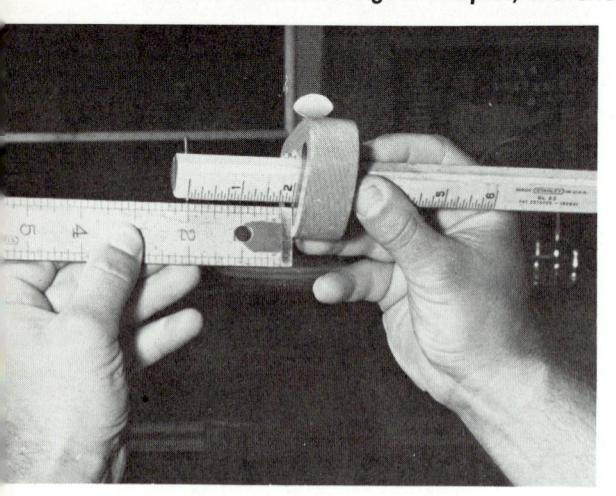

68-11. Setting a marking gauge.

68-12. Using a marking gauge. Push the gauge away from you.

UNIT 69

New Developments in Woodworking

Research in wood technology has contributed much new information on materials and processes. Wood can now be impregnated with plastic resins so that it becomes as hard as metal. New machines have been developed for bending wood and applying finishes. The Forest Products Laboratory in Madison, Wisconsin, continually studies the problems associated with new wood products and the ways of making them. Among the important new developments of scientific research are wipe-on finishes and airless spraying.

WOOD FINISHING

Some new finishes can be applied by wiping them on with a rag instead of by brushing them on. Sealacell, Minwax, and oil finish are some penetrating wipe-on finishes commonly used in school shops as well as in cabinet shops.

Research has also developed a whole family of water-base paints for both inte-

Unit 69: New Developments in Woodworking

rior and exterior use. When you are through painting with these, you simply wash the brush in soap and water.

AIRLESS SPRAYING

This is a method of spraying finish on a surface without using compressed air in the spray gun. Pressure is applied to the liquid in its container, such as a five-gallon paint can. This pressure forces the finish through the connecting hose to the spray gun, then out a slot which produces a fan-shaped spray pattern. Fig. 69-1. The slot may be turned for vertical or horizontal spray. In this method all the finishing solution settles on the object being sprayed. Paint, lacquer, and other synthetic liquid finishes can be applied this way.

WOOD BONDING

Another new development applies electronic principles to woodworking. Radio waves are used in a process called *dielectric* heating to dry glued joints rapidly. Sometimes this process is called wood welding.

Dielectric heating is based on the fact that molecules can be disturbed, or made to move rapidly. These moving molecules cause friction which causes heat. The disturbance is caused by very high frequency radio waves. The radio waves move the glue molecules so quickly that they generate heat which dries the glue. This action is similar to what happens to food when it cooks in a microwave oven.

With this method of drying, glued boards can be ready for working in minutes instead of days, as required by ordinary methods. The dielectric heating machine consists of a high frequency generator and a hand gun. Fig. 69-2. The high frequency waves from the generator are transmitted to the wood by the hand gun. As the hand gun is moved along the glue joint, the high frequency waves excite the glue molecules, causing heat which dries the glue rapidly. Since the heat is generated *inside* the glue, drying is much faster than when the glue is heated by placing the wood in an oven.

The process can be used for gluing in any position where the hand gun can be placed on the glue joint. It can be used for edge to edge gluing, on the edges of boards (Fig. 69-3), or even for repairs (Fig. 69-4).

69-1. *Diagram showing operation of airless spraying. Compressed air forces paint from the container through the hose to the spray gun. The spray gun breaks the paint into a mist for painting.*

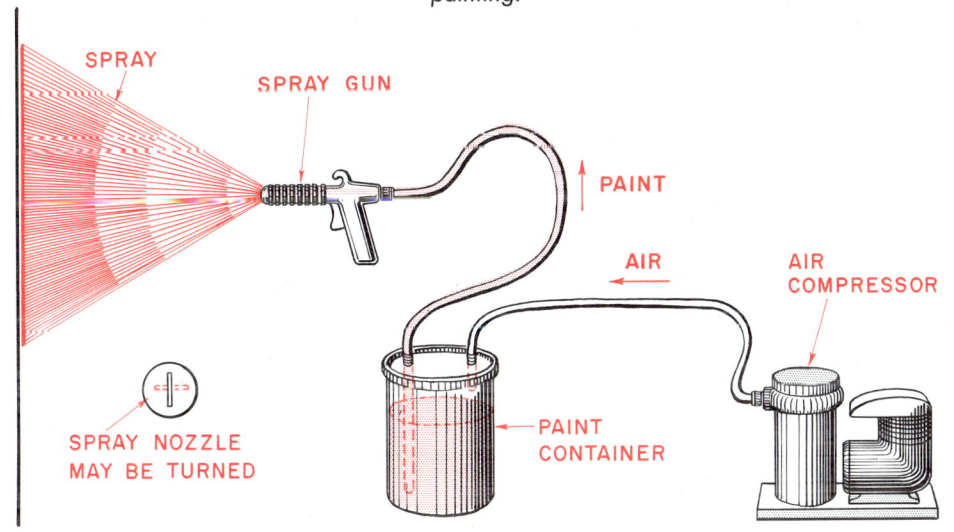

329

Part III: Manufacturing—Principles, Materials, and Processes

Workrite Products Co.
69-2. A dielectric heating machine.

Workrite Products Co.
69-3. Gluing a counter top with roller electrodes on the hand gun.

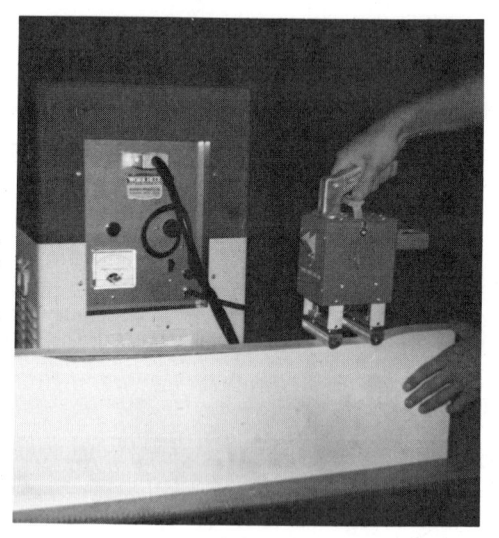

69-4. Repairing furniture. The glued joint is being dried by dielectric heating.

330

UNIT 70
Woodcutting Principles

There are several ways of cutting wood. You may use a saw, a chisel, or a piece of abrasive paper. The common kinds of cutting are shown in Fig. 70-1.

Some woodworking tools are used for more than one kind of cutting. Drills and crosscut saws really cut with a shearing action. The lathe tool also cuts by shearing as it is held against the revolving piece. Probably the most commonly used tool in woodworking is the plane, and it too cuts with a shearing action.

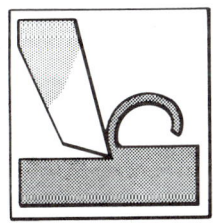

Fig. 70-1

Cutting

Cutting is the process of removing or separating pieces of material from a base material.

KIND OF CUTTING	DEFINITION	EXAMPLES
Sawing	Cutting with a tool having pointed teeth equally spaced along the edge of a blade.	Operations on the circular saw, crosscut saw, ripsaw, coping saw, band saw, jigsaw.
Shearing	Cutting usually between two cutting edges crossing one another, or by forcing a single cutting edge through a workpiece.	Cutting with a wood chisel, knife, plane.

Part III: Manufacturing—Principles, Materials, and Processes

Fig. 70-1 (Continued)

KIND OF CUTTING	DEFINITION	EXAMPLES
Abrading	Cutting by wearing away material, usually by the action of mineral particles.	Hand sanding, belt sanding, disc sanding.
Drilling	Cutting with a cylindrical tool usually having two spiral cutting edges.	Operations using the drill press, auger bit, twist drill.
Milling	Cutting with a tool having sharpened teeth equally spaced around a cylinder or along a flat surface.	Jointer-planer operations; cutting with wood files.
Turning	Cutting by revolving a workpiece against a fixed single-edge tool.	Operations on the wood lathe.

70-1. This chart illustrates the cutting processes you will learn about in the following units.

UNIT 71

Sawing Wood

For cutting stock to size you need a ripsaw and a crosscut saw. The saw used for cutting across the grain is called a **crosscut saw.** The saw used for cutting with the grain is called a **ripsaw.**

CUTTING TO LENGTH

The teeth of the crosscut saw look like little knife blades. The teeth are bent alternately to the right and the left. This is called the "set" of the saw. The outside edges of the teeth cut the wood fibers on either side, and the center of the cutting edges removes these fibers. The groove left by the saw is called the *kerf*. Fig. 71-1. The teeth have "set" to make the cut wider than the saw. This keeps the saw from binding in the cut.

Crosscut saws come in many sizes. The easiest to use is one about 18" to 20" long. A crosscut saw that has 8 to 10 teeth per inch is best for cutting dry wood. Fig. 71-2.

When sawing stock to length, first use a try square to mark the cutting line. If the board is long, lay it across two sawhorses. A short board may be clamped in a vise to hold it. If you have the board on a sawhorse, place your left knee on the board to hold it. Grasp the saw in the right hand. Place the saw just outside of the

71-1. *This drawing shows how the teeth of a saw form a kerf that is wider than the saw.*

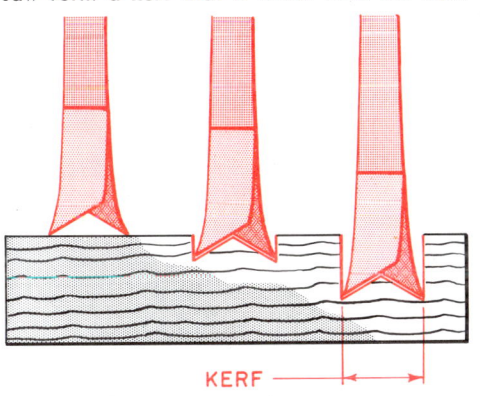

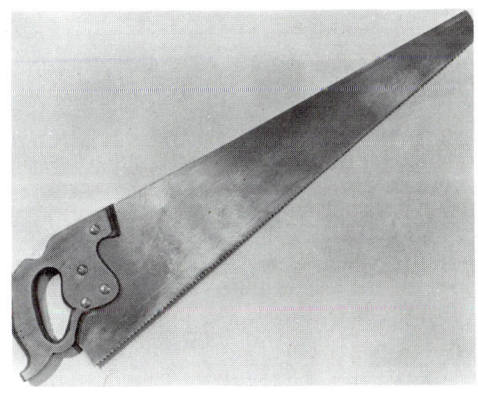

71-2a. *A crosscut saw.*

71-2b. *Close-up of a crosscut saw blade.*

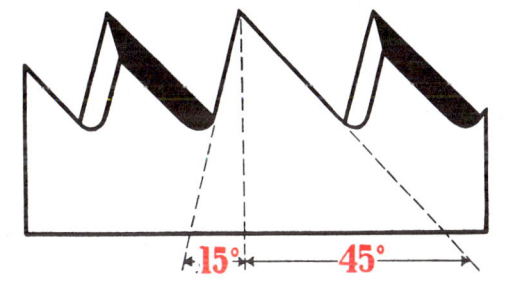

333

Part III: Manufacturing—Principles, Materials, and Processes

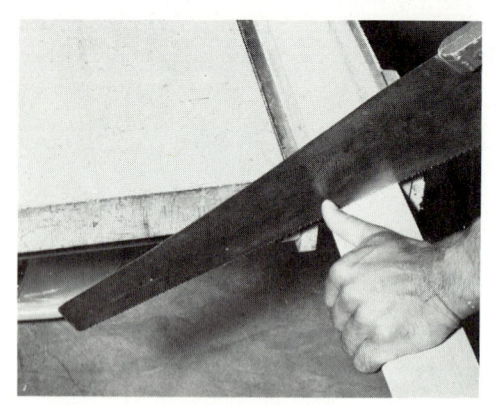

71-3. *Starting a cut. Guide the saw with the thumb until it is started.*

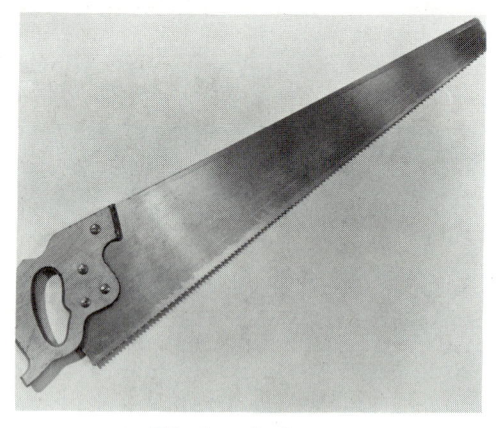

71-4a. *A ripsaw.*

layout line. Place your left thumb against the smooth part of the saw to guide it. Fig. 71-3.

Starting with most of the blade below the board, pull up on the saw to start the kerf. Pull the saw up in this way two or three times before starting to saw. If you try to begin the cut on the down stroke, the saw may jump out of your hand and mar the wood or cut your hand. Hold the saw at an angle of 45 degrees to the stock. Cut with steady, even movement. Do not jerk the saw and do not force it.

Make sure you are cutting square with the board. While sawing, watch the *line*, not the saw. Blow the sawdust off the line so you can see it. If the saw starts to go away from the line, correct this by twisting the handle a little. Hold the end of the board for the last few cuts. This will keep the board from splitting before the saw kerf is complete.

CUTTING TO WIDTH

Sometimes you need to cut boards to width. The ripsaw is used to cut wood with the grain. It has teeth that are like chisels. A ripsaw should be about 24" long. Fig. 71-4. Short stock may be clamped in a vise. If the board is long, you will need to use sawhorses. The ripsaw should be held at an angle of 60 degrees.

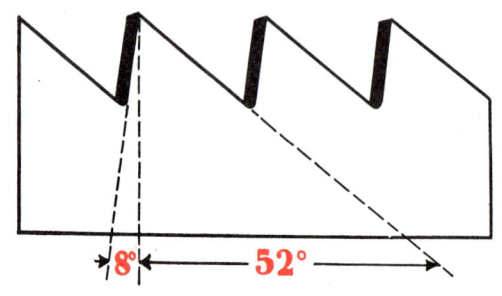

71-4b. *Close-up of a ripsaw blade.*

CUTTING PLYWOOD

Plywood should be cut with a fine-tooth crosscut saw. Place the plywood face up. Support the wood so that it will not sag. With a pencil, mark the line to be cut. Hold the saw at a low angle to the plywood to avoid splitting. Fig. 71-5.

CUTTING CURVES

For making many projects it may be necessary to cut curves or irregular shapes from wood. For such cuts the saw must have a thin blade. The two handsaws most commonly used for irregular cuts are the **coping saw** and the **compass** or **keyhole saw.**

The coping saw has a U-shaped frame into which a blade is fastened. Most coping saws have a screw handle to tighten

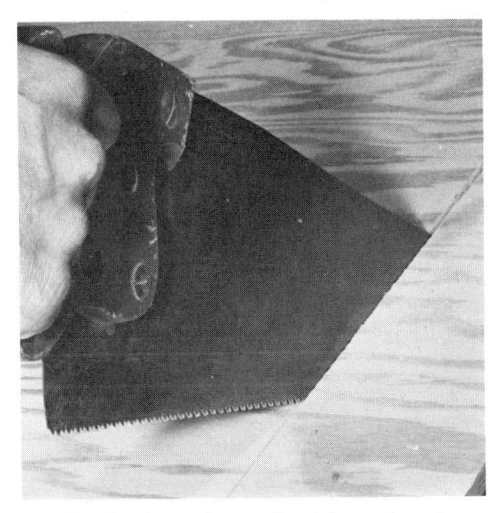

Unit 71: Sawing Wood

71-5. Cutting plywood with a handsaw. Hold the saw at a low angle to the wood.

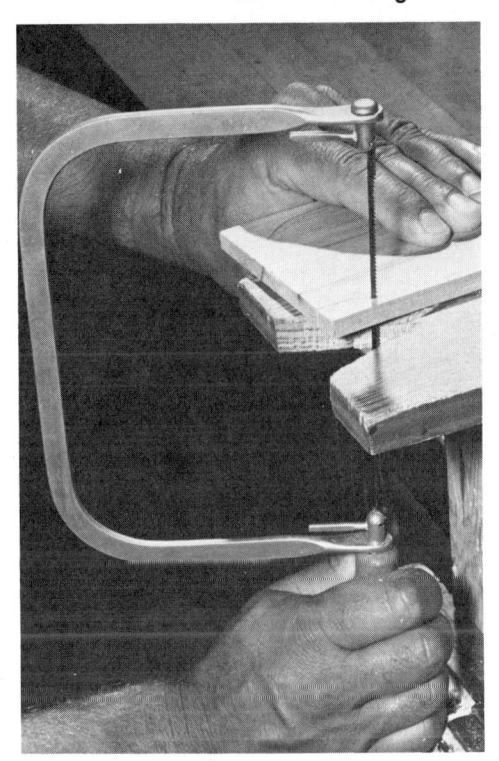

71-6. Using a coping saw to cut a piece of wood held on a saw bracket.

71-7. Using a coping saw with the work held in a vise.

the blade. This kind of saw is easy to use because the blade can be turned. Blades for the coping saw have teeth like those of a ripsaw. For most work a blade with 15 teeth to the inch will be satisfactory.

You can use a coping saw with the work held either over a saw bracket, Fig. 71-6, or in a vise, Fig. 71-7. If you are using a saw bracket, the teeth should point *toward* the handle. If the work is held in a vise, the teeth should point *away* from the handle.

Grasp the handle of the saw in your hand; move the saw up and down or back and forth depending on where you are sawing. Keep the blade moving at a steady, even pace. The blade may break if you jerk it or put too much pressure on it. At sharp corners keep working the saw and turn it slowly in the direction of the line. Twisting or bending the blade at the corners will also usually break it.

Compass and keyhole saws are used when you cannot use a coping saw, as for cutting curves in large boards or in plywood. The compass saw looks like a regular handsaw except that it is much smaller and almost comes to a point at the end. A keyhole saw is smaller than a

Part III: Manufacturing—Principles, Materials, and Processes

71-8. Using a compass saw to cut a circle in a large sheet of plywood.

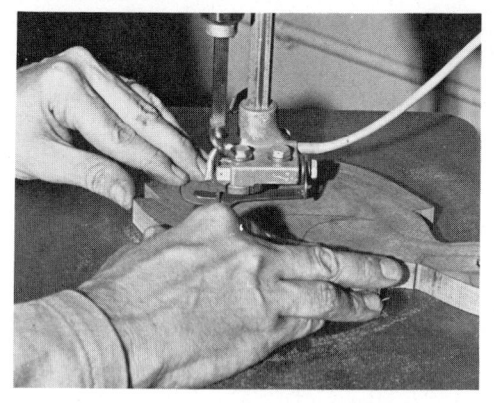

71-9b. The correct way to hold the work when cutting with a jigsaw.

compass saw and is used for cutting keyholes and for similar work. Fig. 71-8 shows a compass saw in use.

The **jig** or **scroll saw** is a machine for cutting curves. Fig. 71-9a. The saw blade moves up and down and is used for the same kind of cutting as the coping saw. The jigsaw is a safe machine if you follow the rules. You will probably use a jigsaw in making some of your projects. Special blades are made for this saw, but a coping saw blade without pins can be used successfully.

Cutting with the jigsaw requires the same care as cutting with a coping saw.

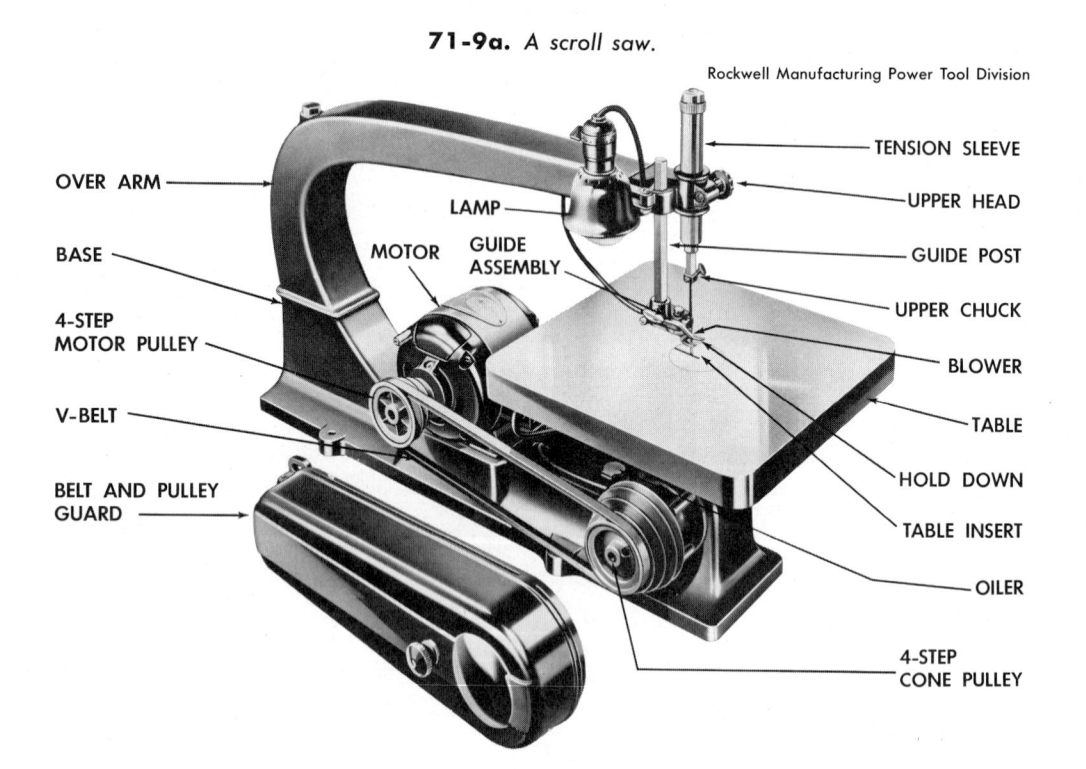

71-9a. A scroll saw.

Rockwell Manufacturing Power Tool Division

- OVER ARM
- BASE
- 4-STEP MOTOR PULLEY
- V-BELT
- BELT AND PULLEY GUARD
- LAMP
- MOTOR
- GUIDE ASSEMBLY
- TENSION SLEEVE
- UPPER HEAD
- GUIDE POST
- UPPER CHUCK
- BLOWER
- TABLE
- HOLD DOWN
- TABLE INSERT
- OILER
- 4-STEP CONE PULLEY

Unit 71: Sawing Wood

Adjust the guide so that the spring tension holds the work firmly against the table. Hold the work with the thumb and fingers as shown in Fig. 71-9b. Don't force the stock into the saw. Use an even pressure. Turn the stock slowly when cutting a curve; if it is turned too sharply or rapidly the blade will break.

If you are going to cut an internal curve or design, drill a hole in the center of the waste stock first. Remove the throat plate from the jigsaw. Unfasten the blade from the plunger. Slip the work over the blade. Fasten the top of the blade back to the plunger. Replace the throat plate. Adjust the guide to the correct pressure. Then take a cut from the hole to the layout line.

CUTTING WITH THE BAND SAW

The **band saw** is also used for cutting curves, circles, and irregular designs. This saw can be used for straight crosscutting and ripping too. The band saw is used for heavier wood than the jigsaw; it has a wider blade and cuts faster. It does not make as smooth a cut as the jigsaw. The band saw has a blade that runs over two large wheels. One of the wheels is on the top of the machine and one on the bottom. The upper wheel is adjustable in order to tighten the blades.

To cut on the band saw, the wood is placed on the table and pushed into the blade. The saw cuts rapidly; so be sure your fingers are out of the way. The band saw should not be used without permission of the instructor.

CIRCULAR SAW

In Fig. 71-10 you see a **circular saw.** This is used for power sawing. Your instructor may use this to do the same work as with a hand saw.

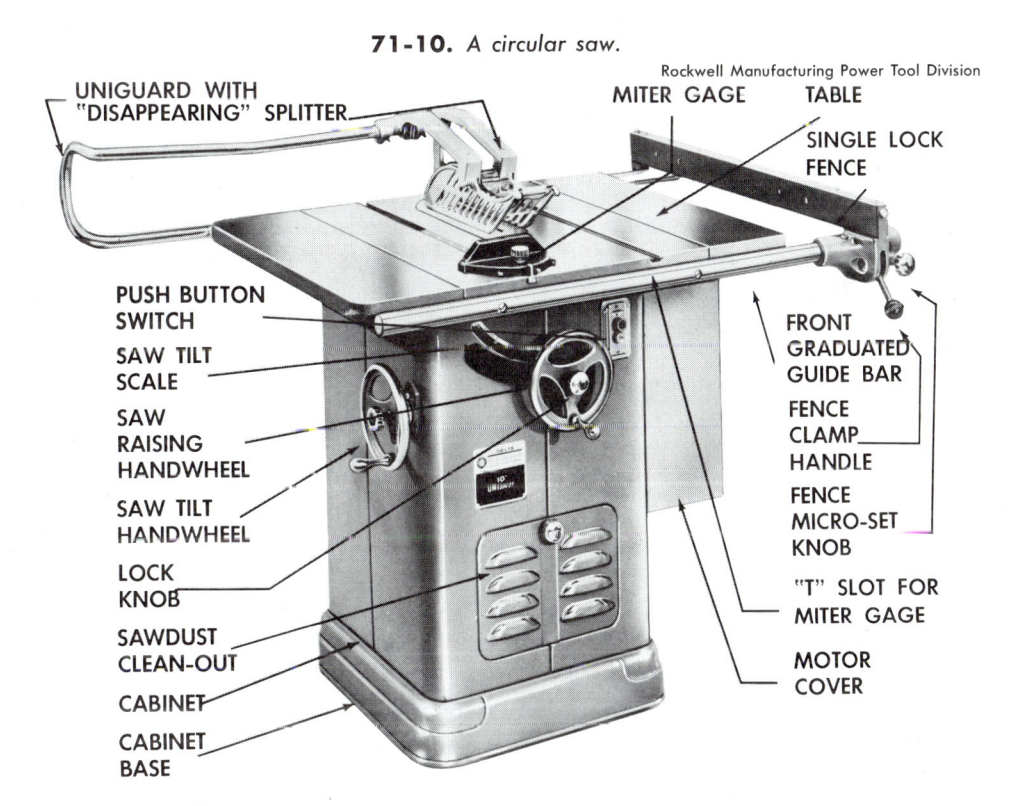

71-10. A circular saw.

ROCKWELL DELTA 10" TILTING ARBOR UNISAW

UNIT 72

Planing and Chiseling Wood

The most common tool used for removing wood is the *plane*. After pieces have been sawed, they are rough. Even surfaced wood still has small knife marks when it comes from the mill. If these are not removed, they will show up when you apply a finish. The hand plane is used to remove marks and smooth rough edges.

The plane is a tool which you must learn to handle correctly. It is the most complicated hand woodworking tool you will use. It takes more care and adjustment than any other tool. Fig. 72-1 shows the major parts of the plane.

PARTS AND TYPES OF PLANES

The *body* of the plane is made of steel. The *base,* or *bottom,* is smooth or sometimes ribbed. Behind the opening in the base is a *frog*. This is the support for the *plane iron.* A brass nut adjusts the depth of cut. A long slender lever is used for making a sideways adjustment of the cutter. The double plane iron consists of the *plane iron* itself and the *plane iron cap.* The plane iron fits over the frog and is held in place by the *lever cap.*

There are four common types of bench planes. They are all much alike. The big difference is in their length. The *jack plane* is from $11\frac{1}{2}''$ to 15'' long. The *smooth plane* is from 7'' to 9'' long. These planes are used for general-purpose planing. The *fore plane* and the *jointer plane* are much longer. These are used for planing large edges such as doors.

Sharpening the Plane Iron

The plane must be sharp. One way to check for sharpness is to sight along the edge. A sharp edge will not reflect any light.

If your plane iron is very dull or has nicks, it will have to be ground. Grinding is the shaping and forming of the cutting edge. Your instructor will grind your plane iron or show you how.

If your plane iron needs touching up or if it has been ground, it must be honed. Honing makes the cutting edge razor-sharp. (The plane iron must of course be removed from the plane for grinding and honing.)

To hone, select an oilstone with a flat, true surface. Apply a few drops of oil to the face of the stone. Place the bevel of the plane iron flat on the surface of the oilstone. Raise the end of the plane iron so just the cutting edge rests on the stone. Move the iron back and forth or in a circular pattern on the face of the stone. A wire edge or feather edge will form on the cutting edge. To remove this, turn the plane iron over and lay it flat on the stone. Move it back and forth a few times. *Be sure to hold the iron flat.* Then turn the plane iron over and give it a few strokes. Turn it over and stroke the back again. Repeat this until the wire edge is gone. The cutting edge should now be sharp.

Assembling the Plane

To assemble, the iron cap is placed on the plane iron as shown in Fig. 72-2. The

Unit 72: Planing and Chiseling Wood

set screw is tightened. The edge of the cap must fit tightly against the top of the plane iron. Otherwise, shavings will get between the cap and the plane iron, and the plane will not cut properly.

Insert the double plane iron into the plane with the bevel side down. Be careful not to hit the edge of the plane iron on the plane and dull it. Once the plane iron is properly in place, secure it with the lever cap. If you need more than thumb pressure to fasten the lever cap, unscrew the lever cap screw a bit.

Adjusting the Plane

Before starting to plane, you should adjust the tool for the correct depth of cut. Hold the plane upside down with the bottom at eye level. Turn the brass adjusting nut until the plane iron just appears beyond the bottom of the plane. Then move the lateral adjustment lever

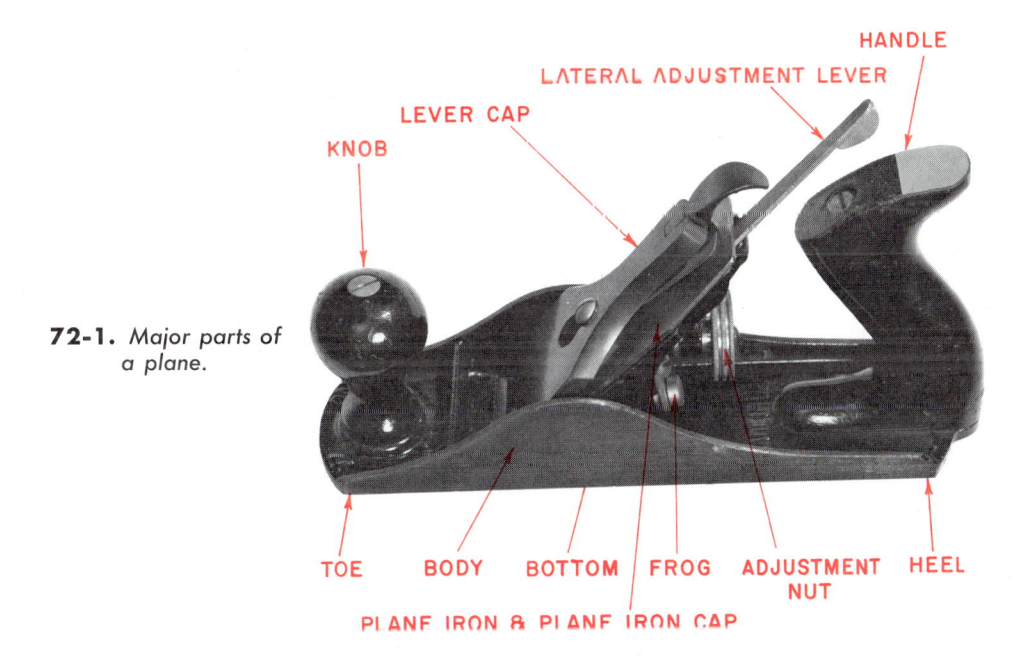

72-1. Major parts of a plane.

72-2. The correct way to assemble a double plane iron.

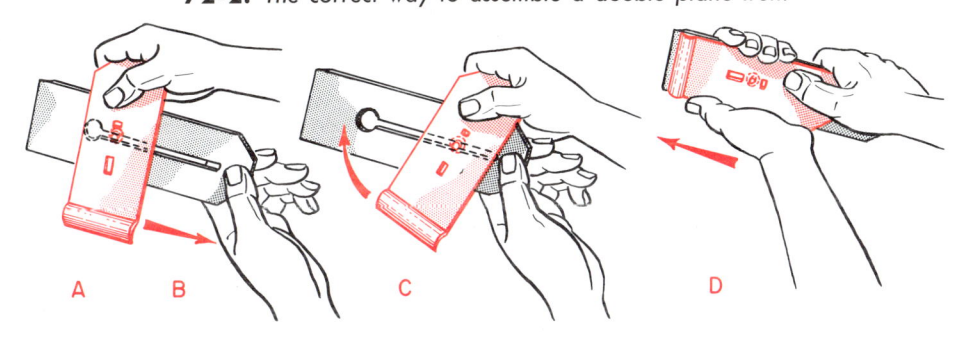

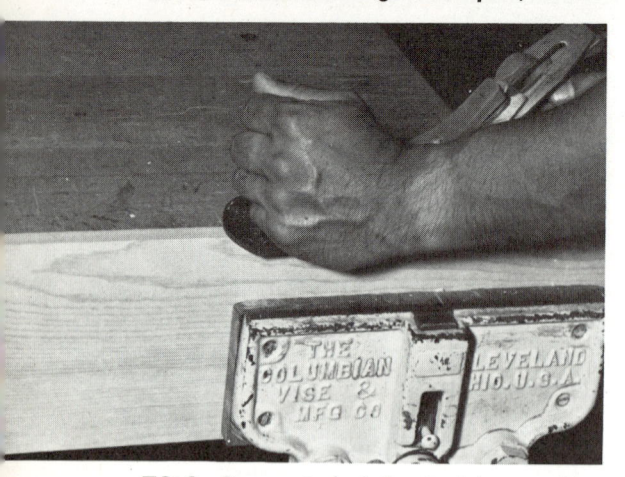

Part III: Manufacturing—Principles, Materials, and Processes

72-3. Be sure to lock the stock in a position that allows you to plane with the grain.

72-4. Checking the edge with a try square. Make sure the edge is square with the face. Move the try square along the board.

until the blade is parallel with the bottom of the plane. For fine work or smoothing a surface, a fine cut is best.

PLANING A SURFACE

Lock the board to be planed in the vise or between the dog of the vise and the bench stop. If the wood is rough, you may need to take a few cuts with the plane to see which way the grain runs. The board should be locked so that you are planing with the grain. Fig. 72-3. Planing against the grain will make the board rougher.

Grasp the knob of the plane in one hand and the handle in the other. Stand just back of your work. Use a back and forth motion with your body. Apply pressure to the front of the plane at the start of the stroke. Apply pressure to the rear of the plane as it begins to leave the surface. Lift the plane off the board on the return stroke. If you take a shearing cut, with the tool at a slight angle to the direction of cut, the plane will work more easily. Work across the board gradually. Plane down the high spots first, as these will require more planing than the rest of the surface. After the surface of the board begins to get smooth, check it with a straightedge to see if it is true. Light will show under the straightedge where there are low spots. It is best to check the entire length and width of the board. The first surface you have planed is called the face surface. This is the surface you use to start squaring stock.

Squaring Stock

To square up stock to width, select the best edge. Fasten the stock in a vise, with the edge extending above the jaws. Fig. 72-3. For short pieces a smooth plane will work nicely. For long pieces a long plane, such as a jointer plane, should be used. Adjust the plane to take a fine cut. Plane with the grain and take long strokes. This will remove a thin shaving all along the stock. Do not remove much wood. Try to get the edge square with the face. With a try square check the edge against the planed face. Fig. 72-4. The edge and face should be square with each other.

Set a marking gauge to the correct width. (Refer back to Fig. 68-11.) Mark the stock along its entire length with the gauge. Remember to push the gauge away from you. If there is much stock to be removed, the board should be ripped to within $\frac{1}{8}''$ of the finished measurement. Lock the stock in the vise, and plane this second edge just as the first. Be sure to check it against the face with a try square.

Unit 72: Planing and Chiseling Wood

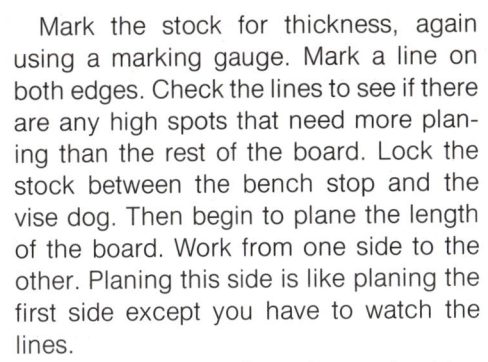

Mark the stock for thickness, again using a marking gauge. Mark a line on both edges. Check the lines to see if there are any high spots that need more planing than the rest of the board. Lock the stock between the bench stop and the vise dog. Then begin to plane the length of the board. Work from one side to the other. Planing this side is like planing the first side except you have to watch the lines.

As you near the lines, keep checking the piece with a straightedge and try square. Check this side against both edges with the try square.

Planing End Grain

Planing end grain is harder than planing the face or edge. When you plane the end of a board, you must cut off the fibers of the wood. The block plane is used for planing end grain. Fig. 72-5. It is much smaller than other planes.

The block plane is held in one hand. Begin from one edge and work toward the middle of the board. Then begin from the other edge and do the same thing. Be sure to hold the block plane square with the work. It is wise to take a shallow cut to keep the plane from jumping. By planing halfway across the end, then starting from the other side, you are not likely to split the wood. Another way to prevent splitting is to take a piece of scrap wood of the same thickness as the stock and place it against the edge of the stock. Still another way is to cut a bevel on the waste edge of the stock, then begin to plane from the other edge all the way across the wood.

USING THE CHISEL

Some cutting jobs that cannot be done with a saw or a plane are done with a **chisel** or a **gouge**. Chisels should be used with great care. They cause more injuries than any other woodworking tool. Always carry the chisel with point down, and never make a cut toward the hands or body.

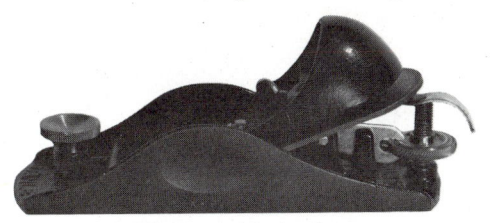

72-5. A block plane.

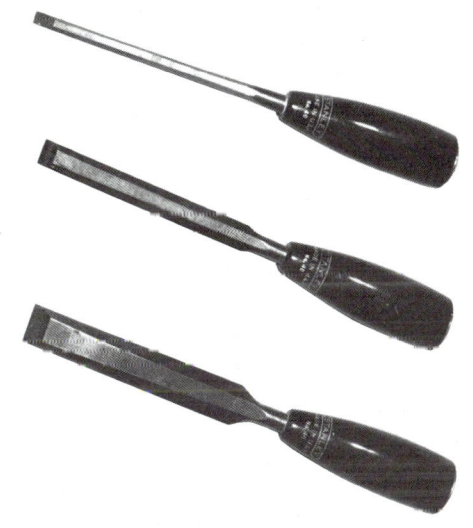

72-6. Some common sizes of wood chisels.

Chisels are of two types—the *socket chisel* and the *tang chisel*. Socket chisels are heavier and will take pounding better than the tang chisels. Chisel sizes range from $\frac{1}{4}''$ to $2''$. Fig. 72-6.

Gouges are chisels with curved blades. They also range in size from $\frac{1}{4}''$ to $2''$. To cut with a chisel, it is often necessary to pound it with a mallet. This mallet has a head of wood, hard rubber, or rawhide.

To use a chisel, fasten the work securely in a vise. Fasten it so you can cut with the grain. For rough cutting hold the chisel with the bevel against the wood. For light cuts, turn the chisel over. A shearing cut is easier to make than a straight cut. When cutting across the grain, it is best to work first from one side and then the other. If you try to cut all the way across the piece from one side, the

Part III: Manufacturing—Principles, Materials, and Processes

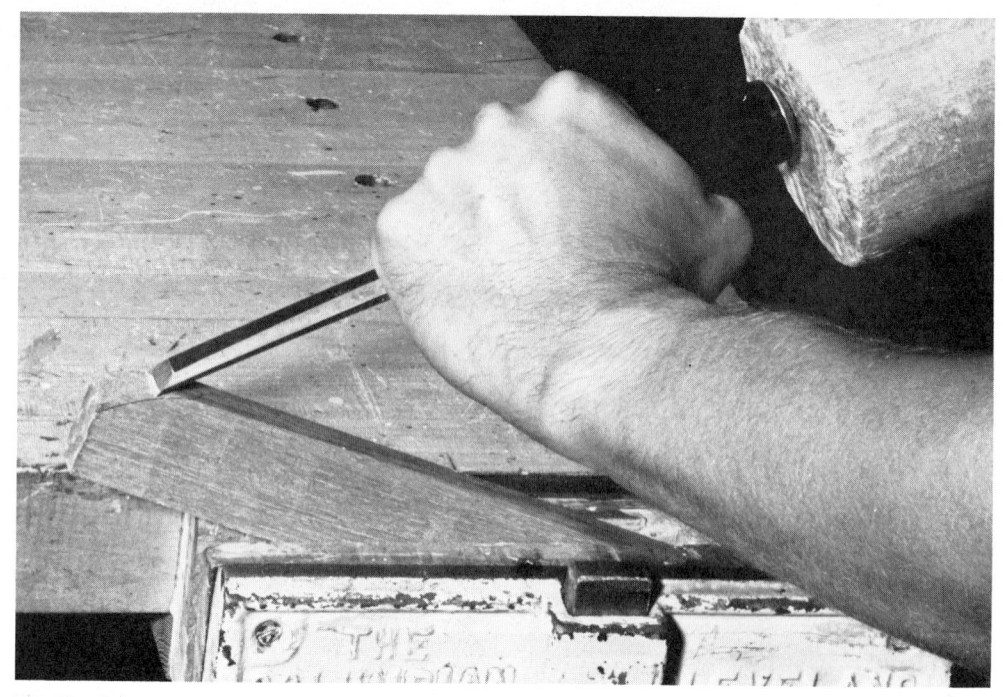

72-7. Cutting a curve with a chisel. Several straight cuts are taken first; then the curve is smoothed out.

72-8. Carving on a bowl with a gouge. Always keep your hands behind the chisel to avoid serious cuts.

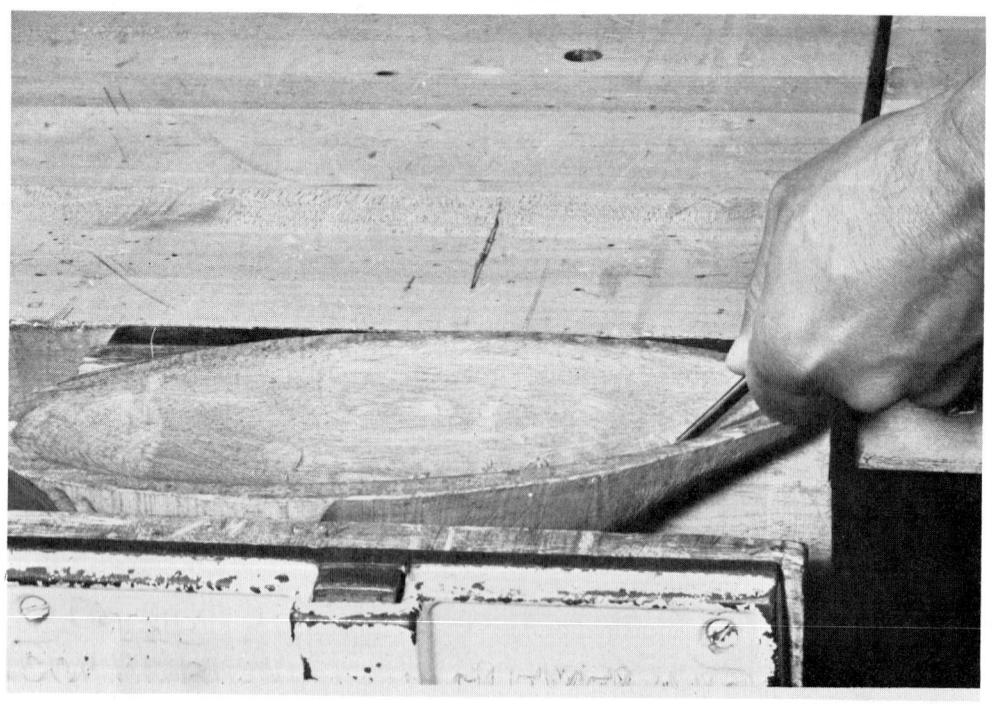

Unit 73: Abrading Wood

opposite side will split. Curves can be cut on boards by starting at a corner and taking several cuts. Fig. 72-7.

Many bowls are made by using gouges. When gouging out a bowl, you may need a mallet to make heavy cuts. It is better to take heavy cuts across the grain. The gouge is less likely to dig in. Gouges are used for wood carving on bowls and model boat hulls. Fig. 72-8.

For some projects it is necessary to form a curved surface. Curves can be formed with a bladed tool such as the **spokeshave.** The spokeshave was originally used for shaping the spokes of wooden wheels. It is used for finishing the edges of curves and molding irregular shapes. The cutter blade is sharpened much like the plane iron. It has two adjusting nuts on the top. Fig. 72-9. The spokeshave may be either pushed away from you or pulled toward you. Files and rasps may also be used for shaping curved surfaces. (See Unit 75.)

72-9. The spokeshave.

UNIT 73 — Abrading Wood

Sanding is the process of cutting the wood fibers with some type of abrasive. *Abrasives* are hard materials that grind or wear away a softer material. The main reason for sanding is to smooth the wood surfaces before the finishing operation. Sanding is very important because finishes make defects show up more. Scratches you can barely see will be noticeable after you apply the finish to your project.

Sanding on either wood or plastic projects is usually not started until all the other work is done. There are times when some shaping can be done with abrasive paper. However, a general rule is never to try to make abrasive paper take the place of a chisel or a plane.

Abrasive papers are sold in many forms. (See Unit 36.) Sheets are most commonly used in the school shop. The grade of abrasive paper you select will make a difference in your work. A carefully planed surface can be sanded with a fine paper (150 or 180) and be ready to finish. If tool marks show on the wood, it

343

Part III: Manufacturing—Principles, Materials, and Processes

73-1. Sanding a flat surface with a sanding block. Be sure to sand with the grain of the wood.

73-2. Sanding the edge of a board. Be sure to keep the sanding block square with the surface.

73-3. Sanding an inside curve with the sandpaper wrapped around a dowel.

will be necessary to use a coarser paper. The coarser grades of paper are usually used for shaping edges of wood.

SANDING WOOD

Each piece of a project should be sanded before assembly. After the project is assembled, light sanding should be done again before the finish is applied.

For sanding flat surfaces a sanding block should be used. Fasten the piece to be sanded in a vise or hold it firmly on a bench. Apply an even pressure to the block, and sand the surface *with the grain.* Fig. 73-1. Move the block back and forth and work from one side to the other. Don't sand the edges too much. Start with a medium paper and finish with a fine paper. When sanding an edge, fasten the piece in the vise so that the edge is showing. Use two hands on the sanding block. Be sure to keep the sanding block square with the face. Fig. 73-2. To sand an end, use the same procedure as for sanding an edge. Sand in one direction only. Sand the corners and arrises lightly. (An *arris* is the edge formed by two surfaces.)

For sanding inside or outside curves, you can simply hold the sandpaper in your hand. For sanding inside or concave surfaces the abrasive paper can be wrapped around a stick such as a large dowel. Fig. 73-3. Round pieces such as stool legs can be sanded by using the paper like a shoeshine cloth. Turned parts that are straight can be sanded with the grain. Very small parts may be sanded by first fastening a piece of abrasive paper to a board. This is clamped in a vise or held on a bench top. Hold the small pieces in

Unit 73: Abrading Wood

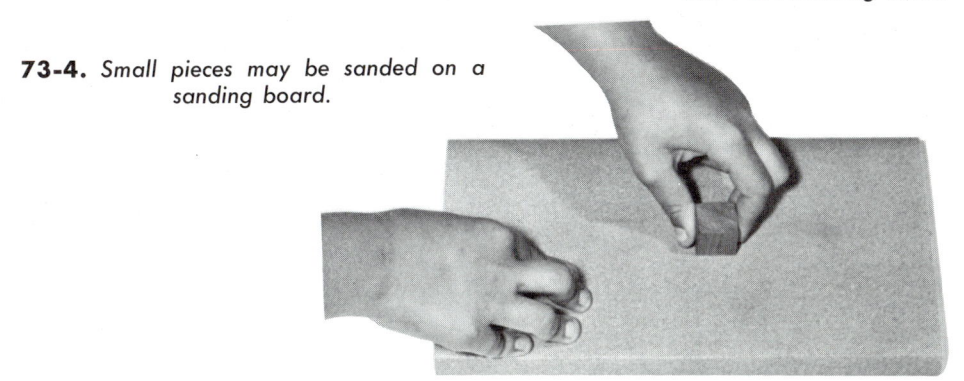

73-4. Small pieces may be sanded on a sanding board.

your hand and rub them back and forth over the paper. Fig. 73-4.

POWER SANDERS

Some shops may have one or more kinds of power sanders. The most popular are **belt sanders** and **disc sanders.** Fig. 73-5. The work is placed on the table and pushed against the belt or disc. The disc sander is best used for coarse sanding or shaping pieces. The belt sander can be used for medium or fine sanding. Belts of different grit can be used on the belt sander.

When you cannot take the work to the sander, a **portable sander** can be used. The portable belt sander, for example, uses a sanding belt like the floor machine. The belt revolves on two wheels. The sander is placed over the work. This sander is hard to use because the belt makes the machine run away from you. The finish sander has a more gentle action. Straight-line action leaves the smoothest finish. Never use any power sander without the permission of the instructor.

Power sanders are occasionally used to sand the edges of plastic pieces. A disc or belt sander can be used to true the edges of plastic. These machines can also be used to shape irregular pieces of plastics.

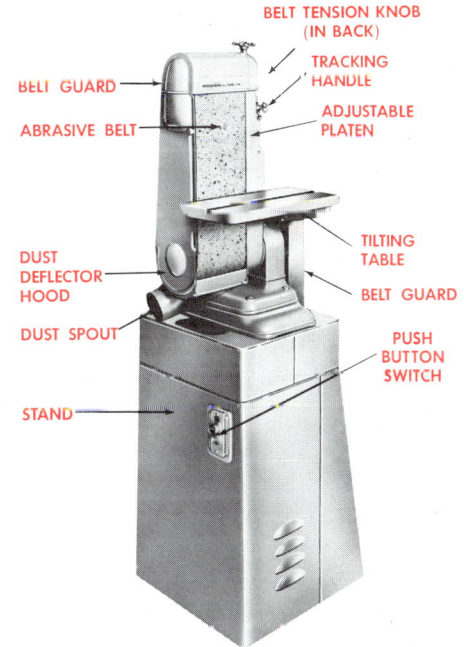

Rockwell Manufacturing Power Tool Division
73-5. A belt sander.

UNIT 74

Drilling Holes in Wood

Many woodworking projects involve the boring of holes. Some common drilling tools are shown in Fig. 74-1. For cutting small holes—$\frac{1}{4}''$ or less in diameter—a **twist drill** is used. For cutting holes larger than $\frac{1}{4}''$ an **auger bit** is used. For still larger holes an **expansion bit** is needed. This tool can be adjusted with different cutters to bore holes from $\frac{7}{8}''$ to 3''. For boring holes partway through a board a **Foerstner bit** is used.

Auger bits come in sizes ranging from No. 4 to No. 32. The number stamped on the tang of the bit indicates the size in sixteenths of an inch. For example a No. 4 would be $\frac{4}{16}''$ or $\frac{1}{4}''$. A No. 7 would be $\frac{7}{16}''$. A set of auger bits has all the numbers from 4 through 16.

Auger bits are used in a **brace.** Fig. 74-2. The size of the brace is measured by the sweep. A good size is 8'' or 10''. Most braces have a ratchet that allows boring holes in a corner even though there isn't room for a complete swing of the handle.

To install a bit in a brace, hold the shell of the chuck in your left hand and turn the handle to the left until the jaw is open. Insert the bit and turn the handle to the right to fasten it. When placing the bit in the brace, be sure to have the corner of the bit in the U grooves of the jaws.

BORING HOLES

Measure and lay out the position of the holes by drawing centerlines. Punch the center of the hole with a scratch awl.

74-1. Tools for drilling: (A) Twist drill (B) Auger bit (C) Expansion bit (D) Foerstner bit.

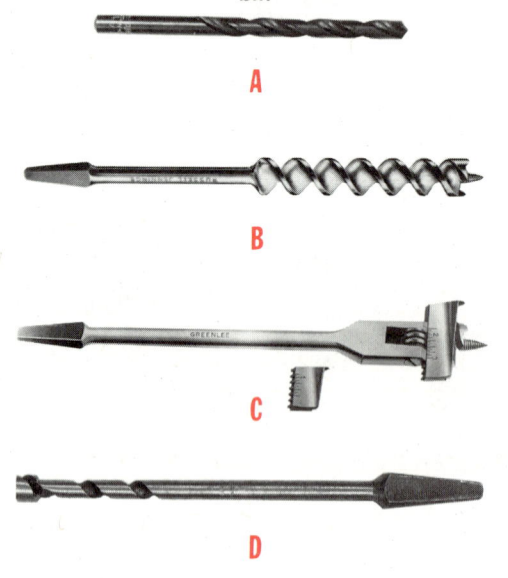

74-2. The brace is used with an auger bit for boring holes.

Stanley Tools

Unit 74: Drilling Holes in Wood

74-3. Small pieces can be clamped in a vise. Be sure to keep the bit square with the work by lining it up with a try square.

Place the stock in a vise so that the brace can be used in a horizontal position. Fig. 74-3. Guide the bit with your left hand and start it in the hole made with the scratch awl. Hold the head of the brace with your left hand. Turn the handle with your right hand. Be sure to keep the bit square with the work. You can sight along the top of the bit. Have another student sight the bit to see if it is straight up and down.

Do not press too hard on the brace. A properly sharpened auger bit will almost feed itself into the wood. Continue to bore until the point of the bit just comes through the stock. Now turn the wood around and bore from the other side. If this is not done, the wood will split when the bit goes through. Another way to keep the wood from splitting is to clamp a scrap block of wood to the back of the stock. Then you can bore all the way through.

Sometimes you need to bore only partway through a board. For this you need a **depth gauge,** Fig. 74-4. A piece of masking tape may also be placed on the bit to show how deep to bore.

To bore a hole at an angle, set a sliding T bevel at the proper angle to use as a guide. Start the auger bit as you did for straight boring. When the screw feeds into the wood, tilt the bit to the proper angle. The bit should line up with the T bevel. Fig. 74-5.

74-4. A depth gauge fastened to an auger bit.

74-5. Using a T bevel as a guide for boring a hole on a slant.

Part III: Manufacturing—Principles, Materials, and Processes

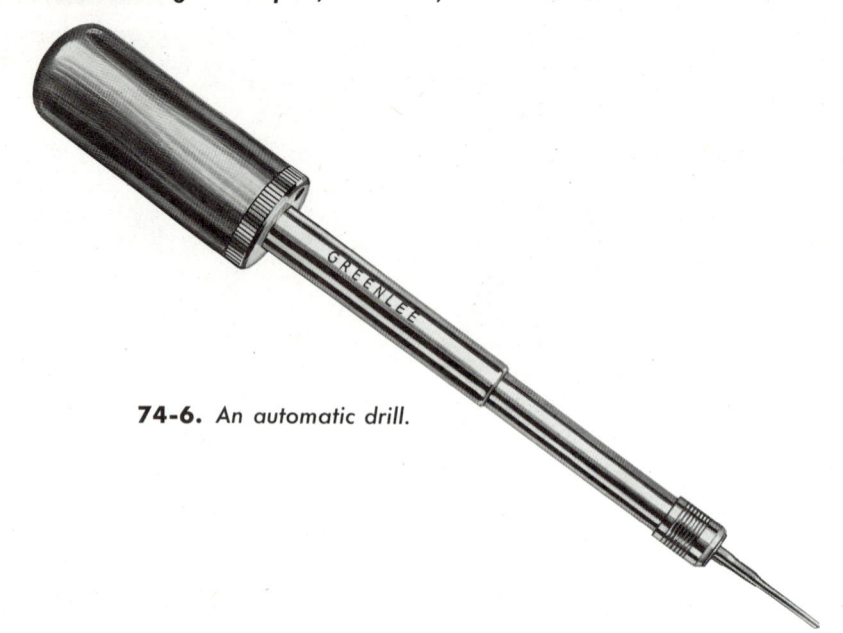

74-6. An automatic drill.

74-7. Using a hand drill for drilling a small hole in a piece of wood.

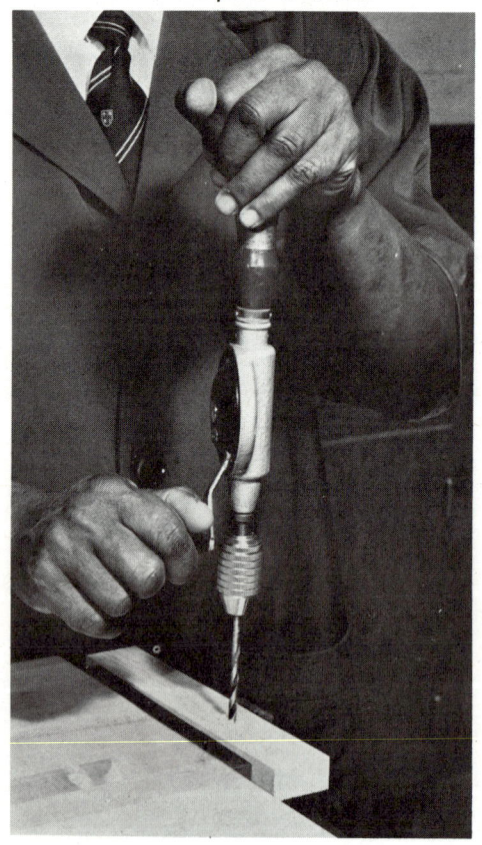

To bore a large hole use an expansion bit. Set the distance from the feed screw to the spur. This will be half the diameter of the hole. This equals the radius of the hole. Be sure to lock the cutter. It is a good idea to bore a hole in a scrap piece to check the size of the hole. When the feed screw comes through the wood, finish the hole from the other side.

As mentioned earlier, Foerstner bits are used for boring holes that go only partway through a board. The sizes range from $\frac{1}{2}$" to 2". Draw a circle where you want the hole.

DRILLING HOLES

Holes $\frac{1}{4}$" or smaller are usually drilled with a hand drill. (See Unit 38 for more information on the hand drill, electric drill, and drill press.) Twist drills have straight shanks. These drills may be used for making holes in either wood or metal. Twist drills in a set range in size from $\frac{1}{16}$" to $\frac{1}{2}$" in intervals of $\frac{1}{64}$".

The **automatic drill** is used for boring small holes in wood. Fig. 74-6. The drill points are carried in the handle. To use this tool, select the desired drill point,

Unit 75: Milling, Shaping, and Filing Wood

place it in the chuck, and tighten. When you push down on the handle, the point turns, thus drilling the hole. The **hand drill** is used with the twist drill. Fig. 74-7. It has three jaws in the chuck. These jaws hold the round shanks of the twist drills.

An electric hand drill is a useful tool. These drills are sized according to the largest drill they will hold. The most common size is $\frac{1}{4}''$.

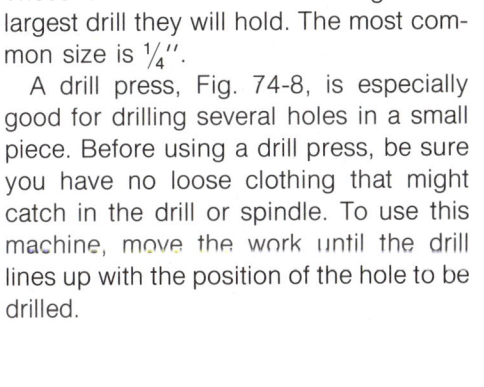

A drill press, Fig. 74-8, is especially good for drilling several holes in a small piece. Before using a drill press, be sure you have no loose clothing that might catch in the drill or spindle. To use this machine, move the work until the drill lines up with the position of the hole to be drilled.

74-8. Using a drill press. Notice that the stock is held firmly in a vise.

UNIT 75

Milling, Shaping, and Filing Wood

Wood milling is a form of wood removal. Rough boards are planed to thickness on a machine called a planer. The edges of wood are often rounded or cut to some other curved shapes. In this unit we will learn of some methods of shaping by both hand and machine.

FILES AND RASPS

Many times, small curves will require the use of a *rasp* or a *file*. Fig. 75-1. Files are available in many sizes and shapes. The most often used files are the half-round cabinet and flat files. The rasp removes large amounts of stock quickly,

Part III: Manufacturing—Principles, Materials, and Processes

75-1. Wood rasp.

75-2. One type of Surform® tool.

but leaves a rough surface. Be sure to use a handle on a file or rasp. See Unit 39 for additional information on files.

The *Surform® tool* is for forming. Its tool steel blade has rasplike teeth that make it easy to cut wood. Fig. 75-2. This tool is used like a rasp, but it really cuts the wood instead of scraping. It produces a smooth, flat surface. It is good for shaping odd-shaped projects.

CUTTING WITH THE JOINTER

Your shop may have a jointer for smoothing the edges and faces of boards.

The jointer is a surfacing machine. Fig. 75-3. It has a base, two tables, and a cutter head. When used improperly, it is a dangerous machine. Probably your instructor will operate the jointer for you. The jointer is usually used for smoothing an edge and making it square with the face. Fig. 75-4.

SHAPING WITH THE ROUTER

The router, Fig. 75-5, is a hand machine that is used for many cutting and shaping jobs. It can cut grooves, round edges, make bead and cove edge cuts,

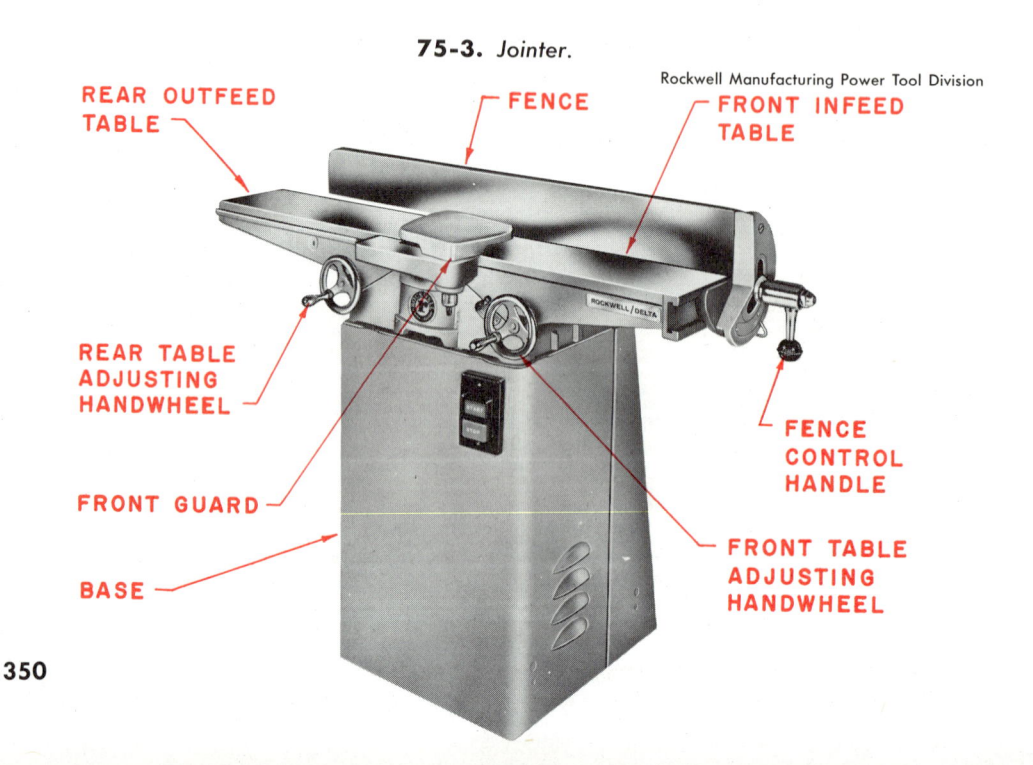

75-3. Jointer.

Rockwell Manufacturing Power Tool Division

REAR OUTFEED TABLE
FENCE
FRONT INFEED TABLE
REAR TABLE ADJUSTING HANDWHEEL
FENCE CONTROL HANDLE
FRONT GUARD
FRONT TABLE ADJUSTING HANDWHEEL
BASE

350

Unit 75: Milling, Shaping, and Filing Wood

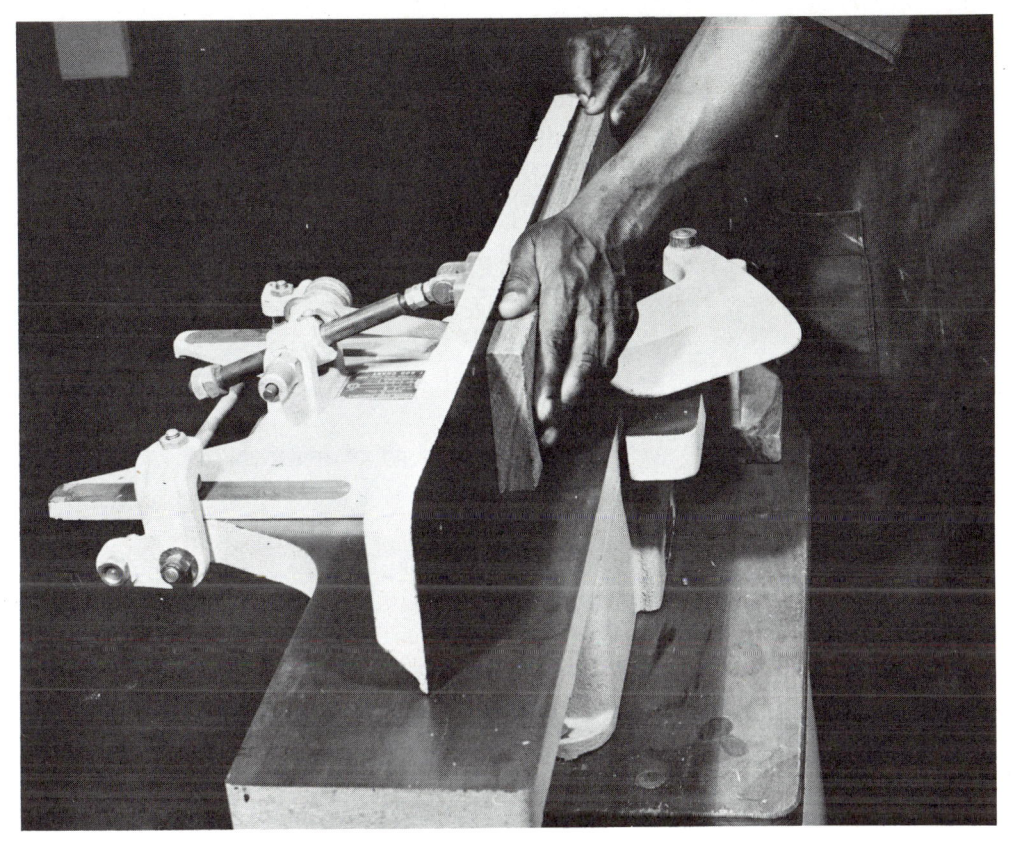

75-4. Using the jointer.

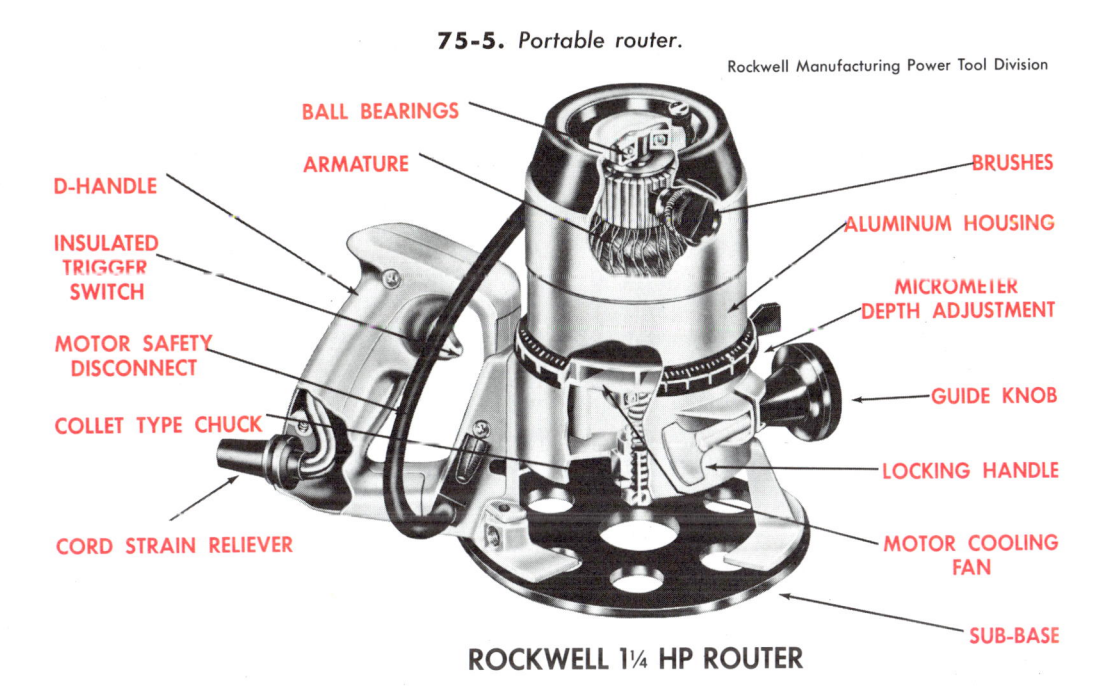

75-5. Portable router.

Rockwell Manufacturing Power Tool Division

- D-HANDLE
- INSULATED TRIGGER SWITCH
- MOTOR SAFETY DISCONNECT
- COLLET TYPE CHUCK
- CORD STRAIN RELIEVER
- BALL BEARINGS
- ARMATURE
- BRUSHES
- ALUMINUM HOUSING
- MICROMETER DEPTH ADJUSTMENT
- GUIDE KNOB
- LOCKING HANDLE
- MOTOR COOLING FAN
- SUB-BASE

ROCKWELL 1¼ HP ROUTER

351

Part III: Manufacturing—Principles, Materials, and Processes

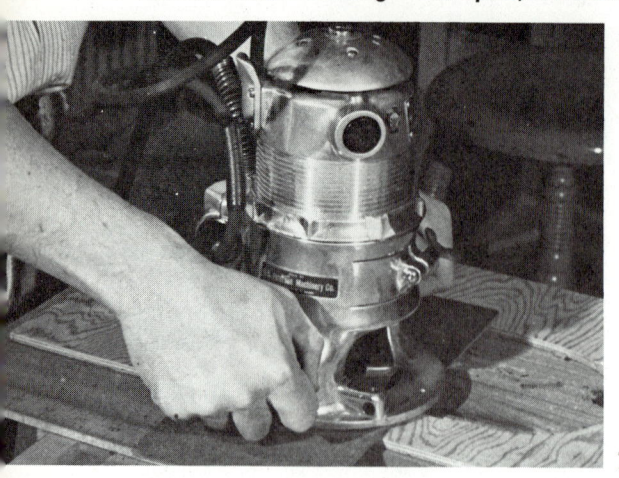

and do much more. It consists of a high-speed motor mounted on an adjustable base. The chuck at the end of the motor shaft can hold a number of differently shaped cutters. It can also be used to dish-out the middle of a board in order to make a serving tray or bowl. Fig. 75-6. The router can be a very dangerous tool in inexperienced hands. **Check with your instructor before using it.**

75-6. *Using the router.*

UNIT 76

Wood Turning

Many projects require turned parts for their construction. The *wood lathe* is the machine used to make these turned parts. The machine has a *bed,* a *headstock,* and a *tailstock.* Fig. 76-1. It also has a *tool rest* that can be moved. The headstock has a hollow taper into which the *live center* is fastened. The tailstock also has a taper, ground to hold the *dead center.*

The common cutting tools include a 1″ gouge, a ½″ gouge, a 1″ skew, a ½″ skew, a roundnose tool, a spear, and a parting tool. Fig. 76-2.

There are two methods of turning wood—namely, *cutting* and *scraping.* In cutting, the tool is held so that the cutting edge digs into the revolving wood. In scraping, the tool is held at right angles and fine particles are worn away. Scraping is easier than cutting.

The piece to be turned should be larger and about 1″ longer than the finished piece. Make a line across the wood to locate the center. Fig. 76-3. Place the live center over the end and tap it with a mallet to force the spear into the wood. With hardwood it may be necessary to make saw kerfs across the corners for the live center.

Hold the stock against the live center and bring the tailstock to within about 1½″ of the end. Lock the tailstock to the bed. Then turn the tailstock handle to bring the tailstock up to the wood. Force the tailstock into the wood about 1/32″. Back the tailstock off and rub some wax

Unit 76: Wood Turning

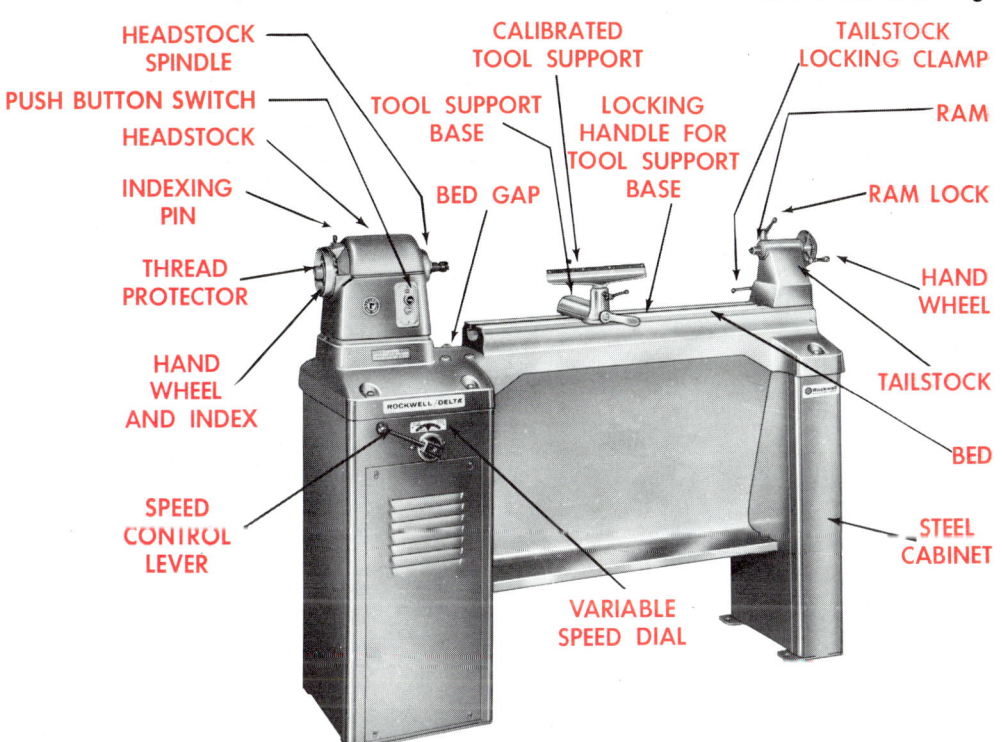

ROCKWELL DELTA 12" HEAVY DUTY VARIABLE SPEED WOOD LATHE

Rockwell Manufacturing Power Tool Division

76-1. The wood lathe.

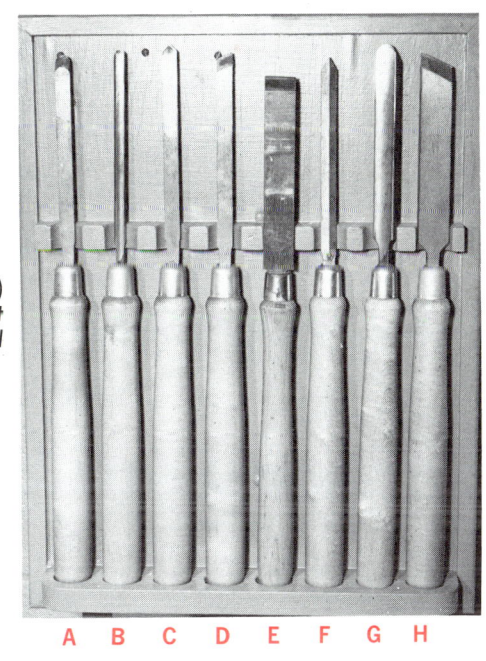

76-2. A set of lathe turning tools: (A) *Roundnose* (B) *Small gauge* (C) *Diamond point* (D) *Small skew* (E) *Flat skew* (F) *Parting tool* (G) *Large gouge* (H) *Large skew*.

353

Part III: Manufacturing—Principles, Materials, and Processes

on the wood. Then tighten the tailstock. Adjust the tool rest to clear the stock by about $\frac{1}{8}''$ and slightly above center. Rotate the stock by hand to make sure the stock clears the tool rest.

To begin, the lathe should be set on the slowest speed. Use the large gouge. Hold it against the wood as shown in Fig. 76-4. The gouge is used for rough turning. For finish turning use a skew; increase the machine speed. Be careful with the skew so as not to catch it in the stock. Always make sure to have a good hold on the lathe tools. Keep the tool rest close to the work. If there is too much space between the tool rest and the work, the tool may catch and be thrown out of your hands.

Faceplate turning is done by fastening a piece of wood to the faceplate with screws. The faceplate is mounted on the bedstock spindle. The piece of wood is sawed out round on a jigsaw or a band saw. The tool rest is turned around in front of the work. Begin turning with the gouge the same as for turning between centers. Lamp bases, bowls, and trays are turned on the faceplate. Fig. 76-5.

76-3. *Marking the center of the stock to be turned.*

76-4. *Turning between centers on the lathe. This student is making a rough cut with the large gouge.*

Do not run the lathe at excessive speeds. This is especially important in the beginning before the work is trued up. Unbalanced pieces running at a high speed may fly out of the lathe and injure you or someone else. Never use the wood lathe without the instructor's permission.

76-5. *Faceplate turning. Scraping tools such as a roundnose tool are especially good for removing material from the inside of a bowl.*

UNIT 77

Wood Forming Principles

As shown in Fig. 77-1, steaming and laminating are the main methods used to bend wood. Skis, toboggans, and certain furniture parts are made this way. Wood can also be bent without heat. All of these methods are described below.

STEAM BENDING

Certain kinds of wood bend more easily than others. These are ash, hickory, birch, and oak. Before bending, wood should be steamed or boiled in hot water. This softens the wood cells so that they can be stretched or compressed; then the wood will bend much more easily than when dry.

To soften the wood, a heating tube is often used. This tube is closed on the lower end and has a cover on the upper end. Water is poured into the tube and heated. The wood is inserted into the tube and the cover placed on the upper end. After the pieces have been heated, they are removed and placed in the bending form. Draw the stock around the form. This must be done slowly and carefully because wood will split when pulled too rapidly. As the wood is bent, it is clamped to hold it until formed. The wood should dry for at least 24 hours in the form. After forming, it is sanded in the usual manner.

BENDING WITHOUT HEAT

Flat stock can be bent without heating, if a saw kerf is cut in one end of the stock. Fig. 77-2. Next, cut pieces of veneer wider than the stock to fit in the saw kerf. Put waterproof glue on both sides of the veneer and slip it into the kerf. Clamp the stock in the bending form and let the glue

355

Part III: Manufacturing—Principles, Materials, and Processes

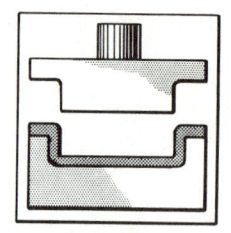

Forming

Forming is the process of shaping wood without adding to or removing any of the material.

KIND OF FORMING	DEFINITION	EXAMPLES
Bending	Forming by uniformly straining wood around a straight axis.	Steam bending and laminating of wood.

77-1. Wood forming.

dry. Spruce and mahogany are good woods to use for this process, which is a variation of the laminating process explained next.

LAMINATING WOOD

Another way of forming wood products is by laminating. This is the process of building up thickness by gluing several layers of wood together. The grain runs in the same direction. (In plywood or veneer the grains of alternate layers run at right angles to each other.) Laminating is done to produce the attractive beams found in buildings such as schools and churches. Fig. 77-3. These beams are very strong and resist fire better than solid pieces. Laminated beams can be made from short pieces.

Laminating can be done in the school shop to make small projects such as salad servers. First, make a full size pattern of the curve to be bent; then decide on the number of thicknesses to use in the project. Usually an odd number is best—three, five, or seven.

Next, make the form from hard maple or birch. It must be wide enough to allow at least 1″ on either side of the veneer. Lay out the curve on the block; then carefully cut the curve. This is best done on the band saw. **Be very careful when using the band saw.** The two halves must fit perfectly. Sand the forms lightly to make a better surface. Fig. 77-4.

Cut several pieces of veneer large enough for the project. You can use one or several kinds of wood for the different layers. Spread glue evenly on all the layers. Do not put glue on the outside of the top and bottom pieces.

Place a piece of wax paper on one-half of the form and lay the veneer on it. Lay a piece of wax paper over the top of the veneer and set the top form in place. Clamp the two forms together with wood clamps. Allow the piece to dry under pressure. When dry, remove the piece from the form; saw out the design with the jig saw, and sand. Fig. 77-5.

If you are making a project that will be used around food, finish with salad oil.

Unit 77: Wood Forming Principles

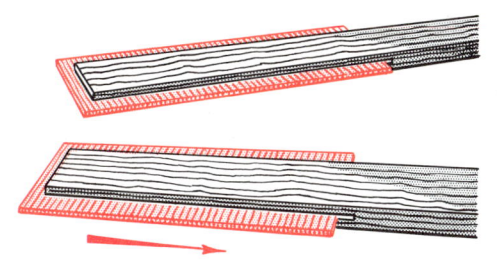

77-2. Veneer inserted in saw kerfs of flat stock. Spruce and mahogany work well for this process.

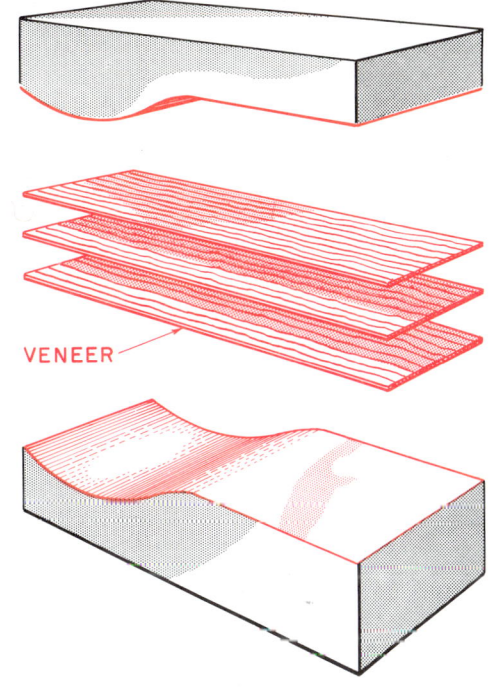

VENEER

77-4. This kind of form is needed for laminating in the school shop. Salad servers could be made using forms like these.

77-3. Laminated wooden beams used in a church building.

77-5. Chair made from laminated walnut and formed in a steam beveler.

357

UNIT 78

Wood Fastening Principles

Mechanical fastenings most frequently used on wood are screws and nails. Machine bolts, special rivets, and spring clips are also used. Fig. 78-1 shows the fastening methods used for wood.

To join by adhesion, a substance which is different from the materials being joined is used. This is usually some kind of glue. Many kinds of glue are used for wood products. Waterproof glues are often used on wood that will be exposed to the weather. Others may be used where the wood will not be exposed to moisture. Two different materials may be fastened together by adhesion. For example, plastic can be cemented to wood by using the newer epoxy cements, or contact cements.

78-1. *Ways to fasten wood.*

Fastening

Fastening is the process of joining materials together. The materials may be joined permanently or semipermanently. Different materials require different types of fasteners. Wood materials used in the shop may be fastened in one of two ways—mechanical fasteners or adhesion.

KIND OF FASTENING	DEFINITION	EXAMPLES
Mechanical	Permanent or semipermanent fastening with special locking devices.	Nails. Screws. Corrugated fasteners. Machine bolts. Rivets.
Adhesive	Permanent fastening by bonding like or unlike materials together with glue or cements.	Glue. Contact cement. Epoxy cement.

UNIT 79

Woodworking Joints

There are many kinds of wood joints. Some are used more often than others, but all joints must be laid out, cut, fitted, and assembled. Most joints are held together by glue. The strength of a joint is determined largely by how much surface of one piece touches the other. Joints which do not have much surface touching are reinforced with nails, screws, or dowels.

The pieces to be joined should first be squared and cut to size. Lay out the parts carefully. Use a sharp pencil to mark the two pieces of a joint so that they will not get mixed up. This is especially important when gluing several pieces edge to edge for a tabletop.

The *butt joint* is used for gluing pieces together edge to edge. This is not a very strong joint; so it is often reinforced with dowels. Fig. 79-1. Dowels are hardwood rods, usually of birch or maple. They are available in a variety of sizes from $\frac{1}{8}$" to 1" in diameter, with or without grooves. Dowel rods are particularly good for reinforcing the joints of tabletops or wide boards built up from several narrower boards. Carpenters use butt joints in house construction and in the construction of boxes and crates.

The *lap joint* is used where two pieces cross. Fig. 79-2. Lap joints are fairly easy to make. One-half the thickness of each piece is cut so that the pieces fit flush together. The lap joint is laid out by marking the width and depth of the wood to be removed. The backsaw is used to make the depth cut. The wood between the cuts

79-1. *Two pieces glued together edge to edge. Dowels are used to make the joint stronger.*

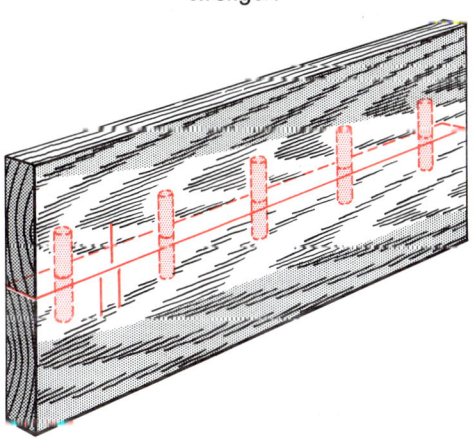

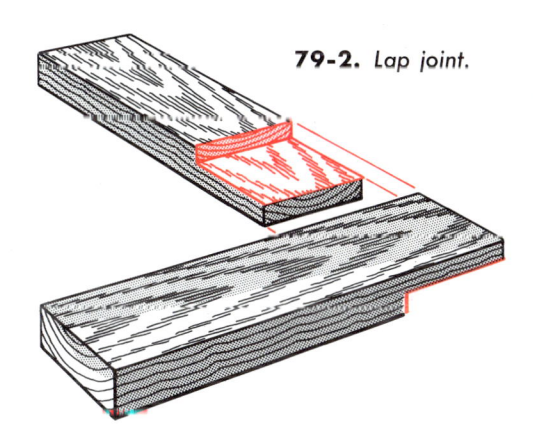

79-2. Lap joint.

Part III: Manufacturing—Principles, Materials, and Processes

is removed with a chisel. The sawing should be done inside the marking lines so as to make a good tight fit.

The *rabbet joint* is used for fitting panels into a frame. This joint is commonly used for making doors for cabinets. A groove is made in the edge, or end, of the wood used for the frame. This groove is the same size as the thickness of the piece that will be fastened to it. Fig. 79-3.

The *dado joint* is commonly used for supporting shelves in bookcases. Fig. 79-4. The width and depth of the dado is marked on the board to be cut. The width depends on the board that is to fit into the joint. The backsaw is used to cut the sides to the proper depth. A chisel is used to remove the excess wood. Be sure to chisel from both sides to avoid splitting the wood. On rough work, the dado joint may be fastened with nails. On finish work the joint is usually fastened with glue.

The *miter joint* is used for cutting and fitting rafters and moldings. It is also commonly used for picture frames. This joint helps eliminate end grain, but it is a rather weak type of construction. Fig. 79-5. A T bevel or a miter square is commonly used to lay out the miter cut on the two pieces of wood to be joined. Then the stock may be clamped in the vise and sawed. If the pieces to be joined are small, they can be sawed with a backsaw. However, the easiest method of cutting miters is to use a miter box. The best miter boxes are adjustable for sawing at many different angles. Fig. 79-6.

Miter joints are usually nailed and glued. The first nail is driven from the outside edge, at a right angle to the miter cut, until the point comes through and makes an impression on the opposite piece. The two bevels of the miter joint are then given an even coating of cabinet glue. One half of the joint is securely

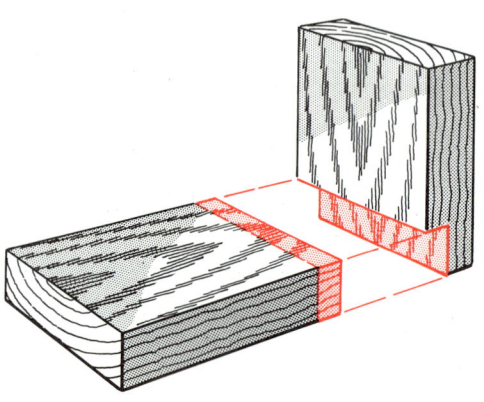

79-3. *Rabbet joint. This joint is used in furniture and doors.*

79-4. *Dado joint. This joint is used for shelves in bookcases.*

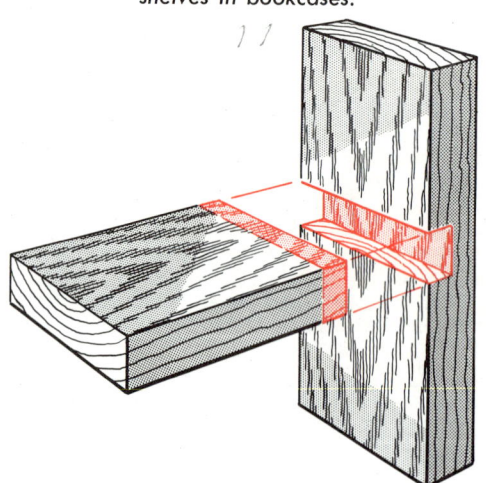

79-5. *Miter joint. This is a common joint for making picture frames.*

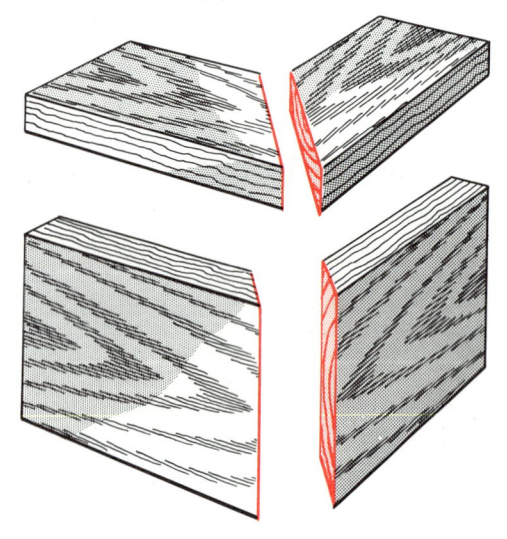

Unit 79: Woodworking Joints

fastened in a vise, then the half which contains the nail is placed in position and the nail driven in. The joint is then removed from the vise and the opposite side is clamped in the vise. Another nail is driven in from the opposite side. This will counteract the slippage that occurred when the first nail was driven in, and will help line up the joint and make an even and square contact. All surplus glue should be wiped from the edges of the joint with a damp cloth before the glue sets.

Mortise and tenon joints are commonly used to fasten legs to the rails of tables and chairs and to join parts in many other types of furniture construction. In the mill, mortise and tenon joints are rapidly made by machines. When properly made and fitted, the mortise and tenon joint is strong. It can be made successfully with hand tools, but it requires more time and more careful workmanship than some other joints. The mortise is the hole, and the tenon is the tongue which fits into it. Fig. 79-7.

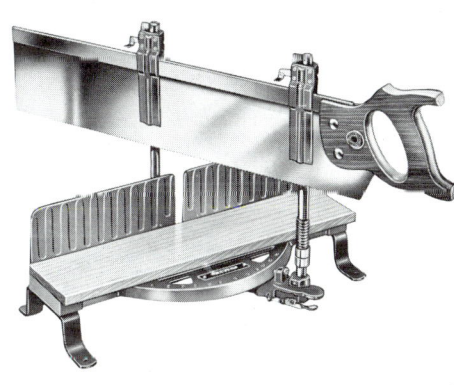

79-6. Miter saw. This is adjustable to any angle for making miter joints.

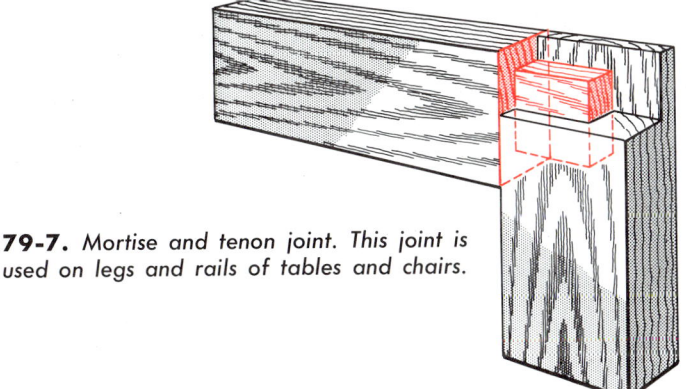

79-7. Mortise and tenon joint. This joint is used on legs and rails of tables and chairs.

UNIT 80

Mechanical Fasteners for Wood

The most common mechanical fastener for wood is the nail. Almost everyone has had some occasion to drive and pull nails. It seems simple, but some skill is needed to drive a nail straight without bending it.

The most common tool for driving nails is the *claw hammer*. Fig. 80-1. Hammers are available in many sizes with heads that weight 5 to 20 ounces. A 10- to 12-ounce head would be about right for most work. The face of the hammer head should be slightly rounded.

The *nail set* is another tool used for nailing. It is a short metal punch with a cup-shaped head used to drive the head of a nail below the surface of the wood. Fig. 80-2.

NAILS AND NAILING

There are many kinds and sizes of nails. Nails are made of aluminum, brass, copper, and steel. Some mild steel nails are coated or galvanized to keep them from rusting. The kinds of nails that you will use most are *common, box, casing,* and *finishing.* Fig. 80-3.

The length of nails is indicated by their penny size. (The letter "d" means penny.) Nails range from 2d to 60d. The larger the number, the bigger the nail.

80-2. *Nail set. This is used to drive the head of a nail about $1/16''$ below the surface of the wood.*

80-1. *Proper way to start a nail. Hold the claw hammer near the head and tap the nail.*

Unit 80: Mechanical Fasteners for Wood

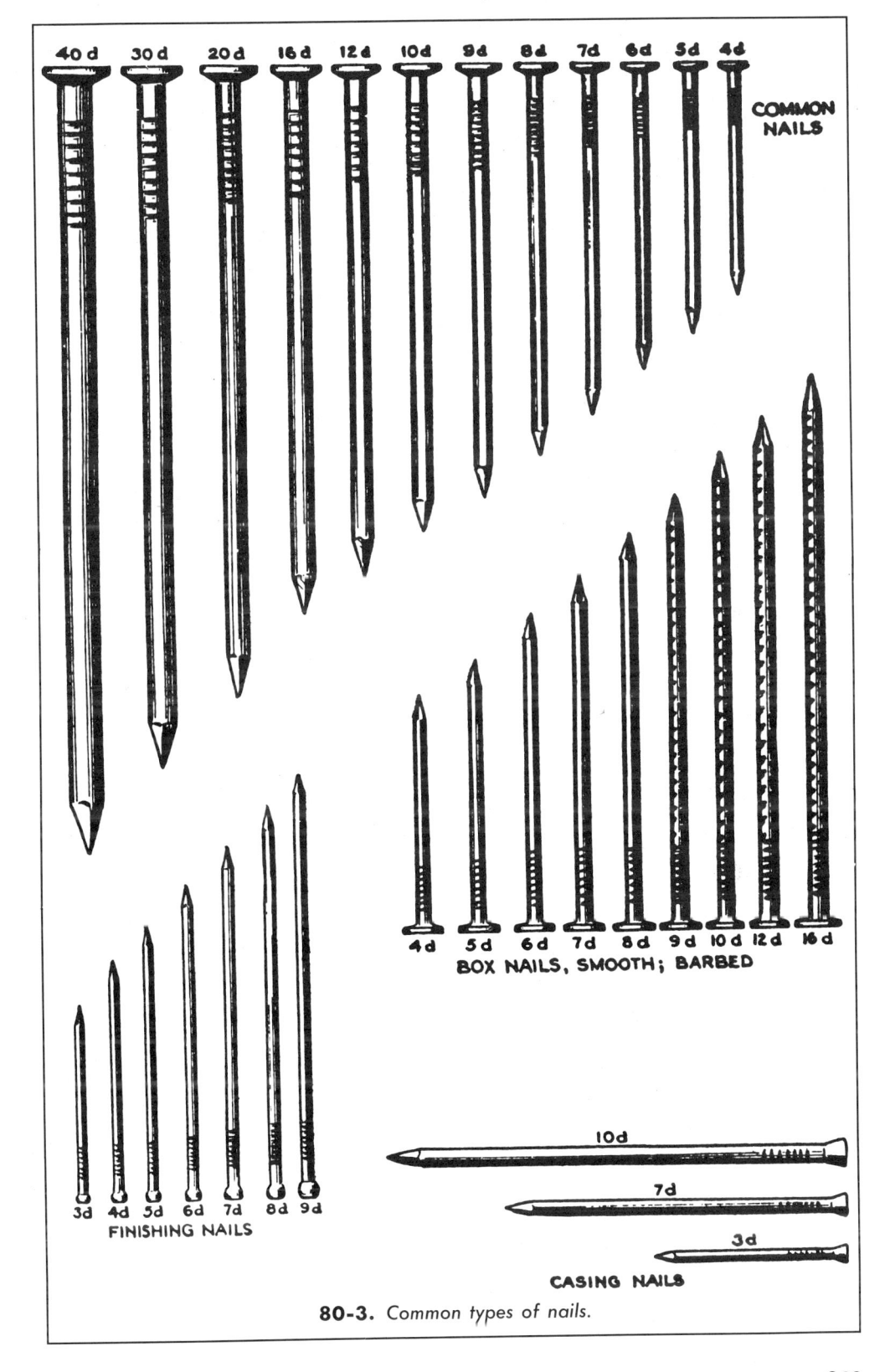

80-3. Common types of nails.

Part III: Manufacturing—Principles, Materials, and Processes

Box nails are thin with flat heads. They were designed for nailing together boxes. The common nail looks like a box nail except it is heavier. Casing nails have small heads. They are used for finish carpentry or sometimes for projects. The finishing nail is the finest of all the nails and is used for cabinetwork.

Brads are really small finishing nails that are used for fastening thin stock. They are indicated by length in inches. The corrugated fastener is used for holding some joints and is good for repair work. Fig. 80-4.

Before driving nails, be sure to choose the correct kind and size for the job. Small nails are chosen for thin stock, heavier ones for thick stock. To make a tight joint, nails are sometimes driven at an angle.

To start a nail, hold it in one hand between the thumb and fingers. Hold the hammer near the head and tap the nail. Fig. 80-1. Remove your fingers from the nail once it is started. To drive the nail, hold the hammer near the end of the handle. Use the wrist, elbow, and arm to swing the hammer. Watch the head of the nail, not the hammer. Try to drive the nail with a few sharp blows rather than many light taps. If a nail bends, pull it out and drive a new one.

Do not place several nails along the same grain marking. This may split the wood. Do not drive casing or finishing nails completely in with the hammer. Use the nail set. Hold the nail set as shown in Fig. 80-2. Then drive the nail until it is about $\frac{1}{16}$" below the surface.

If you are nailing hardwood, you may need to bore holes for the nails. This will keep the wood from splitting and the nails from bending over. The holes should be slightly smaller than the size of the nail. A little wax on the nail will make it drive easier.

If the nails you are using are so long that they will go all the way through the pieces being nailed, you may need to clinch the joints. Drive the nails completely through the pieces and bend over with the grain.

Sometimes you may need to pull some nails. Force the claw of the hammer under the head of the nail. Pull on the handle. When the nail is pulled part way out, slip a scrap of wood under the hammer head. Fig. 80-5.

SCREWS

Screws are another type of mechanical fastener used to assemble wood projects. It takes longer to install screws than nails, but they make a stronger joint. Also, joints made with screws are easy to take apart and reassemble. A few screws will do the work of several nails. (See Unit 51 for further information on screws.)

Screwdrivers come in many sizes and shapes. There are two common types—the plain and the Phillips head. The plain screwdriver is used for slotted-head screws. The size depends on the length of the blade. The tip of the screwdriver should be the same width as the head of the screw. The blade should be flat on the tip and fit properly into the screw head as shown in Fig. 80-6. This is very important. If a screwdriver is ground or worn to a sharp edge, it may slip out of the slot and mar the wood. The Phillips head screwdriver is made for driving screws with *recessed* heads.

There are several things to know about wood screws. These are: The kind of

80-4. *Corner made with corrugated fastener. It should be driven flush with the wood surface.*

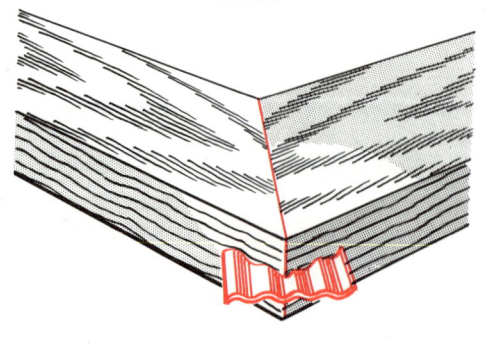

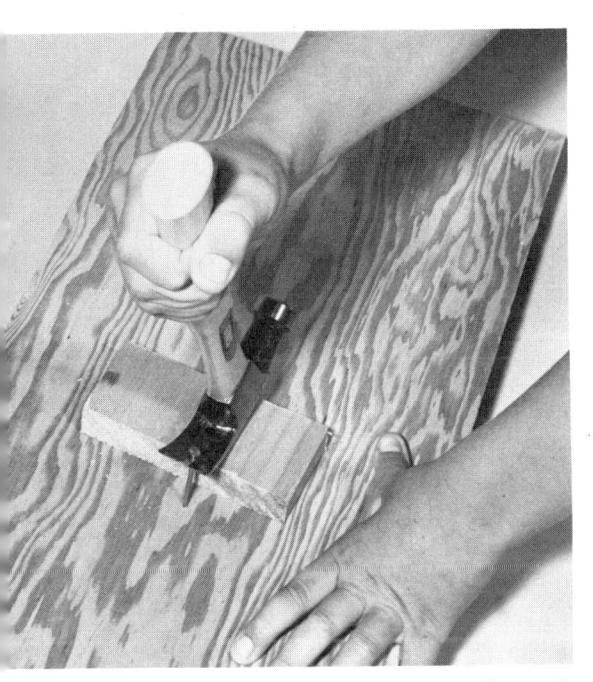

Unit 80: Mechanical Fasteners for Wood

80-5. Using a claw hammer to pull a nail. When the nail is partway out, slip a block of wood under the head.

80-6. A screwdriver should fit properly into the screw head, or damage may result. (Inset) Phillips and slotted-head screws.

head, the diameter or gauge, the length, the kind of metal, and the finish. There are three kinds of screws you may use in woodworking. These are the *flathead,* the *oval-head,* and the *roundhead.* All three are available with either slotted or Phillips heads. The common screws come in almost any length from 1/4" to over 6". Most screws are made of steel. Some are made of aluminum and brass, for use where moisture might rust the steel screws. Most flathead screws have a bright finish. Roundhead screws are usually finished dull blue.

Wood screws are indicated by numbers from 0 to 24. The smaller the number, the thinner the screw. Fig. 80-7 shows that a number 9 screw would be larger than a number 7.

To get the most holding power, you should choose a screw long enough to go into the second piece of wood almost the entire length of the screw threads. This will be about two-thirds the length of the

80-7. Table showing sizes of bits needed for shank and pilot holes.

No. of Screw	For Shank Clearance Holes	For Pilot Holes* Hardwoods	For Pilot Holes* Softwoods	No. of Auger bit to Counterbore for Sinking Head (by 16ths)
0	1/16	1/32	1/64	
1	5/64	1/32	1/32	
2	3/32	3/64	1/32	3
3	7/64	1/16	3/64	4
4	7/64	1/16	3/64	4
5	1/8	5/64	1/16	4
6	9/64	5/64	1/16	5
7	5/32	3/32	1/16	5
8	11/64	3/32	5/64	6
9	3/16	7/64	5/64	6
10	3/16	7/64	3/32	6
11	13/64	1/8	3/32	7
12	7/32	1/8	7/64	7
14	1/4	9/64	7/64	8
16	17/64	5/32	9/64	9
18	19/64	3/16	9/64	10
20	21/64	13/64	11/64	11
24	3/8	7/32	3/16	12

*Sometimes called "anchor holes."

365

Part III: Manufacturing—Principles, Materials, and Processes

screw. End grain wood does not hold very well; so select a longer screw for this.

DRILLING HOLES FOR WOOD SCREWS

To fasten two pieces of wood with screws you need to drill two holes for each screw—one for the screw *shank* and the other, called the pilot hole, for the screw *threads*.

The shank hole should be large enough so that the screw can be pushed in with the fingers. The depth of the pilot hole should depend on the hardness of the wood. Pilot holes in soft wood only need to be about half the length of the screw. In hardwood they should be drilled the entire length of the screw thread.

Flathead and oval-head screws should be countersunk. Countersinking is a way of enlarging the top of the hole so that the top of the screw will be level with the wood surface. A countersink should be used in a brace or a drill press. (See Unit 38). Cut just deep enough so that the screw will be level with the surface of the wood.

To install the screws is a simple job if you have drilled the correct shank and pilot holes. Place the screw in the hole and push it as far as you can without forcing. Grasp the handle of the screwdriver in one hand. Use the other hand to guide the blade of the screwdriver. Turn the screw until it is set. Be careful not to let the screwdriver slip out of the slot and mar the wood. Don't tighten too much, or you might strip the threads or break off the screw.

Plastic can be fastened with the same kind of screws used in wood and metal. A hole must be drilled for the screw, or the plastic will crack. Regular nuts and bolts may be used to fasten pieces of plastic together. Holes must be drilled in the plastic for the bolts.

UNIT 81 — Adhesive Fastening of Wood

To fasten wooden pieces together permanently, use some kind of glue. This type of fastening is done for several reasons. Boards can be glued together edge to edge to make larger surfaces as, for example, a tabletop. Boards can also be glued together face to face to make them thicker, as in making a lamp. Joints that are to be fastened together permanently are also glued.

You should be familiar with six kinds of glue: animal hide glue, casein glue, plastic resin resorcinol, polyvinyl, contact cement, and epoxy glue. The ones most commonly used are *animal hide* glue and *polyvinyl*.

Unit 81: Adhesive Fastening of Wood

81-1. *Boards for a tabletop are glued edge to edge using bar clamps. Notice the scrap pieces to protect the edges of the boards.*

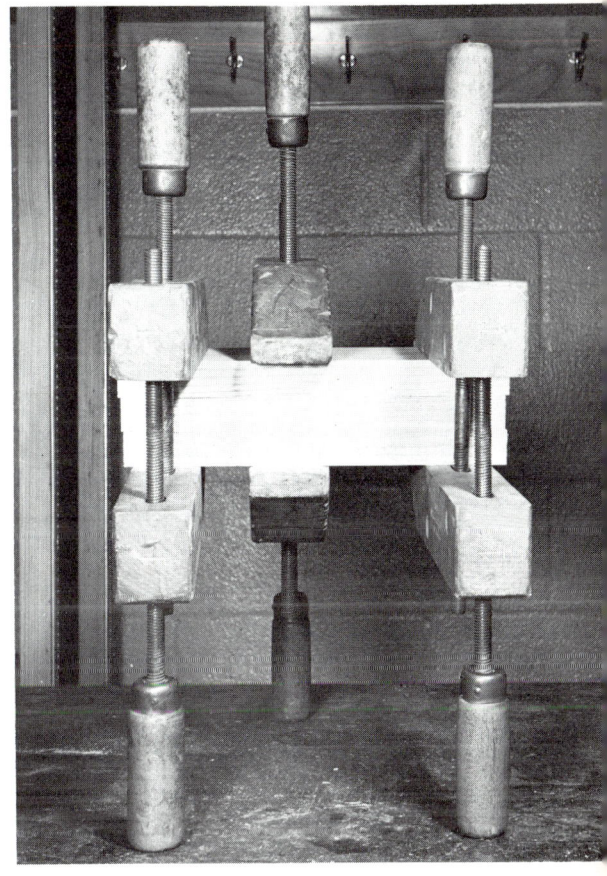

81-2. *Stock glued face to face. The pieces are held with hand screws until the glue is set.*

Animal hide glue, which is usually brown, is made from hoofs, hides, and bones of animals.

Polyvinyl glue is odorless, colorless, and does not stain. It is good for working on furniture. It is always ready to use. However, it is not waterproof; so it cannot be used to glue pieces that will be exposed to the weather.

Contact cement is used for bonding veneer or plastic to plywood. Epoxy cement will stick to almost anything. It can be used on wood, metal, plastic, ceramics, and many other materials.

CLAMPS

There are two types of clamps that are most useful for woodworking. These are the *bar clamp* and the *hand screw*. Each clamp works with a hand screw adjustment. The bar clamp is used for wide pieces. Fig. 81-1. The hand screw is used for smaller pieces. Fig. 81-2. Before starting to glue up a project, be sure to have plenty of clamps handy. When using bar clamps, place a piece of scrap stock between the clamp and the work. This will protect the work from the clamps.

GLUING UP STOCK

First assemble all the parts to be glued. Adjust the clamps and try them on the pieces before applying the glue. There should be a clamp about every 12" to 15" when gluing edge to edge. When using glue on a bench top, be sure to protect the bench with wrapping paper or newspapers.

Using a brush, stick, or roller, apply glue to both the surfaces to be joined. Make sure that both pieces are completely covered. Do not apply too much

367

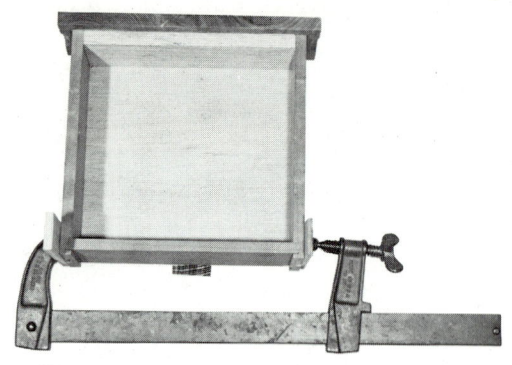

81-3. A drawer being held in a clamp while the glue dries.

glue, or it will squeeze out of the joint when the clamps are tightened.

When gluing edge to edge, place glue on all the edges to be glued. Then lay the pieces on the clamps. Tighten the outside clamps slightly. Tap the ends of the boards until they are even. Make sure that all the faces are even. Then tighten the clamps. *Don't tighten too tight.* You cannot pull a poor joint together by using extra pressure on the clamps. Fig. 81-3.

Remove the surplus glue before it hardens. The more glue you remove now, the less scraping you will have to do later.

For gluing stock face to face, hand clamps are used. First arrange the pieces the way they are to be glued. Set the clamps to the proper opening. Apply the glue to all surfaces to be glued. Clamp the pieces together. Be careful to keep the jaws of the clamps parallel. This will keep the pressure even. Fig. 81-2.

The time it takes glue to dry depends on the kind of glue used. White polyvinyl glue takes only about one-half to one hour to set. It is best to let glue dry overnight with the clamps in place. Any excess glue can be removed with a scraper or chisel.

Many of the joints used in making wood products are fastened with glue. Glue is applied to both parts of the joint. The joints are assembled and either clamped or nailed to hold the pieces until the glue dries. When projects are assembled with glue, they cannot be taken apart.

UNIT 82 Wood Finishing Principles

A well-constructed project deserves a good finish. More projects are ruined by improper finishing than by any other mistake during production. Notice the fine finishes that are applied to commercially constructed pieces of furniture. A properly applied finish brings out the beauty of the wood and gives the completed project a mark of quality.

Wood may be finished in one of several ways, as shown by the chart. Fig. 82-1. A knowledge of the materials used for wood

Unit 82: Wood Finishing Principles

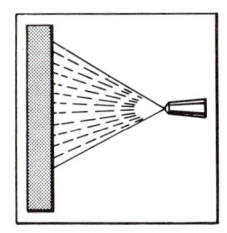

Finishing

Finishing is the process of treating the surface of a material for appearance and/or protection.

KIND OF FINISH	DEFINITION	EXAMPLES
Coloring*	Applying penetrating chemicals or heat to a material to change its color.	Staining. Charring.
Coating*	Applying a layer of finishing substance to the surface of a material.	Painting. Lacquering. Dipping.
Remove Finishing	Finishing by cutting the surface by abrasive action.	Wire brushing. Sandblasting. Rubbing with coated abrasives.

*Coating could be considered a coloring process, since coating usually does change a product's color. However, it is customary to consider coating and coloring to be separate processes, as defined in the chart above.

82-1. *Types of wood finishing.*

finishing is important. Just as important is knowing the right order for using the materials. If the steps in the finishing process are not followed in the correct order, a well-constructed project may be ruined. Many times the finish makes the difference between professional and amateurish workmanship.

Finishes are applied to wood to protect the surface and to change the appearance. Wood will soak up moisture from the air during humid seasons and dry out

369

during dry seasons. Wood used outside is exposed to rain, sun, wind, snow, and cold. Wood used for buildings will last longer if protected by some kind of finish. Such wood is usually painted, but sometimes varnished. Telephone poles, fence posts, railroad ties, and other wood which is used on or in the ground will decay rapidly without some kind of protective coating. Wood used for these purposes is usually treated with creosote. This material is forced into the wood to help preserve it.

As mentioned earlier, a finish not only protects a wood surface but also changes its appearance. It is important to choose the right kind of finish for each job and to apply it well. Otherwise appearance of the wood will not be changed for the better.

Before applying any finish to a product, you must prepare the surface. This is usually done by sanding, as explained in Unit 73.

BASIC FINISHING STEPS

There are certain basic steps in finishing. Although you will not need to perform them all for every wood product you construct, you should become familiar with them:

1. *Bleaching* lightens the color of the wood.

2. *Staining* brings out the grain of the wood. It is also done to change the color of the wood.

3. *Filling* is required for some types of wood. Oak, mahogany, and walnut have large cells which form little troughs when the wood is cut. These must be filled to obtain a smooth finish. Birch and maple have smaller cells; so they require no filler. Neither do pine, cedar, or redwood.

4. *Sealing* is done after staining to keep the stain from bleeding. Sometimes a wash coat of shellac is used. If a lacquer finish is to be applied, a lacquer sealer may be used.

5. *Applying the finish.* Lacquer, varnish, or synthetic finish is applied. These may be applied with a brush or sprayed. Usually more than one coat is needed. Each coat should be sanded before the next is applied. Use a 180-grit abrasive paper. Make sure the finish is dry before sanding.

6. *Rubbing, buffing, and waxing.* These are done after the last coat of finish is applied. The surface may be rubbed with pumice stone or with very fine 380 or 400 wet-or-dry sandpaper. Steel wool may also be used. The surface is rubbed until it is dull. The final step is to apply a coat of good wax and polish.

TEXTURING WOOD

Sanding is a removal process which is usually done to make the wood smooth. However, some types of removal finishing leave the wood rough, or, in other words, give it *texture.*

One method of texturing wood is by *sandblasting.* Sand under high pressure is forced against the wood surface, cutting away part of the wood fiber. The soft part of the wood is removed, leaving the hard parts higher (or *in relief*). Large panels for use in homes, offices, and restaurants are sometimes finished in this way.

Another texturing method is called *charring.* A blowtorch is used to burn away the soft fibers and blacken the wood. Rubbing with a wire brush removes loose material and leaves the wood dark brown or black. Great care must be taken not to burn the wood too much and start a fire.

Panels of certain woods, such as walnut, birch, cherry, maple, and mahogany, are sometimes *grooved* to improve their appearance. The panels are passed through machines which have cutters set at the desired intervals. The resulting grooves are about $1/16''$ deep.

Texturing of wood panels is mostly done in the mills. The equipment is too large and costly for home or school shops. You can purchase wood panels with most finishes already applied. When choosing these materials it is best to consult a good dealer.

UNIT 83

Color Finishing of Wood

STAINS AND BLEACHES

Stain is a transparent finish. (Transparent means you can see through it.) Stain improves the appearance of wood by adding color and bringing out the grain. It also helps preserve the wood. Sometimes stain is used to make a cheaper wood look like a more expensive kind.

There are many kinds of stains. Only *oil stains* and *water stains* are used in most schools. Before you apply stain to your project, test it on a scrap piece of wood to see if it is what you want.

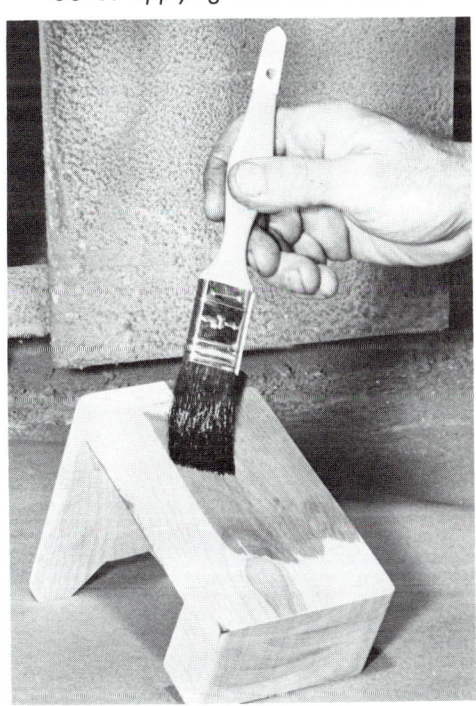

Stains come in many colors and shades. They are usually labeled according to the type of wood they resemble. There are walnut, light oak, dark oak, mahogany, and many others. Oil stain is easier to apply, but water stain is cheaper, has a more even color, and is less likely to fade.

Applying Stain

All sanding should be complete before applying the stain. Wipe the surface of the project and be sure there is no grease or glue left on the wood.

First choose the color stain you wish to use. Apply the stain. A soft, clean brush is best for this, but a rag or a sponge may be used. Fig. 83-1. As soon as the wood is the color you want, wipe off the excess stain with a clean cloth. Fig. 83-2. Allow the stain to dry for 24 hours before you

83-1. *Applying stain with a brush.*

83-2. *Wipe the excess stain off the wood with a clean, soft rag.*

apply any other finish. It is easier to stain large surfaces if they are in a horizontal position. Be careful that no drops of stain fall on the work. Begin at the center and work toward the edges. Inside corners and recessed surfaces should be stained first.

Water stain will raise the grain of the wood. Before applying this stain, sponge the surface lightly with water. After the wood is dry, sand lightly with 2/0 sandpaper. This will help the stain flow on evenly.

End grain soaks up stain rapidly and becomes too dark. To prevent this, coat the end grain with solvent just before applying the stain. Coat with turpentine when using oil stain, with water when using water stain.

Bleaching

Bleaching lightens the color of wood. This is done with chemicals that remove some of the color but do not injure the wood.

Household laundry bleach may be used on light-colored woods. Mix one-half pint of bleach with one gallon of water and apply with a brush or a rag. Let the wood dry, then sand.

For other bleaching, a solution of oxalic acid crystals in hot water can be used—12 ounces of crystals per gallon. Apply with a brush, and let the bleach stay on the wood 10 to 15 minutes. Be careful not to let the solution come in contact with your skin.

After the oxalic acid bleach has been on the wood for the required time, it must be neutralized. To do this, sponge the wood with a solution of three ounces of borax in a gallon of water. Let the wood dry, then sand it.

For large projects it is better to use commercial bleaches. With these it is possible to remove a little color or all of it.

Bleaching solutions are very strong chemicals. Special care should be used when working with them. It is best to wear rubber gloves and an apron.

Safety in the Finishing Room

Most finishing materials will burn. Keep them away from heat and flame. Oil-soaked rags that are wadded together may catch fire by spontaneous combustion. All rags or papers that have been soaked in finishing materials should be put in a metal can.

Many paints contain solvents which may cause sickness. Always do your finishing in a well-ventilated room. Keep containers of materials tightly closed when not in use.

UNIT 84

Coat Finishing of Wood

SHELLAC

Shellac is one of the coat finishes applied with a brush. It is a good finish for many projects because it is easy to apply. However, it turns cloudy if it gets wet; so it is not good to use where there is water. It can be used by itself or as a sealer over a stain or filler. Shellac is often used to seal knots before they are painted.

Shellac is made by dissolving *lac gum* in *alcohol*. Most lac gum comes from India and Thailand where a tiny insect deposits it on trees. The gum is gathered, dried, purified, and ground.

Common mixtures are 3 or 4 pounds of lac gum to a gallon of alcohol. These are called *3 or 4 pound cuts*. Natural shellac is orange. As a result it gives many woods an unattractive appearance. White shellac, a bleached form of the orange shellac, is better for general use, though it does not leave as tough a finish.

Keep shellac in a glass container; it will turn brown if kept in metal. Before applying shellac, wipe the project clean with a cloth that has been dipped in alcohol. It is better to apply several thin coats of shellac than one or two heavy ones. Thinned shellac sinks into the surface of the wood better. A soft bristle brush is best for applying the shellac. Use a clean varnish brush about 1½" to 3" wide. Dip about one-third of the brush length into the shellac and wipe off the sides of the brush on the container. Fig. 84-1.

Begin at the center of a flat surface and work toward the edges. Work quickly using long, light strokes. Fig. 84-2. Don't go over the same area several times. Shellac dries quickly, and the brush will stick and leave marks. It requires about 4 or 5 hours for a coat of shellac to dry completely. Between coats go over the surface with steel wool or 5/0 sandpaper. Be sure to rub with the grain. Before applying the second coat, wipe the surface with a clean rag.

Be careful not to apply the shellac too thick. This will make the wood look yellow. Do not let the shellac build up and run on the edges of the project. After the entire project has been covered, clean

84-1. *Dip about one-third of the bristle length into the shellac and wipe off the sides on the container.*

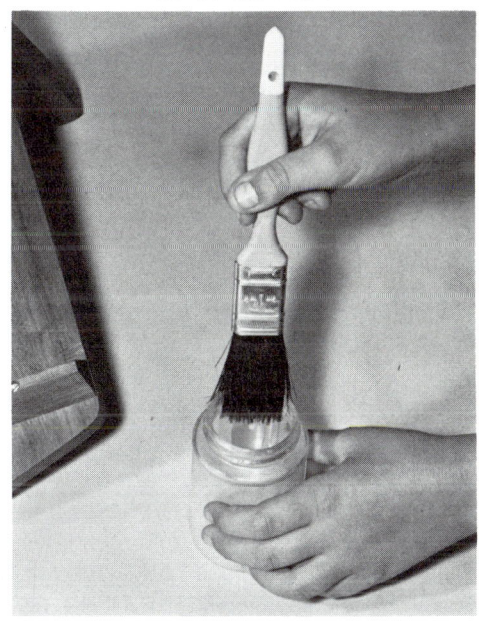

Part III: Manufacturing—Principles, Materials, and Processes

84-2. *Apply shellac quickly with light strokes.*

the brush in alcohol. The brush may be hung in shellac, as no scum forms on the surface. The container should be tightly covered to prevent the alcohol from evaporating and to keep out dirt.

VARNISH

Varnishes are mixtures of gum resins, vegetable oils, and various thinners and driers. When properly applied, varnish is an excellent finishing material. It produces a hard, bright surface. However, it is difficult to get a good varnish finish in the shop. This is because varnish dries slowly and the sticky surface becomes covered with tiny dust particles.

Modern research has eased the problem. Old style natural varnishes took up to 48 hours to dry. Today synthetic varnishes dry overnight and will not collect dust after about two hours. For most work a high gloss or satin finish varnish is used. These are easier to apply than others. For outside finishes where there is moisture, *spar varnish* is best. This is the kind used on boats. It is also used for tabletops and other pieces that will have hard wear or contact with water.

For the small shop, varnish should be bought in small cans. Scum forms on the surface of open cans and is difficult to remove. If you use the varnish from a can that has a scum, be sure it is all removed, or it will mar a good finish.

To apply varnish, first find a dust-free place. If you have no finish room, wait until all the machines are turned off. Do not varnish on cold, damp days, as the varnish will not dry properly. The temperature should be between 70 and 80 degrees F (21–26 °C), where you are varnishing.

Wipe the project with a clean rag. Select a 1½" to 2" varnish brush. Dip the brush in the varnish about one-third the length of the bristles. Do not overload it. Apply the varnish with long, easy strokes. Brush first with the grain, then across the grain. When the brush is "dry" continue brushing easily with the grain. You can brush out varnish more than shellac because it dries more slowly. Work from the center toward the edges. Be careful not to let the varnish build up and run on the edges.

When you finish the first coat, soak the brush in a can of turpentine. Cover the varnish can as soon as you are finished so that a scum will not form. Allow the first coat to dry about 24 hours. After it is dry, rub the surface with 6/0 sandpaper. Use your fingers, not a sanding block, for holding the sandpaper. Wipe the surface clean before applying the second coat. Do not apply the second coat too soon. Make sure the first coat is completely dry.

The second coat is applied the same as the first. If it gives good coverage, you will not need to apply any more. Allow it to dry and, if a third coat is needed, sand with 6/0 sandpaper just as after the first coat. The final coat may be rubbed with pumice stone and water. This will produce a dull (satin) finish. Sometimes rottenstone and oil are used for final rub-

Unit 84: Coat Finishing of Wood

bing. Pumice stone and rottenstone are finely ground abrasive powders. Pumice stone is available in several grades. Rottenstone is very fine.

After the varnish has dried and been rubbed, apply a good paste wax. Polish with a clean cloth. This should provide a professional looking finish that you will be proud of.

LACQUER

Lacquer is used quite often for finishing wood. Both clear and colored lacquers are available. See Unit 55 for more information on lacquer.

PAINTING

Painting is a good way to finish certain projects. Many pieces of furniture and cabinetwork are painted. Paint seals the surface so that it is not affected by moisture. Paint also makes the surface better looking and easier to keep clean.

Many kinds of paint are available. There are exterior and interior house paints, gloss, semigloss, and flat paints, cement paints, screen paints, oil paints, water paints, and many others. The composition varies depending on the use. Almost all paints have a vehicle, pigment, and driers. The *vehicle* is the liquid part of the paint. This might be linseed oil, turpentine, or some other liquid. The *drier* speeds up the drying of the paint. The *pigment* is the solid part of the paint. This provides the color.

Applying Paint

Before painting be sure the surface is clean and smooth. Go over any knots with a light coat of shellac. The first coat of paint may be a *primer*. The primer should be brushed into the pores of the wood.

To apply, brush a small amount at a time onto the wood. Fig. 84-3. (Beginners often apply the paint too thick.) Allow the first coat to dry about 24 hours. Go over the surface with a medium grade sandpaper. Apply the second coat. (In a three-coat process, this is called the undercoat.) If a third coat is to be applied, sand the undercoat with a fine sandpaper. Then apply the third coat, being sure to brush it evenly. On wood which has been painted before, one or two coats of paint are usually enough. On new wood, three coats may be needed.

84-3. *Painting wood with a brush. Be careful not to apply too much paint. You should brush with even strokes.*

Enamels are colored varnish. They are not opaque. That is, they will not cover as well as paints will. Therefore when using enamels, it is usually best to apply a primer coat which is opaque. Enamels dry with a gloss finish. They are available in many colors. Enamels are usually used for small projects which need a colored finish. Enamel is applied with a brush the same way as paint. Use a short, even stroke and work in a small area. Enamel should be allowed to dry 24 hours between coats.

BRUSHES

Good quality brushes are important for a good finish. For each type of finish you

375

Part III: Manufacturing—Principles, Materials, and Processes

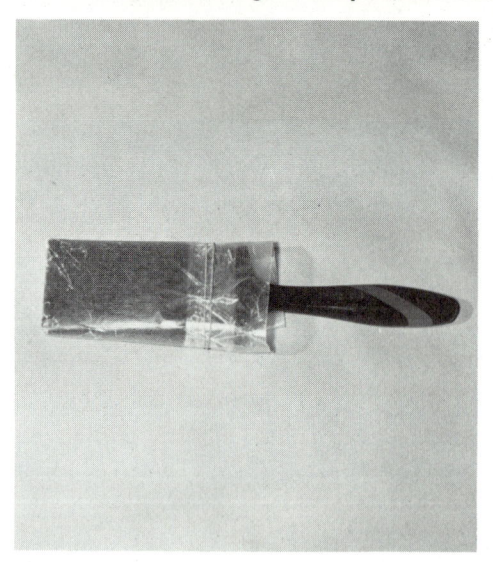

apply, you should have several brushes ranging from 1" to 4" in width. Most bristles are set in rubber.

Cleaning and care of brushes is a very important part of finishing. The same solvents that are used to thin the finish are usually used for cleaning brushes. There are also special brush cleaners. For storing overnight, brushes may be placed in a container of solvent. Brushes should always be suspended, not made to stand on the bristles. When they are going to be stored longer, they should be cleaned in solvent, then washed with soap and water. Then they should be rinsed, dried, and wrapped in wax paper. This way brushes may be stored for long periods. Fig. 84-4. See Unit 55 for more information on brushes.

84-4. *Brushes may be cleaned and wrapped in wax paper for storage.*

DISCUSSION TOPICS

Part 3—Manufacturing—Principles, Materials, and Processes
Section 3—Woodworking
Unit 65
　1. Name some of the ways wood is used today.
　2. Name three building products made from wood.
Unit 66
　1. What is the first step in the lumbering process?
　2. What is the name of the saw that cuts logs into boards?
　3. Why are hardwoods not cut to standard widths and lengths?
　4. What is meant by airdrying? Kilndrying?
　5. What is the purpose of the planing mill?
　6. What are the main differences between softwoods and hardwoods?
　7. List four common softwoods.
　8. List six common hardwoods.
Unit 67
　1. Name several ways in which trees are important.
　2. What is the difference between veneer and plywood?
　3. Why is plywood usually made with an odd number of plies?
　4. What are two common types of board made from the waste of lumber?
Unit 68
　1. Explain what is meant by a board foot.
　2. What measurement is used in selling plywood?
　3. What tool is commonly used for marking width and thickness of a board?

Units 65-84: Discussion Topics

Unit 69
1. In the airless-spray method how does the paint get from the container to the spray gun?
2. List some other new developments in finishing.

Unit 70
1. What is the definition of cutting?
2. What kind of cutting action do the plane and the chisel have?
3. What kind of cutting is done by particles of grit?

Unit 71
1. There are two kinds of handsaws. Can you name them?
2. What is meant by the set of a saw?
3. At what angle do you hold the crosscut saw?
4. Do you push down or pull up to start a saw?
5. What kind of a saw would you use to cut plywood? Why?
6. What kinds of saws may be used for cutting curves?
7. What are the names of the two power tools that are used for cutting curves?

Unit 72
1. What plane is used for general planing?
2. Why must the plane iron cap fit tightly to the plane iron?
3. What does the lateral adjustment lever do to the plane iron?
4. Why should you not plane against the grain?
5. What is the name of the small plane used for planing end grain?
6. What are three ways to keep from splitting the wood when planing end grain?
7. What are the two types of chisels?
8. What should be used for tapping a chisel?
9. What safety precaution should you always remember when using the chisel?

Unit 73
1. What is the main reason for sanding wood surfaces?
2. Should heavy sanding be done after a project is assembled? Discuss.
3. Is it correct to sand across the grain?

Unit 74
1. How are auger bits numbered?
2. What is an expansion bit?
3. Why should you not bore a hole completely through from one side?
4. How do twist drills differ from auger bits?

Unit 75
1. What tool was originally used to shape spokes of wheels?
2. What is the rasp used for?
3. What is a router? What kinds of cuts can it make?

Unit 76
1. What machine is used for making turned parts?
2. What are the two methods of turning wood?
3. What method of turning is used for making bowls?

Unit 77
1. Why must the bending of wood around a form be done slowly?
2. What method may be used to bend flat stock without heating?
3. What is meant by laminating wood?

Unit 78
1. What is fastening?
2. Name the two ways in which wood may be joined.

Part III: Manufacturing—Principles, Materials, and Processes

Unit 79
1. What largely determines the strength of a joint?
2. List the ways a joint may be reinforced.
3. What is the name of the joint used for gluing pieces together edge to edge?
4. Where two pieces cross, what kind of a joint is used?
5. What joint is commonly used for bookshelves?
6. What joint is widely used for picture frames?
7. What joint is commonly used for legs of tables and chairs?

Unit 80
1. What is the simplest method of fastening wood?
2. What tool is used for driving nails?
3. How is the size of nails indicated?
4. What are the most commonly used kinds of nails?
5. What tool is used for installing screws?
6. What three types of screws are most commonly used in woodworking?
7. What materials are screws made of?
8. What is the purpose of a pilot hole?
9. What is countersinking?
10. What might happen if you tighten screws too tight?

Unit 81
1. Name six kinds of glue used in the school shop. What kinds are used most often?
2. What kind of glue can be used on nearly anything?
3. What are the two common types of clamps used in woodworking? When is each used?
4. What will happen if you tighten the clamps too tight?
5. Why should scraps of wood be used with clamps?
6. How may excess glue be removed?

Unit 82
1. Why should wood products be finished?
2. What is done to telephone poles to help preserve them?
3. Why are houses painted?
4. How is a wood surface prepared before the finish is applied?
5. What are the six general steps for finishing a project?
6. What are some processes that may be used to finish wood by removing part of the surface?

Unit 83
1. Why is stain used on wood?
2. Name two common types of stain.
3. What are the advantages of water stain?
4. What is the advantage of oil stain?
5. How are stains applied?

Unit 84
1. What is the source of shellac?
2. What is meant by a 4 pound cut? A 3 pound cut?
3. What is the color of natural shellac?
4. Why is it difficult to get a good varnish finish in the shop?
5. What are the three main ingredients of paint?
6. How many coats of paint are usually used over new wood? Over painted wood?
7. How does enamel differ from paint?

PART IV
Building Construction

Unit 85 Introduction to Building Construction

Unit 86 Foundations

Unit 87 Framing and Roofing the Building

Unit 88 Utilities and Finishing

Discussion Topics

UNIT 85
Introduction to Building Construction

The building of shelter has always been an important part of life. Early human beings lived in caves to obtain shelter from the wind, rain, and snow. The first construction may have been digging to improve the cave. Later, people probably began to build shelters using other materials, such as wood, stone and earth. As their knowledge increased and they learned to use tools, they began to build larger, more comfortable structures. As knowledge of materials increased even further, people learned to use natural materials to build roads, aqueducts, churches, and other buildings as well as homes. One of the first things people did once they learned to use tools was to design and build better housing.

Today construction is a very important part of industry in the United States. Thousands of people make their living working in some part of the construction industry. The total value of buildings constructed in any one year would be several billion dollars.

The construction industry differs from the usual manufacturing industry in the location where the work is performed. In most manufacturing industries there is a factory to which materials are brought. The workers come to the factory to make something such as an automobile or a radio. In the construction industry the workers travel to the location of the work. As soon as one building is completed, they must go to a new site where another building is being constructed.

In the future more and more of the elements of construction may be done away from the site. Even today roof trusses, pipes for plumbing, and some wall sections are built or put together at a central point or factory. They are then taken to the construction site. At the site workers put the pieces together. There are also companies that manufacture complete houses for transportation to the owner's lot. These are called precut houses.

As the population has increased, there has been an increase in the need for new construction. To meet the needs of the people for shelter, millions of new homes and apartments have been built. New office buildings and stores have been built to meet the needs of business and industry. New roads, bridges, dams, and other structures have been built. All of these have required the skills and labor of millions of people working in the construction industry and in industries which supply goods for construction.

UNIT 86

Foundations

BEGINNING THE PROJECT

Before a new home or building is constructed, someone must want it. Someone must decide to build a particular building on a certain lot.

Once a building has been decided upon, there are several things which must be taken into account before the actual building begins. Usually a permit is required. This *building permit* is usually obtained from the city or county building department. The building permit must be posted on the building site. As each phase of the building is completed, inspectors sign the permit. This shows that someone who is familiar with the local building requirements (the *building code*) has inspected the work and found that it meets the requirements.

Once the necessary permits have been obtained, the building site must be prepared. If there are buildings on the site, they must be torn down and the debris hauled away. If there are trees and brush on the site, these must be cleared where the building will be located. Usually only enough trees are cut to make room for the building. The rest of the trees are left for shade and landscaping.

After the site is prepared, the building must be *laid out* (outlined) on the ground. The *plot plan* shows the building in relation to the property. Fig. 86-1. The actual layout of the building is done by using *batter boards*. These are usually 2″ x 4″ stakes driven into the ground with a board fastened to the top of them. Batter boards are located at each corner of the building. A nail is driven into the top of the boards and a cord is stretched between nails. The cord outlines the size and shape of the building. Fig. 86-2.

As you can see in Fig. 86-2, the batter boards themselves are placed outside the construction area in order to allow room for construction machinery to operate without knocking them over.

FOUNDATIONS

Once the building has been laid out, the construction can begin. If the building is to have a basement, this must be dug. Usually this is done with large earthmoving machinery. If the building is to be built on a slab, the land must be leveled.

Next the foundation is built. The foundation supports the weight of the building. Foundations are usually made from concrete. Because the concrete is soft when it is mixed, it must have a *form* to give it shape. The first step in constructing foundations is to *set the forms*. Foundation forms are usually made on the site from wood. Fig. 86-3 (Page 384) shows a foundation form for a wall. Fig. 86-4 shows the forms for a slab foundation. Once the forms are in place, the wet concrete is poured into them. If the foundation is a slab, the concrete is finished smooth. The slab foundation becomes the floor of the house when it is finished. Fig. 86-5 shows a slab foundation with the plumbing.

If the house is to be built over a basement or crawl space, the utilities, such as plumbing and electrical equipment, can

Part IV: Building Construction

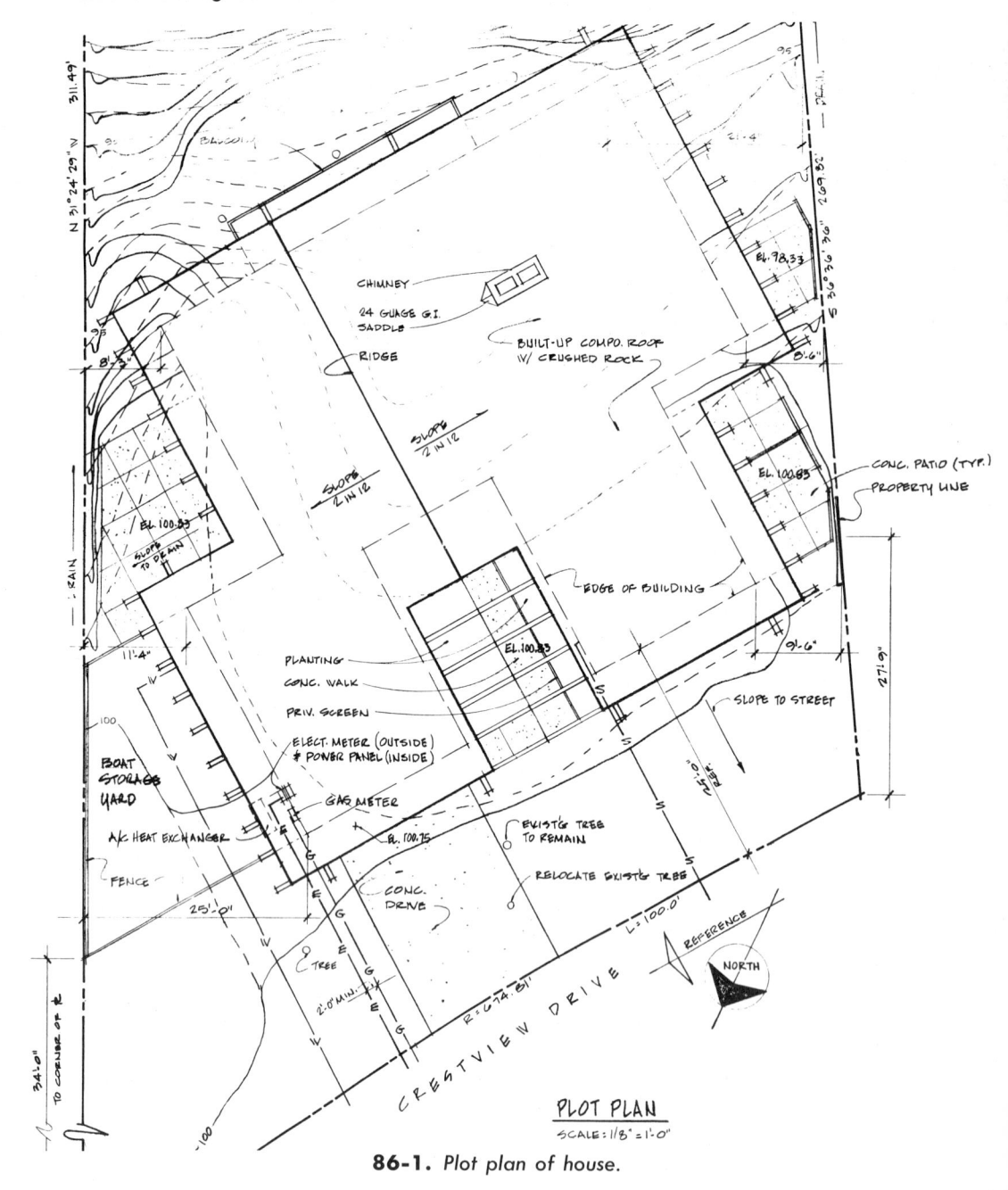

86-1. Plot plan of house.

be placed in position after the foundation is poured. If the house is to be built on a slab such as shown in Fig. 86-5, the utilities must be placed before the foundation is poured.

Once the foundation is poured and set, usually in 24 to 48 hours, the forms are removed. The concrete is allowed to *cure* to become strong. This usually takes about 14 to 25 days. Once the concrete is cured, the rest of the construction may begin.

Unit 86: Foundations

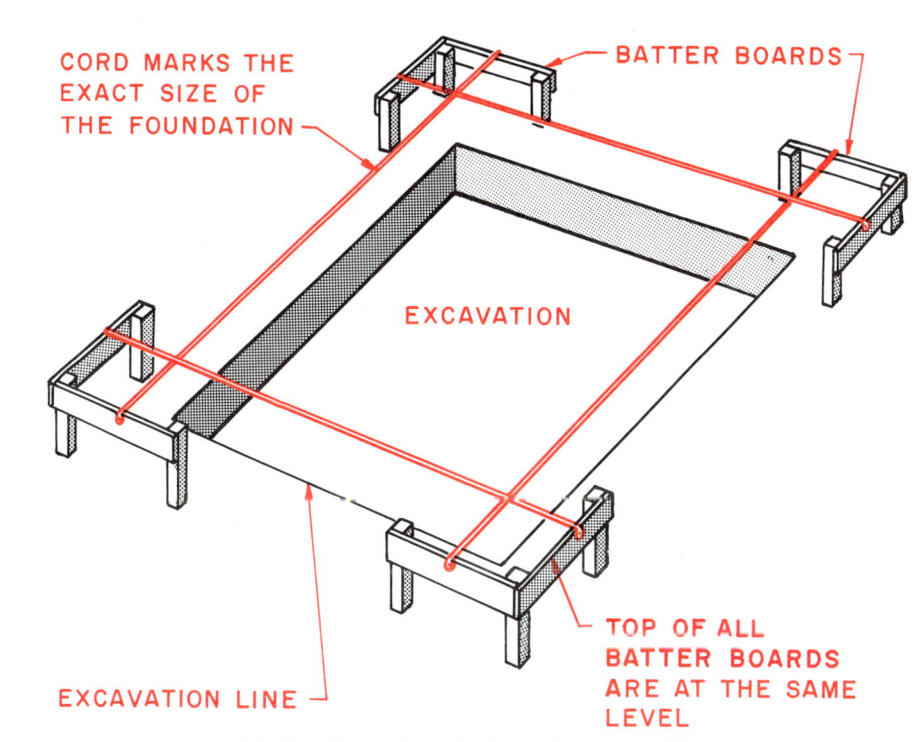

86-2a. Batter boards for laying out building.

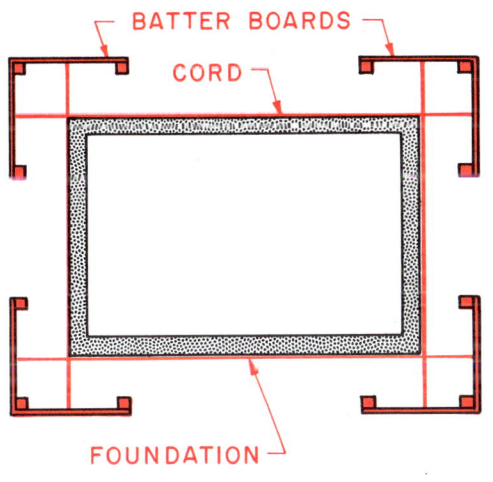

86-2b. Position of foundation in relation to batter boards and cord.

Part IV: Building Construction

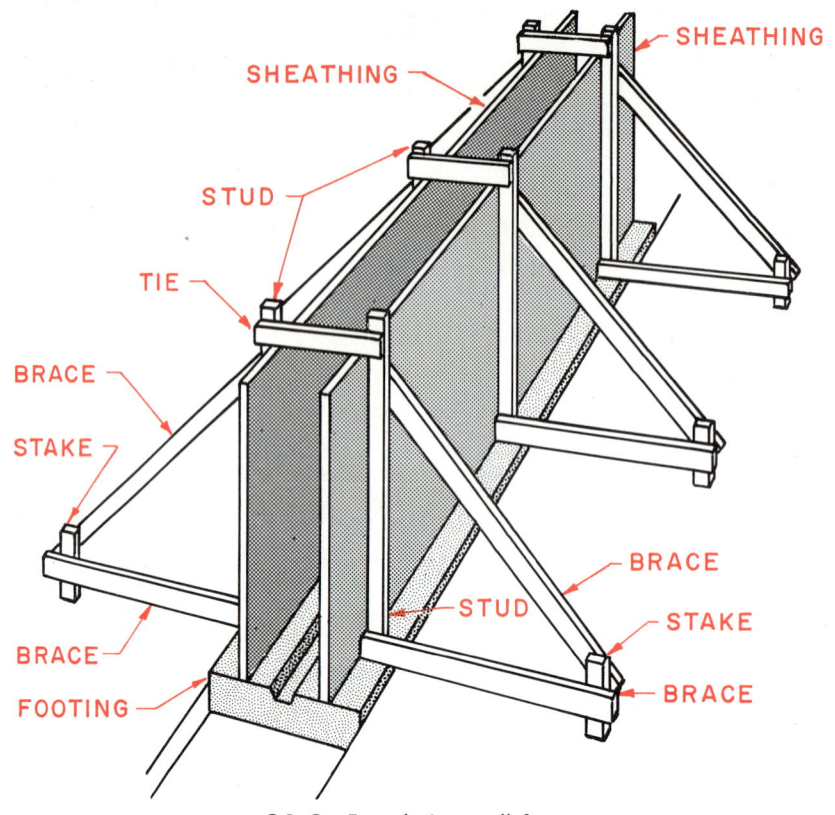

86-3. Foundation wall form.

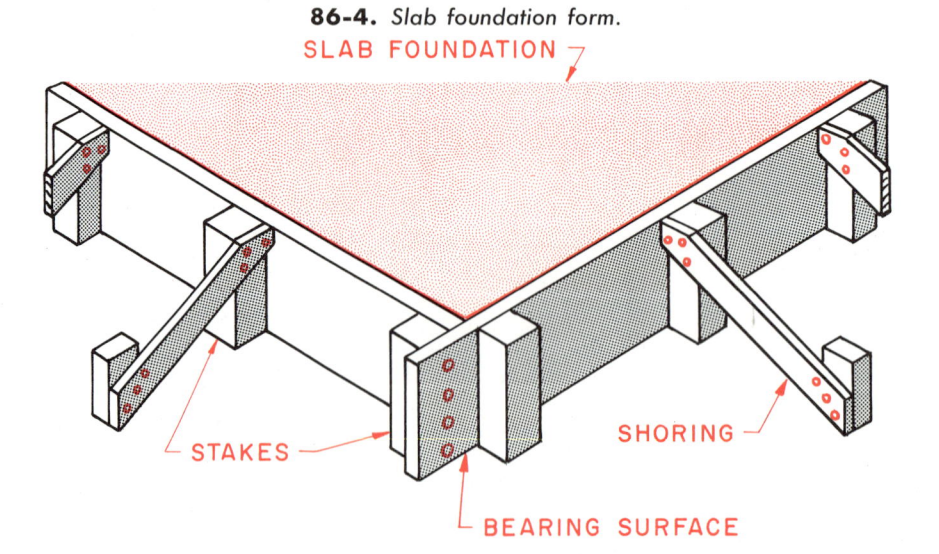

86-4. Slab foundation form.

Unit 87: Framing and Roofing the Building

86-5. Slab foundation with plumbing.

UNIT 87

framing and Roofing the Building

Once the foundation has been poured and cured, the next step in construction is building the *superstructure*. The superstructure is that part of the building that rises above the ground. The superstructure rests on the foundation. The superstructure may take any shape from a high-rise building to a garage. Here we are going to be concerned with wood frame superstructures.

Generally wooden frames are used for small buildings, such as houses. Usually the framing for these buildings is divided into three major parts. These are the floor framing, the wall framing, and the roof framing. Floor framing, where wooden floors are utilized, is made up of horizontal members called *joists*. (Joists are also used for ceiling framing.) Most wall framing is made up of vertical members called *studs,* and most roof framing is made up of sloped members called *rafters*.

To begin framing a house, a *sill* is laid on top of the foundation. The sill is a horizontal piece of lumber. It is the bottom of the frame. The sill is held to the foundation by *anchor bolts* which were placed in the concrete every 5 or 6 feet while the concrete was moist. The threaded end of the bolts points up. Holes are marked and drilled in the sill so that the sill can be placed down over the anchor bolts. Fig.

Part IV: Building Construction

87-1. After the sill is leveled, it is held by tightening the anchor bolts.

In some areas of the United States, termites (wood-eating insects) are a problem. Termites can eat their way through framing and make tunnels which weaken the structure.

In areas where there are termite problems, a *termite shield* made from a strip of metal is placed under the sill. The shield stretches along the full length of the sill and extends on each side. This shield helps to keep the ground-dwelling termites from burrowing through holes or cracks in the foundation and into the wood frame.

Floor joists are planks set on edge. They carry the weight of the floor. The flooring material rests on the floor joists. Joists rest on sills and extend from one foundation wall to another. Generally the joists are spaced 16" on center. That is, the center of one joist is 16" from the center of the next. Fig. 87-2.

The ends of the joists are usually held in place by nailing them to a *header*. A header is a piece of lumber the same dimension as the joist that is set flush with the outside of the sill. Fig. 87-2. To keep the centers of the joists from twisting and turning, *bridging* is used between the joists. Fig. 87-2. Bridging is made from 1" x 4" boards or pieces of metal.

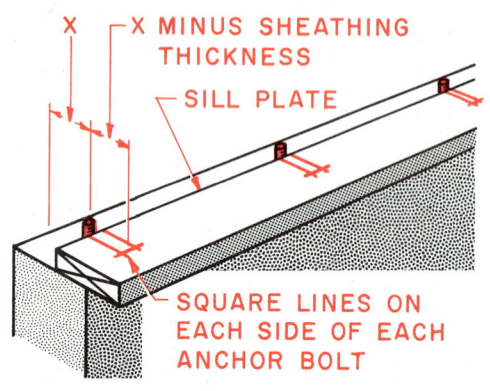

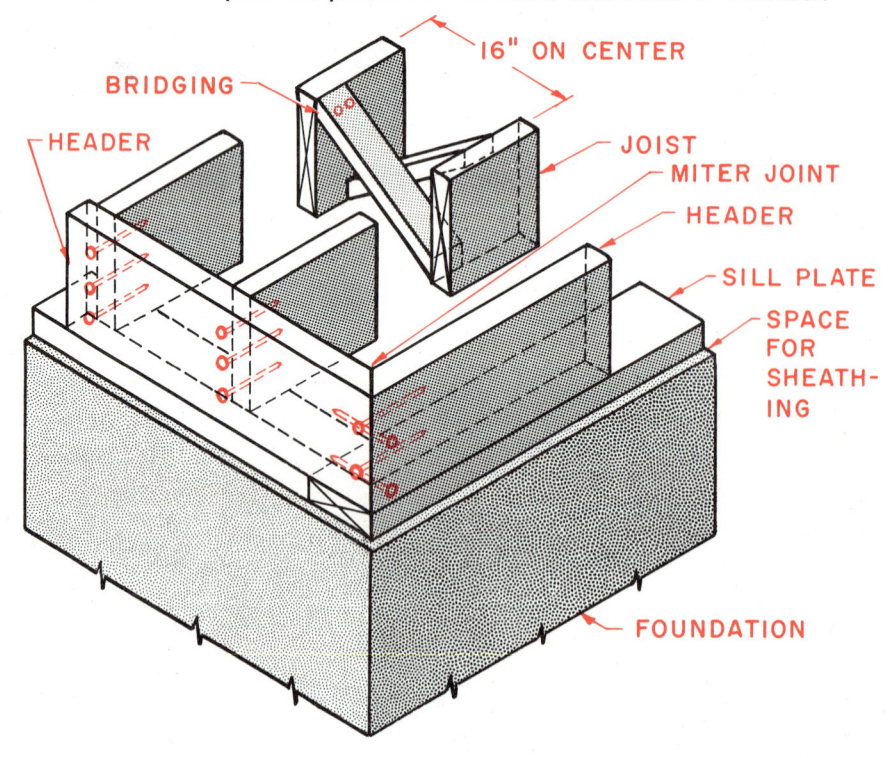

87-1. *Marking the sill for anchor bolts.*

87-2. *Floor joists are placed 16" on center and nailed to a header.*

Unit 87: Framing and Roofing the Building

A subfloor is nailed to the top of the joists. A second floor (the "finish floor") is usually laid over this floor. Plywood or boards are laid diagonally over the joists to form the subfloor. A hardwood floor is usually used over the subfloor.

If the house has a wooden floor, the walls are placed on top of the subflooring. If the house is being constructed on a concrete slab, the walls are placed on a sole plate fastened to the foundation.

Exterior walls are placed directly over the foundation. The interior (partition) walls are usually over an inside foundation wall or over a girder. The walls on the first floor usually are framed with 2" x 4" lumber. A piece of 2" x 4" lumber, laid flat, is nailed to the subflooring (or fastened to the concrete slab) exactly where the wall is to be. This piece of lumber is called the *sole plate*.

To complete the wall framing, pieces of 2" x 4" lumber called *studs* are cut to the length needed and are stood on end 16" on center along the sole plate. They are toenailed in place. Across their tops is nailed a *top plate* of 2" x 4" lumber. A second top plate called a *double plate,* is nailed over the first. The end joints in the two plates are staggered to make the top plate more like one continuous piece.

Another way of building a wall is to first assemble it on the floor. Fig. 87-3. The wall is then tilted up and nailed into position. The double plate is nailed on, overlapping where walls join, to tie the walls together and to strengthen them.

There are two common ways of bracing studs to keep them from bending or twisting. One way is to place short lengths of 2" x 4" lumber, called fire blocks, horizontally between the studs. These fire blocks serve as braces as well as draft stops to prevent the spread of fire in a building. These blocks are nailed in line, or they may be staggered above and below a line for ease in nailing. Another common way to brace studs is to use diagonal let-in braces, usually of 1" x 4" lumber. A brace is set to run from one top

87-3. Wall sections being constructed on the floor.

87-4. Assembled wall sections ready to be nailed in place. Note the let-in brace at the center of the picture. The other braces are temporary.

corner of the frame down to some point on the sole plate at an angle of about 45°. This makes a triangular frame within the wall section and makes the frame rigid and solid. In the studs, notches are cut to the thickness of the diagonal brace so that they do not interfere with the installation of the sheathing material. Fig. 87-4. (Sheathing usually consists of boards or plywood nailed to the outside of the frame. The finish siding will be applied to it.)

387

Part IV: Building Construction

After one story of the frame is completed, a second story may be built in the same way. Joists and headers are placed on the double plate of the first story and covered with a subflooring. Walls are built on top of this to form the second story.

Most wood frame buildings have sloped roofs. The top of the slope is called the *ridge*. The bottom of the slope forms the *eaves*. To frame the roof, *rafters* are used. The rafters rest on the top plates and meet at the ridge. Where the lower end of the rafter hits the top plates, a notch is cut in the rafter so that there will be a flat edge resting on the plate. Fig. 87-5. Usually the rafter goes a foot or more past the face of the wall. This holds the roofing that goes beyond the outside wall to form the eaves. Rafters are set in pairs, sloping down each side of the roof. These pairs meet at a ridge board along the top.

Trussed roof members may be used in place of conventional rafters. Trusses may be made on the site, or they may be

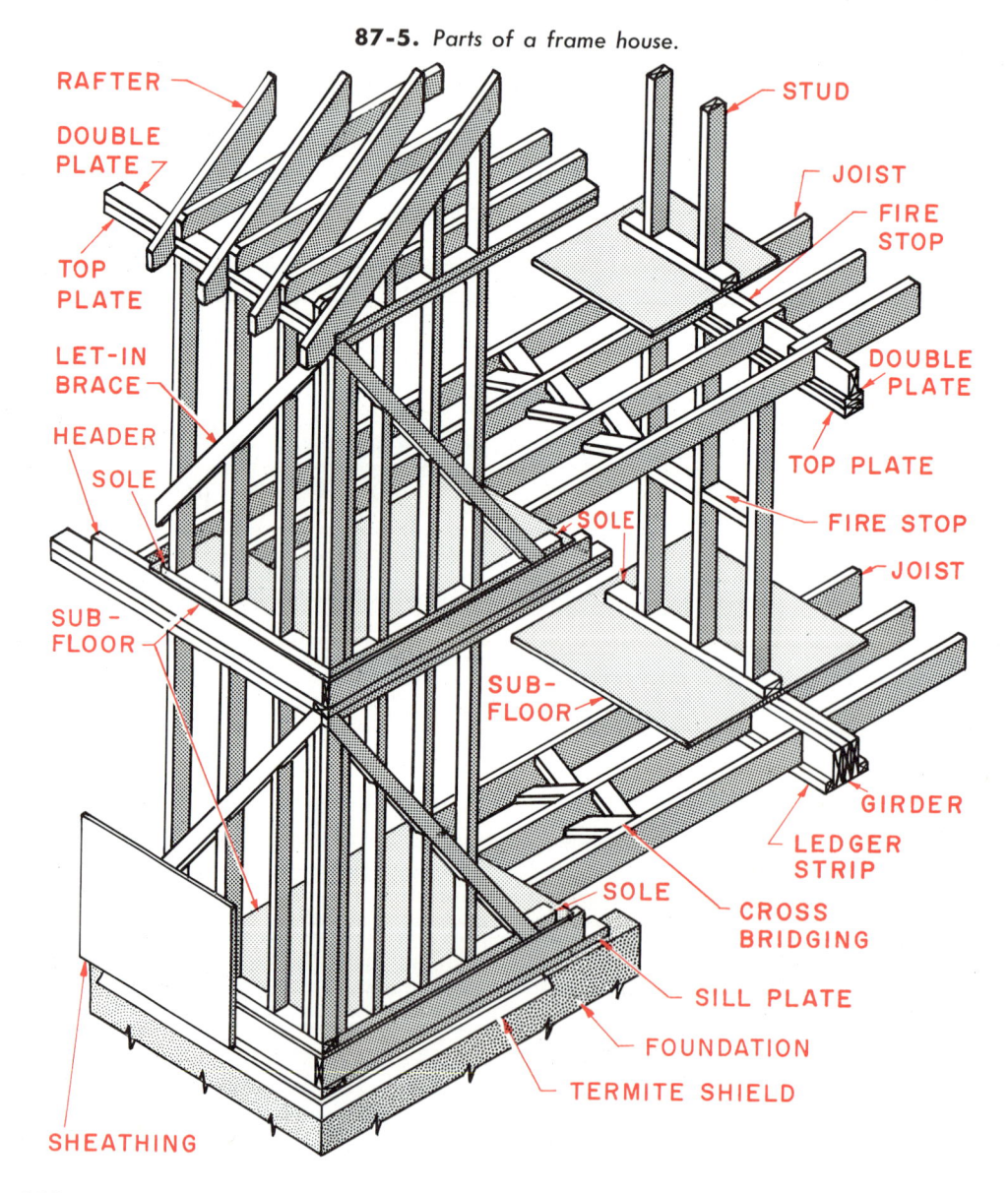

87-5. Parts of a frame house.

manufactured off the site. *Trusses usually combine the rafters and ceiling joists into one triangular piece.* The truss is then installed as a unit.

Roof frames are covered with *roof decking,* which serves the same purpose as sheathing and subflooring. Boards or sheet material are nailed over the rafters. The rafters are usually covered over completely. Sometimes, when wood shingles are used, spaces are left between roof decking to save material and to allow better air circulation to dry the shingles after wet weather.

UNIT 88: Utilities and Finishing

During the construction of a house, the utilities must also be considered. Utilities include heat, electricity, gas, water, and sewage. Even before the foundation or slab is constructed, outside utilities must be installed. The water pipe must be placed from the city main to the house. The gas line from the main to the house must also be installed. The soil pipe to carry the waste from the house to the sewer must be put in. Once all these utilities are "roughed in," the foundation or slab is poured.

HEATING

The utilities in the building itself are installed as the house is being framed. One of the very important utilities is heat. Before installing the heating system, it must be decided what type would be best for the location and the type of house.

There are several ways of heating a building. One uses steam or hot water going through pipes and radiators. Another uses hot air forced through sheet metal ducts. Whatever type of heating system is selected, the piping or ductwork must go in as the house is being framed and before the outside sheathing goes on or the interior walls are finished.

Another heating method uses electricity in resistance wires located in the ceiling. This method is very clean and noiseless. It also eliminates the need for pipes or ductwork. However, the building needs to be well insulated if electric heat is used, as the heating is more gradual than with other methods. Currently the energy crisis and the cost of electricity are discouraging many people from using electric heat. On the other hand, a shortage of natural gas in some areas is leading to increased use of electric heating systems.

PLUMBING

Once the heating pipes or ducts have been installed, the plumbers begin to install the water and sewage pipes. A plumber generally runs the soil pipe, which is the large drain pipe, and the smaller drains first. To run soil pipe, one has to start at the sanitary sewer connec-

Part IV: Building Construction

88-1. Plumbing pipes installed and capped, ready for the finish plumbing.

tion, which is just inside the foundation wall. All drain lines have to slope toward the sanitary sewer. These lines run to the fixtures and continue up through the roof where they act as vents.

Vents allow the fixtures to drain properly and prevent the siphoning of water from the traps under each fixture. If there were no vents, the effect would be the same as turning a bottle full of liquid upside down. The liquid just gurgles out because air can't get into the bottle easily. The same principle applies to a drainage line.

A trap is installed under each fixture to keep sewer gas and odors from entering the room.

Water lines generally start from the water meter, which also is just inside the foundation wall, and run to all the fixtures. To prevent accidental burns, the hot water is always installed on the left side, as you face the fixture. The hot water line starts from the water heater and runs to all the fixtures where hot water is needed. The outlets of water lines are generally shut off with test plugs or nipples and caps until the inside walls and floors are completed. They are removed when the fixtures are installed. Fig. 88-1.

Permanent fixtures such as bathtubs and shower bases are installed at the time the roughing in takes place because they must be built into the walls.

ELECTRICITY

The electrician generally hooks up the service to the house very early in the construction so that other craftsmen working on the house can have electric power.

After the heating and plumbing have been roughed in, the electrician will locate the number of outlets as set by specifications and attach the boxes to the walls. He or she will then drill all the holes (through the framing) needed to run the wire to these boxes. Fig. 88-2. The wires are attached to the boxes and left coiled up in the boxes. The feed end is attached to the panel box, but it is not hooked up to the terminals. This leaves the circuit

Unit 88: Utilities and Finishing

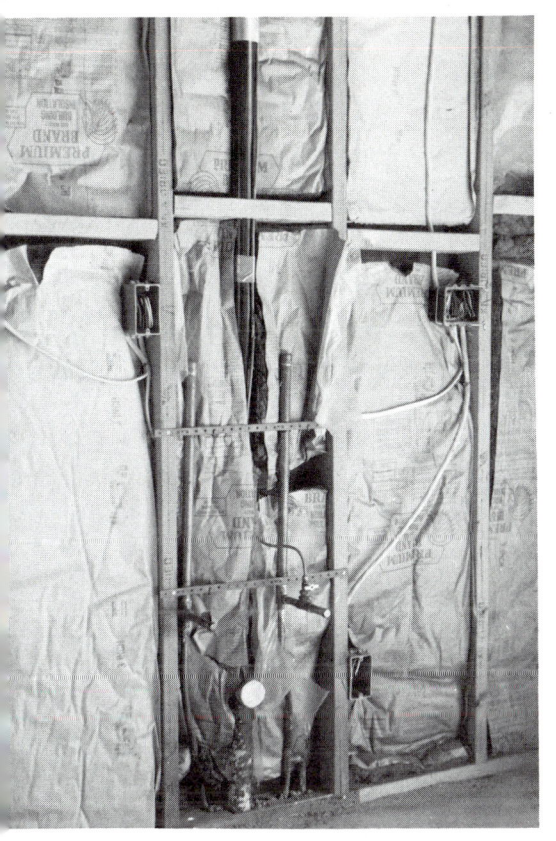

88-2. Wiring roughed in, along with some plumbing.

88-3. Main power panel being wired in. Cables run to outlets and to underground utilities.

88-4. Underground power cables will be run through these plastic pipes. Metal object in illustration is terminal panel for telephone cables.

dead, and no electricity flows through it until the time comes to finish the installation. Fig. 88-3.

There are many other appliances and fixtures that may have to be roughed in. Examples of these are communications lines and ductwork for kitchen fans.

Today many areas specify that all utilities be underground. Communication lines, such as telephone and electrical cables, are run through plastic conduit buried underground. Fig. 88-4 shows conduit through which power cables will be run.

FINISHING

Once the utilities are in, the finishing operations may be completed. In many areas of the country, insulation is installed in the outside walls (the walls that enclose

391

88-5. Insulation stapled in an outside wall along the stair.

88-6. Holes in dry wall for electrical and communication outlets.

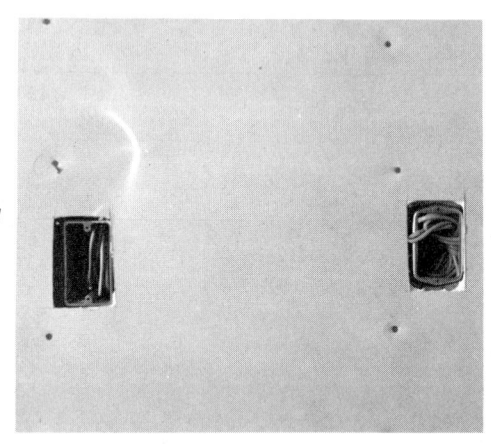

88-7. Hole in dry wall for heating duct.

88-8. House partially wrapped for stucco. Panels of felt paper and chicken wire are fastened to the studs, and stucco is applied to the outside like plaster.

88-9. Finish coat of stucco. House may be painted desired color.

the house). Insulation usually comes in batts with flaps that are stapled to the framing of the outside walls. Fig. 88-5. Insulation should also be placed in the ceiling and in any floors that are above unheated areas, such as crawl spaces.

Inside the house, the walls and ceilings are covered with a coating of plaster or with gypsum board. When plaster is to be applied to the interior, *lath* must be placed over the studs to hold the plaster. Lath may be made of gypsum, wire mesh, or other materials. In the past most walls were of lath and plaster.

In many homes today, sheets of gypsum board are nailed over the studs. This is called drywall construction. The nail holes and joints are covered with a plasterlike material to make a smooth wall. Holes are cut in the gypsum board sheets for electrical outlets and heating ducts. Figs. 88-6 and 88-7.

Other parts of the interior are then finished. Doors are hung and the door casings constructed. The trim is placed around the windows and the windows put in place. The finish floor is installed. This might be hardwood, which is nailed to the subfloor, or asphalt or vinyl tile, which is put down with an adhesive. Carpeting may also be installed.

At the same time the interior is being finished, the outside is receiving its finishing material. There are several ways of finishing the exterior of a house. Wood siding called clapboard or lapped board siding may be used. These are usually boards 6" to 10" wide placed horizontally around the house and lapped over one another to shed water. Another method is to use 4' x 8' textured plywood panels. This method of siding a house is fast, and when the panels are painted, they present a pleasing appearance.

One method of finishing exteriors in many parts of the country uses a masonry material called *stucco*. Stucco is usually made from portland cement, sand, and lime. It is applied over a felt paper and chicken wire reinforcement. Fig. 88-8. A stucco finish has the appearance of rough cement. Fig. 88-9.

The final work on a house consists of finishing the interior. The walls and ceilings are painted the desired colors or covered with wallpaper. The cabinet work is completed in the kitchen and bathrooms, and the faucets and other plumbing fixtures are installed. The light fixtures, outlets, switches, and covering plates are installed. When all this work has been completed, the house is ready for the owner to move in.

As you can see, there are many job specialties in house construction—carpentry, plumbing, and so forth. For large office buildings and factories, even more workers in special fields are needed.

Part IV: Building Construction

DISCUSSION TOPICS

Part 4—Building Construction

Unit 85

   1. How does the construction industry differ from the usual manufacturing industry?

   2. Some companies manufacture complete houses for transportation to a lot. What are such houses called?

Unit 86

   1. Who issues building permits?

   2. After the site is cleared, what is the next step in constructing a building?

   3. What are batter boards?

   4. What are foundation forms?

   5. How long does it take for concrete to cure?

Unit 87

   1. What is the superstructure?

   2. What are the floor framing members called? The wall framing members? The roof framing members?

   3. How is the sill fastened to the foundation?

   4. What is a termite shield and where is it placed?

   5. What is a header?

   6. What is a ridge board?

Unit 88

   1. Name two common heating methods.

   2. Why are vents needed in plumbing?

   3. Why must bathtubs be installed at the same time the plumbing is roughed in?

   4. What is the purpose of lath in finishing walls?

   5. Why is board siding usually overlapped?

   6. What is stucco?

PART V
Power and Energy

Section 1—Electricity

Unit 89 Introduction to Electricity

Unit 90 Electricity and Magnetism

Unit 91 Forms of Electricity

Unit 92 Sources of Electricity

Unit 93 Conductors and Circuits

Unit 94 Electromagnetism

Unit 95 Converting Electricity to Heat

Unit 96 Converting Electricity to Light

Unit 97 Communication

Discussion Topics

UNIT 89

Introduction to Electricity

This is an age of electricity. Without it the efficient factories, the comfortable homes, and the swift transportation and communication of this era could not exist. Fig. 89-1. Electricity is almost always available when you want it. A switch can turn it off and on just as water can be turned off and on with a faucet. Electricity can be changed into other forms of energy. There are appliances to turn it into heat, sound, motion, and light. These appliances include toasters, stoves, bells, motors, electric fans, and light bulbs.

Electricity is as important in industry as it is in the home. Electric motors provide power for almost all industries. For exam-

89-1. *Cockpit of a DC-10 airplane. Notice all the electrical instruments and switches used to control and measure various functions of the plane.*

McDonnell Douglas Corp.

Unit 90: Electricity and Magnetism

ple, changing electrical energy to heat for welding metal is a very important part of industry.

The generation (production) of electrical energy is an industry in itself. With a few exceptions, most of the electrical generators are turned by steam turbines. The steam is usually produced by heat supplied by coal, oil, or atomic power. Today, with the emphasis on conservation of resources, engineers are looking for other heat sources. One possible source is heat from inside the earth. This is called geothermal steam.

Electricity is used for transportation such as the diesel electric trams. A diesel engine powers a generator which produces electricity. This electricity is used to run powerful electric motors attached to the wheels of the engine. These electric motors actually provide the propulsion power for the engine.

Electricity in one form or another is used for communication. The radio, television, telephone, and telegraph all depend on electricity. Thus you can see that it is a very important part of our life.

Electricity has always been with us. However, it is only recently that we have learned how to use it. There are hundreds of jobs related to electricity. Perhaps you will become interested in one of them.

UNIT 90
Electricity and Magnetism

Electricity is all around you. When you walk across a rug, electrons are collected in your body; you can see the electricity when you touch a metal object and the sparks jump.

Everyone uses electricity in some way. Learning how to use and control it is important in your everyday life. You may become interested enough in how electricity works and is controlled to make it your life's work.

Many people make a living in different jobs related to electricity. You may know about some of them. There are electrical engineers and technicians who design electrical devices, from television sets to toasters. There are many craftsmen who build these devices. You may know an electrician in your town who installs wiring in new houses or rewires old houses. There are also electricians and electronic technicians who service electrical devices.

The radio and television industries employ many electricians. Communications companies, like the telephone company, employ thousands of men and women to work with electrical devices. Fig. 90-1 shows a technician checking a communications satellite before it is launched.

MAGNETISM

Electricity and magnetism are related in interesting ways. A magnet can be used

Part V: Power and Energy

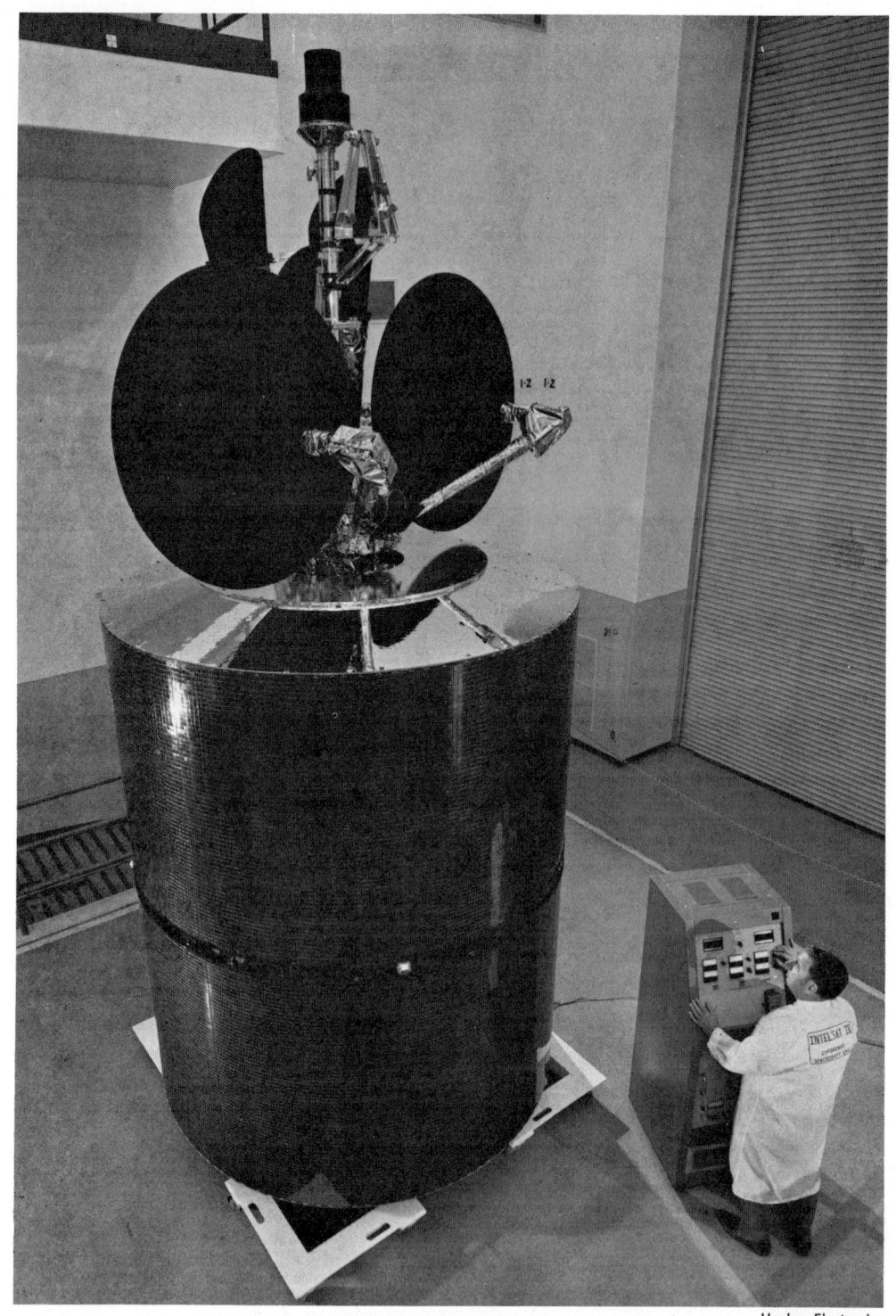

90-1. Worker checking Intelsat IV communications satellite. Satellite will carry 6000 two-way telephone calls or twelve television channels.

Hughes Electronics

Unit 90: Electricity and Magnetism

to produce an electric current, and electricity can also produce magnetism. You will learn more about this in later units. The rest of this unit will help you understand magnetism, as an introduction to electricity.

Magnetism has been known since ancient times. Shepherds noticed that certain small pieces of stone stuck to the iron tips of their staffs. These stones were really iron ore. The ancient Chinese discovered that a small piece of this stone on a string would always point in a northerly direction. The Greeks called these stones *magnetite*. Ancient mariners called them lodestones and used them to aid in the navigation of their ships. These were the first natural magnets.

Basically a *magnet* is a material that attracts iron or steel. A magnet may be made by stroking a piece of steel with a lodestone or another magnet. A piece of soft iron may be magnetized very easily this way, but it loses its magnetism soon. Hard steel is more difficult to magnetize, but it keeps its magnetism. Therefore a magnetized piece of hard steel is called a *permanent magnet*. Permanent magnets may be made in many shapes. Fig. 90-2. Some are straight bars, called *bar magnets*; others are bent like horseshoes and are therefore called *horseshoe magnets*.

The greatest force of a magnet occurs at the ends. These concentrations of magnetic force are called the magnetic poles. Each magnet has a *north pole* and a *south pole*. If you hang a bar magnet on a piece of string so that it can swing freely and there is no other metal or magnet near it, one end will point north and the other south. Fig. 90-3. This happens because the earth acts like a giant magnet with poles close to the north and south geographic poles. The end of a magnet which points north is marked with an N. The other end is marked with an S.

A *compass* is a small magnet balanced on a point so that it is free to turn. The magnetic effect of the earth, mentioned above, causes the end of the compass needle marked N to point north. Fig. 90-4.

The earth's magnetic poles are not in exactly the same place as its geographic

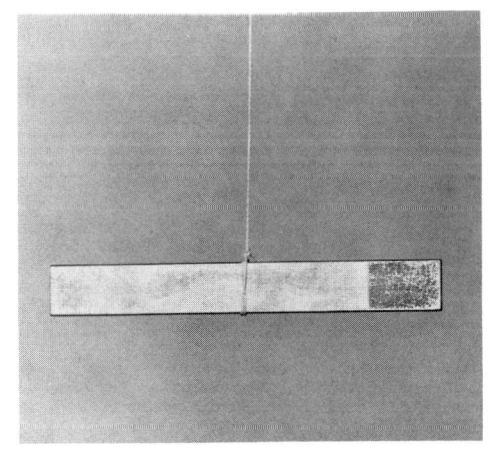

90-3. A bar magnet hung on a string acts like a compass.

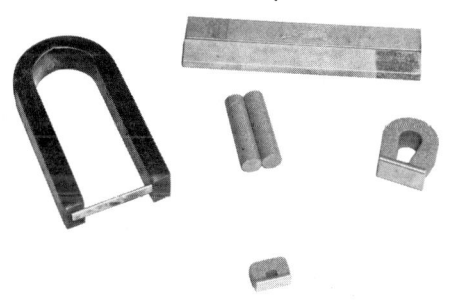

90-2. Permanent magnets are made in many sizes and shapes.

90-4. A compass needle is really a magnet.

Part V: Power and Energy

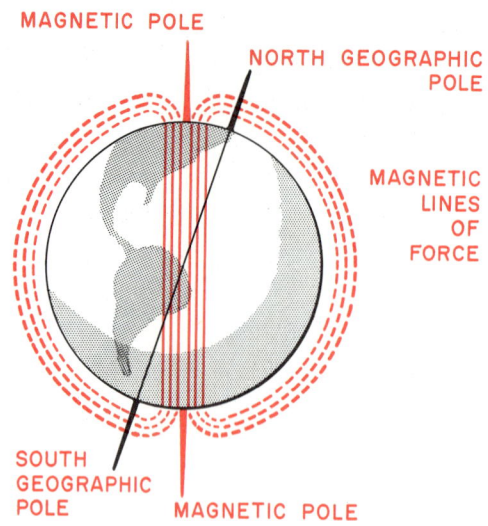

90-5. The earth is really a big magnet. A compass needle points to the earth's magnetic poles.

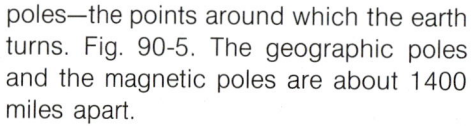

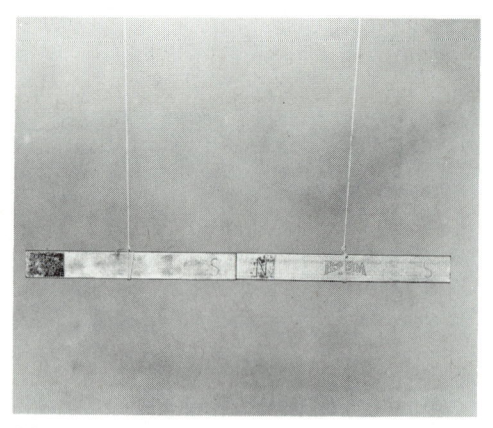

90-6. Unlike poles of magnets attract each other.

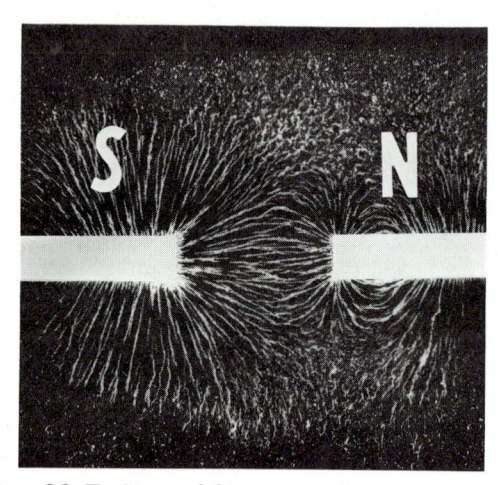

90-7. Lines of force around a magnet.

poles—the points around which the earth turns. Fig. 90-5. The geographic poles and the magnetic poles are about 1400 miles apart.

A compass needle points to the magnetic pole and not to the geographic pole. Navigators must make corrections for this in order to get where they plan to go. This difference between the true geographic pole and the magnetic pole is called the *angle of declination*.

LAWS OF MAGNETISM

As explained, magnets will attract iron or steel. However, they sometimes do the opposite; instead of attracting, they repel. For example, if two bar magnets are suspended by strings, the north pole of one will repel the north pole but attract the south pole of the other. Fig. 90-6. This can be stated as a law:

Unlike poles attract each other; like poles repel each other.

Lines of force flow out of the north pole of a magnet and back into the south pole. You cannot see these lines, but you can prove that they exist. Place a sheet of paper over a magnet, then sprinkle iron filings on the paper. The filings will arrange themselves as shown in Fig. 90-7. These filings show the magnet's lines of force.

These lines make up the *magnetic field of force*. Where the lines of force flow, the magnet exerts its force. The flow or movement of these lines is called *flux*. Flux refers to the flow of magnetism—the stronger the flux, the stronger the magnet.

Iron, steel, and nickel can be magnetized. However, some materials cannot be magnetized. Paper, wood, glass, and

Unit 90: Electricity and Magnetism

90-8a. *Before a bar is magnetized, the molecules are in all directions.*

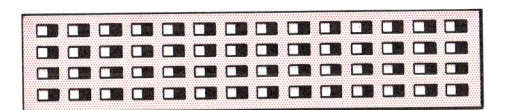

90-8b. *After a bar is magnetized, the molecules are lined up in one direction.*

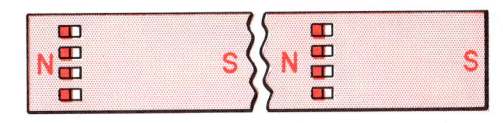

90-9. *If a magnet is broken, we have two magnets. Each time a magnet is broken, the pieces that are left have a north and a south pole.*

copper are examples of nonmagnetic materials.

Magnetism will pass through almost all materials. For instance, air, glass, and paper allow magnetism to pass through. They are called *magnetically transparent*.

What causes an iron bar to become magnetized? No one knows exactly, but many scientists believe that the molecules in the iron bar act as very tiny magnets. Before the bar is magnetized, the molecules are in all directions. Fig. 90-8a. The process of magnetizing makes the north and south poles of the molecules line up. After the bar is magnetized, its molecules are arranged as in Fig. 90-8b.

If a magnetized bar is broken, each piece becomes a magnet with a north and a south pole. Fig. 90-9. A bar may be magnetized by rubbing it with another magnet. Commercially, magnets are made by placing the material to be magnetized in a very strong magnetic field.

CARE OF MAGNETS

Magnets are quite sturdy, but there are some things which may be done to make them last longer. When storing a horseshoe magnet, place a piece of metal, called a *keeper*, across the poles. Bar magnets should be stored in pairs with north and south poles together. Magnets should not be handled roughly or dropped, as this can reduce their magnetism. Also, too much heat will destroy a magnet.

401

UNIT 91

Forms of Electricity

It is not easy to define electricity. It is a form of force, or energy, not a substance you can handle easily like water or earth. Still, despite the difficulties and dangers of working with electricity, people have learned how to produce it, transport it, and control it.

There are two types of electricity: *static* and *current*. Static electricity is not very useful and may even cause great trouble when large amounts of it, such as lightning, are discharged. However, current electricity is valuable because it can be controlled and used to do work.

STATIC ELECTRICITY

The word static means *at rest*. This kind of electricity is at rest, or is stationary. Static electricity was probably the first kind known to people. Not very much was known about it until Benjamin Franklin flew his kite and showed that lightning was really a form of electricity.

Static electricity is generated by friction. You can generate this form of electricity yourself in many ways. You may have combed your hair on a dry day and had the comb crackle or your hair cling to the comb. This is static electricity. So is the little shock you may get if you walk on a carpet on a dry day and then touch a water faucet. The friction of car tires on the road may build up static electricity in the car. At many toll booths there are wires which stick up from the pavement to discharge the electricity so that the toll taker will not get a shock. Paper going through a modern high-speed printing press also builds up static electricity. Many times this causes the sheets of paper to stick together and jam up the press.

As you can see, static electricity is a nuisance. Yet it can be used to demonstrate one of the basic laws of electricity. This law says that *like charges repel each other and unlike charges attract each other*. This can be shown by using two

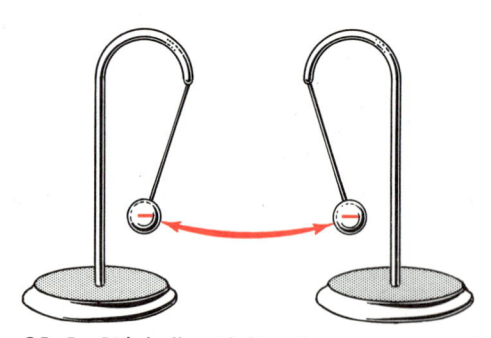

91-1. *Pith balls with like charges repel each other.*

91-2. *Pith balls with unlike charges attract each other.*

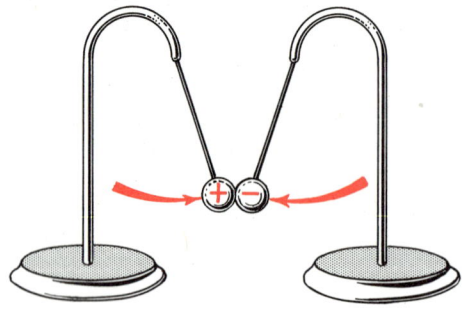

402

Unit 91: Forms of Electricity

pith balls as shown in Figs. 91-1 and 91-2. When the balls are charged alike, they repel each other; they do not touch. When they have unlike charges, they attract each other. Notice how similar this is to the law of magnetism discussed in the previous unit.

CURRENT ELECTRICITY

To be useful, electricity must be thoroughly controlled. Static electricity can scarcely be controlled at all, but current electricity can be made to work for people.

The first person to produce current electricity was an Italian scientist named Alessandro Volta. He made a "sandwich" of copper and zinc discs. Then he placed cloth moistened in salt water between the discs. This pile of copper and zinc discs was called the voltaic cell. When wires were connected to the discs, an electric current flowed through them. The unit of electrical pressure, the *volt,* is named after Volta. Volta discovered that when two different metals were placed in a chemical which acted on them, an electrical current was produced. Flashlight batteries work on this principle.

There are some terms which you must know in order to understand why electricity behaves the way it does. Two of these terms are *voltage* and *amperage.*

A force or pressure is needed to make electricity flow through a wire, just as pressure forces water through a hose. This pressure is measured in volts. For example, a single flashlight battery has a pressure, or voltage, of 1.5 volts.

The amount of electricity flowing through a wire depends on the number of electrons flowing through the wire. Of course you cannot count the electrons themselves, just as you cannot count the molecules of water passing through a pipe. But you can measure the flow of current accurately in terms of *amperes.* An ampere is the amount of current that one volt will cause to flow through one ohm of resistance. (Resistance and electrons will be explained in later units.) The important thing to remember is that amperes are a standard measurement of electrical current flow. The higher the number of amperes, the more current that is flowing.

In the SI metric system the volt and ampere are also used.

UNIT 92

Sources of Electricity

In the last unit you learned that electrical current depends on the flow of electrons. To understand this better you need to know something about atoms, because electrons are parts of atoms.

All matter is made of tiny particles called *atoms*. Though they are much too small to see, atoms themselves are made up of still smaller particles called *protons, neutrons,* and *electrons*.

The center of the atom is called the *nucleus*. It contains the protons and the neutrons. The electrons are in orbit around the nucleus.

Fig. 92-1 gives you some idea of how an atom might look. In the nucleus of this atom there are eight protons and eight neutrons. Eight electrons revolve around the nucleus.

92-1. *An atom of oxygen. The nucleus has eight protons and eight neutrons. There are eight electrons around the outside of the nucleus.*

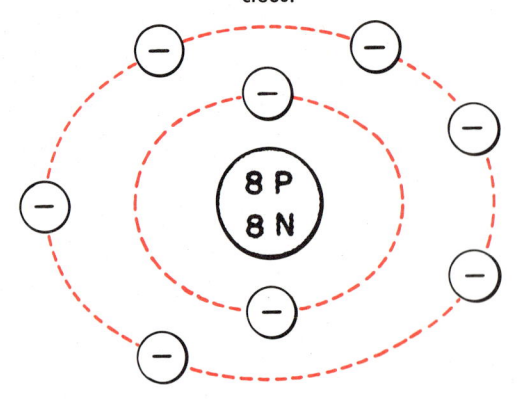

Protons and electrons have electrical charges, like the pith balls shown in the previous unit. Protons have a positive charge; electrons, negative. Neutrons do not have any electrical charge.

Normally the positive and negative forces of an atom equal each other. In other words, there are as many protons as electrons, leaving the atom neutral. When two substances are rubbed together, friction causes electrons from one substance to be transferred to the other. This unbalances the atoms and an electric charge is built up. When the atoms try to balance themselves again, sparks jump from one substance to the other. This explains why friction is one source of electricity.

ELECTRICITY BY CHEMICAL ACTION

One of the most common sources of electricity is a battery made up of two or more cells. Remember that Alessandro Volta made a cell by wiring discs of metal and putting them in a chemical which acted on them. A simple cell may be made by wiring a grapefruit as shown in Fig. 92-2. Make two small cuts in the skin of the grapefruit. In one, place a penny or a small piece of copper; in the other, place a nickel or a small piece of zinc. Connect the two metals to a sensitive meter and you will see that a voltage is being generated.

A stronger cell may be made by placing a strip of copper and a strip of zinc in a

Unit 92: Sources of Electricity

glass of water. Then add a small amount of vinegar or other acid. Again, the electricity that is produced will register on a meter. Fig. 92-3.

The cell just described is called a *voltaic cell*. It is one way of converting chemical energy into electrical energy. Such a cell cannot be recharged because the zinc strip will be eaten away in the chemical action that produces electricity. This type of cell is called a *wet cell* because the acid is in liquid form. Such cells are not in common use because they are not very handy. If tipped, the liquid will run out.

The *dry cell* is more convenient. Such cells are commonly used in flashlights. They have no liquid to spill. A cross section of a dry cell is shown in Fig. 92-4. The dry cell has four main parts. These are the *zinc container,* the *blotting paper liner,* the *carbon rod center,* and the *chemical mixture* which is around the carbon rod. The chemical mixture is made of powdered carbon, manganese dioxide, and sal ammoniac (ammonium chloride). When the cell is discharged (used up), water is formed inside it. Sometimes this makes the cell expand.

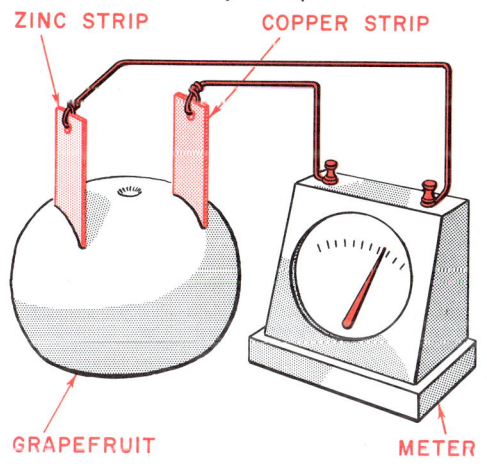

92-3. *A better simple cell can be made with a copper and a zinc strip and an acid like vinegar.*

You will notice two terminals on the cell in Fig. 92-4. One is attached to the zinc can and is called the negative pole, indicated by a minus sign (−). The other is attached to the carbon rod and is called the positive pole. It is indicated by a plus sign. (+).

Some new types of dry cells on the market today have certain advantages

92-2. *The acid in the grapefruit acts on the copper and zinc strips and makes electricity. This is really a simple cell.*

92-4. *The dry cell is more useful than the wet cell. This is a cross section of a dry cell.*

405

Part V: Power and Energy

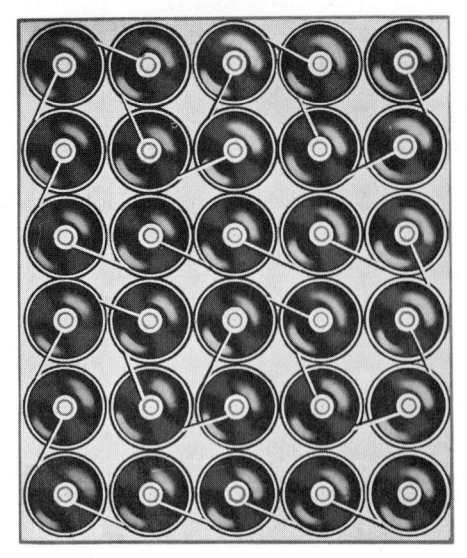

92-5. *A battery is really many single cells connected together.*

over the older types. One, called the *mercury cell,* makes its voltage by the chemical action between zinc and mercuric oxide. This type of cell lasts longer than the ordinary cell and produces almost five times more current. Another new type is the *nickel-cadmium cell.* This type of cell may be recharged. It also has a long life and is light and compact.

You probably have heard people call a single flashlight cell a battery. Technically this is wrong. A *battery* is made up of two or more connected cells. An example is shown in Fig. 92-5. After the cells are connected to form the battery, they are usually enclosed in one case.

It is important to understand how and why to connect cells. Cells are connected either in *series* or in *parallel.* If you had a small toy motor that required nine volts and you wanted to use dry cells to operate this motor, you would connect the cells in series. Fig. 92-6. Each cell produces $1\frac{1}{2}$ volts; so six cells in series will supply nine volts for the motor. By connecting more cells in series, higher voltages may be obtained. This is done for radio batteries.

For many uses you need the voltage of only one cell, but you may need it for long periods of time. All the current of one cell would be used in a short time. To make a battery that will last longer, connect several cells in parallel as shown in Fig. 92-7. The total voltage is the same as the voltage of one cell. The life is increased because current is drawn from more cells.

The dry cell is a *primary cell* because it cannot ordinarily be recharged. Rechargeable cells are called *secondary cells.* The most familiar type of secondary cell is the lead-acid cell used in automobiles.

The *storage battery* is a secondary cell that is a reservoir for electricity. It stores electrical power it receives and makes it available as needed. A storage battery does not make electricity. A cutaway view of a storage battery is shown in Fig. 92-8.

The storage battery is made up of two different kinds of lead plates in an *electrolyte.* The electrolyte is a mixture of distilled water and sulfuric acid. As the battery is charged or discharged, there is a change in the composition of the plates and the electrolyte.

Each cell of a storage battery produces about two volts. To make the twelve-volt battery used in most cars today, six cells are connected in series. Each of the cells has its own little compartment. At the bottom of each compartment is a space called a *sediment chamber.* Here particles from the plates and other material collect. This prevents short circuits.

Each cell has a *filler cap* so that distilled water may be added to the battery. The battery should be checked often to make sure the liquid covers the plates.

The condition of a battery may be tested by the use of a *load test* or a *hydrometer.* For the load test the battery is discharged at a faster than normal rate and the drop in battery voltage is noted. A twelve-volt battery should not drop below nine volts under the load test.

Unit 92: Sources of Electricity

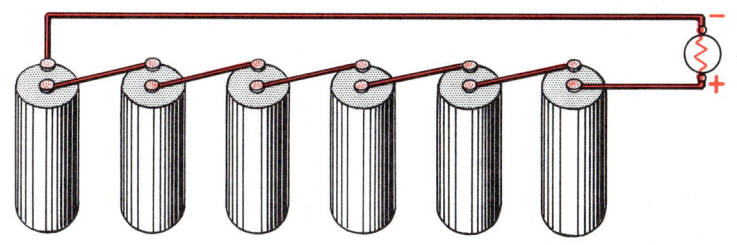

92-6. Single cells connected in series. How much voltage would these six cells provide?

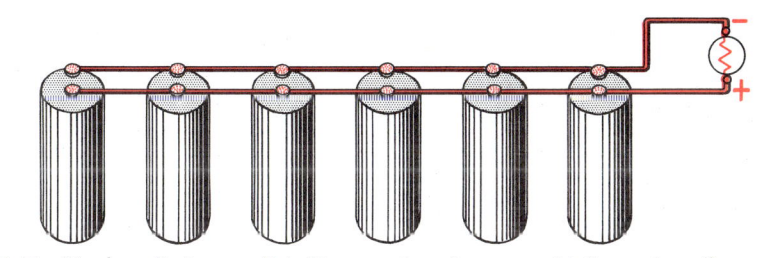

92-7. Single cells in parallel. How much voltage would these six cells provide?

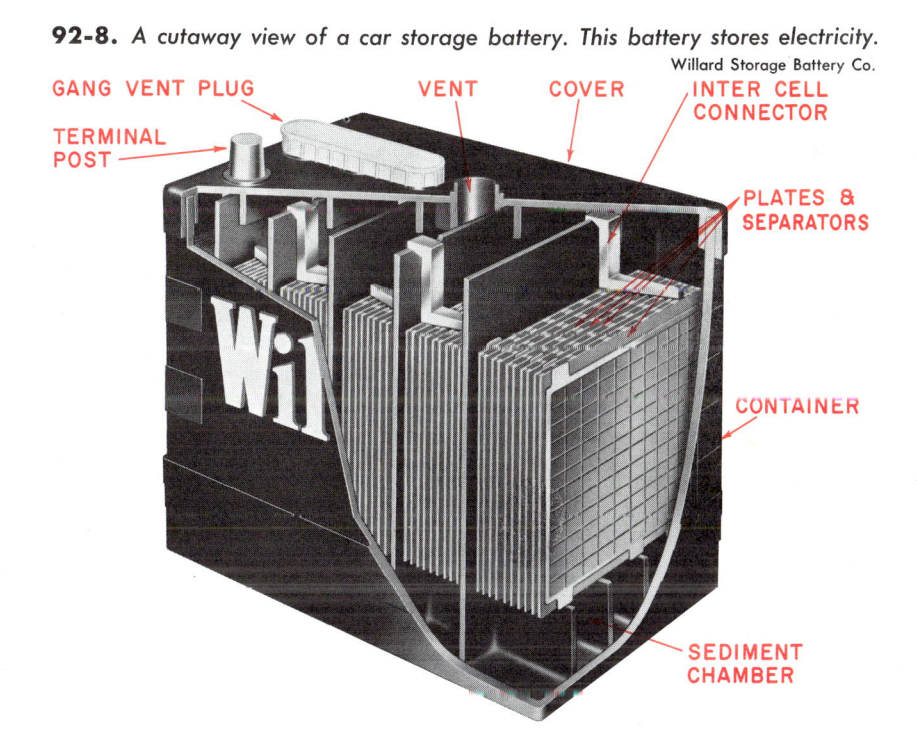

92-8. A cutaway view of a car storage battery. This battery stores electricity.

Willard Storage Battery Co.

GANG VENT PLUG
TERMINAL POST
VENT
COVER
INTER CELL CONNECTOR
PLATES & SEPARATORS
CONTAINER
SEDIMENT CHAMBER

Part V: Power and Energy

A hydrometer is a device that tests the battery by testing the condition of the electrolyte. A fully charged battery will read 1.260 on the hydrometer. Fig. 92-9. A fully discharged battery will read 1.110.

The terminals of the storage battery in a car may become corroded after a period of time. If this happens, a solution of baking soda should be poured on the terminals and allowed to remain for a few minutes. Then it should be washed off and the terminals wiped clean.

When working with storage batteries, you should be careful not to spill the electrolyte. It will eat holes in your clothes and burn your skin. Also, during the charging of storage batteries, highly explosive hydrogen gas sometimes forms. **Do not light matches near charging batteries.**

One of the newer methods of producing electricity is the *fuel cell*. A fuel cell converts the energy of a chemical reaction to electricity. It uses low-cost fuel and an oxidant. The most common type, and the one used in the space program, is the hydrogen-oxygen cell. In this cell, electricity and water are generated from a

92-9. A hydrometer.

FULLY DISCHARGED AT 1.110

FULLY CHARGED AT 1.260

408

Unit 92: Sources of Electricity

controlled reaction of oxygen and hydrogen and an acid electrolyte. Fig. 92-10 shows the action of a fuel cell.

ELECTRICITY FROM HEAT

When two wires of different metals are twisted together and heated as shown in Fig. 92-11, an electric current will flow. Heat causes the electrons to move. *Thermocouples* operate on this principle.

92-10. *A typical fuel cell. Hydrogen reacts at the anode to give up an electron (e$^-$) to the load while releasing hydrogen ions (H$^+$) in the solution. At the cathode, these hydrogen ions combine with oxygen and the electrons from the load circuit to produce water.*

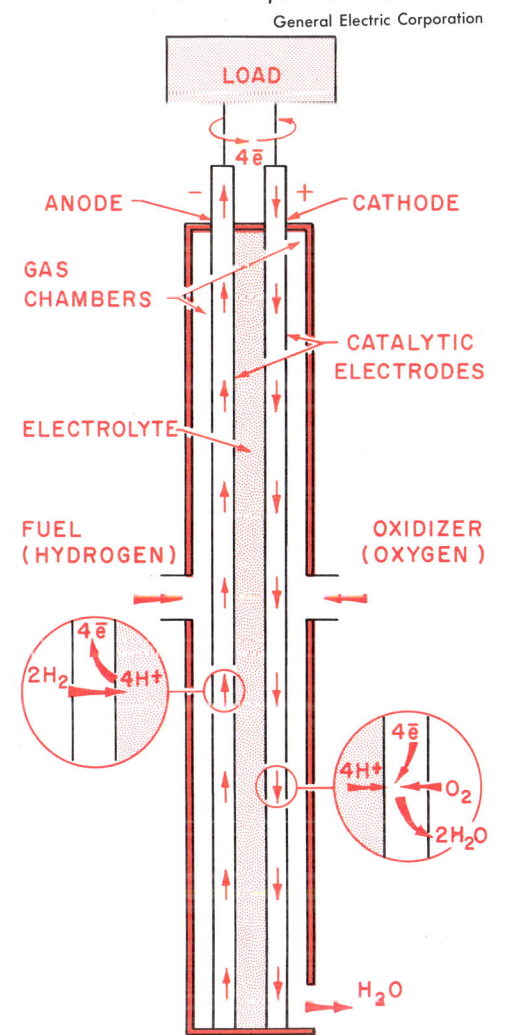

General Electric Corporation

These are commercial devices, made of two different metals, and are used to indicate and control heat in ovens and furnaces. Thermocouples are connected to meters which record the amount of current flowing through the wires—the more heat, the more current. A thermocouple combined with such a meter is called a *pyrometer*. Pyrometers are used for checking the proper pouring temperatures of molten metal.

Thermocouples do not furnish large amounts of electrical current. For this reason they cannot be used to provide electrical power.

ELECTRICITY FROM PRESSURE

When pressure is applied to certain materials, they will produce a slight electric current. One substance that reacts this way is a type of crystal known as *Rochelle salts.* As more pressure is applied to the crystal, more electricity is produced.

One of the most familiar uses of electricity produced this way is in a record player. Fig. 92-12. A needle is attached to the crystal. When the needle slides in the record groove, it vibrates. The vibrations of the needle duplicate the original vibrations that were pressed into the record. The needle vibrations cause pressure on the crystal so that it produces electricity in the same pattern as the original. The

92-11. *Heating a thermocouple will make electricity.*

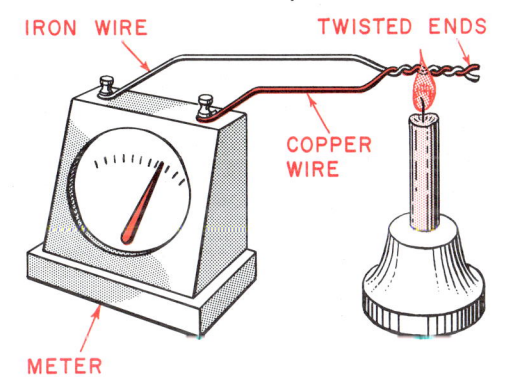

Part V: Power and Energy

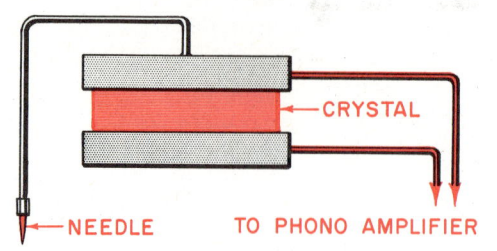

92-12. Grooves in a phonograph record cause pressure on the needle. This pressure is carried to the crystal, which produces electricity.

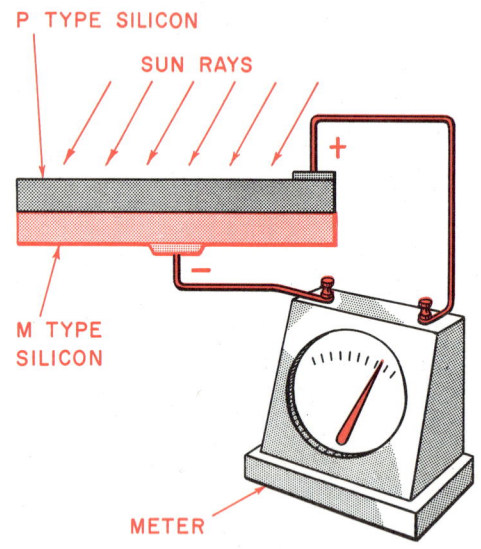

92-13. Drawing of a solar cell. Electrons travel from one type of silicon to the other when the rays of the sun strike the cell.

92-14. Workers installing solar cells on a satellite. The dark squares are small solar cells connected together.

amount of electricity is very weak; so it must be made stronger by an amplifier.

Crystals are also used in microphones. The principle of generating electricity by pressure is the same for the microphone as for the record player. The only difference is that the pressure is applied to the crystal by a voice speaking into the microphone.

ELECTRICITY FROM LIGHT

Some materials will generate small amounts of electricity when light strikes them. This is called the *photoelectric effect.* Some of these materials are sodium, selenium, and potassium. These materials are used to make what are known as photoelectric or solar cells. Fig. 92-13. By controlling the amount of light that strikes one of these cells, the amount of electricity can be controlled.

Most photoelectric or solar cells consist of a metal plate coated with some light-sensitive substance. These light-sensitive cells are used for operating light meters for photography, burglar alarms, and other control devices. One of the newer uses for solar cells is as a source of power for satellites. Because each cell generates only a small amount of electricity, it takes many cells to power a satellite. Fig. 92-14 shows how solar cells are used for satellites.

410

Unit 92: Sources of Electricity

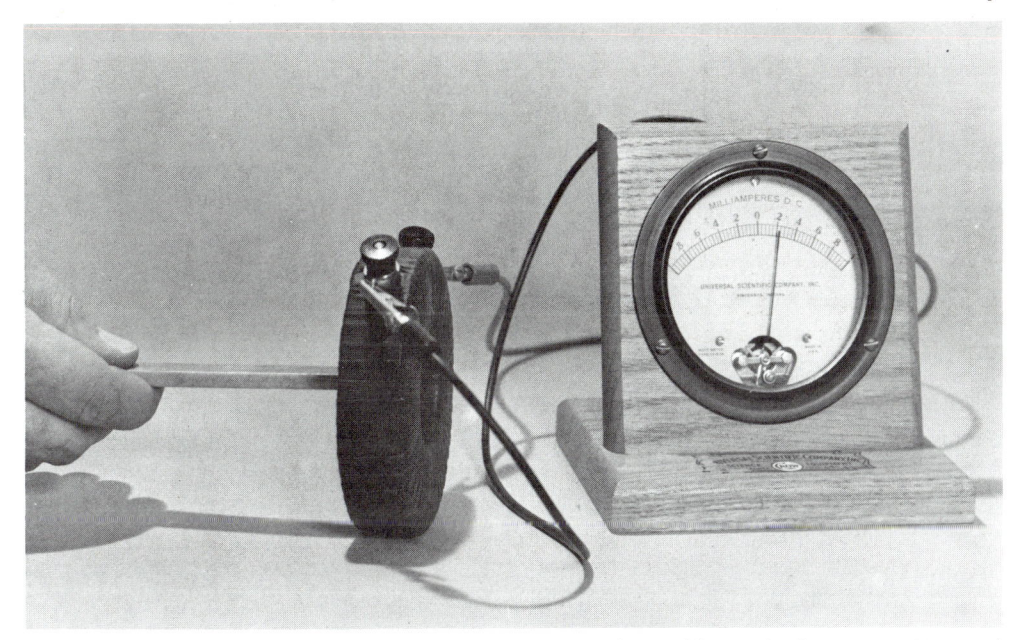

92-15. Electricity is produced by a coil cutting magnetic lines of force. As the magnet is moved in and out of the coil, a current is generated.

Western Electric Corporation
92-16. A generator which is used for supplying emergency power to telephones.

ELECTRICITY FROM MAGNETISM

The most important source of electricity is the generator. The *generator* changes mechanical energy to electrical energy. All generators work on the principle of cutting magnetic lines of force with coils of wire. Fig. 92-15. The generator is a cheap and easy way of producing electricity. It is the way most electricity is produced for your home and for industry. Automobiles also have a form of generator to keep the battery charged. In Unit 94 you will learn more about electrical generators. Fig. 92-16 shows an electrical generator used to provide emergency power for telephones.

UNIT 93

Conductors and Circuits

From Unit 92 you will remember that electrons usually are in orbit around the nucleus of an atom. When an electron is removed from an atom, it is called a *free electron.* The atoms that make up certain metals have electrons which are loosely bound to the nucleus. This means the electrons are free to move from one atom to another if pushed with a small amount of force. The flow of current is really the movement of free electrons through an electrical conductor. Materials which allow the free motion of large numbers of free electrons are called *conductors.* Copper wire is a good conductor.

93-1. *These illustrations show a schematic drawing and a photograph of a simple circuit.*

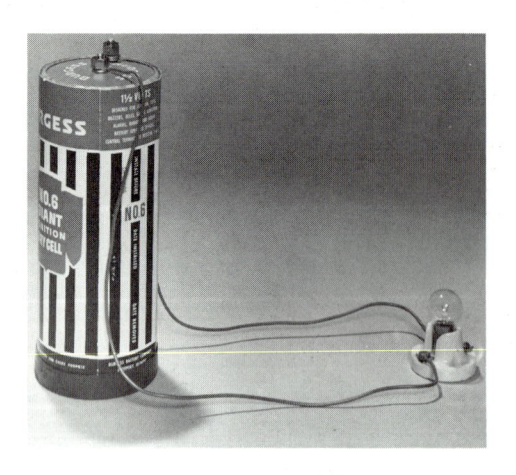

Free electrons move from one atom to another, forcing out other electrons in a kind of chain reaction. The process goes on until the energy is moved the entire length of the conductor. A good conductor is said to have *low resistance* to current flow.

The opposite of a conductor is an *insulator.* Insulators have very few free electrons; so little or no current will flow through them. The best conductors are used as wires to carry electrical energy; the poorest are used as insulators, to prevent current flow. Below is a list of the best conductors and the best insulators.

Conductors	Insulators
Silver	Dry air
Copper	Glass
Aluminum	Mica
Brass	Polystyrene plastic
Zinc	Rubber
Iron	Asbestos

SIMPLE ELECTRICAL CIRCUIT

Most useful electrical energy is transmitted through closed *electrical circuits.* The simplest circuits have a source of electricity, a load (something to use the electricity), and connecting wires. Fig. 93-1.

Wire sizes are indicated by gauge number—the larger the number, the smaller the wire. Electricians usually choose the smallest wire that will safely carry the current and not get hot and burn the insulation. If the wire gets too hot, it

Unit 93: Conductors and Circuits

might start a fire. The smaller the wire, the more resistance it has to flow of electricity. Resistance in a wire also depends on the length, kind, and temperature of the wire. Resistance is measured in *ohms*.

One of the basic laws of electricity is called *Ohm's law*. This law is named after George Simon Ohm, who developed it. Ohm's law is a mathematical way of finding the resistance, the amperage, or the voltage of a circuit. It says that total amperage multiplied by total resistance is equal to the voltage.

Fig. 93-2 makes it easy to remember how to use this formula. The horizontal line (across) means divide; the vertical line (down) means multiply. If you know the amperage (I) and voltage (E) of a circuit and want to find out the resistance (R), cover the R with your finger. What is left? E divided by I. Substitute the numbers for the symbols, divide, and you have the answer.

Now try an actual example. How much voltage would it take to push 2 amperes through a wire that has a resistance of 55 ohms? Cover the E in the circle and you see that you need to multiply I x R, or 2 x 55, for an answer of 110 volts. Engineers who design electrical equipment and appliances use Ohm's law in deciding what materials to use.

Remember, to make current flow there must be a complete circuit. There are four parts to a complete circuit. They are:

- Source of electricity.
- A way of turning the current on and off.
- A way for the current to flow through the circuit.
- The load or device that is to use the current.

The source of current may be a dry cell. The symbol for cell is:

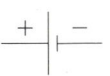

The symbol for a battery is:

One way to turn the current on and off is with a *switch*. Another is with a push button, as for doorbells.

Electrical wires are usually of copper, but aluminum is sometimes used. Joining wires is called *splicing*. The most common splice is the *Western Union splice*. Others are the *tap splice* and *pig-tail splice*. Fig. 93-3.

There are many kinds of circuits. There are open circuits, closed circuits, short circuits, parallel circuits, and series circuits.

A circuit is open when there is a break in the wire or when a switch is not closed. A closed circuit is a complete circuit. For example, when a push button is pushed, this closes the circuit. A short circuit al-

93-3. *Three kinds of wire splices. The Western Union splice (left) is most common. Also shown are the tap splice (center) and the pig-tail splice (right).*

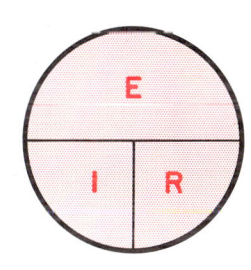

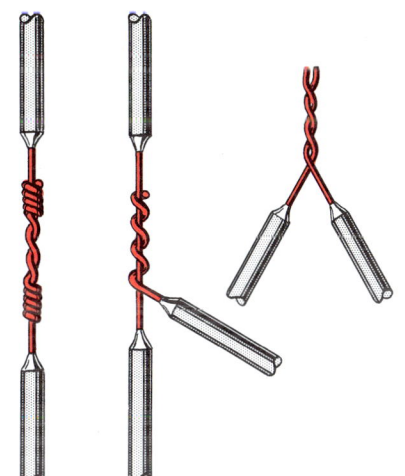

93-2. *Ohm's law diagram. E stands for voltage, I for amperage, R for resistance.*

413

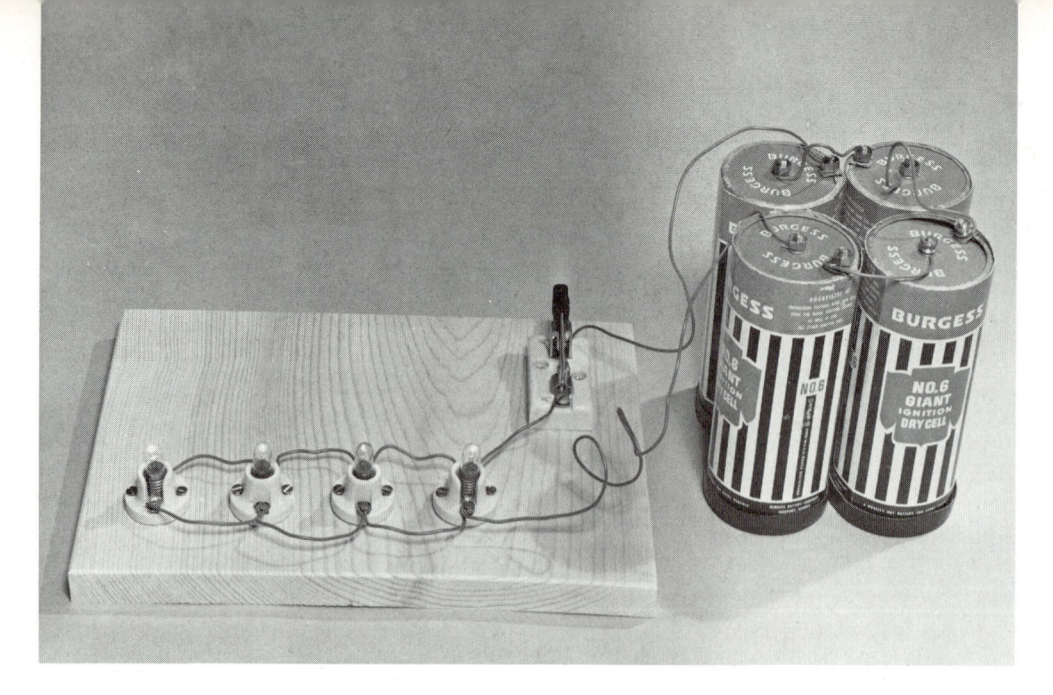

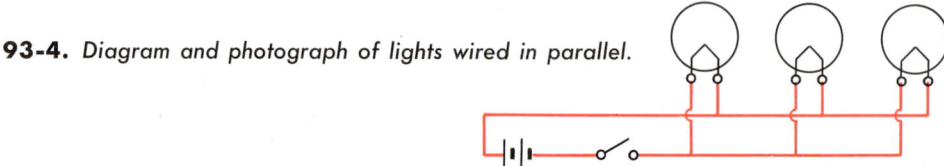

93-4. *Diagram and photograph of lights wired in parallel.*

lows the current to flow where it is not meant to flow. Short circuits can cause damage unless there is a fuse in the circuit.

The parallel circuit is used in connecting lights and other electrical appliances. Parallel circuits are shown in Fig. 93-4. When the switch is closed, the lamps will light. Two switches could also be connected in parallel to turn on the lights from two places. Fig. 93-5.

When lights are connected in series, the current must flow through each light to complete the circuit. If one light burns out, the circuit is open. Fig. 93-6 shows lights connected in series. Why do you suppose this type of circuit is not used for house wiring?

To understand the language of the electrician you will have to learn some symbols. It would take too much time and space to draw pictures of the parts of a circuit; so electricians use symbols instead. Some of the more common electrical symbols are shown in Fig. 93-7.

CORDS, PLUGS, LAMP SOCKETS

Most electrical appliances have an attached cord so that they can be plugged into an electrical outlet. These cords should be inspected frequently and replaced as needed. Especially common problems are broken or frayed wires, and those with cracked insulation.

Wiring a lamp is one of the most common jobs in electricity. Sometimes you may need to put a new cord on the lamp. At other times you may need only to replace the plug.

To wire, first obtain a sufficient length of lamp cord. Attach the socket as shown in Fig. 93-8. Remove $\frac{1}{2}''$ of insulation from the wire ends. Remove the cap from the socket. (This is usually done by pressing as indicated on the socket.) Slip the cap over the wire. Slip the casing from the socket. Fasten the wires under the screws. Put the casing over the socket.

Plugs are of various types. With some the wire is slipped into the plug and held

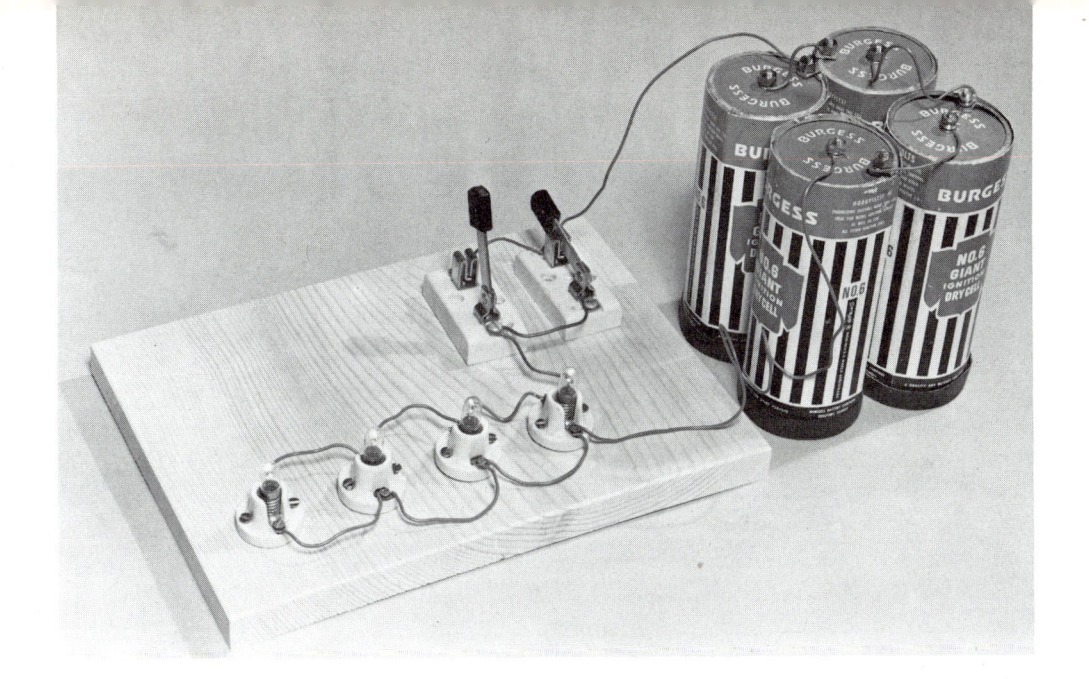

93-5. Diagram and photograph of lights and switches wired in parallel.

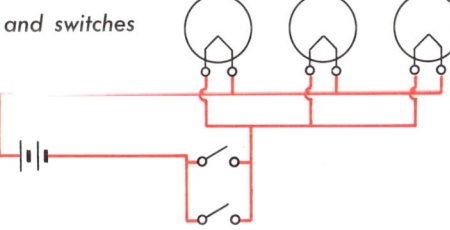

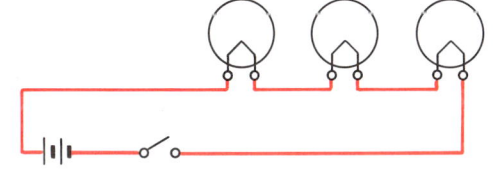

93-6. Diagram and photograph of lights wired in series.

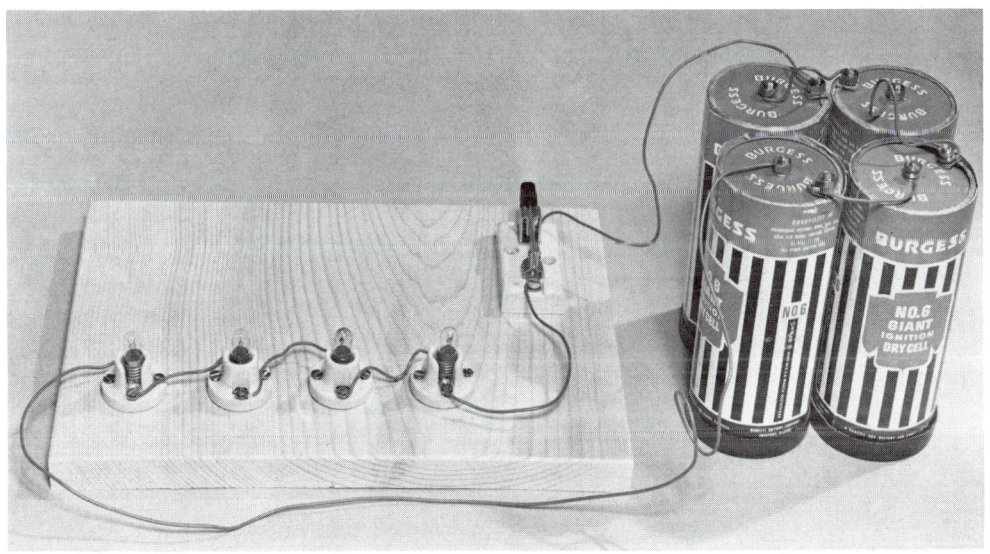

415

Part V: Power and Energy

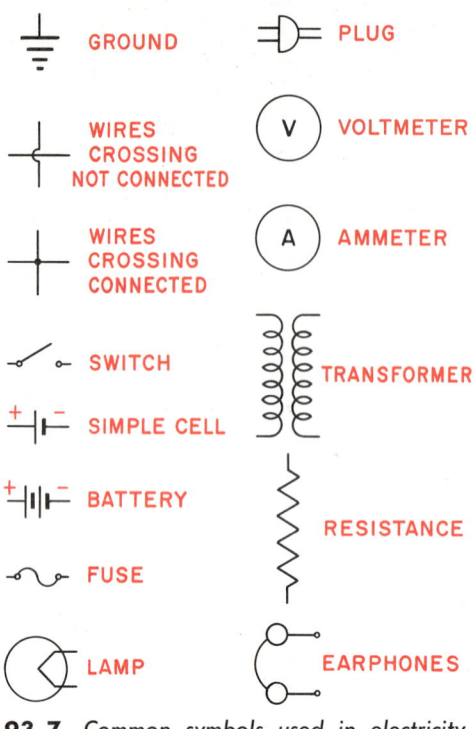

Common symbols: GROUND, PLUG, WIRES CROSSING NOT CONNECTED, VOLTMETER, WIRES CROSSING CONNECTED, AMMETER, SWITCH, TRANSFORMER, SIMPLE CELL, BATTERY, RESISTANCE, FUSE, LAMP, EARPHONES.

93-7. Common symbols used in electricity and radio.

93-8. Light socket with parts separated and cord attached.

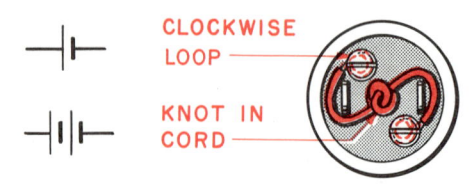

CLOCKWISE LOOP
KNOT IN CORD

93-9. Wiring a plug.

by a clamp. On others the wire is soldered to the prongs of the plug. The most common type uses screws to fasten the wire to the prongs. Fig. 93-9. Fastening a cord to a plug or socket is very easy. However, be careful not to have any of the strands of wire touching, or a short circuit will result.

Some plugs have three prongs instead of the usual two. These *grounded plugs* are especially common on appliances that may be used in moist places or near water. One end of the wire is connected to the case of the appliance; the other end is connected to the third prong. This grounds the case so that if a short circuit occurs, it will not shock the person using the appliance. Special adapter plugs are available for connecting grounded appliances to two-pronged outlets. CAUTION: The grounding wire should be connected to a good ground if an adapter is used.

Always be sure to read the instruction book which comes with the appliance. Never attempt any repairs unless you are qualified.

UNIT 94

Electromagnetism

In Unit 90 you learned about magnetism and permanent magnets. Now you are going to study the effects of a current in a wire. Around every electrical conductor where current is flowing there are magnetic lines of force. Through a piece of cardboard, pass a wire carrying current. Fig. 94-1. Place three compasses on this cardboard and you will see that the needles point in the direction of the magnetic lines of force. If the current is reversed, the compass needles will point in the opposite direction. The direction of the magnetic field depends on the direction of the current flow.

When a wire carrying a current is wound into a coil it is called a *solenoid*. The magnetic fields around each wire join together. A solenoid will have a magnetic north pole at one end and a magnetic south pole at the other. Fig. 94-2. The strength of the magnetic field depends on the number of turns of wire in the coil and the current flowing through the coil.

A typical solenoid is a coil of wire wound on a hollow tube. A piece of soft iron fits into this tube and can be moved in and out. When the coil is connected to a current, the solenoid magnetically sucks the iron core into its center. The solenoid is useful for opening or closing valves and switches, among many other applications. Door chimes use one or more solenoids to strike metal strips and produce musical notes. Automatic washers also use solenoids for turning the water on and off. Fig. 94-3.

The solenoid coil uses air as the only conductor of the magnetic field. Other materials will conduct magnetic lines of force better than air. These materials are said to have better *permeability*. Soft iron is one such material. A coil of wire wound on an iron core is called an *electromagnet*. An electromagnet may be made by winding many turns of No. 24 wire around

94-1. Lines of force around a wire. Notice how the compass needles point in different directions.

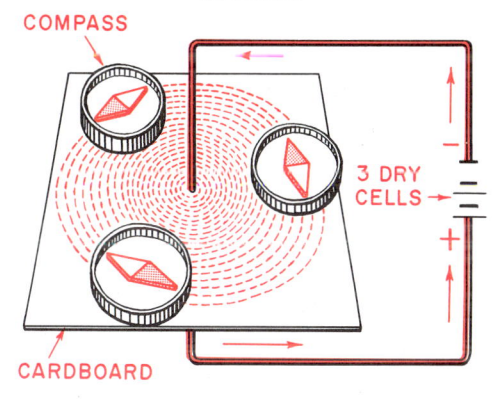

94-2. A solenoid coil. Notice that it has a north and a south pole.

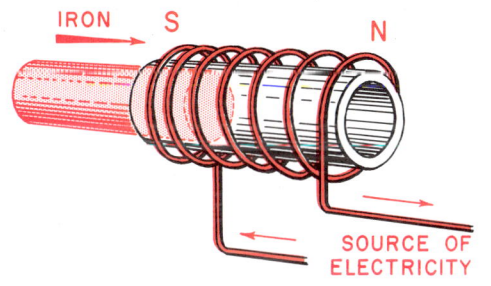

Part V: Power and Energy

a nail, then connecting the wire to a dry cell.

With the electromagnet, iron substances may be picked up. You will notice that when the dry cell is disconnected there is no longer any magnetism; whatever was stuck to the magnet drops off. This explains how large electromagnets are used in junkyards for picking up and loading scrap iron. Electromagnets are also used in relays, in voltage regulators for cars, in doorbells and buzzers, and in magnetic switches.

Still another use of electromagnetism is in the transformer. A *transformer* is a device for transferring electrical energy from one circuit to another. A transformer consists of two coils of wire wound around an iron core. Fig. 94-4. A transformer may increase (step up) the voltage or decrease it (step it down).

The winding in which the current enters the transformer is called the *primary coil*. The winding in which the current leaves the transformer is called the *secondary coil*.

GENERATORS

As mentioned earlier, electric current will produce a magnetic field. Michael Faraday, an English scientist of the 19th century, proved that this works both ways—a magnetic field can be used to produce electricity. His experiments led to the development of the *generator*, a device for changing mechanical energy into electrical energy. Figs. 94-5 and 94-6.

To produce electricity with a generator there must be a magnetic field and a coil of wire (called an *armature*) which moves through the field. As the coil revolves it takes on an electrical charge.

Because the coil turns, it is necessary to connect wires that are not turning to those that are. To do this a small ring, divided into two sections, is fastened to the ends of the coil. This ring is called the *commutator*. Contacts called *brushes* rub against the commutator and transfer the voltage from the revolving coil to the stationary wires. Such a generator produces direct current.

Generators that produce alternating current have two or more *slip rings* instead of a commutator. These rings are not divided into sections as the commutator is.

Simple generators can be improved by using electromagnets instead of permanent magnets. These electromagnets are called *field coils*.

There are two types of generators in use today, *direct current* and *alternating current*. Current from a direct-current generator always flows out of one pole and back into another. Current from an alternating-current generator moves first out of one pole and into the second, then out of the second and back into the first.

94-3. *A solenoid. The iron bar is sucked into the coil when the current is on.*

94-4. *A transformer. The current enters the primary coil and leaves the secondary coil. A transformer either raises or lowers the voltage.*

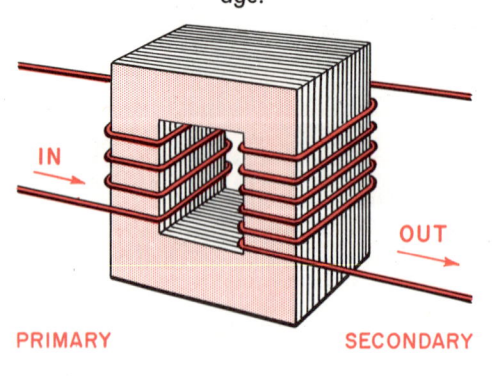

IN → PRIMARY   OUT → SECONDARY

Unit 94: Electromagnetism

94-5. *The control room of a large power-generating station. Workers here regulate the power for many thousands of homes and industries.*

The flow changes direction 120 times a second in a 60-cycle generator. Most of the current used in homes and industry today is 60-cycle alternating current. Alternating current can be changed to higher or lower voltages and carried over wires for long distances. This cannot be done with direct current.

MOTORS

The operation of the electric motor is the reverse of the generator. The motor changes electrical energy to mechanical energy. Besides their use in almost every industry, electric motors have many household uses such as refrigeration, cleaning rugs, ventilation, heating, and keeping time. In school shops motors are used on drills, saws, lathes, jointers, and many other machines.

The operation of an electric motor depends on magnetic fields. It particularly depends upon two principles you have already learned. One is that like poles repel each other and unlike poles attract each other. The second is that a magnetic field exists between the two poles of a magnet.

An electromagnet, called an *armature*, is placed between the north and south poles of the permanent magnets. Like the armature of the generator, this electromagnet rotates and at its ends it has pieces of metal called the *commutator*.

94-6. *A direct-current generator. Broken lines show the magnetic field. The armature turning in the magnetic field generates electricity which is removed by the commutator and the brushes. The colored arrows show which way the current flows. The black ones identify parts.*

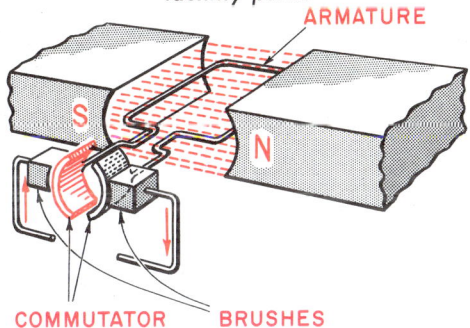

419

Part V: Power and Energy

Brushes contact the commutator sections and provide a way for the current to get to the armature coil. Current from a battery passes through the armature coil, then returns to the battery through the other commutator piece and brush. Fig. 94-7.

Here is how one turn of the armature takes place: The poles of the permanent magnets attract the poles of the electromagnet, causing the armature to turn. As the armature turns, the brushes slide off the commutator and the circuit is broken. Then the armature continues to turn, and the current is reversed in the armature. This causes the poles of the armature to change so that the north pole of the electromagnet is next to the north pole of the permanent magnet. Like poles repel; so the armature continues to turn.

This process of attraction and repulsion continues until the battery is disconnected. The arrangement of the commutator and brushes is very important because the direction of the current must be reversed at just the proper time.

Large electric motors have many coils on both the armature and the field. Each coil on the armature is connected to a commutator segment. Fig. 94-8.

There are many ways of winding and connecting the coils which control the speed of the motor. Motor speed is measured in revolutions per minute (RPM). Refrigerator motors run at about 1725 RPM; some others run as fast as 7000 RPM.

So far you have seen how the motor operates on direct current. Many motors will work on both direct current (DC) and alternating current (AC). One kind of motor, the *induction motor,* is designed to operate only on AC. Fig. 94-9. This motor has no armature coil, no commutator, and no brushes. The rotating part or *rotor* is made of laminated pieces of metal. The change in direction of the alternating current substitutes for the commutator and brushes.

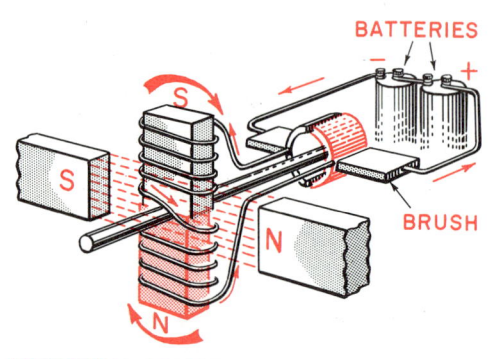

DIRECTION ARMATURE TURNS

94-7. A motor. The attraction and repulsion of the magnets and the armature make the motor turn. The large, colored arrows show the movement of the armature. The smaller ones show current flow. The black arrows identify parts.

WINDINGS

COMMUTATOR SEGMENTS

94-8. Armature and commutator of an electric motor. Notice the many windings and commutator pieces.

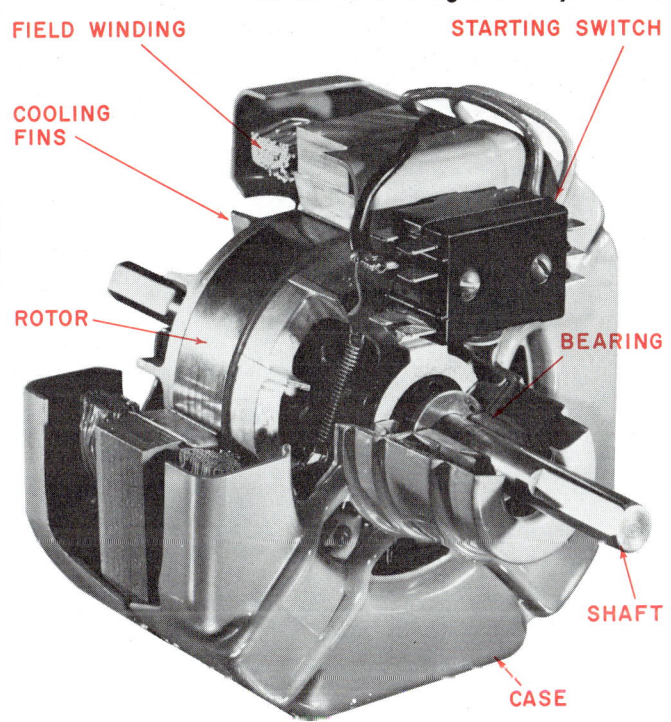

Unit 95: Converting Electricity to Heat

FIELD WINDING
STARTING SWITCH
COOLING FINS
ROTOR
BEARING
SHAFT
CASE

94-9. *Cutaway view of an induction motor. This type of motor does not have brushes or commutator. It will operate only on alternating current.*

UNIT 95

Converting Electricity to Heat

Electricity can be used to produce heat. This makes it useful for many purposes in the home as well as in industry. The toaster, the iron, the water heater, the waffle iron, and the coffee pot are just a few common appliances that depend on electrical heat. Fig. 95-1. How many more can you name?

How does electricity produce heat? To understand this you have to remember a few facts from previous units. Electrical current is really the movement of electrons through a conductor. This movement causes heat.

Electrons move easily through some materials, and cause very little heat. Such materials are called good conductors. However, when electrons pass through a poor conductor they meet more resistance. It takes more pressure (voltage) to

421

Part V: Power and Energy

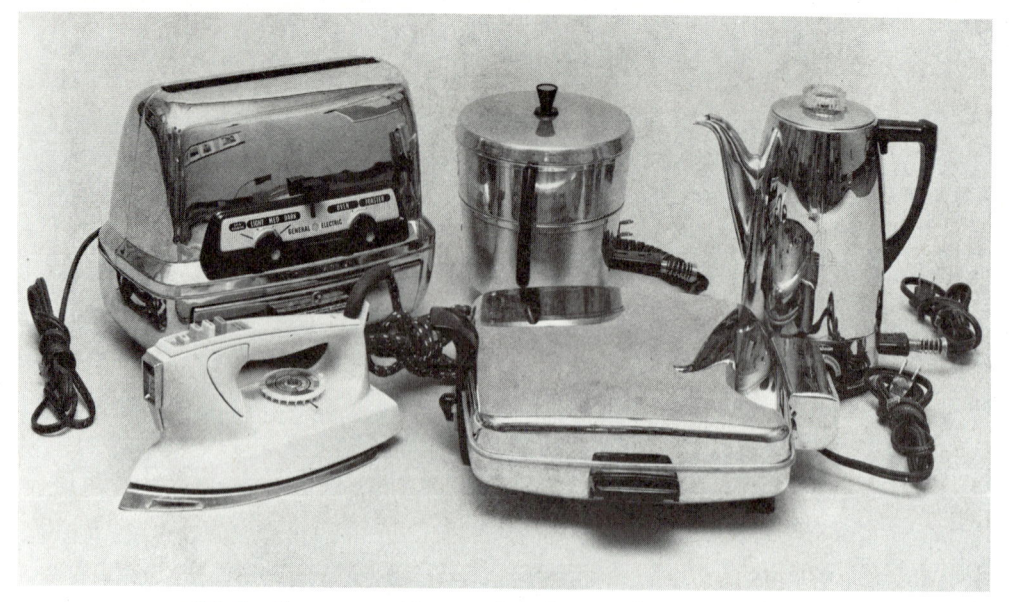

95-1. Common appliances that change electricity to heat.

push them through. As a rule, the more resistance the electrons meet, the more heat they will build up.

To understand this better, think for a moment about a gasoline engine. As long as the engine is properly oiled, its parts move easily and do not get too hot. But if the oil leaks out, the parts do not move easily any longer. They rub against each other and meet a kind of resistance called friction. The engine will soon get very hot. Does this comparison help you to see how resistance in a wire causes heat?

There are special conductors which can be used to control the resistance to the movement of electrons. *Nichrome wire* is such a conductor. By using the correct size and amount of this wire, the desired degree of heat can be produced with a certain amount of electricity. This is the kind of arrangement used to provide heat in the electrical appliances mentioned a few paragraphs earlier. The device that actually produces the heat is called a *resistance-heating element*.

Large appliances that use a great amount of current are usually installed permanently. Smaller ones often are portable so that they can be plugged into electrical outlets wherever they are needed. Whether large or small, these appliances can be dangerous. Both electricity and heat, if used improperly, can cause personal injury and property damage. Before using any heating appliance, be certain to read the instruction book.

FUSES

Fuses guard against one of the chief dangers of using electricity. Like many appliances, they work on the principle that electricity makes heat. Their use is explained more fully in the following paragraphs.

Fuses are safety devices to prevent electrical equipment and circuits from being burned out by an overload. An overload means that the circuit is carrying too much current. The circuit is arranged so that all the current must pass through the fuse. A special conductor in the fuse will carry only a certain amount of current. This conductor grows hot and melts when too much current passes through it. A melted fuse (usually called a "blown"

Unit 95: Converting Electricity to Heat

95-2. Common kinds of fuses. These types are used in home fuse boxes.

95-3. Circuit breaker. Many homes now have these instead of fuses.

fuse) breaks the circuit and prevents the overload from flowing into the rest of the circuit. You can see that the fuse operates on the same principle as electrical heating devices.

The two types of fuses usually used in the home are the *cartridge fuse* and the *plug fuse*, Fig. 95-2. The cartridge fuse is commonly used for 220-volt circuits that carry up to 30 amperes. The plug is usually used for circuits that do not carry over 25 amperes.

For motor circuits, such as on a furnace or air conditioner circuit, you may find a special kind of fuse called a *fusetron*. This type of fuse permits a large current flow for a short period of time. This allows the motor to get started, but prevents the heavy load from lasting too long.

Today many homes are equipped with *circuit breakers* instead of fuses. These devices, which look like switches, will open the circuit like a fuse if the current flow gets too heavy. Fig. 95-3. With this type of protection it is not necessary to replace fuses. The circuit breaker is just reset by pushing or turning it off, then back on.

A blown fuse or a tripped circuit breaker means trouble. It means there is either a short circuit or an overload. In either case the trouble should be corrected before replacing the fuse or resetting the circuit breaker. Never replace a fuse with one of higher current rating. Also never place a piece of metal, such as a penny, under a fuse.

HEAT FROM ELECTRICITY FOR INDUSTRY

Industry also uses electricity for making heat. Some special steels are heated in electric furnaces that use large carbon rods and an arc of electricity. These furnaces use great amounts of electricity and produce very high temperatures.

Another important use of electrical heat in industry is for *arc welding*. The welding rod is held close to the piece to be welded. Current passes through both the rod and the piece to be welded. This

423

Part V: Power and Energy

95-4. *Arc welding is one way electricity is changed into heat in industry.*

makes an arc which melts the rod and the piece being welded. Arc welding is used for such purposes as joining sections of pipelines and fastening the steel members of tall buildings.

Arc welding produces harmful rays which will burn much like the sun. Never look directly at the arc or you will damage your eyes. Welders wear helmets with special glass to protect their eyes. Fig. 95-4.

Industry uses electricity to produce heat in still other ways. One way is by converting electricity to high-frequency radio waves. This process, called *high-frequency heating,* is used for heating parts which a welder cannot reach. Sometimes it is also used on a production line where speed is important.

UNIT 96

Converting Electricity to Light

Probably the most common use of electricity is to provide lighting. Most people are so used to electric light that they never stop to wonder how the light bulb works. Fig. 96-1.

As you remember from the previous unit, electricity produces heat when it flows through a wire with resistance. When the wire gets hot enough it glows, first a dull red, then brighter and brighter. However, most types of wire would get too hot and melt instead of giving a bright and lasting glow.

The man who developed the first practical electrical lighting system was Thomas Edison. He searched a long time before he and his assistants discovered a material that would give light, but would not burn up. He placed a wire made of this material in a glass bulb and removed the air. (Wires used this way are called *filaments.*) Edison's first bulb produced light, but also got very hot and did not last long. He used filaments of carbon and later of bamboo. Now filaments for light bulbs are made from *tungsten*—a metal

Unit 96: Converting Electricity to Light

96-1. Lights are a necessary part of industry. This power station is a good example of a well-lighted industrial plant.

Southern California Edison

that has high resistance and a high melting point. The tungsten filament gives a white light with much less heat than the Edison light bulb.

The light bulb must have a source of electricity. One source is the dry cell which is used in the flashlight. There are many sizes and shapes of flashlights. Most have a battery case, a switch to turn them off and on, a light bulb, a reflector, and some sort of lens over the bulb. Cells in flashlights are usually connected in series to increase the voltage.

There are other types of flashlights. One is a small, one-cell light attached to a key chain. Another is the large lantern-type light which is used by railroad brakemen and construction workers.

Electricity for your home comes from a power station. These stations are often many miles away; so the voltage is increased, or "stepped up," by transformers to many thousand volts. Then it is carried over wires to your home. Before it can be used in your home, it must be reduced, or "stepped down," to 110 or 220 volts. This is done by a transformer usually close to your home. Fig. 96-2.

96-2. A transformer is used to change the high voltage to 110 volts for your home.

425

Part V: Power and Energy

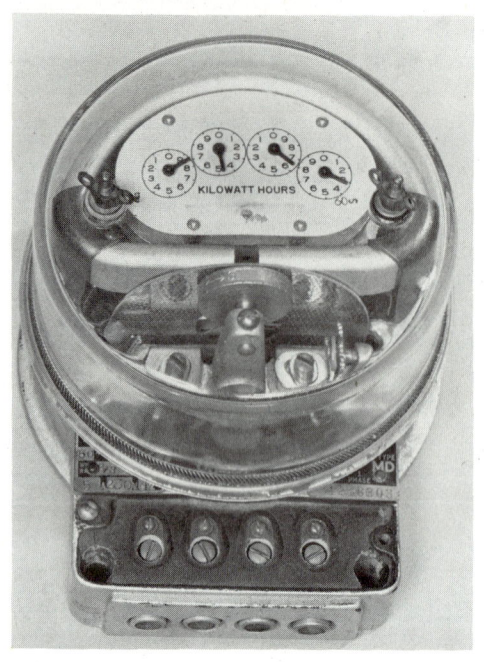

96-3. A watt-hour meter measures the amount of electricity that is used, as in a home or an industrial plant.

This reduced voltage is still dangerous and can cause severe shock or even death under certain conditions; so take no chances with the electricity in your home.

READING METERS

The power company must have some way of measuring the amount of current you use. This is done with a *meter*. Fig. 96-3. As the current goes through the meter, the electricity runs a motor that turns the hands on the meter dials. The faster the current flows, the faster the meter runs.

Notice the dials on the meter in Fig. 96-4. The four dials are read as any four-figure number would be. For example, the number 1649 is read one thousand six hundred forty-nine. The first dial gives the thousands of kilowatt hours, the second gives the hundreds, the third the tens, and the last the units.

Two of the hands move *clockwise;* the other two, *counterclockwise.* The hands are run by the motor through a set of gears. Always read the number which the hand has just passed.

Notice the position of the hands in Fig. 96-5. The thousands hand has just passed 8; so the reading for this hand is 8000. The hundreds hand has passed 5 and is about halfway to 6; so this would be 500. The tens hand is almost to 4, but has not reached it yet; so this would be 30. The units hand has passed 2. The reading for this meter would be 8532.

Meters are not set back to zero each month. The reading for one month is subtracted from the reading for the preceding month. This is the number of *kilowatt hours* of electricity used during that month.

What does the term *kilowatt hours* really mean? Watts, you recall, are a measurement of electrical power, determined by multiplying voltage times amperage. (Review Unit 93.) A watt hour would be the amount of work done by one watt in an hour. It takes 60 watts to light a 60-watt bulb for one hour. This would amount to 60 watt hours. A kilowatt is simply a thousand watts. It is easier to measure large amounts of electrical power in kilowatts than in watts, just as it is easier to count large sums of money in dollars rather than in pennies. A kilowatt hour is the amount of work done by a thousand watts in an hour. Here is a simple example. If it took two kilowatts to operate all the appliances in a home for an hour, and if the appliances were used for four hours, the total electricity used would be eight kilowatt hours.

LIGHTING CIRCUITS

Most of the lights in your house are connected in a parallel circuit, as in Fig. 96-6. This method is best because if one light goes out, they do not all go out.

Some lights are connected in series as in Fig. 96-7. Christmas tree lights often used to be connected this way. When one bulb burns out, all the others go out because the circuit is broken. With this type

426

Unit 96: Converting Electricity to Light

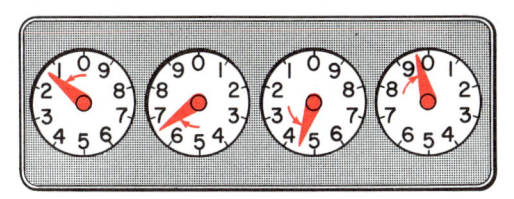

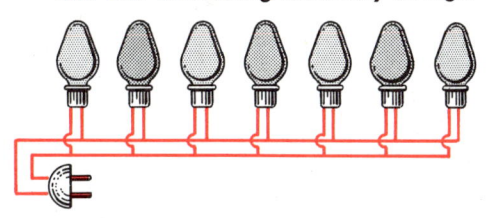

96-4. Dials on a watt-hour meter.

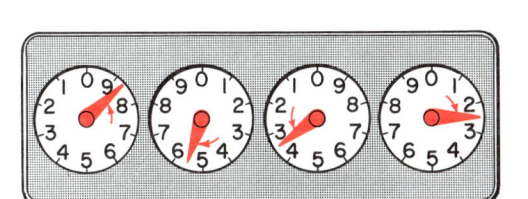

96-5a. The text explains how to read this meter.

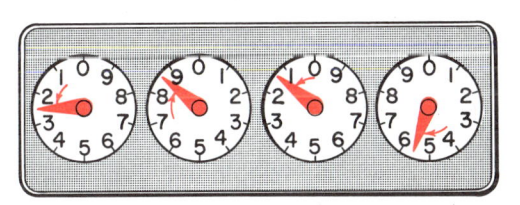

96-5b. Can you read this meter?

96-6. Christmas tree lights connected in parallel.

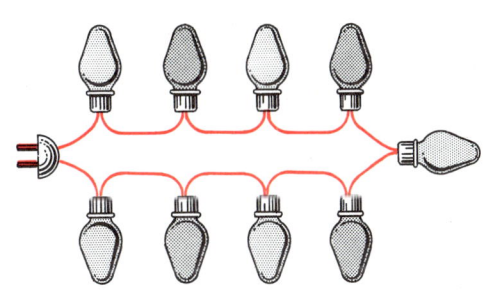

96-7. Christmas tree lights connected in series. What will happen if one light burns out?

of connection there must be just the right number of lights in the circuit. If there are too many lights, they will be dim; if too few, they will be too bright and perhaps burn out.

OTHER LIGHTING METHODS

So far we have been talking about common household light bulbs. There are other ways to change electricity to light. The arc light, for instance, used to be fairly common as a street light and is still used in commercial motion picture projectors. Its light is produced by electricity passing between two carbon electrodes. This causes a great deal of heat as well as light.

Neon and some other gases will glow when an electric current passes through them. The gas is in a glass tube that has a metal electrode attached to each end. An electric current is made to flow through the gas between the electrodes. Different gases glow in different colors. Neon tubes may be bent into many shapes, making them useful for signs.

Fluorescent lights work on a principle similar to neon tubes. A coating on the inside of the tube glows when the current flows between the electrodes.

Smaller tubes filled with a gas called xenon are also used for lighting. These require a high voltage for short periods of time and give off a very bright light. These tubes are used in photographer's flashguns. Because they give off such an intense light, they are used at some airports. In fog and haze, pilots can see them better than other types of lights.

CAUTION: The coating on the inside of fluorescent tubes is dangerous; so when handling, be careful not to break the glass tube.

HOUSE WIRING

More and more electrically operated devices are being used in the home today. Everyone should be aware of some of the important parts of the wiring in a

96-8a. *Typical electric power generating station. This plant operates on natural gas to avoid polluting the air.*

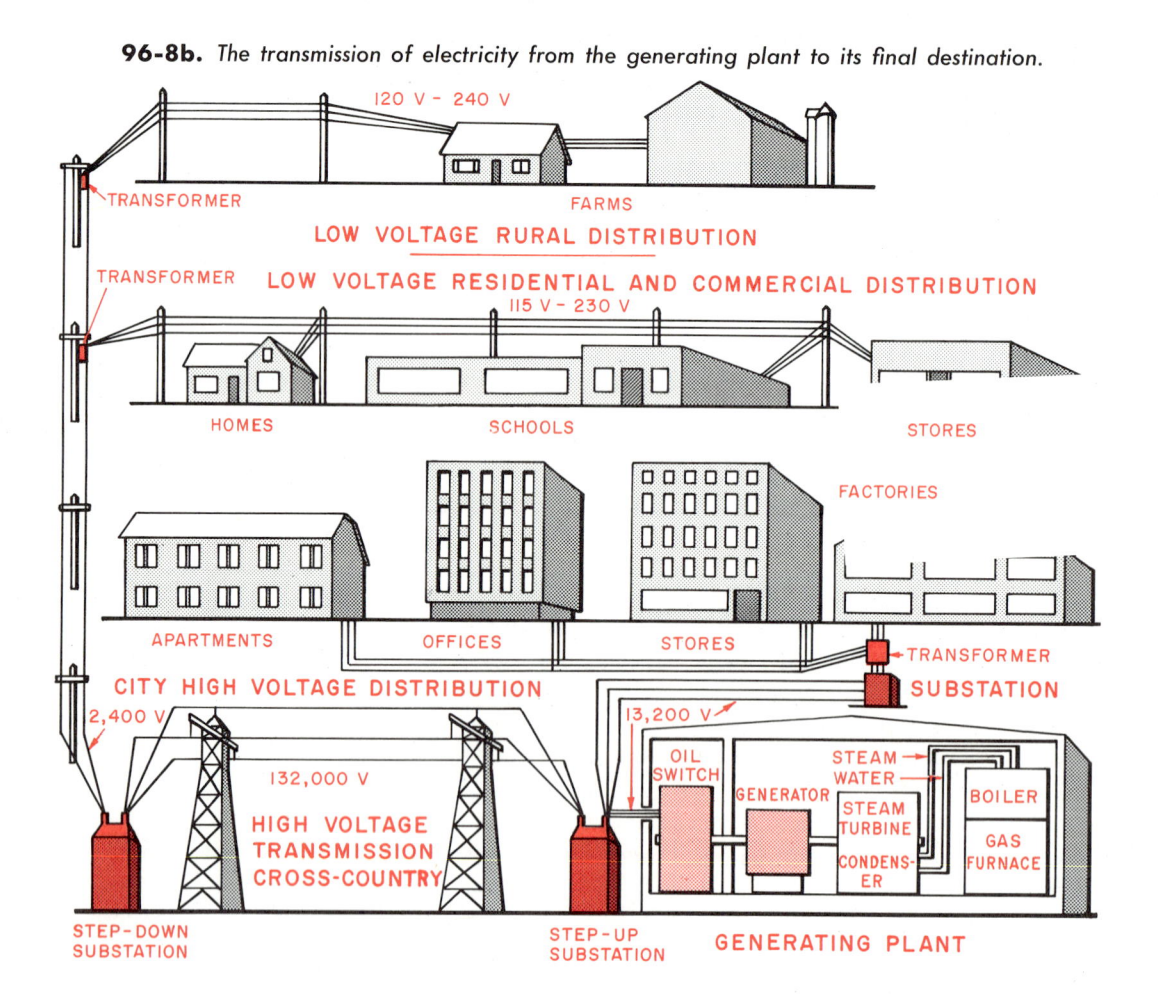

Southern California Edison

96-8b. *The transmission of electricity from the generating plant to its final destination.*

120 V - 240 V
TRANSFORMER
FARMS
LOW VOLTAGE RURAL DISTRIBUTION

TRANSFORMER
LOW VOLTAGE RESIDENTIAL AND COMMERCIAL DISTRIBUTION
115 V - 230 V
HOMES   SCHOOLS   STORES

FACTORIES
APARTMENTS   OFFICES   STORES   TRANSFORMER
CITY HIGH VOLTAGE DISTRIBUTION   SUBSTATION
2,400 V   13,200 V
OIL SWITCH   STEAM WATER
132,000 V   GENERATOR   BOILER
HIGH VOLTAGE TRANSMISSION CROSS-COUNTRY   STEAM TURBINE   GAS FURNACE
CONDENSER
STEP-DOWN SUBSTATION   STEP-UP SUBSTATION   **GENERATING PLANT**

Unit 95: Converting Electricity to Heat

home. CAUTION: Wiring in houses must pass strict inspection when it is installed. A person with limited experience should not attempt to do house wiring. You may be able to make simple repairs and replacements. You should also understand how the electricity gets from the generating plant to the wall outlet.

Electricity is generated in large plants such as shown in Fig. 96-8. The electricity is sent over transmission lines to substations, where the voltage is reduced. From the substation it is sent over power lines to the homes, where it is further reduced for use in lighting and appliances. Fig. 96-9.

At the local substation the electricity is reduced to about 2400 volts. A transformer on the pole outside your house further reduces the voltage to 220–240 for use in your home. In some areas the electrical distribution system is underground. In these areas the wiring and the step-down transformers are both underground, and no wires can be seen overhead.

Electricity is brought into the house by three wires to the watt-hour meter. Fig.

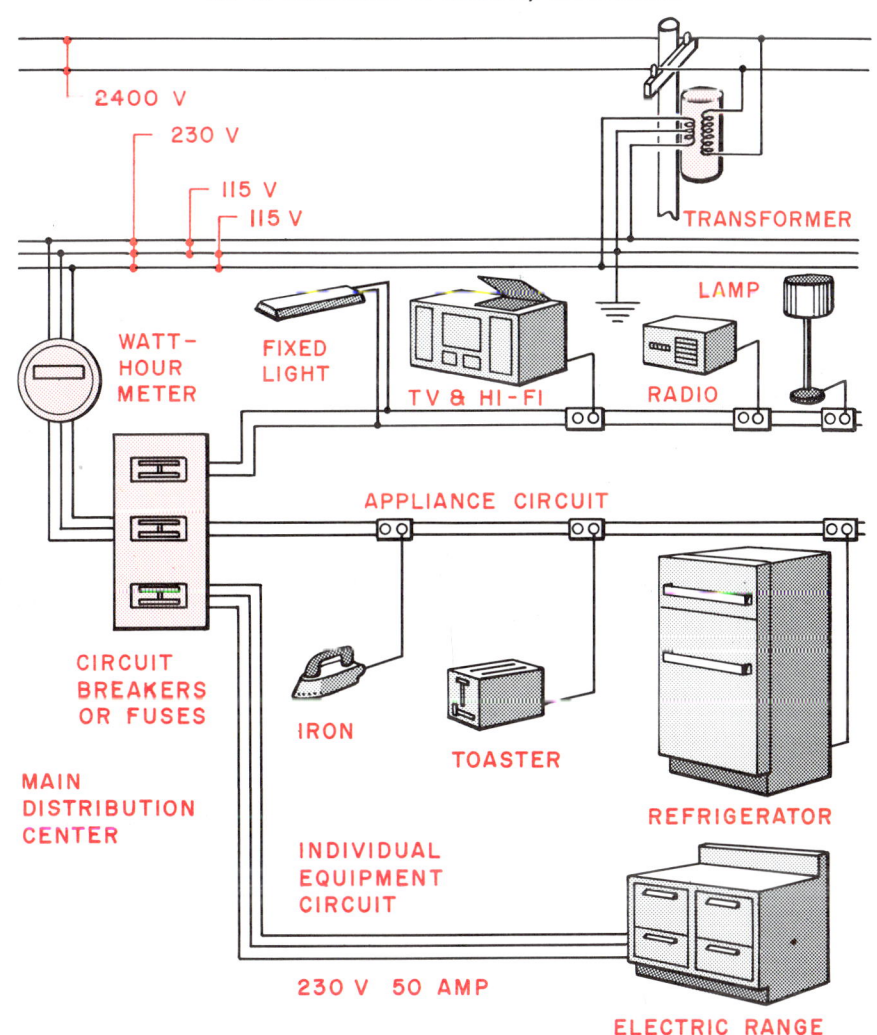

96-9. *Distribution of electricity in the home.*

Part V: Power and Energy

96-3. This meter is usually attached to a service panel which contains circuit breakers to protect the wiring in the house. The service panel also has one main circuit breaker to shut off all power to the house if that is necessary. Some older service panels have fuses such as those shown in Fig. 95-2. When a circuit becomes overloaded, the circuit breaker trips open or the fuse blows. Remember, before resetting the circuit breaker or replacing a fuse, correct the cause of the overload. *Never* replace a fuse with one rated for a higher current.

From the service panel the wiring goes throughout the house. Fig. 96-9.

In homes the branch circuit wiring is one of three kinds. Where local regulations permit, the most common type of wire is nonmetallic sheathed cable (Romex). Other kinds are flexible armoured cable and metal conduit through which wires are placed. Many localities require metal conduit in places where the wire might get damaged, such as in the garage. Fig. 96-10.

Many portable appliances, such as a toaster, are plugged into wall outlets. Fig. 96-11 shows a common duplex outlet and how it would be connected. Outlets are usually wired with No. 12 wire. Several outlets may be connected in parallel.

The lights in a home are usually turned off and on with a wall switch like the one shown in Fig. 96-12. Since lighting circuits do not require as much current as outlet circuits, they are usually wired with No. 14 wire.

When architects draw plans for a building, they indicate where all the lights and outlets will be located. They also show on the floor plan where the service panel and other electrical devices will be located. Typical electrical symbols are shown in Fig. 96-13.

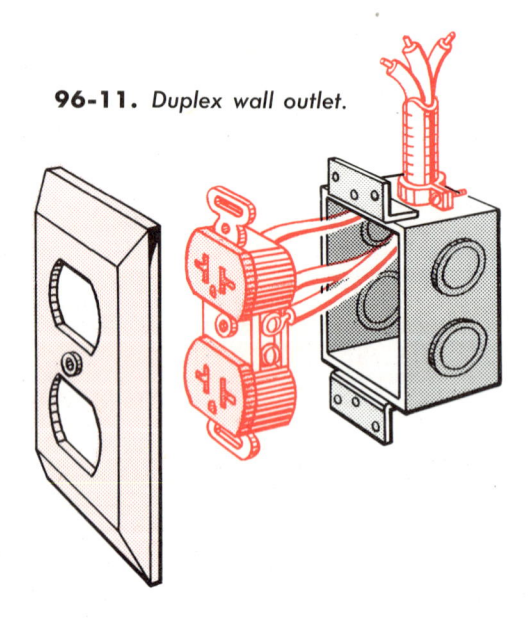

96-10. Three kinds of cable.

ROMEX

FLEXIBLE CONDUIT

CONDUIT

96-11. Duplex wall outlet.

Unit 96: Converting Electricity to Light

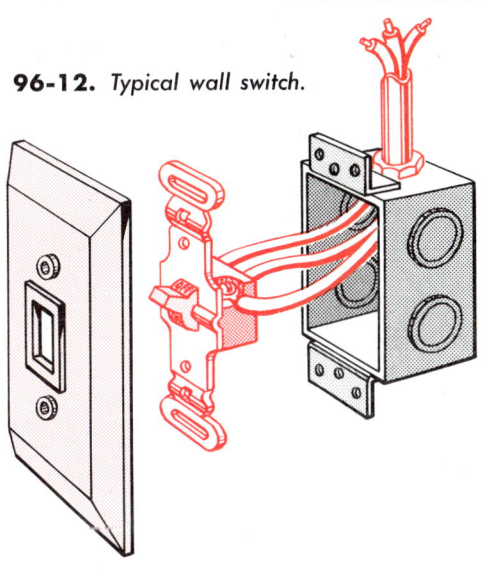

96-12. *Typical wall switch.*

96-13. *Symbols used by architects when drawing house plans.*

SYMBOLS			
	ELECTRIC SWITCH		RECESSED CEILING FIXTURE
	3 - WAY SWITCH		CEILING MOUNTED PENDANT FIXTURE
	DIMMER SWITCH		CUSTOM EXTERIOR HANGING FIXTURE
	TELEPHONE OUTLET		SURFACE MOUNTED CEILING LIGHT
	110 V CONVENIENCE OUTLET		WALL BRACKET LIGHT
	1/2 HOT CONVENIENCE OUTLET		CUSTOM HANGING FIXTURE
	WATERPROOF CONVENIENCE OUTLET		CUSTOM CHANDELIER
	220 V CONVENIENCE OUTLET		HEAT, LIGHT AND EXHAUST FAN
	110 V CONVENIENCE OUTLET (FLOOR MTD)		150 V FLOOD LIGHT
	HOSE BIB		2 TUBE FLUORESCENT LIGHT
	FUEL GAS		
	T V ANTENNA		

431

UNIT 97

Communication

For centuries most information traveled only as fast as people could carry it. The use of carrier pigeons and smoke signals helped a little. However, it was only when people learned to use electricity that fast, effective communication across long distances became possible.

THE TELEGRAPH

The first method of using electric current for communication was the *telegraph.* It was developed about 1837 by Samuel F. B. Morse. In 1844 he sent and received messages between Washington, D.C., and Baltimore, Maryland. The distance was about 40 miles.

His telegraph had an electromagnet with an arm that clicked when a current flowed through the circuit. A spring pulled the arm from the magnet when the circuit was broken. The device to open and close the circuit was called a *key* and was operated like a push button. Fig. 97-1 shows the circuit of a simple telegraph.

Notice that one wire is connected to the symbol for ground. This system needs only one wire because the earth serves as another wire and completes the circuit.

When the key is pressed down, current flows in the circuit. The electromagnet at the other end makes a click. Dots are made by short contact of the key and dashes by longer contact. The International Morse Code is shown in Fig. 97-2.

Today in commercial telegraph systems thousands of messages may be sent over one line in one day. To help speed up these messages, devices other than the hand key are used. Messages may be sent on a machine that looks like a typewriter. It is called a *teletype.* At the receiving end the message may be printed automatically on sheets of paper or a paper tape.

97-1. *Drawing of a simple telegraph circuit.*

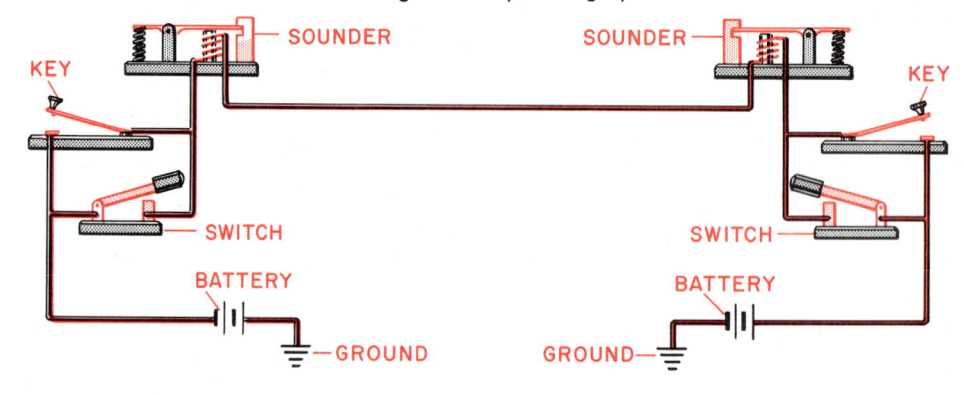

432

Unit 97: Communication

THE TELEPHONE

The second method of using electric current for communication was the *telephone*. It was invented by Alexander Graham Bell. In 1876 he said the first words over a telephone to an assistant in another room. Today we can talk by telephone to almost any place in the world. A cutaway view of a telephone is shown in Fig. 97-3.

Of course, the sound waves do not travel from speaker to listener. Instead, the sound is changed to electricity which travels over the telephone wires. The telephone circuit has four parts. There are a *source of electricity,* a *conductor,* a *transmitter,* and a *receiver.*

The conductor, usually wire, connects telephones in various places.

The transmitter is used for sending messages and the receiver is used for receiving them. When you use a telephone, you talk into the transmitter and listen with the receiver. Fig. 97-4.

Inside the transmitter is a thin metal disc called a *diaphragm*. Attached to the back of this diaphragm is a little cup containing small grains of carbon. Carbon is a conductor of electricity. The amount of current that can flow through the carbon grains depends on how tightly the grains are packed together. The tighter they are packed, the more current will flow.

The receiver also has a thin metal disc inside. It is held in place by a small magnet. Around this magnet are small coils of wire which make an electromagnet. Fig. 97-5.

Here is how the telephone works. When you talk, you make sound waves in the air. These strike the thin metal disc of the transmitter. This disc moves in and out as you talk. As it moves in and out, the disc presses the grains of carbon together. The resistance of the carbon changes as you talk. More or less current flows through the transmitter. The amount of current flowing through the transmitter depends on what you are saying. The sound waves of your voice are changed into electric currents that are sent over the telephone lines.

When the electric current reaches the receiver, it changes the permanent magnet into an electromagnet. The thin metal disc in the receiver moves back and forth

97-2. *International Morse Code.*

INTERNATIONAL MORSE CODE

A •—	N —•	1 •————
B —•••	O ———	2 ••———
C —•—•	P •——•	3 •••——
D —••	Q ——•—	4 ••••—
E •	R •—•	5 •••••
F ••—•	S •••	6 —••••
G ——•	T —	7 ——•••
H ••••	U ••—	8 ———••
I ••	V •••—	9 ————•
J •———	W •——	0 —————
K —•—	X —••—	
L •—••	Y —•——	QUESTION
M ——	Z ——••	••——••
PERIOD •—•—•—	COMMA ——••——	

97-3. *Cutaway view of a telephone.*

AT&T

Part V: Power and Energy

97-4. Cross section of a telephone transmitter.

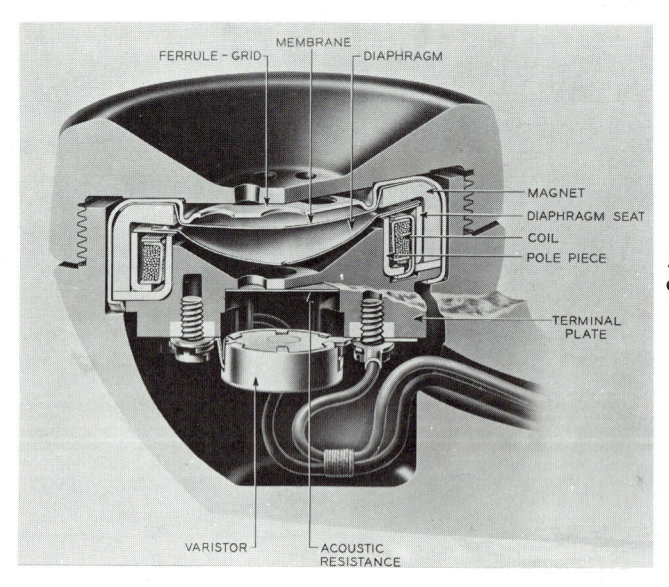

97-5. Cross section of a telephone receiver.

and makes sound waves which your ear hears.

Today many millions of telephones are connected together in one gigantic network. When you dial a telephone number, very complicated switches pick out the correct line and connect your telephone to it. This completes the circuit so that your conversation can take place. Today it is possible not only to dial practically every place in the United States but also to talk with persons at 98 percent of the telephones in the world. Figs. 97-6 and 97-7.

COMPUTERS AND CALCULATORS

From earliest times people have had the need to count. At first they probably counted using fingers and toes. Then devices were invented to help count. One of the earliest was the *abacus*. It is still

Unit 97: Communication

97-6. Men and women working as telephone operators help make it possible to talk with people nearly anywhere in the world.

97-7. The woman in the picture is a frameman for Southwestern Bell. Her work involves soldering new connections, rearranging wires, and doing preventive maintenance for customers' telephones.

used in some parts of the world. Fig. 97-8.

Through the centuries, more and more complex devices were invented to help people count. Today we have two important such devices, the electronic *calculator* and the *computer*. The electronic calculator, such as the one shown in Fig. 97-9 will add, subtract, multiply, and divide, as well as do several other special mathematical calculations. The electronic calculator is made possible by the use of very small electronic circuits such as that shown in Fig. 97-10.

For more complex calculations and for storing information, a computer is used. The computer is a complex electronic machine that rapidly performs routine or complex mathematical and decision-making tasks. The most widely used in the digital computer. This machine can do mathematical problems. Digital computers are also used for decision-making operations.

Computers must be "fed" information in order to solve a problem. The information fed to a computer is called *input*. Electric typewriters, cards, magnetic tape, and paper tape are all ways of feeding a

97-8. An abacus. This was one of the earliest calculating instruments.

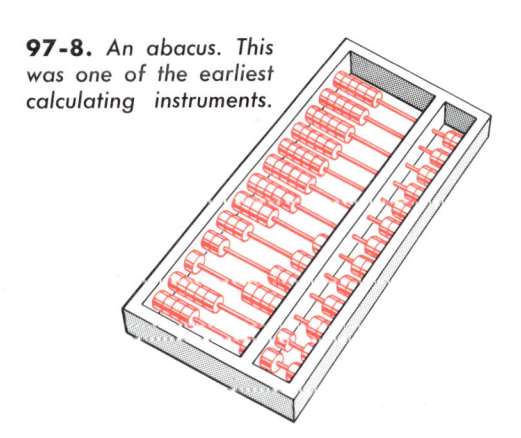

computer information. Magnetic ink is another type of input. This method is used on the bottom of bank checks.

Output from a computer is the finished problem. This is usually some form of printed material like bank checks, typewritten pages, or it may be cards or tape.

435

Part V: Power and Energy

97-9. *A hand-held calculator. The small size is made possible by the use of microelectronic circuit chips such as the one shown in Fig. 97-10.*

97-10. *This is a magnified photograph of a circuit chip in its package. The wires, each about one-third the thickness of a human hair, have been bonded to the circuit pads with an ultrasonic machine.*

Today computers have many and varied uses. They can tell when to pick oranges or when to sell cattle. They are used to keep track of all the items a company has in its warehouse. They calculate the exact orbit of a satellite. Fig. 97-11.

WIRELESS COMMUNICATION

Waves of energy are constantly speeding through space. Sound waves were mentioned earlier. Light also travels by waves. Some of these waves come to us from the sun and the stars. Others start here on earth. There are still other waves which differ in length from light and sound waves. They also differ in the number of vibrations per second, or *frequency.* Electrical devices are used to produce waves of different lengths and frequency. These devices are very complex, but the principle is easy to understand.

When electric sparks jump across a gap, they send electric waves speeding through the air. These waves may be "picked up," or received, at a distant station. The sparks can be made to spell

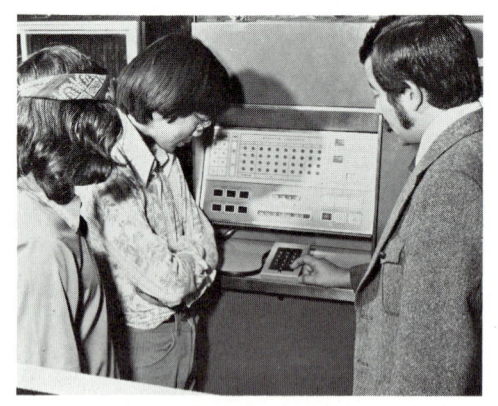

97-11. *An instructor demonstrating computer controls to students*

out a message in dots and dashes as the clicks of the telegraph do.

In voice radio someone talks into a microphone—a device like a sensitive telephone transmitter. Fig. 97-12. The voice makes the air vibrate, and this in turn causes a plate in the microphone to vibrate. The vibrating plate produces an electric current, much the same as in the telephone transmitter. This current is very weak; so it is amplified (strengthened).

Unit 97: Communication

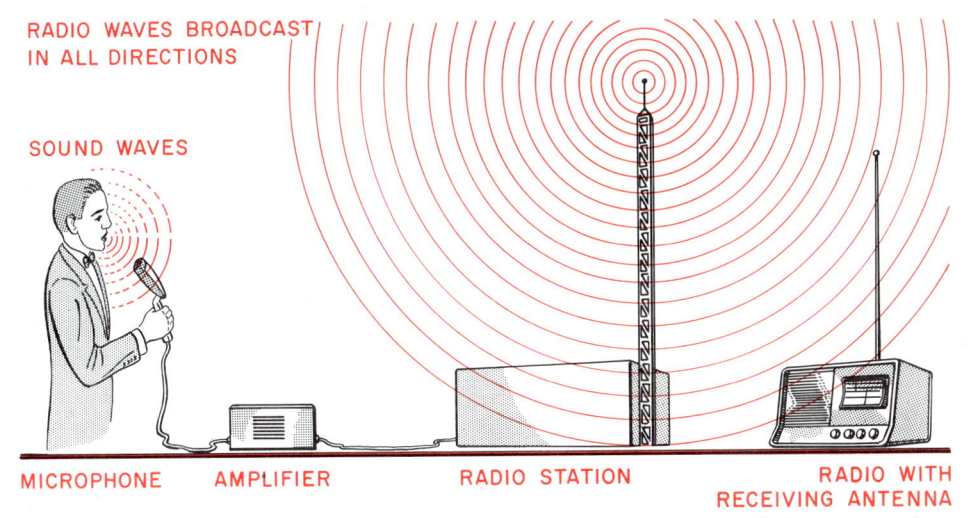

97-12. Wireless communication. The radio waves go out in all directions.

The part of the radio transmitter which actually sends out a signal is called the *antenna*. The amplified current causes radio waves to be sent out from the antenna. These waves, after traveling through the air, are received by the aerial of your radio, and they cause electrical impulses to flow along a wire into the radio. An insulated coil of wire attached to the aerial collects the energy in the receiver. The current collected in this coil alternates within the coil circuit.

Direct current is needed to operate the loud speaker of the receiver. Some of the tubes or transistors furnish this by allowing electricity to travel through them in only one direction. Other tubes or transistors increase the sound volume, and still others increase the range or distance at which the receiver can pick up stations. Fig. 97-13.

You may become interested in radio and want to learn more about it. Many good books on the subject are available. Your teacher or a librarian can probably recommend one. Many times the field of radio, television, and other devices that use vacuum tubes and transistors is called *electronics*.

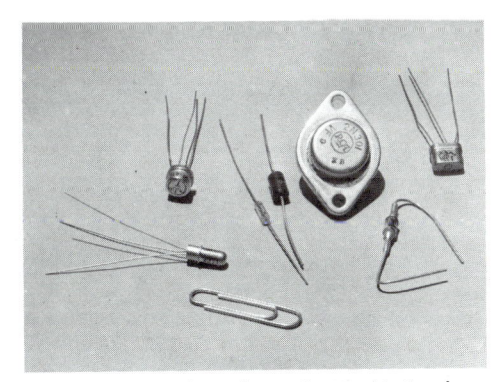

97-13. Examples of transistors. Notice how small they are.

TELEVISION

It is not likely that you will work on a television set in class. However, you will probably be interested in learning something about how television works.

The television camera shoots a scene similar to the way a movie camera does. The camera sends electrical impulses of what it sees to the transmitting station. The transmitting station sends out the sight and the sound to receivers that are within range.

Part V: Power and Energy

The picture tube in a TV receiver has a screen, which is the glass seen by the viewer. This screen is coated with a compound which glows like a fluorescent light when hit by electrons. Each little area glows in brightness according to the amount of light in that part of the picture scanned by the camera. In this way, an image is processed on the screen.

For color television, the camera picks up the scene in color and sends impulses to the transmitter just as in black and white television. The transmitter sends out the signal, which is picked up by the set and changed back to a color scene in the picture tube. Color television is a very complicated field. People who work on television sets must have special training.

DISCUSSION TOPICS

Part 5—Power and Energy
Section 1—Electricity
Unit 89
1. Name three sources of heat for running steam turbines to produce electricity.
2. What is one of the new heat sources being researched today?
3. Name two ways electricity is used for communication.

Unit 90
1. Name the poles of a magnet.
2. What are natural magnets called?
3. Which poles of magnets repel each other?
4. Which poles of magnets attract each other?
5. What is a magnetic field?
6. If a bar magnet is broken in two, what happens?
7. How should magnets be stored?

Unit 91
1. Is lightning a form of static electricity or current electricity?
2. Which is more valuable to people—static electricity or current electricity?
3. What basic law of electricity may be shown by static electricity?
4. What causes a spark to jump from your finger to a water faucet on a cold dry day?
5. Under gasoline trucks there are pieces of leather or chains long enough to reach the road. What do you think is their purpose?
6. What is the unit of measure of electrical pressure?
7. What is the unit of measure of electrical current flow?

Unit 92
1. What is the center of an atom called?
2. What kinds of particles make up the nucleus of an atom?
3. Do protons have a positive or a negative electrical charge?
4. What are the four main parts of a dry cell?
5. Why should you remove dead cells from a flashlight promptly?
6. What are some of the new cells in use today?
7. What type of battery is used in an automobile?
8. What is the electrolyte used in a storage battery?
9. How may the condition of a storage battery be tested?

Units 89-97: Discussion Topics

10. What may be used to clean the terminals of a storage battery?
11. What is the most common type of fuel cell?
12. What, briefly, is a thermocouple used for?
13. What is a common use for electricity generated by pressure on a crystal?
14. How do photographers make use of photoelectric cells?
15. Why are solar cells good sources of power for satellites?
16. On what principle do all generators work?

Unit 93
1. What is an electrical conductor? Name some of these conductors.
2. What is an insulator? Name some insulators.
3. What is the measurement for resistance?
4. See Fig. 93-2. What would you do to find the voltage in a circuit? To find the current? The resistance?
5. How are wires fastened together?

Unit 94
1. What proves that there are magnetic lines of force around a wire carrying electricity?
2. List several uses for a solenoid.
3. What does a transformer do to electrical energy?
4. What does a generator do?
5. What is the difference between direct current and alternating current?
6. What does a motor do to energy?
7. What is the revolving part of an electric motor called?
8. Why can an induction motor be used only on alternating current?

Unit 95
1. Name some household appliances in which electricity is changed to heat.
2. As electrons meet more resistance, will they produce more or less heat?
3. For what purpose are fuses and circuit breakers used?
4. What is the advantage of a circuit breaker over a fuse?

Unit 96
1. Read the meter in Fig. 96-5b. How many kilowatt hours were used?
2. What is a kilowatt?
3. If the lights in your house were wired in a series circuit and one burned out, would anything happen to the others? Explain.
4. Why is tungsten used for the filament of a light bulb?
5. Why must the air be removed from a light bulb?
6. How does electricity get from the generating plant to your home?
7. What three kinds of cable are used in house wiring?

Unit 97
1. Why is only one wire needed for a telegraph system?
2. What is the sound of a dot on the telegraph? A dash?
3. What carries telephone messages through wires?
4. How does a telephone receiver produce sounds?
5. In what part of the telephone are there carbon grains? A permanent magnet?
6. What was one of the earliest calculators?
7. What is one of the main differences between a calculator and a computer?

PART V
Power and Energy

Section 2–Power

Unit 98   Introduction to Power

Unit 99   Power and Machines

Unit 100   Small Gasoline Engines

Discussion Topics

UNIT 98

Introduction to Power

For the cave dwellers the only power available was their own muscles. They traveled, hunted, built shelters, and raised food, all with muscle power. After a time they learned to tame some of the animals they had hunted and put the animals' muscles to work for them.

After many years people learned to use tools to increase their power. The first such tool may have been a tree branch which was used as a lever. Such a lever is an example of what is now called a *simple machine*. The other simple machines include the wedge, the wheel and axle, the pulley, the screw, and the inclined plane.

It is within the last 150 years that we have learned how to add other than muscle power to simple machines. One of the first power sources was the steam engine.

James Watt is given credit for producing the first really workable steam engine about 1800. After that steam was an important source of power for many years. Today steam is still used to power the turbines for producing electricity.

Probably the next great step in the development of power sources came with the invention of the gasoline engine. Dr. Nicholas Otto developed a working engine in 1876. This led to the development of the automobile. Today millions of cars, trucks, and buses use the gasoline engine as a power source.

The steam engine and the gasoline engine are just two of the power sources we use to help us do work. Everyone is familiar with the jet engine on airplanes. Fig. 98-1. Electrical power is used for many

98-1. A DC-10 passenger jet. This airplane can carry up to 380 people.

McDonnell Douglas Corporation

Part V: Power and Energy

jobs which muscle power would not be strong enough to do. Since World War II the use of the atom as a power source has become important. Nuclear reactors generate heat which produces steam to run electrical generators. Nuclear power plants are now quite common in certain parts of the country.

With today's emphasis on conserving our natural resources and environment, there are many people investigating the use of solar power. The sun's rays are used in certain sections of the country for heating and cooling homes and heating the water in swimming pools. Using wind as a source of power for generating electricity is also being researched. The heat within the earth is another possible energy source for the future. All of the power sources and machines were developed to help people do work more easily, better, or faster.

UNIT 99 — Power and Machines

SIMPLE MACHINES

Simple machines make work easier in the simplest way possible. In Unit 98 you learned that there are six simple machines: the lever, the wheel and axle, the inclined plane, the wedge, the screw, and the pulley.

A *lever* is a long bar with something to place it on for support. The place where the lever is supported is called a *fulcrum*. This is where the lever turns. The fulcrum may be at either end of a lever or anywhere between the ends. The *effort* is the amount of push or pull you have to use to move the lever. The *resistance* is what you are moving with the effort. Levers are called *first class, second class,* or *third class* depending on where the fulcrum is. Fig. 99-1 shows the three classes of levers.

A wheel on an axle is a kind of lever. A doorknob, the steering wheel of a car, and an egg beater all use the *wheel and axle*. When you turn the crank on a pencil sharpener, you are using a wheel and axle.

Inclined means sloping or slanted. A plane is a flat surface, such as a floor or the top of a desk. So an *inclined plane* is a sloping or slanted flat surface. A board used to slide a box or barrel from the ground onto a truck is an inclined plane.

Two inclined planes placed back to back form a *wedge*. A chisel is a wedge; so is a knife.

A *screw* may be defined as a wedge that winds around a cylinder. You are familiar with the screws used as fastening devices.

A *pulley* is a simple wheel that is free to turn on an axle. Usually it is a grooved wheel over which a rope is run. Several pulleys may be combined to increase the effort, such as with a block and tackle.

Unit 99: Power and Machines

When you raise a flag by pulling down on a rope, you are using a pulley at the top of the flagpole.

Besides knowing some of the basic machines, today it is becoming necessary to understand the metric units used for measuring power. Presently both the customary units and the metric are being used by people who work with the various power generating devices. Eventually the metric units will become more commonplace. You should know and understand at least the few units given in Fig. 99-2.

WATER POWER

Another way that people learned to make work easier was with water power. A waterwheel placed in a moving stream will change some of the energy of the stream to other types of energy. This energy may be used for grinding grain, sawing wood, or other useful purposes. In the early days of the United States water furnished most of the mechanical power for factories.

People kept looking for improvements. A waterfall, obviously, was a source of more energy than a flowing stream. However, the early waterwheels were not very efficient and could not be used with large waterfalls. Eventually a better waterwheel, called the Pelton wheel, was invented to answer this need. The Pelton wheel was widely used in the western United States.

Today waterwheels or turbines do not supply power directly for running machinery. Instead they change water power to electrical power that can be sent over long distances and used to run machinery. Fig. 99-3.

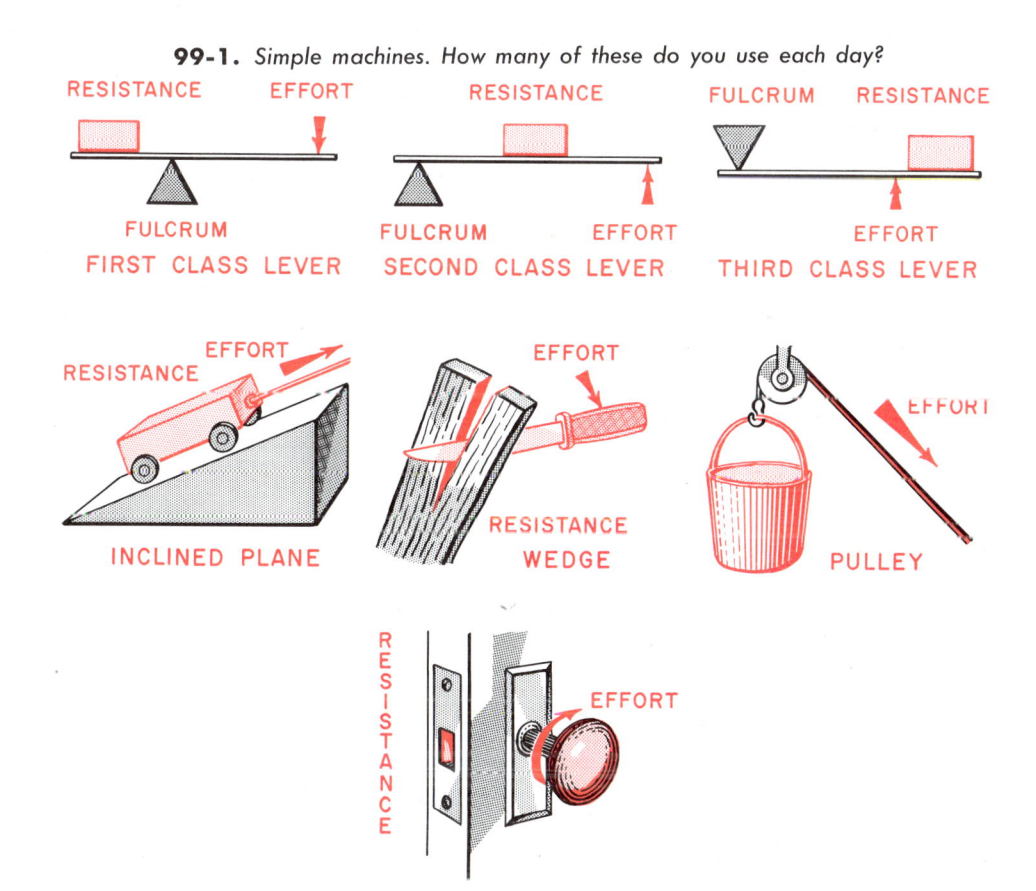

99-1. Simple machines. How many of these do you use each day?

FIRST CLASS LEVER
SECOND CLASS LEVER
THIRD CLASS LEVER
INCLINED PLANE
WEDGE
PULLEY
WHEEL AND AXLE

443

Part V: Power and Energy

Metric Units of Power

Quantity	Unit of Measurement	Symbol
Speed	metre per second	m/s
	kilometre per hour	km/h
Power	watt	W
	kilowatt	kW
Energy	kilowatt-hour	kW·h
Electric Potential Difference	volt	V
Electric Current	ampere	A
Electric Resistance	ohm	Ω
Frequency	hertz	Hz
Pressure	pascal	Pa

99-2. *Metric units used to measure various kinds of power.*

STEAM POWER

The first industrial revolution started when steam power was used to pump water from the coal mines of England. James Watt improved the steam engine which had been invented by Thomas Newcomen.

Not only did the invention of the steam engine change factories, but it also changed transportation. It was the steam engine that George Stephenson used in the locomotive which he invented, and Robert Fulton used it in his steamboat. Until the end of World War II many steam engines were used on the railroads. Now the diesel locomotive has replaced the steam engine.

Steam is still an important source of power. Steam turbines are used for generating much of the electricity used in the United States. The steam turbine is also used for power on large ocean liners. Fig. 99-4.

GASOLINE ENGINES

Probably no invention changed transportation as much as the gasoline engine. About 1876, a German named Dr. Nicholas Otto built what was called a *four-stroke-cycle engine.* It used a gas, not a liquid, for fuel. In 1885 Gottlieb Daimler made an engine that used gasoline as fuel. This is known as an *internal*

99-3. *The water turbine. This is used for changing water power to electrical power.*

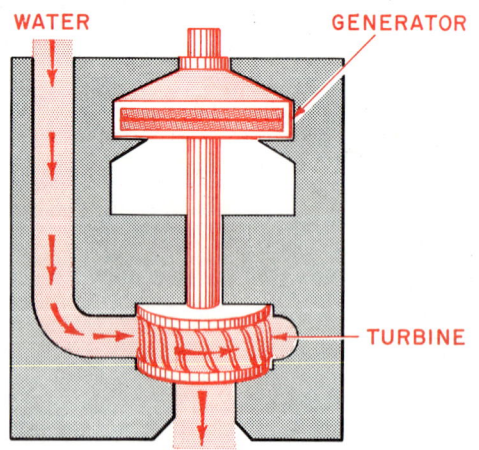

99-4. *The steam turbine. This changes steam power to electrical power.*

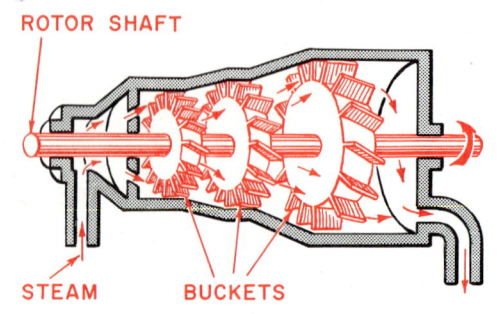

Unit 99: Power and Machines

combustion engine because the fuel is burned inside the engine.

The operation of the four-stroke gasoline engine is quite simple. Fig. 99-5a. During the *intake stroke* the piston moves down. This makes a suction which draws the fuel and air into the cylinder. When the piston reaches the bottom of the stroke, the intake valve closes and makes the chamber airtight.

During the *compression stroke* the piston moves up and compresses the fuel and air. When the piston gets to the top of the stroke, a spark from the spark plug ignites the mixture of fuel and air. The fuel burns very rapidly, almost like an explosion, and produces great force. The force of this explosion pushes the piston down. This downward movement is called the *power stroke*. During this time both the intake and exhaust valves are closed. As the piston gets to the bottom of the power stroke, the exhaust valve opens. The burned gases pass out of the engine through the muffler into the air. During the *exhaust stroke* the piston goes back to the top of the cylinder, forcing the gases out.

When the piston reaches the top of the cylinder during the exhaust stroke, the cycle begins again. When many cylinders are operated together, as in an automobile engine, each cylinder is fired in order to provide smooth operation and more power.

In the United States, the Duryea brothers built the first gasoline automobile in 1893. People at first called this a horseless buggy. A number of people started making automobiles soon after this. Some names of early manufacturers, such as Olds, Ford, and Chevrolet, are still familiar today.

Gasoline engines are made in many sizes. You know how big most automobile engines are. Engines of other sizes provide power for lawn mowers, farm tractors, boats, airplanes, and many other pieces of machinery. Fig. 99-5b shows a small gasoline engine used on a motorcycle.

ROTARY ENGINES

The rotary engine is a new kind of internal combustion engine. It was designed by Felix Wankel of Germany.

99-5a. *The four cycles of a piston engine.*

PISTON ENGINE

1. INTAKE
2. COMPRESSION
3. IGNITION
4. EXHAUST

445

Part V: Power and Energy

99-5b. *Powerful, small gasoline engines have made possible the many types of motorcycles and motor bikes which are popular today.*

Kawasaki Motors Corporation

Today the rotary engine is often called the Wankel engine.

The rotary engine differs greatly from regular piston engines, as shown by Fig. 99-6. It obtains the intake, compression, power, and exhaust cycle by a triangular rotor. This rotor revolves off center, as you can see in Fig. 99-6. The three tips of the rotor remain in snug contact with the chamber walls, dividing the open spaces into three sections. During the intake stroke, fuel and air are drawn into the combustion chamber. As the rotor revolves, the space in the chamber is reduced. This compresses the fuel and air and corresponds to the compression stroke of a four-stroke engine. As the rotor turns with the fuel and air mixture, it passes two spark plugs. One fires a split second after the other to help insure that all the fuel/air mixture is burned. (The more complete the combustion, the fewer pollutants are discharged into the air.) The exploding fuel drives the rotor around to the exhaust portion of the cycle, where the gases are expelled through the exhaust port. See Fig. 99-6. Fig. 99-7 shows the rotor and housing of a typical rotary engine. The only moving parts are the rotor and the crankshaft. There is no vibration as in a piston engine.

99-6. *The four cycles of a rotary engine.*

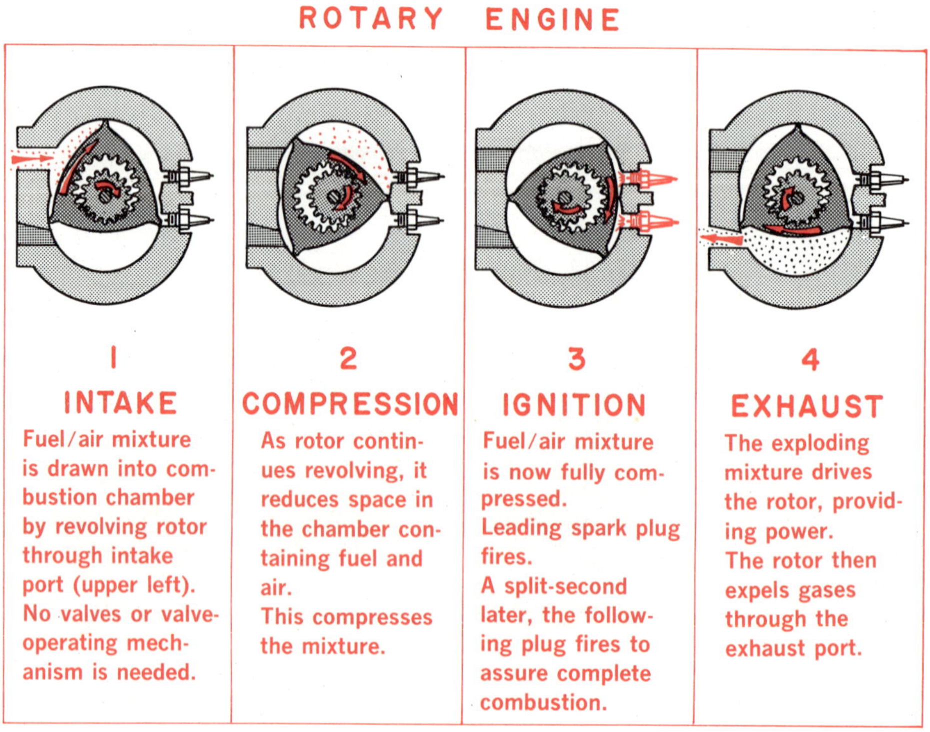

ROTARY ENGINE

1 INTAKE	2 COMPRESSION	3 IGNITION	4 EXHAUST
Fuel/air mixture is drawn into combustion chamber by revolving rotor through intake port (upper left). No valves or valve-operating mechanism is needed.	As rotor continues revolving, it reduces space in the chamber containing fuel and air. This compresses the mixture.	Fuel/air mixture is now fully compressed. Leading spark plug fires. A split-second later, the following plug fires to assure complete combustion.	The exploding mixture drives the rotor, providing power. The rotor then expels gases through the exhaust port.

446

Unit 99: Power and Machines

99-7. Rotor and housing of a rotary engine. Notice the seals on the rotor tips. *Mazda Motor Car Company*

99-8. Fluid power used to operate a piece of machinery. The power is transmitted through these hoses by a liquid under pressure.

The rotary engine is small, lightweight, and inexpensive to manufacture. It can run at high speeds for long periods of time. Some rotary-engine cars are sold in the United States.

DIESEL ENGINES

Another type of internal combustion engine important today is the *diesel engine*. This was invented by Rudolph Diesel. He was trying to make an engine more efficient than the steam engine. He found that if he compressed air enough, it became so hot that it would ignite fuel. To prevent the fuel from exploding too soon, the fuel is shot into the cylinder after the air is compressed. Since the compressed air is hot, as soon as the fuel is shot in (or *injected*) it burns. No spark is needed as on gasoline engines.

At first diesel engines were very large. They had to be used where they could be kept in one place. As the engines were improved, the railroads started using them. Diesels have now replaced all steam locomotives. As the diesel engine was made still smaller, the number of its uses increased. Among other uses, these engines now supply power for trucks, buses, tractors, and boats.

FLUID POWER

Fluid power is becoming very important in industry. Fluid power is really not a source of power like the gasoline engine. Instead it is a way of transmitting power and applying it to do work. Pressure on a fluid will be transmitted equally in all directions. In a hydraulic jack a small force applied to the fluid can lift a heavy object. Today fluid power is used for operating car lifts, power shovels, aircraft wheels, and many other things.

The system that is used today has a pump, a reservoir to store the oil, a pressure relief valve, a control valve, and a cylinder or motor that does the work. These are connected with hoses or pipes to carry the oil. The force is controlled by a valve and is transmitted by the pressure of the oil in the hoses and pipes. Fig. 99-8 shows fluid power equipment for operating a piece of machinery.

Part V: Power and Energy

JET ENGINES

Airplanes powered by jet engines are familiar to everyone today. Giant airliners carrying hundreds of people and tons of freight fly from coast to coast in about five hours. Jet airplanes are relatively new; the first jet was flown by the Germans in 1939. The first jet flight in the United States came during World War II, about 1944. The principle of the jet engine has been known for many years. In the seventeenth century Sir Isaac Newton designed a carriage which was to be driven by shooting a jet of steam out of the back. The principle of a modern fan-jet engine is shown in Fig. 99-9.

The *turbojet* has no propeller. It shoots a jet of hot gases out the back of the engine at high speed. The plane responds by moving forward in much the same way that an inflated balloon shoots forward when you let go of the stem. In the turbojet engine a large amount of air is drawn in the front, compressed, and forced into a combustion chamber. Fuel is shot in and the hot gases try to escape. The only way they can escape is out the back of the engine, and on their way they strike a turbine wheel which drives the compressor, compressing more air. This action continues as long as fuel is injected into the combustion chamber. These engines develop great amounts of power for their weight. They also allow planes to fly higher and faster than propeller-driven airplanes. Fig. 99-10.

McDonnell Douglas Corporation

99-10. *Man working on one of the latest jet engines. These engines are so large, a man can stand up in the intake opening.*

For certain uses, such as for short runway takeoffs and flying below 500 MPH, the propeller has advantages. The turboprop engine combines the jet engine and the propeller. Several turbine wheels are fastened to a shaft. The power of the jet engine is used to turn the shaft, which has a propeller fastened to its end. This jet-propeller combination furnishes about twice as much power as a piston engine of the same weight. Fig. 99-11.

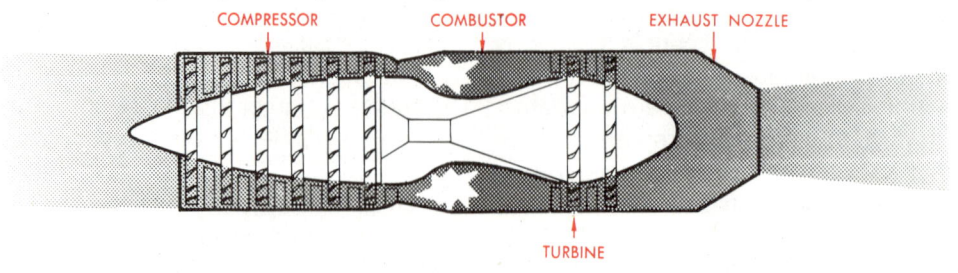

99-9. *The turbojet engine. Hot gases rushing out the exhaust nozzle force the airplane forward.*

COMPRESSOR COMBUSTOR EXHAUST NOZZLE

TURBINE

TURBOJET ENGINE

The prop-jet is one example of how the jet engine can be used to turn a shaft. This principle is used for other purposes than driving a propeller.

Gas turbine engines are now being tested by several automobile manufacturers for use in cars and trucks. Gas turbines differ from those used in airplanes. Instead of fastening extra turbine wheels to the shaft which drives the compressor, a second turbine is fastened to a separate shaft. It is not connected to the first turbine, but is driven by the same gases. This shaft can drive the wheels of a car or locomotive or drive an electric generator.

ROCKETS

One of the fastest growing methods of propulsion is *rocketry*. Many people think of rocket power as new, but the Chinese used rockets in ancient times. For many years rockets were used for military purposes. Then in the nineteenth century, rockets were largely replaced by artillery because it was accurate. However, when the Germans developed the V-2 rocket near the end of World War II, interest was again aroused in the military use of rockets.

About three hundred years ago Sir Isaac Newton, the great British physicist, discovered a law of nature that explains why rockets and jet engines work. This principle is known as Newton's third law of motion. It says: For every action there is an equal and opposite reaction.

Gas rushes out the rear of the rocket. That is the action. The rocket surges forward. That is the reaction. The action and the reaction are opposite, obviously, because the gas and the rocket move in opposite directions. They are also equal, as the law states, but this is harder to understand because other forces, such as gravity, are also acting on the rocket.

The important idea to remember is that since they are equal, the speed of the rocket depends on the speed of the gas leaving the rear of the rocket. This is called the *exhaust velocity* and is related to the heat of the burning fuel. Rockets carry their own oxygen as well as fuel so that they can operate in outer space, where there is no air. Fig. 99-12.

ALTERNATE SOURCES OF MOTOR POWER

With the interest in improving the environment and reducing pollutants, several other forms of power are being investigated. One that has produced great interest from the early days of the automobile is steam power. So far the steam car has not proven practical, even though several

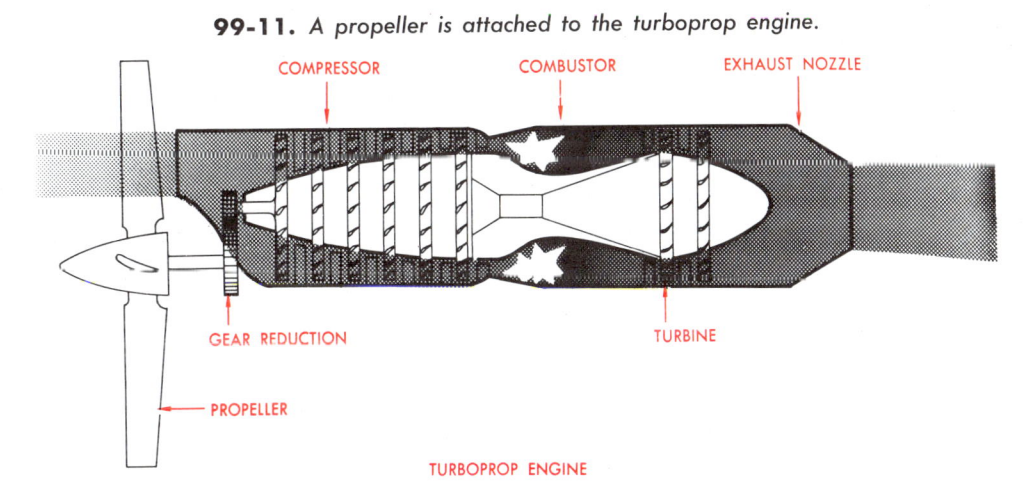

99-11. *A propeller is attached to the turboprop engine.*

COMPRESSOR COMBUSTOR EXHAUST NOZZLE

GEAR REDUCTION TURBINE

PROPELLER

TURBOPROP ENGINE

Part V: Power and Energy

99-12. A Saturn rocket lifts off the launching pad at the Kennedy Space Center.

companies have spent millions of dollars on development work. One of the main problems which must be overcome is the time it takes to produce the steam in a cold engine.

One other form of power that does show potential, and is being used in many

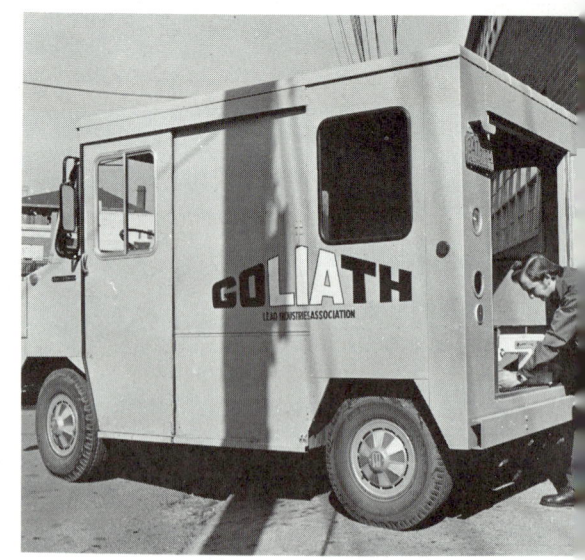

99-13. An electric-powered delivery vehicle.

delivery vehicles, is electric power. Electric-powered vehicles are equipped with batteries, usually lead storage cells. The batteries may be recharged periodically with a charger similar to that used for charging automobile batteries. One example of an electric-powered vehicle is shown in Fig. 99-13. This vehicle is powered by lead acid batteries that supply 112 volts. The batteries can operate the vehicle for 20 miles at 50 miles per hour or 50 miles at 20 miles per hour. Some problems with electric vehicles are the weight of the batteries and the space they require. With further development of the fuel cell and with the diminishing supplies of other forms of energy, the electric vehicle may become popular.

ATOMIC POWER

One of the newest forms of power is developed by using *uranium atoms*. Except that it is more complicated, using atoms for energy is much like using coal or oil. Atomic energy is first changed into heat. This is done in a device called a *reactor*. Fig. 99-14. Then, a liquid goes through pipes and carries the heat from the reactor to a boiler. There the heat is

Unit 99: Power and Machines

used to turn water into steam. The steam runs a turbine to generate electricity.

The atoms of uranium are changed into heat inside a special area that keeps radioactive materials from getting into the air. This *reactor area* has thick walls of steel and several safety devices to keep the reaction from happening faster than is safe. The air around atomic power plants is constantly checked to insure that no radioactivity gets into the air.

Atomic power plants discharge few pollutants into the air. However, there is a problem with the used radioactive material. When it can no longer be used to generate steam, much of the material is remanufactured into material to be used over again in other plants. Some material is waste and must be disposed of where it is of no danger to the public. This waste is usually buried underground in atomic disposal areas where it will remain for many years.

There are several atomic power plants in the United States that are generating power for homes and industry.

SUN POWER

The basic source of almost all energy is the sun. Without the sun neither plant nor animal life would be possible on earth. The sun produces tremendous amounts of energy, of which only a very small part is used. That part is mainly used by plants. Most of the sun's energy is wasted.

People have been looking for ways to use the sun's energy for a long time. Mirrors were used many years ago for starting fires. Recently mirrors have been used for boiling water and melting metals. Fig. 99-15. The energy of the sun is also

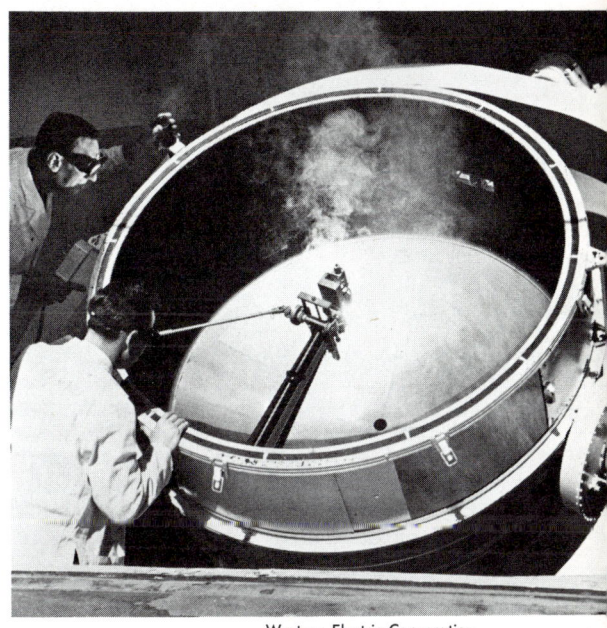

Western Electric Corporation
99-15. Melting metal with a large sun furnace.

99-14. A boiling-water nuclear reactor for generating electricity.
Iowa Electric Light and Power Co.

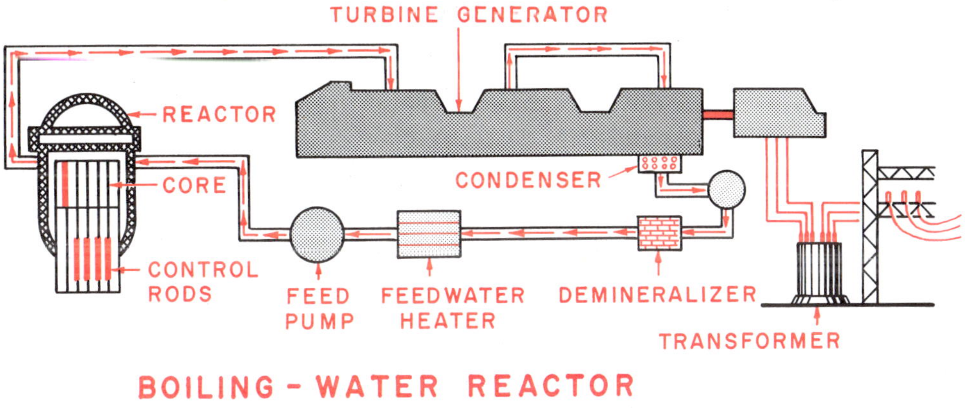

BOILING - WATER REACTOR

Part V: Power and Energy

99-16. *Sun-powered house. Panels to collect heat from the sun are set at a 45° angle to the ground. Heat is stored in water tanks. Electricity is stored in storage batteries housed in small building at the right of the house.*

Lead Industries Association

used to make electricity. This is done with the *solar cell*. This source of electricity is used for powering many of the satellites that are in orbit.

With the diminishing supply of fossil fuels, many scientists are looking for other ways of heating and cooling homes. A home using solar energy is shown in Fig. 99-16. This home was built to test the use of sun power for heating, cooling, lighting, and for running the many appliances we use in the home. Someday many homes and industries may make use of energy from the sun. More information on solar power is found in the Technology Reports at the end of this book.

UNIT 100 — Small Gasoline Engines

Almost everywhere you look today there is some machine that makes use of a small gasoline engine. From lawn mowers to motorcycles, from cement mixers to portable electrical generators, the small engine has many uses. Fig. 100-1a.

The small gasoline engine operates on the same principles as the larger automobile engines. A fuel/air mixture is taken into a cylinder, compressed, and ignited to produce the force to drive the piston down, creating power. This explosive *up and down* power of the *piston* is converted into rotary power by using a *connecting rod* to connect the piston to the *crankshaft*, which rotates. Most small engines in use are either *two-stroke cycle* or *four-stroke cycle* engines.

FOUR-STROKE CYCLE ENGINE

A cutaway view of a four-stroke engine is shown in Fig. 100-1b. You can see that the cylinder block is a casting, usually of aluminum for lightness, with a hole for the piston. The piston is connected to the crankshaft by a connecting rod. Small engines may be either air cooled or water cooled. Outboard motor engines are water cooled. Motorcycle engines are air cooled. In Fig. 100-1b you will notice fins around the part of the casting the piston

Unit 100: Small Gasoline Engines

moves in. These fins help to keep the engine cool.

Fastened to the top of the cylinder block is the head. On air-cooled engines the head also has fins to help in cooling. The head has a threaded hole into which the *spark plug* is placed.

The piston moves up and down in the cylinder and is attached to the connecting rod, which, in turn, is attached to the crankshaft. The piston has several grooves cut around it into which *rings* are placed. The rings help to seal the piston

100-1a. *Typical small gasoline engine.*

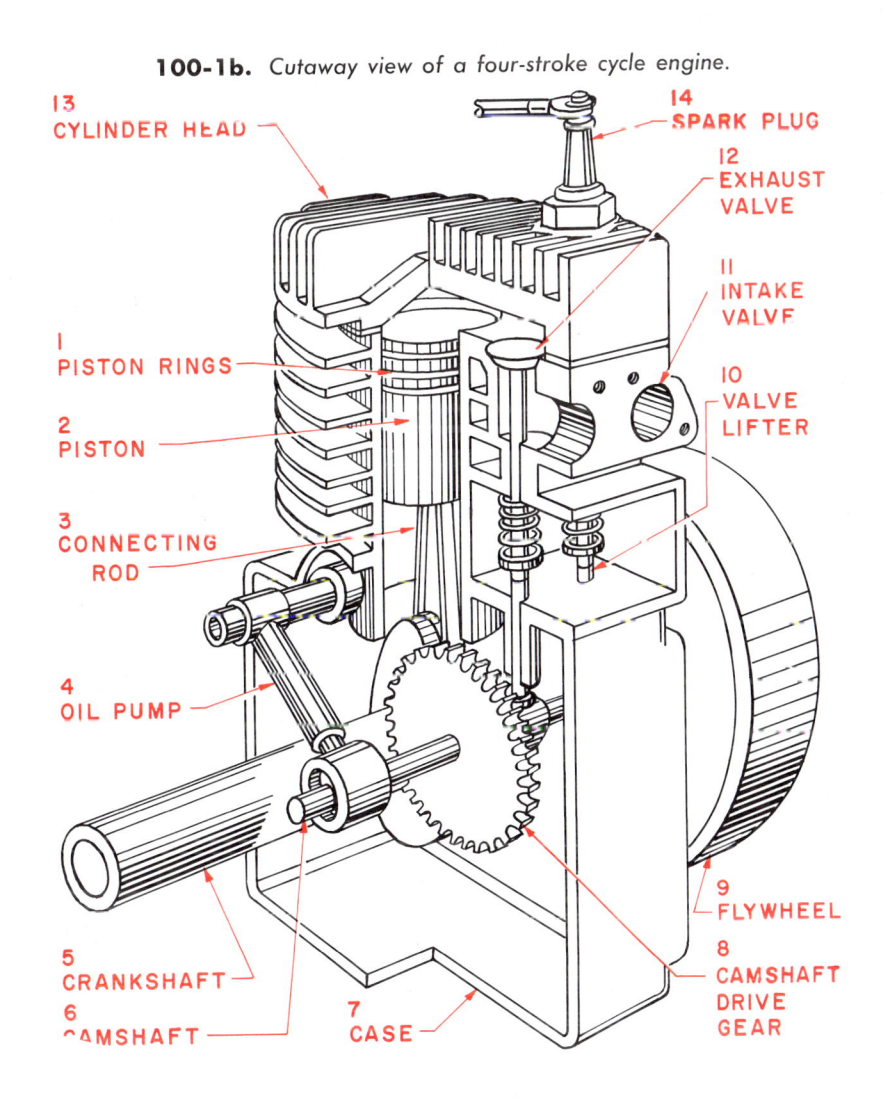

100-1b. *Cutaway view of a four-stroke cycle engine.*

1. PISTON RINGS
2. PISTON
3. CONNECTING ROD
4. OIL PUMP
5. CRANKSHAFT
6. CAMSHAFT
7. CASE
8. CAMSHAFT DRIVE GEAR
9. FLYWHEEL
10. VALVE LIFTER
11. INTAKE VALVE
12. EXHAUST VALVE
13. CYLINDER HEAD
14. SPARK PLUG

453

Part V: Power and Energy

to the cylinder wall and to keep gases and oil from escaping.

The crankshaft has an offset so that as the piston moves up and down it causes the crankshaft to turn. The crankshaft is in the *crankcase,* which also houses the lubricating oil. All the moving parts are lubricated from the crankcase.

The *camshaft* operates from a timing gear from the crankshaft. Fig. 100-1b. On the camshaft are two *cams* that open the valves as they turn. A heavy spring closes the valves. Fig. 100-2. There are two valves, intake and exhaust. The intake valve opens to allow the fuel/air mixture into the cylinder. The exhaust valve opens to allow the burned gases to escape. Fig. 100-2 shows the operation of a small four-stroke cycle engine.

TWO-STROKE CYCLE ENGINE

The two-stroke engine operates without the valves and the camshaft that are needed for the four-stroke engine. Instead, the two-stroke engine uses a *reed valve* to control the entry of the fuel mix-

100-2. Operation of a four-stroke cycle gasoline engine.

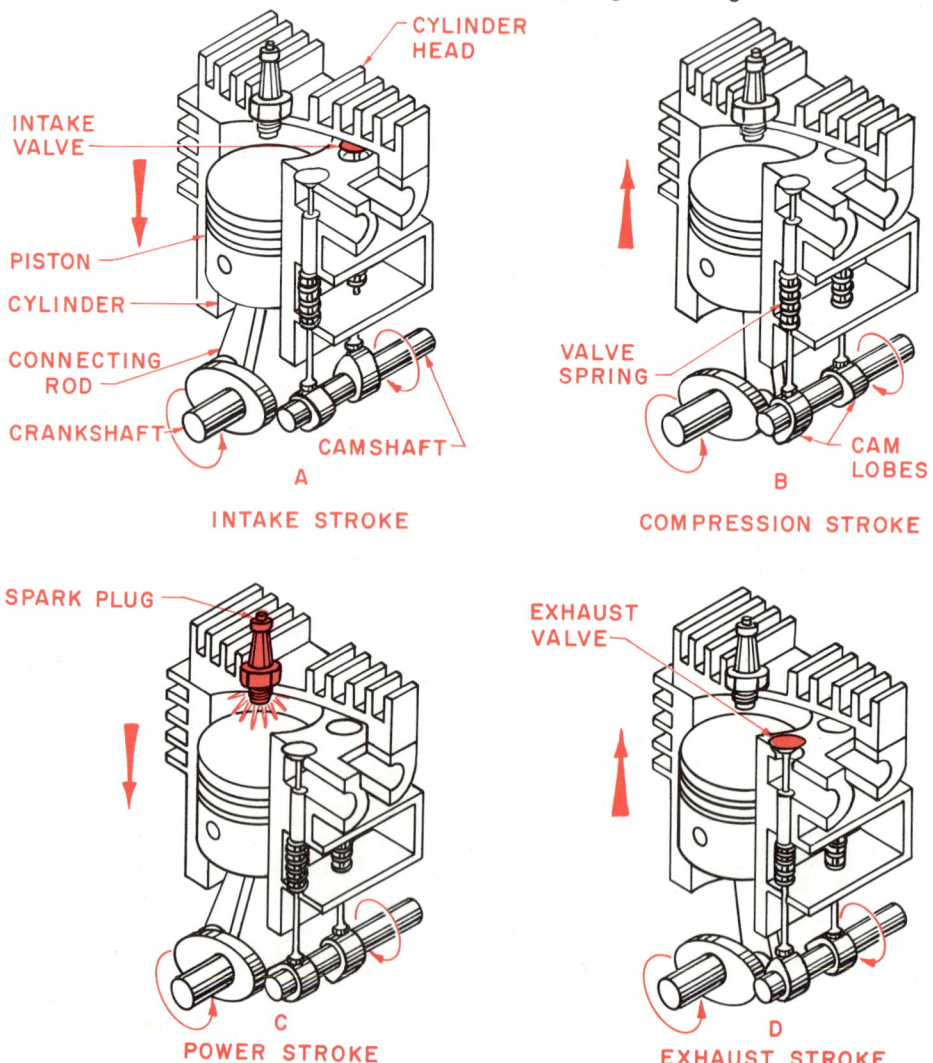

Unit 100: Small Gasoline Engines

ture into the crankcase. Fig. 100-3, A. The crankcase houses the connecting rod and crankshaft as it does with the four-stroke engine. The operation of the two-stroke cycle engine is shown in Fig. 100-3. The fuel mixture is drawn into the crankcase through the reed valve on the compression stroke. When the piston is at the top of the cylinder, the mixture is ignited by the spark plug. On the power stroke the piston is forced down past the exhaust port and the intake port. This allows the exhaust gases to escape and the new fuel mixture to enter the cylinder from the crankcase. Fig. 100-3, D.

OPERATION OF GASOLINE ENGINES

There are two main systems necessary for the operation of any gasoline engine. These are the *fuel system* and the *ignition system*.

Fuel System

The fuel system must provide the air/fuel mixture for combustion. The basic parts of the fuel system include a gasoline tank to store the fuel, a fuel line to carry the fuel to the carburetor, and the carburetor. The fuel must get from the fuel tank to the carburetor before it can be burned. This is done by one of three methods. Fig. 100-4. In the gravity system the fuel tank is placed higher than the carburetor and the fuel flows by gravity. In the suction system the fuel tank is usually placed below the carburetor and the fuel is *sucked* from the tank to the carburetor by the intake stroke of the piston. The forced feed system uses a *fuel pump* that sucks the fuel from the tank and pumps it to the carburetor. This type of fuel feed system is used on automobiles. Small gasoline engines use either gravity or suction feed.

After the fuel arrives at the carburetor, several important things happen. First the fuel is *atomized*, or broken up into small droplets. Then the fuel is moved and mixed with air in the ratio of about 15 parts of air to 1 part of fuel. After the fuel and air are mixed, the carburetor directs the fuel/air mixture into the cylinder

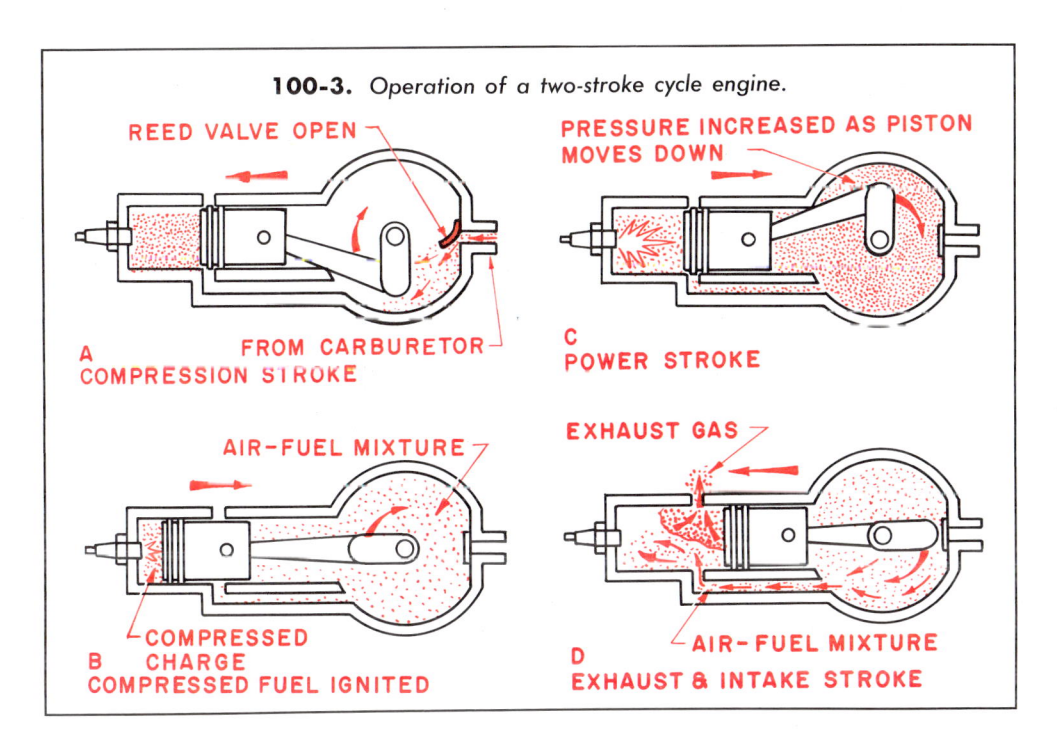

100-3. Operation of a two-stroke cycle engine.

A — COMPRESSION STROKE — REED VALVE OPEN — FROM CARBURETOR

B — COMPRESSED CHARGE COMPRESSED FUEL IGNITED — AIR-FUEL MIXTURE

C — POWER STROKE — PRESSURE INCREASED AS PISTON MOVES DOWN

D — EXHAUST & INTAKE STROKE — EXHAUST GAS — AIR-FUEL MIXTURE

455

Part V: Power and Energy

where it is burned. The essential parts of a carburetor are shown in Fig. 100-5.

CARBURETOR

Fuel enters through an intake valve and flows into a storage area called a *float chamber.* This chamber has a float in it made of hollow brass. When fuel comes into the chamber, the float rises and closes the intake valve. As fuel leaves the chamber, the float drops down. The intake valve opens again, allowing more fuel to enter the float chamber.

Next to the float chamber is the *air horn,* which is the carburetor proper. The air horn is a hollow metal tube connected to the air cleaner at one end and to the engine at the other end. The air cleaner is important because it filters out dust and dirt from the incoming air. If there were no air cleaner, the dust and dirt would be drawn into the engine, causing excessive wear. There are various kinds of air cleaners, grouped into *dry* types and *oil-bath* types.

Air coming through the air horn mixes with fuel from the float chamber to create the proper fuel/air mixture for combustion. This may be done in various ways. Some air horns have a narrower diameter near the middle. This narrow area is called a *venturi.* As air passes through the venturi, its speed increases and its pressure decreases. The decreased pressure around the main discharge hole (Fig. 100-5) causes the fuel to spray out in a fine mist.

The same result can be obtained in some small engines without a venturi. A tube runs from the float chamber to the air horn. When the piston in the cylinder moves down, it causes a partial vacuum in the cylinder. Outside air pressure forces the air through the carburetor (air horn) to create the fuel/air mist.

Between the venturi and the lower part of the carburetor is the *throttle valve* (butterfly). When an engine is idling, the throttle valve is closed, and only a small amount of air flows past it. In fact, the air flow is so small that it cannot pick up enough fuel to keep the engine running.

To supply fuel when an engine is idling or running at low speeds, another fuel passage is used. This passage is a tube which connects with the carburetor below the throttle valve. Fig. 100-5. At higher speeds, the throttle valve is opened, and it does not interfere with the flow of air and fuel.

A cold engine cannot be started on the same fuel mixture it uses for running. It must have a *rich* mixture; that is, one that has more than the normal amount of fuel in the air. To create a rich mixture, a

100-4. *Three fuel feed systems.*

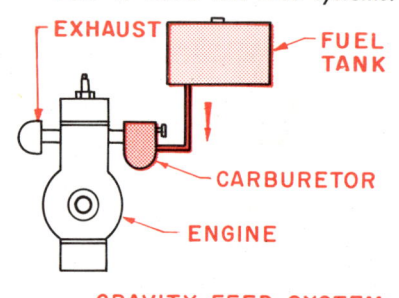

GRAVITY FEED SYSTEM

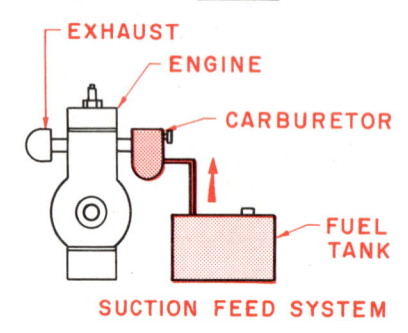

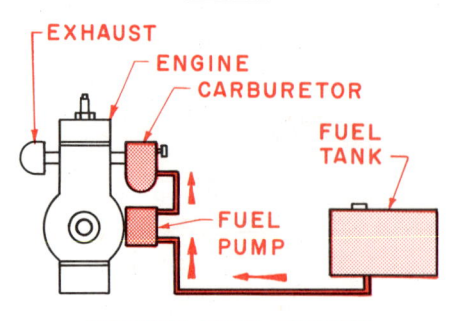

SUCTION FEED SYSTEM

FORCED FEED SYSTEM

Unit 100: Small Gasoline Engines

choke valve is used. The choke valve is located in the upper part of the air horn. By closing the choke, air intake is reduced and a vacuum is formed in the carburetor. The vacuum increases the flow of fuel into the carburetor, creating the rich mixture needed for easy starting.

Once the engine is running, the choke valve should be opened to allow more air to enter. If the choke valve on a small engine remains closed too long, raw fuel will enter the combustion chamber. The raw gasoline can damage the cylinder walls.

Between the carburetor and the cylinder openings is the *intake manifold*. On a four-stroke engine, fuel and air come through the carburetor into the manifold. The fuel/air mixture then passes through a valve and into the combustion chamber. On a two-stroke engine the carburetor is connected with the crankcase. The fuel/air mixture enters the crankcase from the carburetor through a reed valve. From the crankcase, the mixture enters the combustion chamber through ports that open when the piston is at the bottom of the stroke. Fig. 100-3, D.

Four-stroke engines use plain gasoline. Two-stroke engines use a mixture of gasoline and oil, usually 25 parts gasoline to 1 part oil.

Ignition System

An internal combustion engine must have a way of igniting the air/fuel mixture to make it burn. This is done with the aid of the ignition system. The ignition system on most small gas engines is a magneto system. (At this point it might be well to review a few basic electrical principles from Unit 94.)

The magneto system consists of a few very important parts. There is a *rotor*, which is a strong magnet that revolves inside the armature. Fig. 100-6. The *armature* is really a coil with metal laminations. The *condenser* stores electrical energy during the time the breaker points open. The *coil* is really a step-up transformer to change low voltage to the high voltage needed to make the spark at the spark plug. The *breaker points* open and close to interrupt the primary circuit. The *spark plug* produces the spark in the cylinder to ignite the fuel.

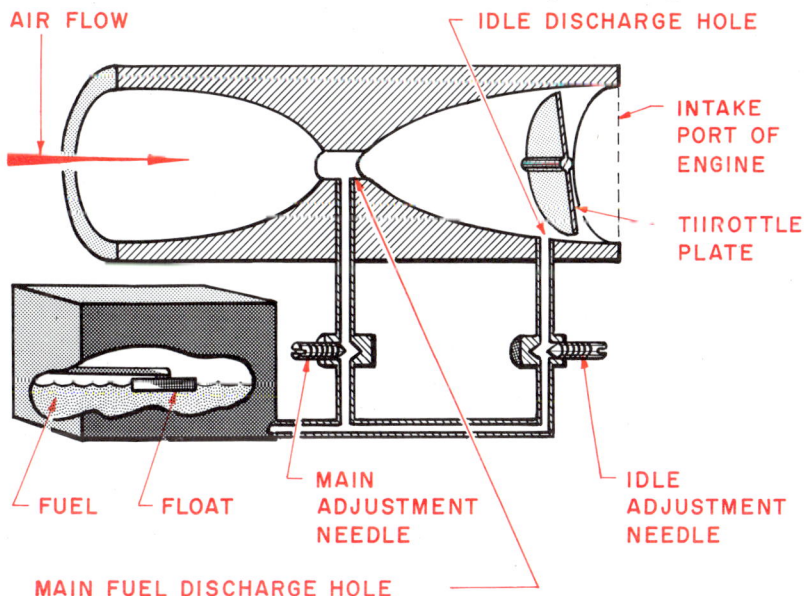

100-5. Parts of a carburetor on a small gasoline engine.

Part V: Power and Energy

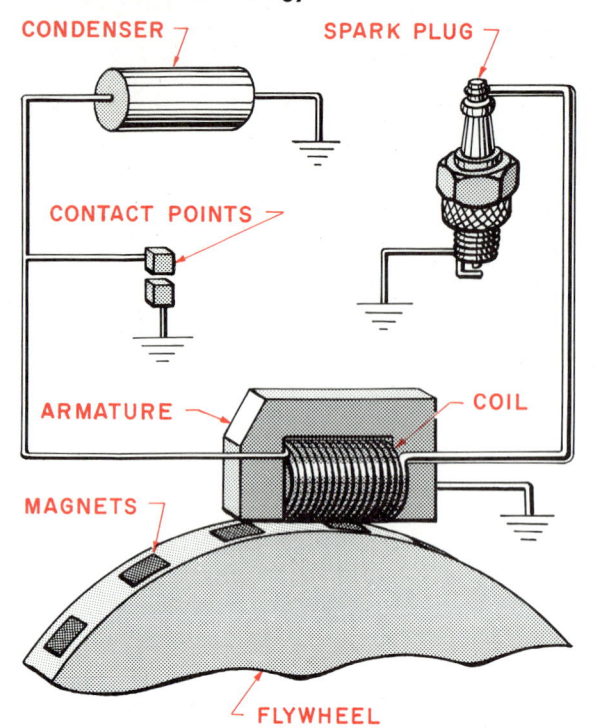

100-6. *Typical magneto ignition system.*

100-7. *Schematic of the primary and secondary circuits of the magneto ignition system.*

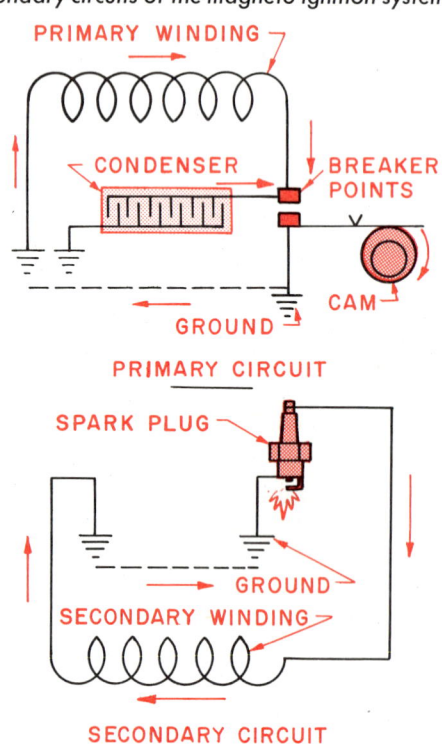

The *primary circuit* consists of the large primary windings on the coil, the breaker points, and the condenser. The *secondary circuit* consists of the fine windings on the coil and the spark plug. Fig. 100-7.

As the rotor revolves inside the laminations of the armature, it causes a magnetic area of force that cuts the coil of the armature. In this way a voltage is built up in the primary circuit.

When the process begins, the breaker points are closed. The current flows freely through the primary circuit. At just the right moment, when the primary current is high, a cam opens the breaker points. This causes the magnetic field in the primary circuit to collapse. In turn, a current begins to flow in the secondary circuit.

The amount of current flow depends partially on the proportion between the number of turns on the primary circuit and the number of turns on the secondary circuit. A small voltage in the primary may be increased to as high as 30 000 volts in the secondary circuit. This high

Unit 100: Small Gasoline Engines

100-8. Checking oil level in a four-stroke cycle engine.

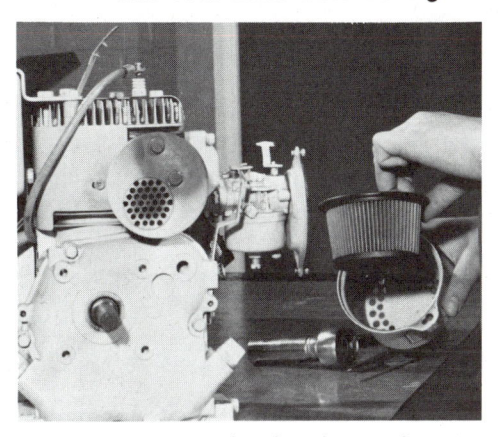

100-9. Removing the dry element from an air cleaner.

voltage in the secondary circuit causes a spark to jump across the terminals of the spark plug.

A condenser in the primary circuit stores electrical energy. Without a condenser, an arc would jump across the breaker points as they opened. With the condenser, however, the electrical energy is temporarily stored in the primary circuit just as the breaker points open.

SMALL ENGINE MAINTENANCE

Small engines, like automobiles, require periodic maintenance and repair. Small engines are built to provide trouble free operation. To insure this, the engine should be used according to the instruction manual, and certain routine maintenance should be performed. The instructions should indicate what fuel is to be used. If the engine is a two-stroke, a mixture of fuel and oil must be used. If the engine is four-stroke, *do not* use a fuel and oil mixture.

There are two important safety rules to follow when working on engines:

1. Work on an engine and add fuel or oil *only* when it is stopped.
2. Keep all flames and heat away from gasoline.

The routine maintenance which should be done includes checking and changing oil, cleaning the air cleaner, and servicing the spark plug. Two-stroke engines receive their lubrication from the oil in the fuel mixture and need no additional lubrication. Four-stroke engines are lubricated with oil in the crankcase. The level of the oil should be checked each time before the engine is used. Check the oil level by taking out the oil plug. Fig. 100-8. If the oil runs out, the level is high enough. If not, oil should be added.

Air entering the carburetor first passes through the air cleaner. The cleaner removes dirt from the air to prevent clogging the carburetor or damaging the engine. Periodically the air cleaner must be removed and cleaned. One type of air cleaner, the dry element, is shown in Fig. 100-9. The air cleaner is removed from the engine. Then the element is removed from the air cleaner. Tap the element sharply on a flat surface to dislodge the dirt. This element may also be cleaned with compressed air.

The spark plug supplies the spark needed to ignite the fuel. It too needs periodic cleaning for best operation. The burning fuel leaves a deposit on the spark plug which must be removed. The deposit may be removed by scraping or with a wire brush. If the electrodes are badly burned or the insulator cracked, the plug should be replaced. If you are going to

Part V: Power and Energy

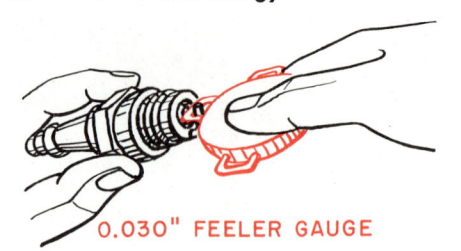

100-10. Adjusting a spark plug with a feeler gauge.

reuse the plug, set the gap to the manufacturer's specifications by using a feeler gauge. Fig. 100-10. Check the spark plug wire to be sure that it is not cracked and that the terminal going to the spark plug is clean.

Probably the most common complaint with a small engine is failure to start. If an engine fails to start, there are certain things to check for:

1. Check to see that there is fuel in the tank.

2. Check for spark. Remove the spark plug wire from the spark plug. Hold it close to the frame of the engine and turn the flywheel. There should be a spark. If not, check the breaker points, the coil, and the condenser.

3. Check to see if there is compression. Pull the starter until there is strong resistance. Then release it and see if the engine rebounds. If there is not strong resistance or if the engine does not rebound, check to see that the spark plug is tight.

4. Check to see that there is gas to the carburetor. Remove the spark plug and crank the engine a few times. There should be gas in the cylinder by now. If there is not, check to see if the fuel line is plugged or if the fuel valve is turned off.

5. Check to see that the engine is not flooded. This can usually be determined by a strong smell of raw gasoline. If the engine is flooded, open the choke and turn off the fuel. Crank the engine until it starts; then open the fuel valve.

Remember: Be sure to follow the manufacturer's directions for the operation and repair of any engine.

DISCUSSION TOPICS

Part 5—Power and Energy
Section 2—Power
Unit 98
   1. Name four of the simple machines.
   2. What are some of the power sources used to run machines today?
Unit 99
   1. What is a lever? An inclined plane?
   2. Who invented the steam engine?
   3. Describe the operation of a four-stroke gasoline engine.
   4. What are some advantages of a rotary engine over a piston engine?
   5. Briefly describe how a turbojet engine works.
   6. What is done with radioactive waste from atomic power plants?
Unit 100
   1. On a two-stroke engine, how is the entry of the fuel mixture into the crankcase controlled?
   2. What two main systems are needed for the operation of any gasoline engine?
   3. What are the three methods of getting fuel to the carburetor?
   4. What is a venturi?
   5. Why is an air cleaner needed on an engine?
   6. Name two safety rules to follow when working on engines.
   7. Describe how to clean a spark plug.

PART VI
Transportation

Unit 101 Introduction to Transportation

Unit 102 Rail Transport Systems

Unit 103 Air Transport Systems

Unit 104 Sea Transport Systems

Unit 105 Automotive Transport Systems

Discussion Topics

Part VI: Transportation

Metric Fact Sheet*

— Automotive —

- Auto design dimensions are in mm.
- Distances measured in kilometres (km): one mile = 1.6 km; one km = 0.6 mile.
- Fuel consumption measured in litres/100 km: 20 mpg = 12 litres/100 km.
- Speed in km/h: 55 mph = 90 km/h (approximately).
- Horsepower replaced by kilowatt (kW): 100 hp engine = 75 kW (approximately).
- Tire pressure in kilopascals (kPa): 32 psi = 220 kPa (approximately).
- Torque measured in newton meters: one pound foot = 1.36 N · m. Torque developed by a compact engine is 110 lb. ft. or 150 N · m.
- Auto mass (weight) in kilograms (kg): 1 kg = 2.2 pounds.
- Typical spark plug gap setting: 0.020″ = 0.5 mm. (See drawing.)

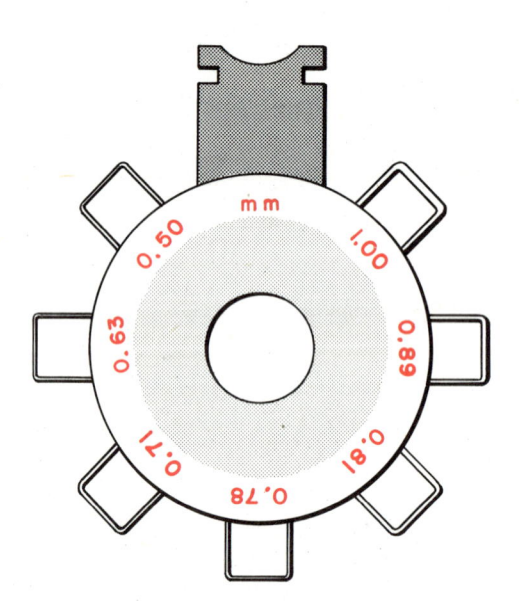

*You will find other information on metrics in the Appendix.

462

UNIT 101

Introduction to Transportation

One of the amazing features of American life is our convenient and efficient transportation system. Goods as well as people are moved from place to place quickly, comfortably, and safely. This is not to say that the system cannot be improved. Trains and planes sometimes run late, and baggage is often lost or delayed. But when you consider the size of this nation, with all its people, one must agree that the system is good. Fig. 101-1.

We take our transportation system for granted today. An air trip from Detroit, Michigan, to Washington, D.C., takes about one hour and fifteen minutes. Think of traveling that distance by carriage, when the trip took many days! Efficient transport has contributed greatly to our economic and industrial growth.

THE TRANSPORTATION SYSTEM

Transportation, like farming or manufacturing, is an important business. Transportation is the business that has to do with travel and communication, with the movement of people and things. It is a type of *service* industry because it serves to move people and materials from one place to another. Raw materials are hauled from the mine to the factory, and products are carried from the factory to the consumer. Fig. 101-2.

In order to do this we need vehicles such as trucks and ships, and highways and waterways on which they can travel. We also need people to operate the sys-

101-1. *Our transportation system moves both people and materials. This electric train speeds passengers between Washington, D.C., and New York at speeds of 120 MPH.*
Amtrak

101-2. *Huge trucks haul products from factories to consumers over the highways of our nation.*
American Trucking Association

Part VI: Transportation

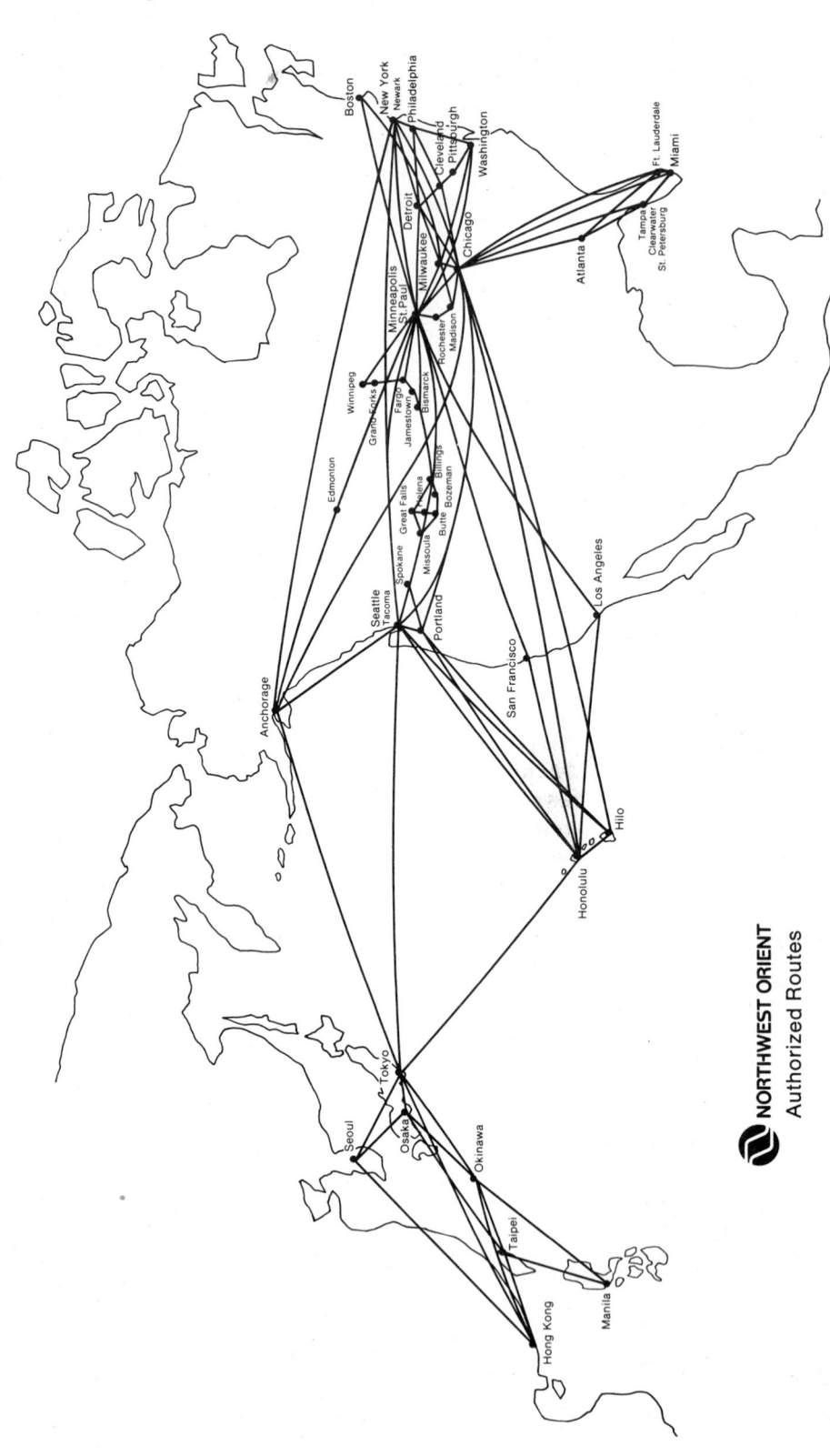

101-3. Airways are not "seen" with the eye, but they exist as air routes of clearly defined air spaces shown on maps and charts.

101-4. Racing cars are competition vehicles of special design and construction. They are not used for normal travel.

Gilmore Racing Team, Inc.

101-5. Earthmoving vehicles do not normally use established travelways. They are built to withstand the rigors of off-road operation.

Caterpillar Tractor Company

tem—drivers, highway engineers, designers, traffic control technicians, and many other skilled workers. Many people play a part in designing, planning, operating, and maintaining our transportation system.

Essentials of Transportation

There are two essential parts to any transportation system: the *way,* or travel space, and the *vehicle,* or carriage unit.

The *way* for travel varies with the type of vehicle. There are highways for trucks and cars, airways for aircraft, railways for trains, and seaways for ships. Some of these ways, such as highways and railways, are clearly visible to us. Seaways and airways are not easily "seen," but they are clearly marked on maps and charts for navigators to follow. Fig. 101-3. Our government maintains 3.25 million miles of highways and 25 000 miles of inland waterways and regulates 230 000 miles of airways. Railways, on the other hand, are usually privately owned and maintained.

The terminals or stations are also important parts of the travelways. Huge airports, bus stations, etc., are needed to provide a scheduled place for loading and unloading people and materials. And, of course, the operations of each travelway must be under the direction of some authority to guard against accidents and to build an efficient and reliable transport system. Control tower operators at airports, signal and control technicians for rail and seaways, a traffic policeman and signal light—all of these serve to direct traffic.

Many types of vehicles haul freight and people. There are airplanes, automobiles, cycles, trucks, buses, ships, barges, and trains. In addition, there are other special types of vehicles which do not usually use travelways. Among these are military vehicles, off-road vehicles such as farm tractors and earthmoving machinery, and experimental vehicles and competition vehicles such as racing cars. Fig. 101-4.

Elements of Vehicle Design

Each vehicle is designed to be used in some special way. In order to perform its specific task or function, its *structure* must conform to this function. For example, earthmoving vehicles must have a strong frame to withstand twisting and turning while pulling or pushing heavy loads. Fig. 101-5. In addition, the vehicle must have a *propulsion* system, or engine, which will supply enough power to move these heavy loads. Finally, the vehicle must have a proper *control* system to maintain its direction, speed, and performance.

The elements of vehicle design, then, are structure, propulsion, and control. These elements, along with the essentials of transportation, will be related to rail, air, sea, and automotive transportation systems in the units to follow. (More information on power systems is found in the units on power and energy in this book.)

465

UNIT 102

Rail Transport Systems

Railroads have played an important part in the development of the United States as a major industrial nation. They opened up the western part of this country. They provided fast and reasonably efficient long distance transport before the days of trucks, buses, and airplanes. Since the opening of the first American public railroad, the Baltimore and Ohio, in 1828, we have seen the railroad grow and prosper, decline, and now begin to grow again.

The railroads remain the most important hauler of freight in the nation. Today's railroads carry over 41 percent of all intercity freight. In terms of ton-miles they carry more than all the trucks, planes, and barges combined. (One ton-mile is equal to one ton of freight moved one mile.) America's railroads serve 45 000 towns and cities on over 200 000 miles of track. They use a fleet of 1.7 million freight cars and 29 500 locomotives. Fig. 102-1.

One reason for their importance is the efficiency of rail operations. The metal wheel on the metal rail produces a minimum of friction and permits railroad locomotives to pull their loads with less energy than other vehicles. A locomotive uses about one-fourth as much energy as a highway truck in moving one ton of material one mile.

Railroads also move three times as much freight per gallon of fuel as big trucks and 125 times as much as cargo aircraft. This is a huge fuel savings, which also reduces air pollution.

102-1. Railroads are an important link in the American transportation system.

Amtrak

Unit 102: Rail Transport Systems

For example, railroads—on a ton-mile basis—give off less than half the amount of exhaust emissions released by diesel trucks. A recent study indicates that railroads—despite carrying the lion's share of the intercity ton-mileage—are responsible for only slightly more than one percent of all air-pollutant emissions from transportation sources. Railroads are truly an important part of our nation's commerce.

THE RAILWAY

The train travels on a bed of ties and steel rails. These *ties* (crossties) are square wooden logs about six feet long and are laid on a bed of gravel or crushed rock called *ballast*. The ties are spaced 21 inches apart, from center to center, and provide support for the steel *rails*. The rails weigh from 60 to 155 pounds to the yard and have a standard length of 39 feet. Modern railways are made of welded track sections a mile long. These sections are smoother, quieter, and require less maintenance. The distance between the rails is called the *gauge*. Rails are spaced 4' 8½" apart in the United States, Mexico, and Canada. The thousands of miles of such track serve many communities in North America. Fig. 102-2.

There are also other types of railways, such as the monorail. Fig. 102-3. Monorail cars run along a track located either above or below them. Cars that ride above the monorail are balanced by a gyroscope or guide wheels. Monorails are less costly to build and are popular for city-to-city travel.

RAILROAD OPERATIONS

An important part of a railway system is the control of its operations. This requires stations, freight terminals, classification yards, signals and control centers. Some of the more important operations are described here.

Railroad stations are familiar to almost everyone. Here passengers board trains which take them to their destinations. But hauling freight by rail is another matter. In the railroad classification yard, loaded freight cars from all over the nation are joined to others to form a train. Fig. 102-4. The classification yard is a massive complex of tracks. A few inbound tracks expand into a dozen or more parallel receiving tracks. Then these merge into a few tracks, which, if it is a "hump" yard, go over the hump. Beyond, the tracks fan out again, this time in the "bowl," where row on row of parallel tracks, in turn, join to handle the outbound traffic.

Obviously, the simplest way to run a railroad would be to make up a full train at Point A and run it straight through, without stopping, to its destination at Point B. There are such trains, called unit trains, and they are, indeed, an efficient way to transport goods. But every car in such a train must be headed for the same place. If railroads tried to make up every train that way, there would either be a lot of very short trains, or locomotives would spend a lot of time at shipping points waiting for a full complement of cars for a single destination. That wouldn't be efficient. Therefore most trains are made up of cars headed for a wide variety of destinations.

That is why a classification yard is needed. The train pulls into a yard and is broken up, with the cars sorted according to final destinations. New trains pick up the sets of reclassified cars and leave the yard in different directions.

Through the years this has mostly been done manually. Workers read the numbers on incoming cars, learned their destinations from advance reports, and then assigned the cars to classification tracks where they awaited pickup. In this system, of course, there's an obvious danger of a yard becoming bottlenecked. In fact, by its very nature, it must be a sort of bottleneck—a place into which incoming trains are squeezed, then separated and sent out in all directions. Railroaders constantly look for ways to reduce the "squeezing" time and cut the period be-

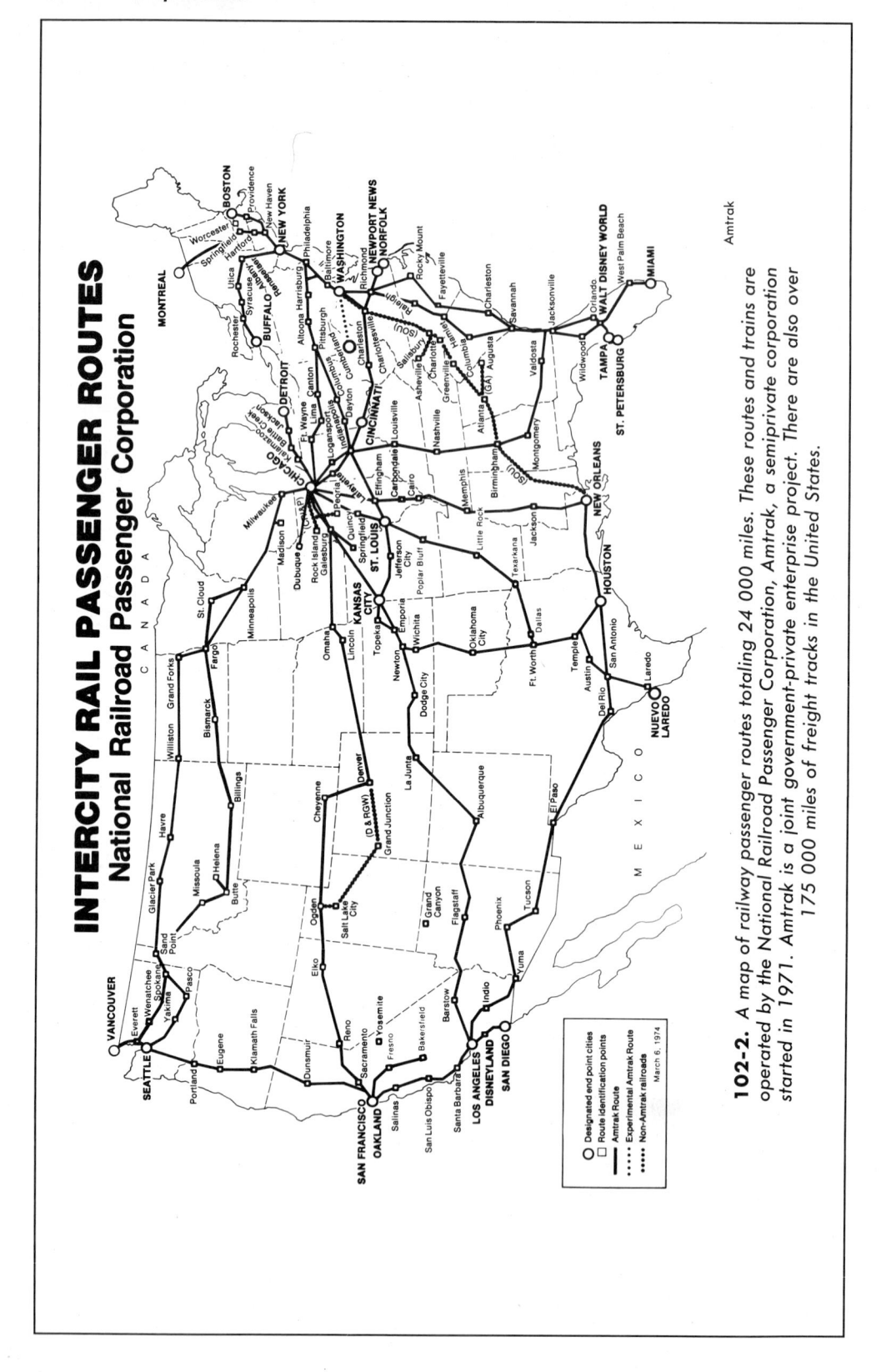

Part VI: Transportation

102-2. A map of railway passenger routes totaling 24 000 miles. These routes and trains are operated by the National Railroad Passenger Corporation, Amtrak, a semiprivate corporation started in 1971. Amtrak is a joint government-private enterprise project. There are also over 175 000 miles of freight tracks in the United States.

Unit 102: Rail Transport Systems

Seattle Center
102-3. Monorail trains ride on only one rail. They are faster and less expensive to operate.

Association of American Railroads
102-4. A railroad classification yard. Here freight cars are joined to become trains.

469

Part VI: Transportation

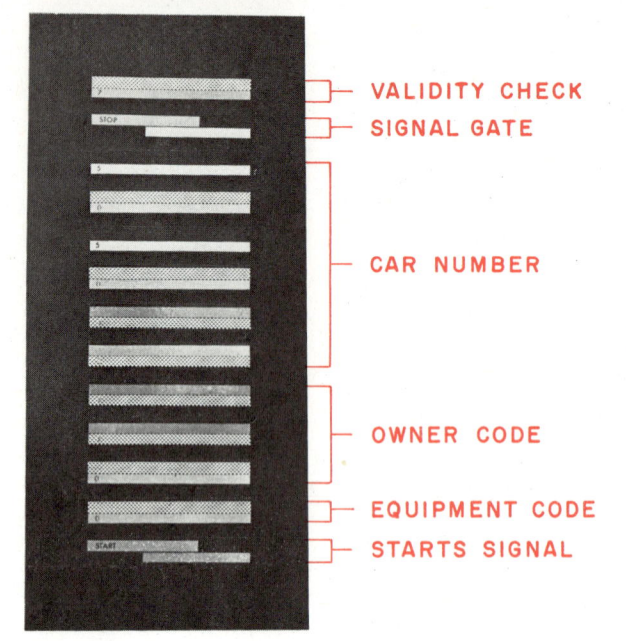

102-5. *This rail car identification label is made from color-coded reflective tape. A scanner reads the label and sends the information directly to a computer control center.*

tween the funneling in of trains on one side and the release of trains on the other.

In modern yards the most important time-saving tool is the computer. It can "see" and "think" faster and "remember" more than any human being. Automatic Car Identification (ACI) scanners can be used to "read" color-coded labels on incoming cars. (The ACI system will be discussed in detail later in this unit.) Because the scanners can read very fast, an incoming train can travel at 15 miles an hour, three times faster than when a person had to read and write down the car numbers. The computer's memory banks also can store the exact location of every car in the yard and make this information available almost instantly. As a series of cars approaches the top of the "hump"—over which they will roll freely to the proper track—scanners transmit the number of each to a screen in the hump yardmaster's office. As a car rolls down the hump, a machine automatically slows its speed to prevent it from damaging the cars it is to join. To do this, the computer must calculate the car's gross weight, the curvature of the track, the distance the car must travel, and even the prevailing weather conditions. Among other things, this means the car may be weighed while in motion. When the cars have been classified, the computer can produce lists of trains ready for departure, along with the total tonnage.

Not every railroad yard is computerized yet. Such yards are very expensive, but the ones that have been constructed are proving their worth. One automated yard in the Midwest cost $12.5 million. It has taken over the operations of four other yards in the area and relieved a burden on yet another, and handling time in that area has been cut in half.

Today's railroaders are constantly looking toward the future—a future when a growing population and economy will need much more of every product than it does now. It is a future when peak efficiency will be essential. There will be no time for unnecessary delays or avoidable errors. The computerized classification

Unit 102: Rail Transport Systems

yard is a giant step toward that peak efficiency.

Still another electronic development on the railroads is CTC—Centralized Traffic Control. CTC enables an operator seated at a remote terminal to "see" and direct traffic on hundreds of miles of railroad track. From the terminal the operator pushes a button or moves a lever, actuating switches and signals miles away. Thus one train can be routed briefly onto a siding while another, coming from the opposite direction along the same track, speeds safely by. One of the values of CTC is that more trains can use fewer tracks, and they can use them safely and efficiently. Other applications for computers and computer-related systems are being developed at a rapid pace.

Automatic Car Identification

As mentioned earlier, the Automatic Car Identification system (ACI) uses computers to speed the process of car classification. This system also makes it possible to give a customer accurate information on the location of a shipment of automobiles, iron ore, or other freight. Before ACI this information was collected visually. This led to many delays and errors. Now both the customer and the manufacturer always know the whereabouts of a freight shipment.

There are three basic parts to ACI. A *label*, Fig. 102-5, is applied to both sides of a railway car. This label is made up of strips of reflective color-coded tape and measures 10 x 22.5 inches. This special tape reflects light in such a way that it is 200 times brighter than paint. The labels contain optical information on car serial numbers and ownership codes. A *scanner*, which reads the labels, is mounted in freight yards. Fig. 102-6. This sensitive instrument can read each label four times when a car is moving at speeds of one hundred miles per hour. The third part of ACI is the *decoder*. This device converts the scanner signal into meaningful numbers suitable for a teletype printout or for input to a computer control center.

The next time you are at a rail crossing, notice the colorful labels on the freight cars. You will know that this label is a part of ACI and that it contributes to a more efficient railroad freight system.

Canadian National

102-6. Automatic Car Identification scanner unit reads the rail car label at speeds of up to 100 MPH.

RAILWAY VEHICLES

Locomotives, freight cars, and passenger cars are the standard railway vehicles. The steam locomotive was the first type of engine used to pull railway cars. Fig. 102-7 and 102-8. Diesel engines, introduced in 1925, were cleaner, more powerful, and more efficient. This added power enabled the railroad companies to increase the number of cars in a train and cut shipping costs. Fig. 102-9. Locomotives of more than 6000 horsepower are used today.

The locomotive of today is actually a diesel-electric. It uses an electric genera-

Part VI: Transportation

102-7. Steam locomotive, 1866. *Southern Pacific Company*

102-8. Steam locomotive, 1906. This powerful "Mallet" engine weighed 350 000 lbs and was used to pull iron ore cars. *Great Northern Railway*

102-9. A modern diesel locomotive. For long trains two or even three locomotives are joined together to provide the needed power. *Santa Fe Railway*

tor and wheel-mounted motors to transfer power from the engine to the drive wheels. It is the most familiar locomotive on today's railroads. Figs. 102-10 and 102-11.

Electric locomotives are also in use. However, at the beginning of the 1970's, there were fewer than 300 all-electric locomotives. The biggest advantage of the electric is simply that it is powered from a central generating station. But the higher unit horsepower and the low maintenance costs are offset by the high cost of transmission facilities along the right-of-way.

Newer gas turbine locomotives have also been developed. The train in Fig. 102-12 has five cars, with a power unit at each end. The total train length is 423 feet. Each power car is propelled by a turbine engine similar to those developed for aircraft use and is rated at 1140 horsepower. A second turbine engine rated at 430 horsepower drives an alternator, which supplies electric power for the train's auxiliary system, lighting, bar-grill unit, and air conditioning.

The transmission is hydraulic-mechanical and also has a hydrodynamic brake. For use in the United States the trains will have three separate braking systems: hydrodynamic, conventional tread brakes, and supplementary disc brakes.

The total seating capacity of a five-car, single class train is 296 plus 24 chairs at tables in the bar-grill dining area. Each of the two power units have 48 seats, one coach has 80 seats, the other 76, and the passenger compartment of the bar-grill car has 44 seats.

Unit 102: Rail Transport Systems

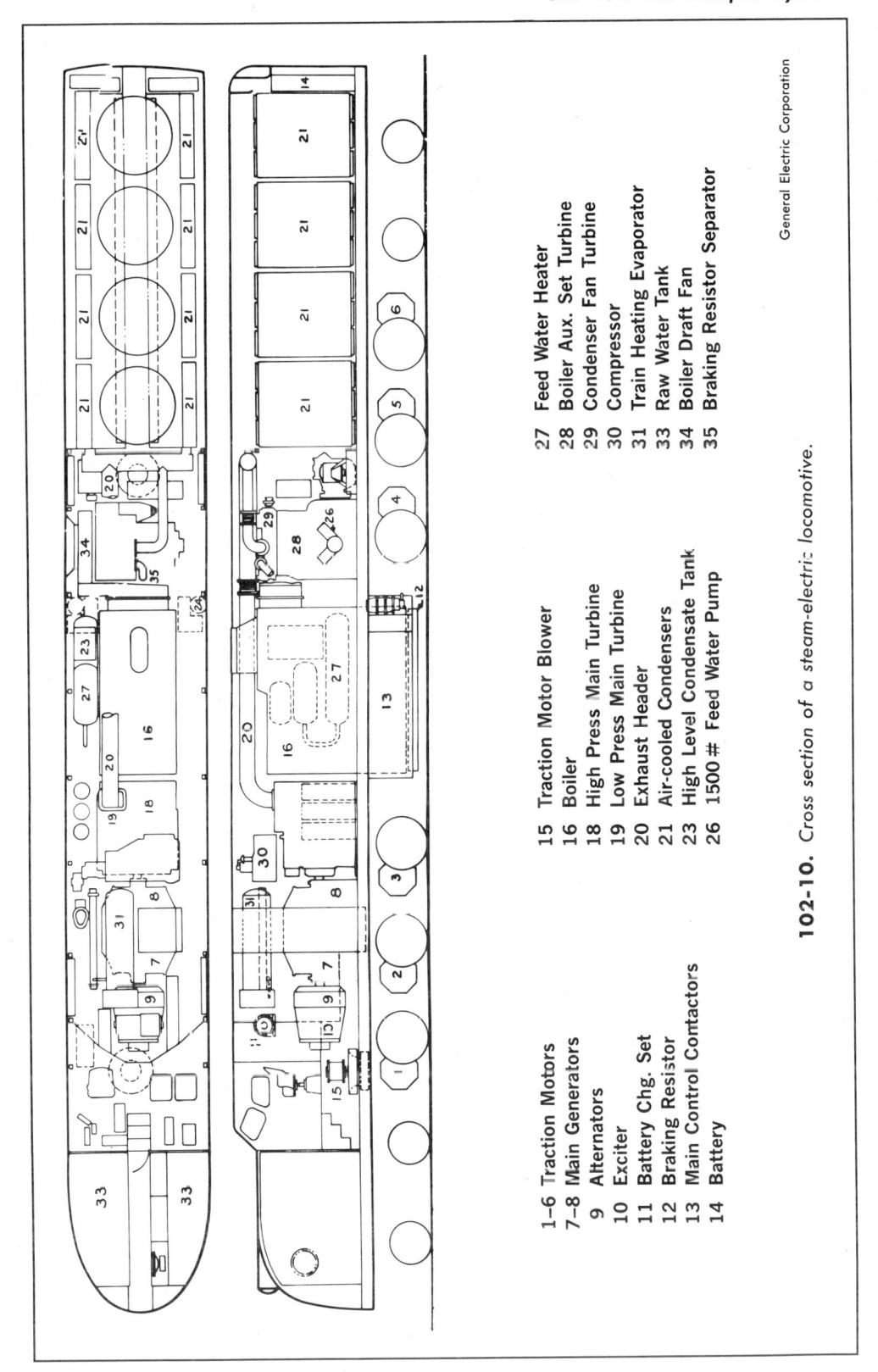

1-6 Traction Motors
7-8 Main Generators
9 Alternators
10 Exciter
11 Battery Chg. Set
12 Braking Resistor
13 Main Control Comtactors
14 Battery
15 Traction Motor Blower
16 Boiler
18 High Press Main Turbine
19 Low Press Main Turbine
20 Exhaust Header
21 Air-cooled Condensers
23 High Level Condensate Tank
26 1500 # Feed Water Pump
27 Feed Water Heater
28 Boiler Aux. Set Turbine
29 Condenser Fan Turbine
30 Compressor
31 Train Heating Evaporator
33 Raw Water Tank
34 Boiler Draft Fan
35 Braking Resistor Separator

General Electric Corporation

102-10. Cross section of a steam-electric locomotive.

473

Part VI: Transportation

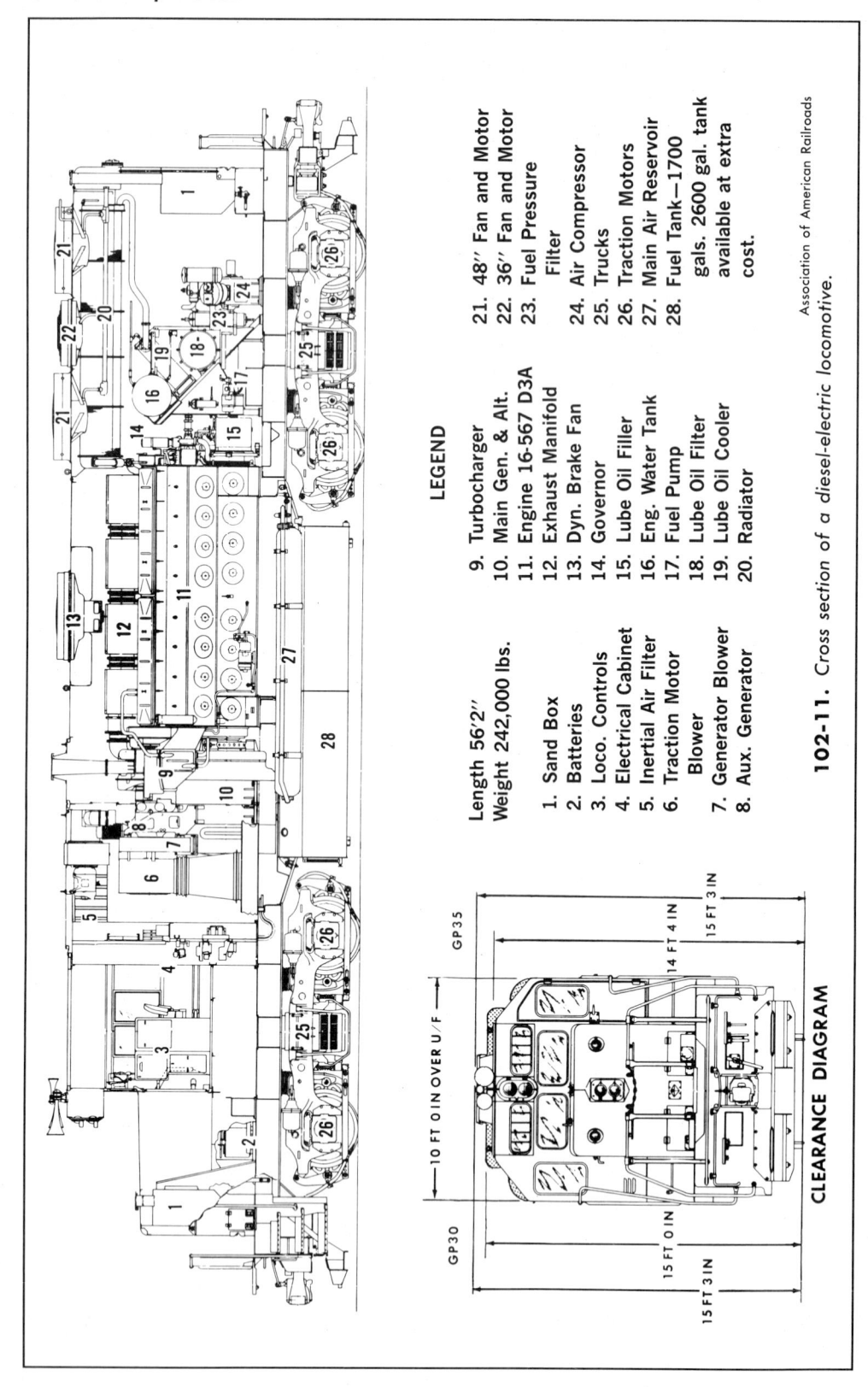

LEGEND

Length 56'2"
Weight 242,000 lbs.

1. Sand Box
2. Batteries
3. Loco. Controls
4. Electrical Cabinet
5. Inertial Air Filter
6. Traction Motor Blower
7. Generator Blower
8. Aux. Generator
9. Turbocharger
10. Main Gen. & Alt.
11. Engine 16-567 D3A
12. Exhaust Manifold
13. Dyn. Brake Fan
14. Governor
15. Lube Oil Filler
16. Eng. Water Tank
17. Fuel Pump
18. Lube Oil Filter
19. Lube Oil Cooler
20. Radiator
21. 48" Fan and Motor
22. 36" Fan and Motor
23. Fuel Pressure Filter
24. Air Compressor
25. Trucks
26. Traction Motors
27. Main Air Reservoir
28. Fuel Tank—1700 gals. 2600 gal. tank available at extra cost.

Association of American Railroads

102-11. Cross section of a diesel-electric locomotive.

CLEARANCE DIAGRAM

102-12. A gas turbine locomotive, capable of speeds up to 125 MPH. It is rated at 1140 horsepower.

Amtrak

standard flat

single deck livestock cars

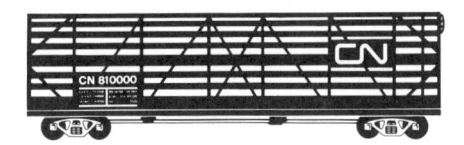

box car

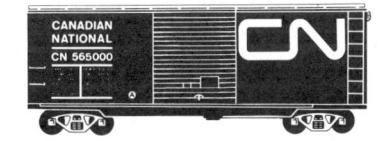

standard refrigerator car

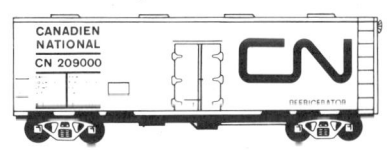

hopper—open

standard gondola

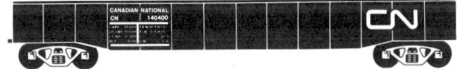

Canadian National

102-14. Railway freight cars. Study the design of each in order to understand what it is used for.

Locomotives have simple control devices for safe, easy operation. Fig. 102-13. Many safety features are built into its controls, such as automatic braking in case the operator has a disabling accident. The all-electric train shown in Fig. 102-1 has only one control to dial train speed from zero to a maximum of 120 MPH.

Other "rolling stock" vehicles include freight and passenger cars. The important freight cars are shown in Fig. 102-14, and each is designed for a special use. Some of these cars are designed to carry truck trailers "piggyback." Trucks pull these trailers to freight yards where the trailers are loaded on special cars. At their destinations the trailers are unloaded, and trucks once again pull them to their customers. Fig. 102-15. Freight cars are strong and durable enough to hold up

102-13. Control panel for a diesel locomotive.

Burlington Northern

102-15. Truck trailers ride "piggyback" on this special freight car.

Santa Fe Railway

475

Part VI: Transportation

how to "read" a freight car

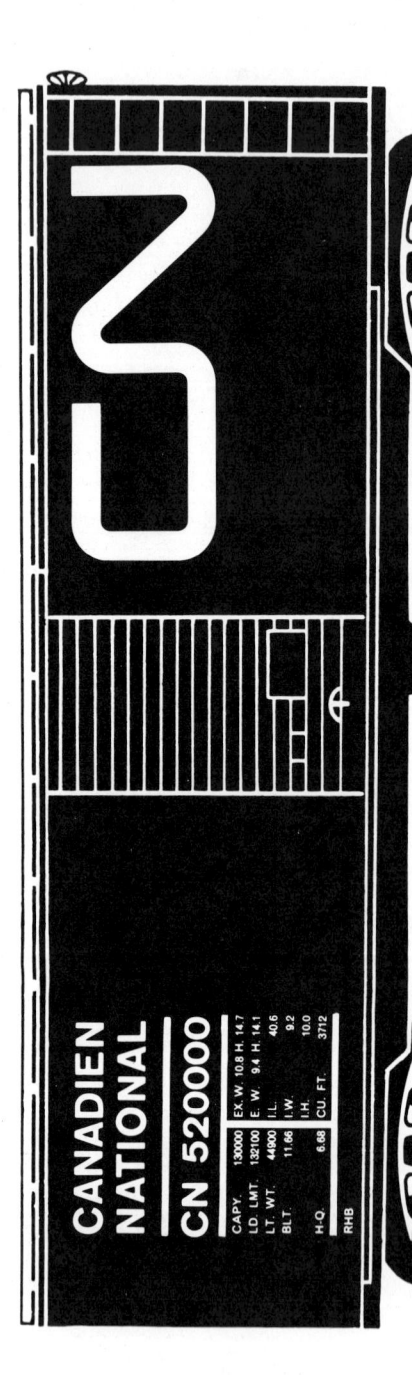

Each of the markings on the sides of the 109,000 CN freight cars at your service contains important information. They help, too, to make sure that the right type of car is in the right place for the right load at the right time. The markings on this box car tell you its size, weight, capacity, as well as other important facts. Here is an explanation of the complete markings.

RHB Mechanical designation of type of car as listed in official railway equipment register.

CAPY. 130000 This car's nominal capacity is a 130,000 pound load.

LD. LMT. 132100 Load limit is 132,100 pounds and must not be exceeded.

LT. WT. 44900 This is weight of car when empty.

BLT. 11.66 Car was built in November, 1966.

H-Q. 6.68 Last shopping of car was in Montreal in June, 1968.

EX. W. 10.8 H. 14.7 Extreme width of car is 10'8" at a height of 14'7" above the rails.

E.W. 9.4 H. 14.1 Width of car at eaves is 9'4" at 14'1" above rails.

I.L. 40.6 Inside length 40'6".

I.W. 9.2 Inside width 9'2".

I.H. 10.0 Inside height 10'.

CU. FT. 3712 Volume of car in cubic feet.

102-16. How to read a freight car.

Canadian National

476

Unit 102: Rail Transport Systems

102-17. *The LIM test vehicle.* 
Department of Transportation

102-19. *The Tracked Air Cushion Research Vehicle.*
Department of Transportation

NEW DIRECTIONS IN RAILROAD VEHICLE TECHNOLOGY

The need for faster, safer, and more efficient rail systems has led to some interesting new vehicles. The Linear Induction Motor (LIM) test car is a lightweight, high speed vehicle designed for intercity rail travel. Fig. 102-17. This vehicle operates at speeds up to 250 MPH. Its propulsion system is almost noiseless and does not pollute the atmosphere. Fig. 102-18. A second experimental vehicle is the Tracked Air Cushion Research Vehicle (TACRV). Fig. 102-19. These vehicles operate over a guideway suspended by air without touching the guideway. They run at speeds up to 300 MPH (483 km per hour). They are very efficient, using a LIM to generate 10 000 lbs of thrust.

102-18. *Structural diagram of the LIM test vehicle.*
Department of Transportation

LINEAR INDUCTION MOTOR TEST CAR

- ELECTRONICS
- ALTERNATOR
- GAS TURBINE
- LIM DYNAMIC BRAKING RESISTOR
- FUEL TANK
- APU
- LINEAR INDUCTION MOTOR (LIM)
- 2 DISC BRAKES PER AXLE
- TRUCK ASSY
- AERODYNAMIC BRAKES
- REACTION RAIL

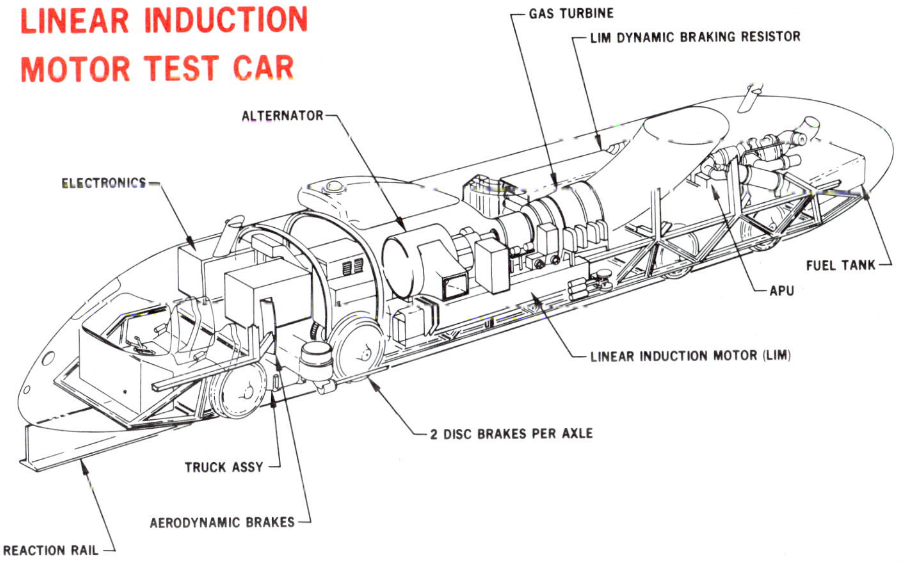

UNIT 103

Air Transport Systems

The carrying of people and materials by aircraft is perhaps the most exciting and interesting form of transportation today. Huge airplanes roaring from runways and climbing into the skies cause people to stop and stare at this marvelous invention. Fig. 103-1.

AIRWAYS

Like other forms of transportation, airplanes need paths or routes to follow. These *airways* are strictly controlled for air traffic so that planes will not collide. Of course, the airways are invisible except on flight maps and charts.

The useful airspace is considered to have a ceiling (top limit) of 75 000 feet. Its base is not even, of course, but follows the contours of the earth. It changes above cities, mountains, tall towers, and other obstructions and reaches down to the ground at airports.

In the sky above the United States, there are more than 280 000 miles of federal airways. These sky highways are divided into two different systems. The low altitude airway system generally begins at 1200 feet above the earth and goes up to, but does not include, 18 000 feet. The high altitude airway system goes from 18 000 feet to 45 000 feet. Airspace above 45 000 feet is reserved for point-to-point flights. Fig. 103-2. Airplanes traveling west or south must fly at even numbered altitudes. Those flying east or north use odd numbered altitudes. Planes must also fly at least 1000 feet above cities and 500 feet above open country.

Airways are the freeways of the sky, complete with an aerial version of signs, access roads, directional guides, and even "parking" places—areas over airports known as holding points. Airplanes hold at these points, flying in an oval pattern, so that they may be spaced in an orderly fashion before moving along the airways or into airports for landing.

In the United States, the agency which controls air traffic is the Federal Aviation Administration (FAA). Its responsibilities begin at the drawing boards where aircraft are designed and at the factories where they are made. It has authority over the people who dispatch the aircraft from airports, the crews who fly the planes, the aviation mechanics who maintain them, and other specialists (parachute riggers, flight instructors, etc.). FAA responsibilities include the airspace, the navigation aids, the airway system, the airports, and the research needed to continually improve the performance and safety of aircraft. FAA also provides inspectors to help the National Transportation Safety Board in accident investigations.

AIR TRAFFIC CONTROL

Air traffic is similar to automobile traffic; it cannot operate helter-skelter. Instead, it must operate according to established rules—Instrument Flight Rules (IFR) and Visual Flight Rules (VFR).

In general, pilots flying IFR navigate mainly by instruments. They rely on them and on the instructions they get by radio from air traffic control specialists to stay

Unit 103: Air Transport Systems

103-1. Airplanes are an important form of modern transportation.

British Airways

103-2. Flight levels separate airplanes' flying altitudes according to their direction of flight.

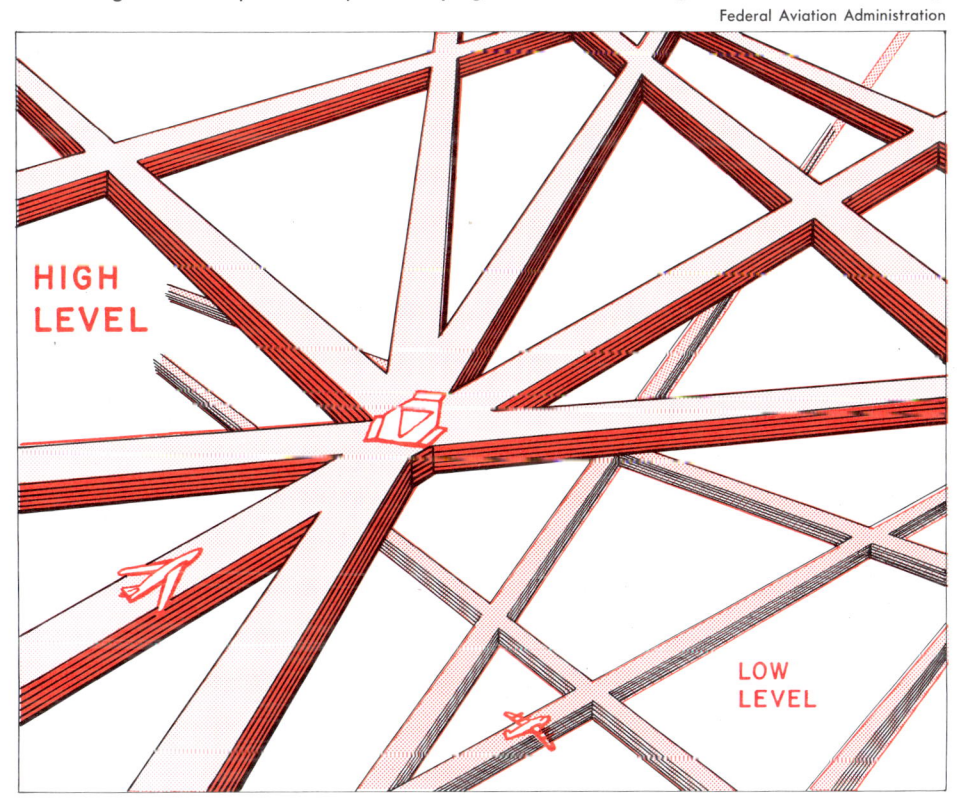

Federal Aviation Administration

HIGH LEVEL

LOW LEVEL

479

Part VI: Transportation

103-4. Mobile lounges are part of the facilities at many modern airports.
Pan American

103-3. Control towers regulate traffic near airports. The operators and technicians must be trained well to handle all emergencies.
Federal Aviation Administration

safely separated from other aircraft. They file a flight plan before taking off and are given a clearance that keeps them away from other planes flying IFR in the same area.

Pilots flying VFR, however, rely on their own sight to avoid other aircraft and must follow the idea of: "See and be seen."

IFR operations are required when weather conditions fall below the minimum for cloud ceiling heights and visibility. In order to fly IFR, a civilian pilot must pass a written and a flight test and receive an instrument rating from FAA. When flying through "positive control" airspace (generally above 24 000 feet), pilots must fly under IFR regulations.

Air traffic in the United States operates under a "common system." This means that military and civilian aircraft are controlled by the same facilities. Traffic near an airport is controlled either by a military control tower or by one of the more than 320 FAA airport control towers. Traffic on the airways is controlled by *Air Route Traffic Control Centers* located throughout the country. Each center and tower handles traffic within its own area, using radar and communications equipment to keep aircraft moving safely. As the flight progresses, control is transferred from center to center and from center to tower. Fig. 103-3.

There is a third air traffic facility, the Flight Service Station, that provides services to civil aviators, air carriers, and military pilots. About 385 of these stations and combined station/towers are scattered around the nation, each covering an area of roughly 400 square miles. Flight Service Station specialists, all of them expert on their area's terrain, provide preflight and inflight briefings, weather information, suggested routes, altitudes, and any other information important to the flight's safety.

If an airplane is overdue at its reporting station or destination, the Flight Service Station starts a search and rescue operation. If a pilot is lost or is having some trouble, it will give instructions and direc-

Unit 103: Air Transport Systems

Northwest Orient Airlines

103-5. *The DC-3 was considered to be the first of the modern airliners. It carried 28 passengers and a crew of 3. Many of these airplanes are still used throughout the world.*

Northwest Orient Airlines

103-6. *The Boeing 377 Strat-o-cruiser, 1949. This aircraft carried 80 passengers 3000 miles at a speed of 340 MPH. This was one of the last of the generation of propeller-driven aircraft.*

tions to the nearest emergency landing field.

Providing communities and airport owners with planning and engineering advice is another important FAA function. The FAA also provides these services to other countries. There are about 11 050 airports on record with the FAA.

FAA operates two major airports—Washington National Airport and Dulles International Airport. Washington National is located in Arlington, Virginia, four miles from downtown Washington, D.C. Dulles, one of the world's largest jetports, is located near Chantilly, Virginia, 26 miles west of the nation's capital. Mobile lounges are used for transporting passengers to jet planes, parked far from the terminal building where noise and fumes cannot cause discomfort. Fig. 103-4.

AIRCRAFT

The first powered flight took place at Kitty Hawk, North Carolina, on December 17, 1903. There the Wright brothers flew an airplane some 120 feet, a flight which lasted 12 seconds. Since then, considerable progress has been made in the design of aircraft. The first commercial airplanes were slow, drafty, and noisy, flying at speeds of a little over 100 MPH (160 km per hour).

One of the most remarkable airplanes was the famous Douglas DC-3. It entered service in 1936, had a top speed of 230 MPH, and a range of about 1500 miles. Fig. 103-5. Following World War II, faster and larger airplanes with greater ranges were developed. Fig. 103-6. All were driven by turbine or piston-powered engines. The first jet engines were used on military aircraft. The first commercial jet airliner was a British airplane, the Hawker-Siddley Comet, which flew in 1958. It traveled at a speed of 526 MPH, carried 81 passengers, and had a range of 3225 miles. This plane ushered in a new air age. Since that time, a number of modern jetliners have been designed. Several in use today are shown in Figs. 103-7 through 103-10.

Aircraft are designed for carrying both freight and passengers on short and long hauls. Fig. 103-11. While most airplanes carry both passengers and freight, there are models designed for carrying freight only. These are able to carry large pieces because they have specially made cargo

481

Part VI: Transportation

103-7. The Boeing 707 was introduced in 1958 and is one of the most popular jet airliners in operation.

103-9. This huge Boeing 747 "Jumbo Jet" is the largest commercial jet aircraft.

103-8. The Boeing 727 is smaller than the 707 and is used for shorter flights.

103-10. The Douglas DC-10 is another of the large modern jet aircraft.

doors and compartments. Fig. 103-12. Loading is done mechanically, and the cargo is placed in containers to speed up loading and unloading. Airplanes can also be converted to carry only passengers, only freight, or both. Fig. 103-13. Air freight is, of course, very fast and is growing in popularity.

There are many other types of aircraft designed for special uses. Light airplanes are for business and recreational travel. Fig. 103-14. Both light and heavy helicopters serve as a means of passenger travel, as well as for construction work. Fig. 103-15. Military aircraft are used for our nation's defense. Fig. 103-16.

Aircraft Structures

Airplanes are built of lightweight, tough alloys of aluminum and titanium. They are

Unit 103: Air Transport Systems

Comparative Aircraft Data Chart

Manufacturer	Boeing	Boeing	Boeing	Douglas
Type	Commercial Transport	Commercial Transport	Commercial Transport	Commercial Transport
Configuration	Psgr.	Psgr.	Psgr.	Psgr.
Seating Capacity	18/108	12/138	58/304	40/196
Cabin Width (ft.-inches)	11'7"	11'7"	20'1.5"	18'7"
Over-all Length	153'2"	152'11"	231'4"	182'3"
Height to Top of Tail	34'	42'5.5"	63'5"	58'1"
Wing Span	108'	145'9"	195'8"	161'4"
Wing Area (sq. ft.)	1650	2892	5500	3647
Engine Manufacturer	Pratt & Whitney	Pratt & Whitney	Pratt & Whitney	Pratt & Whitney
Engine Designation	JT8D-7	JT3D-3B	③ JT9D-7W	JT9D-20
Engine t/o Thrust	14 000 lbs	18 000 lbs	47 000 lbs	48 500 lbs
Number of Engines	3	4	4	3
Type of Fuel	Kerosene	Kerosene	Kerosene	Kerosene
Maximum Taxi Weight (lbs)	173 000	336 000	③ 778 000	532 000
Maximum Landing Weight (lbs)	150 000	215 000	564 000	380 000
Empty Weight (lbs)	98 900	142 900	365 000	266 300
Fuel Capacity (gal)	7680	23 855	51 000	36 239
Maximum Certificated Altitude (ft)	42 000	42 000	45 000	42 000
Maximum Cert. Cruise Speed (mph)	631	628	636	610
Normal Operating Altitude (ft)	27 000–31 000	29 000–37 000	31 000–39 000	29 000–37 000
Normal Cruise Speed (mph)	550	545	555	555
Maximum Structural Payload (lbs)	37 100	52 100	159 500	101 700
Passenger Payload (lbs)	25 010	29 110	74 210	49 610
Range with Pass. P.L. (st. mi)	1760	5850	6740	5100

103-11. *This chart compares the size and operation of some of the modern jet passenger aircraft.*

Boeing Company

103-12. *The nose of this huge 747 freighter lifts up to make loading more convenient.*

483

Part VI: Transportation

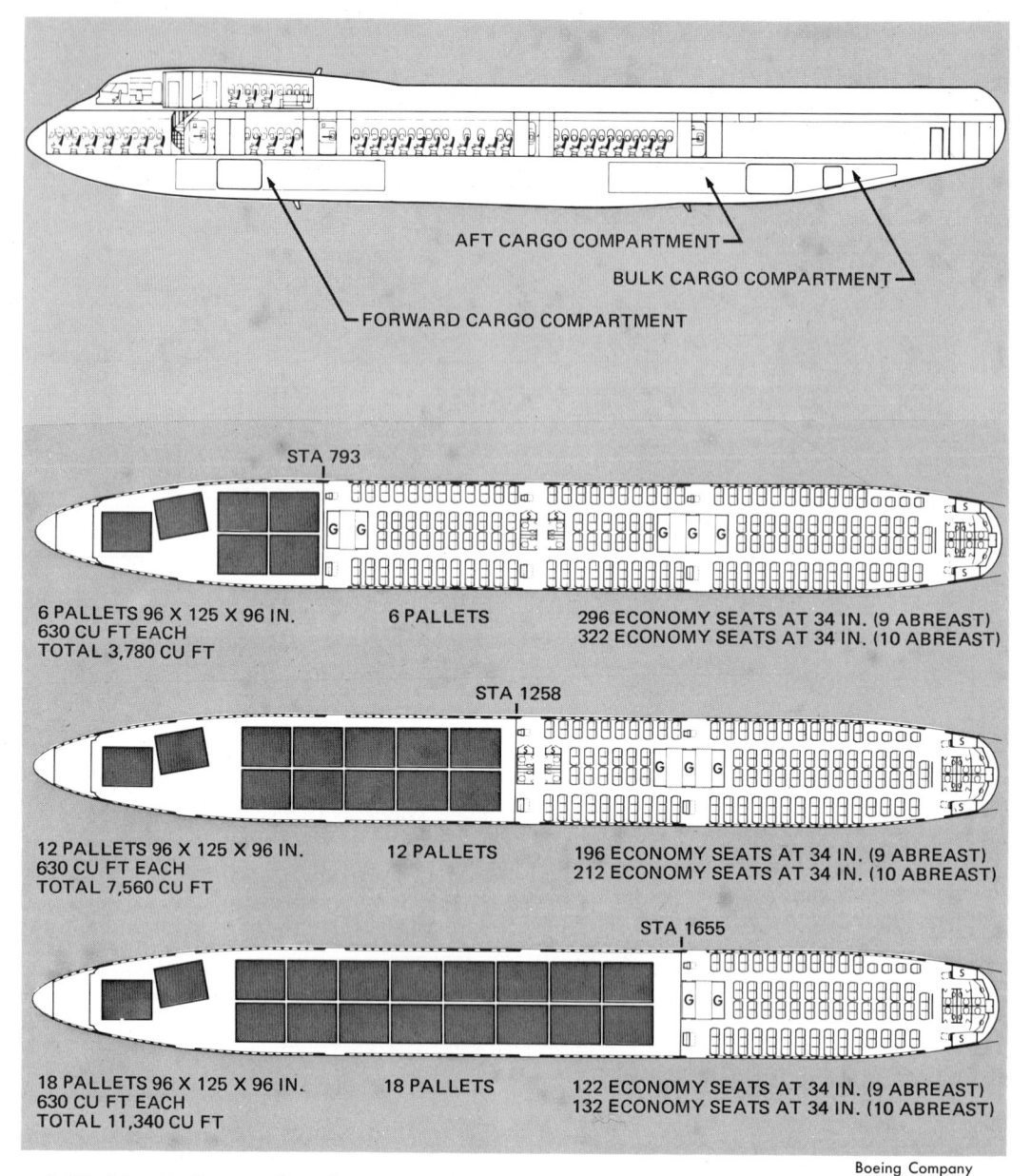

AFT CARGO COMPARTMENT
BULK CARGO COMPARTMENT
FORWARD CARGO COMPARTMENT

STA 793

6 PALLETS 96 X 125 X 96 IN.
630 CU FT EACH
TOTAL 3,780 CU FT

6 PALLETS

296 ECONOMY SEATS AT 34 IN. (9 ABREAST)
322 ECONOMY SEATS AT 34 IN. (10 ABREAST)

STA 1258

12 PALLETS 96 X 125 X 96 IN.
630 CU FT EACH
TOTAL 7,560 CU FT

12 PALLETS

196 ECONOMY SEATS AT 34 IN. (9 ABREAST)
212 ECONOMY SEATS AT 34 IN. (10 ABREAST)

STA 1655

18 PALLETS 96 X 125 X 96 IN.
630 CU FT EACH
TOTAL 11,340 CU FT

18 PALLETS

122 ECONOMY SEATS AT 34 IN. (9 ABREAST)
132 ECONOMY SEATS AT 34 IN. (10 ABREAST)

Boeing Company

103-13. *Airplanes such as this 747 can be converted to carry different amounts of cargo and passengers.*

designed to be strong to withstand the forces of flight such as wind and pressure. Fig. 103-17 shows a typical aircraft structure. Note how the frames and ribs are covered with a thin, strong metal sheathing, or skin. Riveting is the process generally used to fasten aircraft sections together. Recently, computerized riveting has been developed. Huge machines clamp the skin to an entire wing frame section. An automatic riveting machine is programmed to locate a rivet position, drill a hole, insert a rivet, head the rivet, and then mill it flush with the surface of

Cessna Aircraft Company
103-14. Light aircraft are designed to carry passengers and cargo for business and pleasure travel.

Rotor Way, Inc.
103-15. This lightweight helicopter is designed to carry two passengers.

Department of the Air Force
103-16. The modern jet fighter is part of our air defense. These aircraft are fast and maneuverable and heavily armed.

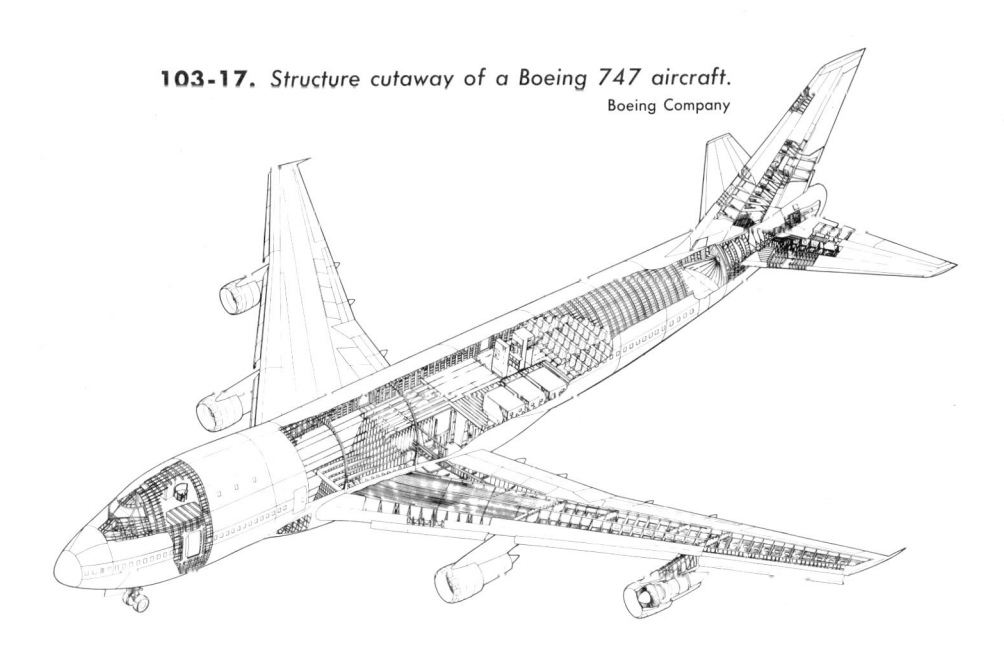

103-17. Structure cutaway of a Boeing 747 aircraft.
Boeing Company

485

Part VI: Transportation

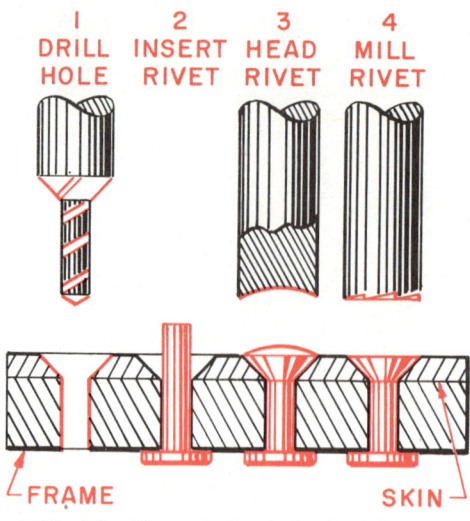

103-18. *Computerized riveting diagram.*

the skin. Fig. 103-18. This is a fast, efficient way to set the 1 800 000 rivets contained in a Boeing 747.

Once built, newly designed aircraft are tested in huge structure test frames. Fig. 103-19. Here they are twisted, pulled, and shaken to test the airworthiness of the craft.

Modern aircraft are powered by piston, turbine, and jet engines. More information on these engines can be found in Unit 99.

Much research is taking place on rocket engines and supersonic aircraft. Supersonic commercial aircraft, or SSTs, have been built by Russia and as part of a joint French-British program. In addition, research is being done by the National

103-19. *Structural testing takes place in huge frames such as this.*

Boeing Company

Unit 103: Air Transport Systems

Aeronautics and Space Administration (NASA). Much has been learned about flight, structure, power, and electronic guidance systems through NASA research.

Aircraft Controls and Instruments

The first airplanes had simple controls to guide them in flight. Today, the larger the aircraft, the more engines and electronic gear (such as radar) there are to control. Larger aircraft, therefore, have larger, more complicated instrument panels. Shown in Fig. 103-20 are the parts of a light airplane; its instrument panel is shown in Fig. 103-21. Compare this with the complicated instrument panel of a modern jet transport, which takes three people to fly it. Fig. 103-22.

Flying is safe and exciting, but it requires much training to fly large aircraft. Some small helicopters have a few simple instruments to control them in flight. Figs. 103-23 and 103-24.

Aircraft are an important part of our transportation system. They join with rail, land, and sea vehicles to provide this nation with a fast, efficient, and safe way to move people and materials.

103-20. *The main parts of a light airplane: (1) Propeller (2) Landing gear (3) Wing strut (4) Wing (5) Right wing aileron (6) Right wing flap (7) Fuselage (8) Horizontal stabilizer (9) Fin and dorsal (10) Rudder (11) Elevator (12) Left wing flap (13) Left wing aileron (14) Door (15) Seat (16) Windshield (17) Engine cowl.*

Cessna Aircraft Company

Part VI: Transportation

Cessna Aircraft Company
103-21. Instrument panel of the airplane shown in Fig. 103-20.

103-22. Cockpit and instrument panel of a DC-10 jet airplane.

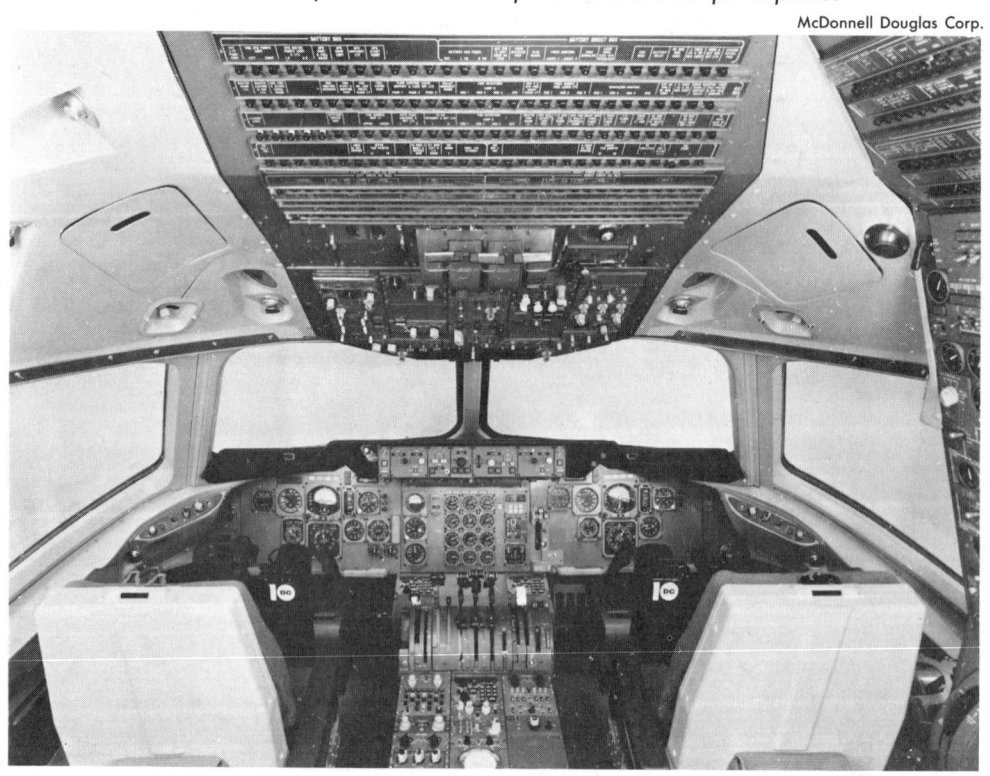

McDonnell Douglas Corp.

Unit 103: Air Transport Systems

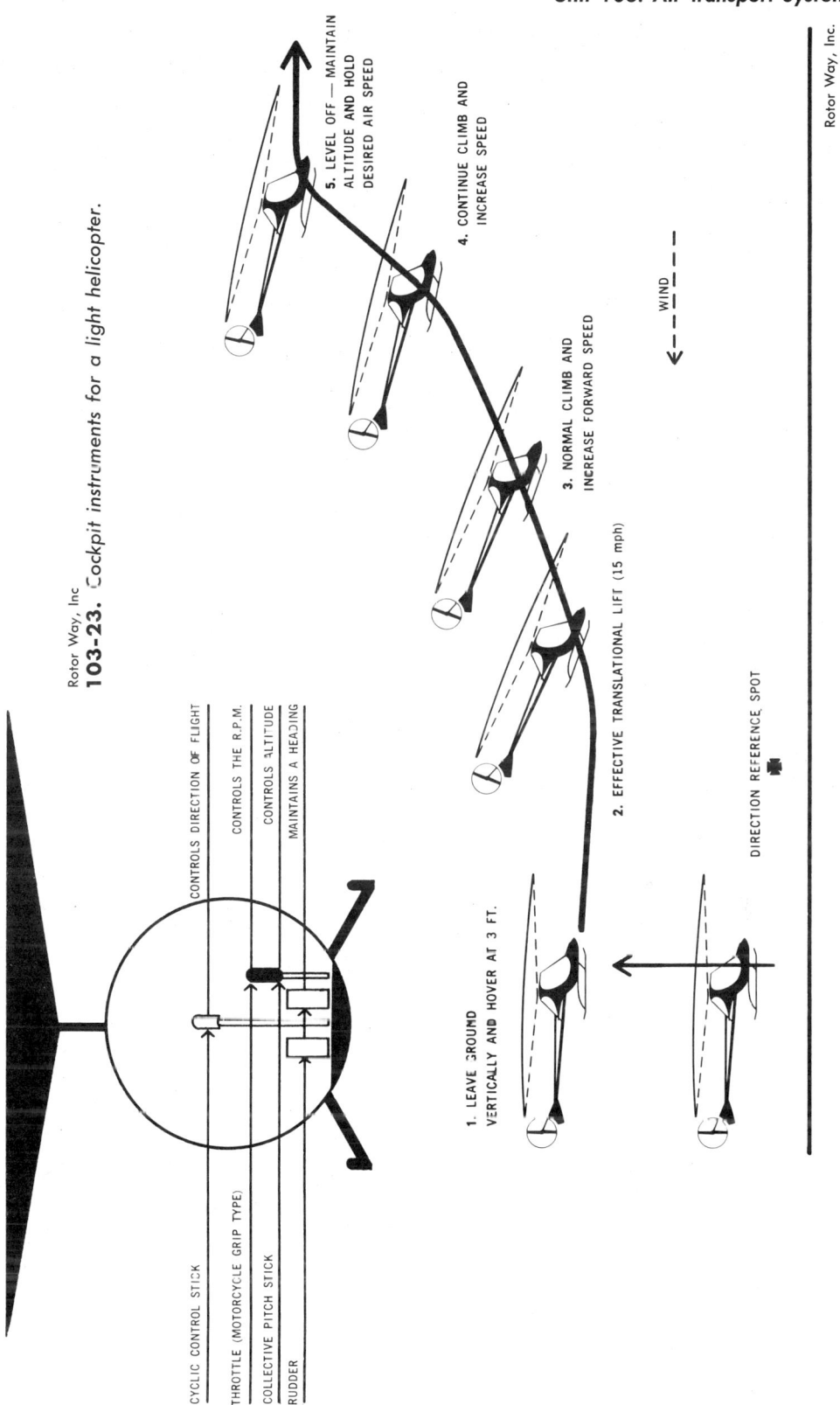

103-23. Cockpit instruments for a light helicopter.

CYCLIC CONTROL STICK — CONTROLS DIRECTION OF FLIGHT
THROTTLE (MOTORCYCLE GRIP TYPE) — CONTROLS THE R.P.M.
COLLECTIVE PITCH STICK — CONTROLS ALTITUDE
RUDDER — MAINTAINS A HEADING

Rotor Way, Inc

103-24. Normal take-off diagram for a light helicopter.

1. LEAVE GROUND VERTICALLY AND HOVER AT 3 FT.
2. EFFECTIVE TRANSLATIONAL LIFT (15 mph)
3. NORMAL CLIMB AND INCREASE FORWARD SPEED
4. CONTINUE CLIMB AND INCREASE SPEED
5. LEVEL OFF — MAINTAIN ALTITUDE AND HOLD DESIRED AIR SPEED

WIND

DIRECTION REFERENCE SPOT

Rotor Way, Inc.

489

UNIT 104

Sea Transport Systems

The carrying of people and materials by water is one of the oldest forms of transportation. Even though traveling by water dates back to the ancient Egyptians, it is still an important method of moving materials between countries, as well as within countries. Fig. 104-1.

MATERIALS TRANSPORT

By far the greatest number of ships that are in use today carry cargo. Ships carry everything from safety pins and plastic dolls to automobiles and large machinery.

Since 1950 cargo shipping has changed greatly. Before this time all the cargo was carried inside the ship into large compartments called *holds* which were loaded and unloaded by workers called *stevedores*. Since the early 1950s a new type of cargo ship called the container ship has been growing in use. Fig. 104-2 shows a container ship with containers stacked on the deck as well as in the holds.

Container ships have structures in the holds which permit the containers to be stacked one on top of the other. The containers are the size and shape of semitrailers. They can therefore be transferred from the boat to a truck and driven to their final destination. This eliminates the handling of individual items on the dock and reduces both the cost of cargo and the time it takes to load and unload a ship.

Special cranes on the docks load and unload the containers. Fig. 104-3. An all-container ship may spend one day in port as compared with six or more days for a conventional ship handling non-containerized cargo. Fig. 104-4 shows a container port facility.

104-1. *Modern container freighter on the open sea.*

Sea-Land Service

Unit 104: Sea Transport Systems

Port of Long Beach
104-2. Container ship with containers stacked on the deck.

Sea-Land Service
104-3. Loading a container onto a ship. Note the wheels from which the container has been lifted.

104-4. Container port facility.

Port of Long Beach 491

104-5. A supertanker.

104-6. River tow on the Mississippi.
Union Mechling Corporation

Today other types of cargo, like liquids and ore, are handled by large "super ships." For carrying crude oil and gasoline, supertankers have been developed. These are so large that they cannot use port facilities. The tankers anchor outside the harbor and unload through pipes and hoses or to smaller tankers which can use the port facilities. Fig. 104-5.

On the inland waterways such as the Mississippi River much bulk cargo, such as petroleum products, coal, and ore, is still shipped by river barge. The old river steamboat has been replaced by diesel vessels and barges.

On the Mississippi, towboats push barges that are tied securely together and then fastened to the towboat. The largest tows of barges carry up to 40 000 tons of cargo. Fig. 104-6.

Another of the important inland waterways is the Great Lakes. Iron ore mined in Minnesota is shipped in large ore carriers to the smelters in Illinois and Pennsylvania. Now with the St. Lawrence seaway open, oceangoing vessels can travel all the way to Chicago to unload their cargo.

PASSENGER TRANSPORT

Before the invention of the airplane, the only way to cross the ocean was by ship. Passenger ships were an important part of shipping companies' fleets. Before World War II the passenger ships achieved a status they have not had since. Ships such as the "Queen Mary," the "United States," and the "Queen Elizabeth" provided luxurious ways to cross the ocean. Fig. 104-7. With the coming of the airplane, the numbers of passengers on ships declined until today most of the passenger ships that are still in service are holiday cruise ships. Fig. 104-8.

SHIPS

A ship is a powered vessel designed for navigation on the sea. A ship is larger than a boat. A boat is small enough to be carried on a ship. A vessel that sails the ocean is called a ship.

A ship's size is measured by tonnage. Originally the term was used to measure how much the ship could carry. Now weight is measured by *deadweight* tonnage, which describes the capacity of tankers, and *displacement* tonnage, which is the weight of the ship as it floats.

In ancient times ships were powered by slaves manning oars. Later the wind was harnessed as a power source. The history of ships as a means of transportation for passengers and cargo really began with the sailing ship. Sailing ships dominated the sea lanes from about 1450 until the Civil War. The greatest advantage of the sailing ship was that wind costs nothing. The one big disadvantage of the sailing ship was that it depended on the wind. For this reason shippers were never sure

104-7. The "Queen Mary," one of England's passenger ships, sailed between England and New York.

104-8. This passenger ship sails to the Far East.

Pacific Far East Lines

when the ships or goods would arrive. Sailing ships were difficult to maneuver in battle because one was never sure of the wind.

The sailing ship reached its peak during the nineteenth century with the streamlined, fast *clipper ships.* One of the most famous of the clipper ships was the "Flying Cloud." Fig. 104-9.

By the late 1860s ships powered by steam were replacing the sailing ships. The last large-scale service of sailing ships came during World War I. By the 1920s there were practically no large sailing ships competing with steamships.

The first successful steamboat in the United States was the "Clermont," built by Robert Fulton. This boat carried cargo and passengers on the Hudson River. Early oceangoing steamships used both steam and sail for power. Many early steamships suffered mechanical failures and had to use sails to finish their voyages.

The first steamships were powered by *reciprocating* steam engines. As power plants were improved, a new type of engine was developed: the steam turbine. The turbine engine was more efficient and used less fuel. Another advance in power plants was the use of the diesel engine in ships. Today many ships are powered by diesel engines.

Smithsonian Institution

104-9. "Flying Cloud," one of the most famous clipper ships. It set a record of 89 days from New York to San Francisco.

Modern ocean ships are made of steel. Ships are constructed on land in shipyards. They are launched into the water after completion. Fig. 104-10 shows a partly finished tanker in a shipyard.

Since the beginning of sea transportation, ships have been used for military purposes. Some famous naval battles were fought using sailing ships. One such battle was fought in 1588 between English and Spanish forces. The defeat of the Spanish fleet (the Armada) marked the

493

104-10. Tanker under construction in a shipyard. Today ships are constructed of steel which is welded together.
Todd Shipyard Corporation

104-11. Modern navy ship.
United States Navy

104-12. The nuclear submarine "Bluefish." Using nuclear power enables ships like this one to remain underwater for many weeks at a time.
United States Navy

104-13. Roll on/roll off cargo vessel. Vehicles are driven onto the stern of the ship and transported on deck. On reaching port they are driven back off the stern.
Matson Navigation Company

104-14. *Cable-laying ship "Long Lines." This ship is used for laying telephone cable on the ocean floor.*

104-15. *Hydrofoil vessel running on its three fins, or foils.*

beginning of England's rise as a world power.

With the advent of steam power, navies began designing new ships. The combination of steam power and metal construction brought about new ships and new battle tactics. Fig. 104-11. Today's navies have ships which travel under the sea as well as on top. Some ships today are powered by nuclear reactors. This type of power is used mostly on submarines to enable them to remain underwater for a long time. Fig. 104-12 shows a nuclear submarine.

Ships have changed greatly since the days of sail power. Today they can carry thousands of tons of cargo or millions of barrels of oil. New methods of loading and unloading have shortened the time a vessel must remain in port. Fig. 104-13 shows one other new type of cargo vessel. With this ship, cargo containers or vehicles can be driven onto the ship, transported, then driven off.

SPECIAL PURPOSE VESSELS

In addition to the ships that carry cargo and passengers and the navy vessels, some ships have been developed for very special uses. One such ship, named "Long Lines," is used by the Western Electric Company to lay cable under the ocean. Fig. 104-14. The cable is fed out the stern, or rear, of the ship and falls to the ocean floor. The "Long Lines" can carry 2000 miles of cable at one sailing.

Because of a decrease in the number of passengers, there are very few passenger ships now crossing the Atlantic or Pacific. However, a need has developed for fast, economical water transport between land areas separated by small areas of water, such as the Hawaiian Islands. One new type of ship to meet this need is the jet hydrofoil developed by the Boeing Company.

A hydrofoil vessel actually rides above the water on fins called *foils*. Fig. 104-15. The boat is propelled by jets of water from pumps driven by gas turbines. As the speed of the boat increases, the hull of the boat lifts out of the water. The boat settles into the water at the dock to board passengers. The Boeing Jetfoil has a cruising speed of 51 MPH even over 12-foot waves. In shallow water the foils are retracted against the hull. A drawing of the Boeing Jetfoil is shown in Fig. 104-16.

Another type of craft using a special propulsion system is the *surface effect ship*, often called a *hovercraft*. The hov-

Part VI: Transportation

ercraft operates on a cushion of air which is created under the craft by large fans. The air is pumped down from above and comes out the sides. This craft can operate on both land and water. Fig. 104-17 shows the principle of the surface effect ship.

Sea transportation is an important part of our total transportation system. As ships and propulsion systems continue to improve, this form of transportation will continue to compete with air and land transportation systems for both cargo and passengers.

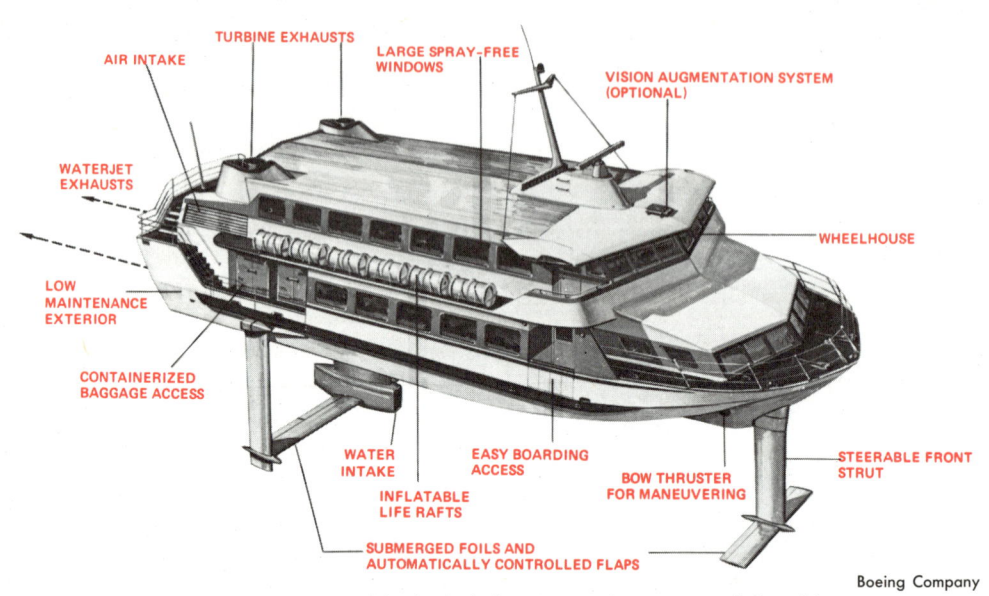

104-16. Drawing of hydrofoil showing various parts of the ship.

104-17a. Drawing of a surface effect ship showing how the stream of air moves.

Bell Aerospace Division of Textron
104-17b. This is the SES-100B, the first surface effect ship launched. It was lowered into the water by crane for the first time in 1971 for testing and evaluation.

UNIT 105

Automotive Transport Systems

Probably no single invention has changed the United States as greatly as did the automobile. Think of all the ways in which cars, and other vehicles such as buses and trucks, affect your life. Perhaps you ride a bus to school. Probably your parents drive to work in cars. When you go on a vacation, you probably travel by car.

Because it is a quick, convenient form of transportation, the automobile contributed to the growth of suburbs and shopping centers, thus changing the makeup of our cities. We have drive-in movie theaters, restaurants, and banks. The road system, the oil industry, the steel industry—all of these have been greatly affected by the automobile.

Before the development of the automobile, travel was often slow and difficult. The roads in the United States were trails used by horseback riders to travel from one town to another. Most early settlements were on river banks or bays, which were used for transportation. The first long hard-surfaced road was completed in 1795. It was the Lancaster Turnpike in Pennsylvania. It was surfaced with broken stones and gravel and extended 62 miles. In 1830, the steam locomotive was used successfully; so road building slowed. Railroads were to be the transportation of the future. Thus from 1850 to 1900, there was little change in the way that roads were built.

With the coming of the automobile, there was a demand for better roads. Farmers were asking for more roads so that they could get their products to the railroad for shipment to market.

The first concrete road was built in Detroit in 1908. By 1924 there were 31 000 miles of concrete roads in the United States. In 1925 a system of numbering highways was established. From 1924 until after World War II, little was done about building more concrete highways. Following World War II, truckers and automobile clubs realized something must be done to improve the highway system. To help solve the problem of rapid highway transportation, the National System of Interstate and Defense Highways was established. Today there are over 42 000 miles of this superhighway.

The interstate highway system connects 90 percent of the United States cities of over 50 000 population with multi-lane divided highways. Fig. 105-1.

Today there are more than 86 million automobiles and 19 million trucks and buses in the United States operating on nearly 4 million miles of streets and highways. The United States is a nation on wheels, and the automotive vehicle has become a necessity.

THE AUTOMOBILE

The automobile is a self-propelled, wheeled vehicle, designed to carry passengers on highways and streets. Automotive vehicles that carry a large number of people are buses, and those that carry freight are called trucks.

The automobile was invented in Europe, but it has had its greatest develop-

497

105-1. Six-lane divided highway. *Wisconsin Division of Highways*

ment in the United States. In 1892 the Duryea brothers built the first successful gasoline-powered automobile in the United States. A Duryea car won the first American automobile race in 1895. Fig. 105-2.

By 1900 there were a number of successful cars being made in the United States. Some of these cars were made by men whose names are still familiar: Ford, Olds, and Dodge. About this same time automobile racing and transcontinental runs became popular.

Experiments continued with types of locomotion other than the internal combustion engine. One was the steam car. The Stanley Steamer (built by the Stanley brothers) set a world speed record of 127.66 miles (205.4 kilometres) per hour in 1906. Propulsion by electricity was also tried and achieved a measure of success. Still, the internal combustion engine proved the most satisfactory. It became the standard engine for cars.

Until about 1900, automobiles were built by hand. Each varied from the other, and parts had to be hand-fitted to the machine, a slow and costly process. Henry Ford began to standardize parts. He also used the conveyor assembly line to speed up production. When the car reached the end of the line, it was driven off on its own power. With these improvements, the time needed for producing a car was greatly reduced, and the price was lowered so that the average person could afford one. The Ford Model T car was the first mass-produced automobile. Fig. 105-3.

During the early 1900s, a number of engineering improvements took place. The electric self-starter replaced the hand crank and made it easier for women to drive a car. Multiple cylinders, better tires, all-steel bodies, steel disc wheels, and closed bodies were features of the new cars.

TRUCKS AND BUSES

The automobile, like the railroad, was built to carry passengers. But the car companies soon discovered a demand for rapid shipment of freight. Larger cities were the first to use trucks. Bakers, dair-

105-2. Duryea car. *Smithsonian Institution*

105-3. Model T Ford. *Smithsonian Institution*

105-4. Half-ton pickup truck. These are used for hauling small loads. *GMC Truck & Coach Public Relations*

105-5. Large over-the-road semitrailer truck. These are used for hauling freight from one city to another. *GMC Truck & Coach Public Relations*

ies, and finally the post office began to use trucks. Until after World War II, the truck did not really compete with the railroad for business. Today, however, almost everything you use has been transported by a truck at some point. Manufacturers make trucks in many sizes, from small half-ton pickups (Fig. 105-4) to large semitrailers that can carry thousands of pounds of freight. Fig. 105-5.

While the large trucks were changing freight transportation, passenger transportation was being affected by motor buses. Before World War I there was a slow beginning to the bus industry. During the period from 1920 to World War II, the bus industry grew, but it did not really reach great importance until after World War II. Today almost every city has buses as part of its rapid transit system. Fig. 105-6.

The railroads once carried passengers from city to city. Motor buses have taken over much of this service. Large buses travel from city to city, carrying passengers in comfort unknown to early bus travelers. Fig. 105-7.

499

Part VI: Transportation

105-6. New transit bus for use in city transportation systems.

Greyhound Bus Lines, Inc.
105-7. Large overland bus. These buses can carry 50 to 60 passengers in comfort between cities.

THE MODERN AUTOMOBILE

After World War II, travel by car increased greatly. What was most needed was a dependable car that could travel at a good speed and would sell at a reasonable price. From the 1940s to the 1970s, the manufacture of cars and improvement of highways increased at a rapid pace. The car of today is a far cry from Henry Ford's Model T. Modern cars may have FM, AM radios, tape players, four-wheel disc brakes, air conditioning, and steel-belted tires. Many of the changes in the automobiles of the 1960s and 1970s were closely related to safety. Today, laws require safety glass, seat and shoulder belts, and front bumpers that can withstand collision at 5 MPH. At the same time, manufacturers have developed other safety features such as the collapsible steering column, dual braking systems, inflatable air bags, and stronger passenger compartments.

In the early 1900s there were many automobile manufacturers. Today, four giant manufacturers account for most of the United States' production of cars: General Motors, Ford, Chrysler, and American Motors. Cars are produced on moving production lines. As the chassis moves along the line, parts are added until the finished car is driven off at the end of the line. Fig. 105-8. Today's car is sleekly designed, highly engineered, and available in many models and styles. Fig. 105-9.

ENVIRONMENTAL IMPACT

The automobile has been a mixed blessing. It has made Americans the most mobile people in the world. As its numbers have increased, however, it has added to the world's pollution problem. As gasoline is burned in the engine, carbon monoxide, nitrous oxide, and hydrocarbons are produced. These are the main ingredients of the pollution we call smog. In 1970 Congress enacted the Clean Air Act, which limits the amount of pollutants an automobile may emit.

To comply with these rules and reduce the pollutants, automobile manufacturers have changed their engines in several ways. Fuel metering devices have been added to *pace* the amount of fuel fed to the engine. Since 1975, new cars have had to use *unleaded* gas. To avoid the wrong fuel being used, the filler pipe of the cars accepts only the fuel nozzle of unleaded gas. Fig. 105-10.

The use of unleaded gas is required because of the addition of another smog

Unit 105: Automotive Transport Systems

105-8. Attaching the grille and bumper to a car on the production line. 
General Motors Corporation

105-9. Modern automobiles have streamlined designs.
General Motors Corporation

reducing device. New cars have a *catalytic converter* added to the exhaust system. This converter is a device that resembles a muffler but is filled with platinum and palladium materials. Fig. 105-11. The converter works at a very high temperature, around 1000°F (538°C), and changes carbon monoxide and hydrocarbons into carbon dioxide and water.

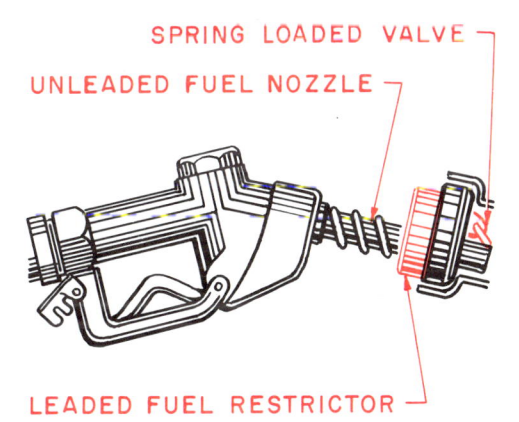

105-10. Fuel nozzle for unleaded gas.
— SPRING LOADED VALVE
— UNLEADED FUEL NOZZLE
— LEADED FUEL RESTRICTOR

— CATALYST CONTAINER
— EXHAUST OUTLET
— EXHAUST INTAKE
— OXIDIZING BED
— INSULATION

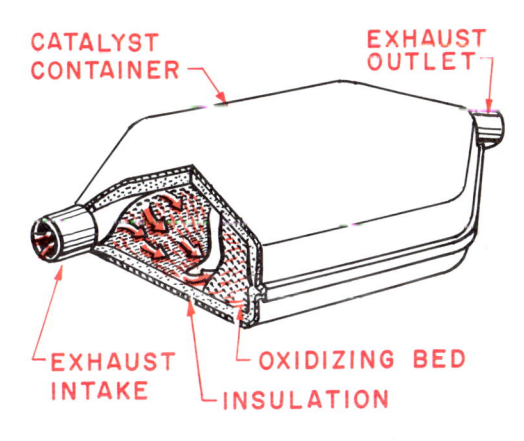

105-11. Example of catalytic converter used by General Motors
— ENGINE
— CROSS-OVER PIPE
— EXHAUST PIPE
— CATALYTIC CONVERTER
— MUFFLER
— INTERMEDIATE PIPE
— TAIL PIPE

501

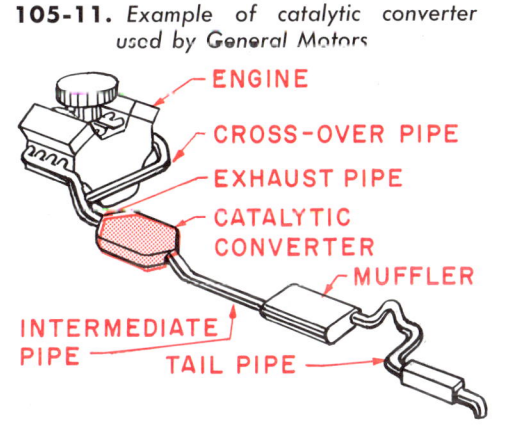

Part VI: Transportation

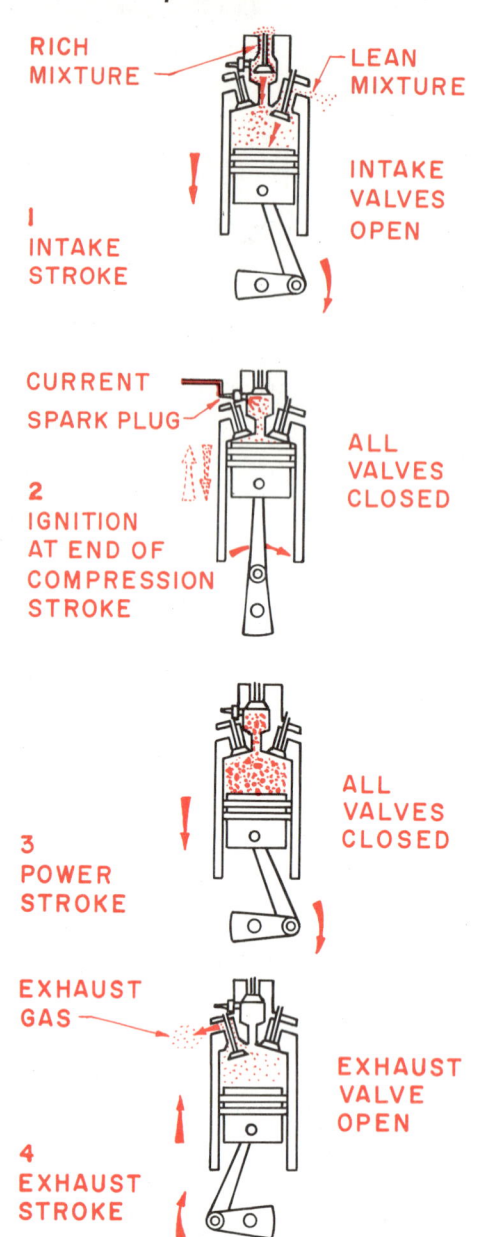

105-12. *Stratified charge engine: (1) A rich mixture and a lean mixture enter the cylinder; (2) the rich mixture is ignited by the spark plug. This ignites the lean mixture. The power stroke and the exhaust stroke (3 & 4) are the same as on a regular engine.*

General Motors Corporation
105-13. *Electric-powered vehicle, one alternative to the gasoline automobile.*

Another solution to the problem of making a car burn fuel more efficiently and cleaner is called a *stratified charge*. A *rich* mixture and a *lean* mixture enter the combustion chamber. Fig. 105-12. The piston compresses the mixture. The rich mixture fires, igniting the lean mixture. The leaner the mixture, the fewer pollutants. Using this type of combustion, an engine will meet the Clean Air Standards for 1975. Several of the American car makers are considering the stratified charge engine as an alternative to the catalytic converter.

Another alternative is the return of the electric car, in an improved form. A number of experimental vehicles have been built, one of which is the General Motors 512 Experimental Vehicle. Fig. 105-13.

Much research remains to be done. Scientists, manufacturers, and governments must work together to eliminate the pollution problems of the world.

DISCUSSION TOPICS

Part 6—Transportation

Unit 101
1. Why is transportation called a *service* industry?
2. What are the two essentials of any transportation system?
3. What are the elements of vehicle design? Why are these elements needed in a vehicle?

Unit 102
1. How did railroads help to open up the West to settlement?
2. What is a ton-mile?
3. Discuss some advantages of railroads over other forms of transportation.
4. Describe the operation of a railroad classification yard.
5. What is ACI and how does it work?

Unit 103
1. Describe the two airway systems over the United States.
2. What are some of the Federal Aviation Administration's responsibilities?
3. What does IFR stand for? What does VFR stand for?
4. When did the first successful powered flight take place? Who were the builders of the airplane used in this flight?
5. Which countries have built supersonic commercial aircraft?

Unit 104
1. What is the major use of ships today?
2. What is a container ship? How does it differ from earlier cargo ships?
3. How do barges move on the water?
4. Discuss some advantages and disadvantages of the sailing ships.
5. What was the "Clermont"?
6. How does a hydrofoil differ from a hovercraft?

Unit 105
1. From 1850 to 1900 there was little change in the way roads were built. Why?
2. Where was the automobile invented?
3. Today most cars are run by internal combustion machines. What were two other methods of propulsion used in early automobiles?
4. Discuss some of the safety features that have been added to cars in recent years.
5. Why must cars built since 1975 use unleaded gas?

PART VII
Modern Industry

Unit 106 What Is Modern Industry?

Unit 107 The Essentials of Industry

Unit 108 The Elements of Industry

Unit 109 Mass Production in the School

Unit 110 Careers

Discussion Topics and Activities

UNIT 106

What Is Modern Industry?

There are few materials which people can use as they find them in nature. Cotton, for instance, must be spun into yarns, then woven into cloth which is used to make clothing. The people and companies that do this work are part of an *industry*—the textile industry.

There are many industries. You have probably heard of the steel, petroleum, automobile, and entertainment industries, to name just a few. Fig. 106-1.

An industry may be defined as all the activities involved in producing a certain type of goods or services and making those goods or services available to the people who need or want them. *Goods* are material things such as clothes and tools. *Services* are nonmaterial items. For instance, the television and radio programs you enjoy are a service provided by the entertainment industry.

Think for a moment of the working men and women that you know. How many of them have jobs related to one of the industries in Fig. 106-2? Probably many of

106-1. *Modern industry is an organization of people, materials, and machines. This woman is attaching a microscopic wire to a part of a telephone.*

Western Electric Corporation

106-2. *Industries can be classified in many ways. The manufacturing and construction groups shown in this chart are based on the ones used by the United States Bureau of Labor Statistics.*

American Industries

Goods Producing		Services
Manufacturing	**Construction**	Advertising
Chemical	Homes	Appliance repair
Raw materials	Commercial buildings	Banking and finance
Food	Structures (Bridges, TV towers, etc.)	Education
Transportation equipment		Entertainment
Communication equipment		Food distribution
Power		Health
Consumer products (Non-food items, such as clothing, furniture)		Importing
		Insurance
		Publishing
		Sanitation
Heavy machinery		Shipping

Part VII: Modern Industry

106-3. *Technology is solving environmental problems. These automotive technicians are working on emission control.*

them do, because most people in the United States and other advanced nations are employed in the production of goods and services.

Ours has not always been an industrial society. In past centuries most people worked at providing food. In some underdeveloped nations this is still true today. However, as farm machinery and methods have improved, fewer people have been needed to operate farms. Steadily growing numbers of people have given up farming to take jobs in industry.

Products were not always made by mass production. Eli Whitney is generally recognized as the first person to use this technique in this country. In 1798 he was given an order for 10 000 muskets. He used special patterns, fixtures, and jigs to produce these weapons with interchangeable parts. Before then, guns were hand crafted, one at a time, and the parts for one could not be used for another.

Henry Ford developed mass production to the point that, in the 1920s, a Model T Ford car was coming off the production line every ten seconds. The main ideas of mass production are:
- Interchangeability of parts.
- Automatic conveyors to move the parts.
- Specialized labor.
- Elimination of wasted effort and motion.

The result is that today, a nut made in New Jersey will fit a bolt made in California. Mass production has made it possible for people to enjoy more and better products at lower cost. In the future, automation and computerized manufacturing may make production even more efficient.

The growth of industry has changed our society tremendously. Not all of the changes have been desirable. Crowded cities and smog, for example, are problems related to industry. Still, most people would agree that industry does far more good than harm to our society. For instance, who would want to do without electricity, automobiles, and modern plumbing? Today many nations have the highest standard of living they have ever known, as a result of industry.

It is interesting to note that some of the problems connected with an industrial society are also being solved by industries themselves. For instance, low-cost housing units can be mass-produced to improve living conditions in crowded cities. Air pollution, partly a result of factory smoke and automobiles, is being relieved by air-purifying systems also developed by industry. Fig. 106-3.

Throughout the centuries, people have constantly tried to find more efficient ways of producing the goods and services they have wanted and needed. The resulting progress can be called *industrial-technological advancement*. This advancement shows progress toward the kind of life most people want. Historically, nations and societies have ceased to exist when they have been unable to provide

Unit 106: What Is Modern Industry?

the products which their people needed and wanted. Thus industrial efficiency is important for keeping our society going.

Another name for this efficiency is *productivity*. This term refers to the ability to turn out a maximum of high quality goods and services with a minimum of effort.

People become more productive when they are better trained and have better tools and machinery to use. For example, it takes a lot of time and effort to dig a ditch with a hand shovel and a pick. But someone who has a power shovel, and the skill to use it, can dig a ditch faster, with far less effort. The same holds true for those working in factories; better equipment, and the skill to use it, make better workers. This is why productivity has increased over the years.

A nation may have great natural resources, but only when they are made useful to people do those resources add to the nation's real prosperity. Therefore a nation's wealth can be measured by the productivity of its workers. The total value of goods and services produced by a nation's workers is called the *gross national product,* or GNP. Generally speaking, nations with the largest GNPs are those with the highest standards of living.

Fig. 106-4 shows how the productivity of a typical worker in the United States has grown since the start of this century. Note that in a ten-hour day, common in 1900, a worker produced very little more than what a worker in 1970 turned out in a single hour.

PEOPLE AND TECHNOLOGY

The period in which you are now living is often called the machine age, the age of automation, or the age of technology. These are accurate descriptions, for all about us we see evidence of machines and automation. In recent years, people have gone to the moon, passenger aircraft have flown at twice the speed of sound, and we have seen remarkable changes in medicine, and in a vast number of other materials and products.

It would seem that there is very little that people cannot do if they set their minds and hands to the task. In a sense this has always been so. People have always been inventing, and finding better ways of doing things. Today, however, changes take place much faster than in past years. This is because people are better trained and educated and have better tools and materials. In other words, our technology is better.

Some authorities estimate that human beings, the toolmakers, have been on earth for roughly 240 000 years. If we take this figure and set it to the scale of a 24-hour clock, we would get a drawing like that in Fig. 106-5. Note that people spent 22 of the 24 "hours" in the Paleolithic, or Old Stone Age. During this time they lived in caves and first used crude stone tools. Just a short *two hours* ago they entered the Neolithic, or New Stone Age. At this time they made tools of polished stone, began to farm and raise animals for food, and invented the all-important wheel.

One hour and twenty-four minutes ago they discovered copper. *One hour* ago they learned how to make and use bronze. Fig. 106-6. Now they had tools far superior to those of stone—stronger

106-4. *This chart shows how a typical worker's productivity has grown since 1900. Note that the dollar amounts do not refer to the worker's wages, but to the value of what the worker produces. These figures are based on the United States, but similar growth has taken place in Canada and other industrial nations.*

Our Changing Productivity

Year	Value of Goods and Services, Per Hour	Average Number of Hours of Work Per Week
1900	$.56	60
1920	$.70	54
1930	$.80	47
1950	$3.15	40
1970	$5.44	37

Part VII: Modern Industry

and sharper, lighter and easier to use. *Forty-eight minutes* ago people discovered iron, and learned to cast and shape it into even better tools. With the discovery of metals, people could make more efficient and dependable machines, and a variety of excellent products. Printing was invented just *six minutes* ago. Fig. 106-7.

Two minutes ago the Industrial Revolution began. During this period appeared some of the most significant inventions: Watt's steam engine; Hargraves' spinning machine (Fig. 106-8); Whitney's cotton gin; and Maudslay's screw-cutting lathe (Fig. 106-9). The factory emerges here, and machines become more efficient because of steam power. People learned to produce and use electricity only *one minute and 18 seconds* ago. About *25 seconds* ago the first airplane was flown. Atomic power, computers, and space flight were born just a few *seconds* or *fractions of a second* ago.

People no sooner learn to use a machine or a material, than a new one comes along for them to master. Along with new materials, skills, and ideas, many new tools have also been perfected to help people work more quickly and efficiently. Fig. 106-10. From simple clay pots made by hand, people have moved to dishes mass-produced by machine. And whereas people once had to hew logs to make boards by hand, with great effort, they now do it simply, with the aid of machines. Fig. 106-11. Steadily im-

106-5. *Each "hour" of this 24-hour clock represents 10 000 years. The time before the Neolithic is called the Paleolithic Age. This primitive era occupies nearly all of human existence on earth.*

106-6. *This primitive forge from Africa was one of the first successes in heating metal so that it could be shaped. The bellows are made of animal skins. These are pumped by hand to force air to the charcoal fire.*

The Science Museum, London

508

106-8. The "Spinning Jenny" was invented by James Hargraves around 1855. It improved textile production because it could spin several threads at the same time.

106-7. Treadle lathe used in the early 1700s. Can you figure out how it works?

106-9. Maudslay's screw-cutting lathe, early 1800s.

106-10. A modern metalworking lathe.

509

Part VII: Modern Industry

106-11. People once made furniture by hewing logs. Now they use machines.

proving technology has made our work easier, and given us better food and clothing, and made us more comfortable and healthier (as shown by longer life spans).

However, there are some serious problems which come to us with technology. Following is a list of some important characteristics of a technological society, with some discussion of how they affect us.

• Technology causes people to become more *detached* from their work. This means that they have less physical contact with the materials they are making into products. For example, at a numerically controlled (or automated) milling machine, a technician operates buttons and levers, and the machine does all the work. In some cases, the operator does not even see the material being worked. Fig. 106-12. And in some automated factories, the materials and the machines may be well away from the control panel, often in another part of the building. In these situations, it is hard for people to become personally involved and interested in their work. Fig. 106-13.

• Technology demands a very high degree of accuracy in the production of goods. In many cases, a machine can do jobs that people cannot possibly do; machines are in some ways more accurate and reliable. This changes the types of jobs that are available, as the machines take over the jobs that people once did. The result is that many people must learn to live with the fact they will probably change jobs, or at least be retrained, several times during their working years.

• The efficiency of technology is directly related to repetitive actions (actions which are done over and over). In other words, technology is most effective in mass-production situations, which can use automatic devices to make goods. Not only does this result in great numbers of identical products, but the production line jobs become very specialized. This is called "division of labor," and while it makes for production line efficiency, it can become very boring.

• Technical societies use great amounts of raw materials and cause serious pollution problems. Whenever people live together, such problems occur. However, in technical societies they are much more common and serious.

PEOPLE AND ECOLOGY

One of the main purposes of this course is to help you better understand the technical society in which you live. You learned in this unit that technology aids us in many ways. You also read that it causes some problems, such as the need to train for new jobs. However, there is another great problem that we face today, perhaps more serious than any other—*pollution*.

Pollution in all its forms is a critical issue in technical societies. One reason for this is that such societies create a large amount of waste. This may seem surprising at first, since efficient production would seem to eliminate waste. However, such efficiency is not the whole story. There is a point at which it becomes cheaper and more profitable to waste a material rather than reuse it.

For example, labor costs have become so high that it is cheaper to throw away "tin" cans than it is to collect them, melt them down, and reuse the scrap metal. Likewise, it is easier for a beverage firm to

Unit 106: What Is Modern Industry?

Bethlehem Steel Corporation

106-12. *Automation removes people from their work. They no longer shape material by hand in factories.*

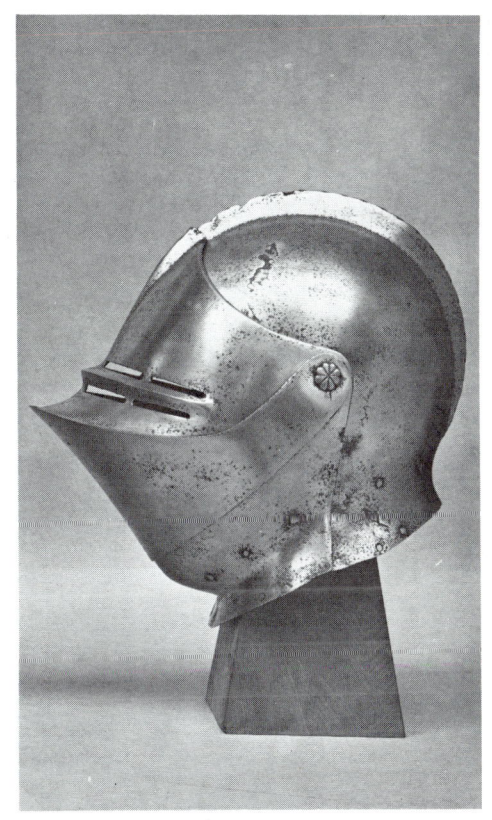

106-13. *Metal craftsmen of the Middle Ages made armor by hand. How would this headpiece be made today?*

use throwaway bottles rather than the type that must be returned to the store, hauled to the bottling factory, washed, inspected, and refilled.

Although these methods save money for the canner and the bottler, they pose a big problem for society: What to do with a huge accumulation of cans, bottles, and other junk? It is interesting to note that in nonindustrial, developing nations, waste disposal problems are practically nonexistent. Every material is too valuable to throw away. By contrast, every year Americans discard 7 million automobiles, 1 million tires, 20 million tons of paper, 28 million bottles, 48 billion cans, and 165 million tons of solid waste. We also dirty the air we breathe by gushing incredible amounts of smoke and fumes into it each year. Because of our carelessness, we dump many tons of waste into our waterways, polluting the water we need for drinking, washing, transportation, and recreation. A word used often in connection with this problem is *ecology*, which is simply the study of how people (and other living things) live in their environment.

The chart in Fig. 106-14 describes this situation visually. It shows that when our natural resources are used to produce

106-14. *Material flow and recycling diagram.*

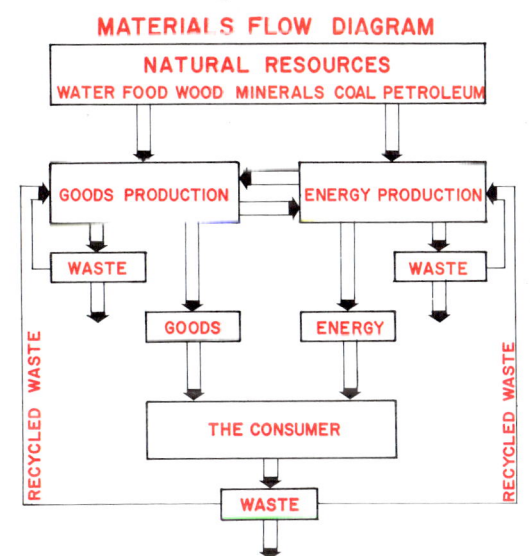

MATERIALS FLOW DIAGRAM

NATURAL RESOURCES
WATER FOOD WOOD MINERALS COAL PETROLEUM

GOODS PRODUCTION — ENERGY PRODUCTION

WASTE — WASTE

GOODS — ENERGY

RECYCLED WASTE — THE CONSUMER — RECYCLED WASTE

WASTE

511

Part VII: Modern Industry

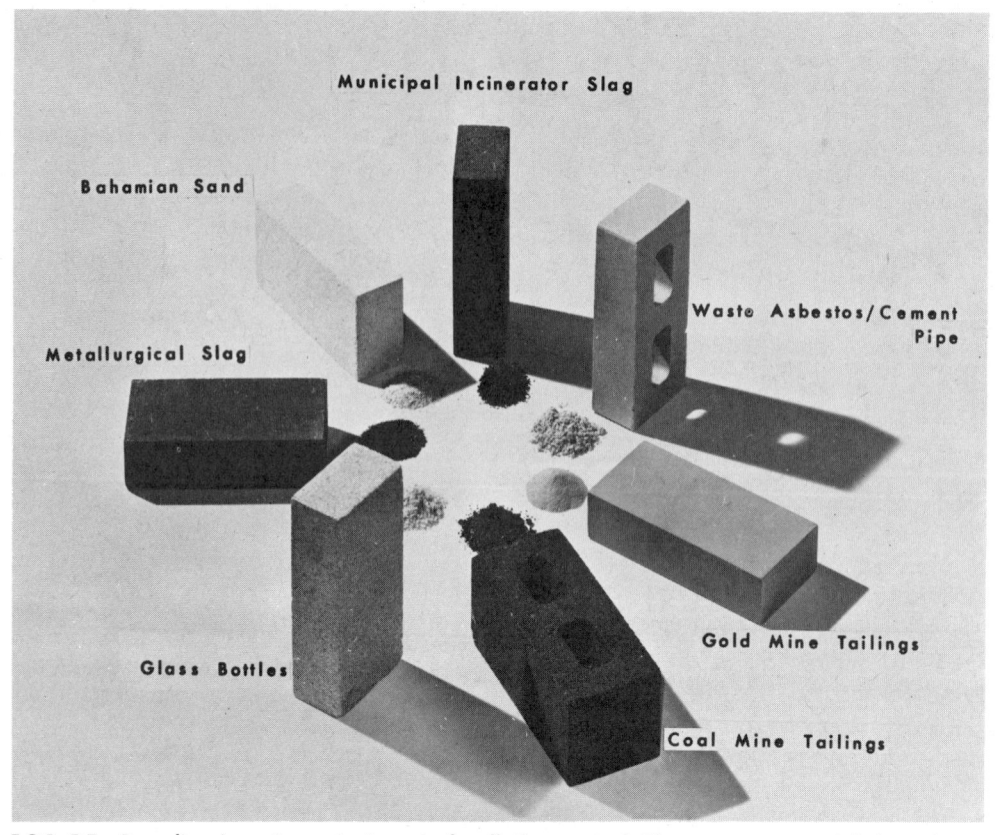

106-15. Recycling is an important part of pollution control. These waste materials have been recycled into building bricks.

goods and energy, some waste results before the product reaches the consumer, and still more waste occurs after the consumer has the product. Some of the waste materials are reused, but much is not. For example, when we burn coal to produce heat, we get ashes and smoke as waste products. When we convert iron ore to steel, we also get gases and slag. When we burn gasoline in our cars, we also produce smoke, fumes, and carbon deposits. When we finish a candy bar, we throw away the wrapper.

In other words, although *consume* means to use up, a consumer actually uses up only a part of many products and discards the rest. Recycling materials is an important answer to this problem. Fig. 106-15.

In this unit you have learned about the background, achievements, and problems of industry. No one knows the future, but it seems very likely that our society will continue to become more mechanized and specialized. Some people worry that machines may change our environment or our economy so much that we will be ruined. However, we can solve these problems, because people are greater than any machine. Your task in building a better, more humane society is to understand and appreciate technology for what it is and can do; to do this you must be informed. Machines cannot think; people can. The more you understand about technology, the better you will be able to help in solving the problems caused by industrialization.

UNIT 107

The Essentials of Industry

As said in Unit 106, productivity has increased because skilled workers with improved equipment have turned raw materials into useful products more efficiently. Fig. 107-1. This points out the three basic resources which are necessary to all industry. They are:

- Material resources—such as timber and iron ore.
- Human resources—people, everyone from machine operators to top management, whose work helps produce goods and services.

107-1. *Modern industry is made up of people, materials, and machines. Electronic units are typical industrial products.*

Design Center, Copenhagen

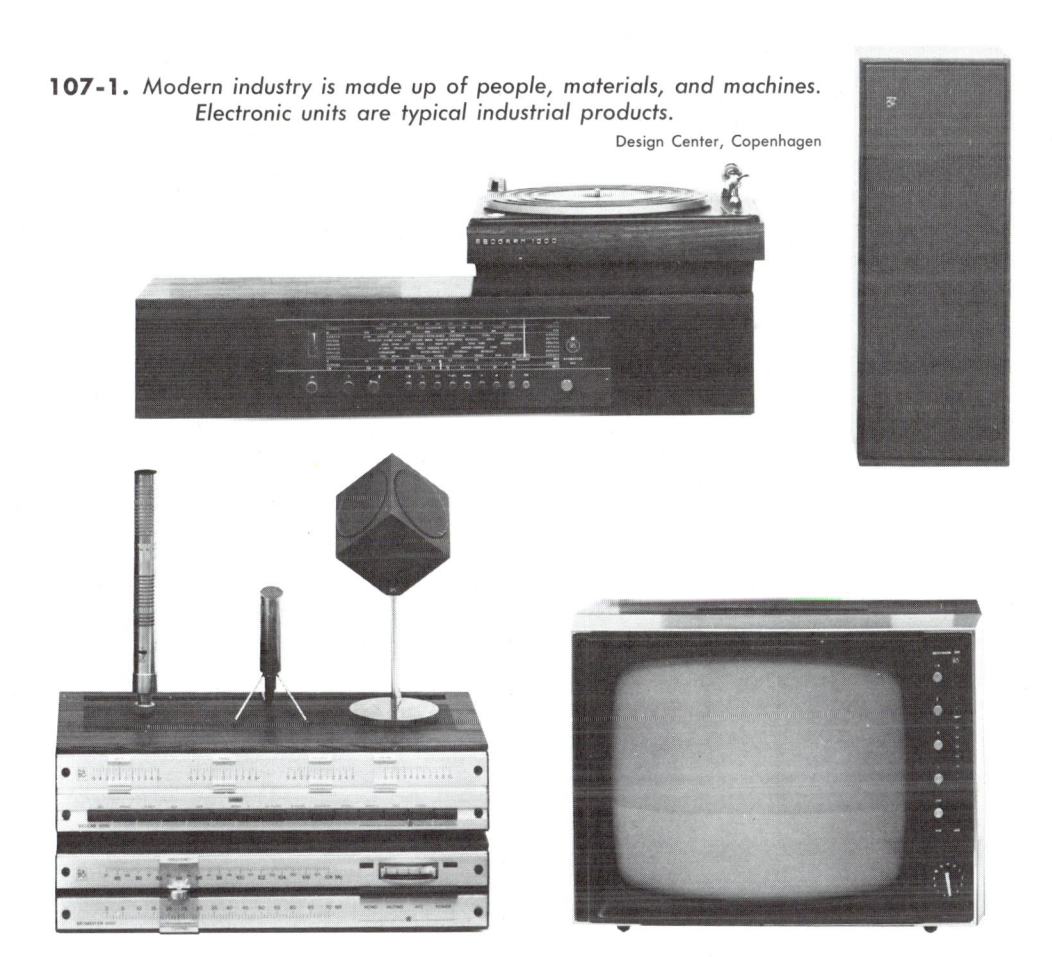

513

Part VII: Modern Industry

THE ESSENTIALS OF INDUSTRY

MATERIAL RESOURCES   **HUMAN RESOURCES**   **CAPITAL RESOURCES**

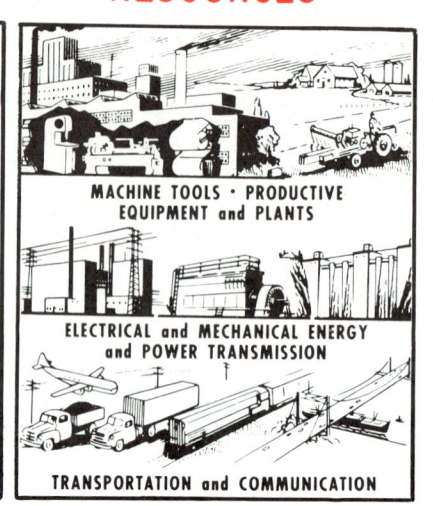

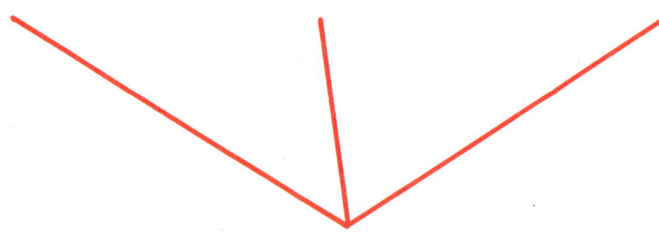

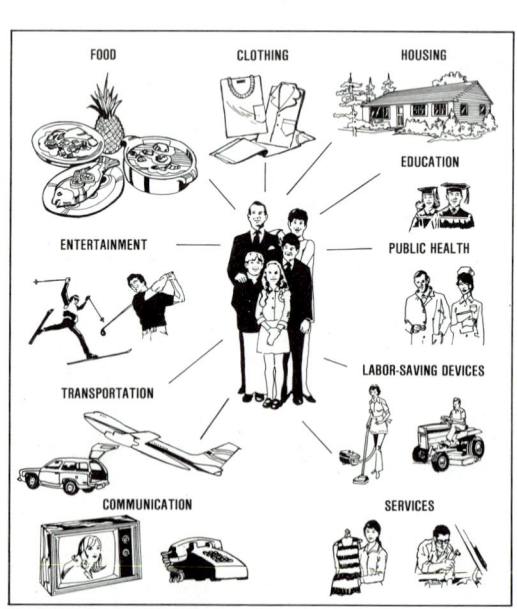

107-2. The essentials of industry—material resources, human resources, and capital resources. Every industry combines these to provide goods and services for the benefit of people.

- Capital resources—such as factories and equipment.

Without these resources, industry could not exist. That is why these resources are called the *essentials of industry*. Fig. 107-2.

Obviously, even with these essentials, an industry needs a system and a team in order to meet the needs and wants of millions of people. In this unit you will learn more about this system (mass production) and the team (a corporation).

MATERIAL RESOURCES

When we think of the material resources a country has, we usually consider only those used to make products. The common types that come to mind are wood and metals. But nations have many other material resources which contribute to their wealth. Some examples are coal, petroleum, water, soil, raw chemical deposits, and even air.

A nation which has great supplies of natural resources is fortunate, for it does not have to rely upon other countries to provide the raw materials needed for manufacturing. The United States is rich in natural materials. In this unit we shall be learning about them, and what we must do to insure a continuing supply. This textbook contains several units devoted to wood, metals, and plastics; so they will not be further discussed here. Instead, let us examine some of the other materials found in this country.

Coal

Coal is a soft black or brown rock used mainly as a fuel. It is called a *fossil fuel* because it was formed from decaying plants. These plants, layer upon layer of them, were covered by rocks and soil. Millions of years of heat and pressure caused them to turn into the coal we use today. There are two main classes of coal:

Bituminous, or *soft*, *coal* is the most plentiful type. It is used mainly by steam plants that generate electricity, and as coke in making steel.

Unit 107: The Essentials of Industry

Anthracite coal is harder than bituminous. Sometimes it is simply called *hard coal*. It burns cleaner and with less smoke, and it is used mainly in heating homes. It is more expensive than soft coal.

Other types of coal include *lignite* and *peat*. Lignite and peat are low grade coals with very high moisture content. They must be dried before burning and are used as fuels in some countries.

Because oil and gas were cleaner and more convenient, coal became less valuable. However, because of fuel shortages in this country, more coal is again being used. Research has led to cleaner coal fuels. Coal is also a source of chemicals for making plastics, dyes, and fertilizers. About 35 percent of the world reserve of coal is found in North America. Most of it is bituminous.

Petroleum

Petroleum comes from the earth and is a thick, dark liquid called oil or crude oil. No one knows exactly how it was formed. Many scientists say is comes from decayed remains of prehistoric plant and animal life. The same kinds of heat and pressure that formed coal probably formed oil. The difference is that the liquids were forced through porous soils into reservoirs deep under the ground and under the seas. Fig. 107-3. Today oil wells are sunk deep into the earth to tap these pools. Petroleum is made into fuels such as gasoline and kerosene. It is also made into lubricants and chemicals. Natural gas also collects underground and is a valuable fuel. Petroleum and natural gas provide more than $3/4$ of all the energy used in the United States. About $1/4$ of the world's petroleum is found in Canada and the United States. Huge deposits are also found in the Middle East, Africa, and Mexico.

Water

Water is vastly important. Not only is it needed for drinking, cleaning, and farm-

515

Part VII: Modern Industry

107-3. *Oil drilling takes place on land and sea. This huge offshore rig is used to pump oil from the ocean floor.*

107-4. *Water is a necessity of life and an important resource for industry. It also provides us with recreation.*

ing, but also it is a key industrial resource. Industries use water for generating electric power, as a cleaning and cooling agent, and as an ingredient in many products. Water is basic to sewage disposal. It is a major factor in the transportation and recreation industries. Fig. 107-4.

It is easy to take water for granted, because our mighty rivers and lakes seem to provide an endless supply of it. However, the supplies are unevenly distributed. As a result there are many areas which suffer severe water shortages. Our need for water rises each year, and some cities must transport it through hundreds of miles of pipelines and waterways. Also, many of our rivers and lakes are polluted.

Clean water is becoming more difficult to obtain.

Making the most of our water supplies is an important task. Many industries recirculate water through their plants so that is can be used more than once. Some cities have found ways of recovering water from treated sewage plant flows. Increasing attention is being given to the crucial task of stopping the pollution of our lakes and streams.

Soil

Topsoil is the uppermost layer of soil. It is a light, crumbly material which can store much water. Plants need it because it is rich in the materials they need in order to grow.

Topsoil is formed through the decay of plants and animals, minerals, and bacteria. This is a slow process. Even in many

Unit 107: The Essentials of Industry

good farming areas, topsoil is only seven or eight inches deep. Therefore erosion—the wearing away of topsoil by water, wind, and fire—is a serious problem. Soil conservation is the study of ways to protect this valuable resource.

Chemical Deposits

Many industries make products from chemicals, which is why chemicals are so valuable. Many basic chemicals come from other materials familiar to us all. For example, from petroleum we get xylene for paint and ethylene for antifreeze. Phosphates come from certain types of rock and are used in fertilizers and detergents. Common salt is converted to chlorine gas and caustic soda. Chlorine in turn is used as a water purifier and caustic soda is used in making soap. Chemical research leads to the development of better paints and fuels, medicines and foods, and many other useful things.

Materials Research and Development

Scientists study our natural resources. They try to find ways to make better use of these materials. An example of successful research is the use of *lignin.* Lignin is a chemical which holds wood fibers together in a tree. This material used to be wasted in the process of making paper. Now lignin is saved and used in food flavoring, perfume, drugs, and fuels.

Another example is *taconite,* a very low-grade iron ore found in abundance in this country. With a special process called *pelletizing,* it is now possible to produce a concentrated form of taconite which can be used by the steel industries.

Our natural resources fall into two main categories—*renewable* and *nonrenewable.* The renewable ones, such as forests and water, are restored by nature, but this takes time. We must be careful not to use up such materials faster than they can be restored. The nonrenewable materials are called *one-crop resources.* Coal, petroleum, and metallic ores are some examples. It is important to realize that good conservation must be practiced for both the renewable and the nonrenewable kinds of materials.

E. I. duPont de Nemours & Co., Inc.
107-5. *People are the most important resource we have. Their education and training are important to this world's progress.*

HUMAN RESOURCES

Of all the resources essential to industry, the human ones are the most important. Fig. 107-5. People plan products, dig ore, manage businesses, operate machines, and consume products. Without people, industries could not exist, and there would be no reason for them to exist. People make industry work.

The process of starting a business is described later in this unit. People pool their money and form a corporation. Then they may hire other people. Some may be hired to manage the company on a day-to-day basis. They are called the *management.* Others, the *nonmanagerial employees,* do such work as planning

Part VII: Modern Industry

107-6. Managers work with employees to solve industrial production problems.

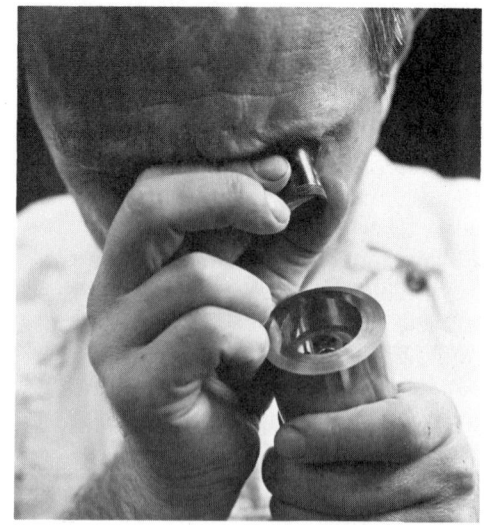

107-7. Skilled employees are the backbone of industry. This tool and die maker is checking a metal molding die.

Western Electric Corporation

products, making out the payroll, and operating machines. This unit is about both kinds of employees and the part they play in manufacturing. More information on employees and careers is found in Unit 110.

Management

The main job of management is to organize and direct the natural, human, and capital resources of a company for effective operation. Managers have a broad variety of professional backgrounds. They may have worked as salespeople, accountants, engineers, scientists, or in many other jobs. Each is promoted to management because she or he has some special ability. Some are chiefly concerned with such matters as finance or personnel. Fig. 107-6. Others—the engineers and scientists—deal with technical problems.

Many managers are promoted from within the company. In this way, a capable machine operator can become a foreman or a department manager, provided he or she has the right training for the new job. Some managerial employees need college education. Others get their skills in technical schools, on the job, or in training programs run by the corporation.

Nonmanagerial Employees

While there are many managers and supervisors in factories, most of those who work there are not managers. They are the clerks, the technicians, and the machine operators who are directly responsible for the production of goods. Such persons perform their tasks as directed by the managers.

Some industrial workers are *unskilled*. This means they have fairly simple jobs that require little training. Most workers are semiskilled. Some training is needed to do such jobs as vehicle driving, assembling parts, and certain machine operations such as metal stamping.

Those in the *skilled* occupations must attend schools to learn welding, drafting, toolmaking, business-machine operation, or cabinetmaking. It seems likely that there will always be a shortage of skilled workers in industry. Fig. 107-7.

Finally, there are the *technicians*. They serve as engineering or laboratory assistants. Generally, they must have two or more years of college work, usually in a technical school or community junior college. This is the fastest growing group of nonmanagerial workers.

Employee Organizations

Most groups of workers—professional and nonprofessional—form unions or other associations. Teachers, doctors, plumbers, nurses, and carpenters are just a few of many such groups. The associations are formed for two important reasons: to set and maintain high standards of performance, and to look after the welfare of the group.

For example, an organization of carpenters sets standards of basic training, experience, and continuing education so that the members will be able to turn out work of high quality. It also, through *collective bargaining,* arranges for fair wages, vacations, pensions, and medical benefits, in discussions with management. Such worker organizations are called *unions*.

There are many unions in the United States today. The American Federation of Labor was created to include skilled machinists, printers, welders, and others. The Council of Industrial Organizations was formed to represent the interests of mass-production workers, regardless of skill. These two groups joined in 1955 to become the AFL-CIO. Some other important unions are the Teamsters, United Mine Workers, and United Automobile Workers.

The professions have formed organizations such as the National Association of Manufacturers, the American Medical Association, and the American Vocational Association. All such groups, in management, labor, and the professions, are concerned that each member gets a fair share of America's industrial wealth.

Industrial Employment

According to recent statistics, over half of the working people in the United States are employed in manufacturing or related industries. See Fig. 107-8 for more information on workers in manufacturing and other occupations.

Employment figures are always changing. By studying such changes, one can get a picture of which groups are growing and which are not. Such information is important, for it tells us what kinds of human resources will be needed in the future.

CAPITAL RESOURCES

When you visit a factory, look carefully at the many pieces of equipment there. Workers are using hand tools such as hammers and screwdrivers. There are also many machines and other tools, as well as automatic conveyors to carry finished products. You will see telephones and adding machines, and furniture, in the offices. And of course there is the building itself, with its electric lights and heating system.

All of the above are examples of industry's *capital resources.* These resources are commonly called the "tools" of industry, for they are all required in order to make products. Let us take a closer look at some of these capital resources needed by industry.

Tools and Other Equipment

Machines and tools are used to make usable products out of materials such as wood and metal. Fig. 107-9. A bicycle frame, for example, is made of steel tubing. Some machines are used to cut the pieces of tubing to length, and others to bend them to shape. A special fixture holds the pieces in proper position, and another machine welds them together. The welded joints are ground smooth, holes are drilled where necessary, and the frame is painted—all mechanically. Many different pieces of equipment and machines are needed to make these frames. Factories need many kinds of special tools, depending upon the product being made.

519

Part VII: Modern Industry

Factory Buildings

Most industrial work is done in buildings that are specially designed and equipped for the purpose. There are *production buildings*, where materials are made into parts which are then assembled. *Warehouses* are used to store raw materials and finished products. Adminis-

107-8. *This chart is based on figures from the U.S. Bureau of Labor Statistics. Notice how many of the workers are either directly or indirectly connected with the manufacturing industries.*

PERSONS EMPLOYED BY GROUP*

GROUP	EMPLOYEES	PERCENT
MANUFACTURING	18,567,000	23.7
WHOLESALE AND RETAIL TRADE	17,753,000	22.6
GOVERNMENT	15,223,000	19.4
SERVICES	14,180,000	18.1
TRANSPORTATION AND PUBLIC UTILITIES	4,481,000	5.7
FINANCE, REAL ESTATE, AND INSURANCE	4,238,000	5.4
CONTRACT CONSTRUCTION	3,321,000	4.2
MINING	766,000	0.9

*EXCLUDING AGRICULTURE

Unit 107: The Essentials of Industry

tration or *office buildings* house the clerks, typists, and managers. There may be still other buildings for the heating plant, for vehicles, for miscellaneous storage, and for many other uses. Some corporations are housed in one building, but many of the larger ones require a number of them, even hundreds, all needed for effective production.

Energy and Power

The heating systems, lights, and machines in a factory need power to operate. The energy requirements of many industries are varied and great. Gas, fuel oil, electricity, and coal are used in large amounts to satisfy these needs. Atomic power plants are being used in some regions to supply energy, and may become even more important in the future. Research is also being done on other sources of energy.

Communications

Materials and tools must be ordered, and the finished products sold. These activities require communication between people, over great distances. Telephones, mail, and telegraph are common means of communication. Fig. 107-10. Transportation can also be considered as a form of communication, in which goods instead of messages are carried from one place to another. More information on transportation systems can be found in Part 6.

Equipment, buildings, power, communications, transportation—all of these are capital resources of industry. When a corporation is formed, much of the money that has been raised will usually go toward the purchase of capital items such as these. Later, a large part of the corporation's income will also be spent on capital goods—for instance, repairing and replacing equipment, and continuing to buy power. A corporation must meet these expenses before it can show a profit; so its products must be priced accordingly.

107-9. Machine tools and buildings are a part of industry's capital resources.

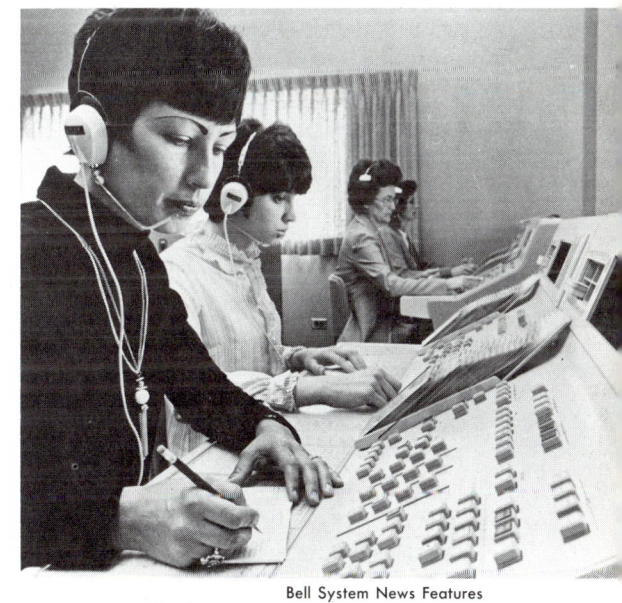

107-10. Telephone communications are important to business, industry, and the private citizen.

THE MANUFACTURING CORPORATION

Most of the goods that you need to buy are readily available. For instance, if you want a coat, you go to a store and choose one from a large supply. You pay for it and take it home. Even major items such as new cars and homes can be pur-

521

Part VII: Modern Industry

107-11. *Mass production involves work on an assembly line. Each trained person performs one important operation.*

Western Electric Corporation

chased ready-made, available for almost immediate possession. This process is so common that you probably do not think about it very much.

However, it was not always easy to obtain needed products. Before this century, most items were *custom built*—that is, made to order, individually, by craftsmen. If a man needed a coat, he went to a tailor, selected a fabric, described the style he wanted, and was measured. The tailor would then begin to make the coat and would notify the customer when it was finished.

There were advantages to custom production. A craftsman could fashion a product nearly like an artistic creation. The customers could get almost exactly what they wanted (if they could afford it). But the system also had disadvantages. If you lost your coat in November, it might be January before the tailor could get a new one ready for you.

A bigger problem was that custom production could not meet the needs of a growing population. There were not enough craftsmen to produce all the items that people needed and wanted, at prices that most people could pay.

Perhaps the best example of this is shown by the automobile. Henry Ford was not the first one to build a car, but he was the first to make cars available to large numbers of people. He devised a way of making automobiles in large numbers and at fairly low cost. Ford's cars were not custom built; they were mass-produced.

Mass Production is making of goods in quantity, using assembly-line methods and involving the interchangeability of parts. Fig. 107-11. Mass production also involves the division of labor—that is, each member of a production line performs a single operation. An especially important part of this method is that wasted effort and motion are reduced through careful planning and training. Briefly stated, the four principles of all mass-production systems are:

- Assembly-line method.
- Interchangeable parts.
- Labor specialization.
- Time and motion studies.

Industrial mass production is big business. It involves many people and extensive amounts of money and facilities. It also requires an effective system of organization. The type of organization which starts and maintains most mass-production operations is a *corporation*. In order to understand giant industrial corporations, we will first compare them with smaller, simpler business organizations.

Small Businesses

There are a number of ways to start and operate a business. For example, in an art metal course you might learn to make beautiful medallions which people would like to buy. You might buy equipment and supplies with your own money, make the medallions in your basement, and sell them yourself. The profits would be all yours. This form of business is called a *proprietorship*.

Perhaps you would not have enough money to buy the equipment and supplies. Then you might ask a friend to put up half the money and come into the business with you. You might make the medallions and your friend might sell them. You would share the profits. This type of business is called a *partnership*.

Together you and your partner would make the decisions about how to run the business. You would have to decide on the kind of equipment and the amount of supplies to buy, how many medallions to make at once, and how much to charge for your product. You would also have to decide whether to advertise, whether to add other products to the "line," and countless other questions.

As you see, starting and running even a small business is not a simple matter. For a large mass-production operation, the problems are complex.

The Manufacturing Operation

To set up an operation for the mass production of automobiles, a company needs far more money than one or two people could get together. A large number of people invest their money to set up such an operation. The kind of business they form is called a *corporation*. The investors own the business. Fig. 107-12.

There may be hundreds or even thousands of people who own part of a large corporation. Obviously, they cannot all sit down together to discuss how to run the business. Therefore these owners, called *stockholders,* elect a small group of people to provide the top-level management. This group is called the *board of directors*. A board must have at least three members, but a typical large corporation might have as many as 15 directors. Usually directors are persons with considerable business experience, and often they are people who have invested large amounts of money in the corporation.

The board chooses one of its members to be the *president* of the corporation. It also appoints other top corporation offi-

Unit 107: The Essentials of Industry

Corporate Organization

Stockholders
Board of Directors
President
General Manager
Manager
Assistant Managers
Operators

107-12. *This chart shows how a corporation is set up.*

cers, such as a *secretary* and a *treasurer*. The secretary keeps records of the board's decisions and also of who the stockholders are. The treasurer is in charge of handling the company's money. The board may also name one or more vice presidents, but the chief executive is the president. It is his or her job to manage the company so that the board's decisions are carried out.

For instance, the board may decide that the company should manufacture only the engines for the cars they plan to make. It would be the president's responsibility to see that the right kind of manufacturing operation is set up. The president would also be in charge of arrangements for buying the automobile bodies and other parts to go with the engines.

The president cannot handle all the details of these jobs alone; so other employees are hired. At first, most of the people employed will be executives. Later, when the company is ready to begin operation, employees will be hired to operate and maintain the machines, and others to sell the finished products.

It would be hard to find any two large corporations which have exactly the same management setup. However, the typical arrangement would be for the president to have one chief assistant. In some corpo-

Part VII: Modern Industry

107-13. Management is responsible for the safe and efficient operation of industry.

Eastman Kodak

rations this person is called the *executive vice president;* in others, the *general manager.*

Next in line would be a group of *managers,* each in charge of a department. The general manager sees that the president's instructions are passed along to the managers, makes sure that the instructions are carried out, and reports back to the president about anything that is causing a major problem. Fig. 107-13.

For instance, the board might decide that a computer should be installed to regulate certain machines. The president and the consultants would decide which kind of computer would be best. This information would then be given to the general manager who in turn would tell the manager of the purchasing department to buy the computer. Some weeks later the general manager might report back to the president that the computer has been purchased and installed. Or the president might have to report that some difficulty has arisen—perhaps a shortage of qualified computer operators. The president would then have to think of ways to cope with this problem—perhaps offer higher salaries or send some employees through a training program for computer operators. Fig. 107-14.

The larger the corporation, the more levels of management there are. In the largest corporations, only the most serious problems are brought to the attention of the president. On the other hand, in some small businesses the president makes nearly every executive decision, including whom to employ as office helpers.

Next in order under the department managers are the foremen. A foreman may be responsible for a large or small crew of workers (operators), making sure that they work safely and accomplish their assigned jobs. It should be noted that the term "foreman" is often associated more with the factory operations than with the front office. Thus a worker in personnel management, with the same level of responsibility as a foreman, may be given a different title. This worker's title might be assistant manager or assistant supervisor.

Unit 107: The Essentials of Industry

Western Electric Corporation
107-14. *The computer is a key machine in the operation of industry. Computers do everything from keeping track of orders to preparing payroll checks.*

How to Start a Corporation

You can start a simple corporation in school to mass produce a product. If you were ever to start a real public corporation, you would have to work with a lawyer. The lawyer would tell you about the laws in your state which govern corporations. However, for your school corporation, you won't have to bother about these details. You will be mainly concerned with setting up an organization which can make quality products safely, with minimum expense and labor.

If you wish to learn something more about public corporations, you might ask a business or social studies teacher in your school. You could also talk with a lawyer or business executive in your city.

The members of your class will be the stockholders in the corporation. Each member will own one share of stock. The stockholders should elect three of their members to the board of directors. The board should prepare a simple *charter* for the corporation. (A copy of a charter may be obtained from your Secretary of State.) The charter should list the name of the corporation (the class can decide on a name), its location, how long it will operate, and what kinds of products it will make. The board will then appoint a president and general manager for the corporation. The class as a whole may now proceed to the assignment of jobs for the rest of the company positions.

Enter the names on a corporate organization chart. Fig. 107-15. Some people will have to hold more than one job.

The group can then decide on a product to make and assign the necessary jobs. See Unit 109, "Mass Production in the School."

525

Part VII: Modern Industry

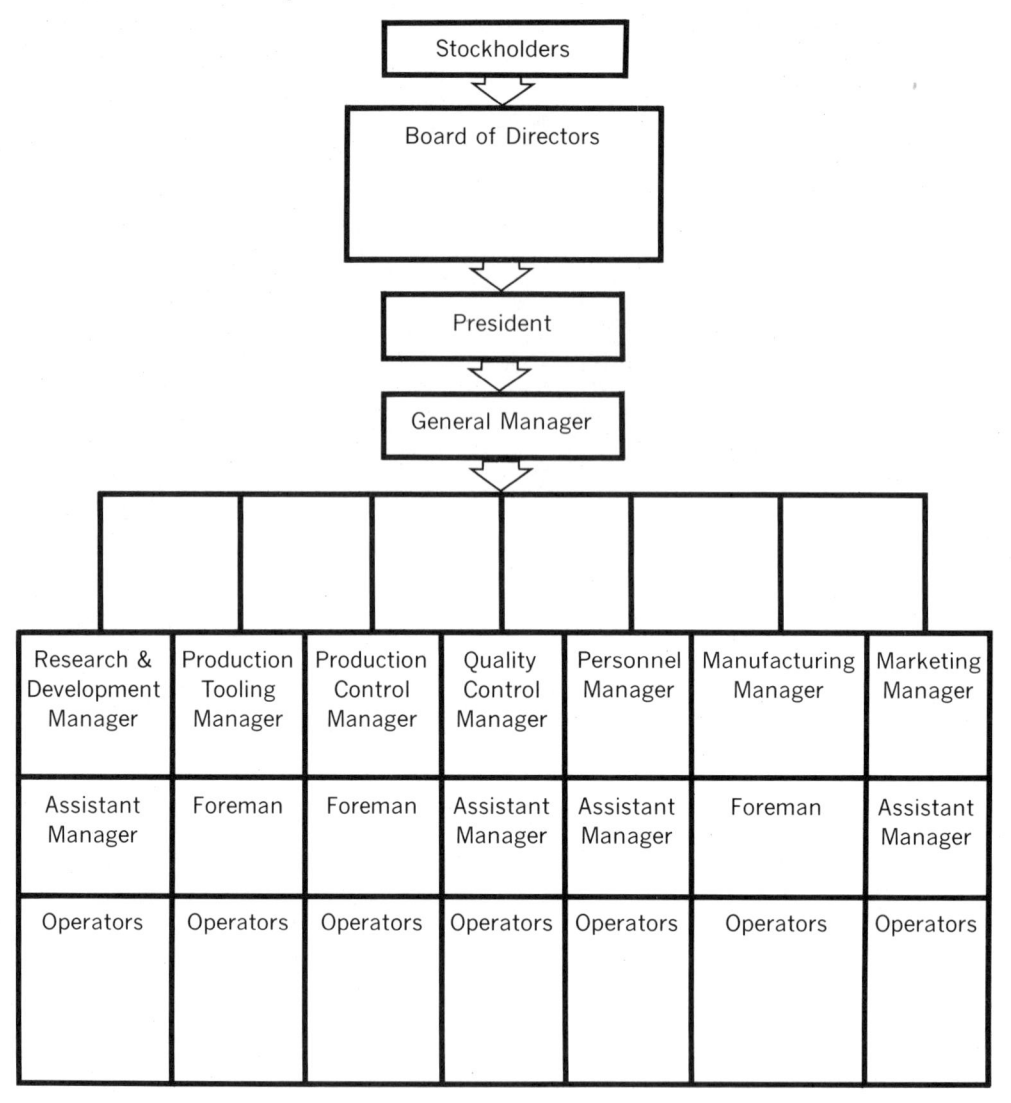

```
                        Stockholders
                             ↓
                     Board of Directors
                             ↓
                         President
                             ↓
                     General Manager
                             ↓
```

Research & Development Manager	Production Tooling Manager	Production Control Manager	Quality Control Manager	Personnel Manager	Manufacturing Manager	Marketing Manager
Assistant Manager	Foreman	Foreman	Assistant Manager	Assistant Manager	Foreman	Assistant Manager
Operators	Operators	Operators	Operators	Operators	Operators	Operators

107-15. *Use an organization chart like this one to form your classroom corporation. Write the names of the people to do the jobs in the spaces on the chart. (Do not write in this book.)*

UNIT 108

The Elements of Industry

This book is chiefly concerned with those industries which produce goods. In other words, it concentrates on the manufacturing industries and on the ways in which raw materials are changed into usable products.

Hundreds of familiar products, which you probably take for granted, are the result of much planning and effort by many people. Your desk, your pencil, the book you are reading, all were once nothing more than ideas. How does a product get from the idea stage to the consumer—the person who uses it? Fig. 108-1 shows the elements of industry. This is a graphic record of how products

108-1. The elements of industry are a way of organizing people, materials, and machines to produce the things we use every day.

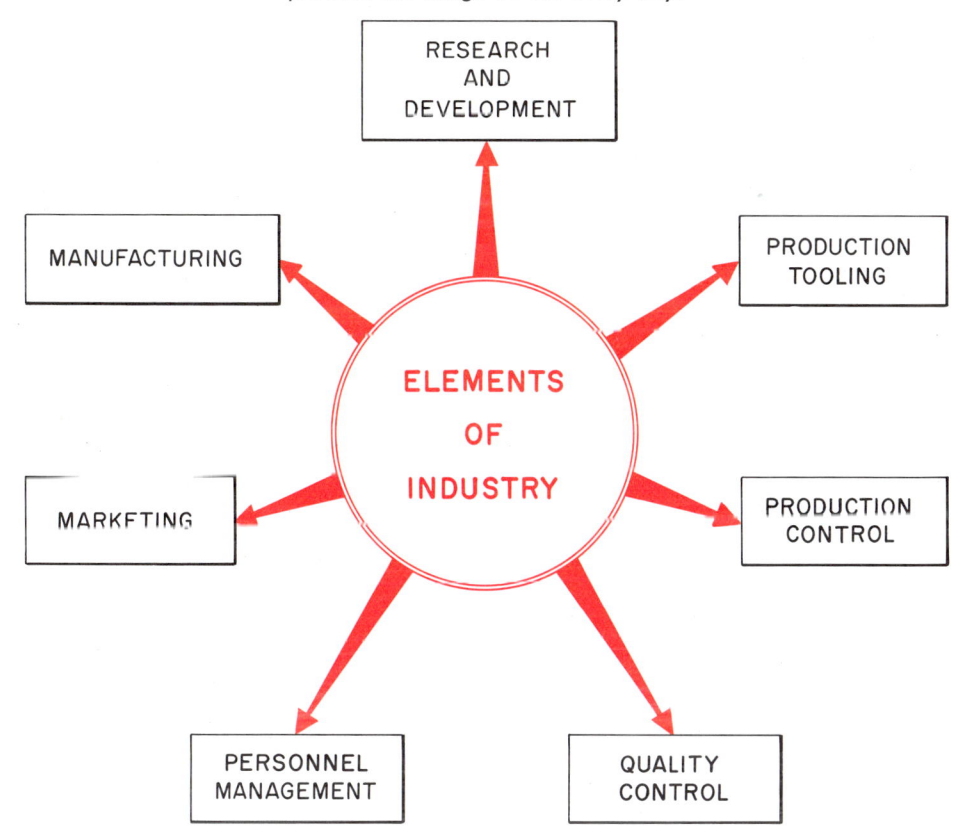

```
                    RESEARCH
                      AND
                  DEVELOPMENT

   MANUFACTURING                    PRODUCTION
                                     TOOLING

                    ELEMENTS
                       OF
                    INDUSTRY

   MARKETING                        PRODUCTION
                                     CONTROL

      PERSONNEL                      QUALITY
      MANAGEMENT                     CONTROL
```

527

Part VII: Modern Industry

are planned, made, and sold in large amounts.

In this unit you will learn what these elements are and how they work in production.

THE ELEMENTS OF INDUSTRY

As with management setups, hardly any two corporations have exactly the same departments. However, no matter what departments are called or how they are organized, in nearly every corporation, they are basically alike. This is because certain steps are needed to take a product from the designer's mind to the user's hands. The departments of a manufacturing corporation accomplish these key steps. As shown on the chart in Fig. 108-1, there are seven of these key steps, often called the *elements of industry:*

- Research and Development (RD)—the inventing and designing of products.
- Production Tooling (PT)—the designing and making of special tools used to manufacture the product.
- Production Control (PC)—the study and planning necessary to insure the proper flow of materials through the assembly line.
- Quality Control (QC)—the setting and maintaining of standards of acceptability for a product.
- Personnel Management (PM)—the selection and training of workers for industry.
- Manufacturing (MF)—the changing of raw materials into usable products by cutting, forming, fastening, and finishing the materials.
- Marketing (MK)—the distribution of finished products to the people who are to use them.

You can see that the operation of a corporation is a difficult task which involves many persons. The president, general manager, and managers of the various departments work together in the long-range planning for the corporation. They decide which products to make, how many to make, what to charge for them, and how to be more efficient in making them. They must also plan for the employee benefit programs and make certain that the company profits are used wisely. The administration of the corporation is to business what the brain and the central nervous system are to the body. Its purpose is to figure out the best ways of doing things and send instructions to all the employees so that the corporation runs smoothly, efficiently, and at a profit.

Research and Development

The new products, materials, and processes which help us to live better do not just happen accidentally. They are invented and perfected by persons who are trained in art, science, and engineering. These are the people who work in research and development. Research and development (or RD for short) is the planning of new products and the improvement of old ones to meet the needs of people who use them. RD is sometimes called "the industry of discovery" because it is such a large, important part of the industrial world and requires so many people with different talents.

People have always been involved in RD work. Cave dwellers learned how to drill holes in stones. They found they could chip a stone to give it a sharp edge. This was the primitive RD work which led to inventing the stone axe.

Throughout the ages people from all parts of the world have shown their inventiveness. Five thousand years ago the Egyptians already were using the potter's wheel, and the Chinese had a workable loom before the time of Christ.

Today's technology is very complex. In order to bring together all of the abilities needed for research and development, corporations often rely on the team approach. In the development of a modern automobile, for example, engineers work on the engine and drive system. Artist/designers deal with body styling. Similar RD teams design products such as refrig-

108-2. Recreational vehicles such as this dune buggy result from the work of RD teams.

erators, motor scooters, and mechanical toys. Fig. 108-2.

KINDS OF RD

RD is concerned with new processes and materials as well as products. Let's take a closer look at each type. *Process RD* involves experimenting with new methods of cutting, forming, fastening, and finishing the raw materials of industry. Good examples here are the developing of continuous casting, and the basic oxygen process in steelmaking. Process RD is also concerned with improving material-working methods through automation.

Materials RD creates new materials for use in industry. Think of the many plastics which have been developed in recent years—plastics for squeeze bottles, automobile bodies, fishing rods. In the space program we have also seen many new materials such as titanium frames for electronic gear, special plastic-ceramic nose cones, and metal honeycomb cabin sections.

Product RD is directed toward creating new products for the manufacturing industries. The system used in product development is illustrated in Fig. 108-3.

The people who work on product development are called *industrial designers.* They are trained in art and engineering. Usually they work as teams to solve problems related to new products. Since they must design products which can be sold at a profit, they need to know something about marketing. The marketing element of industry is discussed later in this unit.

Production Tooling

You may have heard the term, "tooling up." These words are used in the manufacturing industries. For example, when a

Part VII: Modern Industry

Management comes up with an idea.	**R & D team takes the problem and analyzes the possible product.**	**Market research studies the demand for the product and its salability.**
Designers sketch possible solutions, evaluate them, and make prototype drawings.	**Prototype is built of the final solution.**	**Prototype is tested, and final corrections are made.**
Final model is inspected and passed.	**Detail and assembly drawings are made for production.**	**Scooter is ready for production.**

108-3. *The research and development activities necessary in planning a new motor scooter.*

company comes out with a new model automobile, it must "tool up" for the product. This means that special tools must be made to stamp out the newly designed bodies. New bumpers, wheels, and headlights also require new tools to make them.

Production tooling (PT) is the element of industry concerned with these tools. Simply, it involves the assembling of all the tools, machines, and equipment needed to make some product. Fig. 108-4. If you were to make a coffee table, you would need hand tools and machines to make the parts, and perhaps some special devices to hold the pieces together while gluing them. Deciding what tools you need, and then getting or making them is all a part of "tooling up."

PT, therefore, involves (1) deciding what tools are needed that are already in the shop; (2) ordering the tools you need but don't have; and (3) designing and making any special tools you need.

Earlier units of this book described many common hand and machine tools. This unit will discuss the special tools that are used in mass production.

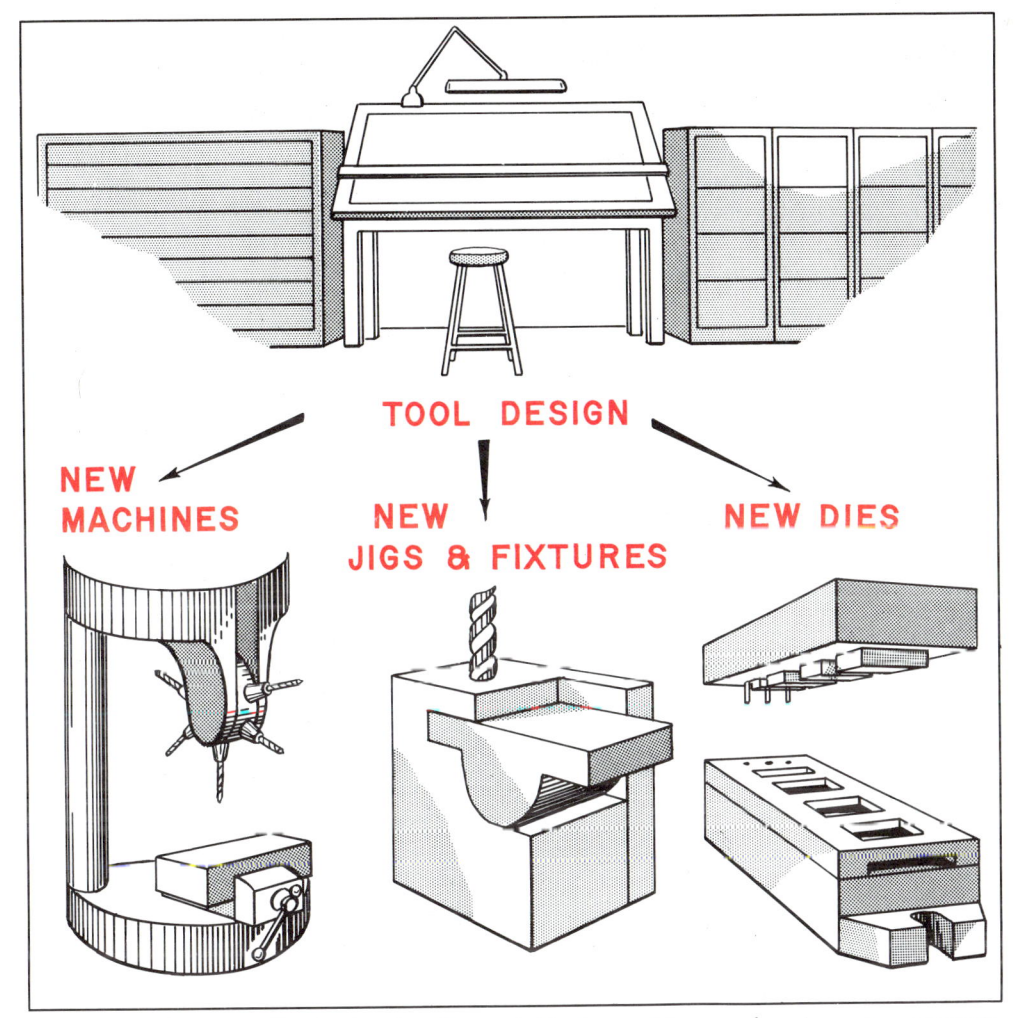

Unit 108: The Elements of Industry

108-4. Production tooling is planning the special tools, machines, and equipment necessary to manufacture a new product. These pictures show some of the things which have to be planned and made.

108-5. This drilling jig holds the workpiece so that it can be drilled.

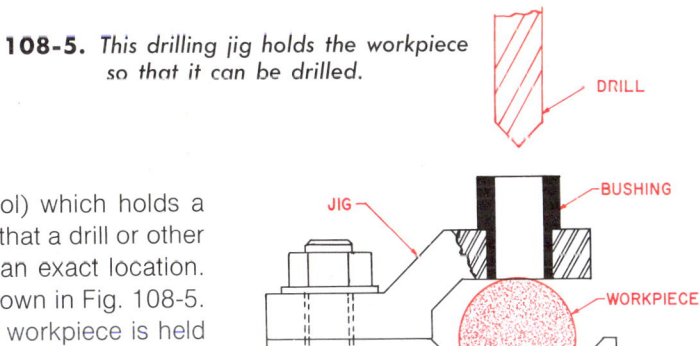

JIGS

A jig is a device (tool) which holds a workpiece securely so that a drill or other tool can be guided to an exact location. Study the drilling jig shown in Fig. 108-5. Note that the steel rod workpiece is held in such a position that a hole will always be drilled exactly through the diameter of the rod. This jig eliminates the task of having to locate the hole with a center

531

Part VII: Modern Industry

punch and clamping the piece in a vise before drilling. Jigs are valuable tools in production work. As a safety measure, small jigs are not usually fastened to the drill press table, except for holes above $\frac{1}{4}''$ in diameter. The drill bushing prevents the guide hole from enlarging.

FIXTURES

A fixture is a device which holds workpieces during machining or assembly. Fixtures are usually attached to a specific machine. They are therefore associated with that machine. Thus we have milling fixtures, lathe fixtures, grinding fixtures, assembly fixtures, and others. Fig. 108-6 shows a fixture which clamps a workpiece securely in place during milling. With fixtures, workpieces can be fastened quickly and easily, and the finished pieces will always be alike.

OTHER TOOLS

While jigs and fixtures are two of the most important kinds of tools used in industry, there are many others which are also necessary. Pressing punches and dies, extrusion and drawing dies, and casting patterns are some further examples. The people who make these devices are called *tool and die makers*. Fig. 108-7. They are highly skilled craftsmen and must work and study for many years before becoming qualified.

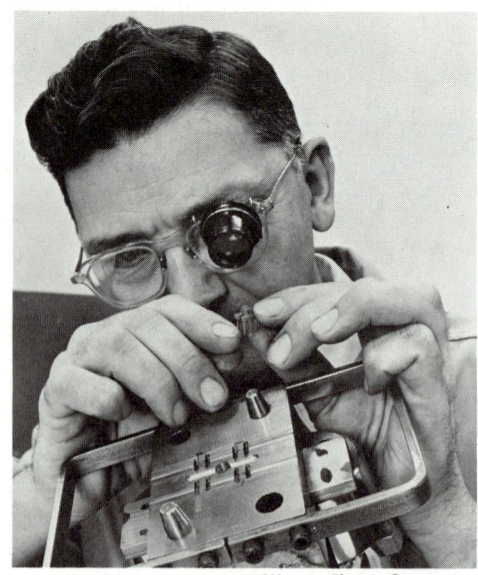

Western Electric Corporation
108-7. *A molding die (foreground). Making the die was part of the tooling up process for producing tiny transformer parts like the one in the tool and die maker's hands.*

Production Control

If you were building a table, you would not glue the legs and rails together until the dowel holes had been drilled. Neither

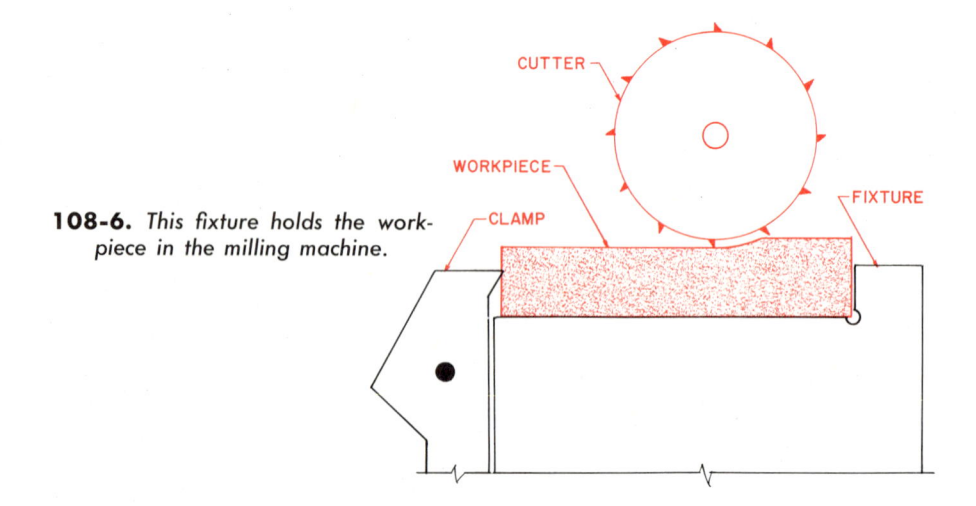

108-6. *This fixture holds the workpiece in the milling machine.*

Unit 108: The Elements of Industry

would you paint the top if it had not been cut to shape and sanded. The same kind of clear thinking is necessary when making automobiles. The wheels are not put on until the frame has been completely assembled.

In order to make certain that a product will be made properly, the right materials must arrive at the right place, in the right amounts, and at the right time. This kind of careful planning is called *production control*, or PC. Fig. 108-8. PC deals with the organization of the manufacturing processes. Its most important aspects are *routing*, *scheduling*, and *dispatching*.

Closely related to production control is *plant layout*. The machinery and equipment must be arranged in a well-planned way within the factory. Usually this kind of layout is done by engineers who understand the production process. Fig. 108-9.

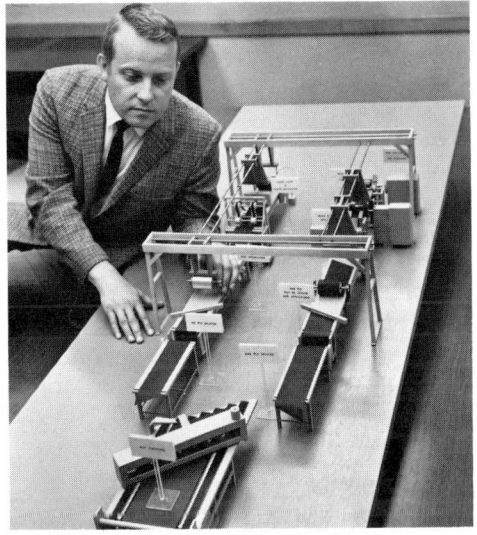

The Firestone Tire & Rubber Company
108-9. Production control specialists (also called methods engineers) study the production steps. This helps them in planning the layout for the production line.

108-8. Production control is the routing of materials and the scheduling of people and machines to manufacture a product. Getting the right materials to the right place for manufacturing, assembling, and inspecting is an important part of industry. The illustrations describe this activity.

The number of products to be made is decided.

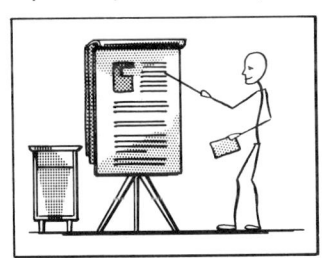

The manufacturing operations are studied.

The routing of materials and the scheduling of machines is planned.

Plans are made for inspection and supervision.

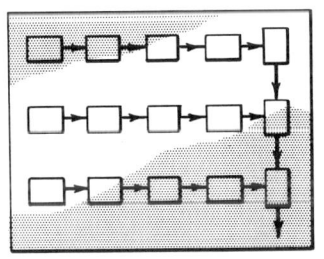

A final plant layout is made, locating the machines and assembly areas.

533

Part VII: Modern Industry

PRODUCTION PLANNING

It is obvious that PC begins long before one starts to make a product, and that the planning activities are many. To begin with, the product plans and production figures (market forecast) must be studied. This information is needed to determine how many products (units) must be made. It is also needed to write *bills of materials* so that the proper raw materials and special parts can be ordered. Fig. 108-10. This is the same kind of bill of materials you prepare when making a project.

Another important activity is to determine how much the products will cost. Here one must study the actual production costs, plus the time required for setting up the line.

ROUTING

Routing is preparing a plan of the steps required to make something. A *route sheet* (or *plan of procedure*) is usually prepared for every kind of part to be made. For example, if you were making a simple footstool with a top and four legs, you would need one route sheet for the stool top and one for the legs.

A typical route sheet is shown in Fig. 108-11. One begins by studying the product to determine how it is made. Every step is then listed in proper order, and the route sheets are prepared from these.

Routing also involves making an *assembly-line layout* (sometimes called a *production control chart* or *process chart*). This layout gives a picture of how the materials and parts will move on the production line. One such chart is shown in Fig. 108-12. These layouts must be kept up to date so that management can get a clear picture of how production is going and what changes have been made in the assembly line. The *process symbols* in Fig. 108-13 are used in keeping the layout up to date.

SCHEDULING

Scheduling is fitting specific jobs or operations into a general timetable so that materials and parts enter the production line at the right place and time. A schedule, then, is simply a method of relating facilities, orders, materials, and time.

A chart commonly used to prepare schedules is a *Gantt Chart*. One such chart is shown in Fig. 108-14. Note that it shows not only the quantities of parts but also the dates for ordering and receiving materials, for starting production, and for sub- and final assemblies. Schedules are also called operation or progress charts.

Schedules, in order to be useful, must be based on realistic estimates of the time

108-10. Bill of materials for a bookcase. A route sheet and an assembly-line layout for the bookcase are also shown in this unit.

Bill of Materials

Product: Vista Bookcase
Model Number: 2000-A
Drawing Number: 1100
Date: Jan. 12, 19--

Part Number	Description	Material	Quantity	Unit	Code
2000-A-1	Shelf, 3/4 × 12 × 48	Walnut	18,000	B/Ft.	361
2000-A-2	Leg, 1 × 1 × 60	CRS Angle	20,500	L/Ft.	484
2000-A-3	Bracket, J68	CRS	4,100	Ea.	616
2000-A-4	Leg Cap, T6	ABS	4,100	Ea.	241
2000-A-5	Screws, #10 × 3/4	Steel	10,000	Ea.	107

Unit 108: The Elements of Industry

PROGRAM	PART NAME		ISSUE DATE	PART NUMBER		
VISTA BOOKCASE	SHELF		MAY 18, 197-	2000-A-1		
FOR MODELS	MATERIAL	WT./LBS. RGH. FIN.	DRAWING NO.	SHEET OF	HOURLY CAPACITY	
2000-A	WALNUT	RELEASE 197-	1117		GROSS	NET

LINE NO.	OPER. NO.	OPERATION DESCRIPTION	TOOL - MACHINE - EQUIPMENT DESCRIPTION	UNITS REQ'D.	TOOL OR B.T. NUMBER	GROSS	NET
1	1	CUT TO LENGTH	CUT-OFF SAW	2	1412		
2	2	SHAPE EDGES	ROUTER	3	801		
3	3	DRILL SCREW HOLES	DRILL PRESS	3	612		
4					USE DRILL JIG 1971-A-J4		
5							
6	4	SAND SURFACES	DRUM SANDER	1	406		
7							
8							
9							
10							
11							
12							
13							
14							
15							
16							
17							
18							
19							
20							

108-11. Route sheet for the bookcase.

535

Part VII: Modern Industry

108-12. Assembly-line layout for the bookcase.

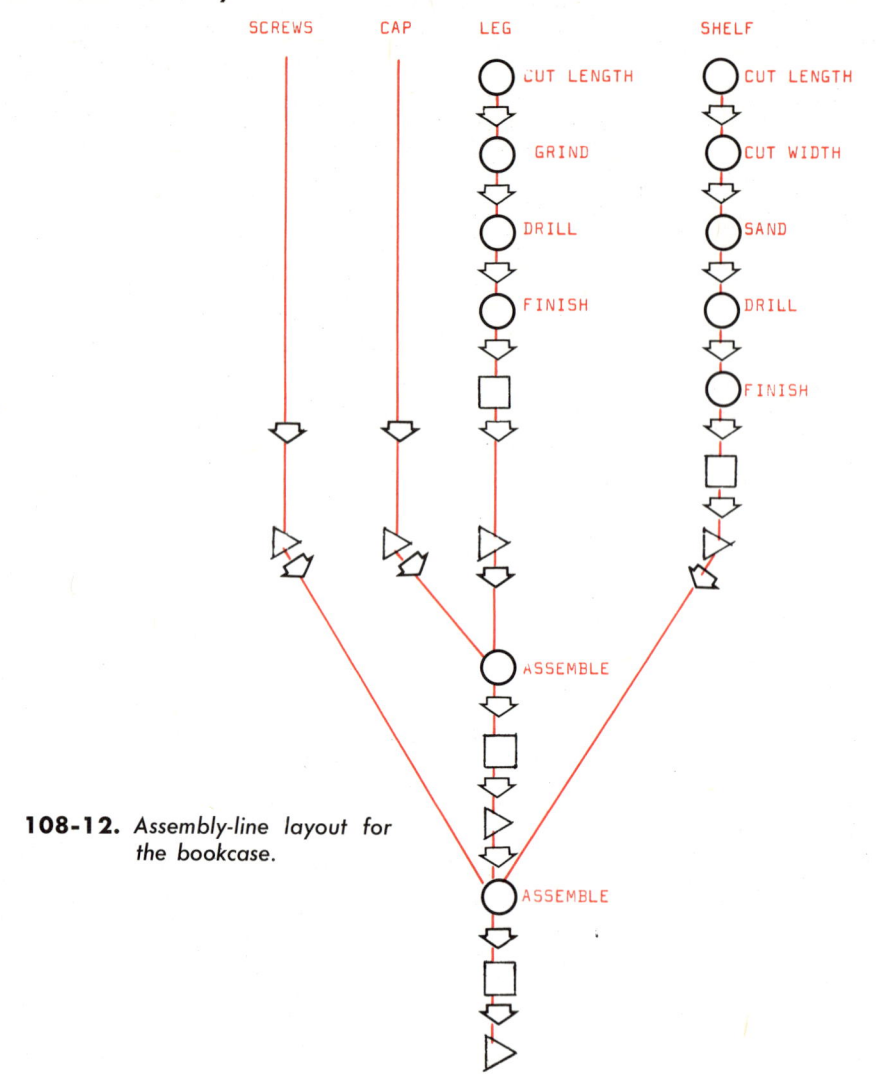

SYMBOL	MEANING
○ OPERATION	CHANGING OR WORKING A MATERIAL
⇨ TRANSPORTATION	MOVING A PART FROM ONE PLACE TO ANOTHER
□ INSPECTION	EXAMINING A PART FOR QUALITY
▽ STORAGE	KEEPING A PART SAFELY UNTIL NEEDED
D DELAY	HOLDING A PART, DUE TO UNEXPECTED EVENT

108-13. Process symbols. Study the assembly-line layout to see how these symbols are used.

Unit 108: The Elements of Industry

JOB	MON	TUE	WED	THU	FRI			
BRACKET Form		G						
Drill		R						
Weld								
Grind				V				

SYMBOLS USED

A — operator absent M — materials holdup
G — green (inexperienced) operator R — machine repair
I — poor instructions T — tools lacking
L — slow operator V — holiday

Planned Work: ─────
Actual Work: ▬▬▬▬▬

108-14. Example of a Gantt Chart. The number of hours worked or the number of units produced can be shown in this chart. Henry L. Gantt, who developed this type of chart, was an American industrialist in the 19th and early 20th centuries.

537

Part VII: Modern Industry

Management clearly defines the standards of quality to be maintained.

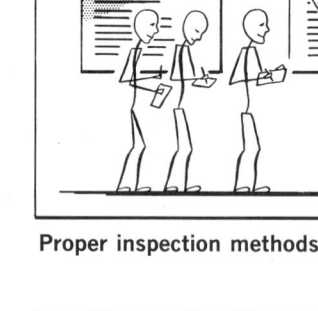

Proper inspection methods are planned.

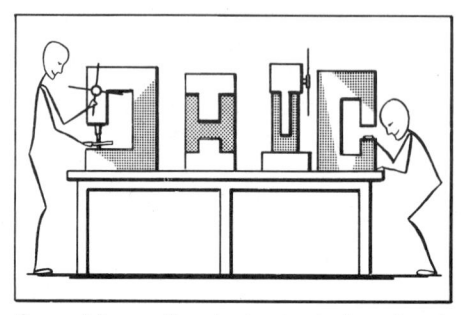

Correct inspection tools are designed and used.

Good records are kept showing the results of quality control. Improvements are made when necessary.

108-15. *The purpose of quality control is to set and maintain the standards for raw materials, in-process materials, and the finished product. This system of inspection eliminates defective products and makes possible the interchangeability of manufactured parts. This chart shows typical QC activities.*

required for each operation. Time-and-motion-study technicians are responsible for these estimates.

DISPATCHING

Dispatching is issuing work orders to set the production line in motion. For example, the foremen on the assembly line are told when production should begin, and how many units must be made each day. These orders are important, for they tell when materials should be released from storage and when production should begin.

In summary, it should be said that PC is a very important activity. The smooth operation of the production line depends greatly upon the PC planners having done their jobs well. They must keep a constant watch on the line. All departments must report any changes or corrections in the scheduled operations. In this way the line will continue to run efficiently.

Quality Control

Products made in a factory must meet certain standards. Otherwise they will not be useful, and people will not buy them. The element of industry concerned with this part of production is quality control, or QC. QC can be defined as those activities which prevent defective articles from being produced or, if they are produced, prevent them from reaching the market. In this way management tries to insure that a product will be acceptable to the buyer. Fig. 108-15.

Unit 108: The Elements of Industry

A QC program is rather broad. It begins with an inspection of incoming raw materials and parts. It also involves constant regulation of the production process and evaluation of products coming from it.

There are two main groups of activities for QC—those concerned with acceptance, and those concerned with prevention. *Acceptance* activities include inspecting raw materials and parts to be used in production, designing inspection devices, inspecting gauges and tools, and inspecting finished goods.

Some typical *prevention* activities include studying defect or rejection records, examining customer complaints, inspector training, and employee morale meetings.

Briefly, QC attempts to prevent defects by study and training, and by inspection of raw materials and finished goods. When successful, this saves money for the corporation in many ways. It reduces the amount of waste material and it saves the time needed to replace or readjust defective products.

When interchangeability of parts is important, QC has one other very important function. It is QC's job to assure that all of the parts will fit together in the final assembly. This is done by setting rigid controls on the sizes of the parts. For example, a company might have to make 10 000 gears to be used in fishing reels. If the gears are just a tiny bit too large or too small, they will not fit in with the other parts of the reel. QC assures that any one of those gears can be used in making any one of the 10 000 reels. This is what interchangeability is. A further example is that a $\frac{1}{2}$" nut made in Minnesota must fit a $\frac{1}{2}$" bolt made in Michigan.

There are three steps or phases in a QC program: specifications, tooling, and inspection.

Specifications are detailed descriptions of the requirements for a product. Some typical requirements might be size, material, function, roundness, squareness, or flatness. For example, you might specify that a cutting board must be $\frac{3}{4}$" thick, 7" wide, and 12" long, and be made out of basswood.

You might further state that you will accept boards that are $\frac{1}{8}$" smaller or larger ($\pm \frac{1}{8}$"), in any of the dimensions. This specifies the amount of error you will tolerate in each piece. It is important that the correct tolerance be allowed, because tool wear and operator error make it impossible for all the boards to be exactly the same size.

With specifications you describe exactly what the product must be like, and how much error you will tolerate.

Tooling in QC refers to the special devices required to measure the accuracy of parts. A "go/no-go" gauge is an example of such a tool. By slipping a part into this device the inspector can tell at a glance whether or not it is the right size.

Some very complex automatic measuring machines are used in industry. The one in Fig. 108-16a is being used to check the accuracy of automobile parts merely by watching the machine dials and meters. It is the responsibility of the QC

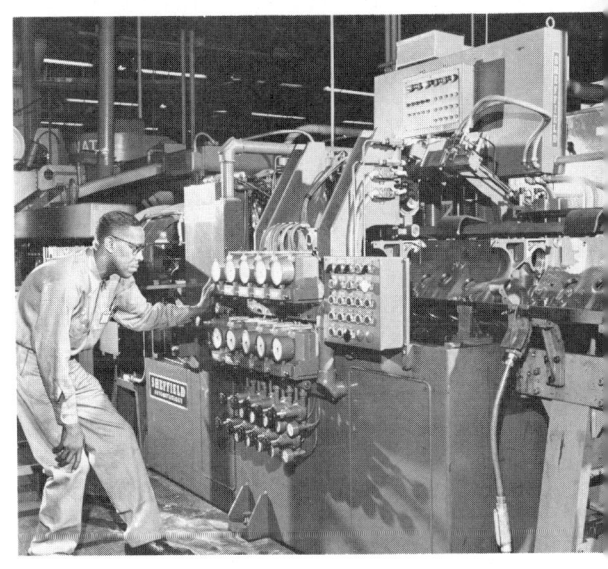

108-16a. *An elaborate testing machine used in the automobile industry.*

Part VII: Modern Industry

108-16b. Nondestructive tests (NDT) include X rays of products. This X ray of a motorcycle will reveal any flaws in welded parts. *Sandia Laboratories*

staff to design and build, or purchase, these inspection devices.

Inspection of parts takes place after the specifications have been written and the special tools prepared. Inspectors must be trained to do their jobs at specified intervals in the production line. As stated before, this is an acceptance activity of QC. In addition to special inspectors, machine operators are expected to examine their own work. They are qualified to do this because they know what the part should look like, and they can detect flaws early.

INSPECTION METHODS

In a good QC program, every automobile made is inspected thoroughly. However, it is not practical to examine every vitamin pill or every electrical fuse. The kind of product being made determines

108-17. Industry must have skilled workers to operate the machines and move the materials on the assembly line. Personnel management is the hiring, training, and supervising of these workers. The pictures describe how people are selected for their jobs.

The work is studied and the jobs are described. Lists of duties and responsibilities are made.

When a person is hired he or she is interviewed and tested. He or she may have another interview and more tests when promoted.

Employees are placed in the right jobs to match their qualifications or abilities.

Employees are trained to work safely and efficiently.

Supervisors observe and evaluate the work of the employees.

540

Unit 108: The Elements of Industry

the method by which it is inspected. The main methods are described here.

Complete or 100 percent inspection is performed on items such as machines, vehicles, and appliances. Fig. 108-16b. Very complex products such as these need close attention. This method is highly expensive, and though it is very reliable, it is not foolproof.

Random sampling is a method by which decisions about the quality of a product are made by examining a small number of the items, taken from a larger batch. For example, from a batch of 10 000 table tennis balls, 100 are selected at random for testing. If 90 of them meet the production specifications, the whole batch is accepted. If not, the batch is rejected as scrap. Most of the product inspection is done by sampling methods. This is reliable and far less expensive than 100 percent inspection.

Destructive testing is a sampling method in which the sample is destroyed in order to test it. Electrical fuses are an example here. The samples must be destroyed to see if they do, in fact, work. Chairs are also inspected this way. They are "torture-tested" for strength and durability, and are destroyed in the process.

Personnel Management

Personnel management (PM) is concerned with the selection, hiring, training, and supervising of workers for industry. The production line cannot operate efficiently unless the right person, properly trained, is doing the right job. Fig. 108-17.

SELECTION

Some people are recruited to fill job openings. Others are hired because they have asked (applied) for a job. In *recruiting,* members of a company's personnel department look for someone to hire. They go to schools and employment agencies and talk to people who might be interested in working for their company. Those who are recruited, as well as those who apply, are interviewed and tested to see if they have the qualifications for the job.

HIRING

On the basis of the interview and the employment tests, the possible employee fills out an application and has further tests and interviews with the personnel staff. These staff members are interested in learning what education an applicant has, what his or her interests are, and whether or not he or she can get along with people. The personnel staff will explain the company benefit policies, such as sick leave, retirement, insurance, and vacations. They also tell the applicant about salary and promotion opportunities with the company.

If the interviews are satisfactory to all, the applicant or recruit will be hired. It is most important that the employee be happy with the company, and the company must be satisfied that the employee can do a good job.

TRAINING

Different jobs have different education and training requirements. Unskilled and semiskilled workers usually can be trained on-the-job for their work. Some factories hold special classes for these people. For example, a maintenance worker will be taught what is expected of him or her in keeping the shop clean and safe. There will be instruction about the schedule for trash collections and about the proper use of the sanitation chemicals and cleaning compounds.

Just because these jobs require little training does not mean that they are not important. A factory that is not clean, safe, and well maintained cannot operate.

Skilled workers come to the factory with skills they have learned in schools, in the armed forces, or at other factories. For example, machine operators must know how to read blueprints or plans, must understand the different materials they work with, and must know hand and

108-18. One task of the personnel management department is to train people to do certain jobs. Classroom work, as well as work on machines, is a part of this training.

machine tool skills. Still, they too must go through some training in the factory in order to learn how things are done there. The same would be true of the technicians. They are skilled persons, but must also have some basic plant training. Fig. 108-18.

You can see that setting up training programs is an important task for those who work in PM. They must decide which person is best suited to a particular job.

They must decide what additional training the person needs. If a person is to be hired as an assembler of small radios, she or he must know how to solder and use small hand tools, and perhaps test various circuits while putting the radio together. The applicant may already know some of this. The training she or he needs will be determined by what prior training was received, and by the specific job to be done.

108-19. After the designing, planning, and tooling have been done, the next step is to make the product. This is called manufacturing, and it involves four operations: cutting, forming, fastening, and finishing. Often the materials used in manufacturing have already been partially processed. Still they are considered raw materials because they are not yet a finished part of a useful product.

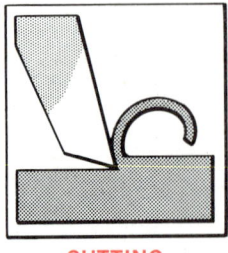

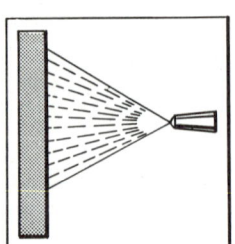

CUTTING   **FORMING**   **FASTENING**   **FINISHING**

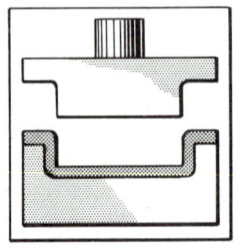

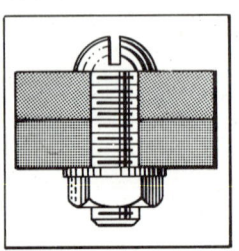

108-20. *Manufacturing changes raw materials into useful products. Here continuous lengths of pipe are being made from steel.*

SUPERVISION

After a person has been trained to do a job, supervisors from his or her own department and from PM will visit regularly to see whether he or she is doing the job properly. If the worker is making mistakes, these must be corrected. If the job changes, the worker may require some extra training, or retraining. The supervisor also identifies those workers who are doing an especially good job, for promotion purposes.

Manufacturing

Earlier in this unit you learned that the manufacturing industries are those which produce goods or products for people to use. This is done by changing raw materials, such as wood or metal, into usable products. You have also learned that not every department does the actual work of making the product. For example, personnel management and production control are not responsible for the actual working of the raw materials.

Those departments which actually convert the raw material into finished products make up the manufacturing (MF) element of industry. It is in these departments where the industrial processes of cutting, forming, fastening, and finishing take place. Fig 108-19.

For example, a basketball hoop is made from a piece of $\frac{1}{2}''$-diameter steel rod, which is cut to length and bent to form a large ring. A piece of steel sheet is also cut to shape, holes are drilled in it, and then it is formed to make the supporting brace. The ring and brace are welded together, then painted to complete the product. The above example shows how the various cutting, forming, fastening, and finishing operations are used to make a piece of sports equipment. Other products are made by similar techniques. Manufacturing is an important element of industry because it is the step by which the raw materials of nature are made into products needed by people.

The process of changing raw materials begins when iron ore is dug out of the ground and made into steel shapes such as sheets, bars, and rods. The same kinds of things are done to plastic, wood, and ceramics to produce the stock materials used in the factory. Fig. 108-20.

Part VII: Modern Industry

Cutting, forming, fastening, and finishing operations are shown in chart form in many sections of this book. Study these to learn about the many ways in which raw materials are made into the products we use every day.

Marketing

Marketing (MK) is the process of getting products from those who make them to those who use them. Marketing helps to deliver the right kinds of goods and services to us, in the right form and amount, at the right time and price. Fig. 108-21. In order to do this, the people in marketing have certain jobs to perform. These are described in the following paragraphs.

PRICING

Although the pricing of goods is often done by a separate division of a company, marketing has a part in it. And sometimes the marketing department has this as a main responsibility. Prices are arrived at by considering all of the costs involved in making and selling a product. Raw materials, machines, tools, building rental, repayment of borrowed money, energy, employees' salaries, advertising,

108-21. *Marketing is the distributing and selling of the manufactured product. The task of getting the goods from those who make them to those who use them involves many people in many kinds of jobs. These illustrations show how this is accomplished.*

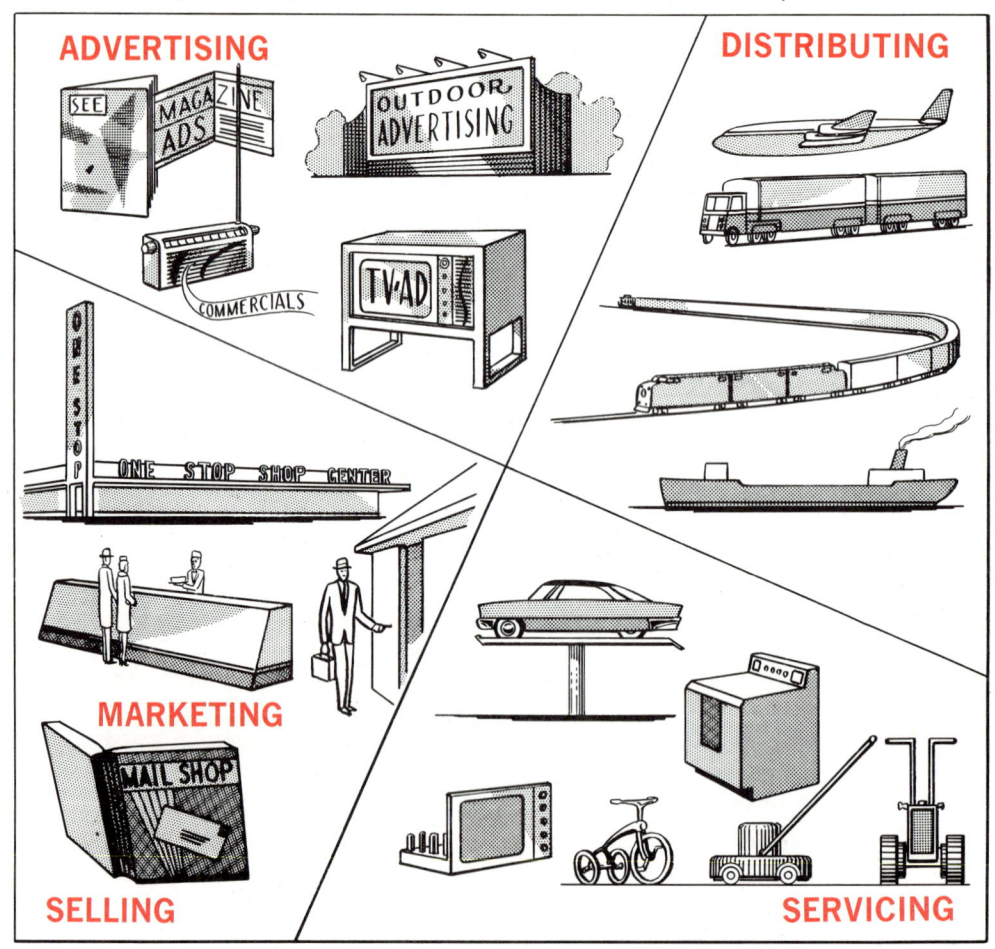

and distributing—all these have to be figured into the price of goods. Above all, the company must make a profit in order to pay stockholders a dividend on their shares of stock and to invest in new equipment and in RD. In our society, profit is important to keep businesses efficient, and to keep them producing the goods we need.

PACKAGING

In industry, packaging refers to the containers used to hold products. You see and use many kinds of packages each day. The gum you chew comes in a wrapper; the shoes you buy come in a box; the soda you drink comes in a can or bottle. The purpose of these packages is to protect and identify their contents. Food wrappers keep foods clean and safe for you to eat. The wrapper also serves to tell about the kind of food in the wrapper. Of course, it is very important that the design of the package be attractive so that people will want to buy it.

ADVERTISING

The usual purpose of advertising is to make the public aware of and interested in certain goods and services. Manufacturers advertise in the *communications media,* which include television, radio, newspapers, and magazines. They buy time or space in these media to inform people of new products, and remind them of the value of older ones. Advertising can perform valuable services. For instance, through advertising we can learn about different brands of the same kind of product so that we may select the one which suits us best. Of course, we must realize that advertisers tell us only the best things about a product. It is always best to make up our own minds about a product rather than buy it strictly because we are told it is good.

DISTRIBUTING

Distributing refers to all the activities involved in getting a product from the manufacturer to the place where it will be used. For most of the world's history, people used products and materials which originated in or near their own area. Many types of goods could not be transported over long distances, and those which could were very costly. Now much of what we use—food, clothes, even our homes—may have been brought from far away.

Trucks and trains, ships and barges, all play an important role in distribution, but perhaps the greatest advance has come through air travel. For example, one company that makes earthmoving equipment promises delivery of replacement parts anywhere in the world in 48 hours or less. Without air delivery, a road construction project in a distant place—India, for instance—could be delayed for weeks because of a defective part.

Goods often have to be stored for long periods of time. Christmas gift items, for example, may have to be made months in advance of the season. Storing them is also a part of distribution.

SELLING

After the product reaches the retail store or shop, someone has to sell it to the consumer. Salespeople serve an important function for the customer in this way. They also perform other valuable services such as keeping doctors up to date on new medicines, making small manufacturers aware of new equipment, and informing teachers about new books. Selling is the final step in the making-using cycle.

SERVICING

To service a product is to maintain and repair it when needed. Servicing is becoming more and more important to the consumer. The reason for this is that so many of the things we use are becoming more complicated, and we cannot always repair them ourselves. Electric appliances, automobiles, power mowers—all need regular attention so that they will

Part VII: Modern Industry

108-22. Modern marketing includes installing and servicing as important parts of its program. *Weyerhaeuser Company*

work properly. Service representatives do these jobs for us. Good service helps to sell products because people want to know that they can get items repaired without too much trouble. As more and more of our products require regular servicing, more people to service them are needed. This is why the service industries are among the fastest growing occupational group. Fig. 108-22.

MARKET RESEARCH

The aim of market research is to collect and study facts about customer needs and reactions to products. This is done through market or product preference surveys and by studying product sales. This information helps management to decide which kinds of products to make and how products should be changed. Market research people must therefore work very closely with a company RD program in making certain that the public gets the kinds of products it wants.

STUDYING OCCUPATIONS

In this unit you have learned about some of the kinds of jobs available in the manufacturing industries. You and many of your classmates will be working at such jobs when you leave school. What kind of job would you like? You can help yourself to prepare for a job in industry by studying some of these occupations.

Most important, you must get to know yourself. What are your likes and dislikes? What school subjects do you like the best? What kinds of hobbies do you have? What are the educational requirements for some specific occupations which interest you? In which occupations can you earn the most money, and which offer the best future in other ways?

These are the kinds of questions you must answer in studying an occupation. By learning about occupations and about yourself, you can make an intelligent career choice.

UNIT 109

Mass Production in the School

In Units 106, 107, and 108 you learned of the ways in which industry works to produce great quantities of products for better living. As you know, this is called mass production. This mass production can be done in the school shop on a smaller scale. You will make a smaller number of products, but you will be using the same elements of industry that are used in large factories. Fig. 109-1. Such activities will help you to learn a lot about industry and production.

The mass production experience demands a lot of planning by the teacher and the entire class. The work begins by discussing the organization of industry (Units 107 and 108). You may wish to form a "corporation" or operate less formally as a class business. Teams of students are organized to plan each element of production. Fig. 109-2. Remember that these elements are research and development (RD), production tooling (PT), production control (PC), quality control (QC), personnel management (PM), manufacturing (MF), and marketing (MK). Study Unit 108 for more information about the duties of each team.

109-1. *Mass production activities in the school are an opportunity to learn about modern industry and careers.*
Republic Steel Corporation

109-2. *Planning is an important part of mass production.*

547

Part VII: Modern Industry

In this unit we will be studying how to mass-produce a trouble light for an automobile. This light can be used as an aid in changing a tire at night, or to make an engine repair. The light is plugged into the car's cigarette lighter, and the long cord will permit the light to be used where it is needed outside the car.

RESEARCH AND DEVELOPMENT (RD)

The first step in production is planning or designing the product. You may remember this as the element of industry called research and development. The trouble light was chosen by a group of

109-3. *The product—an automobile trouble light.*

109-4. *Trouble light side panel detail.*

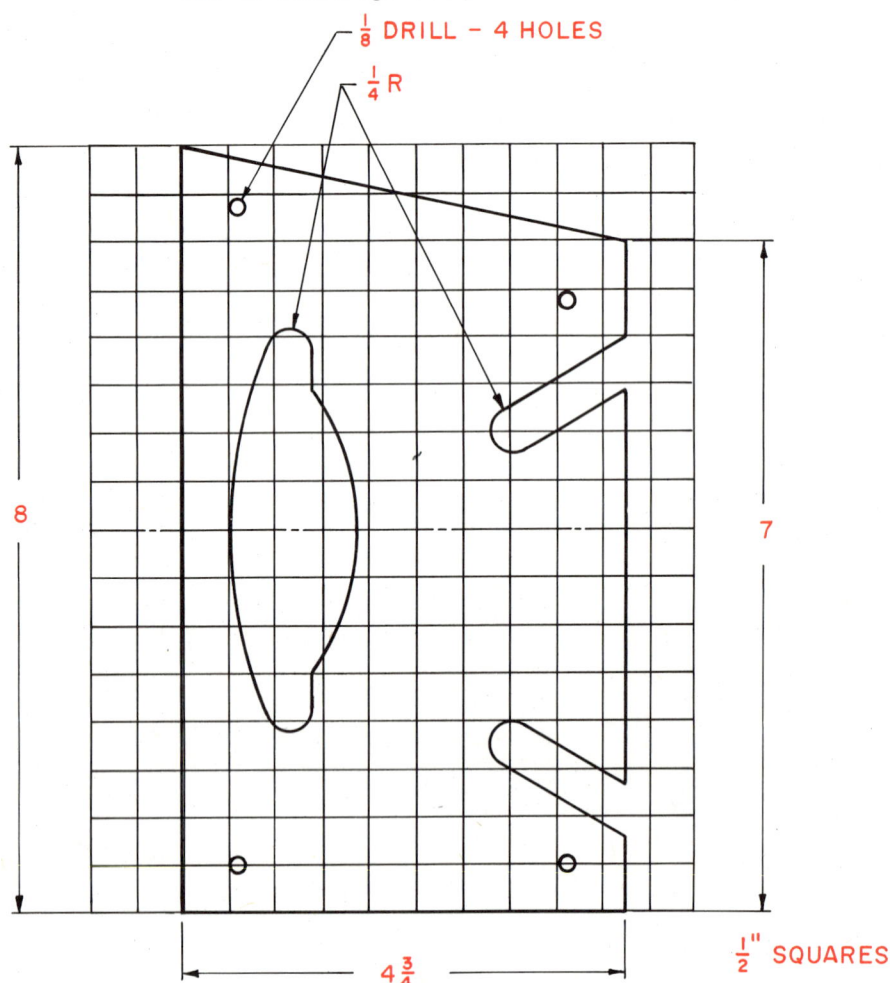

$\frac{1}{8}$ DRILL – 4 HOLES

$\frac{1}{4}$ R

8

7

$4\frac{3}{4}$

$\frac{1}{2}''$ SQUARES

548

Unit 109: Mass Production in the School

students in an industrial education class. They studied the problem carefully and sketched some ideas. They found that all that was needed was a simple case, some electric wire, a sealed beam automobile headlamp, some screws, and a special plug that would fit into the cigarette lighter on a car's instrument panel.

The total cost of the project was low. The sealed beam lamp was free. Such a lamp has a high *and* a low lighting element inside. When one element burns out, the lamp must be replaced. You only need a lamp with one good element for the trouble light project. Most garage mechanics will give you those which they remove from cars.

After several lights had been designed and improved, a *prototype,* or sample, was made. Fig. 109-3. The RD team then made drawings of the parts as well as an assembly drawing showing how the parts fit together. Figs. 109-4 through 109-6.

PRODUCTION TOOLING (PT)

This team is responsible for designing and making the special jigs and fixtures needed to mass-produce the project. Fig. 109-7. The trouble light is very simple and does not need any special tools. The PT team decided that only one was

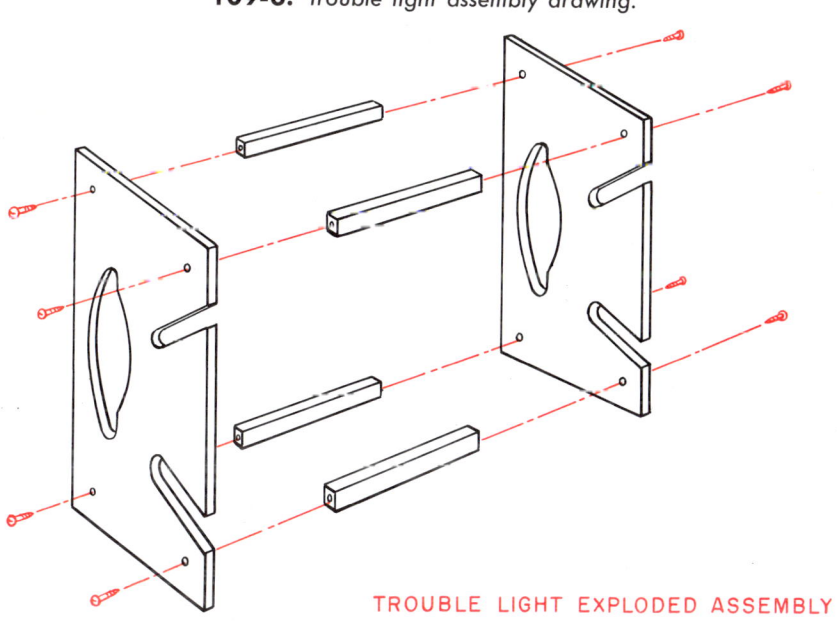

109-5. *Trouble light spacer detail.*

TROUBLE LIGHT SPACER

MATERIAL – HARDWOOD

4 REQ'D.

109-6. *Trouble light assembly drawing.*

TROUBLE LIGHT EXPLODED ASSEMBLY

Part VII: Modern Industry

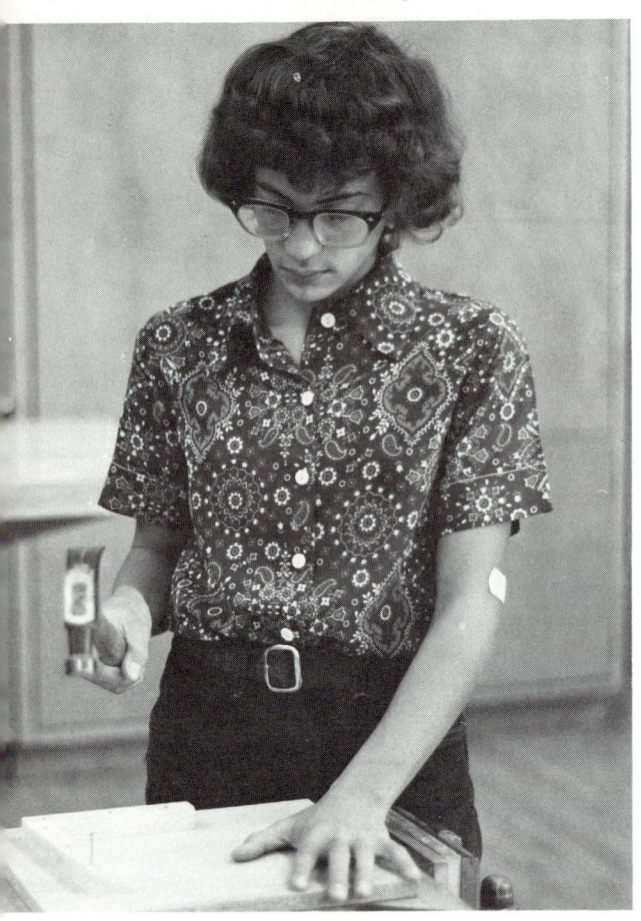

109-7. Production tooling—designing jigs and fixtures for making the trouble light.

109-8. The drill jig is used by placing the side panel pattern on top of the side panel to be drilled. The holes are drilled with a hand drill or drill press.

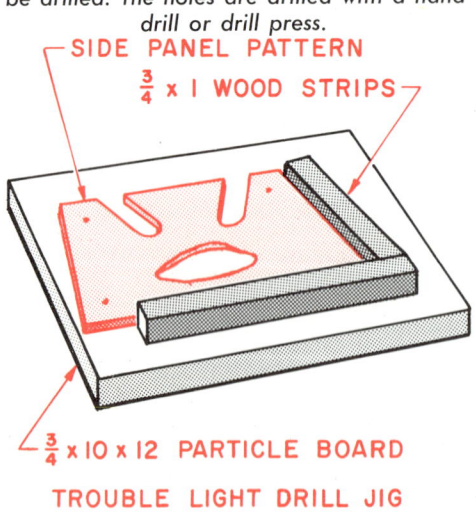

SIDE PANEL PATTERN
¾ x 1 WOOD STRIPS
¾ x 10 x 12 PARTICLE BOARD
TROUBLE LIGHT DRILL JIG

109-9. Production control—preparing bills of materials and flow charts.

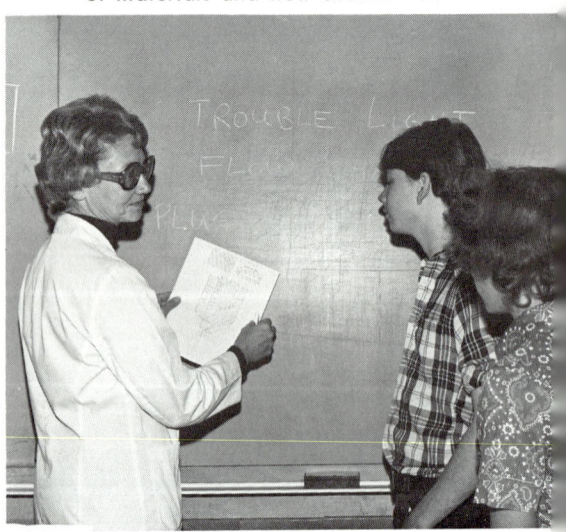

550

Unit 109: Mass Production in the School

needed—the jig to locate the holes in the side panels. Fig. 109-8.

PRODUCTION CONTROL (PC)

The task of this team is to prepare a bill of materials, route sheet (or plan of procedure), flow chart, and a Gantt Chart. You can learn how to make these charts by studying Unit 108. They are made from the drawings prepared by the RD team (Figs. 109-4 through 109-6). The tools designed by the PT team are also important. The complete charts are shown in Figs. 109-9 through 109-13. Note that these plus the drawings show all of the information you need in order to make the project.

QUALITY CONTROL (QC)

The purpose of quality control is to make sure that the trouble light is made correctly. Parts must fit together properly, and the paint must not be chipped or scratched. The lamp must also work properly; a 12-volt battery can be connected to a cigarette lighter to check this. No special quality control devices or tools need to be made. Most of the inspections are visual. Fig. 109-14 (Page 555).

PERSONNEL MANAGEMENT (PM)

An important part of manufacturing is to train workers for jobs on the production line. By studying the production control sheets, the personnel manager can see what operations have to be done at machines or work stations. Your teacher will help by demonstrating how to do these tasks. The students on the personnel management team are helpers. Students in the class are assigned jobs and trained to perform them. It is very important to stress safety. The student workers must also learn to read the detail drawings and to follow the procedures necessary to make each part. Their work must be checked from time to time to make sure they know their jobs. Only then can the work move smoothly. Fig. 109-15.

MANUFACTURING (MF)

The manufacturing phase of the mass production activity is where "it all comes together." Here all the planning and

109-10. *Trouble light bill of materials.*

Bill of Materials

No.	Size T	Size W	Size L	Name of part	Material	Unit cost	Total cost
2	$1/8$	$4\,3/4$	8	Side	Masonite		
4	$1/2$	$1/2$	$4\,1/4$	Spacer	Maple		
8	#6	—	$3/4$	Screws RH	Brass		
1			12'	2-Strand Lamp Wire	Copper		
1				Sealed Beam Auto Head-Lamp-12 V			
1				Auto Cigarette Lighter Plug 12 V			

PROGRAM Trouble Light		PART NAME Side			ISSUE DATE		PART NUMBER 1	
FOR MODELS		MATERIAL	WT./LBS.	RGH.	FIN.		SHEET 1	OF 1
		Masonite	RELEASE				HOURLY CAPACITY	
LINE NO.	OPER. NO.	OPERATION DESCRIPTION	TOOL–MACHINE–EQUIPMENT DESCRIPTION		UNITS REQ'D	TOOL OR B.T. NUMBER	GROSS	NET
1	1	Cut to Size	Band Saw					
2	2	Sand	Disc Sander					
3	3	Trace Pattern	Pencil					
4	4	Cut to Shape	Drill, Jig Saw					
5	5	Sand	Files, Sandpaper					
6	6	Drill Holes	Hand Drill					
7	7	Clean	Thinner					
8	8	Paint	Paint and Brush					
9								
10								

PROGRAM Trouble Light		PART NAME Spacer			ISSUE DATE		PART NUMBER 2	
FOR MODELS		MATERIAL	WT./LBS.	RGH.	FIN.		SHEET 1	OF 1
		Maple	RELEASE				HOURLY CAPACITY	
LINE NO.	OPER. NO.	OPERATION DESCRIPTION	TOOL–MACHINE–EQUIPMENT DESCRIPTION		UNITS REQ'D	TOOL OR B.T. NUMBER	GROSS	NET
1	1	Cut to Length	Band Saw					
2	2	Sand Ends	Disc Sander					
3	3	Lay Out Holes	Rule, Scriber					
4	4	Drill Holes	Lathe, Chuck, $3/32$ Drill					
5								
6	5	Sand	Sandpaper, Fine					
7	6	Clean	Thinner					
8	7	Paint	Paint and Brush					
9								
10								

109-11. *Trouble light route sheet (plan of procedure).*

Unit 109: Mass Production in the School

training that have gone on are used to change raw materials into a usable product—the trouble light. The production line is set up; student workers move into their work positions or stations. Fig. 109-16. They read their plans and do their jobs. Quality control checks are made. The product is assembled and the final tests are made. Each lamp is tested to make sure it works and meets the standards of quality. The product is ready for marketing.

MARKETING (MK)

Marketing is the last step in the production process. Here the product is gotten to the person who needs it. Fig. 109-17.

There are several different plans you can use to market the trouble light. You

109-12. *Trouble light flow chart.*

SIDES (2)	SPACERS (4)	SCREWS (8)	WIRE	LAMP	PLUG
CUT SIZE	CUT LENGTH				
SAND	SAND ENDS				
TRACE PATTERN	LAY OUT HOLES				
CUT SHAPE	DRILL HOLES				
SAND	SAND				
DRILL HOLES	CLEAN				
CLEAN	PAINT				
PAINT					

ASSEMBLE

ASSEMBLE

Part VII: Modern Industry

could make one lamp for each student in the class. Divide the total cost of the lamps by the number of lamps made to get the cost per unit. This is the amount each person must pay for a lamp. For example, suppose you produced 25 lamps. The costs might read as follows:

$$
\begin{aligned}
50 \text{ side panels} &= 6.00 \\
100 \text{ spacers} &= 2.00 \\
100 \text{ screws} &= 1.00 \\
300 \text{ feet of wire} &= 16.00 \\
25 \text{ plugs} &= 12.50 \\
25 \text{ sealed beams} &= \text{no cost} \\
\text{TOTAL} & \quad \$37.50
\end{aligned}
$$

$$\frac{\$37.50}{25} = \frac{\$1.50}{}$$

Each student must then pay $1.50 for his or her lamp.

Another plan could be to advertise the lamp in the school, take orders, and produce them for sale. In this case the cost per lamp could be increased to perhaps $2.00. Then the profit could be used to decrease the cost of the lamp each class worker would buy.

Still another scheme could be to sell the lamps at a reasonable profit to raise money for some school project or for an organization such as the Red Cross, United Fund, or a children's hospital.

If advertising is to be used in selling the lamp, this also becomes a cost. The cost of paper and paint for posters must be figured in the total cost.

109-13. *Trouble light Gantt Chart. This chart will show the number of pieces produced.*

JOB Trouble Light	MON	TUE	WED	THU	FRI
Side					
Spacer					
Assembly					

Planned Work: ────
Actual Work: ▬▬▬

SYMBOLS USED

A—operator absent
G—green (inexperienced) operator
I—poor instructions
L—slow operator

M—materials holdup
R—machine repair
T—tools lacking
V—holiday

Unit 109: Mass Production in the School

109-14. Quality control is necessary to make sure that the lights are made correctly.

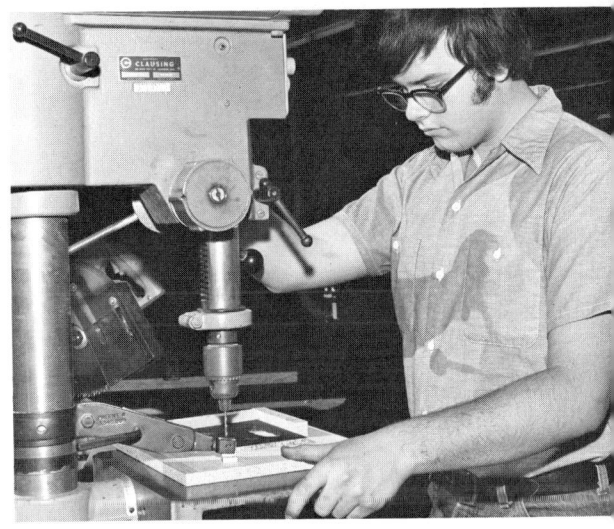

109-16. Manufacturing—converting raw materials to usable products. This person is using a drill press to drill the screw holes in the side panels of the trouble light.

109-15. Training people to work on the production line is the job of the personnel management team.

109-17. Marketing the trouble light—getting the quality product into the hands of the consumer.

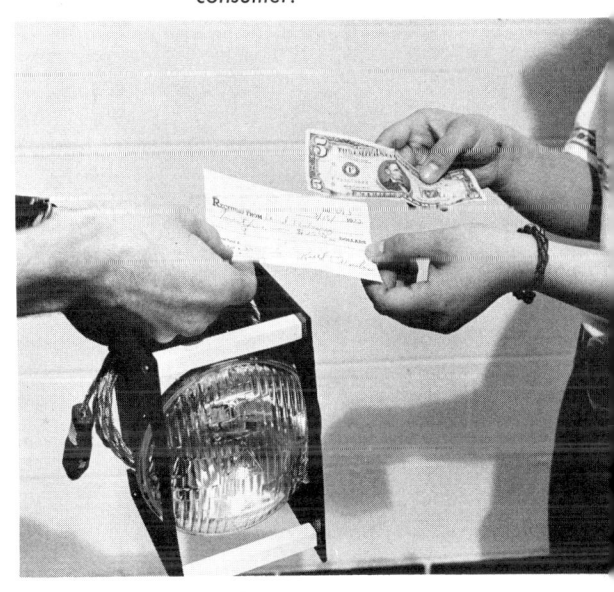

555

UNIT 110

Careers

Men and women in the United States have over 30 000 jobs to choose from when considering a career. These jobs can be clustered, or grouped, into a number of different areas, as shown in Fig. 110-1. Note the variety of job areas shown in the chart. Each of the clusters shows an area of interest and skills. Many of these jobs are in industry. Others are in recreation or transportation or public service. This unit will discuss the jobs related to industry. Other kinds of jobs will be studied in other career education classes in your school.

One of the most important things you can get from your experience in school is to discover your job interests. This is called career awareness and career exploration. What do you want to be doing in five years? Ten years? What kinds of jobs are available in industry? Fig. 110-2. If you could pick any job, what would it be? What do you have to do in order to prepare for it? How do you go about getting a job? These are some of the questions which will be discussed in this unit.

CRAFTS

Industry depends heavily on people skilled in the crafts to produce goods. These workers have the training and the experience necessary to do difficult tasks. They make the drawings, patterns, models, and tools and dies needed for production. They operate machines and use tools and measuring instruments. These skilled workers also print newspapers, build cabinets, install electrical wiring, and repair and adjust machines and instruments. You can see that the crafts include many different kinds of jobs in industry. Some examples of the careers available are described here.

Machinists are people skilled in using metalworking machines such as lathes, milling machines, and drill presses. They must know how to set the workpieces in the machine, read blueprints, and use measuring tools. Their work must be very accurate, and they must check their work against the blueprint to make sure it is done properly. Tool and die makers are skilled machinists who specialize in making devices and instruments used in production, such as jigs and fixtures. The machinists of today must also work with numerically controlled automatic machines of many types. Fig. 110-3.

Sheet metal workers must know how to read blueprints and lay out shapes on sheet metal. They are skilled in using sheet metal cutting and forming tools and machines. They know how to use layout tools and measuring devices. Sheet metal workers make aircraft and automobile parts, heating ducts, and metal containers.

Cabinetmakers use woodworking tools, machines, and layout instruments in making furniture and cabinets. They know how to select the proper woods for a job and are skilled in constructing and finishing the pieces according to the plans given to them. Theirs is an interesting and

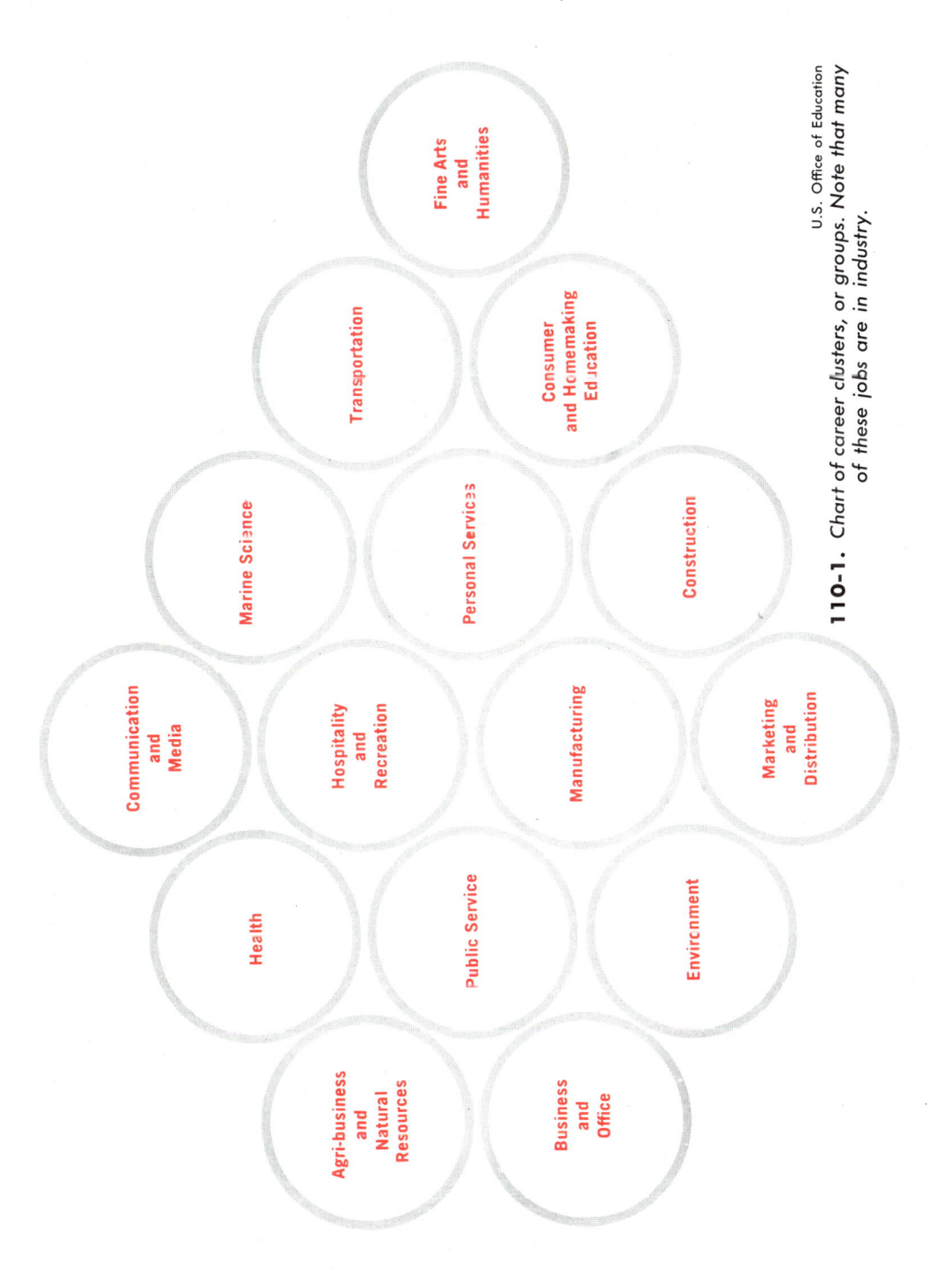

110-1. Chart of career clusters, or groups. Note that many of these jobs are in industry.

U.S. Office of Education

- Fine Arts and Humanities
- Transportation
- Consumer and Homemaking Education
- Marine Science
- Personal Services
- Construction
- Communication and Media
- Hospitality and Recreation
- Manufacturing
- Marketing and Distribution
- Health
- Public Service
- Environment
- Agri-business and Natural Resources
- Business and Office

Part VII: Modern Industry

Careers in Industry*

CRAFTSMEN	TECHNICIANS	ENGINEERS & SCIENTISTS	OTHER
Machinist	Drafting	Chemical	Machine repair
Welder	Designing	Mechanical	Plant maintenance
Tool & die maker	Mechanical	Aerospace	Office worker
Sheet metal worker	Electronic	Metallurgical	Manager
Carpenter	Graphic arts	Civil	Education & training
Cabinetmaker	Computer	Industrial	Sales & marketing
Printer	Automotive	Basic research	
Electrician	Industrial	Applied research	
Auto mechanic	Welding		
Auto body repairman	Building construction		

*This is a partial listing. There are many others.

110-2. These are some of the kinds of jobs you can get in industry. Each one requires education and training. Your experiences in school will help you to select the kind of job which interests you.

110-3. This machinist is working with a numerically controlled turret lathe. The workpiece is locked in the chuck (a). The machine is programmed to automatically select tools (b) to drill, bore, ream, tap, or mill the workpiece. The program tape is stored in the control unit (c).

Jones & Lamson

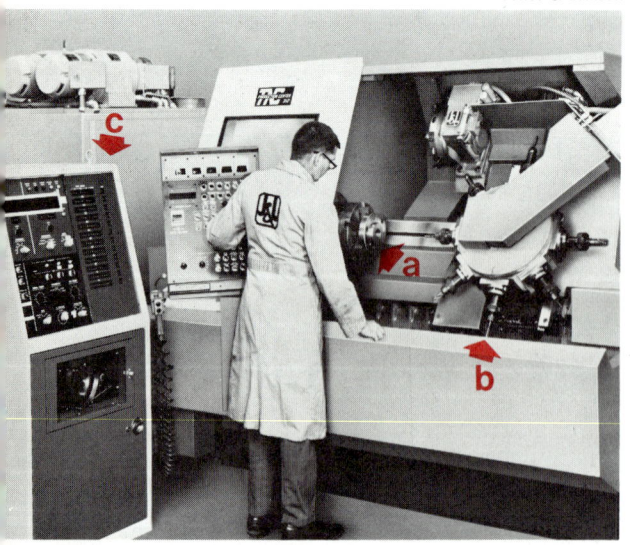

110-4. The cabinetmaker is a highly skilled woodworker who works from drawings to produce quality furniture and cabinets.

Jens Risom Design, Inc.

demanding job. They often are called upon to restore, repair, or duplicate furniture. Fig. 110-4.

Printers must know a great deal about the graphic arts industry. They operate many different machines, such as offset presses, linotype machines, and photographic equipment. They set type, make plates, run proofs, and do layout and design work. They print on many different materials such as paper, plastics, wood, leather, and metals. Fig. 110-5.

Auto mechanics are valuable workers who keep automobiles, trucks, and other vehicles operating. They must know how to read service manuals, figure out what is wrong with an engine, and proceed to repair it. Mechanics use many tools, instruments, machines, and test equipment in their work. Today especially, they have to know about emission control in engines to reduce the pollution of our environment. A closely related trade is that of the auto body technician, who straightens dents, replaces parts, and refinishes automobile equipment. Fig. 110-6.

From these descriptions of jobs in the skilled crafts you can see that these jobs require special training. You can get this training in a number of ways. The industrial shop courses you take in school will give you a good background in tool and machine skills. After you graduate from high school, you can go to a vocational or technical school for further work. Many high schools also offer vocational education courses in metalwork, woodwork, drafting, graphic arts, electricity-electronics, and automechanics.

110-5. People in the printing trades use photographic equipment in their work.
Lockheed Corporation

110-6. Auto mechanics must know how to use many different kinds of tools and instruments in their jobs.
Gulf Oil Corporation

Part VII: Modern Industry

110-7. Apprentice craftsmen must return to school as a part of their training programs. They study such subjects as blueprint reading and shop mathematics.

Many workers learn their skills in apprenticeship programs. These vary in length from three to five years. There is a training program set up for each apprentice trade. You can get information on these programs from your local trade unions. Most apprenticeship programs include classroom training in blueprint reading, mathematics, and various skills related to that trade, as well as shop experience. Fig. 110-7.

TECHNICAL CAREERS

Technicians work closely with scientists and engineers, and their importance and recognition are growing daily. Their main responsibility is to carry out the details of projects which are planned by a scientist or engineer. Technicians work in industrial laboratories and manufacturing plants, medical research centers, and experimental engineering programs. In fact, any place where there is work of a scientific or technical nature, it is almost certain that technicians also are there, working in some important job.

Today's technicians are usually graduates of technical institutes or of junior or community colleges having two-year technology programs.

In addition to technicians with formal training, some others have become technicians because of training received during military service. Some technicians began as workers on regular production or skilled jobs. Their mechanical ability, along with a good grasp of math and science, led to a technical job. These people also prepared themselves for their technical jobs by going to night school or taking approved correspondence courses in technical subjects. Some technicians have obtained their present jobs after completing part of a regular engineering course at a college or university. Technicians with this background and even technicans with formal training sometimes attend evening classes at a local college or university with the idea of some day completing the requirements for a degree in engineering or science. Experience has shown them that additional education often helps in becoming better qualified for promotion into jobs with more responsibility. An engineer needs from three to five technicians as assistants.

In summary, then, formal training at a technical institute or junior or community college provides the best route for becoming a technician. Other ways are open, however, if the basic qualifications and desire are present. Some typical technician jobs are described here.

Drafting and design technicians are first of all skilled drafters. They know layout and detail work and are neat and accurate. They prepare drawings from specifications (written descriptions of details not shown on a drawing), sketches, or notes furnished by engineers or scientists. They must have some knowledge of manufacturing machines and production methods to construct layout drawings quickly and accurately. In design work, engineering ideas come to life. As they gain experience, designers work more closely with engineers, architects, and scientists. Their knowledge of machines and the operating principles of mechanisms is a big help in developing the details of any design. Sometimes designers work from sketches made by engineers. On other occasions they may develop their design "right on the board" with oral instructions from the engineer as their only guide. Fig. 110-8.

Automotive technicians must know much about mechanical and electronic equipment. They use electronic equipment to control automobile engine tests. In such tests the engine runs just as if it were supplying power to a car traveling along a road. All this is done by automatic controls without the engine leaving the laboratory. In fact, the engine isn't even installed in a car. Instead, it is attached to a power measuring device called a dynamometer. The fuel flow to the engine and the load produced by the dynamometer are controlled by electrical equipment such as oscilloscopes, digital voltmeters, potentiometers, and electronic counters. Such instruments are typical of equipment used by automotive technicans. They must also know how to develop special equipment for testing emission control in automobiles.

The *welding* technicians stand between the welding engineers, who originate the work, and the welders, who complete the work. They adapt theory to production. They use drawing instruments and gauges, collect data, perform laboratory tests, build, supervise, and control machinery and testing equipment. They perform a function which would otherwise require the services of a trained engineer. These technicians can complete their education and become engineers. They can become the head of a department, the chief testing technician, or start a welding business of their own. There are many opportunities for technicians in all fields.

The *building construction* technicians work closely with civil engineers. They do

Teledyne Post, Des Plaines, IL
110-8. *Drafting and design technicians work from architects' and engineers' notes to design products for manufacturing.*

design work, test materials, survey, estimate, supervise construction, and write reports. Many things once done by civil engineers are now done by building construction technicians. They are not usually responsible for the design or construction of engineering projects. However, they do assist and are accountable to the professional engineer. They may act as the chief of party for a surveying crew, or supervise the materials testing laboratory as well as hold other responsible positions. They must have a knowledge of all types of construction: wood, metal, and concrete. They may be building bridges, dams, or buildings. Fig. 110-9.

ENGINEERING AND SCIENCE

Engineers and scientists invent, develop, design, and refine ideas and things that are used in production processes. They are leaders in the production team made up of crafts workers and technicians. Fig. 110-10.

How do you know if you can become a scientist or an engineer? First take a look

Part VII: Modern Industry

110-9. Building construction technicians work with precast concrete structures as well as wood and metal.

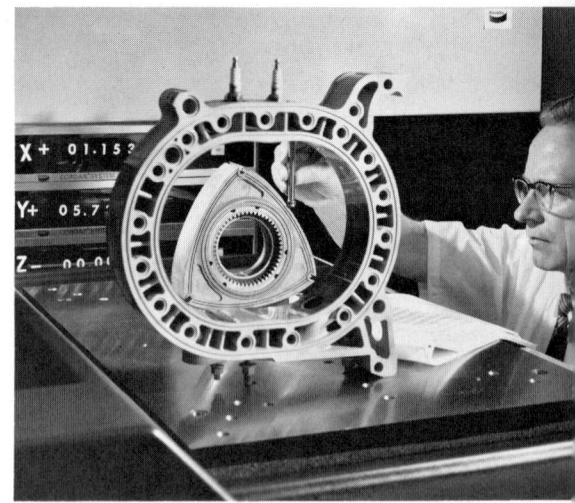

110-10. Engineers and scientists are the leaders of the production team. This mechanical engineer is working on a quality control inspection device for Wankel engines.

at you and school. How are your grades in science and mathematics? Good marks are required for college admission. Prospective engineers and scientists are usually interested in these subjects and may find themselves active in scientific projects or science fairs. Good grades usually reflect the type of study habits and mental discipline required for success in both college and career.

The scientist or engineer has an inquisitive mind, wanting to know why as well as how. Such a person may like to tinker with things such as model aircraft, automobiles, or radios—discovering how they work or trying to improve them. He or she should have the ability to design and create—to put ideas into sketches and, in turn, be able to visualize a form or device from drawings.

These are some of the signs. Don't be discouraged if they don't all fit your situation. Some people do not display all these traits early in life, while others who do possess them become successful in other fields. But these signs can be used as a rough guide.

If you think you are interested in this field, your goal in high school should be to build a firm foundation for training in college. To qualify for most professional schools you must take several basic subjects, many of which you would probably take anyway. These provide the groundwork for any field of science or engineering and represent their basic tools—mathematics, science, and communication.

The following section tells about some of the careers in science and engineering.

The primary concern of the *chemical engineer* is changing raw materials into useful products. These engineers study unit operations to learn about physical properties like fluid flow, thermodynamics, and heat and mass transfer. By combining this information with their knowledge of chemistry, they can design and develop the processes which make possible the large-scale production of fuels, industrial chemicals, food-stuffs, paints, and glass. They are largely responsible

Unit 110: Careers

110-11. *Electrical engineers design communication equipment used in telephone systems.*

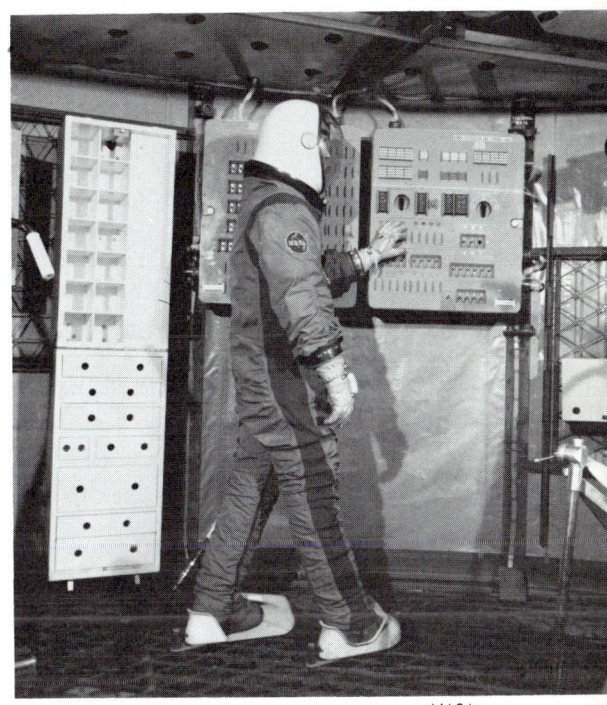

110-12. *Aerospace scientists develop and plan the tests for space exploration equipment.*

for the development and manufacture of many artificial materials such as rubber substitutes, synthetic fibers, and plastics.

Electrical engineers work in the production, control, and application of electrical energy in the fields of power and electronics. They design and develop the circuits, systems, and electrical components that provide electricity for homes, industry, and transportation. Electronics uses electricity to extend human capabilities in such fields as communication, instrumentation, and computer technology. Current research in atomic energy and solid state physics has opened new areas for growth in electrical engineering. Fig. 110-11.

Aerospace engineers are interested in extending travel into space. Fig. 110-12. Aeronautical and aerospace engineers apply many areas of engineering to all types of flight vehicles, from aircraft to missiles. These engineers study aerodynamics, hydraulics, electronics, structural design, material strength, and flight mechanics. They develop and test guidance and propulsion systems for airplanes and spacecraft. This field demands a broad base of scientific and engineering knowledge so that the engineer can adjust to the rapid changes and discoveries now being made.

Civil engineers are interested in people's relationship to their physical environment. They design and build structures and systems that add to the comfort, convenience, and safety of people. They are trained in soil mechanics, building material, structure analysis, hydrodynamics, fluid mechanics, and environmental health. Civil engineers are key persons in developing commercial buildings, expressways, pipelines, waterways, sanitary systems, bridges, and dams.

THE PRODUCTION TEAM

The scientist on the production team serves as the discoverer since she or he is a person who seeks new knowledge. The scientist is an inquirer—a person trained in the laws of nature who investigates the world and its secrets to learn more about

Part VII: Modern Industry

110-13. Managers plan and direct work in such operations as sales, training, and purchasing.

110-14. The work of the secretary is essential in keeping an office running smoothly.

why and how things behave as they do. He or she is interested in both basic and applied research. Scientific study areas include physics, chemistry, mathematics, and biology.

The builder on this team is the engineer. He or she applies knowledge gained from scientific discoveries to the practical problems of life to create things that people can use. A basic knowledge of science and mathematics is combined with judgment and experience to design new products and systems. Some people call engineering the art of making science useful.

Technicians on the team act as assistants to both scientists and engineers by helping them convert their ideas into accomplishments. They possess certain skills which enable them to perform many tasks in support of the scientist's work, such as building test equipment, conducting tests, and recording data.

The worker skilled in a craft is an important member of the team who puts into practice the results of development and planning. Goods roll off the production line through her or his efforts. All together—the scientist, the engineer, the technician, and the skilled worker produce the goods and services which provide us with the things we must have in order to live safely, healthfully and comfortably.

BUSINESS CAREERS

Many persons are needed in industry aside from those skilled in crafts, technical jobs, and engineering. Persons are needed to manage and supervise sales and marketing as well as other activities.

Management personnel work as supervisors of departments, managers of divisions, or vice-presidents or presidents of companies. These people work together

Unit 110: Careers

110-15. Office business machine operators may work with small adding machines or with large computers such as the units shown here.
Remington Rand Univac

in planning and managing the operation of the industry. Such operations include sales, production, services, purchasing, accounting, research and development, and training. These people are trained in business schools and colleges. Their jobs require the ability to work closely with people and to understand the finance and management of industry. Fig. 110-13.

Office workers are another important class of business people. Secretaries, accountants, typists, general clerks, and business machine operators are examples.

Secretaries, in addition to being good typists, must be able to understand the thought behind their bosses' correspondence and dictation. They must handle much of the general correspondence on their own, and they may be called upon to supervise the work of other clerical employees. By relieving their bosses of many details and routine clerical duties, they serve in a minor executive capacity as a personal assistant. Secretaries set up appointments for their bosses and remind them of important engagements as they arise. They interview visitors, handle confidential reports and personal mail, and see that the office work runs smoothly. Fig. 110-14.

Although their jobs may vary from office to office, bookkeepers generally record business transactions in journals and ledgers. They prepare reports and statements from these entries. Their responsibilities range from keeping track of cash received and paid out to closing the books and preparing financial statements. In smaller offices a single bookkeeper, cashier, or clerk may handle all of these duties. Bookkeeping in larger offices often requires a number of separate departments and the services of many bookkeepers and other office workers.

Business machine operators and technicians are important in industry. Modern offices use a number of special machines—calculators, bookkeeping machines, billing and posting machines, tabulators, keypunches, duplicators, and many others. Fig. 110-15. Banks, large department stores, industrial concerns, and government offices often have entire departments equipped with them. They make possible the smooth and efficient processing of a tremendous amount of data. Their usefulness has made the field

Part VII: Modern Industry

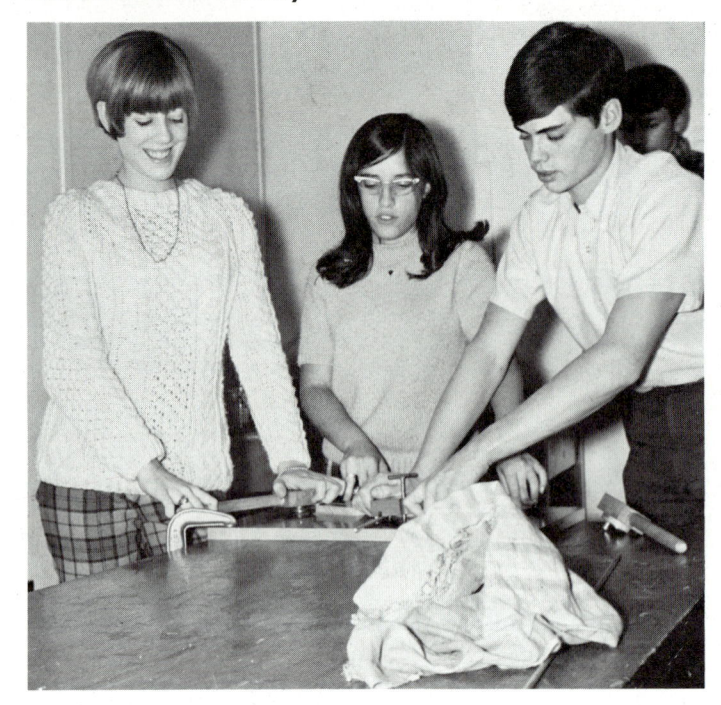

Aluminum Company of America
110-16. Mass-production activities in school will help you to learn something about industry and yourself.

of business machines the fastest growing of all office groups. Special schooling is required to learn how to operate these machines.

Many different kinds of clerical workers are needed in industry. For example, a file clerk keeps correspondence and other office paperwork on hand for ready reference and record. A billing clerk checks payments due from customers for goods and services, makes out invoices, and records payments when received. An order clerk makes out and processes purchase orders for merchandise, materials, and other supplies. A stock clerk takes charge of storerooms and stockrooms and handles orders for supplies, stationery, tools, and instruments and also keeps track of inventories, advising supervisors when stock items need to be reordered. A shipping and receiving clerk handles the paperwork (shipping orders, bills of lading, freight or mail charges and regulations) connected with the shipment and receipt of goods. A mail clerk runs the company's post office, handles incoming and outgoing mail, deliveries, and packages.

Many office workers start out as messengers, mail deliverers, or helpers in office mailrooms.

These brief descriptions of different kinds of jobs should help you to understand what your career interests are. The experience you have in school is also important. The courses you study, such as writing, mathematics, science, history, and industrial arts, are all important. Each will help you to discover what your talents and interests are. A mass-production activity in industrial arts will give you the experience of designing, making, and selling a product. This will also help you to learn about your career interests. Fig. 110-16.

LEARNING ABOUT YOURSELF

You should begin to think seriously about your future and your career while you are in school. The classes you select in high school can and should relate to your occupational interests. One good way of beginning the search for a career is to think about your interests and school activities. You should begin to learn as

I. Work Preferences

Check your likes with a plus (+) and your dislikes with a circle (○).
1. Work indoors. ____
2. Work where I would sell things. ____
3. Work involving mathematics and science. ____
4. Work where I can be my own boss. ____
5. Work with tools and machines. ____
6. Work in drafting. ____
7. Work requiring patience and accuracy. ____
8. Work with other people. ____
9. Work which is clean and neat. ____
10. Work involving original thinking. ____
11. Work directed by someone else. ____
12. Work depending on my writing skill. ____
13. Work which is physical. ____
14. Work where I would meet people. ____

II. School Subjects

Use check marks to indicate the subjects you like, and also how well you do in them.

Subject	Like it	Below Average Grades	Average Grades	Above Average Grades
1. Science				
2. Mathematics				
3. Social studies				
4. English				
5. Drafting				
6. Shop courses				
7. Business				
8. Art				
9. Physical education				
10. Others				

III. Activities

List the clubs, teams, or other groups to which you belong.

_____
_____
_____
_____
_____

List your hobbies.

_____
_____
_____
_____
_____

IV. Work Experience

List the jobs you have held. Check those you liked.

_____
_____
_____
_____
_____

If you could choose anything, what kind of job would you like to have?

_____
_____
_____

110-17. *Personal inventory of interests and school activities. This inventory will help you in choosing a career.*

much about yourself as you can. The classes you take, the spare-time jobs you have had, and your hobbies will all help in learning about yourself. Look at the form in Fig. 110-17. Answer the questions as accurately and honestly as you can. (Do not write in the book.) Think carefully about the question before you answer it. When you have completed the form, show it to your parents, teachers, and counselor. Discuss it with them. They can help you in planning a school program which will help you to prepare for your career.

STUDYING OCCUPATIONS

At this point you have learned about typical kinds of jobs in industry. You have also learned something about yourself. The next step is to select an occupation

Part VII: Modern Industry

Occupational Study Form

1. What is the occupation which interests you? (Carpenter? Mechanic? Other?)

2. How much education or training is required for this job?

3. Is there now, or will there be in the future, a great demand for workers in this occupation?

4. What are the promotion possibilities?

5. Describe the salary, pension, vacation, and other benefits.

6. How many persons are now employed in this type of work?

which interests you and to study it. You may feel that a career in drafting is one you wish to explore. The form in Fig. 110-18 will aid you in this study. There are many ways to get information on the occupation or job you have chosen to study. Talk to your teacher and to drafters in industry. Go to your counselor and get a booklet on careers in drafting. Look in magazines and newspapers. These will have articles on drafting; your librarian can help you to get these. Look at the job advertisements in newspapers. They will give you an idea of how much money a beginning drafter will make. Talk to persons who employ drafters to learn about promotions, the kinds of work drafters do, and the kind of people they want to hire. In short, learn all you can about the job that interests you. In this way you can begin to think and plan for the career you may work in when you finish your schooling.

110-18. *This form will help you learn something about a job which interests you.*

DISCUSSION TOPICS AND ACTIVITIES

Part 7—Modern Industry
Unit 106
  1. What is an industry?
  2. Who is generally recognized as the first person to use mass production techniques in the United States?
  3. What do the letters GNP stand for?
  4. Who invented the steam engine?
  5. Prepare a bulletin board display on pollution problems in your city.
Unit 107
  1. List the three essentials of industry.
  2. List the three types of coal used as fuel throughout the world.
  3. What percentage of the world's petroleum is found in North America?
  4. List two important labor unions in the United States.

Units 106–110: Discussion Topics and Activities

   5. List four types of capital resources found in industry.
   6. What is a corporation?

Unit 108
   1. List the seven elements of industry.
   2. List three main types of research and development found in industry.
   3. What is the difference between a jig and a fixture?
   4. List the three parts of production control.
   5. List three inspection methods used in quality control programs.
   6. List the seven parts of a marketing program.

Unit 109
   1. Design a simple project that you can mass-produce in the school.

Unit 110
   1. List three types of crafts jobs in the world of work.
   2. Does an engineer need more education and training than a craftsman? Why?
   3. List some typical careers in the world of business.
   4. Fill out the two career information sheets shown in Figs. 110-17 and 110-18. (Do not write in the book.) After you have filled out these forms, discuss them with your teacher and your parents.

TECHNOLOGY REPORT 1
Welding

Gas Metal-Arc Welding. Gas metal-arc welding is done with the heat of an electric arc discharged between a workpiece and a consumable electrode. The electrode melts and thus supplies the filler metal. The process is a method of gas-shielded arc welding. No flux or coating is used on the filler metal. An inert gas is used to shield the metal from the air. The process is often called MIG (for metal inert gas) welding. Fig. 1-A.

Gas Tungsten-Arc Welding. Gas tungsten-arc welding is done with the heat from an electric arc discharged between a workpiece and a nonconsumable electrode made of tungsten. The gas tungsten-arc process, like the gas metal-arc process, is gas-shielded arc welding. An atmosphere of inert gas surrounds the arc. No flux is used. The process is often called TIG (for tungsten inert gas) welding. Tungsten is used for the electrode because of its resistance to high temperatures and for its electrical characteristics. Fig. 1-B.

Submerged-Arc Welding. Submerged-arc welding is flux-shielded arc welding. The heat for fusion is furnished by an electric arc discharged between a workpiece and a consumable electrode. Filler metal is supplied by the electrode wire. The weld metal is shielded from the air by a loose, granular mixture of flux that surrounds the arc. Fig. 1-C.

Submerged-arc welding is somewhat similar to MIG welding. A long rod of bare filler metal is used as the electrode, and the filler metal is fed automatically into the joint.

1-A. *Gas metal-arc welding.*

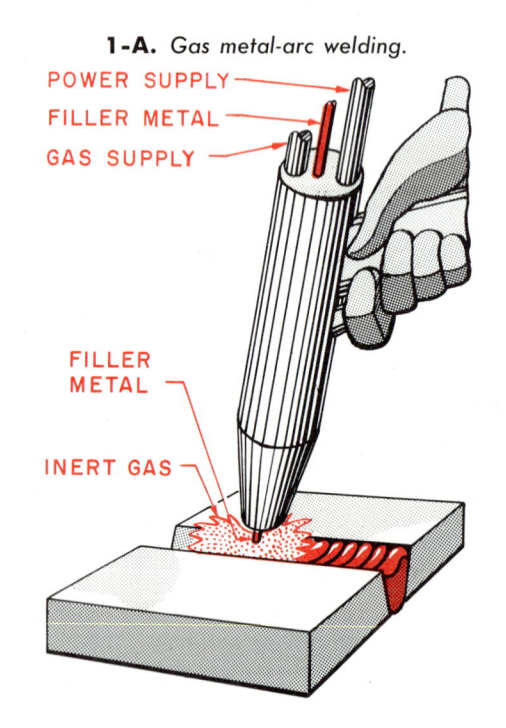

1-B. *Gas tungsten-arc welding.*

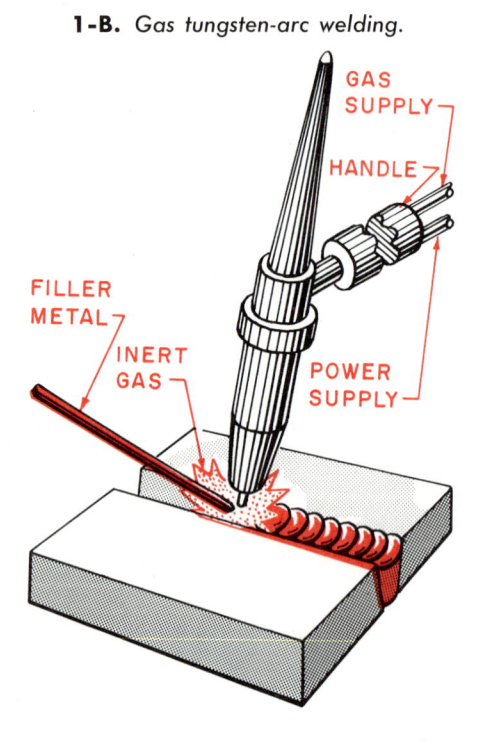

Plasma-Arc Welding. Plasma-arc welding is similar to TIG welding in that an electric arc is discharged between a workpiece and a nonconsumable tungsten electrode. The arc for plasma-arc welding, however, is conducted to the base metal by a controlled stream of plasma (electrically charged gas capable of conducting electricity). Fig. 1-D.

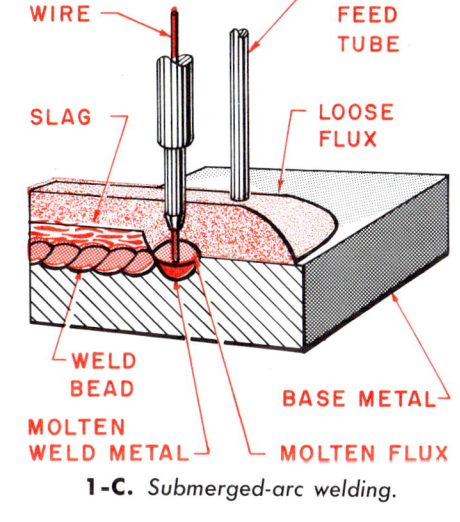

1-C. *Submerged-arc welding.*

1-D. *Plasma-arc welding.*

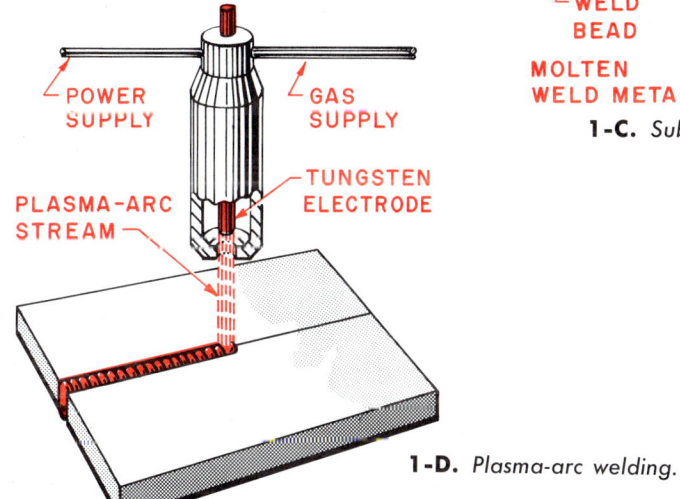

TECHNOLOGY REPORT 2
Composite Materials

When two or more materials are combined but retain their original identities, the result is called a *composite*. This means that the basic materials do not dissolve into each other, but remain as metal, plastic, or whatever they originally were. Composites have their own set of properties. These properties are unlike those of any one of the materials from which the composite was formed.

The materials combined are called the *constituents* of the composite. Since the constituents retain their individual identities, the properties of the composite are influenced by the properties of the constituents. Thus, a composite can have the strength of one constituent; the light weight of another; and the chemical, thermal, and electrical properties of a third. Many property combinations are

571

Technology Report 2

possible. One very familiar composite is glass-reinforced plastic, or fiberglass. This is a mixture of glass fibers and polyester resin. Another is concrete, which is a mixture of cement and gravel. There are many other composites. Four of these are described here.

Cermets. Ceramic and metal particles are bonded together by heat and pressure to produce cermets (meaning *ce*ramic *met*als). The particles are mixed, pressed, and sintered (heated without melting). They are sometimes applied to a backing material. Cermets can withstand high heat because of the presence of ceramic particles. They are used for high-speed metal-cutting tools, clutch plates, and high-temperature valves. Fig. 2-A.

Composite Plastic-Sand Flooring. This industrial flooring is made up of several urethane resin base coatings. These are covered with a top coat of resin and sand and a final resin seal coat. This material provides a rugged skidproof floor with high impact resistance. The floor is resistant to fungi and chemical solvents. It is used in factories, commercial kitchens, and meat-packing plants. Fig. 2-B.

Composite Plastic-Ceramic Flooring. This composite flooring material is used in offices, schools, hospitals, and shopping centers. It is made by laying a urethane resin coat over a base material such as concrete. Ceramic tiles are then laid in the liquid resin. After setting, it is polished to an attractive, lightweight, and durable finish. Fig. 2-C.

Plastic Laminates. The familiar plastic coverings for kitchen counters, desks, and tables are composites made from paper, polyester resin, and melamine sheets. These sheet materials are impregnated with liquid resins and cured with heat and pressure. The result is a very tough, hard, smooth decorative surfacing material. It resists heat, moisture, and solvents. Fig. 2-D.

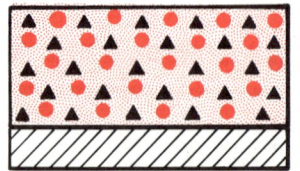

2-A. Composition of cermets.

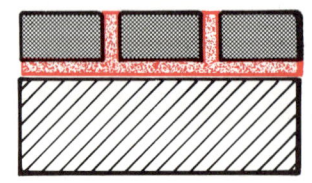

2-C. Plastic-ceramic flooring.

2-B. Plastic-sand flooring.

2-D. Plastic laminate.

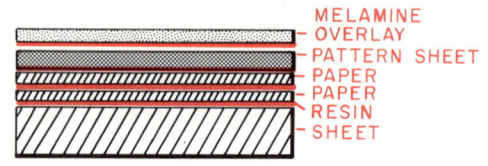

TECHNOLOGY REPORT 3
Automatic Harvesting of Trees

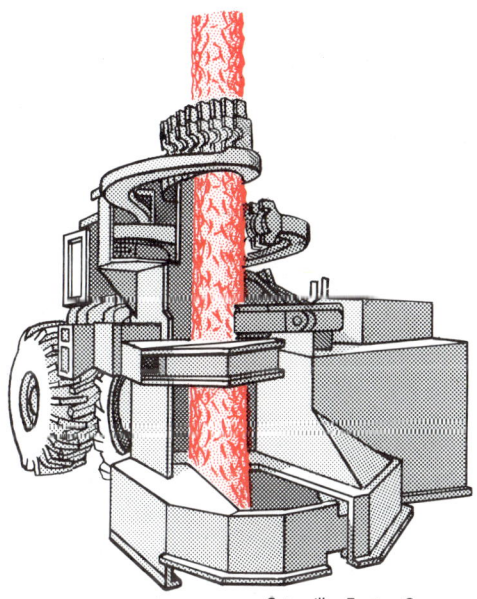

Caterpillar Tractor Company

3-A. *Harvester approaches tree.* As the shear is activated, grapple arms grip the tree with constant hydraulic pressure and hold it steady for shearing. Delimber knives also wrap around the tree.

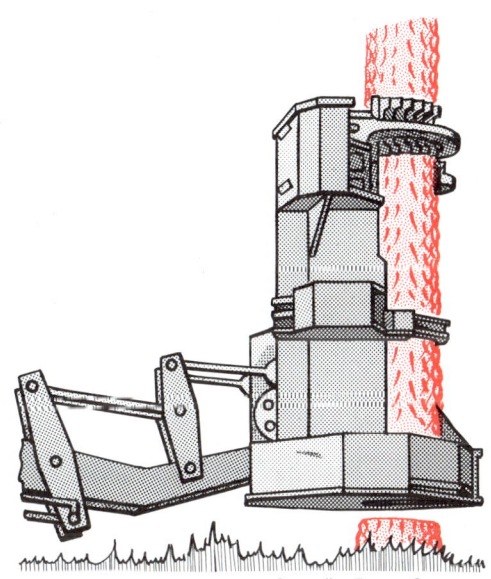

Caterpillar Tractor Company

3-B. *Shear cuts tree.* The 1" (25 mm) thick steel shear powered by a vane-type hydraulic pump cuts through the trunk of the tree. The cut is made within 4" (100 mm) of ground level.

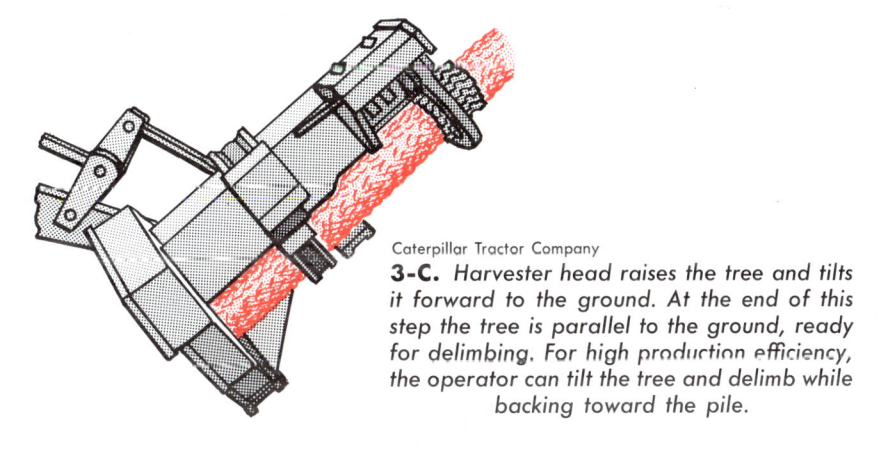

Caterpillar Tractor Company

3-C. *Harvester head raises the tree and tilts it forward to the ground.* At the end of this step the tree is parallel to the ground, ready for delimbing. For high production efficiency, the operator can tilt the tree and delimb while backing toward the pile.

Technology Report 3

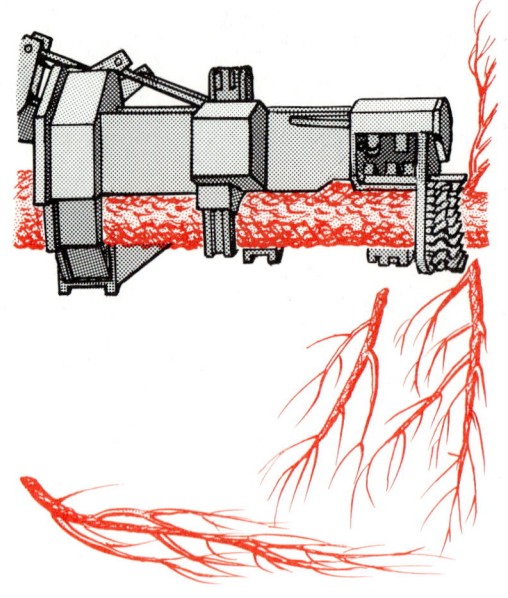

Caterpillar Tractor Company
3-D. *Hydraulically driven chain pulls the tree through the harvester. Cross beams with sharpened grousers engage tree trunk and drive the tree as grapple arms guide and hold it against the chain. Hard steel knives cut the limbs flush with the tree trunk.*

Caterpillar Tractor Company
3-E. *Shear snips off tree top. Delimbing is effective down to 2.5" (64 mm) diameter top. The felling shear removes the top at any given length. Operator can also use the shear to cut any desired shorter lengths during delimbing.*

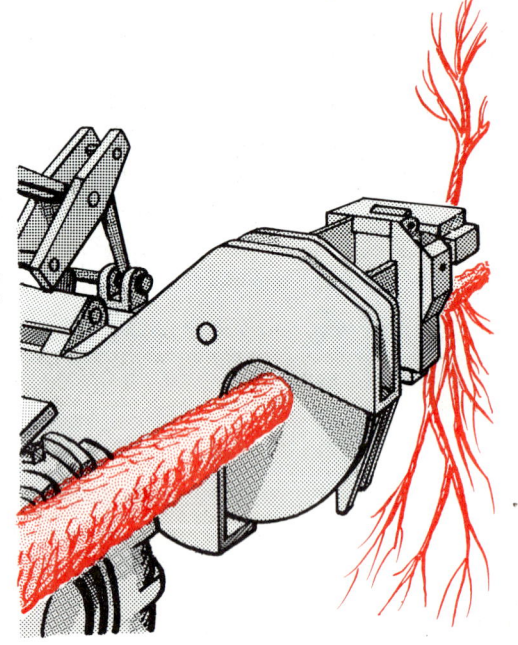

Caterpillar Tractor Company
3-F. *Operator drops the harvested tree onto a bunched pile. Delimbed tree drops on bunched pile. In a minute or less the trimmed and topped tree is bunched and the operator moves to the next tree.*

3-G. An automatic tree harvester in operation. *Caterpillar Tractor Company*

TECHNOLOGY REPORT 4
Modified Wood

Modern technology has developed a number of ways to treat wood to change its structure, improve its properties, and increase its range of applications. This is called wood modification. Materials with properties quite different from those of the original wood are obtained by chemically treating wood, compressing it, radiating it, or combining these and other treatments.

Wood is treated with chemicals to increase its resistance to decay, fire, and moisture. Another chemical treatment gives wood a high degree of dimensional stability (shrink prevention). This is the polyethylene glycol (PEG) process. The treatment consists of soaking rough-sized green wood in the PEG solution for several weeks, thus preventing the cell walls from shrinking during the drying process.

Plasticization. Some wood modification processes involve a pretreatment of the wood to soften it. Such a process, called plasticization, acts on the lignin-cellulose structure of wood to loosen it.

575

Technology Report 4

Plasticization is followed by the application of heat and pressure, generally between forming dies, to produce a desired contour. The resultant product is excellent for such applications as forming rounded corners on desk legs. Two other wood modification methods are illustrated and described here.

Wood Plastic Composition. An important modification treatment is *wood plastic composition* (WPC). In this process, wood is placed in a vacuum chamber where air is removed from the cells of the wood. Fig. 4-A. A plastic monomer such as methacrylate is then introduced into the chamber, where it enters the wood cells. Next the wood is bombarded with radioactive isotopes, causing polymerization to take place. Fig. 4-B. This process in effect converts the wood into plastic.

The moisture resistance, strength, and dimensional stability are improved greatly. This material is used for small wooden parts, door and tool handles, and furniture parts.

Compreg. Improved properties can also be obtained by applying chemical and compression treatments to wood. Wood treated with a thermosetting resin, such as a phenolic, then compressed and cured is known as *compreg.* Figs. 4-C, D, and E. Through this process, a penetrating, bulking agent is deposited in the fibers of veneers, improving their stability. Additional advantages are improved appearance and moldability. Typical applications include antenna masts, small airplane propellers, and products for which electric insulation characteristics are important. Wood treated in a similar manner but without compression is called *impreg.*

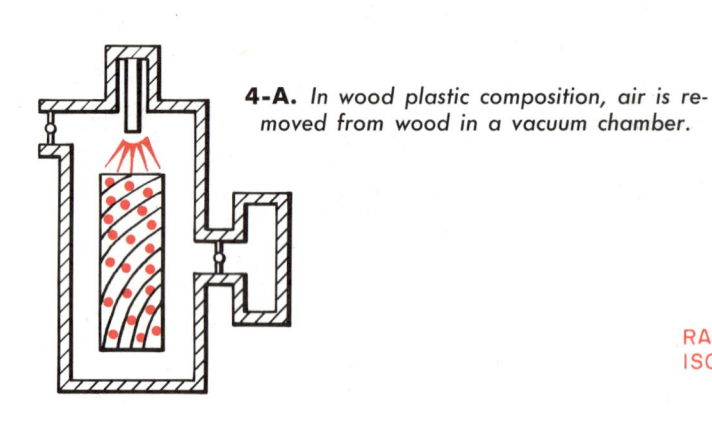

4-A. In wood plastic composition, air is removed from wood in a vacuum chamber.

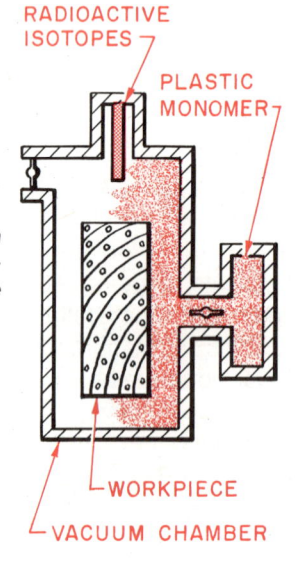

4-B. The radiation causes polymerization. In polymerization, groups of identical small molecules (monomers) join together to form large molecules (polymers).

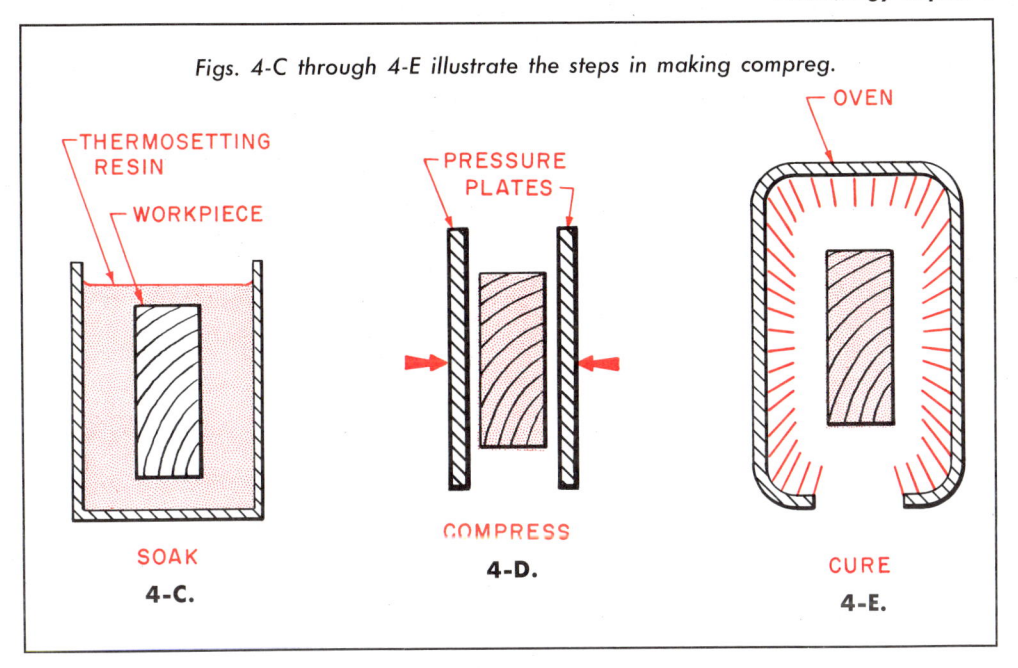

Figs. 4-C through 4-E illustrate the steps in making compreg.

4-C. SOAK

4-D. COMPRESS

4-E. CURE

TECHNOLOGY REPORT 5

Numerical Control

Numerical control (N/C) is a method of running machines automatically. Numerical instructions are written in code. These instructions, or programs, are prepared in advance. The coded instructions are recorded on punched cards, magnetic tape, or punched tape. They can control the order of machining operations, machine positions, distance and direction of movements of the tool or workpiece, flow of coolant, and the selection of the proper cutting tool for each operation.

The tapes are placed on a control unit, which is a simple computer. The control unit can drive the machine tool through the programmed operations and movements automatically. The machine operator starts, stops, loads, unloads, and observes the tool. The operator can change instructions after each job by replacing the tape on the control unit with another tape containing a different program.

There are two main types of N/C. *Point-to-point positioning* moves the tool from place to place to drill, ream, etc. *Continuous path contouring* moves a milling tool along a cutting path to shape a workpiece. Both systems use X, Y, and Z rectangular coordinates to position the tool. Figs. 5-A through 5-E.

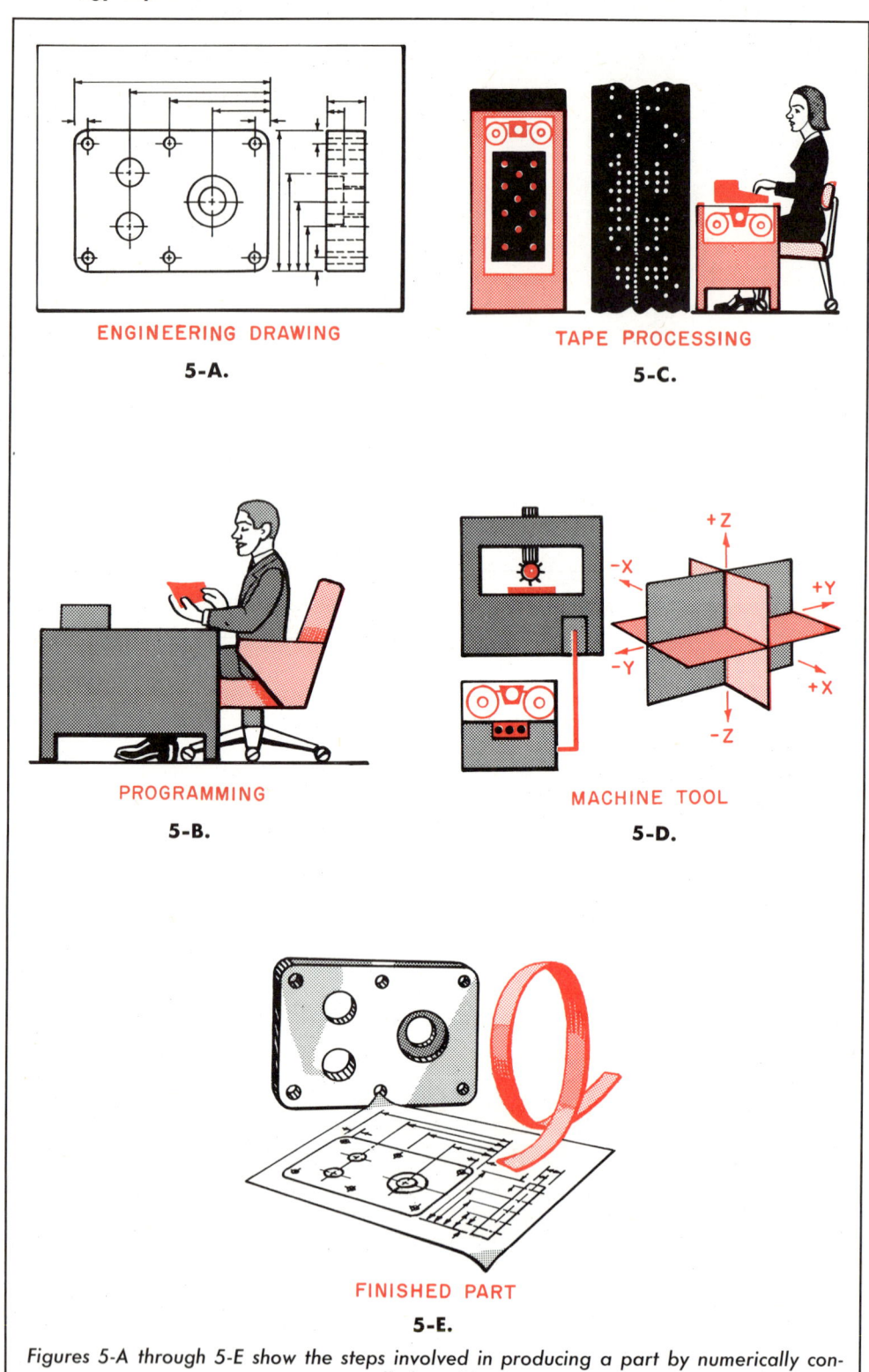

Technology Report 5

ENGINEERING DRAWING
5-A.

TAPE PROCESSING
5-C.

PROGRAMMING
5-B.

MACHINE TOOL
5-D.

FINISHED PART
5-E.

Figures 5-A through 5-E show the steps involved in producing a part by numerically controlled machines.

578

TECHNOLOGY REPORT 6
Alternate Power Sources

Traditionally America has relied on wood, coal, oil, and gas as sources of power. These power sources have run factories, heated homes, and propelled our transportation. America now is faced with a shortage of some of these power sources. New sources or new uses for old sources may need to be found. This technology report describes some of the alternatives we may be using in the future.

Wind Power. For centuries wind has furnished free power to the world. Windmills have long been used by the Dutch to pump water from their land. In the early days of this country, windmills were used to pump water for use on farms.

Today, windmills can be used to generate electricity. Surveys have shown that there is tremendous potential in wind power, but that it is not a very reliable source of energy. The development of high efficiency windmills that will work with little wind will make the use of wind power practical.

In the 1940s there was a unit in Vermont which generated power to be fed into the regular electrical system of a town. When the wind velocity was between 20 and 70 miles per hour, the wind generators cut into the line. This unit at Grandpa's Knob, Vermont, could generate up to 1500 kilowatts of electricity. Fig 6-A. Damage to the blades of the windmill caused it to be shut down and later dismantled. Now, however, windmills are again being considered as a source of energy.

Geothermal Power. Geothermal power means using natural steam from within the earth to run electrical generators. In some places the *magma*, or molten rock, which is normally deep within the earth is close to the surface. Steam is formed from water which comes in contact with the magma. Wells are drilled which tap this steam. Geologists say that these steam wells may last for a thousand years.

Areas in which geothermal power is available include the western United States, Iceland, and New Zealand, as well as other areas. Fig. 6-B.

Steam from the wells is carried by pipes to turbine generators. From this point on,

6-A. *The windmill at Grandpa's Knob, Vermont.*
Central Vermont Public Service Corp.

Technology Report 6

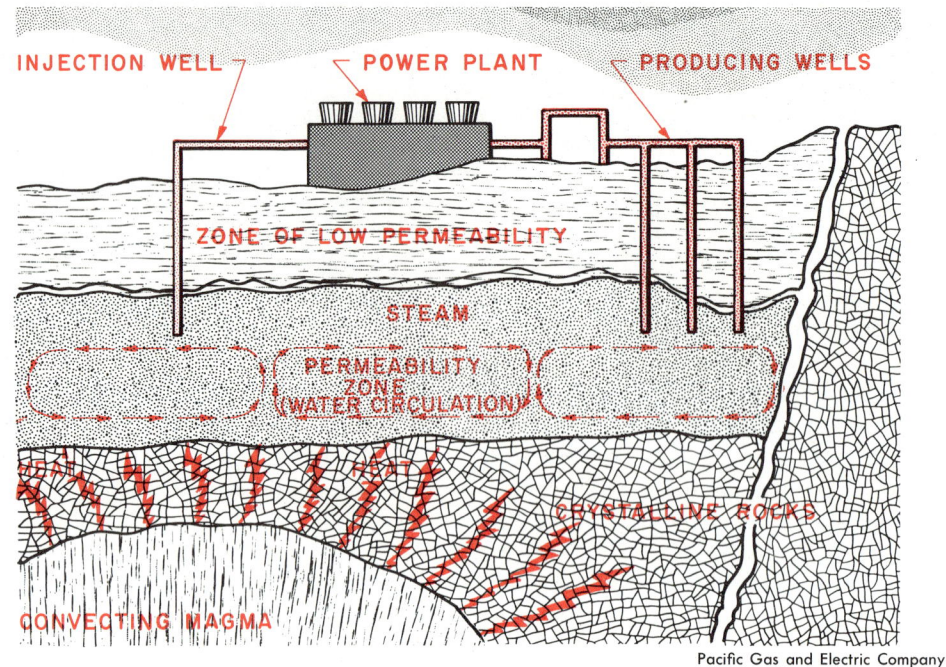

6-B. A geothermal power plant uses steam from the earth to produce electricity.

Pacific Gas and Electric Company

6-C. Producing fuel gas from waste. Shown here is the Purox® system, developed by Union Carbide.

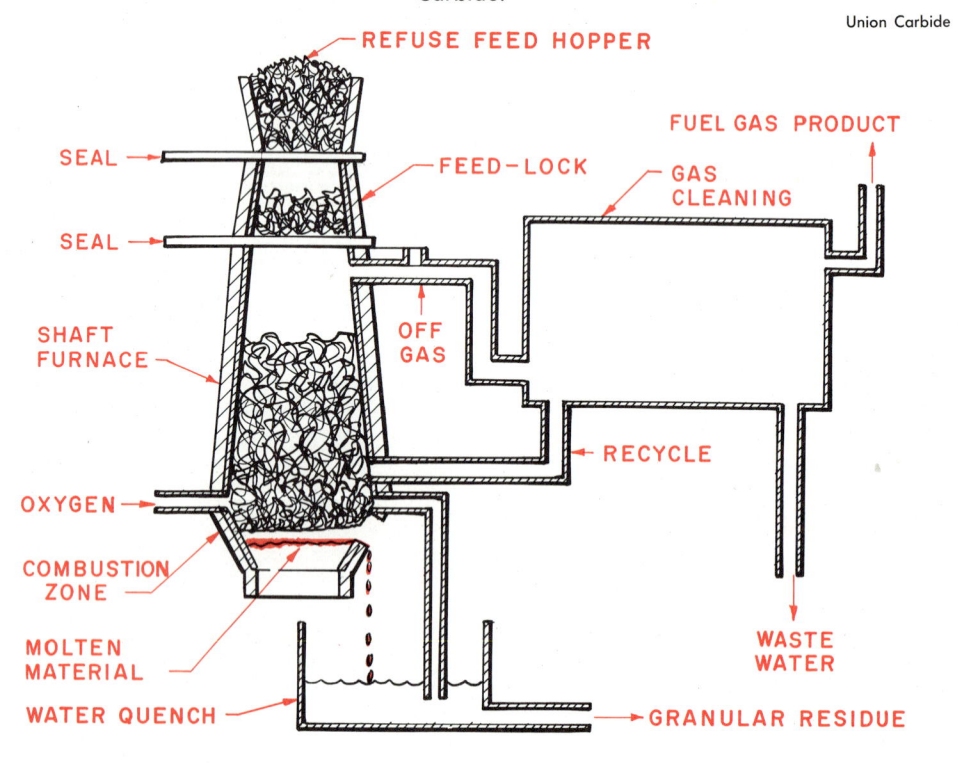

Union Carbide

Technology Report 6

an electrical generating station run by geothermal steam is the same as a plant using steam from any other source, such as coal.

Energy from Waste. When organic wastes are allowed to decompose, or rot, carbon dioxide and methane gas are produced. Methane gas can be burned in boilers to produce steam for running electrical generators.

A more efficient method of producing gas from solid organic waste involves the use of heat. When organic materials are heated in the absence of oxygen, they break down into several gases, liquids, and tars. Wastes are placed into a chamber, or reactor, and hot inert gas is used to heat the wastes. (An inert gas is one that will not react chemically with the wastes.) This process is called *pyrolysis*. This process can be run continuously. The gas that is produced is taken off, cleaned, and used for heating homes, cooking, or for generating electricity. The solid material that is left is used for landfill. Fig. 6-C.

Solar Power. Of all the sources of power available today, solar power—offers the best alternative to the sources in common use. The radiation received from the sun over the total surface of the earth is many times larger than the world's energy needs. The problem is how to harness this energy efficiently and economically. Another problem is its irregularity due to clouds and the changing seasons. When these problems are taken care of, solar energy can be used for a variety of purposes.

Home Heating. A solar heating system in a home needs an energy collection system, a heat storage system, and a pump to distribute the heat. The energy collectors are usually flat panels located on the roof of a house. The energy is used to heat water in large tanks or to heat rocks. The water or rocks will hold the heat for quite a while. When it is needed, the heat is distributed by water which is pumped through the system or by air which is moved through ducts by fans. Fig. 6-D.

While the sun shines, heat is collected by the rooftop panels and stored. During the night and on cloudy days, the stored heat is used to warm the home.

6-D(1). *Heating a home with solar energy. When the sun shines on the solar collectors on the roof, warm air is circulated through the house. The cool air is sent up to the roof to be warmed by the sun.*

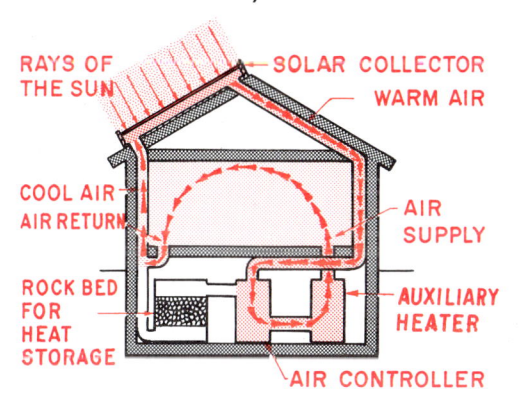

6-D(2). *Once the home is at the desired temperature, the warm air from the rooftop can be diverted to the rock bed. Here the heat can be stored for future use.*

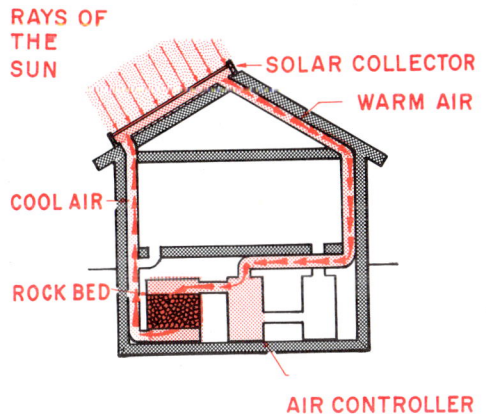

Technology Report 7

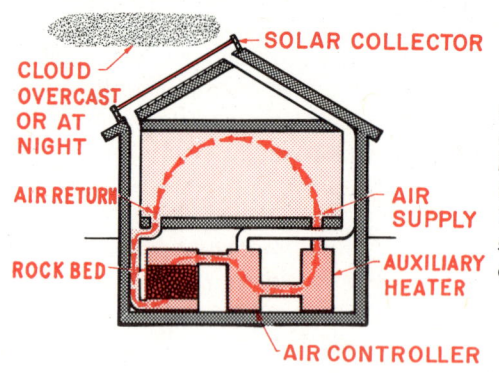

6-D(3). *During the night and on cloudy days, the stored heat is used to warm the house. As you can see in this drawing and in the two before it, there is an auxiliary heater. This is a regular gas or electric heater. It supplements the solar heat and can take over completely when solar heat is not available.*

TECHNOLOGY REPORT 7

Automotive Engines

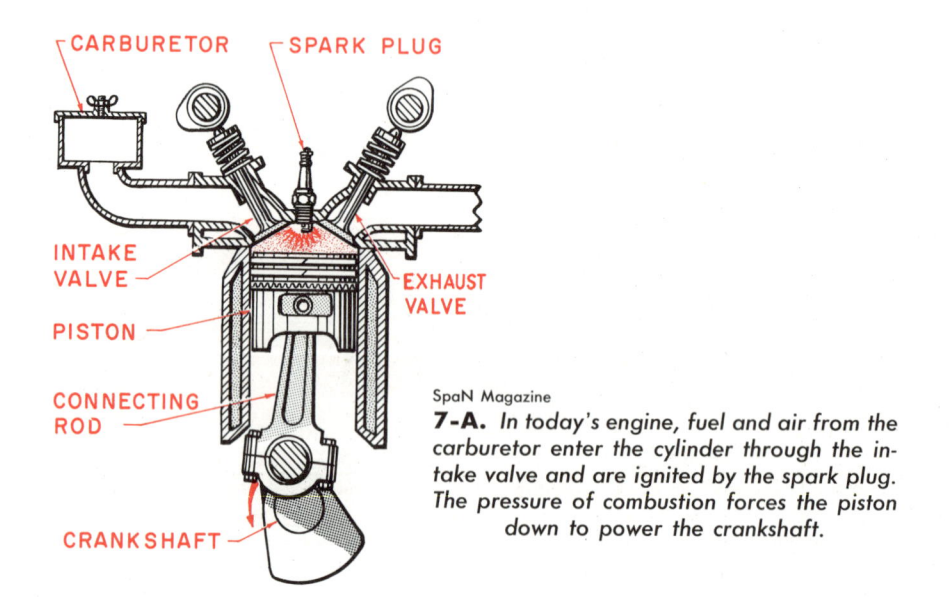

SpaN Magazine

7-A. *In today's engine, fuel and air from the carburetor enter the cylinder through the intake valve and are ignited by the spark plug. The pressure of combustion forces the piston down to power the crankshaft.*

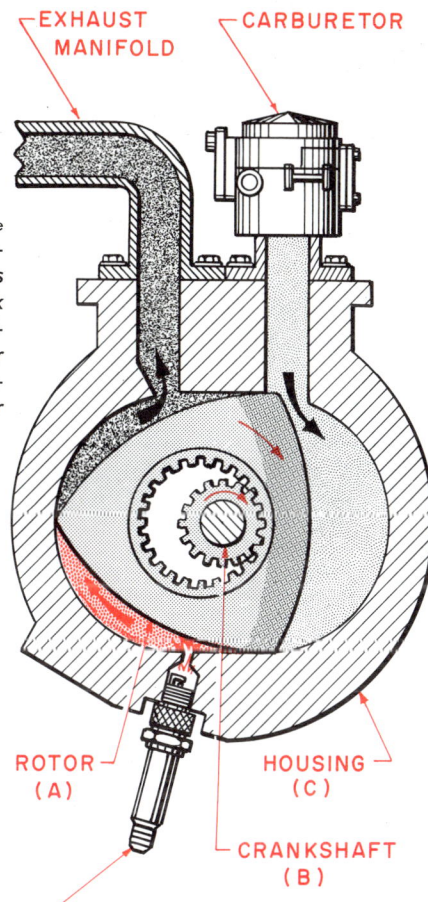

Technology Report 7

7-B. A Wankel engine uses a rotor (A) instead of pistons to develop power. Fuel is drawn in, compressed, and fired by the spark plug. Exhaust gases are forced out the manifold. The energy of combustion turns the rotor inside the housing (C), driving the crankshaft (B) attached to a transmission and rear axles. Rotary engines burn gasoline.

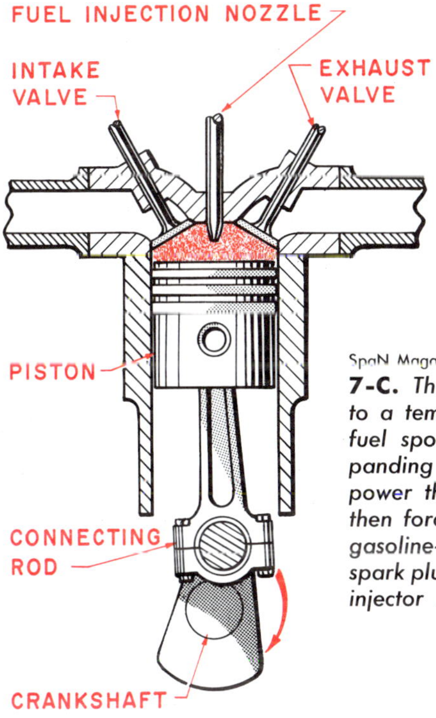

SpaN Magazine

7-C. The diesel compresses air in the cylinder to a temperature high enough to ignite the fuel spontaneously when it is injected. Expanding hot gases drive the piston down to power the crankshaft, and the rising piston then forces exhaust gases out, as in present gasoline-fueled engines. No carburetor or spark plugs are needed, but an expensive fuel injector is required. Diesels are heavy and expensive to build.

SpaN Magazine

Technology Report 7

SpaN Magazine

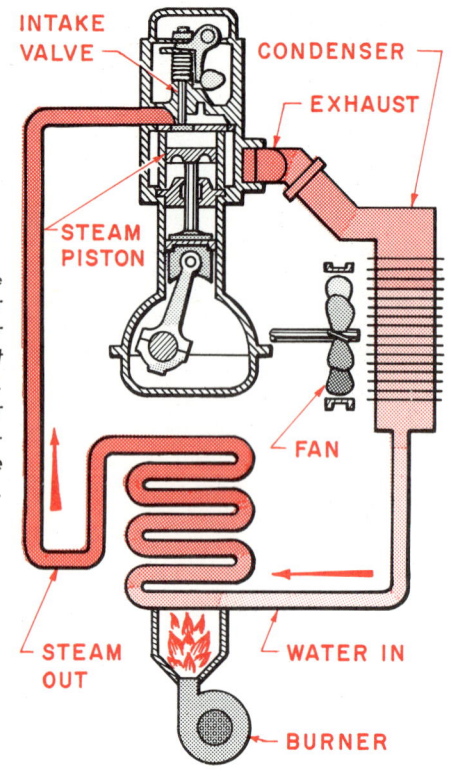

7-D. Steam or vapor systems use water or other fluid to develop power. The burner heats the fluid to high pressure and expands it through a piston that drives a crankshaft. Spent fluid is then cooled in the condenser before being reheated in the boiler and repeating its journey. Vapor cycle systems are too costly, bulky, and heavy for auto use.

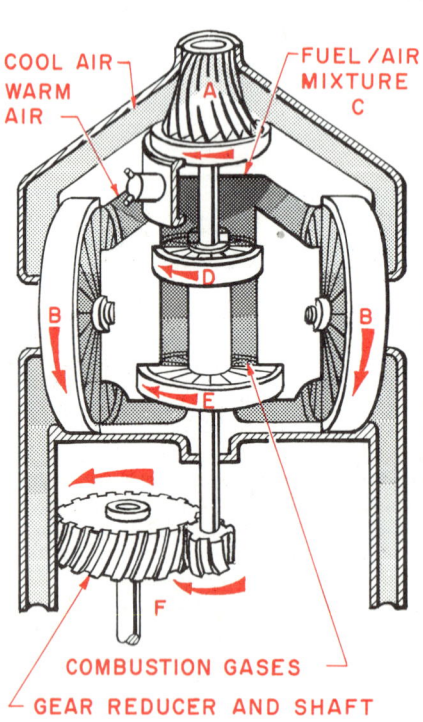

SpaN Magazine

7-E. In the gas turbine, the compressor (A) forces air through the heat exchanger (B), where it is warmed. Fuel is burned in the combustion chamber (C), and combustion gases expand through the turbine (D) that drives the air compressor and through the turbine (E) that powers the car via a gear speed reducer (F) and a shaft. Gas turbines for cars were road- and driver-tested years ago, and proved uneconomic.

Technology Report 7

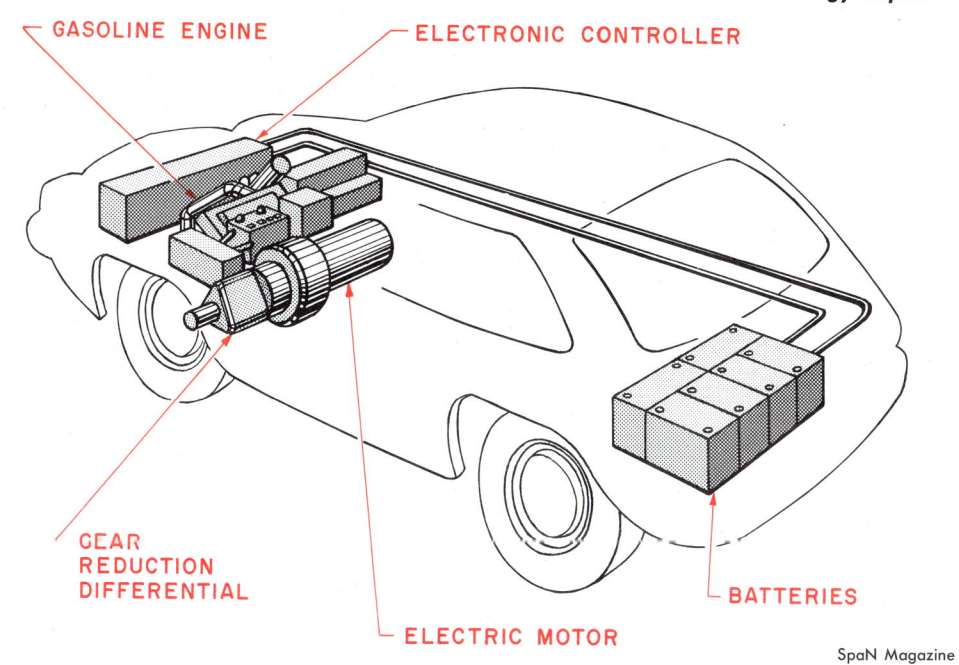

7-F. This hybrid car uses an engine that drives a generator that charges batteries. The batteries power an electric motor that moves the car. The small car can run on electricity alone or use both power sources. In the latter case, the gasoline engine provides a steady source of power to charge the batteries. An all-electric car, on the other hand, has no engine. Its batteries must be charged from electric power lines.

APPENDIX

Table 1
Approximate Conversions
(Customary to Metric; Metric to Customary)

From	To	Multiply By
LENGTH		
inches	millimetres	25
feet	millimetres	300
yards	metres	0.9
miles	kilometres	1.6
millimetres	inches	0.04
millimetres	feet	0.0033
metres	yards	1.1
kilometres	miles	0.6
AREA		
square inches	square millimetres	650
square inches	square centimetres	6.5
square feet	square metres	0.1
square yards	square metres	0.8
square miles	square kilometres	2.6
acres	square hectometres (hectares)	0.4
square millimetres	square inches	0.001 6
square centimetres	square inches	0.16
square metres	square feet	11
square metres	square yards	1.2
square kilometres	square miles	0.4
square hectometres (hectares)	acres	2.5
VOLUME		
cubic inches	cubic millimetres	16 000
cubic inches	cubic centimetres	16
cubic feet	cubic metres	0.03
cubic yards	cubic metres	0.8
fluid ounces	millilitres	30
pints	litres	0.47
quarts	litres	0.95
gallons	litres	3.8
cubic millimetres	cubic inches	0.000 06
cubic centimetres	cubic inches	0.06
cubic metres	cubic feet	35
cubic metres	cubic yards	1.3
millilitres	fluid ounces	0.03
litres	pints	2.1
litres	quarts	1.06
litres	gallons	0.26
MASS (Weight)		
ounces	grams	28
pounds	kilograms	0.45
tons	metric tons	0.9
grams	ounces	0.04
kilograms	pounds	2.2
metric tons	tons	1.1
TEMPERATURE		
degrees Fahrenheit	degrees Celsius	(°C × 1.8) + 32
degrees Celsius	degrees Fahrenheit	(°F − 32) × 0.6

Appendix

Table 2
A- and C-Series Paper and Envelopes

A-Series Paper-Trimmed Sizes			C-Series Envelopes		
Size	Millimetres	Inches*	Size	Millimetres	Inches*
A0	841 × 1189	$33\frac{1}{8} \times 46\frac{3}{4}$	C0	917 × 1297	$36\frac{1}{8} \times 51$
A1	594 × 841	$23\frac{3}{8} \times 33\frac{1}{8}$	C1	648 × 917	$25\frac{1}{2} \times 36\frac{1}{8}$
A2	420 × 594	$16\frac{1}{2} \times 23\frac{3}{8}$	C2	458 × 648	$18 \times 25\frac{1}{2}$
A3	297 × 420	$11\frac{3}{4} \times 16\frac{1}{2}$	C3	324 × 458	$12\frac{3}{4} \times 18$
A4	210 × 297	$8\frac{1}{4} \times 11\frac{3}{4}$	C4	229 × 324	$9 \times 12\frac{3}{4}$
***					
A5	148 × 210	$5\frac{7}{8} \times 8\frac{1}{4}$	C5	162 × 229	$6\frac{3}{8} \times 9$
A6	105 × 148	$4\frac{1}{8} \times 5\frac{7}{8}$	C6	114 × 162	$4\frac{1}{2} \times 6\frac{3}{8}$
			**DL	110 × 220	$4\frac{5}{16} \times 8\frac{5}{8}$
A7	74 × 105	$2\frac{7}{8} \times 4\frac{1}{8}$	C7	81 × 114	$3\frac{1}{4} \times 4\frac{1}{2}$
A8	52 × 74	$2 \times 2\frac{7}{8}$	C8	57 × 81	$2\frac{1}{4} \times 3\frac{1}{4}$
A9	37 × 52	$1\frac{1}{2} \times 2$			
A10	26 × 37	$1 \times 1\frac{1}{2}$			

*To nearest $\frac{1}{8}$ inch.
**Standard commercial envelope, takes size A4 sheet.
***Two intermediate sizes, 210 × 280 mm ($8\frac{1}{4}'' \times 11''$) and 210 × 198 mm ($8\frac{1}{4}'' \times 7\frac{3}{4}''$) are under consideration.

Table 3
B-Series Paper—Trimmed Sizes

Size	Millimetres	Inches*
B0	1000 × 1414	$39\frac{3}{8} \times 55\frac{5}{8}$
B1	707 × 1000	$27\frac{7}{8} \times 39\frac{3}{8}$
B2	500 × 707	$19\frac{5}{8} \times 27\frac{7}{8}$
B3	353 × 500	$13\frac{7}{8} \times 19\frac{5}{8}$
B4	250 × 353	$9\frac{7}{8} \times 13\frac{7}{8}$
B5	176 × 250	$6\frac{7}{8} \times 13\frac{7}{8}$
B6	125 × 176	$4\frac{7}{8} \times 6\frac{7}{8}$
B7	88 × 125	$3\frac{1}{2} \times 4\frac{7}{8}$
B8	62 × 88	$2\frac{1}{2} \times 3\frac{1}{2}$
B9	44 × 62	$1\frac{3}{4} \times 2\frac{1}{2}$
B10	31 × 44	$1\frac{1}{4} \times 1\frac{3}{4}$

*To nearest $\frac{1}{8}$ inch.

Appendix

Table 4
Customary-Metric Drill Sizes and Conversion Chart

Fractional Inch	Decimal Inch	Number or Letter	mm	Fractional Inch	Decimal Inch	Number or Letter	mm	Fractional Inch	Decimal Inch	Number or Letter	mm
1/64	0.0156				0.0610		1.55		0.1285	30	
	0.0157		0.4	1/16	0.0625				0.1299		3.3
	0.0160	78			0.0630		1.6		0.1339		3.4
	0.0165		0.42		0.0635	52			0.1360	29	
	0.0173		0.44		0.0650		1.65		0.1378		3.5
	0.0177		0.45		0.0669		1.7		0.1405	28	
	0.0180	77			0.0670	51		9/64	0.1406		
	0.0181		0.46		0.0689		1.75		0.1417		3.6
	0.0189		0.48		0.0700	50			0.1440	27	
	0.0197		0.5		0.0709		1.8		0.1457		3.7
	0.0200	76			0.0728		1.85		0.1470	26	
	0.0210	75			0.0730	49			0.1476		3.75
	0.0217		0.55		0.0748		1.9		0.1495	25	
	0.0225	74			0.0760	48			0.1496		3.8
	0.0236		0.6		0.0768		1.95		0.1520	24	
	0.0240	73		5/64	0.0781				0.1535		3.9
	0.0250	72			0.0785	47			0.1540	23	
	0.0256		0.65		0.0787		2.0	5/32	0.1562		
	0.0260	71			0.0807		2.05		0.1570	22	
	0.0276		0.7		0.0810	46			0.1575		4.0
	0.0280	70			0.0820	45			0.1590	21	
	0.0292	69			0.0827		2.1		0.1610	20	
	0.0295		0.75		0.0846		2.15		0.1614		4.1
	0.0310	68			0.0860	44			0.1654		4.2
1/32	0.0312				0.0866		2.2		0.1660	19	
	0.0315		0.8		0.0886		2.25		0.1673		4.25
	0.0320	67			0.0890	43			0.1693		4.3
	0.0330	66			0.0906		2.3		0.1695	18	
	0.0335		0.85		0.0925		2.35	11/64	0.1719		
	0.0350	65			0.0935	42			0.1730	17	
	0.0354		0.9	3/32	0.0938				0.1732		4.4
	0.0360	64			0.0945		2.4		0.1770	16	
	0.0370	63			0.0960	41			0.1772		4.5
	0.0374		0.95		0.0965		2.45		0.1800	15	
	0.0380	62			0.0980	40			0.1811		4.6
	0.0390	61			0.0981		2.5		0.1820	14	
	0.0394		1.0		0.0995	39			0.1850	13	
	0.0400	60			0.1015	38			0.1850		4.7
	0.0410	59			0.1024		2.6		0.1870		4.75
	0.0413		1.05		0.1040	37		3/16	0.1875		
	0.0420	58			0.1063		2.7		0.1890		4.8
	0.0430	57			0.1065	36			0.1890	12	
	0.0433		1.1		0.1083		2.75		0.1910	11	
	0.0453		1.15	7/64	0.1094				0.1929		4.9
	0.0465	56			0.1100	35			0.1935	10	
3/64	0.0469				0.1102		2.8		0.1960	9	
	0.0472		1.2		0.1110	34			0.1969		5.0
	0.0492		1.25		0.1130	33			0.1990	8	
	0.0512		1.3		0.1142		2.9		0.2008		5.1
	0.0520	55			0.1160	32			0.2010	7	
	0.0531		1.35		0.1181		3.0	13/64	0.2031		
	0.0550	54			0.1200	31			0.2040	6	
	0.0551		1.4		0.1220		3.1		0.2047		5.2
	0.0571		1.45	1/8	0.1250				0.2055	5	
	0.0591		1.5		0.1260		3.2		0.2067		5.25
	0.0595	53			0.1280		3.25		0.2087		5.3

588

Table 4 Continued

Frac-tional Inch	Dec-imal Inch	Number or Letter	mm	Frac-tional Inch	Dec-imal Inch	Number or Letter	mm	Frac-tional Inch	Dec-imal Inch	Number or Letter	mm
	0.2090	4			0.3160	O		17/32	0.5312		
	0.2126		5.4		0.3189		8.1		0.5315		13.5
	0.2130	3			0.3228		8.2	35/64	0.5469		
	0.2165		5.5		0.3230	P			0.5512		14.0
7/32	0.2188				0.3248		8.25	9/16	0.5625		
	0.2205		5.6		0.3268		8.3		0.5709		14.5
	0.2210	2		21/64	0.3281			37/64	0.5781		
	0.2244		5.7		0.3307		8.4		0.5906		15.0
	0.2264		5.75		0.3320	Q		19/32	0.5938		
	0.2280	1			0.3346		8.5	39/64	0.6094		
	0.2283		5.8		0.3386		8.6		0.6102		15.5
	0.2323		5.9		0.3390	R		5/8	0.6250		
	0.2340	A			0.3425		8.7		0.6299		16.0
15/64	0.2344			11/32	0.3438			41/64	0.6406		
	0.2362		6.0		0.3445		8.75		0.6496		16.5
	0.2380	B			0.3465		8.8	21/32	0.6562		
	0.2402		6.1		0.3480	S			0.6693		17.0
	0.2420	C			0.3504		8.9	43/64	0.6719		
	0.2441		6.2		0.3543		9.0	11/16	0.6875		
	0.2460	D			0.3580	T			0.6890		17.5
	0.2461		6.25		0.3583		9.1	45/64	0.7031		
	0.2480		6.3	23/64	0.3594				0.7087		18.0
1/4	0.2500	E			0.3622		9.2	23/32	0.7188		
	0.2520		6.4		0.3642		9.25		0.7283		18.5
	0.2559		6.5		0.3661		9.3	47/64	0.7344		
	0.2570	F			0.3680	U			0.7480		19.0
	0.2598		6.6		0.3701		9.4	3/4	0.7500		
	0.2610	G			0.3740		9.5	49/64	0.7656		
	0.2638		6.7	3/8	0.3750				0.768		19.5
17/64	0.2656				0.3770	V		25/32	0.7812		
	0.2657		6.75		0.3780		9.6		0.7874		20.0
	0.2660	H			0.3819		9.7	51/64	0.7969		
	0.2677		6.8		0.3839		9.75		0.808		20.5
	0.2717		6.9		0.3858		9.8	13/16	0.8125		
	0.2720	I			0.3860	W			0.8268		21.0
	0.2756		7.0		0.3898		9.9	53/64	0.8281		
	0.2770	J		25/64	0.3906			27/32	0.8437		
	0.2795		7.1		0.3937		10.0		0.847		21.5
	0.2810	K			0.3970			55/64	0.8594		
9/32	0.2812				0.4040	X			0.8661		22.0
	0.2835		7.2		0.4062	Y		7/8	0.8750		
	0.2854		7.25	13/32	0.4130	Z			0.886		22.5
	0.2874		7.3		0.4134		10.5	57/64	0.8906		
	0.2900	L		27/64	0.4219				0.9055		23.0
	0.2913		7.4		0.4331		11.0	29/32	0.9062		
	0.2950	M		7/16	0.4375			59/64	0.9219		
	0.2953		7.5		0.4528		11.5		0.926		23.5
19/64	0.2969			29/64	0.4531			15/16	0.9375		
	0.2992		7.6	15/32	0.4688				0.9449		24.0
	0.3020	N			0.4724		12.0	61/64	0.9531		
	0.3031		7.7	31/64	0.4844				0.965		24.5
	0.3051		7.75		0.4921		12.5	31/32	0.9687		
	0.3071		7.8	1/2	0.5000				0.9843		25.0
	0.3110		7.9		0.5118		13.0	63/64	0.9844		
5/16	0.3125			33/64	0.5156			64/64	1.000		25.4
	0.3150		8.0								

Appendix

Table 5
Drill Chart
(Boring Approximate Metric Holes with Customary Drills)

mm	Customary Drill Size	mm	Customary Drill Size	mm	Customary Drill Size
1.00	60	5.00	9	9.00	T
1.20	3/64	5.20	6 or 13/64	9.20	23/64
1.40	54	5.40	3	9.40	U
1.60	1/16	5.60	2 or 7/32	9.60	V
1.80	50	5.80	1	9.80	W
2.00	47	6.00	B or 15/64	10.00	X or 25/64
2.20	44	6.20	D	10.20	Y
2.40	3/32	6.40	1/4 or E	10.50	Z
2.60	38	6.60	G	10.80	27/64
2.80	34 or 35	6.80	H	11.00	7/16
3.00	31	7.00	J	11.20	*
3.20	1/8	7.20	9/32	11.50	29/64
3.40	29	7.40	L	11.80	15/32
3.60	9/64	7.60	N	12.00	*
3.80	25	7.80	5/16	12.20	31/64
4.00	22	8.00	O	12.50	*
4.20	19	8.20	P	12.80	1/2
4.40	17	8.40	O or 21/64	13.00	33/64
4.60	14	8.60	R		
4.80	12 or 3/16	8.80	S		

* no equivalent size

Appendix

Table 6
Steel Temperature Chart Using Color to Indicate Temperature

Color	Temperature °F	Temperature °C
White	2200	1204
Lemon	1825	1096
Orange	1725	941
Cherry red	1325	718
Dark red	1175	635
Faint red	900	482
Pale blue	590	310

Table 7
Tempering Chart for Steel Tools

Tools	Color	Temperature °F	Temperature °C
Scribers, Hammer faces	Pale yellow	450	232
Center punches	Full yellow	470	243
Cold chisels	Brown	500	260
Screw-drivers	Purple	530	277

Table 8
Softwood Lumber
(Possible Metric Replacement Sizes)

NOMINAL (inch)	ACTUAL (inch)	REPLACEMENT (mm)
1 × 4	3/4 × 3 1/2	19 × 89
1 × 6	3/4 × 5 1/2	19 × 140
1 × 8	3/4 × 7 1/4	19 × 184
1 × 10	3/4 × 9 1/4	19 × 235
1 × 12	3/4 × 11 1/4	19 × 285
2 × 4	1 1/2 × 3 1/2	38 × 89
2 × 6	1 1/2 × 5 1/2	38 × 140
2 × 8	1 1/2 × 7 1/4	38 × 184
2 × 10	1 1/2 × 9 1/4	38 × 235
2 × 12	1 1/2 × 11 1/4	38 × 285

Sheet materials: 4' × 8' replaced by 1200 × 2400 mm (47.24" × 94.48" or approximately 3/4" narrower and 1 1/2" shorter).

Metric lumber lengths in metres: 2, 2.4, 3, 3.5, 4, 5, 5.5, and 6.

Index

A

Abacus, 434–435
Abrading
  of metal, 176, 187–192
  of plastic, 303
  of wood, 332, 343–346
Abrasives
  defined, 343
  grading of, 187–188
  kinds of, 187
  using, 188–192
ACI. *See* Automatic car identification (ACI)
Acids, in etching, 215
Adhesion, and plastics, 305
Adhesives
  for metal, 174
  for plastics, 304
Advertising, 545
AFL-CIO, 519
Aircraft, 481–489
Airdrying, of lumber, 318
Air traffic control, 478–481
Airways, 478
Alloys, 149, 154–155
Aluminum, 150–152, 161
Aluminum oxide, 187
American Federation of Labor, 519
American Medical Association, 519
American Vocational Association, 519
Amperes, 403
Anchor bolts, 385
Angle(s)
  bisecting of, 60
  of declination, 400
Angular developments, in sheet metal patterns, 167–168
Annealing, 235
Antenna, 437
Anvil, 233
Anvil hardy, 233
Apprenticeship programs, 560
Aprons, 38
Architects, 18
Armature, 418, 419, 457
Arris, 344
Arrowheads (on lines), 79
ASA rating, 129
Automatic car identification (ACI), 471
Auto mechanics, 559
Automobile, 497–502

B

Balance (measuring device), 32
Bales, 119
Ballast, 467
Bar folders, 221
Basswood, 319
Batter boards, 381; illustrated, 383
Battery
  general discussion, 406–407
  symbol for, 413
Bauxite, 150
Bell, Alexander Graham, 433
Bellows, illustrated, 228
Bending
  of metal, 217, 220–226
  of plastics, 298–299
  steam, 355
Billets, illustrated, 151
Bill of materials, 35, 534, 551
Birch, 319
Bit
  auger, general discussion, 346
  auger, sizes for shank and pilot holes (table), 365
  expansion, 346
  Foerstner, 346
Blast furnace, 149; illustrated, 151
Blasting, abrasive, 279–280
Bleaching, of wood, 372
Blooms, 149–159; illustrated, 151
Blueprints, 98–100
Board feet, figuring, 325
Board of directors, 523
Boat builders, 324
Bonding
  explosive, 173–174
  of wood, 329–330
Bookrack, design of, 23–25
Braces, 346
Brads, 364
Brake, box and pan, 222
Brass, 161
Brazing, 262–264
Breaker points, 457
Breaks, conventional (in drawing), illustrated, 59
Bridging, 386
Bronze, 161
Bruning process, 99
Brushes, generator, 418

592

Index

Buffing, of metal, 187, 277
Buildings, planning of, 91–92
Building construction, 379–393
Building permit, 381
Bulb (in casting), illustrated, 228
Buses, 498–499
Businesses, small, 522–523

C

Cabinetmakers, 324, 556–559
Cable
  electrical, 430
  underwater, laying of, 495
Calculator, electronic, 434–436
Calendering, 292–293
California job case, 112
Caliper
  hermaphrodite, 165
  use of, illustrated, 209
Camera
  process, 122, 123
  types of, 128
Camshaft, 454
Car, electric, 502
Carburetor, 456–457
Careers
  in business, 564–566
  general discussion, 17, 556–568
  in industry (table), 558
  and interests, 567–568
  in plastics industry, 290
  technical, 560–561
  in wood industry, 324
Career clusters (chart), 557
Carpenters, 324
Carriage (in lumbering), 316
Case hardening, 235
Casting
  continuous, 149, 151
  of metal, 217, 227–231
  of plastics, 296, 299
  sand, 227–231
Catalytic converter, 501
Cell, electrical
  general discussion, 405–410
  symbol for, 413
Cell (in rotogravure process), 109
Celluloid, 289
Cementing, 265
Cermets, 572
Chairs, design of, 21
Charring, 370
Chart
  Gantt, 534, 537, 554
  process, 534
  production control, 534
Chase, 116
Chasing, 241–243
Chemical deposits, 517
Cherry, 319
Chisels, 184–185, 341–343
Chlorine, 517
Chucks
  collet, 213
  lathe, 207
Circuit breaker, 423
Circuits, 406–407, 412–415, 426–427
Clamps, 367
Clean Air Act, 500
Clipper ships, 493
Coal, 515
Coating
  of metal, 174, 272
  of plastics, 293, 308, 310
  of wood, 369
Cohesion, and plastics, 305
Coil, electrical, 418
Coil, ignition, 457
Cold composition, 121
Collective bargaining, 519
Color finishing, 282–283
Coloring
  of metal, 272
  of plastics, 308–310
  of wood, 369
Combination set, 165
Communications
  general discussion, 432–438
  in industry, 521
  wireless, 436–437
Communications media, 545
Commutator, 418, 419
Compass (directional), 399
Compass (drawing instrument), 53–54
Composing stick, 112, 114
Composite materials (technology report), 571–572
Composition, wood plastic, 576
Compreg, 576
Computers, 434–436
Concrete, curing of, 382
Condenser, 457
Conductors, electrical, 412–416
Conical developments, in sheet metal patterns, 169
Connecting rod, 452
Contact printing, 133–135
Continuous tone copy, 121

Index

Conversion chart method (of dual dimensioning), 83–84
Conversion tables
  approximate conversions (customary to metric; metric to customary), 586
  customary-metric drill sizes, 588–589
Cope (in casting), 229
Copper, 152–153, 159, 161
Cords, electrical, 414, 416
Corporation, 523, 525–526
Cotton gin, 508
Council of Industrial Organizations, 519
Countersinks, 195
Course objectives, 16–17
Crafts, 556–560
Crankcase, 454
Crankshaft, 452
Creosote, 370
Crucible, illustrated, 228
CTC. See Traffic control, centralized, (CTC)
Cubit, 26
Curves, irregular, 49–50
Customary system (measurement), 26
Cutting
  electro-chemical, of metal, 177
  flame, of metal, 215–216
  laser, of metal, 172
  of metal, general discussion, 171–172, 175–177
  of plastic, 302–303
  rough, on the lathe, 212
  thermal, 214
  of wood. See Woodcutting
Cylinder press, 107–108
Cylindrical developments, in sheet metal patterns, 168–169

D

Daimler, Gottlieb, 444
Design
  general discussion, 18–25
  and metrics, 85–87
  of vehicles, 465
Designers, 18, 529
Developer (for offset plates), 122
Dies, 292; illustrated, 252
Diesel, Rudolph, 447
Die stock, illustrated, 252
Digit, 26
Dimensioning
  on drawings, 46
  dual, 82–84
  general discussion, 78–81

location, 79
metric, 82–87
rounding off, 85
Dispatching, 538
Distributing, 545
Dividers, 54, 165
Doctor blade, 110
Double plate, 387
Draft (in casting), 227
Drafting, 45–97
Drafting machines, 55
Drafting templates, 55
Drag (in casting), 228
Drawing (industrial process), 218, 244
Drawing (drafting), 45–97
Drawing(s)
  assembly, 36, 88–90
  body, 45
  building construction, 91–98
  cabinet oblique, 77
  cavalier oblique, 77
  detail, 37, 88–90
  isometric, 75
  mechanical, 45
  multiview, 68–71
  oblique, 75–77
  perspective, 74–75
  pictorial, 74–77
  working, 35
Drawing boards, 48
Drawing instruments, 53–55
Drier
  in ink, 106
  in paint, 375
Drill(s)
  automatic, 348–349
  customary, boring metric holes with (table), 590
  customary-metric conversion (table), 588–589
  hand, 194, 196, 349
  parts of, illustrated, 199
  sharpening, 196
  tap, for various thread sizes (table), 253
  twist, 195, 346
Drilling
  of metal, 177, 194–199
  of plastic, 303
  of wood, 332, 346–348
Drill press, 196; illustrated, 197
Dry-diazo process, 99
Duplicating processes, office
  electrostatic, 138–139
  general discussion, 138–142

594

spirit, 139–140
Duryea brothers, 445, 498
Dye, layout, 164–165

E

Ear protection, 41
Eaves, 388
Ecology, 510–512
Edison, Thomas, 424
Electrical outlets, 390–391
Electricity
   and building construction, 390–391
   by chemical action, 404–409
   conductors of, 412–416
   converting to heat, 421–424
   converting to light, 424–431
   current, 402, 403
   distribution of, in home, illustrated, 429
   forms of, 402–403
   from heat, 409
   from light, 410
   and magnetism, 397–401
   from magnetism, 411
   and photoelectric effect, 410
   from pressure, 409–410
   sources of, 404
   static, 402–403
   symbols used, 416
   transmission of, illustrated, 428
Electrolyte, 406
Electromagnet, 417
Electromagnetism, 417–421
Electrons, 404, 412
Electronics. *See* Communications
Electroplating, 274; illustrated, 275
Emery, 187
Employee organizations, 519
Employees
   hiring of, 541
   managerial. *See* Management
   nonmanagerial, 517, 518–519
   selection of, 541
   supervision of, 543
   training of, 541
Em quad, 112
Enamel
   for metal, 274
   for wood, 375
Enameling, of metal, 274–276
Energy
   general discussion, 440–460
   in industry, 521
   from waste, 580–581

Engineers
   aerospace, 563
   chemical, 562
   civil, 563
   electrical, 563
   methods, 533
   plastics materials, 290
Engineering, careers in, 561–563
Engines
   automotive, 582–585
   diesel, 447, 471; illustrated, 583
   electric automotive, illustrated, 585
   gasoline, four-cycle, 452–454
   gasoline, fuel system of, 455–457
   gasoline, general discussion, 441, 444–445, 452–460
   gasoline, ignition system of, 457–459
   gasoline, maintenance of, 459–460
   gasoline, operation of, 455–459
   gasoline, small, 452–460
   gasoline, two-cycle, 454–455
   gas turbine, 449; illustrated, 584
   internal combustion, 444–447
   jet, 448–449
   prop-jet. *See* Engines, turboprop
   rotary, 445–447
   steam, 441, 508; illustrated, 584
   stratified charge, 502
   turbojet, 448
   turboprop, 448
   Wankel, 445–447; illustrated, 583
Enlarger, photograph, illustrated, 135
Envelopes, C-series sizes (table), 587
Erasing shield, 53
Etch (for offset plates), 122
Etching, 214–215
Ethylene, 517
Exhaust velocity, 449
Extruding
   of metal, 218, 245
   of plastic, 292, 299

F

FAA. *See* Federal Aviation Administration (FAA)
Faceplate, lathe, 207
Factories, 520–521
Faraday, Michael, 418
Fasteners
   mechanical, 304
   threaded, 250–255
Fastening
   adhesive, of metal, 249, 259–265

Index

adhesive, of wood, 358, 366–368
cohesive, of metal, 249, 266–270
mechanical, of metal, 249, 250–258
mechanical, of plastics, 305
mechanical, of wood, 358
of metal, 173–174, 248–270
of plastic, 304–307
of wood, 358–367
Federal Aviation Administration (FAA), 488
Fiberglass, 307
Filaments, 424
Files
  general discussion, 202–203, 349–350
Filing
  on a lathe, 214
  of metal, 200–204
  of wood, 349–352
Film, photographic, developing of, 130–132
Film, plastic, 292
Finishing
  color, of wood, 371–372
  displacement, of metal, 272, 281–282
  mechanical, of metal, 271, 281
  of metal, 174, 271–283
  of plastic, 308–310
  remove, of wood, 369
  of wood, 328–329, 368–376
Finishing operations (construction), 391–393
Fire blocks, 387
Fixtures, 532
Flammable liquids, storage of, 41
Flask (in casting), illustrated, 228, 230
Flight service stations, 480
Flint, 187
Flooring, 572
Floor plans, 91–97
Flow chart, illustrated, 553
Fluorescent lights, 427
Flux, 400
Ford, Henry, 498, 506, 522
Forging, 217, 232–233
Form(s), building construction, 381; illustrated, 384
Form, printing, 116–118
Forming
  of metal, 172–173, 216–219
  of plastics, 300
  of wood, 355–357
Forming machine, slip roll, 222
Fossil fuel, 515
Foundations, 381–385
Framing, 385–389
Franklin, Benjamin, 402

Freight cars, railroad, 475–476
French curves. *See* Curves, irregular
Frequency, 436
f-stop, 128
Fuel pump, 455
Fulcrum, 442
Fulton, Robert, 444
Furniture, printing, 116
Fuses, 422–423
Fusetron, 423

G

Galley, 114
Gantt, Henry L., 537
Garnet, 187
Gauge
  depth, 347
  drill, 195
  feeler, 460
  line, 111–112
  marking, 326
  rail, 467
  screw pitch, illustrated, 253
  sheet and wire, 164
  wire, illustrated, 159
Gauge pins, 119
Generators, 411, 418–419
Geometric patterns, drawing, 56–61
Geothermal steam, 397
Glues
  epoxy, 264, 265
  general discussion, 366–367
  in woodworking, 367–368
GNP. *See* Gross national product (GNP)
Gothic, single-stroke, 65–66
Gouges, 341–343
Graphic arts, 104–107
Gravure printing, 109–110
Grinder, floor, 188–189; parts of (illustrated), 192
Grinding, 187, 188–189, 191
Grit number, 187–188
Gross national product (GNP), 507
Gutenberg, Johann, 105

H

Hacksaw, 178–180
Halftones, 121
Hammer(s)
  for bending light metals, 220
  ball-peen, 163

Index

claw, 362
cross peen, illustrated, 233
engineer's or sledge, illustrated, 233
Hand groover, 258
Hand screw, 367
Hardboard, 324
Hardening, 235
Hardness testing, 157
Hardwoods, 318, 319, 320
Header, 386
Head rig, 316
Heating
   dielectric, 329–330
   general discussion, 389
   high-frequency, 424
Heat-treating, 233–235
Height, measurement of, 31
Helicopter, 489
Hexagon, constructing, in a circle, 60–61
House, frame, parts of (illustrated), 388
House plans, drawing, 92–97
House wiring, 427, 429–431
Hovercraft, 495–496
Hydrofoil, 495–496
Hydrometer, 406, 408
Hydrospinning, 172–173

I

IFR. *See* Instrument flight rules (IFR)
Imposing surface, 116
Impreg, 576
Impression cylinder, 108
Industrial Revolution, 508–509
Industry
   careers in (table), 558
   elements of, 527–546
   essentials of, 513–526
   general discussion, 504–568
Ink, 105–106
Inspection, 540–541
Instrument flight rules (IFR), 478
Insulators, 412

J

Jigs, 531–532
Jigsaw, 336–337
Jointer, 350, 351
Joints
   sheet metal, 256–258
   welding, illustrated, 267
   woodworking, 359–361

Joists, 385
Justification, 114

K

Kerf, 333
Kilns, 318
Kilowatt hours, 426
Kitchen arrangements, illustrated, 93
Knurling tool, 208

L

Lac gum, 373
Lacquer, 273–274, 375
Laminates, plastic, 572
Laminating
   high-pressure, of plastics, 296
   of wood, 356–357
Lath, 393
Lathe
   metal-cutting, accessories for, 207–208
   metal-cutting, parts of, illustrated, 42
   metal-cutting, use of, 208–214
   screw-cutting, 508–509
   wood, 352–354
Lathe dogs, 207–208
Layout
   assembly-line, 534; example, 536
   of metal, 163–170
Layout tools, for metal, 163–165
Leads, 112; illustrated, 113
Lettering, 65–67
Lettering sets, 80–81
Letterpress printing, 107–108, 115–120
Lever, 442
Light, electricity from 410
Light table, 121
Lignin, 517
Lignite, 515
LIM. *See* Test car, linear induction motor (LIM)
Line copy, 121
Lines
   in drawing, 56–61
   in sketching, 62–63
Linoleum block printing, 120
Lithographic prints, 108
Lithographic stones, 108
Locomotives, 471–475
Lodestones, 399
Lumber
   airdrying of, 318

597

Index

kilndried, 318
softwood, metric replacement sizes (table), 591
surfaced, 325
Lumbering, 316–320

M

Machines
  bending, 224–226
  general discussion, 442–452
  simple, 441, 442–443
Machining, 171–172
Machinists, 556
Magma, 579
Magnetism
  and electricity, 397–401
  electricity from, 411
  laws of, 400–401
Magnetite, 399
Magnets, 397–401
Mahogany, 319
Makeready, 120
Management
  careers in, 564–565
  in corporations, 524
  general discussion, 518
Manufacturing, 523–525, 528, 543–544, 551–553
Maple, 319
Marketing, 528, 544–546, 553–555
Market research, 546
Mass production, 506, 522, 547–555
Measurement
  general discussion, 26–34
  customary, standard units of, 26
  SI metric, standard units of, 26–30
Measuring devices, 31–32
Metal
  abrading of, 187–192
  abrasive blasting of, 279–280
  adhesive fastening of, 259–265
  base, 259
  bending of, 217, 220–226
  buffing of, 277–279
  casting of, 217, 227–231
  coating of, 272
  coat finishing of, 273–277
  cohesive fastening of, 266–270
  color finishing of, 282–283
  coloring of, 272
  common, melting temperatures of (table), 231
  common ferrous (table), 162
  cutting of, 171–172
  displacement finishing of, 272, 281–282
  drawing of, 218, 244
  drilling, 194–199
  electroplating of, 274
  enameling of, 274–276
  extruding of, 218, 245–246
  fastening of, 248–270
  ferrous, 156–159
  filing of, 200–204
  finishing of, 271–283
  forging of, 217, 232–233
  forming of, 172–173, 216–219
  general discussion, 154–165
  heat-treating of, 233–235
  kinds of, 156–165
  layout of, 163–170
  measuring of, 165–167
  milling of, 200–201
  nonferrous, 159, 161
  pattern development of, 163–170
  peening of, 281
  planishing of, 281–282
  polishing of, 277
  pressing of, 218, 236–243
  properties of, 155–156
  raising of, 238–239
  remove finishing of, 272, 277–280
  rolling of, 218, 246–248
  sawing of, 178–181
  shapes and sizes, 156, 158
  shaping of, 193
  shearing of, 182–186
  sheet, thicknesses of (table), 159
  sinking of, 236–238
  spinning of, 243
  stamping of, 241
  tooling of, 239–241
  turning of, 205–214
Metal bars, common sizes of (table), 160
Metallurgy, 155, 173
Metalworking, 144–283
Meters, reading, 426, 427
Metric system. *See* SI metric system
Micrometer
  parts of, 33; illustrated, 210
  reading of, 34; illustrated, 210
  use of, 32–34
Mill, planing, 318
Mills, lumber, 324
Milling
  chemical, 172
  of metal, 177, 200–201

Index

of wood, 332, 349–352
Mill pond, 316
Mimeograph, 140–142
Mining, 149–153
Model T, 498
Moist-diazo process, 99
Molding, of plastics, 293–296, 299, 300
Mold maker, 290
Monorails, 467
Mordants, 215
Morse, Samuel F. B., 432
Morse code, international, 432; illustrated, 433
Motors. *See also* Engines
  electric, 419–421
  induction, 420–421

N

Nailing, 362–364
Nails, 362–364
Nail set, 362
National Aeronautics and Space Administration (NASA), 486–487
National Association of Manufacturers, 519
National Transportation Safety Board, 478
N/C. *See* Numerical control (N/C)
Neolithic age, 507–508
Neon, 427
Neutrons, 404
Newcomen, Thomas, 444
Newton, Sir Isaac, 448, 449
Nichrome, 422
Normalizing, 235
Nucleus, 404
Numerical control (N/C), technology report, 577–578

O

Oak, 319–320
Occupational Safety and Health Act, 41, 42
Occupations. *See also* Careers
  by group, 520
  studying of, 546
Office workers, 565
Offset lithography, 108–109, 121–124
Ohm, George Simon, 413
Ohm's law, 413
Oil. *See* Petroleum
Opaquing solution, 122
Ores, 149
Orthographic projection, 68. *See also* Drawing, multiview
OSHA. *See* Occupational Health and Safety Act (OSHA)
Otto, Dr. Nicholas, 441, 444
Oxyacetylene flame, patterns of, illustrated, 263
Ozalid process, 99

P

Packaging, 545
Paintbrushes, 275, 375–376
Painting, 375
Paints, in coat finishing of metals, 274
Paleolithic age, 507–508
Paper
  A-series sizes (table), 587
  B-series, trimmed sizes (table), 587
  drawing, 55
  making of, 105
  tympan, 118
Papyrus, 105
Parison, 293
Particle board, 324
Partnership, 523
Pattern development, of metal, 163–170
Patternmakers, 324
Patterns
  enlarging, 169–170
  for sheet metal, 167–170
Peat, 515
Peening, 281
Pelletizing, 517
Pelton wheel, 443
Pencils, drawing, 51–53
Personnel management, 528, 541–543, 551
Petroleum, 515
Pewter, 161
Phosphates, 517
Photoelectric effect, 410
Photographs
  printing, 133–137
  taking, 128–130
Pica, 111
Piercing (in sawing), 181
Pigment
  in ink, 105
  in paint, 375
Piston, 452
Pith balls, 402–403
Plain-sawing, 316
Plane, inclined, 442

Index

Plane, wood, 338–341
Planishing, 281–282
Planning, product, 35–37
Planning sheet, 36
Plan of procedure, 534
Plan view, 69
Plant layout, 533
Plastic(s)
  abrading of, 303
  and adhesion, 305
  adhesives for, 304
  bending of, 298–299
  blow forming of, 300
  blow molding of, 293–294
  calendering of, 292
  casting of, 296, 299, 300
  coating of, 293, 308, 310
  and cohesion, 304–306
  coloring of, 308–310
  compression molding of, 294, 300
  cutting of, 302–303
  and design, 21–22
  drilling of, 303
  extrusion of, 292, 299
  fastening of, 304–307
  finishing of, 308–310
  foamed, 297
  foam molding of, 300
  forming in school shop, 298–301
  general discussion, 289–310
  industrial processing of, 292–298
  injection molding of, 295, 300
  laminated, 306–307
  high-pressure laminating of, 296
  mechanical fastening of, 305
  molding of, 299
  reinforcing of, 297
  rotational molding of, 295–296
  sawing of, 302
  shaping of, 303
  shearing of, 302
  smoothing of, 303
  solvent molding of, 296
  thermal welding of, 304
  thermoforming of, 294–295
  thermosetting, 291
  transfer molding of, 294
  turning of, 303
  vacuum forming of, 300
Plasticization, 575–576
Plastics industry, 289–290
Platen press
  general discussion, 107–108
  preparing, 118–119
  printing with, 119–120
Pliers, illustrated, 252
Plot plan 381; example, 382
Plugs, electrical, 414, 416
Plumbing, 389–390
Plywood, 321–322
Points (in carbon content), 156
Point system (printer's measuring system), 111–112
Polishing, of metal
  general discussion, 187, 188, 277
  on a lathe, 214
Pollution, 500–502, 506, 510–512
Power
  atomic, 450–451
  electrical, 395–438
  fluid, 447
  general discussion, 440–460
  geothermal, 579–581
  in industry, 521
  and machines, 442–452
  motor, alternate sources of, 449–450
  solar, 442, 451–452, 581
  steam, 444
  water, 443
  wind, 579
Pressing, 218, 236–243
Pressure, electricity from, 409–410
Pricing, 544–545
Primer, 375
Printers, 559
Printing, 102–127
Printing frame (silk-screen), 125
Printmaking, 98–100
Production, custom, 522
Production control, 528, 532–538, 551
Production control specialists, 533
Production planning, 534
Production team, 563–564
Production tooling, 528, 529–532, 549–551
Productivity, changes in, 507
Projection printing, 135–137
Proof, printing, 115–116
Proof press, illustrated, 115
Prop-jet. *See* Turboprop
Proprietorship, 522
Protons, 404
Prototype, 549
PT. *See* Production tooling
Pulley, 442
Pumice stone, 375
Punches, 163–164, 184
Pyrolysis, 581
Pyrometer, 409

Index

Q

QC. *See* Quality control (Qc)
Quality control (Qc), 528, 538–541, 551
Quarter-sawing, 316
Quoins, 116

R

Radio
  general discussion, 436–437
  symbols used in, 416
Rafters, 385, 388
Railroad classification yard, 467–471
Railroads, 466–477
Rails, railroad, 467
Raising, 238–239
Rammer, illustrated, 228
Random sampling, 541
Range finders, camera, 130
Rasps, 349–350
RD. *See* Research and development (RD)
Reactors, nuclear, 442, 450–451
Reaming, 196
Rectangle, dividing, 60, 61
Recycling, 510–512
Reglets, 116
Relief printing, 107–108
Removing (of metal), 175
Repoussé. *See* Chasing
Reproduction proof, 121
Research and development (RD), 528–529, 548–549
Research vehicle, tracked air cushion (TACRV), 477
Resist, 215
Resources
  capital, 519–521
  human, 517–519
  material, 515–517
  natural, 517
Riddle, illustrated, 228
Ridge, roof, 388
Rings, piston, 453–454
Ripsaw, 333
Riveting
  of aircraft, 484, 486
  general discussion, 255–256; illustrated, 257
Rochelle salts, 409
Rockets, 449
Rolling, 218, 246–247
Roof decking, 389
Rotary press, 107–108; illustrated, 109

Rotogravure process, 109–110
Rottenstone, 374
Routers, 350–352
Route sheet, 534; examples, 535, 552
Routing (planning), 534
Rule(s)
  bench, 325
  general discussion, 31
  metal, 164
  metric, 326
  zigzag, 325

S

Safety
  in color finishing of metals, 282
  in the finishing room, 372
  general discussion, 38–42
  in use of hacksaw, 180
Safety glasses, 38, 40
Sand blasting, 279, 370
Sanders, power, 345
Sanding. *See* Abrading
Sanding pad, 53
Saw(s)
  band, metal-cutting, 180
  band, wood-cutting, 337
  compass, 334–336
  coping, 334–335
  circular, 337
  crosscut, 333
  hole, 180–181
  jeweler's, 181
  keyhole, 334–336
  miter, 360
  scroll, 336–337
Sawing
  of metal, 176, 178–181
  of plastic, 302
  of wood, 331, 333–337
Sawmills, 316
Sawyer, 316
Scales, architect's (table), 50
Scales, customary and metric (table), 51
Scales, drafting, 50–51. *See also* Rule(s)
Scheduling, 534–538
Screen, silk-screen printing, 125–126
Screw (simple machine), 442
Screwdrivers, 364–366
Screws (in woodworking), 364–366
Scriber, 165
Seamer, hand, 221
Sediment chamber, battery, 406
Selling, 545

Index

Separating, of metal, 175
Servicing, 545–546
Shaping
   of metal, 176, 193
   of plastic, 303
   of wood, 349–352
Shearing
   of metal, 176, 182–186
   of plastic, 302
   of wood, 331
Shears, 183, 185–186
Sheeting, plastic, 292
Sheet metal
   joints in, 256–258
   developing patterns for, 167
Sheetmetal workers, 556
Shellac, 373–374
Ships
   container, 490–491
   sailing, 492–493
   surface effect, 495–496
Shutter speed, 128–129
Silicon carbide, 187
Silk-screen printing, 110, 125–127
Sill, 385
Silver, 161
SI metric system
   boring approximate metric holes with customary drills (table), 590
   conversion tables, 29, 30, 586
   customary-metric drill sizes and conversion chart (table), 588–589
   designing in, 85–87
   fact sheet (automotive), 462
   fact sheet (graphic arts), 103
   fact sheet (metalworking), 146
   fact sheet (woodworking), 314
   general discussion, 26–34
   replacement sizes of softwood lumber (table), 591
   standards for lumber, 326–327
   first choice numbers used in designing metric projects (table), 87
   A- and C-series paper and envelope sizes (table), 587
   B-series paper—trimmed sizes (table), 587
   base units (table), 27–28
   units of power (table), 444
   unit prefixes (table), 29
Sinking, 236–238
Sketching, 61–65
Skimmer, illustrated, 228
Slabs, illustrated, 151

Slip rings, 418
Slugs, 112; illustrated, 113
Slurry, 171
Smoothing, of plastic, 303
Snips, 182–183
Softwoods
   characteristics of (table), 320
   general discussion, 318
Soil, 516–517
Soil pipes, 389–390
Soldering
   general discussion, 259–262
   hard, 264–265
   ultrasonic, 174
Solenoid, 417; illustrated, 418
Sole plate, 387
Spark plugs, 457
Sparks, identification of steel by, 165
Spinning, 243
Spinning machine, 508–509
Splices, wire, 413
Spokeshave, 343
Spoon slick, illustrated, 228
Spraying
   airless, of wood, 329
   electrostatic, 174
Sprue pin, illustrated, 228
Squares
   framing, 326
   general discussion, 165
   T-, 48–49
   try, 325
Squeegee, 110, 126
Stains, for woods, 371–372
Stakes, metal-bending, 220–221
Stamping, 241
Stanley Steamer, 498
Steamboats, 493
Steamships, 493
Steel
   common angle sizes, 161
   making of, 149–151
   spark identification of, 165
   temperature and color (tables), 235, 591
Stencil printing, 110
Stencil (silk-screen), 126
Stephenson, George, 444
Stevedores, 490
Stock (wood), estimating, 325–327
Stockholders, 523
Stretchout, 167
Stripping, 122; illustrated, 123
Stucco, 393
Studs, 385

602

Index

Superstructure, 385
Supertanker, 492
Supervision, 543
Surform® tool, 350
Symbols
   architectural, illustration, 97
   in drawing, 56–61
   electrical, 416; illustrated, 431
   process, 534; illustrated, 536

T

Table (furniture), design of, 23
Tables
   abrasive grit numbers, 188
   architect's scales, 50
   approximate customary-metric conversions, 30
   customary and metric scales, 51
   sizes of bits needed for shank and pilot holes, 365
   coloring solutions, 283
   conversion chart for common units, 29
   approximate conversions (customary to metric; metric to customary), 586
   corporate organization, 523, 526
   customary-metric drill sizes and conversion chart, 588–589
   drill chart (boring approximate metric holes with customary drills), 590
   tap drill chart, 253
   first choice sizes (used in designing metric projects), 87
   flat metal bars, common sizes, 160
   hand groover sizes, 258
   possible metric replacement sizes of softwood lumber, 591
   common ferrous metals, 162
   metal properties, 155
   metal sheet thicknesses, 159
   melting temperatures of common metals, 231
   OSHA safety checklist (table), 42
   A- and C-series paper and envelopes, 587
   B-series paper—trimmed sizes, 587
   comparative sizes of drawing paper, 55
   base units of the SI metric system, 27–28
   ISO metric threads, 254
   table of SI unit prefixes, 29
   common steel angle sizes, 161
   steel temperature chart, 235
   temperature of steel related to color, 591
   tempering chart, 235

   tempering chart for steel tools, 591
   common woods and their characteristics, 320
Taconite, 150, 517
TACRV. See Research vehicle, tracked air cushion (TACRV)
Tank method (film developing), 130–132
Tape, metric steel, 326
Taps, illustrated, 252
T-bevel, sliding, 325–326
Technicians, 518–519, 559–561
Technology, effect of, on society, 507–510
Technology reports
   alternate power sources, 579–582
   automotive engines, 582–585
   composite materials, 571–572
   automatic harvesting of trees, 573–574
   numerical control, 577–578
   welding, 570–571
Telegraph, 432
Telephone, 433–434
Teletype, 432
Television, 437–438
Temperature, measurement of, 32
Tempering
   of common shop tools (table), 235
   of steel tools (table), 591
Termite shield, 386
Test car, linear induction motor (LIM), 477
Testing, destructive, 541
Texturing, of wood, 370
Thermocouples, 409
Thermometer, 32
Thermoforming, of plastics, 294–295
Thermoplastics, 291
Threads
   cutting, 254–255
   external, drawing of, 59
   metric, 253–254
   types of, 251–253
Ties, railroad, 467
Tongs, illustrated, 233
Tonnage, 492
Tooling, 239–241
Tools
   casting, illustrated, 228
   for cutting threads, illustrated, 252
   design of, 18, 20
   lathe turning, 353
   measuring, in machine shop work, 208
   sharpening of, 191
   shop, tempering colors and temperatures (table), 235
   steel, tempering of (table), 591

603

Index

for turning threaded fasteners, 251
Tool and die makers, 532
Tool bits, lathe, 208
Toolholders, lathe, 208
Tool post, lathe, 208
Top plate, 387
Topsoil, 516–517
Traffic control, centralized (CTC), 471
Transformer, 418, 425
Transport systems. *See also* Transportation
   air, 478–489
   automotive, 497–502
   rail, 466–477
   sea, 490–496
Transportation, 461–502
Trees, automatic harvesting of (technology report), 573–574
Triangle (drawing instrument), 49
Triangle (geometric shape), finding the center of, 60
Triangulation, in sheet metal patterns, 169
Trucks, 498–499
Tungsten, 424
Turbojet, 448
Turboprop, 448
Turning
   of metal, 177, 205–214
   of plastic, 303
   of wood, 332, 352–354
Type
   composing, 111–114
   foundry, 111
   hand-setting of, 112–114
   movable, invention of, 105
Type bank, 112; illustrated, 113
Type case, 112
Type spacing material, illustrated, 113

U

Unions, labor, 519
Uranium atoms, 450
Utilities, 389–393

V

Valve, reed, 454
Varnishes, 374–375
Vehicle
   in ink, 105
   in paint, 375
Veneers, 321–323
VFR. *See* Visual flight rules (VFR)
Views (in drawings), 72–73

Vinyl-dip process, 174
Vise, metal, 221
Visual flight rules (VFR), 478
Volt, 403
Volta, Allessandro, 403, 404
Voltage, 403
Voltaic cell, 405

W

Walnut, 320
Wankel, Felix, 445
Watt, James, 441, 444
Watt, 508
Wax, in coat finishing of metal, 274
Wedge, 442
Weight, measurement of, 31–32
Welding
   of metal, 266–270, 423
   of plastics, 304
   technology report, 570–571
Wheel and axle, 442
Whitney, Eli, 506, 508
Width, measurement of, 31
Windmills, 579
Wiring, lamp, 414, 416
Wood
   abrading of, 332, 343–346
   adhesive fastening of, 366–368
   bleaching of, 372
   characteristics of (table), 320
   chiseling of, 338–343
   coat finishing of, 373–376
   coating of, 369
   color finishing of, 371–372
   coloring of, 369
   drilling of, 332, 346–348
   fastening of, 358–367
   filing of, 349–352
   forming of, 355–357
   identification of, 318–320
   laminating of, 356–357
   mechanical fasteners for, 362–366
   milling of, 332, 349–352
   modified (technology report), 575–576
   planing of, 338–343
   remove finishing of, 369
   sawing of, 331, 333–337
   shaping of, 349–352
   shearing of, 331
   texturing of, 370
   turning of, 332, 352–354
Woodcutting, 331–355
Wood industry, occupations in, 324

Index

Wood products, 321–324
Woodworking
  general discussion, 312–376
  new developments in, 328–330
Wrench, tap, illustrated, 252
Wright brothers, 481

X

Xenon, 427
Xerography, 138
Xylene, 517